YO-EIJ-071

Financial Accounting
Sixth Edition

JAMES J. BENJAMIN
Texas A&M University

ARTHUR J. FRANCIA
University of Houston

ROBERT H. STRAWSER
Texas A&M University

1986

dame publications, inc.
P.O. Box 35556
Houston, Texas 77235-5556

©dame publications, inc.—1986

All rights reserved. No part of this publication may be reproduced, stored in a retrieval system, or transmitted, in any form or by any means, electronic, mechanical, photocopying, recording, or otherwise, without the prior written permission of the publisher.

ISBN 0-87393-039-8

Library of Congress Catalog Card No. 83-70548

Printed in the United States of America.

Preface

THIS TEXTBOOK introduces the student to all aspects of accounting from the basic concept of the transaction, through the financial information system to financial statements and special reports, into the interpretation of these statements and reports. It is intended for use in the beginning or principles of accounting course for business and non-business majors. The text includes a balanced presentation of the procedures, techniques and fundamental principles underlying accounting, reporting and decision making. Up-to-date pronouncements of the accounting profession (FASB, SEC, etc.) are considered throughout the text and integrated in a clear illustrative manner, not just quoted verbatim. A clear and concise introduction to the accounting process is developed in the early chapters of the text as a basis for special consideration given in later chapters to contemporary topics such as the uses of managerial accounting information, constant dollar accounting, current value accounting, business combinations, and income tax considerations. The text is intended to present a balanced perspective of accounting practice, theory and decision making using accounting information. The approach used is straightforward; completeness of coverage is achieved using simple but accurate terms and examples. It is a teachable text geared to student understanding of the basic concepts and practices—not a reference manual.

The initial chapter introduces the functions of accounting and includes a brief discussion of the objectives of financial accounting, the qualitative characteristics of accounting information and basic accounting concepts. The accounting process is presented and illustrated in the next three chapters. The transactions of a single company for the initial month of its operations are used in illustrating transaction analyses and, then, the entire accounting process. The authors have found that this repetition greatly enhances student understanding of the basic concepts. An outline of the text, with comments on chapter content, follows:

1. Introduces the basic accounting concepts.
2. Discusses the balance sheet, income statement and statement of capital.
3. Traces and explains the basic steps in the recording process.
4. Illustrates the use of the worksheet in facilitating statement preparation and discusses the common types of adjusting entries.
5. Discusses the accounting for a merchandising business and considers the basic concepts of revenue and expense recognition, alternative methods of revenue recognition and illustrates certain of the operational differences among companies, with special emphasis on the differences between retailing and service organizations.
6. Introduces a model of an accounting system and discusses the basic components of such a system.
7. Discusses the accounting procedures used to record and control cash.
8. Discusses the procedures used to account for receivables and payables.
9. Considers the alternative methods of accounting for inventories.
10. Discusses the accounting procedures used for recording and allocating the cost of plant and equipment.
11. Considers the accounting for the disposition of plant and equipment and the procedures for accounting for intangible assets and natural resources.
12. Considers the issues related to the accounting for sole proprietorships and partnerships.
13. Discusses issues relating to the formation of a corporation and the issuance of capital stock.
14. Considers matters relating to the retained earnings and dividends of a corporation.
15. Discusses the accounting for bonds payable and investments in corporate securities.
16. Discusses and illustrates the use of consolidated financial statements.
17. Illustrates the procedures used in preparing the statement of changes in financial position.
18. Examines the issues relating to the inclusion of current value and constant dollar or price-level information in financial statements.
19. Discusses common techniques of analyzing information presented in financial statements.
20. Presents a general discussion of the federal income tax including "inter" and "intra" period tax allocation.
21. Introduces and discusses the objectives of financial reporting, the qualitative characteristics of accounting information and the elements of financial statements.

Acknowledgments

We have received invaluable assistance, ideas, comments and constructive criticisms from both our students and our colleagues. A necessary ingredient in the writing of any textbook is the environment in which the effort took place. Our special thanks go to James McFarland and A. Benton Cocanougher of the University of Houston, William Mobley of Texas A&M University, and William V. Muse of the University of Akron and John E. Pearson, formerly of Texas A&M University and Gulf Research, Inc. for their roles in providing this environment.

Numerous professors and graduate students have provided invaluable help, ideas, comments, and constructive criticisms. We are especially indebted to the following professors for their advice and support in the preparation of this text: R. Mark Alford, Donald T. Anderson, Craig E. Bain, James J. Beecher, James Bryant, Janice Lee Carpenter, Clairmont P. Carter, Mary T. Casey, Michael N. Cassell, Jeanne M. David, Thomas L. Dickens, Thomas P. Edmonds, James M. Emig, Michael L. Fetters, Edward S. Goodhart, James W. Greenspan, Lawrence Gulley, Paul A. Janell, Jai Kang, Larry Klein, Michael R. Lane, Harold O. Lee, Michael P. Licata, Richard Lindhe, James J. Mackie, James E. Meddaugh, William G. Mister, Kate Mooney, D. Robert Okopny, Kenneth N. Orbach, Thomas H. Oxner, Jane Park, William R. Pasewark, Richard Pitre, C. Douglas Poe, Mattie C. Porter, Richard A. Rivers, Gary L. Schugart, David E. Stout, Jerry R. Strawser, Joyce A. Strawser, Forrest Thompson, Daniel Verrault, Ralph E. Viator, Robert B. Welker, Nancy L. Wilburn, Joanne P. Williams and David R. Wright.

We appreciate the permissions received from the American Institute of Certified Public Accountants and the Institute of Management Accounting of the National Association of Accountants which allow us to use problem materials from past Uniform CPA Examinations and CMA Examinations, respectively. Of course, the authors are responsible for any shortcomings of this text.

July 1986

James J. Benjamin
Arthur J. Francia
Robert H. Strawser

P.S.: For sake of brevity, the authors would also like to again thank everybody who might adopt this text at any time in the future. Many people assisted us in the development of this text. Of course, any errors are their responsibility. Finally, a special thanks to our families who have spent sufficient money to require us to earn additional income.

Contents

1. Accounting: An Introduction   1

    Accounting as a Process of Communication. Accounting vs. Bookkeeping. Financial Accounting and Managerial Accounting. Financial Reporting and Financial Statements. Assumptions and Basic Accounting Principles. Entity Assumption. Going-Concern Concept. Monetary Unit Assumption. Stable Dollar Assumption. Time Period Assumption. Historical Cost Concept. Consistency Concept. Matching Concept. Revenue Realization. Materiality Concept. Conservatism. Full Disclosure Concept. Underlying Concepts. Influences on Accounting Principles. American Institute of Certified Public Accountants. Committee on Accounting Procedure. Accounting Principles Board. Financial Accounting Standards Board. Securities and Exchange Commission. Internal Revenue Service. National Association of Accountants. Governmental Accounting Standards Board. Cost Accounting Standards Board. American Accounting Association. Congress. Opportunities in Accounting. Summary. Key Definitions. Questions.

2. Financial Statements   23

    The Balance Sheet. Transaction Analysis. Balance Sheet Classifications. Assets. Liabilities. Owners' Equity. The Income Statement. Transaction Analysis. Income Statement Classifications. Statement of Capital. Summary. Key Definitions. Questions. Exercises. Problems.

3. The Recording Process   59

    The Account. An Illustration. General Journal Entries. Posting. Trial Balance. Adjusting Entries. Posting the Adjusting Entries. Trial Balance After Adjustment. Closing Entries. After-Closing Trial Balance. Financial Statements. Summary. Key Definitions. Questions. Exercises. Problems.

4. The Worksheet and Adjustments   95

    An Illustration. Adjusting Entries. Prepaid Expenses. Accrued Expenses. Depreciation. Unearned Revenues. Accrued Revenues. Accrual Basis of Accounting. Preparation of the Worksheet. Summary. Key Definitions. Questions. Exercises. Problems.

5. Accounting for a Merchandising Firm and Income Determination   135

    Accounting for Merchandising Operations. Accounting for Cost of Goods Sold. Cost of Merchandise Purchased. Sales of Merchandise. Determination of Cost of Goods Sold and Net Income. Objective of Inventory Accounting. Inventory Costs. Periodic and Perpetual Inventories. Inventory Losses. Basis of Accounting. Purchase Discounts. Freight-in, Returns and Allowances. Worksheet for a Merchandising Firm. Time Period of Revenue and Expense Recognition. Revenue Recognition. Revenue Recognition at Completed Production. Revenue Recognition During Production. Revenue Recognition When Cash is Received. Recognition of Expenses. Summary. Key Definitions. Questions. Exercises. Problems.

6. Accounting Systems and Internal Control — 169

Model of a Financial Accounting System. The Chart of Accounts. Coding the Chart of Accounts. The General Journal and General Ledger. Subsidiary Ledgers. Special Journals. An Example—Special Journals and Subsidiary Ledgers. Proving the Control Accounts. Internal Accounting Control. The Audit Trail. Automated Accounting Systems. Computer Hardware. Computer Software. Summary. Key Definitions. Questions. Exercises. Problems.

7. Cash — 201

Cash Receipts. Cash Disbursements. The Bank Reconciliation Statement. Petty Cash Funds. The Voucher System. Summary. Key Definitions. Questions. Exercises. Problems.

8. Receivables and Payables — 233

Classification of Receivables and Payables. Control over Receivables. Accounts Receivable. Bad Debt Expense. Income Statement Approach. Balance Sheet Approach. Balance Sheet Presentation. Writing-Off an Uncollectible Account. Direct Write-Off Method. Accounts Payable. Notes Receivable and Payable. Issuance of the Note. Accrual of Interest. Payment of the Note. Dishonored Note. Notes Issued at a Discount. Discounting Notes Receivable. Statement Presentation of Receivables. Payroll Accounting. Summary. Key Definitions. Questions. Exercises. Problems.

9. Inventories — 271

Control over Inventories. Objective of Inventory Accounting. Basis of Accounting. Inventory Cost Flow Methods. Average Method. First-in, First-out (Fifo) Method. Last-in, First-out (Lifo) Method. Differences in Methods. Lower of Cost or Market. Gross Profit Method. Retail Inventory Method. Summary. Key Definitions. Questions. Exercises. Problems.

10. Long-Term Assets Plant and Equipment: Depreciation — 291

Control over Tangible Long-Term Assets. Types of Plant and Equipment. Accounting for Tangible Fixed Assets. Depreciation. Elements Affecting the Determination of Periodic Depreciation. Useful Life. Salvage Value. Depreciation Methods. Accelerated Cost Recovery System. Recording Long-Term Assets. Assets Acquired during the Period. Interest Costs. Disclosure in the Financial Statements. Costs Incurred After Acquisition. Plant and Equipment in the Financial Statements. Summary. Key Definitions. Questions. Exercises. Problems.

11. Plant and Equipment, Intangible Assets and Natural Resources — 321

Trade-Ins. Natural Resources. Depletion Base and Amortization. Accounting for Oil and Gas Producers. Intangible Assets. Summary. Key Definitions. Questions. Exercises. Problems.

12. Unincorporated Business Organizations — 341

The Sole Proprietorship. Accounting for a Proprietorship. The Partnership. Characteristics of a Partnership. Evaluation of the Partnership Form of Organization. Accounting for a Partnership. Formation of a Partnership. Division of Profits and

Contents xi

Losses. Partnership Financial Statements. Admission of a Partner. Withdrawal of a Partner. Liquidation of the Partnership. Summary. Key Definitions. Questions. Exercises. Problems.

13. The Corporation: Organization and Capital Stock — 375

Characteristics of the Corporation. Forming a Corporation. Capital of a Corporation. Nature of Capital Stock. Rights of Stockholders. Par Value and No-Par Value. Issuance of Par Value Stock. Issuance of Stock for Noncash Assets. Issuance of No-Par Stock. Subscriptions for Capital Stock. Stockholders' Equity in the Balance Sheet. Summary. Key Definitions. Questions. Exercises. Problems.

14. The Corporation: Earnings and Dividends — 401

Nature of Earnings. Extraordinary Items. Discontinued Operations. Prior Period Adjustments. Accounting Changes. Earnings per Share. Dividends. Important Dates Related to Dividends. Cash Dividends. Stock Dividends. Stock Splits. Treasury Stock. Retained Earnings. Appropriation of Retained Earnings. Statement of Retained Earnings. Book Value per Share of Common Stock. Summary. Key Definitions. Questions. Exercises. Problems.

15. Long-Term Liabilities and Investments — 437

Bond Obligations. Classes of Bonds. Bonds Issued at Face Value. Issuance between Interest Dates. Issuance of Bonds at a Discount. Issuance of Bonds at a Premium. Convertible Bonds. Retirement of Bonds. Bond Sinking Fund. Restriction on Dividends. Balance Sheet Presentation. Investments in Corporate Securities. Investments in Bonds. Amortization of Premium. Amortization of Discount. Sale of Bonds. Investments in Stocks. Temporary Investments. Control Over Investments. Accounting for Acquisition of Temporary Investments. Valuation of Temporary Investments. Long-Term Investments in Stock. Summary. Key Definitions. Questions. Exercises. Problems. Appendix: Interest and Present Value Concepts. Interest. Present Values of a Future Sum. Compound Interest and Present Value on a Series of Equal Payments. Application of Present Value Concepts to Bonds Payable. Accounting for Premium or Discount on Bonds—The Interest Method. Bonds Sold at a Premium. Bonds Sold at a Discount. Table A-1: Present Value of $1. Table A-2: Present Value of Annuity of $1 Per Period. Exercises—Appendix.

16. Consolidated Financial Statements — 487

Consolidated Balance Sheet at Date of Acquisition. Consolidated Balance Sheet after the Date of Acquisition. Other Reciprocal Accounts. Pooling of Interest. Usefulness of Consolidated Statements. Consolidated Income Statement. Minority Interest. Profit on Intercompany Sales. Summary. Key Definitions. Questions. Exercises. Problems.

17 The Statement of Changes in Financial Position — 519

Definition of Funds. Sources and Uses of Working Capital. Sources of Funds. Funds from Operations. Other Sources of Funds. Uses of Funds. Determining Sources and

Uses of Working Capital. Changes in Working Capital. Changes in Noncurrent Accounts. Working Capital Provided by Operations. Form of the Statement of Changes in Financial Position. Transactions Not Affecting Current Accounts. Cash Flow Analysis. Cash Flow from Operations. Cash Used for Dividends. Cash Flow Statement. Summary of Mechanics on the Statement of Changes in Financial Position. Preparation of Statement—Funds Defined as Working Capital. Preparation of Statement—Funds Defined as Cash. Summary. Key Definitions. Questions. Exercises. Problems.

18. Accounting for Changing Prices — 565

Constant Dollar Accounting. Measure of the Instability of the Dollar. Effects of General Price-Level Changes. Monetary Items. Nonmonetary Items. Price-Level Adjusted Financial Statements. Illustration of Price-Level Adjusted Financial Statements. Preparation of the Restated Income Statement. Revenues. Expenses Which Affect Monetary Items. Allocated Expenses. Monetary Gains and Losses. Preparation of the Restated Balance Sheet. Current Status of General Price-Level Adjusted Statements. Current Value Accounting. Current Value Approaches. FASB Statement No. 33. Summary. Key Definitions. Questions. Exercises. Problems.

19. Financial Statement Analysis — 603

Comparative Financial Statements. Basic Analytical Procedures. Horizontal Analysis. Vertical Analysis. Common-Size Statements. Ratio Analysis. Comparison with Standards. Analysis for Common Stockholders. Rate of Return on Total Assets. Rate of Return on Common Stockholders' Equity. Earnings per Share of Common Stock. Price-Earnings Ratio on Common Stock. Debt-to-Equity Ratio. Analysis for Long-Term Creditors. Analysis for Short-Term Creditors. Current Ratio. Acid-Test or Quick Ratio. Analysis of Accounts Receivable. Analysis of Inventories. Interpretation of Analyses. Summary. Key Definitions. Questions. Exercises. Problems.

20. Income Tax Considerations — 639

The Federal Income Tax. Classes of Taxpayers. Individual Federal Income Tax. Corporate Income Tax. Differences between Accounting Income and Taxable Income. Interperiod Tax Allocation. Allocation of Income Tax within a Period. Income Taxes and Management Decisions. Summary. Appendix: Tax Tables. Key Definitions. Questions. Exercises. Problems.

21. Basic Accounting Theory — 672

A Conceptual Framework. Objectives of Financial Reporting. Qualitative Characteristics of Accounting Information. Pervasive Constraint. User-Specific Qualities. Ingredients of Primary Qualities. Secondary and Interactive Qualities. Threshold for Recognition. Elements of Financial Statements of Business Enterprises. Elements. Recognition and Measurement in Financial Statements of Business Enterprises. The Role of Financial Statements. Recognition and Measurement. Developing Generally Accepted Accounting Principles. The Accounting Standard Setting Process. International Aspects. Key Definitions. Questions.

Financial Statement — 693
General Motors Corporation

Index — 711

Learning Objectives

Chapter 1 introduces certain basic accounting concepts. Studying this chapter should enable you to:

1. Describe the basic accounting definition and discuss accounting as a process of communication.

2. Describe the role of the accountant and explain why this role has increased in significance.

3. Compare and contrast accounting and bookkeeping.

4. Contrast financial accounting with managerial accounting and identify the primary users of each.

5. Describe the objectives of financial reporting.

6. Identify the basic financial statements and explain the purpose and use of each.

7. Describe the qualitative characteristics of accounting information.

8. Explain "generally accepted accounting principles" and discuss the major concepts underlying these principles.

9. List and briefly decribed certain of the more important influences on accounting principles.

10. Discuss the extent and nature of opportunities in accounting.

Accounting: An Introduction

INTRODUCTION

Accounting has been described as ". . . the art of recording, classifying, and summarizing in a significant manner and in terms of money, transactions and events which are, in part at least, of a financial character, and interpreting the results thereof."[1] This definition emphasizes the ". . . creative skill and ability with which the accountant applies his knowledge to a given problem."[2] Another view of the function of accounting, very similar to that reported above, is that "the primary function of accounting is to accumulate and communicate information essential to an understanding of the activities of an enterprise, whether large or small, corporate or non-corporate, profit or non-profit, public or private."[3] The importance of this second definition is the direct relevance of accounting to many and varied types of undertakings, both private and public, and profit and not-for-profit.

Implicit in any definition of accounting is the importance of the accountant's role in the reporting function. In fact, the primary role of the accountant is reporting and communicating information which will aid various users in the financial community in making economic decisions. These users of accounting information include current and potential owners, managers, creditors, and others.

It should be noted however, that "financial reporting is not an end in itself but is intended to provide information that is useful in making business and economic decisions."[4]

In the past, when businesses were less complex than they are today, there were usually only a very limited number of users of accounting information. For example, at the turn of the century, most businesses in the United States were managed and operated by their owners. Since these owners were intimately involved in the day-to-day operations of their businesses, there was little or no need for accounting reports. The owner or decision-maker already had firsthand knowledge of the information he required in order to operate the business effectively. Today, however, the situation is quite different. Many organizations have increased in both size and complexity. In many instances, the ownership and the management of a business have been separated. Firms are frequently managed by professional managers for their absentee owners who exercise a minimal amount of formal control over the operations of the business except in the most general sense. These owners often have virtually no involvement in the day-to-day activities of the

---

[1] American Institute of Certified Public Accountants, *Accounting Terminology Bulletin No. 1—Review and Resume* (New York: AICPA), p. 9.

[2] *Ibid.*

[3] *Accounting and Reporting Standards for Corporate Financial Statements* (Columbus, Ohio: American Accounting Association, 1957), p. 1.

[4] "Objectives of Financial Reporting by Business Enterprises," FASB Statement of Financial Accounting Concepts No. 1 (Stamford, Conn. FASB, 1978), para. 9.

business. Even professional managers (at all but the most basic levels of authority in the firm) have little *firsthand* involvement in the most fundamental of these activities. Their decisions are, more often than not, made on the basis of reports and summaries which are prepared by their subordinates. It should be noted here that these reports and summaries are prepared using accounting estimates. Too often, managers and other users of financial information may overlook this fact.

Although the above discussion might overstate the case just a bit (the corner pizza parlor may still be owner-operated, but it could well be a franchise operation), the basic point is that most decisions are made on the basis of summary-type reports rather than firsthand information.

What is the role of accounting and the accountant in this process? One observation that has been made is that the task of the accountant is to observe, interpret, summarize, and communicate information in a form which will enable the user of the data to evaluate, control, plan, and even predict performance. It is essential to note the importance of the term "user" in this context. A user could be a manager involved in the evaluation and direction of the continuing operations of the business; a present or a potential stockholder (owner) seeking information for an impending investment decision; a bank officer in the process of reviewing a loan application; a supplier making a decision with regard to a credit application; a federal, state, or local revenue officer evaluating the propriety of a tax return; or even a citizen attempting to assess the performance of some governmental unit. In each of the circumstances mentioned above, and in countless other situations as well, user needs are met, at least in part, by a report prepared by an accountant on the basis of accounting information.

Not to be overlooked is the impact of accounting on our society. The transfer and distribution of the economic resources of society are often related to the actions of the users described above, taken in response to accounting information. Thus, the failure of accounting information systems to report information on an accurate and timely basis could alter the decisions made by various users and thereby create undesirable economic consequences for society.

ACCOUNTING AS A PROCESS OF COMMUNICATION[5]

Accounting may be regarded as a process of communication in a very real sense. Events occur on a continuing basis which affect the operations of an organization. The accountant acts as an observer-reporter, observing events or transactions as they take place, evaluating the significance of these events, then recording, classifying, and summarizing the events in an accounting report. The user receives the report, analyzes its content, and

---

[5] This discussion is based on Norton M. Bedford and Vahe Baladouni, "A Communication Theory Approach to Accountancy," *The Accounting Review*, October 1962, pp. 650-59.

utilizes the information in making economic decisions. Of course, these decisions made by the user cause new events to take place setting the chain in process again through another cycle.

Two factors are of major importance in this communication. First, there should be mutual understanding and agreement between the accountant preparing the report and the persons using the report on the basis of its preparation and content. The accountant must know the user's needs and perceptions and prepare the report so that what the user understands the report to express will indeed correspond with what the accountant intended to express in the report. Bedford and Baladouni call this fidelity—the relationship between what is understood by the user of accounting statements and what the accountant intended to express in his report.

The second factor is that the accountant's report should show a reliable and relevant relationship to the events it attempts to summarize. The report should, to the degree possible and/or practicable, include and describe all the significant events which did, in fact, take place. In the ideal situation, a user would make the same decision based on the analysis of a report that would have been made if firsthand information obtained on a personal basis was used. Bedford and Baladouni refer to this factor as significance—the relationship between the events which take place and the accounting report which attempts to summarize these events.

ACCOUNTING VS. BOOKKEEPING

Often, the distinction between accounting and bookkeeping is not understood. Bookkeeping refers to the actual recording of business transactions. This clerical recordkeeping function may be done manually or electronically with the use of computers. Accounting goes far beyond bookkeeping. The accounting function encompasses the design of the recordkeeping system, the preparation of reports, and the analysis and interpretation of financial and quantitative data. The decision-making involved in the accounting function requires a much greater knowledge and comprehension than the clerical skills which are needed in bookkeeping.

FINANCIAL ACCOUNTING AND MANAGERIAL ACCOUNTING

Although there is considerable overlap between the two, accounting may be thought of as consisting of two basic segments, financial accounting and managerial accounting. The basic difference between these two segments or divisions of accounting lies in their orientation.

Financial accounting is primarily concerned with users who are *external* to the firm and managerial accounting is concerned with *internal* users. Financial accounting attempts to provide external user groups such as current or potential owners, creditors, government agencies, and other interested parties with information concerning the status of the firm and the results of its operations. The objective of financial accounting is to provide these users with the information they require for making decisions.

Managerial accounting attempts to provide the information which is necessary for internal decision making to those who are charged with this responsibility within the firm. Managerial accounting, unlike financial accounting, is not constrained by the requirements of standard setting bodies discussed later in this chapter.

This text is concerned with both financial accounting and managerial accounting. Again, it is important to note that the two overlap. For example, the determination of the cost of the products which are produced by a manufacturing firm may be regarded as a problem that lies within the domain of managerial accounting; however, it is also a concern of financial accounting, because determining the cost of inventory is an important consideration for financial reporting purposes.

FINANCIAL REPORTING AND FINANCIAL STATEMENTS

The objective of financial reporting is to ". . . provide information that is useful to present and potential investors and creditors and other users in making rational investment, credit, and similar decisions."[6] In order to accomplish this goal, it is necessary that the information communicated must be understood; this information ". . . should be comprehensible to those who have a reasonable understanding of business and economic activities and are willing to study the information with reasonable diligence."[7] The users of financial information are concerned with the past and current performance of a business, as well as its future expectations. Recognizing these needs, the primary focus is on reporting information concerning the earnings of a business, although information about the resources of an enterprise are also emphasized.

Financial statements are the reports in which the accountant summarizes and communicates basic financial data. The purpose of financial statements is to provide the information which is required in the decision making process. The basic financial statements which are included in typical accounting reports issued to external users are: the balance sheet, the income statement, the statement of owners' equity, and the statement of changes in financial position. Each of these statements is considered and described in detail in separate chapters later in this text, but we will introduce them in general terms at this point.

Balance Sheet. The balance sheet, or statement of financial position, is the accounting statement that provides information regarding the *financial position* of the firm at a particular *point in time*. The balance sheet provides information about the economic resources of an enterprise (cash, receivables, inventories, equipment, etc.), the claims to those resources (obli-

---

[6] FASB Statement of Financial Accounting Concepts No. 1, para. 34.
[7] *Ibid.*

gations of the enterprise to transfer resources to other entities such as accounts payable, loans, etc.) and owners' equity. The balance sheet is described in detail in Chapter 2 of this text.

The Income Statement. The income statement provides data as to the *results of operations* of the firm for a specific *period of time*, usually a year. The primary focus of financial reporting is the disclosure of information concerning earnings and its components, so the income statement of a business is very important to the users of financial data. The income statement is also discussed in Chapter 2.

The Statement of Owners' Equity. The statement of owners' equity reports the details of the changes in the equity of the owners in the business. The equity of a business is equal to the direct investments made by the owners plus the earnings of the business and less any withdrawals made by owners. In the case of a business organized as a corporation, this statement is referred to as the statement of retained earnings. The statement of owners' equity for a proprietorship, referred to as a statement of capital, is described in Chapter 2 and the statement of retained earnings, the equivalent statement for a corporation, is discussed in Chapter 14.

The Statement of Changes in Financial Position. The users of financial statements are interested in the effects of transactions, events, and circumstances that change the resources of a business and the claims to those resources. The statement of changes in financial position indicates the sources from which the firm obtained its resources and the uses which were made of these resources during an accounting period. It describes how the financial resources of the firm have changed during the accounting period and discloses how these changes were made. Used in combination, the statement of changes in financial position and the other financial statements provide information intended: "... to help present and potential investors and creditors and other users in assessing the amounts, timing, and uncertainty of prospective cash receipts from dividends or interest and the proceeds from the sale, redemption, or maturity of securities or loans. Since investors' and creditors' cash flows are related to enterprise cash flows, financial reporting should provide information to help investors, creditors, and others assess the amounts, timing, and uncertainty of prospective net cash inflows to the related enterprise."[8] The statement of changes in financial position is described in Chapter 17.

These brief comments, which will be elaborated upon in detail in subsequent sections of this text, provide the reader with a thumbnail sketch of the basic financial statements which appear in a typical annual report of a business, a major end product of the accountant's work. We will now introduce and discuss certain of the basic accounting principles, assumptions,

---

[8] *Ibid.*, para. 32.

and concepts which underlie financial reporting and the preparation of financial statements by the accountant.

BASIC ACCOUNTING PRINCIPLES, UNDERLYING ASSUMPTIONS AND CONCEPTS

Underlying the practice of accounting are what is referred to as "generally accepted accounting principles." It is important to note that these "principles" are general rules or guides to action which have evolved over time and have gained acceptance by the consensus of the accounting profession and the financial community. Underlying these principles are several basic concepts which will be briefly described in the paragraphs that follow. These concepts will also be discussed in detail and elaborated upon throughout the remainder of the text.

Entity Assumption

The entity assumption is the basis for the distinction which is made by the accountant between a business and its ownership. In accounting, an organization, often referred to as an entity, is treated as a unit which is separate and distinct from its ownership and is accounted for as such. The affairs and transactions of the owners of a business are not combined or comingled with those of their firms. This is true irrespective of the legal form of organization which is used by the business.

There are three basic forms of business enterprises. A *proprietorship* is an enterprise which is owned by a single person who is personally liable for all of the debts of the business. A *partnership* is a business which is owned by two or more persons who share profits or losses according to an agreement, and who are personally liable for all of the debts of the business. A *corporation* is a business which has a legal identity separate from its owners, or stockholders. Therefore, the stockholders are not personally liable for the debts of the corporation.

The entity assumption is a distinction which always is made in accounting, even though the distinction may not be true in a legal sense for businesses which are organized as either single proprietorships or partnerships. In addition, the accounting entity could be a department or a division, or the accounting entity could be a group of companies even though each one is a legal entity.

Going-Concern Concept

The going-concern concept means that it is assumed that an entity will continue its operations for an indefinite future period of time, at least long enough to fulfill its plans and commitments. This assumption is used in accounting unless there is conclusive evidence to the contrary—for example, if a firm is in the process of bankruptcy proceedings.

Monetary Unit Assumption

The monetary unit assumption means that the transactions and events which occur in a business should be recorded in terms of money. As its definition indicates, accounting is ". . . the art of recording, classifying, and summarizing in a significant manner and *in terms of money* . . ."[9] The monetary unit is a useful means to communicate financial results.

Stable Dollar Assumption

The stable dollar assumption is closely related to the monetary assumption. *The stable dollar assumption assumes that all dollars are of equal worth or value, that is, of the same purchasing power.* Thus, the relevant transactions of an entity are recorded and its accounting reports are prepared on the assumption that a dollar is a stable unit of measure. Under the stable dollar concept, a dollar spent in 1930 is assumed to be equal to a dollar spent in 1975, or a dollar spent in 1985, etc. In other words, any changes which may have occurred in the purchasing power of the dollar due to either inflation or deflation are ignored.

Time Period Assumption

The most accurate determination of an enterprise's performance would be made at the time in which the business ceases to function. However, investors, creditors, and other interested parties need financial information concerning an enterprise on a much more timely basis. *Therefore, financial statements are prepared for such time intervals as a year or a quarter.* Of course, because of estimates and other factors the resulting information becomes less reliable as the time period is shortened, although the relevance of the information is increased.

Historical Cost Concept

The historical cost concept is the assumption that the original cost (acquisition price) of a resource, and not its current market value or replacement cost, is the basis which normally is used to account for the resources of an entity. This assumption has been justified by accountants on the grounds of its reliability. Its proponents argue that historical cost is a fact, whereas, in many instances, alternative measures such as market values or replacement costs may be somewhat subjective and must be determined each time that the financial statements are prepared. Historical cost also has been justified on the basis of the going-concern concept. An entity is assumed to have an indefinite life, and many (if not most) of its resources are acquired for use rather than for resale. Therefore, there is little need to consider the amount which might be realized if these resources were sold.

Of course, there have been serious objections to the use of historical cost, especially when prices have risen substantially. Under these circumstances, critics believe that the historical cost of an asset has no relation to its "value".

---

[9] American Institute of Certified Public Accountants, Accounting Terminology Bulletin No. 1 "Review and Resume," *op. cit.*, para. 9 (emphasis added).

1 | Accounting: An Introduction

Consistency Concept

As indicated previously, accounting principles do not comprise a detailed set of rules and procedures that apply to each and every situation. Rather, they are more in the nature of general guidelines. This is the reason why the accountant may record a particular transaction in alternative ways. Also, different firms may use different accounting methods. For this reason the concept of consistency is essential.

Briefly stated, *the consistency concept requires that once an entity adopts a particular accounting method for its use in recording a certain type of transaction, the enterprise should continue to use that method for all future transactions of the same category.* Note that this concept applies only to the accounting methods used by a particular entity. It does not apply to the methods used by different companies, even though these firms may be engaged in the same line of business or industry.

Consistency, for example, would require that General Motors use the same accounting methods in its reports from one year to the next so that the users of its financial statements are able to make comparisons of the financial position of the company, the results of its operations, and the changes in its financial position between and among years. It would not require, however, that General Motors and Chrysler use the same accounting methods, even though these firms may be somewhat similar in many respects. The financial statements of General Motors and Chrysler may or may not be readily comparable, depending upon the accounting methods which are selected by each of these firms.

Matching Concept

The matching concept is related to the measurement of the earnings or income of an entity. It provides that expenses that can be associated with revenue should be matched with that revenue when the revenue is realized and recognized during a particular period. Thus, the matching concept emphasizes a cause and effect association in which efforts are matched with accomplishments.

Revenue is recorded in accordance with the realization principle (discussed below), not necessarily as cash is received. For example, assume that an accountant prepares a tax return for her client during the month of March, bills the client for this service in April, and is paid in May. The revenue which is earned by the accountant from the preparation of this tax return is included in income for the month of March, because that is the month in which the accountant performed the work which entitled her to the fee.

Likewise, expenses are recorded as they are incurred, not necessarily as they are paid. The expenses incurred by the accountant in performing her work in March should be recorded in March. When she pays for these expenses is not relevant. From the viewpoint of the client, the cost of having the tax return prepared by the accountant is an expense. This expense should be recorded by the client at the point in time in which it was incurred (in March) rather than when it was actually paid (in May).

Revenue Realization

Revenue from sales usually is recognized as a component of earnings when it is realized or realizable and earned. A revenue is earned when the "... entity has substantially accomplished what is must do to be entitled to the benefits represented by the revenue."[10] Recognition differs from realization. *Recognition is the process of formally recording an item in the financial statements; realization is the process of converting noncash resources and rights into cash or claims to cash.*[11]

Revenue from sales usually is recognized at the time that both an exchange transaction takes place and the earnings process is complete or virtually complete. Revenue from sales usually is recognized at the time of delivery of the product; revenue from services is recognized when the service has been performed. Recognizing revenue at these times is objective and verifiable, because the sales price provides a measure for the amount of revenue realized.

Revenue which is earned by allowing others to use the enterprise's resources is recognized as time passes (examples of such revenue includes interest and rent). The amount of revenue which is recognized is determined by the amount which is received or is expected to be received.

Cash may be received prior to production and delivery. Revenue is recognized as the goods are produced and delivered. An example of recognizing revenue in this manner is magazine subscriptions. A publisher may receive payment from subscribers either before or after the subscription period but would recognize income as the magazine is produced and distributed to subscribers.

Materiality Concept

The materiality concept indicates that the accountant should be concerned primarily with those transactions which are of real significance or concern to the users of financial information. For example, assume that a company acquires a pencil sharpener at a cost of $10. It is expected that this sharpener will be used by the business over a five-year period before it will be replaced. In theory, a portion of the cost of the pencil sharpener should be considered as an expense of each year in which it will be used, because it will be of benefit to the company during each of these years. In practice, however, this would be neither realistic nor practical. The benefits which might be obtained by allocating the cost of the pencil sharpener over the five-year period simply would not be worth the cost that this procedure would involve. This example is, of course, a clear-cut case. A precise definition of what is or is not material is often elusive in particular circumstances.

---

[10] FASB Statement of Financial Accounting Concepts No. 5, "Recognition and Measurement in Financial Statements of Business Enterprises," (Stamford: FASB, December, 1984). para. 83.

[11] FASB Statement of Financial Accounting Concepts No. 6, "Elements of Financial Statements," (Stamford: FASB, December, 1985), para. 143.

A general understanding of the basic concept of materiality may be obtained from the following example. Assume that a transaction occurs. It is recorded in Accounting Report #1 in a manner that is theoretically correct. In alternative Accounting Report #2, it is recorded in a way that is expedient, but not necessarily correct in terms of accounting theory. If a user of an accounting report would make the same decision irrespective of whether it was based on Accounting Report #1 (theoretically correct) or Accounting Report #2 (expedient, but not necessarily theoretically correct) then the item obviously does not affect the decision at hand and is, therefore, clearly immaterial or insignificant in amount. On the other hand, if the user would make a different decision on the basis of Accounting Report #1 than might be made using Accounting Report #2, then the item would be considered to be material, because it affected the decision which was made by the user.

Clearly then, decisions as to whether a particular item is or is not material must be made by the accountant and depends on the exercise of professional judgment. Quantitative factors alone are not sufficient to judge the materiality of an item. The nature of the item and the circumstances under which the judgement is to be made must be considered.

Conservatism

Conservatism traditionally has meant that accountants who are selecting an alternative from two equally possible ones choose the accounting alternative that is least likely to overstate assets and income. APB Statement No. 4 stated the following:

> Frequently, assets and liabilities are measured in a context of significant uncertainties. Historically, managers, investors, and accountants have generally preferred that possible errors in measurement be in the direction of understatement rather than overstatement of net income and net assets. This has led to the convention of conservatism...[12]

The FASB believes that such a preference not only introduces a bias into financial reporting, but also conflicts with such qualitative characteristics as representational faithfulness, neutrality, and comparability. The Board discussed conservatism in its Statement of Financial Accounting Concepts No. 2 and stated that "[c]onservatism in financial reporting should no longer connote deliberate, consistent understatement of net assets and profits."[13] Continuing, the Board stated the following:

---

[12] APB Statement No. 4, "Basic Concepts and Accounting Principles Underlying Financial Statements of Business Enterprises," (New York: AICPA, 1970), para. 171.

[13] FASB Statement of Financial Accounting Concepts No. 2, "Qualitative Characteristics of Accounting Information," (Stamford: FASB, 1978), para. 93.

Conservatism is a prudent reaction to uncertainty to try to ensure that uncertainties and risks inherent in business situations are adequately considered. Thus, if two estimates of amounts to be received or paid in the future are about equally likely, conservatism dictates using the less optimistic estimate; however, when two amounts are not equally likely, conservatism does not necessarily dictate using the more pessimistic amount rather than the more likely one. Conservatism no longer requires deferring recognition of income beyond the time that adequate evidence of its existence becomes available or justifies recognizing losses before there is adequate evidence that they have been incurred.[14]

Full Disclosure Concept

Full disclosure means that information which is needed by the users of financial statements should be disclosed in an understandable form. The information may be presented in the main body of the financial statements or in the related notes. In addition to the required financial statements, information should be presented on such items as the following:

1. Details pertaining to elements within the financial statements.

2. Summary of accounting policies.

3. The effect of current value on earnings.

4. Management's discussion of the significance of the company's performance and of future prospects.

5. The effect of changes in accounting principles.

Full disclosure is very important to the efficient operations of the securities market. Efficiency means that security prices react quickly to published financial information.

INFLUENCES ON ACCOUNTING PRINCIPLES

As previously indicated, accounting principles derive their authority from their general acceptance and use by the accounting profession and the financial community. Some of the more important influences on accounting are described in the paragraphs which follow.

American Institute of Certified Public Accountants

The American Institute of Certified Public Accountants (AICPA) is the primary professional association of certified public accountants (CPAs) in the United States today. For CPAs, it is the accounting profession's equivalent of the American Bar Association (for attorneys) and the

---

[14] *Ibid.*, para. 95.

American Medical Association (for physicians). The AICPA is responsible for the preparation of the Uniform CPA Examination that is used in all states and which must be completed successfully in order for an individual to become a certified public accountant. For a number of years this organization has been involved actively in research, which is intended to improve accounting practices and procedures, through its numerous committees and by the publication of *The Journal of Accountancy*, the most widely read professional publication of the practicing CPA.

Within the last decade, the role of the AICPA has changed. An example of this increased activity is the formation of the Auditing Standards Executive Committee (ACSEC). *ACSEC represents the AICPA in the area of financial accounting and reporting.* It issues Statements of Position (SOP) in response to the pronouncements of other accounting governing bodies. SOPs have the dual purpose of providing guidance where none previously existed and of influencing the standard-setting process. ACSEC also attempts to bridge the gap between the accounting standard setting bodies and practicing accountants with the use of issue papers which identify current financial reporting problems, present alternative treatments, and recommend solutions.

The Committee on Accounting Procedure

The Committee on Accounting Procedure (CAP) was formed by the AICPA in 1939 to establish, review, and evaluate accepted accounting procedures. During the period 1939-1959, the CAP issued 51 Accounting Research Bulletins dealing with a variety of accounting practices, problems, and issues. The success of this committee was limited somewhat, because it dealt with specific problems as they arose, rather than establishing an overall framework to deal with these issues, and because the authority of its pronouncements depended solely upon their general acceptance. As the need for additional research into accounting principles intensified, the reasons for the continued existence of the CAP were less evident.

The Accounting Principles Board

In 1959, the AICPA replaced the CAP with the Accounting Principles Board (APB). The APB attempted to establish the basic postulates of accounting as a basis for the formulation of a set of broad accounting principles that would be used to guide the accountant in the specific circumstances of his or her practice. An accounting Research Division was established simultaneously to assist the Board with the research which was necessary to carry out its assigned tasks.

During its fourteen years of existence, the APB issued a total of thirty-one Opinions and four Statements. *APB Opinions are authoritative pronouncements which established generally accepted accounting principles; APB Statements are designed to increase the understanding of financial reporting.*

The APB's membership ranged from eighteen to twenty-one. Although all of the members belonged to the AICPA and were CPAs, not all were practicing public accountants; some members were selected from industry, government, and the academic community.

The Accounting Reseach Division issued fifteen research studies during its term of existence. However, the Division did not interact with the APB in selecting the topics to analyze, nor did the APB request the Division to examine specific accounting problems. This lack of coordination resulted in the Board's issuance of Opinions on topics for which little or no prior research had been conducted.

Prior to 1964, the enforcement of APB Opinions depended primarily on the prestige and influence of the AICPA and the support of the Securities and Exchange Commission, an independent regulatory agency of the Federal government responsible for administering the Federal laws governing the trading of securities. Then the AICPA issued *Rule 203 of the Rules of Conduct of the Code of Professional Ethics. This rule prohibits a member of the AICPA from expressing an opinion that financial statements have been prepared in accordance with generally accepted accounting principles if there is any material departure from the pronouncements of the APB (and now the FASB as well), unless the member can demonstrate that the financial statements otherwise would be misleading due to unusual circumstances.* In addition, all material departures from these pronouncements must be disclosed and the reasons for such departure must be explained in the financial statements.

The APB was criticized for its structure. In addition, the APB's positions on several controversial topics were perceived to be compromises. In 1971, the AICPA established the Study Group on Establishment of Accounting Principles to examine the organization and operation of the APB and to determine the improvements which were necessary. Its recommendations were accepted and led to the creation of the Financial Accounting Standards Board.

Financial Accounting Standards Board

The Financial Accounting Standards Board (FASB) came into existence in July of 1973 as the successor to the APB. Unlike its predecessor, the APB, *the FASB is an independent board whose membership consists of seven full-time, well-paid, distinguished accountants who are experienced in industry, government, education, and public accounting.* FASB members must sever all ties with former employers or private firms. Like its predecessor, the FASB conducts research in accounting matters using its own full-time technical staff members or commissions outside researchers from the academic and financial communities to work on specific projects of interest to the Board.

The research activities of the FASB serve as the basis for an invitation to comment or a discussion memorandum, which is prepared to outline the key issues involved in a particular accounting problem and to invite public comment. After further consideration, the discussion memorandum or invitation to comment is modified and an exposure draft is issued for additional public comment. Depending upon the reaction to the initial exposure draft, the Board may issue a new exposure draft for additional comment or, if it is satisfied at this point, may issue its final Statement, or may do neither. A majority vote of the seven members is required for a Statement to be issued.

The major types of pronouncements which are issued by the FASB are: (1) *statements of financial accounting standards,* which define GAAP; (2) *interpretations of financial accounting standards,* which modify or extend existing standards and which have the same authority as standards; (3) *statements of financial accounting concepts,* which set forth the fundamental objectives and concepts to be used by the FASB in developing financial accounting standards; and (4) *technical bulletins,* which provide guidance on financial accounting and reporting problems. To date, the FASB has issued over 150 statements, interpretations and technical bulletins.

Securities and Exchange Commission

The Securities and Exchange Commission (SEC) was established as an independent governmental regulatory agency with the authority to prescribe accounting practices and standards for the financial reporting of firms that offer securities for sale to the public through national (and interstate) securities exchanges, such as the New York Stock Exchange and the American Stock Exchange. The Securities Act of 1933 and the Securities Exchange Act of 1934 require that these companies file registration statements, periodic reports, and audited annual financial statements with the SEC.

The SEC has worked closely with the accounting profession in establishing and improving accounting practices, particularly in the area of financial reporting. The SEC has stated that the standards issued by the FASB are considered to have authoritative support, and that practices which are contrary to the positions taken by the FASB are considered to be lacking in such support.

Internal Revenue Service

Although in most cases the Internal Revenue Service (IRS) influences accounting in an indirect rather than a direct manner, the income tax code and regulations do affect accounting procedures and methods. The effects of income taxes on accounting information will be discussed throughout this text.

National Association of Accountants

The National Association of Accountants (NAA) is the professional association of accountants who are employed in industry, and as such, is concerned normally with matters which are primarily related to managerial accounting. Of course, many of these issues also have an effect on financial accounting matters as well. Like the AICPA, the NAA sponsors research in accounting and issues periodic reports to its membership.

Governmental Accounting Standards Board

The Governmental Accounting Standards Board (GASB), which was formed in 1984, is an independent organization in the private sector. *The GASB establishes standards for activities and transactions of state and local governmental entities.* The GASB's pronouncements are applicable to such entities and activities as utilities, authorities, hospitals, colleges and universities, and pension plans. If the GASB has not issued a pronouncement applicable to such entities or activities, the FASB's standards should be used.

Like the FASB, the GASB follows due process procedures to provide for broad public participation at all stages of the standard-setting process. The GASB, like the FASB, issues invitations to comment, discussion memorandums, exposure drafts, statements, interpretations, and technical bulletins.

Cost Accounting Standards Board

The Cost Accounting Standards Board (CASB) was the managerial accounting equivalent of the FASB. The CASB was charged with establishing uniform cost accounting standards for defense contractors awarded government contracts. The CASB was established in 1971, and the costs of research and investigation into defense contract problems were paid by the U.S. Government. Reports of the Board were presented to the Congress of the United States. Although its standards are still in effect, the CASB ceased to exist in 1980 when Congress failed to fund its operations.

American Accounting Association

The American Accounting Association (AAA) is concerned primarily with matters relating to accounting education. A sizable portion of its membership consists of accounting faculty of colleges and universities. Like the other professional organizations mentioned above, the AAA sponsors research in accounting and related matters and issues reports from time to time.

Congress

Congress also has involved itself directly in the rule-making process. In 1971, the APB adopted a rule concerning the accounting for the investment tax credit. At that time, the SEC stated its support for the APB's position. However, Congress then passed legislation that stated that no particular method of accounting for the investment tax credit is required. The APB subsequently rescinded its earlier pronouncement.

The brief descriptions which were included above are intended to provide a general indication of the major thrust and composition of these organizations. In many cases, there is considerable overlap in the objectives and even the membership of these groups. All of these organizations (with the possible exception of Congress) share the common objective of seeking to improve accounting practice and financial reporting on both a national and multi-national basis.

OPPORTUNITIES IN ACCOUNTING

The accounting profession in the United States has achieved a professional status that is comparable to that of both the legal and medical professions. Certified Public Accountants (CPAs) are accountants who have completed educational requirements specified by the state in which they are licensed and who have successfully completed the uniform CPA examination. Accountants are employed in a wide variety of positions; any organization, regardless of its purpose, that requires information to be recorded, processed, and communicated usually needs the services of an accountant.

CPAs, in large and small public accounting firms, render a wide variety of services to their clients on a professional basis, much as do attorneys. The services offered by CPA firms include: auditing—the conducting of examinations and rendering of professional opinions as to the fairness of the financial statements of organizations; taxes—tax planning and preparation of local, state, and federal tax returns; SEC work—assisting organizations in filings with the Securities and Exchange Commission; and management services—assisting in the design and installation of accounting systems and, in general, services of an advisory nature that do not fall under any one of the other categories mentioned above.

Many accountants are employed by industry and other profit and not-for-profit organizations. These accountants work in maintaining and improving the information systems of their organizations and are engaged in a wide variety of other tasks and duties.

Accountants also find employment in local, state, and federal government, ranging from small local municipal agencies to large federal organizations such as the Internal Revenue Service, Securities and Exchange Commission, and the General Accounting Office. It may interest the reader that special agents of the Federal Bureau of Investigation are often either trained attorneys or accountants.

At the turn of the present century there were fewer than 250 certified public accountants in the United States. Today there are more than 150,000 CPAs, and the accounting profession continues to grow at an astonishing rate. An indication that this growth is likely to continue is the increasing demand for accounting graduates reflected in the starting salaries paid to accounting graduates. Along these same lines it is interesting to note that presidents of large U.S. corporations more often have a background in accounting than in any other single functional area. Clearly, there is a future in accounting.

SUMMARY

The accounting profession has grown rapidly in recent years both in terms of the number of accountants demanded and employed and in terms of professional stature. Accounting is basically a process of reporting and communicating financial information to a variety of internal and external users. As more and more decisions are based on information obtained from accounting reports, the communication aspect of accounting is of particular significance.

Financial accounting is concerned primarily with providing financial information to users who are external to the firm. Managerial accounting provides necessary information to those individuals responsible for internal decision making. Information is typically provided to external users in the form of four basic financial statements: the balance sheet, the income statement, the statement of owners' equity, and the statement of changes in financial position.

Underlying all accounting practices are certain basic accounting concepts. The entity assumption, the going-concern concept, the monetary unit assumption, the historical cost concept, the stable dollar assumption, time period assumption, the consistency concept, the matching concept, and the materiality concept are among the most important accounting concepts. Once accounting principles based on these concepts are accepted and used by the accounting profession, they become authoritative and are referred to as "generally accepted accounting principles." Many groups influence the acceptance of accounting principles.

Chapter 1 has discussed certain of the basic accounting concepts and definitions that will form a framework for the more detailed explanations included in subsequent chapters.

KEY DEFINITIONS

Accounting Principles Board The Accounting Principles Board (APB) was formed in 1959 to replace the Committee on Accounting Procedures (CAP) as the primary agency responsible for establishing, reviewing and evaluating accounting principles. The APB was replaced in 1973 when criticisms of its structure and positions created the Financial Accounting Standards Board (FASB).

American Accounting Association The American Accounting Association (AAA) is an accounting organization which is primarily concerned with accounting education and research. Its membership consists of accounting faculty of colleges and universities as well as the practicing accountants.

American Institute of Certified Public Accountants The American Institute of Certified Public Accountants (AICPA) is the primary professional association of Certified Public Accountants (CPAs) in the United States. It is involved in research intended to improve accounting practices and procedures.

Balance sheet The balance sheet or statement of financial position is a general purpose financial report which presents the financial position of the firm as of a particular point in time.

Bookkeeping Bookkeeping is the actual recording of business transactions. It is a clerical function which may be done manually or electronically with the use of computers.

Committee on Accounting Procedure The Committee on Accounting Procedure (CAP) was established in 1939 by the AICPA for the role of establishing, reviewing, and evaluating accepted accounting principles. The CAP's successor in this role was the Accounting Principles Board (APB).

Comparability Comparability is the quality of information that enables users to identify similarities in and differences between two sets of economic phenomena.

Conservatism Conservatism is a prudent reaction to uncertainty to try to ensure that uncertainty and risks inherent in business situations are adequately considered.

Consistency concept This concept requires that once a firm adopts a particular accounting method for its use in recording a certain type of transaction, it should continue to use that method for all future transactions of the same category.

Corporation A corporation is an artificial being which has a legal identity that is separate and distinct from its owners or stockholders.

Cost Accounting Standards Board The CASB, which went out of existence in 1980, was the managerial accounting equivalent of the FASB. It was charged with establishing uniform cost accounting standards for defense contractors awarded government contracts. Its standards are still in effect.

Entity assumption This assumption is the basis for the distinction which is made between the entity and its owners. The entity is treated as a unit separate and distinct from its ownership and is accounted for as such.

Expenses Expenses are the costs which are incurred in the process of generating revenues.

Fidelity of accounting information Fidelity of accounting information is the correspondence between the information the accountant wishes to convey and the user's perception of the meaning of the information the accountant reports. The accountant and the user must have a mutual understanding as to certain basic concepts in order for the communication to be valid.

Financial accounting The segment of accounting primarily concerned with the needs of users who are external to the firm.

Financial Accounting Standards Board The Financial Accounting Standards Board is an independent board which conducts research and issues opinions as to the correct treatment and presentation of financial information. Its membership includes accountants from industry, government, education, and public accounting. It is the successor to the Accounting Principles Board of the AICPA.

Full disclosure concept The full disclosure concept requires that all information needed by the users of financial statements should be disclosed on an understandable form.

Going-concern concept This concept is the assumption made by the accountant that the business will operate indefinitely unless there is evidence to the contrary.

Governmental Accounting Standards Board The Governmental Accounting Standards Board (GASB) establishes standards for activities and transactions of state and local governmental entities.

Historical cost concept The historical cost concept is the assumption that the original acquisition cost of a resource, not its current market value nor replacement cost, is the basis to be used in accounting for the resources of an entity.

Income statement The income statement is a summary of the operations of a firm. It reports the income (or loss) of the company during a specified period of time.

Internal Revenue Service The Internal Revenue Service (IRS) is a government agency which is charged with the collection of taxes. The income tax code and regulations often affect the procedures and methods of accounting.

Managerial accounting The segment of accounting concerned with the needs of users who are internal to the firm.

Matching concept The matching concept requires the accountant to match the revenues earned during the accounting period with the expenses which were incurred to generate these revenues during this period.

Materiality concept This concept indicates that the accountant should be primarily concerned with those transactions which are of real significance to the users of his report. No specific value can be assigned to any transaction to determine materiality, but if the information would affect a financial statement user's decisions, then it is material. It is the magnitude of an omission or misstatement of accounting information that, in the light of surrounding circumstances, makes it probable that the judgment of a reasonable person relying on the information would have been changed or influenced by the omission or misstatement.

Monetary unit assumption This is the assumption made by the accountant that all transactions of the business can be recorded in terms of dollars.

National Association of Accountants The National Association of Accountants (NAA) is a professional association of industrial accountants which is concerned primarily with managerial accounting.

Partnership A partnership is a business owned by two or more persons who share profits or losses according to an agreement and who are personally liable for all of the debts of the business.

Proprietorship A proprietorship is a business owned by one person who is individually liable for all of the debts of the business.

Revenues Revenues are the proceeds received or to be received from the sale of goods or services by a business.

Securities and Exchange Commission The Securities and Exchange Commission (SEC) is a government regulatory agency which reviews the financial reporting practices of companies that offer securities for public sale through any national or interstate stock exchange. It works closely with the accounting profession to improve financial accounting practices.

Significance of accounting information Significance of accounting information is the relationship between the actual transactions of the company and the reports which summarize them. The accounting statements should disclose the events which occurred in a manner such that the user would reach the same decision based on the report that he would have made with firsthand information.

Stable dollar assumption This concept assumes that any fluctuation in the purchasing power of the dollar is not significant. For this reason, changes in the purchasing power of the dollar are not recognized in the accounts.

Statement of changes in financial position This statement indicates the sources from which the resources of a company were obtained and the uses which were made of these resources during an accounting period. It shows how the company's financial position has changed.

Statement of changes in owners' equity The statement of changes in owners' equity summarizes investments made by the owners, additions to equity from earnings, and withdrawals made by owners during the accounting period.

Time period assumption The time period assumption requires the preparation of financial statements at such intervals as a year or a quarter to meet users' needs on a timely basis.

Users of accounting information A user of accounting information is anyone who will read and analyze the financial statements in order to use the information contained therein to meet his own needs.

QUESTIONS

1. What is the purpose of accounting?

2. Is accounting useful for both profit and not-for-profit businesses? Explain.

3. Has the need for accounting (and accountants) increased in the United States since the turn of the century? Explain.

4. Who are some of the users of financial statements? Do their needs differ? Why?

5. Explain the similarities and differences between managerial accounting and financial accounting.

6. What are the basic financial statements issued by the typical business? (Briefly describe each statement.)

7. Why is the entity assumption necessary in accounting?

8. Discuss the relationship between the monetary concept, the historical cost concept, and the stable dollar assumption. Are these assumptions realistic?

9. Why have accountants adopted the consistency concept?

10. How can the accountant determine whether a particular item is material in amount?

11. What is the role of the Financial Accounting Standards Board in accounting?

12. Financial statements are prepared in accordance with "generally accepted accounting principles." What are "generally accepted accounting principles" and how are they determined?

13. If you were uncertain as to whether a particular procedure was in accordance with "generally accepted accounting principles," what would you do to find out?

14. What is meant by the term "certified public accountant (CPA)"? How does one become a CPA?

15. What is the purpose of financial reporting?

Learning Objectives

Chapter 2 discusses three of the major financial statements prepared by the accountant. Studying this chapter should enable you to:

1. Present and explain the accounting equation.

2. Identify the two basic sources of a firm's assets.

3. Discuss the purpose, format, and major classifications of the balance sheet.

4. Distinguish between current assets and fixed assets and give examples of each.

5. Discuss the purpose and major classifications of the income statement.

6. Analyze transactions as to the effect on balance sheet and income statement accounts.

7. Identify the basic purpose and format of the statement of capital.

Financial Statements

2

INTRODUCTION

Financial statements are the end product of the financial accounting process. The basic objective of the financial statements of a business is to provide the information which is required by various users for making economic decisions. As was indicated in Chapter 1, the basic accounting statements which are included in the accounting reports normally issued to users are the balance sheet, the income statement, the statement of capital, and the statement of changes in financial position. We will discuss the balance sheet, income statement, and statement of capital in this chapter. The statement of changes in financial position will be considered in Chapter 17.

THE BALANCE SHEET

The balance sheet or statement of financial position is the accounting statement which provides information regarding the financial position of the firm at a particular point in time. It includes information as to the assets, liabilities, and equities of the business as of a given date.

Assets are probable future economic benefits obtained or controlled by a particular entity as a result of past transactions or events.[1] They are the economic resources of the business. An asset is an economic right or a resource that will be of either present or future benefit to the firm. In general, assets are things of value that are owned by the business. The assets of a business may take various forms. For example, assets include: cash, merchandise held for sale to customers, land, buildings, and equipment. In other words, assets are the resources which are used by the business in its continuing operations.

At any point in time, the total of the assets of a business are, by definition, equal to the total of the sources of these assets. A business obtains its assets from two basic sources: its owners and its creditors. Creditors lend resources to the firm. These debts, referred to as liabilities, must be repaid at some specified future date. Liabilities may be defined as probable future sacrifices of economic benefits arising from present obligations of a particular entity to transfer assets or provide services to other entities in the future as a result of the past transactions or events.[2] Owners invest their personal resources in the firm. Investments by owners are increases in net assets of a particular enterprise resulting from transfers to it from other entities of something of value to obtain or increase ownership interests (or equity) in it. Assets are most commonly received as investments by owners, but that which is received may also include services or satisfaction or conversion of liabilities of the enterprise.[3] In other words, the investments of

---

[1] "Elements of Financial Statements of Business Enterprises," FASB Statement of Financial Accounting Concepts No. 3 (Stamford, Conn. FASB, 1980), p. xi.
[2] *Ibid.*
[3] *Ibid.*

owners in the firm and any profits retained in the business are its equity (or capital). Equity is the residual interest in the assets of an entity that remains after deducting its liabilities. In a business enterprise, the equity is the ownership interest.[4] Thus, the sources of a firm's assets are its liabilities and owner's equity.

The relationship among the assets, liabilities, and owners' equity of a business may be summarized by the accounting equation: Assets = Liabilities + Owners' Equity (A = L + OE). The concept expressed in this simple equation underlies the recording process of accounting and also serves as the basis of one of the principal financial statements, the balance sheet. In other words, the balance sheet includes a listing of the assets owned by the firm and the sources from which these assets were obtained, liabilities and owners' equity.

$$\frac{\text{Assets}}{\text{A}} = \frac{\text{Sources}}{\text{L + OE}}$$

The balance sheet or statement of financial position is a statement which reports the financial position of the firm at a particular point in time. The balance sheet discloses the three major categories included in the above equation: assets, liabilities, and owner's equity.

The accounting equation also indicates that the owners' equity is equal to the interest of the owners in the net assets (assets − liabilities) of the business. That is, by transposition, the accounting equation may be restated as follows:

$$A - L = OE$$

Transaction Analysis

A transaction is an event which takes place during the life of a business. In order to illustrate the process of recording transactions and the effect this has on the financial position of a business, we will review the transactions of a small service organization, Kilmer Contractors, during May 19x1, the initial month of its operations.

May 1. Bill Kilmer organized Kilmer Contractors and invested cash of $10,000 in the business.

This increase in the asset cash and the corresponding increase in the investment by the owner, referred to as capital, would be reflected in the balance sheet as follows:

	Assets	=	Liabilities	+	Owner's Equity
	Cash	=			Capital
May 1	$10,000	=			$10,000

---

[4] *Ibid.*

This transaction is an investment of funds in a business by its owner. The asset cash was received by the firm and the owner's equity or capital was increased. Note that the basic accounting equation balances.

May 2. The company purchased painting supplies, paying the $3,000 purchase price in cash.

The increase in supplies and the offsetting decrease in the cash of the business would be reflected in the balance sheet as follows:

	Assets			=	Liabilities	+	Owner's Equity
	Cash	+	Supplies	=			Capital
Balance	$10,000			=			$10,000
May 2	(3,000)		$3,000				
	$ 7,000	+	$3,000	=			$10,000

This transaction represents an exchange of one asset for another. The asset supplies was increased while the asset cash was decreased. Capital was not affected. The equation is still in balance.

May 5. Kilmer Contractors borrowed $2,000 from the Virginia National Bank.[5]

This increase in both assets (cash) and liabilities (notes payable) would affect the balance sheet as follows:

	Assets			=	Liabilities	+	Owner's Equity
					Note		
	Cash	+	Supplies	=	Payable	+	Capital
Balance	$7,000	+	$3,000	=			$10,000
May 5	2,000				$2,000		
	$9,000	+	$3,000	=	$2,000	+	$10,000

This transaction is the receipt of an asset, cash, in exchange for a liability, the promise to pay a creditor at some future time. It reflects the promise of the business to repay $2,000 at a future date in order to have cash on hand and available for use at this time. Again, capital is not affected; what has occurred is an exchange of a promise to pay the liability, notes payable, for the asset cash. The basic accounting equation remains in balance.

May 10. Kilmer signed a contract whereby he agreed to paint two houses sometime during the next few weeks. The customer paid the fee of $1,100 per house in advance.

---

[5] For purposes of illustration, it will be assumed that this is a non-interest bearing note.

This increase in cash and the corresponding increase in liabilities, unearned fees, would be reflected by the business as follows:

	Assets			=	Liabilities			+	Owner's Equity
	Cash	+	Supplies	=	Note Payable	+	Unearned Fees	+	Capital
Balance	$ 9,000	+	$3,000	=	$2,000			+	$10,000
May 10	2,200						$2,200		
	$11,200	+	$3,000	=	$2,000	+	$2,200	+	10,000

The company has agreed to paint two houses at a future date and has received its fee now, before it has done the work. The receipt of the $2,200 increases cash and the liability, unearned fees, by the same amount. Unearned fees is not a liability in the sense that the company will be required to repay the money. Rather, it represents an obligation on the part of Kilmer Contractors to perform a service at some future date. Capital is not affected by this transaction, and the accounting equation, A = L + OE, remains in balance.

May 12. Bill Kilmer, the owner, withdrew $1,000 from the business for his personal use.

This decrease in cash and the corresponding decrease in the owner's equity balance would be reflected in the balance sheet as follows:

	Assets			=	Liabilities			+	Owner's Equity
	Cash	+	Supplies	=	Note Payable	+	Unearned Fees	+	Capital
Balance	$11,200	+	$3,000	=	$2,000	+	$2,200	+	$10,000
May 12	(1,000)								(1,000)
	$10,200	+	$3,000	=	$2,000	+	$2,200	+	$ 9,000

This transaction represents a withdrawal of a portion of the owner's investment from the business. Cash and capital were both decreased by $1,000. The accounting equation is still in balance.

May 15. Kilmer Contractors repaid $500 of the $2,000 it borrowed from the Virginia National Bank.

This decrease in both cash and liabilities would affect the balance sheet as follows:

	Assets			=	Liabilities			+	Owner's Equity
	Cash	+	Supplies	=	Note Payable	+	Unearned Fees	+	Capital
Balance May 15	$10,200 (500)	+	$3,000	=	$2,000 (500)	+	$2,200	+	$9,000
	$ 9,700	+	$3,000	=	$1,500	+	$2,200	+	$9,000

This transaction is a reduction of both liabilities and assets. The business repaid $500 of the $2,000 it owed to the bank. Both cash and the note payable decreased by this amount. Capital is not affected and the accounting equation remains in balance. (Recall that it was assumed that this was a non-interest bearing note.)

The transactions of Kilmer Contractors for the first fifteen days of May are summarized in Illustration 1.

Illustration 1

Kilmer Contractors
Total Transactions
May 1 to May 15, 19x1

	Assets			=	Liabilities			+	Owner's Equity
	Cash	+	Supplies	=	Note Payable	+	Unearned Fees	+	Capital
May 1	$10,000								$10,000
May 2	(3,000)		$3,000						
May 5	2,000				$2,000				
May 10	2,200						$2,200		
May 12	(1,000)								(1,000)
May 15	(500)				(500)				
	$ 9,700	+	$3,000	=	$1,500	+	$2,200	+	$ 9,000

At this point in time, we will prepare a balance sheet for Kilmer Contractors. This balance sheet appears in Illustration 2.

Illustration 2

Kilmer Contractors
Balance Sheet
May 15, 19x1

Assets		Liabilities + Owner's Equity	
Cash	$ 9,700	Note Payable	$ 1,500
Supplies	3,000	Unearned Fees	2,200
		Capital	9,000
	$12,700		$12,700

The balance sheet example for Kilmer Contractors was overly simplified for purposes of illustration. Illustration 3 presents an actual balance sheet for General Motors and includes far more additional account titles and classifications. The reader should note that these classifications are not arbitrary distinctions made by the accountants who prepared the balance sheet. They represent generally followed classifications which are intended to assist the user of the balance sheet in analyzing and interpreting it for his use.

BALANCE SHEET CLASSIFICATIONS

The various classifications included in the balance sheet are intended to assist the user of the statement in acquiring as much information as possible concerning the business. The individual elements of the financial statements are the building blocks with which financial statements are constructed —the classes of items that financial statements comprise. The items included in financial statements represent in words and numbers certain enterprise resources, claims to those resources, and the effects of transactions and other events and circumstances that result in changes in those resources and claims.[6]

It might appear that if a firm desired to provide the user of its statements with the maximum information possible, it could supply him with a listing of all transactions which took place during the period so that the user could perform his own analysis. However, large firms routinely enter into hundreds of thousands or even millions of transactions during any given period. It is therefore highly unlikely that any user would have either sufficient time, the inclination, or the ability to analyze this type of listing. To simplify the analysis of financial statements, firms group similar items in

---

[6] "Elements of Financial Statements of Business Enterprises," *op.cit.*, p. xii.

Illustration 3

CONSOLIDATED BALANCE SHEET

December 31, 1985 and 1984 (Dollars in Millions Except Per Share Amounts)

ASSETS	1985	1984
Current Assets		
Cash	$ 179.1	$ 467.5
United States Government and other marketable securities and time deposits—at cost, which approximates market of $4,933.1 and $8,108.7	4,935.3	8,099.9
Total cash and marketable securities	5,114.4	8,567.4
Accounts and notes receivable (including GMAC and its subsidiaries—$4,038.7 and $3,868.5)—less allowances (Note 10)	7,282.0	7,357.9
Inventories (less allowances) (Note 1)	8,269.7	7,359.7
Contracts in process (less advances and progress payments of $2,525.3 in 1985) (Note 1)	1,453.8	—
Prepaid expenses	2,136.1	428.3
Total Current Assets	24,256.0	23,713.3
Equity in Net Assets of Nonconsolidated Subsidiaries and Associates (principally GMAC and its subsidiaries—Note 10)	5,718.5	4,603.0
Other Investments and Miscellaneous Assets—at cost (less allowances)	3,069.8	2,344.4
Common Stocks Held for the GM Incentive Program (Note 3)	190.2	144.2
Property		
Real estate, plants and equipment—at cost (Note 11)	47,267.1	39,354.1
Less accumulated depreciation (Note 11)	24,325.0	21,649.8
Net real estate, plants and equipment	22,942.1	17,704.3
Special tools—at cost (less amortization)	1,710.9	1,697.2
Total Property	24,653.0	19,401.5
Intangible Assets—at cost (less amortization) (Note 1)	5,945.3	1,938.5
Total Assets	$63,832.8	$52,144.9

Illustration 3 Continued:

LIABILITIES AND STOCKHOLDERS' EQUITY		
Current Liabilities		
Accounts payable (principally trade)	$ 7,322.2	$ 4,743.5
Loans payable (Note 13)	2,655.2	3,086.0
United States, foreign and other income taxes payable	243.1	618.9
Accrued liabilities and deferred income taxes (Note 12)	12,078.0	8,988.2
Total Current Liabilities	22,298.5	17,436.6
Long-Term Debt (Note 13)	2,500.2	2,417.4
Capitalized Leases (including GMAC and its subsidiaries—$76.1 and $113.2)	367.0	355.5
Other Liabilities (including GMAC and its subsidiaries—$300.0 in 1985 and 1984)	7,179.8	5,971.9
Deferred Credits (including investment tax credits—$1,328.8 and $1,259.9)	1,962.6	1,749.2
Stockholders' Equity (Notes 3, 4 and 14)		
Preferred stocks ($5.00 series, $169.3 and $169.8; $3.75 series, $81.4 and $85.8)	250.7	255.6
Common stocks:		
$1-2/3 par value common (issued, 318,853,315 and 317,504,133 shares)	531.4	529.2
Class E common (issued, 66,227,137 and 29,082,382 shares)	6.6	2.9
Class H common (issued, 65,495,316 shares in 1985)	6.6	—
Capital surplus (principally additional paid-in capital)	6,667.8	3,347.8
Net income retained for use in the business	22,606.6	20,796.6
Subtotal	30,069.7	24,932.1
Accumulated foreign currency translation and other adjustments (Note 1)	(545.0)	(717.8)
Total Stockholders' Equity	29,524.7	24,214.3
Total Liabilities and Stockholders' Equity	$63,832.8	$52,144.9

Reference should be made to notes on pages 28 through 38.

order to reduce the number of classifications which appear on the balance sheet. For example, a chain store may own many buildings of different sizes, at various locations and serving different functions, but instead of listing these assets separately, all buildings will normally be grouped and presented as a single amount on the balance sheet.

Assets

When assets are acquired by a business they are initially recorded at the cost of acquisition or original purchase price. This is true even if the business has paid only a portion of the initial cost in cash at the time of acquisition and owes the remaining balance to the seller of the asset.

Assets will vary somewhat in their characteristics such as their useful life in relationship to the business' operating cycle, physical attributes, and frequency of use. Accountants attempt to describe certain of the relevant characteristics of assets on the balance sheet by the use of general classifications such as current assets, long-term (or fixed) assets, and other assets. Within these broad categories there are also several sub-classifications. The usual ordering of assets on the balance sheet is in terms of liquidity—the order in which the assets would normally be converted into cash or used up.

Current Assets. Generally, current assets include cash and other assets which are expected to be converted into cash, sold, or used in operations or production during the current accounting period. The accounting period is usually considered to be one year for most businesses. The general sub-classifications of current assets normally found in the balance sheet include cash, marketable securities, accounts receivable, inventories, and prepaid expenses. These individual asset categories are briefly described below.

Cash. Cash includes all cash which is immediately available for use in the business including cash on hand, in cash registers, and in checking accounts. Cash is discussed in detail in Chapter 7.

Marketable Securities. Marketable securities are temporary investments in stocks, bonds, and other securities which are readily salable and which management intends to hold only for a relatively short period of time. Marketable securities are discussed in Chapter 15.

Receivables. The accounts receivable balance represents the amount which is owed to the business by its customers. If a business has a significant amount of receivables from sources other than its normal trade customers, the receivables from customers are normally classified as trade accounts receivable and the amounts owed by others are classified as other accounts receivable.

A balance sheet may also include notes receivable. Notes receivable are the receivables (from customers or others) for which the business has received written documentation of the debtors' intent to pay. Both accounts receivable and notes receivable are discussed in Chapter 8.

Inventories. Inventories represent the cost of goods or materials which are held for sale to customers in the ordinary course of business, in the process of production for such sale, or to be used in the production of goods or services to be available for sale at some future date. Inventories are described in Chapter 9.

Prepaid Expenses. Prepaid expenses represent expenditures which were made in either the current or a prior period and which will provide benefits to the firm at some future time. For example, a fire insurance policy which protects the assets of a firm for a three-year period may be purchased during the current year. Although the policy was paid for and a portion of the protection used during the current year, the firm benefits from the insurance protection in future years as well. Therefore, the portion of the cost of the policy which is applicable to future years would be considered a prepaid expense at the end of the current year.

Fixed Assets. Fixed or long-term assets are those assets which are acquired for use in the business rather than for resale to customers. They are assets from which the business expects to receive benefits over a number of future accounting periods. Since fixed assets are used in the operations of the firm, and benefits are derived from this use or availability, the cost of these assets is considered an expense of those periods which benefit from their use.

The actual classifications which may be included in the balance sheet under the fixed asset caption will, of course, vary depending upon the type of business and the nature of its operations. The accounting for fixed assets is described in Chapters 10 and 11.

Other Assets. The classification, other assets, includes those assets which are not appropriately classified under either the current or the fixed asset categories described above. This classification may include both tangible and intangible assets. Tangible assets are those that have *physical* substance, such as land held for investment purposes. Intangibles are assets *without* physical substance, such as patents, copyrights, goodwill, etc. This distinction will be discussed in detail in Chapters 10 and 11.

Liabilities

Liabilities are debts. They represent claims of creditors against the assets of the business. Creditors have a prior legal claim over the owners of the business. In the event a business is liquidated, creditors will be paid the amounts owed them before any payments are made to owners. Creditors are, of course, concerned with the ability of the business to repay its debts. In certain instances, creditors may earn interest on the amount due them. Normally, a liability has a maturity or due date at which time it must be satisfied.

Liabilities, just as assets, fall into several descriptive categories. The two basic classifications which are usually employed in the balance sheet are current liabilities and long-term liabilities. Both of these general classes may also have sub-classifications.

Current Liabilities. Current liabilities include those obligations for which settlement is expected to require the use of current assets or the origination of other current liabilities. Examples of current liabilities include accounts payable, notes payable, taxes payable, and unearned revenues. These are described in the following paragraphs.

Accounts Payable. Accounts payable are claims of vendors who sell goods and services to the company on a credit basis. Accounts payable are usually not evidenced by a formal, written document such as is the case with a note.

Notes Payable. Notes payable normally arise from borrowing or, on occasion, from purchases, and are evidenced by a written document. Notes payable may or may not be interest bearing. Notes usually have a fixed or determinable due date.

Taxes Payable. This liability includes any local, state, and federal taxes which are owed by the business at the end of the accounting period but are payable in the next period.

Unearned Revenues. Unearned revenues are amounts collected from customers for goods which have not been shipped or services which have not yet been performed.

Long-Term Liabilities. Long-term liabilities generally represent claims which will be paid or satisfied in a future accounting period (or periods). Examples of long-term liabilities are bonds payable and mortgages payable.

Owners' Equity

Owners' equity, also referred to as capital, represents the claims of the owners against the net assets of the firm. Owners normally assume risks which are greater than those of creditors since the return on investment to the owners is usually undefined. In the event of bankruptcy, claims of creditors take priority over those of owners and must be satisfied first. After all creditors have been paid, any assets that remain will then be available to the owners of the firm.

Accounting for owners' equity is influenced by the legal status of the company—the form of its organization. The legal forms of business recognized and used most extensively in the United States are the sole proprietorship, the partnership, and the corporation. There are certain legal differences associated with these types of organizations which will be considered in Chapters 13 and 14. Basically, the owners' equity of a business is normally divided into two major classifications based on the source of the equity: direct investments made by the owner and profits retained in the business. Owners' equity accounts will be discussed in detail in later chapters.

THE INCOME STATEMENT

The income statement or operating statement provides data concerning the results of operations of the firm for a specific period of time, usually a year. The results of the operations of a business are determined by its revenues, expenses, and the resulting net income.

Revenues and expenses are defined as follows:

> Revenues are inflows or other enhancements of assets of an entity or settlements of its liabilities (or a combination of both) during a period from delivering or producing goods, rendering services, or other activities that constitute the entity's ongoing major or central operations.[7]
>
> Expenses are outflows or other using up of assets or incurrences of liabilities (or a combination of both) during a period from delivering or producing goods, rendering services, or carrying out other activities that constitute the entity's ongoing major or central operations.[8]

Put simply, revenues are the gross increases in assets or gross decreases in liabilities which are recognized and result from the sale of either goods or services. Expenses are gross decreases in assets or gross increases in liabilities that occur as a result of the operations of a business. Net income is the excess of revenues over the related expenses for an accounting period. The revenues, expenses, and the resulting net income for a period are presented in the firm's income statement.

The usual accounting concept of income is based on determining, as objectively as possible, the income earned during a particular accounting period by deducting the expenses which were incurred from the revenues earned. Revenues are the proceeds received from the sale of goods and the rendering of services. Expenses are the costs which are incurred in the process of generating revenues. The accounting concept of income assumes that various rules and principles will be followed. These principles require the accountant to exercise his professional judgment in their application since the accounting concept of income measurement stresses the fair determination of income. The reader should note that fair presentation of income does not mean precise presentation. Accounting is an estimating process that requires the accountant to view transactions as objectively as possible in determining both the financial position of a firm and its income for the period.

Since the income statement presents the results of operations for an accounting period, information included in this statement is usually considered to be among the most important data provided by the accountant. This is because profitability is a major concern of those interested in the economic activities of an enterprise.

Transaction Analysis

The operations of Kilmer Contractors for the first fifteen days of May, 19x1, were analyzed earlier. None of the transactions which occurred during this period were relevant to the income statement since they affected neither

---

[7] *Ibid.*
[8] *Ibid.*

the revenues earned nor the expenses incurred. We will now follow the activities for the remainder of May to see how revenue and expense transactions affect *both* the income statement and the balance sheet. The balance sheet of Kilmer Contractors as of May 15, 19x1 was:

Kilmer Contractors
Balance Sheet
May 15, 19x1

ASSETS		LIABILITIES AND OWNER'S EQUITY	
Cash	$ 9,700	Note payable	$ 1,500
Supplies	3,000	Unearned fees	2,200
		Capital	9,000
	$12,700		$12,700

This balance sheet is the starting point for the continuation of our example. Before proceeding, however, certain fundamental relationships should be reexamined. Recall that all assets are obtained from two basic sources, creditors and owners. At this point, we are concerned with the latter, the assets contributed by owners.

Owners may contribute assets either: (1) directly, that is, by investment; or (2) indirectly, by allowing the *income* earned by the firm to remain with the business and not withdrawing it for their personal use. In other words, just as a direct investment made by the owner increases his equity, the income earned by the firm also increases both the assets and the owners' equity of the firm. Since income is the excess of revenues over expenses (R − E), the basic accounting equation expressed earlier in the chapter may be expanded and restated for purposes of illustration as follows:

$$\text{Assets} = \text{Liabilities} + \text{Owners' Equity} + \text{Revenue} - \text{Expense}$$

$$A = L + OE + R - E$$

Keep in mind that this restatement is made for purposes of illustration only and does not really change either the substance or the meaning of the equation itself. It merely emphasizes the fact that one way in which the owners' equity of a business may be increased is by income—that is, revenues less expenses. Nothing else is changed. Now let us return to the Kilmer Contractors example.

May 17. Kilmer Contractors painted its first house and billed and collected cash of $700 from the customer.

This transaction was a sale of services for cash. It would affect Kilmer Contractors as follows:

	Assets			=	Liabilities			+	Owner's Equity		
	Cash	+	Supplies	=	Note Payable	+	Unearned Fees	+	Capital	+	Revenue (Expense)
Balance May 17	$9,700	+	$3,000	=	$1,500	+	$2,200	+	$9,000		
	700										$700
	$10,400	+	$3,000	=	$1,500	+	$2,200	+	$9,000	+	$700

This transaction reflects the fact that the firm has begun to earn revenue. Cash was received and the owner's equity of the business was increased by the amount of the revenue earned, $700. The basic accounting equation is still in balance.

May 19. Kilmer Contractors painted a second house and billed (but did not collect) its fee of $900.

This transaction was a sale of services to a customer on a credit basis. It would affect the business as indicated below:

	Assets					=	Liabilities			+	Owner's Equity		
	Cash	+	Accounts Receivable	+	Supplies	=	Note Payable	+	Unearned Fees	+	Capital	+	Revenue (Expense)
Balance May 19	$10,400			+	$3,000	=	$1,500	+	$2,200	+	$9,000	+	$ 700
			$900										900
	$10,400	+	$900	+	$3,000	=	$1,500	+	$2,200	+	$9,000	+	$1,600

Again, this transaction records the revenue earned by the firm in painting a customer's house. Unlike the previous transaction, however, cash was not received. The customer was billed for the service and will pay Kilmer Contractors at some future date. Accounts receivable have increased and owner's equity (revenue) has increased by $900, the fee which was charged for painting the house. This transaction illustrates the very important point that revenue is recorded as it is earned, not necessarily as cash is received. This concept reflects the *accrual* basis of accounting.

May 25. Kilmer paid his employees salaries of $400.

This transaction was the payment of an expense in cash. It would affect Kilmer Contractors as follows:

	Assets					=	Liabilities			+	Owner's Equity		
	Cash	+	Accounts Receivable	+	Supplies	=	Note Payable	+	Unearned Fees	+	Capital	+	Revenue (Expense)
Balance	$10,400	+	$900	+	$3,000	=	$1,500	+	$2,200	+	$9,000	+	$1,600
May 25	(400)												(400)
	$10,000	+	$900	+	$3,000	=	$1,500	+	$2,200	+	$9,000	+	$1,200

Expenses of $400 were incurred and paid in cash. This transaction reduces both cash and owner's equity. The reduction in owner's equity is due to the fact that an expense has been incurred, thereby reducing income. (Remember that revenues less expenses equals income.) The accounting equation is still in balance.

May 31. Kilmer Contractors painted one of the two houses contracted for on May 10.

By painting one of the two houses, Kilmer Contractors has partially satisfied a non-cash liability by the rendering of services and therefore earned income. This transaction would be reflected as follows:

	Assets					=	Liabilities			+	Owner's Equity		
	Cash	+	Accounts Receivable	+	Supplies	=	Note Payable	+	Unearned Fees	+	Capital	+	Revenue (Expense)
Balance	$10,000	+	$900	+	$3,000	=	$1,500	+	$2,200	+	$9,000	+	$1,200
May 31									(1,100)				1,100
	$10,000	+	$900	+	$3,000	=	$1,500	+	$1,100	+	$9,000	+	$2,300

On May 10, Kilmer signed a contract to paint two houses and received his fee of $1,100 per house in advance. No income was earned at the point the cash was received because no work had been done at that time. Kilmer Contractors had an obligation to paint the two houses at some future date. This was a liability to perform services, which was previously recorded as unearned fees. Now one of the two houses contracted for has been painted and that portion of the income has been earned. The liability, unearned fees, has been reduced by $1,100 and the income for the current period has been increased by the same amount. These facts require that the statements be adjusted in order to reflect the current status of the contract. Again, this transaction emphasizes the point that income is recorded as it is earned, *not* as cash is received. The accounting equation remains in balance.

May 31. The unused painting supplies on hand at this date had an original cost of $2,000.

The facts of this transaction indicate that an expense has been incurred and should be recorded. It will affect Kilmer Contractors as indicated below:

	Assets						=	Liabilities			+	Owner's Equity		
	Cash	+	Accounts Receivable	+	Supplies	=		Note Payable	+	Unearned Fees	+	Capital	+	Revenue (Expense)
Balance May 31	$10,000	+	$900	+	$3,000 (1,000)	=		$1,500	+	$1,100	+	$9,000	+	$2,300 (1,000)
	$10,000	+	$900	+	$2,000	=		$1,500	+	$1,100	+	$9,000	+	$1,300

During the month of May, Kilmer Contractors used supplies that had an original cost of $1,000. This amount was determined by subtracting the $2,000 cost of the supplies which were on hand at May 31 from the $3,000 total cost of supplies available for use (that is, the supplies on hand at the beginning of the month plus the supplies purchased during the month). As in the previous May 31 transaction, an adjustment is required. The asset, supplies, was decreased by $1,000 (the cost of the supplies used) from $3,000 (the total supplies available for use during the month of May) to $2,000 (the cost of supplies on hand at May 31). This transaction reflects the fact that expenses, like revenues, are recorded as they are incurred or used rather than when cash is disbursed. The accounting equation remains in balance.

All of the transactions of Kilmer Contractors for the month of May are summarized as follows:

Kilmer Contractors
All Transactions
For the Month of May, 19x1

	Assets			=	Liabilities			+	Owner's Equity	
	Cash	+ Accounts Receivable	+ Supplies	=	Note Payable	+ Unearned Fees		+	Capital	+ Revenue (Expense)
May 1	$10,000								$10,000	
May 2	(3,000)		$3,000							
May 5	2,000				$2,000					
May 10	2,200					$2,200				
May 12	(1,000)								(1,000)	
May 15	(500)				(500)					
	$ 9,700	+ $ 0	+ $3,000	=	$1,500	+ $2,200		+	$ 9,000	+ $ 0
May 17	700									700
May 19		900								900
May 25	(400)									(400)
May 31						(1,100)				1,100
May 31			(1,000)							(1,000)
	$10,000	+ $900	+ $2,000	=	$1,500	+ $1,100		+	$ 9,000	+ $1,300

We are now in a position to prepare a balance sheet and an income statement for Kilmer Contractors. The balance sheet would be as follows:

Kilmer Contractors
Balance Sheet
May 31, 19x1

Assets		Liabilities and Owner's Equity	
Cash	$10,000	Note payable	$ 1,500
Accounts receivable	900	Unearned fees	1,100
Supplies	2,000	Capital	10,300
	$12,900		$12,900

The income statement for the month of May would appear as follows:

Kilmer Contractors
Income Statement
For the Month Ended May 31, 19x1

Revenue..............................		$2,700
Less: Expenses:		
Supplies used.................	$1,000	
Salaries.....................	400	
Total Expenses..............		1,400
Income................................		$1,300

The revenues reported in the income statement include $700 earned by painting the house on May 17, $900 earned on May 19 by painting a second house, and $1,100 earned by painting one of the two houses contracted for on May 10 ($700 + $900 + $1,100 = $2,700). The expenses of $1,400 include the salaries of $400 paid to Kilmer Contractors' employees on May 25 and the cost of the painting supplies used during the month of May. The cost of the supplies used was determined by subtracting the cost of the supplies on hand at May 31, $2,000, from the $3,000 cost of the supplies which were available for use during the month ($3,000 − $2,000 = $1,000). Again, note that revenues are recorded as they are earned and expenses are recorded as they are incurred, not necessarily as cash is either paid or received. As previously indicated, this practice is referred to as the accrual basis of accounting.

The income for the month is the difference between the total revenues earned ($2,700) and the total of the expenses ($1,400) which were incurred in order to generate these revenues ($2,700 − $1,400 = $1,300). At the end of the period, this income is added to the owners' equity account.

INCOME STATEMENT CLASSIFICATIONS

As was the case with the balance sheet, classifications which appear in the income statement are intended to be descriptive, functional categories of revenues and expenses. There are many different formats employed for income statements. Variations among industries are substantial and, to compound this problem, variations among firms in the same industry can also be significant. Consequently, the classifications which are used in the income statement will be discussed in detail in later chapters of this text.

STATEMENT OF CAPITAL

At this point, it might be helpful to examine the changes between the balance sheet of May 15 and that of May 31 in order to fully understand the relationship between the income statement and the balance sheet. Balance sheets at May 15 and May 31 are reported in a comparative format below:

Kilmer Contractors
Comparative Balance Sheets

	May 15	May 31	Change
ASSETS			
Cash	$ 9,700	$10,000	$ 300
Accounts receivable	0	900	900
Supplies	3,000	2,000	(1,000)
	$12,700	$12,900	$ 200
LIABILITIES AND OWNER'S EQUITY			
Note payable	$ 1,500	$ 1,500	$ 0
Unearned fees	2,200	1,100	(1,100)
Capital	9,000	10,300	1,300
	$12,700	$12,900	$ 200

Each change in the comparative balance sheets can be explained by the transactions that affected the particular asset, liability, or the owners' equity. (These were summarized previously.)

The change in owner's equity is particularly important because it represents the net increase or decrease in the owner's investment in the firm. This change can be explained by the transactions which occurred on May 17, 19, 25, and the two adjustments which were made on May 31. These same transactions are the ones which appear in a summarized form in the income statement. In other words, the change in capital or owner's equity which took place during the period May 15 to 31 is due to the earnings of the company. These changes in owner's equity are included in a statement of capital (referred to as a statement of retained earnings for a corporation). The statement of capital reports the details of the equity of the owners in the business. Capital is equal to the direct investments made by the owners plus the earnings of the business and less any withdrawals made by owners.

> Withdrawals or distributions to owners are decreases in net assets of a particular enterprise resulting from transfering assets, rendering services, or incurring liabilities by the enterprise to owners. Distributions to owners decrease ownership interests (or equity) in an enterprise.[9]

---

[9] *Ibid.*

Note that the statement of capital for Kilmer Contractors, which covers the entire month of May, includes the investment made by Kilmer on May 1 and the withdrawal made on May 12. In other words, it summarizes all of the transactions which affected owner's equity during the month of May.

A statement of capital for Kilmer Contractors is presented below:

Kilmer Contractors
Statement of Capital
For the Month Ending May 31, 19x1

Capital at May 1, 19x1...................		$ 0
Add:		
Investment.......................	$10,000	
Income for May..................	1,300	11,300
Deduct:		
Withdrawal.....................		(1,000)
Capital at May 31, 19x1.................		$10,300

As indicated above, this statement of capital indicates how and why the owner's equity of Kilmer Contractors changed during the month of May.

The balance sheet, income statement, and statement of capital presented above were deliberately kept brief and simple for purposes of illustration. They do, however, illustrate the basic principles and procedures which are followed in the preparation of financial statements. An income statement for General Motors is presented in the following example.

SUMMARY

The balance sheet, income statement, and statement of capital are three of the basic accounting statements that provide data to various external users to be used in making economic decisions. These and other financial statements are the end products of the accountant's work. Although companies may vary somewhat in the exact detail and format of the data provided, all companies will include essentially the same type of information in their financial statements.

The balance sheet reflects the financial position of a firm at a particular point in time by providing information regarding the economic resources (assets) of the firm and the sources of these resources (liabilities and owners' equity). The format of the balance sheet reflects the basic accounting equation: Assets = Liabilities + Owners' Equity. By convention, the assets of the firm are generally presented on the balance sheet in the order of their

STATEMENT OF CONSOLIDATED INCOME

For the Years Ended December 31, 1985, 1984 and 1983 (Dollars in Millions Except Per Share Amounts)

	1985	1984	1983
Net Sales and Revenues (Notes 1 and 2)			
Manufactured products	$95,268.4	$83,699.7	$74,581.6
Computer systems services	1,103.3	190.2	—
Total Net Sales and Revenues	96,371.7	83,889.9	74,581.6
Costs and Expenses			
Cost of sales and other operating charges, exclusive of items listed below	81,654.6	70,217.9	60,718.8
Selling, general and administrative expenses	4,294.2	4,003.0	3,234.0
Depreciation of real estate, plants and equipment	2,777.9	2,663.2	2,569.7
Amortization of special tools	3,083.3	2,236.7	2,549.9
Amortization of intangible assets (Note 1)	347.3	69.1	.8
Total Costs and Expenses	92,157.3	79,189.9	69,073.2
Operating Income	4,214.4	4,700.0	5,508.4
Other income less income deductions—net (Note 6)	1,299.2	1,713.5	815.8
Interest expense (Note 1)	(892.3)	(909.2)	(1,352.7)
Income before Income Taxes	4,621.3	5,504.3	4,971.5
United States, foreign and other income taxes (Note 8)	1,630.3	1,805.1	2,223.8
Income after Income Taxes	2,991.0	3,699.2	2,747.7
Equity in earnings of nonconsolidated subsidiaries and associates (dividends received amounted to $100.5 in 1985, $706.1 in 1984 and $757.3 in 1983)	1,008.0	817.3	982.5
Net Income	3,999.0	4,516.5	3,730.2
Dividends on preferred stocks	11.6	12.5	12.9
Earnings on Common Stocks	$ 3,987.4	$ 4,504.0	$ 3,717.3
Earnings attributable to:			
$1-2/3 par value common stock	$ 3,883.6	$ 4,498.3	$ 3,717.3
Class E common stock (issued in 1984)	$ 103.8	$ 5.7	—
Average number of shares of common stocks outstanding (in millions):			
$1-2/3 par value common	316.3	315.3	313.9
Class E common (issued in 1984)*	66.5	36.3	—
Earnings Per Share Attributable to (Note 9):			
$1-2/3 par value common stock	$12.28	$14.27	$11.84
Class E common stock (issued in 1984)*	$1.57	$0.16	—

Reference should be made to notes on pages 28 through 38. Certain amounts for 1984 and 1983 have been reclassified to conform with 1985 classifications.
Earnings and earnings per share attributable to common stocks have been restated to reflect the Class E common stock amendment approved by the stockholders in December 1985.
*Adjusted to reflect the two-for-one stock split in the form of a 100% stock dividend distributed on June 10, 1985.

liquidity. The usual subcategories include current assets, fixed assets, and other assets. Similarly, the liabilities (or debts) of the firm are generally subdivided into current and long-term liabilities. The owners' equity section of the balance sheet contains information regarding the direct investment of the owners as well as the income earned by the firm and not withdrawn by the owners.

The income statement is of particular importance to many users of financial statements because it provides information regarding the results of operations of the firm for a specified period of time, usually a year. Only those transactions involving revenues (the proceeds received from the sale of goods and the rendering of services) and expenses (the costs incurred in the process of generating revenues) will be reflected on the income statement. Net income is the excess of revenues over related expenses for an accounting period.

The statement of capital presents a summary of the transactions that affected owners' equity in a given time period. Any change in owners' equity that occurred in that time period will be reflected and explained in the statement of capital.

This chapter has introduced and discussed three of the basic financial statements that are the end products of the accountant's work. The next two chapters will present discussions regarding the process by which these statements are obtained.

KEY DEFINITIONS

Accounting equation or dual-aspect concept The accounting equation may be expressed as follows: *assets = sources of assets* or *assets = liabilities + owners' equity*.

Accounting cycle The length of the accounting or operating cycle of any company is the period of time required for the company to acquire the basic resources to produce, manufacture goods, receive purchase orders, ship goods, and collect cash from the sale. This cycle depends on many factors and could vary from a short period of time for a company in the grocery industry to a long period of time for a company in the liquor industry.

Accounting period The accounting period is the longer of one year or one accounting cycle.

Accounts payable Accounts payable represent amounts the company owes to its creditors for purchases of goods or services in the ordinary course of business.

Accounts receivable Accounts receivable represent the amounts owed by customers to the company for goods or services which were sold in the ordinary course of business,

Assets Assets are probable future economic benefits obtained or controlled by a particular entity as a result of past transactions or events. An asset is something of value owned by the business.

Cash Cash is any medium of exchange which is readily accepted and used for transactions. Besides currency or demand deposits, cash usually includes certain negotiable instruments, such as customers' checks.

Current assets Current assets include cash and other assets which are expected to be converted into cash, sold, or used in operations or production during the current accounting period.

Current liabilities Current liabilities include those obligations for which settlement is expected to require the use of current assets or the creation of other current liabilities.

Elements of Financial Statements Elements of financial statements are the building blocks with which financial statements are constructed—the classes of items that financial statements comprise. The items in financial statements represent in words and numbers certain enterprise resources, claims to those resources, and the effects of transactions and other events and circumstances that result in changes in those resources and claims.

Equity Equity is the residual interest in the assets of an entity that remains after deducting its liabilities. In a business enterprise, the equity is the ownership interest.

Expenses Expenses are outflows or other using up of assets or incurrences of liabilities (or a combination of both) during a period from delivering or producing goods, rendering services, or carrying out other activities that constitute the entity's ongoing major or central operations.

Fixed assets Fixed or long-term assets are those assets which are acquired for use in the continuing operations of a business over a number of accounting periods rather than for resale to customers.

Intangibles Intangibles are assets without physical substance, such as patents.

Inventory Inventories include materials which are used in production, goods which are in the process of production, and finished products held for sale to customers.

Investments by owners Investments by owners are increases in net assets of a particular enterprise resulting from transfers to it from other entities of something of value to obtain or increase ownership interests (or equity) in it. Assets are most commonly received as investments by owners, but that which is received may also include services or satisfaction or conversion of liabilities of the enterprise.

Liabilities Liabilities are probable future sacrifices of economic benefits arising from present obligations of a particular entity to transfer assets or provide services to other entities in the future as a result of past transactions or events. Liabilities represent claims of creditors against the assets of a business.

Liquidity Liquidity normally refers to the order in which assets would be converted into cash or used up.

Long-term liabilities Long-term liabilities generally represent claims which will be paid or satisfied in a future accounting period.

Marketable securities Marketable securities are temporary investments in stocks, bonds, and other securities which are readily salable and which management intends to sell within a relatively short period of time.

Net income Net income is the excess of revenues earned over the related expenses incurred for an accounting period.

Notes payable Notes payable normally arise from borrowing and are evidenced by a written document or formal promise to pay.

Owners' equity Owners' equity, also referred to as net worth or capital, represents claims against the assets by the owners of the business. The total owners' equity represents the amount that the owners have invested in the business including any income which may have been retained in the business since its inception. See also equity, above.

Owners' withdrawals Distributions to owners are decreases in net assets of a particular enterprise resulting from transfering assets, rendering services, or incurring liabilities by the enterprise to owners. Distributions to owners decrease ownership interests (or equity) in an enterprise. Owners' withdrawals are the removal from the business of cash or other assets by the owners of that business.

Prepaid expenses Prepaid expenses represent expenditures which were made in either the current or a prior period and which will provide benefits to the firm at some future time.

Revenues Revenues are inflows or other enhancements of assets of an entity or settlements of its liabilities (or a combination of both) during a period from delivering or producing goods, rendering services, or other activities that constitute the entity's ongoing major or central operations.

Tangible assets Tangible assets are those assets that have physical substance.

Transactions Transactions are events which occur during the life of a business.

Unearned revenues Unearned revenues are amounts collected from customers for goods which have not been shipped or services which have not yet been performed.

QUESTIONS

1. What are the main sources of assets for a company? Why does each source provide assets?
2. A = L + OE expresses what accounting concept? Explain the concept.
3. What is a transaction?
4. What is an asset? Distinguish between current and long-term assets.
5. What is a liability? Distinguish between current and long-term liabilities.
6. Explain the difference between liabilities and owners' equity.
7. What does the balance in the capital account represent?
8. What are some advantages of preparing a balance sheet?
9. What periods of time are covered by the income statement, the statement of capital, and the balance sheet? How is this recorded in the headings of the statements?
10. What is the relationship between the balance sheet and the income statement at the end of the accounting period?

EXERCISES

11. Using these abbreviations, classify each of the following account titles as to what section of the balance sheet they would appear in.

    1. CA — Current assets
    2. FA — Fixed assets
    3. OA — Other assets
    4. CL — Current liabilities
    5. LTL — Long-term liabilities
    6. OE — Owners' equity

CA	Cash	CL	Taxes payable
___	Capital	___	Inventory
___	Note payable	___	Wages payable
___	Prepaid insurance	___	Accounts payable
___	Accounts receivable	CA	Marketable securities
FA	Plant and equipment	FA	Land
OA	Investments	___	Goodwill
OA	Patents	CL	Interest payable

12. Fill in the missing amounts:

	Company Allen	Company Barr
Assets — January 1, 19x1	$120	(d)
Liabilities — January 1, 19x1	80	$ 55
Owner's equity — January 1, 19x1	(a)	95
Assets — December 31, 19x1	130	(e)
Liabilities — December 31, 19x1	(b)	70
Owner's equity — December 31, 19x1	(c)	120
Revenues in 19x1	15	(f)
Expenses in 19x1	19	24

13. Give an example of a transaction which will:

a. Increase an asset and increase owners' equity.
b. Increase an asset and increase a liability.
c. Increase one asset and decrease another asset.
d. Decrease an asset and decrease owners' equity.
e. Decrease an asset and decrease a liability.

14. Given the following information, answer the questions below:

Revenue, 19x1	$24,000
Liabilities — December 31, 19x1	25,000
Investments by owner, 19x1	4,000
Withdrawals, 19x1	12,000
Owners' equity — January 1, 19x1	27,000
Owners' equity — December 31, 19x1	35,000

a. What are the Total Assets on December 31, 19x1?
b. What is Net Income for the year?
c. What is Total Expense for 19x1?

15. Fill in the missing figures in the information below:

	19x1	19x2	19x3
Assets — January 1	$100,000	$120,000	(f)
Liabilities — January 1	60,000	(c)	$72,000
Owners' equity — January 1	(a)	(d)	75,000
Withdrawals	20,000	15,000	17,000
Investments by owners	18,000	16,000	0
Owners' equity — December 31	(b)	(e)	57,000
Income (loss)	20,000	16,000	(g)

16. For each transaction listed below, indicate the effect on the total assets, total liabilities, and owners' equity of the business. Identify the effect of each transaction by using a (+) for an increase, a (−) for a decrease and a (0) for no effect.

		Assets	Liabilities	Owners' Equity
a.	The owner invested cash in the business	(+)	(0)	(+)
b.	Purchased a building for cash	( )	( )	( )
c.	Borrowed cash from the bank	(+)	(+)	(0)
d.	Purchased equipment on credit	( )	(+)	( )
e.	Provided a service and collected cash	(+)	(0)	(+)
f.	Paid wages in cash to employees	(−)	(0)	(−)
g.	Paid a bank loan	(−)	(−)	(0)

17. Classify each of the following items as to whether they would be found on the balance sheet (B), income statement (I), or statement of capital (C).

_____	Cash	_____	Insurance expense
_____	Revenue	_____	Building
_____	Wages payable	_____	Supplies
_____	Withdrawal	_____	Rental expense
_____	Accounts payable	_____	Rental income
_____	Goodwill	_____	Accounts receivable
_____	Unearned fees	_____	Bonds payable
_____	Salary expense	_____	Prepaid insurance

18. Fill in the missing amounts:

Lee Company
Balance Sheet
June 30, 19x1

Assets		Liabilities and Owner's Equity	
Cash	$ 12,000	Accounts payable	$33,000
Marketable securities	31,000	Taxes payable	(b) 11,000
Accounts receivable	7,000	Bonds payable	76,000
Inventory	44,000	Total Liabilities	$120,000
Buildings	193,000		242,000
Land	75,000	Capital	(c)
	(a)		362,000 (d)
	362 —		

19. Longhorn Company had sales revenue of $5,700 for the month of October 19x1. Total expenses incurred during this period were $2,900; including rent for the store of $400; salaries amounting to $900; and the cost of the supplies used of $1,600. Prepare an income statement for the month.

20. Fill in the missing amounts:

Nourallah Company
Comparative Balance Sheets

	April 30	May 31	Change
ASSETS			
Cash	$13,500	$20,000	(a) 6500
Accounts receivable	7,000	(b) 10,300	$3,300
Inventory	(c) 7800	2,700	(5,100)
	(d)	(e)	(f)
	28300	33000	4700
LIABILITIES & OWNER'S EQUITY			
Accounts payable	$14,900	(h) 15000	$ 100
Unearned revenue	(g) 0	$ 8,000	8,000
Capital	(i) 13400	(j) 10000	(k) (3400)
	(d)	(e)	(f) 4700

PROBLEMS

21. Certain transactions of the Ricketts Company for September 19x1 are shown below in equation form. Give a short explanation of the probable nature of each transaction.

	Assets				=	Liabilities	+	Owner's Equity
	Cash	+ Accounts Receivable	+ Supplies	+ Equipment	=	Accounts Payable	+	Capital
Beginning Balance	$10,000	+ $5,000	+ $3,000	+ $12,000	=	$10,000	+	$20,000
(a)				+ 8,000		+ 8,000		
(b)	+ 1,000							+ 1,000
(c)	− 3,000					− 3,000		
(d)	+ 2,000	− 2,000						
(e)	− 4,000		+ 4,000					
(f)	− 3,000							− 3,000
Ending Balance	$ 3,000	+ $3,000	+ $7,000	+ $20,000	=	$15,000	+	$18,000

22. Certain transactions of the Kreuger Company for the month of October are shown below in equation form. Provide a description of the probable nature of each transaction.

	Assets				=	Liabilities		+	Owner's Equity	
	Cash	+ Accounts Receivable	+ Supplies	+ Equipment	=	Accounts Payable	+ Wages Payable	+	Capital	+ Revenue (Expense)
Beginning Balance	$ 8,000	+ $ 9,000	+ $3,000	+ $ 8,000	=	$7,000	+ $1,000	+	$20,000	+ $ 0
(a)		+ 6,000								+ 6,000
(b)	− 2,000								− 2,000	
(c)			+ 2,000			+ 2,000				
(d)	− 5,000			+ 5,000						
(e)	+ 10,000	− 10,000								
(f)	− 4,000					− 4,000				
(g)			− 3,000							− 3,000
(h)							+ 2,000			− 2,000
Ending Balance	$ 7,000	+ $ 5,000	+ $2,000	+ $13,000	=	$5,000	+ $3,000	+	$18,000	+ $1,000

23. Dave Karwin opened a roofing business on June 1 and during the month of June completed the following transactions.

June 1 Dave Karwin formed the Karwin Roofing Service with an initial investment of $15,000.

3 The company purchased roofing shingles, paying the $4,000 purchase price in cash.

7 Karwin received $3,500 as advance payment on a contract to roof two houses during the month of July.

12 Karwin Roofing Service borrowed $3,000 from the Sharpstown State Bank.

June 15 Dave Karwin withdrew $2,500 from the business for personal use.
     30 Karwin Roofing Service made its first payment of $1,000 on the $3,000 loan from Sharpstown State Bank.

Indicate the effects of the transactions on the equation provided below.

Assets	=	Liabilities	+	Owners' Equity
Cash + Roofing Supplies	=	Notes Payable + Unearned Fees	+	Karwin, Capital

24. The following transactions occurred during the initial month of operations of Kingsbery Automotive Service.

> The owner contributed $15,000 cash.
> Auto parts purchased on account, $5,000.
> Paid rent for the first month, $2,500.
> Repaired cars for a $2,200 fee and billed the customers.
> Auto parts used, $1,150.
> Collected $850 on customers' accounts.
> Paid $1,000 to creditors.

a. Indicate the effects of these transactions on the equation provided below.

Assets	=	Liabilities	+	Owners' Equity
Cash + Auto Parts + Accounts Receivable	=	Accounts Payable	+	Kingsbery, Capital + Revenue (Expense)

b. Prepare a balance sheet and an income statement at the end of the month.

25. Sam Jones opened an auto repair business on January 1, 19x1. At the end of 19x1, Jones Auto Repair had the following balances of assets, liabilities, and owners' equity:

Accounts payable	$ 5,000
Accounts receivable	20,000
Building	30,000
Capital	?
Cash	10,000
Land	12,000
Notes payable	12,000
Prepaid insurance	5,000
Supplies	8,000
Unearned fees	16,000
Wages payable	2,000

Required:

Determine the amount in the capital account at year-end and prepare a balance sheet at December 31, 19x1.

26. Below is a balance sheet for Rich Exterminator Company at October 31, 19x1.

Rich Exterminator Company
Balance Sheet
October 31, 19x1

Assets		Liabilities and Owners' Equity	
Cash	$7,500	Note payable	$2,200
Supplies	2,000	Unearned fees	300
		Capital	7,000
	$9,500		$9,500

The unearned fees are the result of receiving in advance a $100 fee for each of three jobs to be performed in the future.

During the month of November, the following transactions occurred.

Nov. 2 Rich Company exterminated a house and billed and collected $100 cash from the customer.
       7 Rich Company exterminated a house and billed but did not collect its fee of $150.
     11 Rich paid his employees salaries of $200.
     17 Rich Company exterminated two of the three houses contracted for in October.
     30 The unused supplies on hand at this date had an original cost of $1,500.

Required:

1. Prepare an income statement for Rich Exterminator Company for the month of November.
2. Prepare a balance sheet at November 30, 19x1.

27. Given the following information, prepare an income statement, a statement of capital and a balance sheet for Pate Company on December 31, 19x1.

Prepaid insurance	$ 500	Wages payable	$ 1,550
Cash	16,600	Goodwill	2,000
Accounts payable	8,800	Equipment	7,900
Unearned revenue	3,840	Salary expense	15,000
Utility expense	750	Rent expense	3,200
Withdrawals	3,000	Office furniture	4,000
Accounts receivable	8,160	Marketable securities	1,200
Revenues	25,000	Capital, January 1, 19x1	17,860
Building	20,000	Bonds payable	20,000
Supplies expense	2,600	Capital, December 31, 19x1	26,310
Supplies	140		

28. The following information was taken from the books of the Dawson Company on December 31, 19x1:

Withdrawal	$ 3,000	Revenue	$60,000
Insurance expense	2,400	Prepaid rent	18,000
Cash	28,000	Wages expense	13,400
Utilities expense	1,900	Supplies expense	1,500
Rent expense	10,200		

Required:

Prepare an income statement for 19x1.

29. Prepare a balance sheet for the Kang Company as of June 30, 19x1.

Kang Company
Balance Sheet
January 1, 19x1

Assets		Liabilities and Owners' Equity	
Cash	$13,000	Accounts payable	$20,000
Accounts receivable	49,000	Salaries payable	9,000
Inventory	1,000	Capital	34,000
	$63,000		$63,000

Transactions which occurred between January 1, 19x1 and June 30, 19x1 were:

a. Accounts receivable of $19,000 was collected in cash.
b. Accounts payable increased by $10,000 due to a purchase of inventory.
c. Salaries payable of $9,000 were paid in cash.

30. Prepare a statement of capital for the Hoffmans Company as of October 31, 19x1, given the following information:

a. On March 27, 19x1, Anne Hoffmans invested $20,000 in the business.
b. Anne Hoffmans invested an additional $57,000 on June 26, 19x1.
c. The capital balance as of January 1, 19x1 was $79,000.
d. The owner withdrew $13,000 on March 8, 19x1.
e. The net income for the period from January 1, 19x1 until October 31, 19x1 was $44,000.

31. The effects on the accounting equation of The Hartford Company are shown on the next page. Write a short explanation of the probable nature of each of the transactions.

2 | Financial Statements 55

	ASSETS					LIABILITIES			OWNERS' EQUITY	
	Cash	Accounts Receivable	Land	Supplies	Prepaid Insurance	Accounts Payable	Unearned Fees	Wages Payable	Capital	Revenue (Expense)
Beginning Balance	$4,320	$9,370	$19,780	$470	$1,400	$5,460	$1,500	$1,320	$27,060	0
(a)					− 400					− 400
(b)				− 290						− 290
(c)							− 300			+ 300
(d)								+ 1,200		− 1,200
(e)	+ 4,000	− 4,000								
(f)	− 3,000					− 3,000				
(g)	+ 2,000									+ 2,000
Ending Balance	$7,320	$5,370	$19,780	$180	$1,000	$2,460	$1,200	$2,520	$27,060	$ 410

32. John King began operating a tax return preparation service on January 1. During the month of January, the following transactions were completed.

Jan. 2 The owner invested $10,000 cash in the business.
      4 The business acquired $3,000 of supplies on account.
      5 Rent of $500 was paid for an office building.
     11 Prepared tax returns on credit for a $3,000 fee.
     15 Salaries of $1,000 were paid to employees.
     25 Collected $1,500 on customer accounts.
     30 Cash of $1,000 was paid to creditors.
     31 Supplies of $1,000 were used.

a. Show the effects of these transactions on the equation provided below.

Assets	=	Liabilities	+	Owners' Equity
Cash + Supplies + Accounts Receivable	=	Accounts Payable	+	Capital + Revenue (Expense)

b. Prepare an income statement for the month of January.
c. Prepare a balance sheet as of January 31.

33. The following information was taken from the records of J.S. Wylie and Company as of July 31, 19x1. Prepare the balance sheet at that date.

Wages payable	$ 5,000
Cash	2,345
Land	30,000
Prepaid rent	300
Accounts payable	1,470
Capital	?
Inventory	5,990
Equipment	15,200
Buildings	33,450
Accounts receivable	1,350
Patents (just purchased)	7,000
Mortgage payable (due January 31, 19x9)	40,000
Marketable securities	1,035
Estimated taxes payable	3,000
Unearned revenue	750

Refer to the Annual Report included in the Appendix at the end of the text:

34. What was the income for the most recent year?

35. Did the most recent year's income increase or decrease from the prior year?

36. Were the increases/decreases in income because of a change in revenue, a change in expenses, or both?

37. What was the largest expense in the most recent year?

38. Which expense increased the most during the most recent year? What expense decreased the most?

39. Which current asset is the largest at the end of the most recent year?

40. Comparing the two years presented, what was the change in long-term debt? What factors might have caused these changes?

41. What is the largest asset amount in the balance sheet at the end of the most recent year?

42. Comparing the two years presented, how much did total stockholders' equity increase/decrease?

43. Comparing the two years presented, did dividends increase or decrease for stockholders?

Learning Objectives

Chapter 3 traces and explains the basic steps in the recording process. Studying this chapter should enable you to:

1. Explain what an account is and how it is used in the recording process.

2. Discuss the use of debits and credits and how they affect asset, liability, and owners' equity accounts.

3. List the basic steps in the recording process.

4. Describe a trial balance and identify the types of errors it will (and will not) detect.

5. Explain the use of adjusting entries.

6. Discuss the purpose and illustrate the process of closing the temporary accounts.

3

The Recording Process

INTRODUCTION

Because the number of transactions which occur in even a small business causing its assets, liabilities, equities, revenues, and expenses to increase and decrease occur much too frequently to prepare a new set of financial statements each time a transaction takes place, an alternative method of recording information must be employed. The description of this recording process, which is basic to every accounting system, is the subject matter of this chapter. The accounting system described, referred to as the "double-entry" system, is applicable to all situations in which financial information must be collected and processed. In small firms the system may be maintained by hand, just as described in this chapter, while in larger organizations it will usually be implemented using mechanical or electronic data processing equipment. In any situation, however, the basic principles involved are the same.

THE ACCOUNT

For purposes of reporting and analysis, the transactions of an entity are summarized or grouped in individual accounts. An account is simply a place or means of summarizing all of the transactions that affect a particular asset, liability, equity, revenue, or expense item. The accounting system of a firm includes an individual account for each type or classification of individual asset, liability, owners' equity, revenue, and expense. The increase or decrease in each of these items will be recorded in its own account using "debits" and "credits." At this point we cannot overemphasize the fact that the words "debit" and "credit" are simply terms used to identify *left* and *right* sides of an account, respectively, and have absolutely no other meaning in their accounting usage. (The reader who accepts this statement as a fact and keeps it in mind will save himself untold grief and will greatly enhance his understanding of the recording process.) For purposes of discussion, a typical account may be illustrated as follows:

(Account Title)

(debit side)	(credit side)

This form of presentation is often referred to as a "T-account."

It was indicated earlier that the "double-entry" method is used in accounting in order to record transactions. To understand the double-entry method a simple rule must be kept in mind: for every transaction recorded, the total dollar amount of the debits must be equal to the total dollar amount of the credits. Since we already know that assets must be equal to liabilities plus owners' equity, the following rules of "debit" and "credit" may be established and used in recording the transactions of an entity:

Assets		Liabilities		Owners' Equity	
debit (+)	credit (−)	debit (−)	credit (+)	debit (−)	credit (+)

Because of the equation:

$$\text{Assets} = \text{Liabilities} + \text{Owners' Equity}$$

and the rule:

$$\text{Total Debits} = \text{Total Credits}$$

the procedures (or rules) for recording increases and decreases in the accounts logically follow:

> To increase an ASSET, debit the account.
> To decrease an ASSET, credit the account.
>
> To increase a LIABILITY or OWNERS' EQUITY, credit the account.
> To decrease a LIABILITY or OWNERS' EQUITY, debit the account.

Since revenues and expenses increase and decrease owners' equity respectively, the rules of debit and credit for owners' equity apply to revenue and expense accounts. Because revenues increase owners' equity, the rule for recording increases or decreases in this account is the same as that for owners' equity:

> To increase REVENUE, credit the account.
> To decrease REVENUE, debit the account.

On the other hand, since expenses decrease owners' equity, the rule for recording expenses is opposite of that for owners' equity:

> To increase an EXPENSE, debit the account.
> To decrease an EXPENSE, credit the account.

In order to illustrate the operation of these rules, assume that a firm obtains a $2,000 cash loan from its bank. This transaction would increase the firm's cash, an asset, by $2,000 and also increase its loans payable, a liability, by the same amount. In order to record this transaction, the firm would debit (increase) its cash account for $2,000 and, at the same time, credit (increase) its loans payable account for $2,000. This transaction would be summarized in the accounts of the firm as follows:

Cash		Loans Payable	
2,000			2,000

Note that the total of the debits (in this instance a debit to the cash account of $2,000) is equal to the total of the credits (a credit to the liability account, loans payable for the same amount). In addition, the accounting equation, $A = L + OE$ remains in balance since the assets and liabilities were both increased by $2,000 (owners' equity was not affected).

When the firm repays its loan to the bank, the payment of $2,000 would decrease the firm's asset, cash, by $2,000 and decrease its liability, loans payable, by the same amount. This transaction would be recorded in the accounts by a debit (decrease) to loans payable of $2,000 and a credit (decrease) to cash of $2,000. The effects of the two transactions, the loan and its repayment, are recorded in the accounts as follows:

Cash		Loans Payable	
(1) 2,000	(2) 2,000	(2) 2,000	(1) 2,000

(1) Borrow $2,000 from bank.
(2) Repay $2,000 to bank.

Again the total debits are equal to the total credits and the accounting equation remains in balance.

It is often useful to consider, analyze, and record the transactions of a business as they occur. The simplest example of this process is the use of the general journal entry, which could be used to record the two transactions explained above as follows:

	Debit	Credit
Cash	2,000	
Loans Payable.		2,000
Loans Payable.	2,000	
Cash		2,000

A general journal entry, usually referred to as a journal entry, is a simple means of recording the transactions of a firm in terms of debits and credits. As illustrated above, the format for each journal entry is to write the title of the account to be debited and the amount of the debit on the first line, then indent and write the title of the account to be credited and the amount of the credit on the second line. This is simply a matter of convention.

For purposes of illustration, transactions will be recorded initially in general journal form and then transferred to the individual "T-accounts" (as illustrated in the foregoing). This latter process is referred to as "posting," transferring information from the general journal to the ledger (the book of entry which contains all the accounts of the firm). The same data which were used in Chapter 2 in order to illustrate the preparation of financial statements for Kilmer Contractors will be employed again in this example.

AN ILLUSTRATION

To illustrate the recording process described above, we will again follow the activities of Kilmer Contractors, the small painting contractor described in Chapter 2, through May, the initial month of its operations. In this process we will review the procedures which are involved in:

1. The preparation of general journal entries.
2. Posting these general journal entries to the ledger.
3. The preparation of a trial balance before adjustment.
4. The preparation of adjusting journal entries.
5. Posting these adjusting entries to the ledger.
6. The preparation of the adjusted trial balance.
7. The preparation of closing entries.
8. Posting these closing entries to the ledger.
9. The preparation of the after-closing trial balance.
10. The preparation of the financial statements.

General Journal Entries

The transactions of Kilmer Contractors which occurred during the month of May 19x1, would be recorded as follows:

May 1. Bill Kilmer organized Kilmer Contractors and invested cash of $10,000 in the business.

This transaction is an investment of funds in a business by its owner. Cash held by the firm and the owner's equity account, capital, were both increased. It would be recorded as follows:

```
Cash ..................................... 10,000
    Bill Kilmer, Capital......................      10,000
```

Cash		Capital	
5/1 10,000			5/1 10,000

As indicated above, the increase in the asset cash would be recorded by a debit to the cash account and the corresponding increase in the investment by the owner would be recorded by a credit to the capital account. This entry illustrates the rule that increases in assets are recorded by debits and increases in equities are recorded by credits. Note that the basic accounting equation, $A = L + OE$, is in balance and the total debits are equal to the total credits. This will hold true for each of the transactions of the business as they are recorded.

May 2. The Company purchased painting supplies, paying the $3,000 purchase price in cash.

This transaction represents an exchange of one asset for another. The asset supplies was increased while the asset cash was decreased. It would be recorded as follows:

```
Supplies ................................... 3,000
    Cash ................................... 3,000
```

Cash				Supplies	
5/1 10,000	5/2 3,000		5/2 3,000	

The increase in the asset supplies would be recorded by a debit to the supplies account while the cash outlay would be recorded by a credit to the cash account. This entry follows the rule that increases in assets are recorded by debits while decreases in assets are recorded by credits.

May 5. Kilmer Contractors borrowed $2,000 from the Virginia National Bank.[1]

This transaction is the receipt of an asset, cash, in exchange for a liability, the promise to pay a creditor at some future date. It reflects the promise of the business to repay $2,000 at a future date in order to have cash on hand and available for use at this time. It would be recorded by the following entry:

```
Cash ....................................... 2,000
    Note Payable ........................... 2,000
```

Cash		Note Payable
5/1 10,000 5/2 3,000		5/5 2,000
5/5 2,000		

---

[1] For purposes of illustration, it was assumed that this was a non-interest bearing note.

The increase in the asset cash is recorded by a debit to the cash account and the increase in the liability, note payable, is recorded by a credit to the note payable account. This transaction illustrates the rule that increases in assets are recorded by debits and increases in liabilities are recorded by credits.

May 10. Kilmer signed a contract whereby he agreed to paint two houses sometime during the next few weeks. The customer paid Kilmer the fee of $1,100 per house in advance.

The company has agreed to paint two houses at a future date and has received its fee now, before it has done the work. The receipt of the $2,200 increases cash and the liability, unearned fees, by the same amount. Unearned fees are not a liability in the sense that the company will be required to repay the money. Rather, this account represents an obligation on the part of Kilmer Contractors to render a service at some future date. This transaction would be recorded by the following entry:

```
Cash ..................................... 2,200
    Unearned Fees ........................      2,200
```

Cash				Unearned Fees	
5/1	10,000	5/2	3,000	5/10	2,200
5/5	2,000				
5/10	2,200				

The increase in the asset cash would be recorded by a debit to the cash account while the increase in the liability, unearned fees, would be recorded by a credit to the unearned fees account. Again, this entry illustrates the rule that increases in assets are recorded by debits and increases in liabilities are recorded by credits.

May 12. Bill Kilmer, the owner, withdrew $1,000 from the business for his own personal use.

This transaction is a withdrawal of a portion of the owner's investment from the business. Cash and capital were both decreased by $1,000. It would be recorded as follows:

```
Withdrawals ............................. 1,000
    Cash .................................      1,000
```

Cash				Withdrawals	
5/1	10,000	5/2	3,000	5/12	1,000
5/5	2,000	5/12	1,000		
5/10	2,200				

The withdrawal of $1,000 in cash from the business by the owner would be recorded by a debit to the withdrawals account and a credit to the cash account. This entry illustrates the rule that decreases in equity accounts are recorded by debits and decreases in asset accounts are recorded by credits.

May 15. Kilmer Contractors repaid $500 of the $2,000 it borrowed from the Virginia National Bank.

This transaction is a reduction of both liabilities and assets. The business repaid $500 of the $2,000 it owed to the bank. Both cash and the note payable decreased by this amount. (Recall that it was assumed that this note was not interest bearing.) The following entry would be made:

Note Payable 500
    Cash 500

	Cash				Note Payable		
5/1	10,000	5/2	3,000	5/15	500	5/5	2,000
5/5	2,000	5/12	1,000				
5/10	2,200	5/15	500				

The repayment of $500 to the bank would be recorded by a debit to the liability account, note payable, and a credit to the asset account, cash. This entry illustrates the rule that decreases in liabilities are recorded by debits while decreases in assets are recorded by credits.

May 17. Kilmer Contractors painted its first house and billed and collected a fee of $700 from the customer.

This transaction indicates that the firm has begun to earn revenue. It is a sale of services for cash. Cash was received and the owner's equity of the business was increased by the amount of the revenue earned. It would be recorded by the following entry:

Cash 700
    Painting Fees 700

	Cash			Painting Fees	
5/1	10,000	5/2	3,000	5/17	700
5/5	2,000	5/12	1,000		
5/10	2,200	5/15	500		
5/17	700				

The sale of services for cash would be recorded by a debit to the cash account and a credit to the revenue account, painting fees. This entry illustrates the rule that increases in assets are recorded by debits and increases in revenues are recorded by credits.

May 19. Kilmer Contractors painted a second house and billed (but did not collect) its fee of $900.

Again, this transaction records the revenue earned by the firm in painting a customer's house. Unlike the previous transaction, however, cash was not received. The customer was billed for the service rendered and will pay Kilmer Contractors at some future date. Accounts receivable have increased and owner's equity (revenue) has increased by $900, the fee charged for painting the house. This transaction illustrates the very important point that revenue is recorded as it is earned, not necessarily as cash is received. This concept reflects the *accrual* basis of accounting. The transaction would be recorded by the following entry:

```
Accounts Receivable . . . . . . . . . . . . . . . . . . . . . . . . . . . . . .  900
    Painting Fees . . . . . . . . . . . . . . . . . . . . . . . . . . . . . . . .        900
```

Accounts Receivable		Painting Fees	
5/19 900		5/17 700	
		5/19 900	

This sale of services to a customer on a credit basis would be recorded by a debit to the asset, accounts receivable, and a credit to the revenue account, painting fees. Again, this transaction illustrates the rule that increases in assets are recorded by debits and increases in revenues are recorded by credits.

May 25. Kilmer paid salaries of $400 to his employees.

Expenses of $400 were incurred and paid in cash. This transaction reduces both the cash balance and owner's equity. The reduction in owner's equity is due to the fact that an expense has been incurred, thereby reducing income. (Remember that revenues less expenses equals income.) The transaction would be recorded by the following entry:

```
Salaries . . . . . . . . . . . . . . . . . . . . . . . . . . . . . . . . . . . . . .  400
    Cash . . . . . . . . . . . . . . . . . . . . . . . . . . . . . . . . . . . . .        400
```

Cash				Salaries	
5/1	10,000	5/2	3,000	5/25 400	
5/5	2,000	5/12	1,000		
5/10	2,200	5/15	500		
5/17	700	5/25	400		

The payment of salaries to employees would be recorded by a debit to the expense account, salaries, and a credit to the asset account, cash. This entry illustrates the rule that increases in expenses are recorded by debits and decreases in assets are recorded by credits.

Posting

The second step in the recording process would be to post each of the journal entries to the appropriate ledger accounts. Posting is the process of transferring the individual debits and credits of each entry to the appropriate account or accounts in the ledger. This step enables the accountant to summarize and group the transactions which occurred according to the individual accounts which they affect. For each transaction, the debit amount in the journal entry is posted by entering it on the debit side of the appropriate ledger account and each credit amount in the entry is posted by entering it on the credit side of the appropriate ledger account. This process was illustrated in the previous section on general journal entries. Recall that the initial transaction of Kilmer Contractors was as follows:

May 1. Bill Kilmer organized Kilmer Contractors and invested cash of $10,000 in the business.

This transaction was recorded by the following general journal entry:

```
Cash .................................. 10,000
    Bill Kilmer, Capital........................    10,000
```

It would be posted to the ledger as follows:

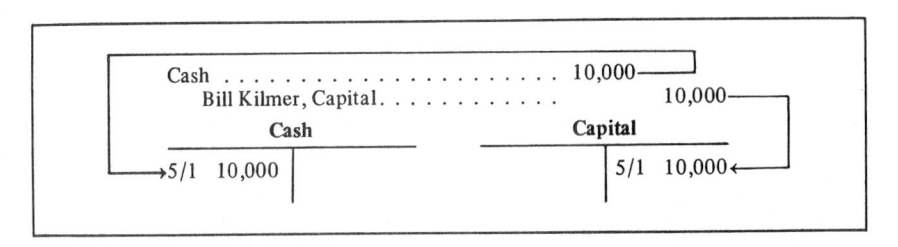

```
Cash .................. 10,000
    Bill Kilmer, Capital...........    10,000

       Cash                    Capital
  5/1  10,000           |              5/1  10,000
```

The debit to cash of $10,000 in the journal entry is posted to the debit side of the cash account in the general ledger and the credit to capital of $10,000 is posted to the credit side of the capital account in the general ledger. The date in the ledger accounts provides a reference back to the original source of the posting, the general journal. Usually, a page reference will also be provided by each entry in the journal and each account in the general ledger in order to facilitate the cross-referencing of transactions.

Each of the transactions of Kilmer Contractors would be posted in this manner. In our example, the transactions journalized in the previous section are posted to the "T-accounts" included below. The dates of the transactions appear by each amount and are included for reference purposes.

Cash			
5/1	10,000	5/2	3,000
5/5	2,000	5/12	1,000
5/10	2,200	5/15	500
5/17	700	5/25	400
	10,000		

Accounts Receivable			
5/19	900		
	900		

Supplies			
5/2	3,000		
	3,000		

Note Payable			
5/15	500	5/5	2,000
			1,500

Unearned Fees			
		5/10	2,200
			2,200

Capital			
		5/1	10,000
			10,000

Withdrawals			
5/12	1,000		
	1,000		

Painting Fees			
		5/17	700
		5/19	900
			1,600

Salaries			
5/25	400		
	400		

Trial Balance

After all of the transactions which were initially recorded in the general journal have been posted to the general ledger, the next step in the accounting process would be to prepare a trial balance. A trial balance is simply a listing of all of the accounts included in the general ledger along with the balance, debit or credit, of each account. The purpose of a trial balance is simply to prove the equality of the debits and credits and to "catch" or detect any obvious errors which may have occurred in either the recording or the posting process. The reader should note, however, that even if the total of the debits in the trial balance is equal to the total of the credits, this only proves that the accounts are "in balance"; it does not indicate that errors have not been made. (For example, a posting could have been made to the wrong account.)

The trial balance of Kilmer Contractors at May 31, 19x1, before adjustments would be as follows:

Kilmer Contractors
Trial Balance Before Adjustment
May 31, 19x1

	Debit	Credit
Cash	$10,000	
Accounts receivable	900	
Supplies	3,000	
Note payable		$ 1,500
Unearned fees		2,200
Capital		10,000
Withdrawals	1,000	
Painting fees		1,600
Salaries	400	
Total	$15,300	$15,300

Adjusting Entries

As previously indicated, the accrual basis of accounting requires that revenues be recorded as they are earned and expenses be recorded as they are incurred. This procedure is followed without regard to either the receipt or disbursement of cash. At the end of any period, then, there will usually be transactions which are still in the process of completion or which have occurred but have not yet been recorded. These transactions require adjusting entries. In the case of Kilmer Contractors, adjustments are required for: (1) the revenue which was earned by painting one of the two houses contracted for on May 10, and (2) the painting supplies which were used during the month of May. These adjustments, referred to as adjusting entries, would be recorded in the accounts by the general journal entries presented below.

May 31. Kilmer Contractors painted one of the two houses contracted for on May 10.

This adjustment records the partial satisfaction of a non-cash liability by the rendering of services (that is, painting one of the two houses) and the earning of income. It would be recorded by the following journal entry:

Unearned Fees	1,100	
Painting Fees		1,100

Unearned Fees		Painting Fees	
5/31 1,100	5/10 2,200		5/17 700
			5/19 900
			5/31 1,100

Recall that on May 10 Kilmer signed a contract whereby he agreed to paint two houses at a future date and received his fee of $1,100 per house in advance. No income was earned at the point the contract was signed and the cash received, because no work had been done at that time.

Kilmer Contractors had an obligation to paint the two houses at a future date. This was a liability to perform services, which was reflected as unearned fees. Now, at the end of May, one of the two houses contracted for has been painted and that portion of the income has been earned. The liability, unearned fees, has been reduced by $1,100 and the income for May has been increased by the same amount. These facts require that the financial statements be adjusted in order to reflect the current status of the contract. Again, this transaction emphasizes the fact that income is recorded as it is earned, *not* as cash is received.

The decrease of $1,100 in the liability, unearned fees, would be recorded by a debit to the unearned fees account and the increase in the revenue, painting fees, would be recorded by a credit to the painting fees account. This adjusting entry illustrates the rule that decreases in liabilities are recorded by debits and increases in revenues are recorded by credits.

May 31. The unused painting supplies on hand at this date had an original cost of $2,000.

The facts of this transaction indicate that an expense has been incurred during the month which has not yet been recorded in the accounts. The following adjusting entry would be required at May 31:

```
Supplies Used . . . . . . . . . . . . . . . . . . . . . . . . . . . . . . . . . 1,000
    Supplies . . . . . . . . . . . . . . . . . . . . . . . . . . . . . . . . . .         1,000
```

Supplies Used		Supplies	
5/31 1,000		5/2 3,000	5/31 1,000

During May, Kilmer Contractors used supplies that had an original cost of $1,000. This amount was determined by subtracting the $2,000 cost of the supplies which were still on hand at May 31 from the $3,000 total cost of supplies that were available for use (that is, the supplies on hand at the beginning of the month plus the supplies purchased during the month). As in the previous May 31 transaction, an adjusting entry was required. The asset, supplies, was decreased by $1,000 (the cost of the supplies used), from $3,000 (the total supplies available for use during the month of May) to $2,000 (the cost of supplies still on hand at May 31). This transaction reflects the fact that expenses are recorded when incurred or used rather than when cash is disbursed.

The increase in the supplies used expense would be recorded by a debit to the supplies used account. The decrease in the asset, supplies, would be recorded by a credit to the supplies account. This adjusting entry illustrates the rule that increases in expenses are recorded by debits and decreases in assets are recorded by credits.

After these two journal entries have been made, all of the transactions of Kilmer Contractors which occurred during the month of May have been recorded in the accounts.

Posting the Adjusting Entries

The adjusting entries would then be posted to the ledger in the same manner as were the regular journal entries. This has been done below. Again, the dates of the transactions are included for the use of the reader for purposes of reference. (Note that the two adjusting entries are dated May 31.)

Cash			
5/1	10,000	5/2	3,000
5/5	2,000	5/12	1,000
5/10	2,200	5/15	500
5/17	700	5/25	400
	10,000		

Accounts Receivable	
5/19 900	
900	

Supplies			
5/2	3,000	5/31	1,000
	2,000		

Note Payable			
5/15	500	5/5	2,000
			1,500

Unearned Fees			
5/31	1,100	5/10	2,200
			1,100

Capital	
	5/1 10,000
	10,000

Withdrawals	
5/12 1,000	
1,000	

Painting Fees			
		5/17	700
		5/19	900
		5/31	1,100
			2,700

Salaries	
5/25 400	
400	

Supplies Used	
5/31 1,000	
1,000	

Trial Balance After Adjustment

The next step in the recording process would be the preparation of a trial balance *after* adjustment. This trial balance is simply the trial balance which was prepared after the adjusting entries were made and posted to the general ledger. The trial balance after adjustment for Kilmer Contractors is presented below.

Kilmer Contractors
Trial Balance After Adjustment
May 31, 19x1

	Debit	Credit
Cash	$10,000	
Accounts receivable	900	
Supplies	2,000	
Note payable		$ 1,500
Unearned fees		1,100
Capital		10,000
Withdrawals	1,000	
Painting fees		2,700
Salaries	400	
Supplies used	1,000	
Totals	$15,300	$15,300

Again, the only difference between the trial balance after adjustment and the trial balance before adjustment presented previously is the inclusion of the effect of the adjusting entries which were made.

Closing Entries

The purpose of closing entries is to close out the temporary accounts (revenues, expenses, and withdrawals) into the owners' equity (capital) account. This process is facilitated by the introduction of a temporary account created solely for the closing process. This account is known as the *income summary account* and is used to collect or summarize all of the revenues and expenses of the firm in a single account which is then, in turn, closed to the capital account (or the retained earnings account for a corporation).

The purpose of the closing process is to systematically reduce all of the balances in the temporary accounts to a zero balance at the end of the accounting period. This means that at the beginning of the next period all revenues, expenses, and drawing accounts will have a zero balance so that these accounts can again be used in order to record the results of operations of that period.

The closing process is accomplished by the preparation of journal entries known as closing entries. These entries are recorded in the general journal and posted to the ledger in the same manner as all other transactions are processed.

We will now illustrate the closing process for Kilmer Contractors. The journal entries which are required to close out the revenue and expense accounts would be made at the end of the month of May, the accounting period used in this illustration. Referring back to the trial balance after adjustment for Kilmer Contractors, the temporary accounts were as follows:

	Balance	
	Debit	Credit
Withdrawals	$1,000	
Painting fees		$2,700
Salaries	400	
Supplies used	1,000	

The entry to close out the revenue account would be:

May 31. Painting Fees 2,700
         Income Summary......................... 2,700

Painting Fees		Income Summary
	5/17 700	5/31 2,700
	5/19 900	
	5/31 1,100	
5/31 2,700	2,700	
	0	

Revenue accounts have credit balances. Therefore, the entry which is required in order to close out the balance in a revenue account consists of a debit to the revenue account for the total revenue for the period and a credit to the income summary account for the same amount. This entry closes out (i.e.—brings the account balance to zero) the revenue account and transfers the total for the period to the credit side of the income summary account.

In our illustration, the painting fees account is now closed and has a zero balance, and the $2,700 revenue from painting fees has been transferred to the credit side of the income summary account.

The two expense accounts would be closed out by the following entry:

May 31. Income Summary........................ 1,400
         Salaries................................. 400
         Supplies Used........................... 1,000

Salaries	Supplies Used	Income Summary
5/25 400		5/31 1,000		5/31 1,400	5/31 2,700
400	5/31 400	1,000	5/31 1,000		
0		0		

Expense accounts have debit balances. Therefore, the entry which is required in order to close out the balance in an expense account credits the account for the total expense for the period and debits the income summary account for this amount. This closing entry reduces the expense account balance to zero and transfers the expense for the period to the debit side of the income summary account.

In our example, both the salaries and the supplies used expense accounts are now closed out and the total of these two accounts ($400 + $1,000) which is the total expense for the period has been transferred to the debit side of the income summary account.

The balance in the income summary account ($2,700 − $1,400 = $1,300) is then transferred to Kilmer's capital account by the following closing entry:

May 31. Income Summary.................... 1,300
            Capital........................ 1,300

Income Summary				Capital	
5/31 1,400	5/31	2,700		5/1	10,000
5/31 1,300		1,300		5/31	1,300
		0			

As indicated above, all revenue and expense accounts are closed to the income summary account. Therefore, the credit side of the income summary account will include the total revenue for the period while the debit side of the account will include the total expenses. The account balance will be the income or loss of the business for the period. If the total of the credits (revenues) in the income summary account exceeds the total of the debits (expenses), revenues are greater than expenses and the difference is the income for the period. On the other hand, if the total of the credits (revenues) is less than the total of the debits (expenses), expenses exceed revenues and the difference is the loss for the period. In either case the balance in the income summary account after all of the revenue and expense accounts have been closed is transferred to the capital account.

In the Kilmer Contractors example the balance in the income summary account, a credit of $1,300 (revenues of $2,700 less expenses of $1,400), was closed out and the income for the period was transferred to the capital account.

As a final step in the closing process the balance in any drawing or withdrawals account is closed out to owner's equity. In the Kilmer Contractors illustration this step would be to close the balance in the withdrawals account directly to capital.

May 31. Capital........................ 1,000
            Withdrawals.................... 1,000

	Withdrawals				Capital		
5/12	1,000			5/31	1,000	5/1	10,000
	1,000	5/31	1,000			5/31	1,300
	0						

Withdrawals made by the owner do not pass through the income summary account since they are not an expense of the period and therefore do not enter into the determination of income. Withdrawal or drawing accounts have debit balances. Therefore, the closing entry which is required to close withdrawals credits the withdrawal account and debits the capital account for the drawings made by the owner during the period.

In the Kilmer Contractors example, the withdrawals of $1,000 are closed out and transferred to the capital account as a reduction of the end-of-period capital balance.

The closing process can be depicted graphically as follows:

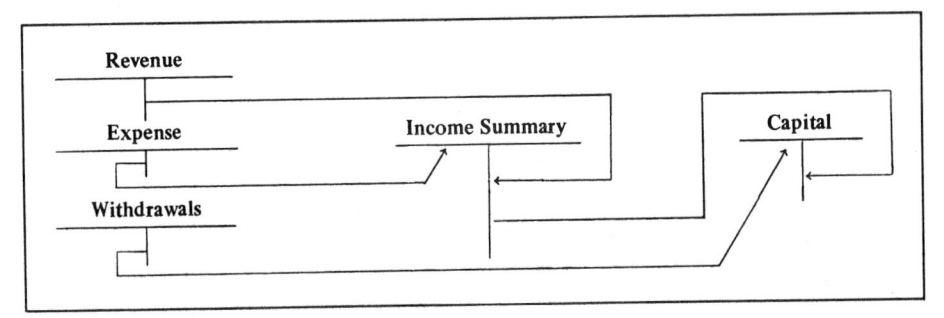

[Diagram showing Revenue, Expense, and Withdrawals flowing into Income Summary, which flows into Capital]

In terms of the specific accounts which were used in the Kilmer Contractors illustration, the closing process is shown below, after all of the closing entries are posted to the accounts.

After-Closing Trial Balance

After all of the temporary accounts have been closed out, a trial balance, referred to as an after-closing trial balance, may be prepared as a test of the equality of the total debits and credits. The after-closing trial balance of Kilmer Contractors is presented below. Since all of the temporary accounts have been closed out, the after-closing trial balance includes only the permanent or balance sheet accounts.

Financial Statements

After all of the adjusting and closing entries have been prepared and made and the posting process has been completed, the general ledger account balances will be up to date as of the end of the period. The information regarding the assets, liabilities, capital, revenues, and expenses included in the general ledger will be used as a basis for preparing the financial statements. Asset, liability, and capital balances as of the end of the period

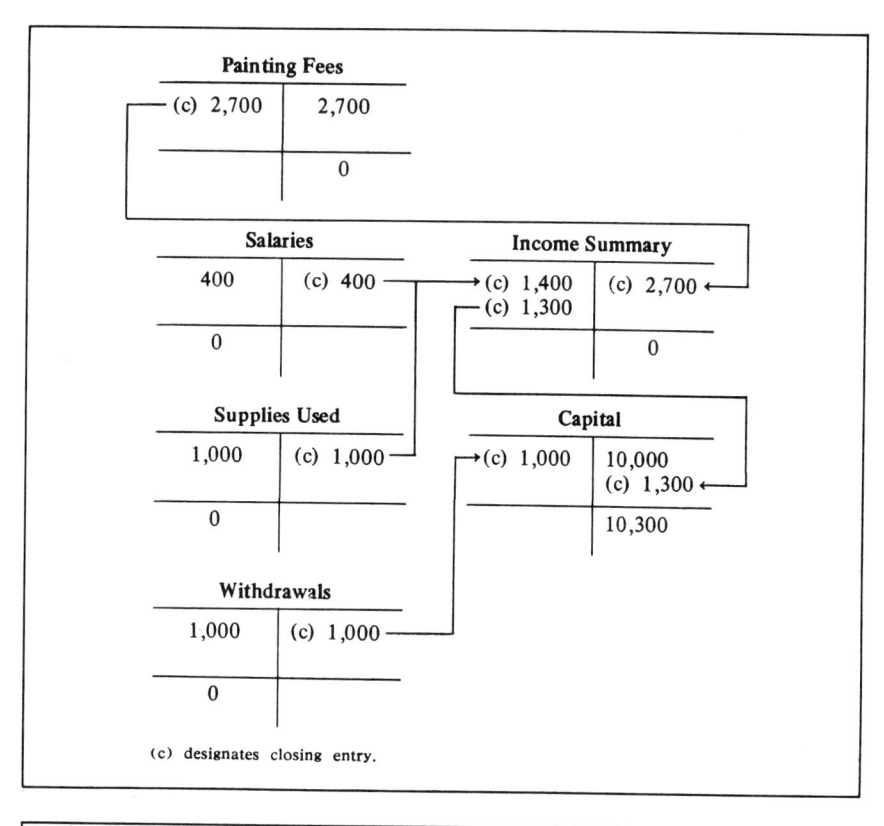

```
                Painting Fees
    ┌─ (c) 2,700  │  2,700
    │
    │              │    0

         Salaries              Income Summary
       400  │  (c) 400 ──→ (c) 1,400 │ (c) 2,700 ←──┐
                          ─(c) 1,300                │
         0  │                                       │
                                     │      0       │
       Supplies Used                 Capital        │
     1,000  │ (c) 1,000 ──→ (c) 1,000 │ 10,000      │
                                     │ (c) 1,300 ←──┘
         0  │                        │ 10,300

        Withdrawals
     1,000  │ (c) 1,000 ─────────────┘

         0  │

    (c) designates closing entry.
```

Kilmer Contractors
After-Closing Trial Balance
May 31, 19x1

	Debits	Credits
Cash	$10,000	
Accounts receivable	900	
Supplies	2,000	
Note payable		$ 1,500
Unearned fees		1,100
Capital		10,300
	$12,900	$12,900

will be taken from the general ledger accounts and used to prepare the balance sheet or statement of financial position. As previously indicated, the after-closing trial balance may be used to check the accuracy of the balance sheet since it includes all permanent accounts which appear in the balance sheet.

The revenues and expenses for the period will also be taken from the general ledger and used to prepare the income statement. The trial balance after adjustment and the detailed amounts which are included in the income summary account may be used as a check on the accuracy of the income statement since both of these sources include the details of the revenues and expenses for the period.

The statement of capital will also be prepared using the capital account from the general ledger as a source. The financial statements for Kilmer Contractors for the month of May are included below.

Kilmer Contractors
Balance Sheet
May 31, 19x1

ASSETS		LIABILITIES AND OWNER'S EQUITY	
Cash	$10,000	Note Payable	$ 1,500
Accounts Receivable	900	Unearned Fees	1,100
Supplies	2,000	Capital	10,300
	$12,900		$12,900

Kilmer Contractors
Income Statement
For the Month Ending May 31, 19x1

Revenue from painting services		$2,700
Supplies Used	$1,000	
Salaries	400	
Total Expenses		1,400
Income		$1,300

Kilmer Contractors
Statement of Capital
For the Month Ending May 31, 19x1

Capital at May 1, 19x1		$ -0-
Add:		
Investment	$10,000	
Income for May	1,300	11,300
Deduct:		
Withdrawal		(1,000)
Capital at May 31, 19x1		$10,300

At this time, several points should be noted by the reader in review. First, the general journal entries were prepared as the transactions occurred. These entries represent a chronological record of the transactions of the company which took place during the month of May. These journal entries were then posted to the ledger accounts. At the end of the month, a trial balance was prepared and the transactions and the status of the company at that point in time were reviewed. All adjustments which were necessary to bring the accounts up to date were made.

The next step in the process was the preparation of a trial balance after adjustment. Again, it is important to note that any trial balance only proves the equality of the totals of the debits and the credits; it gives no other assurance as to the absence of errors.

Entries were then prepared to "close-out" all temporary accounts, the revenues, expenses, and withdrawals for the period. These are the only accounts closed. The permanent accounts, assets, liabilities, and capital, which appear in the balance sheet, are not closed out. The closing entries summarize the balances of the revenue and expense accounts in an income summary account.[2] The balance in the withdrawals account is then closed out to the capital account. The closing entries were then posted to the ledger and the after-closing trial balance. Then the financial statements were prepared.

SUMMARY

Transactions that affect the financial statements of a firm occur much too frequently to permit a revision of the statements after each transaction takes place. Therefore, firms use various "accounting systems" that record and accumulate the essence of these transactions. This allows the accountant to use the summarized data provided by the accounting system to prepare financial statements at designated points in time. The most commonly used accounting system, and the one discussed in this chapter, is the "double-entry" system.

The basic element of the double-entry system, as well as other systems, is the account. An account is simply a place or means of collecting and summarizing all of the transactions that affect a particular asset, liability, or owners' equity account. Each account is increased or decreased by use of debits (left-side entries) and credits (right-side entries). A debit entry increases assets and expenses, but decreases liabilities, owners' equity, and revenue accounts. Conversely, a credit entry increases liabilities, owners' equity, and revenues, but decreases assets and expenses.

The actual recording process involves a number of separate but related steps. The initial step is the preparation of general journal entries at the time the transactions take place. These general journal entries are then posted to the individual accounts in the ledger. After these two steps are

---

[2] The reader will note that the income summary is, in fact, a duplication of the income statement itself. That is, the credits to the summary are the revenues for the period and the debits are the expenses for the period. The difference, or balancing figure, is, of course, the income (or loss) for the period.

completed, the accountant prepares a trial balance before adjustment. This trial balance is simply a listing of each account and the corresponding debit or credit balance in the account. This listing will only detect the most obvious errors and does not guarantee that other errors have not been made.

The next step in the recording process is the preparation of adjusting entries. These entries are necessary to adjust the accounts so that the final balances will reflect the proper updated balances as of the end of the accounting period. The adjusting entries are then posted to the appropriate ledger accounts and a trial balance after adjustment is prepared.

The next phase in the recording process is the preparation of closing entries. These entries are required to close the temporary accounts (revenues, expenses, and withdrawals) so that these accounts can be used to accumulate similar data for the next accounting period. To accomplish this, all revenues and expenses are closed to the income summary account. The income summary account and the withdrawal account are then closed to the capital account. Once the closing entries are prepared and entered into the general journal, they are then posted to the ledger accounts and an after-closing trial balance is prepared.

The final step is the actual preparation of the financial statements. As indicated in previous chapters, the primary financial statements prepared by the accountant are the balance sheet, income statement, and statement of capital.

This chapter has introduced and traced the basic recording process used by most accounting systems. The next chapter illustrates and discusses the worksheet, one of the primary tools employed by the accountant in this recording process, and provides more information regarding the nature and function of adjusting entries.

KEY DEFINITIONS

Account An account is a place or means of summarizing all of the transactions that affect a particular asset, liability, equity, revenue, or expense item.

Adjusting entries At the end of an accounting period, adjusting entries record the transactions which are in process or have been completed but not yet recorded. These entries are necessary in order to record revenues when they are earned and expenses when they are incurred, and not when cash is received or paid. This is in accordance with the accrual concept of accounting.

Closing entries The purpose of closing entries is to close out or transfer the balances in the temporary accounts (revenues, expenses, and withdrawals) into the capital account.

Credit "Credit" is the term used to identify the right-hand side of an account. A credit decreases an asset and increases a liability, equity, or revenue account.

Debit "Debit" is the term used to describe the left-hand side of an account. By debiting an asset or expense account, the account is increased and by debiting a liability or equity account, the account is decreased.

Double-entry method This method requires that for every transaction recorded, the total dollar amount of debits must be equal to the total dollar amount of the credits.

General journal entry The general journal entry is a means of recording the transactions of a firm chronologically in terms of debits and credits.

General ledger The general ledger is a compilation of all the accounts of a firm and their balances.

Posting Posting to ledger accounts is the process of transferring the information from the general journal to the individual accounts of the general ledger. This enables the accountant to review and summarize all changes in the accounts.

Trial balance The trial balance is a listing of all the accounts in the general ledger. If the accounts are "in balance," the total of the accounts with debit balances will equal the total of those with credit balances. The trial balance only indicates that the accounts are in balance. It does not prove that errors have not been made in the recording process.

QUESTIONS

1. What is the purpose of the double-entry system of recording business transactions?

2. Explain the terms "debit" and "credit." What effect does each of these have on asset and liability accounts?

3. What is the general rule of the double-entry system?

4. Describe a general journal entry.

5. What is a T-account?

6. What is "posting"?

7. What is the purpose of a trial balance?

8. What concept of accounting requires adjusting entries? Explain.

9. What type of accounts do closing entries affect? Why are these accounts closed?

EXERCISES

10. The first nine transactions of a newly formed business, Smart Company, appear in the T-accounts below. For each set of debits and credits, explain the nature of the transaction. Each entry is designated by the small letters to the left of the amount.

Cash		Accounts Receivable		Equipment	
(a) 10,000	(c) 2,000	(d) 6,000	(g) 2,000	(b) 3,000	
(g) 2,000	(e) 4,000				
(i) 2,500	(f) 1,000				
	(h) 1,500				

Accounts Payable		Unearned Fees	
(f) 1,000	(b) 3,000		(i) 2,500

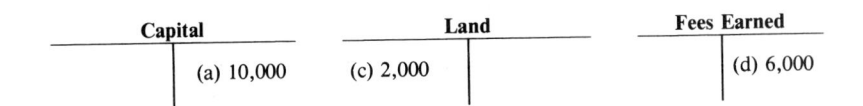

Capital		Land		Fees Earned	
	(a) 10,000	(c) 2,000			(d) 6,000

Wage Expense		Rent Expense	
(e) 4,000		(h) 1,500	

11. Assume that the ledger accounts given in Exercise 10 are for the Smart Company as of December 31, 19x1. Prepare a trial balance for Smart Company as of that date.

12. Prepare the closing entries, the income statement for 19x1 and the balance sheet as of December 31, 19x1, for the Smart Company assuming the data given in Exercise 10.

13. Bob Feller opened a driving range and the following transactions took place in July, 19x1:

    July 1   The owner invested $10,000 cash in the business.
          5   Purchased fixed assets for $5,000; made a cash down payment of $2,000 and signed a 60 day note for the balance.
         10   The total revenue for the month was $1,500; $1,200 in cash was collected and the balance was owed on account by customers.
         15   The total expenses for the month were $1,100; $900 was paid in cash and the balance was owed on account.
         25   The owner withdrew $100 in cash.

    Required:

    Prepare the journal entries to record these transactions and enter the debits and credits in T-accounts.

14. After recording and posting the transactions from Exercise 13, prepare a trial balance for Feller Company as of July 31, 19x1.

15. Given the following T-accounts, prepare the closing entries for the White Company for the month of August, 19x0.

Cash		Accounts Receivable		Supplies	
B.B. 20,000	1,100 (2)	B.B. 4,000	2,000 (1)	B.B. 800	1,000 (8)
(1) 2,000	5,000 (4)	(6) 7,000		(2) 1,100	
(3) 35,000	2,800 (5)				
	14,000 (9)				
	900 (10)				
	500 (11)				
32,700		9,000		900	

Note Payable		Unearned Fees		Capital	
(5) 2,800	2,800 B.B.	(7) 30,000	7,000 B.B.		15,000 B.B.
			35,000 (3)		
			12,000		15,000

Withdrawals		Fees Earned		Supplies Used	
(4) 5,000			7,000 (6)	(8) 1,000	
			30,000 (7)		
5,000			37,000	1,000	

Salaries		Utilities		Property Taxes	
(9) 14,000		(10) 900		(11) 500	
14,000		900		500	

16. Using the information in Exercise 15, prepare an After-Closing Trial Balance for White Company.

17. From the information given in Exercise 15, prepare a balance sheet, income statement, and statement of capital for White Company.

18. Prepare the journal entries for the Wicks Company for the month of December.

Dec. 1 Office supplies were purchased on credit for $5,000.
      3 A new machine was purchased for $15,000 cash.
      4 Revenues of $7,500 were received in advance of services being rendered.
      7 Services were performed on credit for $400.
      9 The bank loaned Wicks Company $10,000.
     12 Ivan Ingot invested $25,000 in the company.
     16 The $400 credit extended for services performed was collected.
     18 A remittance was sent for the office supplies.
     19 Services were performed for one-half of the revenues received in advance.
     21 Ivan Ingot withdrew $3,000 from the company.

Dec. 24 Performed services and collected amount due of $600 in cash.
27 Repaid one-fourth of the bank loan.
30 Salaries of $2,500 were paid to employees.

19. Post each journal entry in Exercise 18 to the appropriate ledger account and prepare closing entries.

PROBLEMS

20. Presented below are the transactions of the Home Finder Realty Company for the month of May, 19x1.

May 1 The owner invested $20,000 cash in the business.
3 Purchased office equipment for $1,800 on account.
5 Purchased a car for $3,000, giving $1,000 in cash and a note payable of $2,000.
10 Purchased $500 of office supplies on account.
15 Paid $300 office rent for the month of May.
16 Paid for office supplies purchased on May 10.
18 Received a bill for $200 for radio advertising.
20 Earned and collected $1,500 commission for the sale of a house.
21 Paid bill for advertising that was received on May 18.
23 Earned but did not collect an $800 commission.
25 Paid salaries of $400.
27 Received payment in full from customer of May 23.
29 Paid the telephone bill, $50.

Required:

Prepare the general journal entries that would be required to record the above transactions.

21. On September 1, 19x1 Mark Walls, a bookkeeper, organized a bookkeeping service business. The following events occurred during September.

Sept. 1 Walls withdrew $10,000 from his personal savings and invested this amount in the business.
2 Paid September rent of $250.
4 Purchased office furniture for $2,000 on account.
6 Received and paid a bill for $200 for advertising in the local newspaper.
9 Received cash of $1,400 as payment for services to customers.
15 Paid the $300 salary of a part-time secretary.
17 Paid for office furniture purchased on account.
18 Purchased $150 of office supplies on account.
20 Received a utilities bill for $75.
21 Completed $600 of services on credit for customers.
23 Collected $200 of receivables for credit services provided.
27 Walls withdrew $600 from the business.

Required:

1. Prepare the general journal entries to record the above transactions.
2. Post the above journal entries to T-accounts.
3. Prepare a trial balance as of the end of September.
4. Prepare closing entries.

22. The following transactions involving the Mantle Company occurred during the month of July, 19x1:

    July 1 Mantle organized the company, contributing $1,000 as an initial investment.
          3 Purchased office supplies paying $100 in cash.
          6 Performed services for his first customer and collected $500 in cash.
          9 Performed services for another customer and agreed to accept his payment of $700 later in the month.
         13 Contracted to perform certain services for a third customer and received the full payment of $1,000 in advance.
         18 Received the payment from the customer for whom services were performed on July 9.
         24 Paid the following operating items:

             Salaries for July........................ $250
             Office rent for July and August.......... 300
             Other July expense......................   75

             (Mantle will prepare financial statements at the end of July.)
         31 Noted that exactly one-fourth of the services contracted for on the thirteenth by a customer had been performed. Counted the office supplies on hand and ascertained that supplies with an original cost of $65 were still on hand.

    Required:

    1. Record the above transactions with general journal entries.
    2. Post the journal entries by entering debits and credits in T-accounts.
    3. Prepare a trial balance as of July 31, 19x1.
    4. Prepare closing entries.

23. Below is the trial balance of the Nittany Lion Company as of October 31, 19x1.

Cash	$10,000	
Accounts receivable	4,000	
Notes receivable	2,500	
Supplies	1,000	
Accounts payable		$ 4,500
Note payable		3,000
Unearned revenue		1,500
Capital		7,500
Withdrawals	500	
Revenues		3,000
Expenses	1,500	
	$19,500	$19,500

    Required:

    1. Prepare the entries which are necessary to close the accounts as of October 31, 19x1.
    2. Prepare the following statements:

        a. Balance sheet
        b. Income statement
        c. Statement of capital

24. Certain data relating to River Corporation are presented below:

Trial balance data as of June 30, 19x1.

Advertising expense	$ 75
Capital	3,195
Cash	895
Commissions earned	1,900
Commissions receivable	950
Interest earned	5
Land	2,000
Mercantile Company bonds	1,000
Notes payable	700
Office rent	80
Salaries expense	800

Adjusted trial balance data as of June 30, 19x1.

Accrued interest receivable	5
Accrued interest payable	7
Accrued rent receivable	55
Accrued salaries payable	100
Advertising expense	75
Capital	3,195
Cash	895
Commissions earned	1,960
Commissions receivable	1,010
Interest earned	10
Interest expense	7
Land	2,000
Mercantile Company bonds	1,000
Notes payable	700
Office rent	80
Rent earned	55
Salaries expense	900

Required:

Compare the unadjusted and adjusted account balances and prepare the adjusting journal entries made by River Corporation as of June 30, 19x1. Also prepare the closing entries as of June 30, 19x1. (No withdrawals were made during the period ending June 30, 19x1.)

25. The following information has been developed by the bookkeeper of the Sneed Company. It relates to the company's operations for 19x1.

Cash receipts		
From customers	$46,100	
Cash disbursements		
For expenses	10,600	
Account balances as of December 31	*19x0*	*19x1*
Accounts receivable from customers, (all collectible)	$10,400	$9,600
Accrued expenses payable	1,900	1,600

Required:

Prepare the company's income statement for the year ended December 31, 19x1.

26. On June 30, 19x1, the Repertory Theater Co. was organized. On that date the owners invested $25,000 in cash and the company manager signed a 10-year lease on a building. The lease called for a monthly rental of $4,000. The first payment under the lease was made immediately; all future rentals were to be paid on the last day of each month. The theater capacity was 800 seats which were to be sold for $3 at each performance. A 3-year comprehensive insurance policy was paid for on July 1, 19x1, at a cost of $600.

   The theater opened on August 1, 19x1. There were 8 performances each week (each evening Monday through Saturday and matinees on Wednesday and Saturday). Through December 31, 19x1, there had been exactly 22 full weeks of performances. The player companies who were engaged to perform received 40 percent of the gate with settlement to be made after each Saturday evening performance for the 8 performances of the week then ending. At the beginning of the 19th week of business a smash hit opened. This show played to capacity crowds and was sold out through the first 7 weeks of 19x2.

   A refreshment counter in the lobby dispensed soft drinks, candy, etc., and proved to be most lucrative. This was the only source of revenue other than ticket sales. Refreshments with an invoice cost of $19,000 had been purchased during 19x1. The inventory of refreshments on hand at December 31, 19x1, had an invoice price of $2,200. All purchases had been paid for except one made on December 27, 19x1, at a cost of $1,200.

   Prior to the opening of the smash hit, the theater enjoyed good success, averaging exactly 75 percent of capacity of all performances. All receipts during the year had been deposited intact and deposit slips showed a total of $517,400 deposited through December 31, 19x1.

   Salaries for ushers, ticket-takers, the manager, and other employees were paid after each Friday evening performance for work done through that performance. These salaries averaged $900 per week. Advertising had been run in local newspapers and $2,900 had been paid for as of December 31, 19x1. The bill for ads run during the last week of 19x1 had not been received by December 31, but based upon knowledge of the rates it was estimated that it would be $150. Utilities bills through December 31 totaled $2,700 and had been paid.

   There were no liabilities at December 31, 19x1, other than those which have been specifically mentioned or alluded to above. No additional investments by the owners had been made and no withdrawals were made.

   Required:

   1. A statement of financial position as of December 31, 19x1.
   2. An income statement for the six months ended December 31, 19x1.

27. Following are given the *total debits* and *total credits* for the year (which include beginning-of-the-year balances) in certain accounts of the Ace Company, *after the closing entries have been posted to the accounts* as of December 31, 19x1.

	Debits	Credits
Advertising expense	$ 210	$ 210
Salaries expense	700	700
Telephone expense	48	48
Prepaid insurance	90	15
Insurance expense	15	15
Fees earned	1,880	1,880
Drawings	600	600
Income summary	1,880	1,880
Accounts receivable	2,330	2,330
Capital	600	19,257

Required:

Reconstruct the December 31, 19x1, *closing entries* (in general journal form).

28. Given the following T-accounts, prepare the following items for the Cowens Company for the month of January, 19x1:

   a. Closing entries
   b. After-closing trial balance
   c. Balance sheet
   d. Income statement
   e. Statement of capital

Cash		Accounts Receivable	
25,000	(1) 3,500	11,710	(2) 4,700
(2) 4,700	(3) 2,300	(7) 1,000	
(4) 12,000	(5) 9,000	8,010	
	(6) 1,000		
25,900			

Note Payable		Supplies	
(1) 3,500	3,800	1,090	
	300	(3) 2,300	(8) 1,900
		1,490	

Unearned Fees		Fees Earned	
(9) 7,000	4,000		(7) 1,000
	(4) 12,000		(9) 7,000
	9,000		8,000

Capital		Withdrawals	
	30,000	(6) 1,000	
	30,000	1,000	

Salaries		Supplies Used	
(5) 9,000		(8) 1,900	
9,000		1,900	

29. Given the following data for the Havlicek Company for March, 19x1, prepare the following items:

    a. Adjusting entries
    b. Closing entries
    c. Income statements
    d. Statement of capital
    e. Balance sheet

Havlicek Company
Trial Balance Before Adjustment
March 31, 19x1

	Debit	Credit
Cash	$57,000	
Accounts receivable	4,500	
Supplies	2,000	
Note payable		$ 7,000
Unearned fees		20,000
Capital		33,000
Withdrawals	2,000	
Earned fees		12,000
Salaries	6,500	
	$72,000	$72,000

Additional data:

1. Supplies on hand at the end of March were $1,500.
2. Unearned fees decreased by $10,000 in March.

30. Presented below are the transactions of the Goodson Realty Company for the month of June, 19x1.

    June 2 The owner invested $15,000 cash in the business.
          5 Purchased office furniture for $1,500 cash.
          7 Paid $300 in cash for June rent.
          9 Office supplies of $200 were purchased on account.
         10 Received and paid a bill for $300 for advertising in a local newspaper during June.
         13 Paid wages of $200 in cash for the month of June.
         15 Received a cash advance of $500 from a customer for services to be rendered during July.
         16 Sold a house and collected $800 commission.
         17 Sold a house and will collect the $600 commission in July.
         21 The owner withdrew $500 from the business.
         23 Received and paid the June telephone bill for $100.
         25 Paid for office supplies purchased on June 9.
         27 Paid the utilities bill for the month, $35.

    Required:

    Prepare the general journal entries necessary to record the above transactions.

31. On August 1, 19x1, Bill King began operating a bicycle repair shop. The transactions of the business during the month of August were as follows:

Aug. 2   King began the business by investing $15,000 in cash and repair equipment with a fair value of $2,000.
      4   Purchased land for $4,000 cash.
      7   Purchased a building for $20,000. The terms of the purchase required a cash payment of $5,000 and the issuance of a note payable for $15,000.
     11   Purchased supplies on account in the amount of $700.
     13   Completed repair work for customers and collected $700 cash.
     15   Paid the $400 salary of an employee.
     17   Completed repair work of $500 on credit.
     19   Paid for supplies purchased on account.
     21   Withdrew $300 from the business to be used for personal expenses.
     25   Received $500 cash for repair work previously completed.
     27   Paid a $50 utility bill.
     30   Made first payment of $1,000 on the note payable.

Required:

1. Prepare the general journal entries to record each of the above transactions.
2. Post the above journal entries to T-accounts.
3. Prepare a trial balance as of the end of August.
4. Prepare closing entries.

32. Below is given certain data relating to the operations of Maxwell Company for the year ended December 31, 19x1.

Trial balance data as of December 31, 19x1:

	Before Adjustment	After Adjustment
Advertising expense	$ 210	$ 210
Salaries expense	700	750
Accrued salaries payable	0	50
Telephone expense	48	58
Accrued telephone expenses payable	54	64
Capital	19,350	19,350
Land	5,600	5,600
Cash	365	365
Prepaid insurance	90	55
Fees earned	1,880	1,960
Insurance expense	30	65
Unearned fees	175	95
Withdrawals	600	600
Accounts receivable	2,330	2,330

Required:

Prepare adjusting entries as of December 31, 19x1 by comparing the above data. Also, prepare the closing entries as of December 31, 19x1.

33. The Maryland Wholesale Company has kept no formal books of accounts. The owner has, however, made up a statement of assets and liabilities at the end of each year. For 19x1 and 19x2, a portion of this statement appears as follows, as of December 31:

	19x1	19x2
Cash	$3,000	$ 5,000
Accounts receivable	7,000	5,000
Accounts payable for expenses	8,000	10,000

An analysis of the checkbook for 19x2 shows (1) deposits of all amounts received from customers totaling $50,000 and (2) cash payments to creditors for expenses amounting to $33,000.

Required:

Prepare the company's income statement for the year ended December 31, 19x2.

34. On January 1, 19x1, the Rowe Realty Company began operations. On that date, Rowe executed a contract for the purchase of five apartment buildings costing $30,000 each. Rowe paid $40,000 of the total purchase price and gave a mortgage note payable for the balance. This note was to be paid in equal installments of $10,000 due each December 31. In addition to the $10,000 principal payment, Rowe must also pay interest of $1,000 each year on December 31.

Additional information:

1. Each apartment building consisted of 24 apartments, each apartment renting for $150 a month including all utilities. During the year, every apartment was rented for the full 12 months, and all rent had been collected to date. Cash receipts were immediately deposited in a checking account when collected, and all cash disbursements were made by check.
2. Salaries for the year consisted of $200 per week for maintenance and $10,000 per year for the apartment manager. Utilities expense paid by Rowe Realty amounted to an average of $500 per month for six months out of the year and $700 for the other six months. Property taxes paid were $6,000. Other expenses paid were $3,500.
3. All expenses have been paid to date and there have been no additional investments or withdrawals made by Rowe.

Required:

1. An income statement for the year ended December 31, 19x1.
2. A balance sheet as of December 31, 19x1.

35. Below are two trial balances for the Bing Company, one before and the other after closing entries have been posted to the accounts as of December 31, 19x1. You are required to reconstruct the closing entries for December 31, 19x1.

	Before Closing	After Closing
Rent expense....................	$ 500	$ 0
Accounts receivable..............	2,200	2,200
Capital.........................	350	2,600
Withdrawals....................	425	0
Fees for services.................	4,543	0
Income summary................	0	0
Accounts payable................	1,350	1,350
Insurance expense................	110	0
Salaries expense..................	1,200	0
Prepaid insurance................	25	25
Supplies used....................	58	0

Refer to the Annual Report included in the Appendix at the end of the text:

36. Which account *does not* appear in the financial statements, but *is* used in the closing process?

37. Were more debits or credits made to the cash account during the most recent year?

38. Referring to the previous question, why is this the case?

39. Were more debits or credits made to the accounts payable account during the most recent year?

40. Referring to the previous question, why is this the case?

41. At the end of the most recent year, how much of that year's net income was not in the equity accounts?

42. Where did the net income mentioned in the previous question go?

Learning Objectives

Chapter 4 illustrates how the worksheet is used to facilitate financial statement preparation and discusses in detail the common types of adjusting entries included on the worksheet. Studying this chapter should enable you to:

1. Explain the purpose of the worksheet and how it assists in the preparation of financial statements.

2. Complete a worksheet when given the essential data.

3. Identify when revenues and expenses are recognized in an accrual system of accounting.

4. List the five common types of adjusting entries and give examples of each.

4

The Worksheet and Adjustments

INTRODUCTION

Most businesses prepare annual reports for the use of their owners, creditors, and other interested parties. In addition to these reports, many companies also provide interim reports which cover periods of less than a year such as a month or a quarter. In order to prepare financial statements at a date other than at the end of the accounting period, a worksheet is often used. The use of a worksheet avoids the necessity of many of the detailed procedures which are normally required in the adjustment and closing process. A worksheet summarizes the trial balance, adjusting entries, and, in effect, closing entries in one simple document. It facilitates the preparation of interim financial statements without recording the adjusting entries in the accounts, if the accountant so desires. A worksheet may also be prepared and used in conjunction with the regular year-end closing process. Even if the accountant intends to record adjusting and closing entries in the accounts, as would be the case at year-end, a worksheet may still be used as a valuable check on the recording process.

An understanding of the worksheet is also important for quite a different reason; it provides an excellent perspective as to the preparation of the income statement, statement of capital, and balance sheet. In short, a critical review and understanding of the worksheet will provide the reader with an excellent overview of the entire reporting process and is particularly useful in developing an understanding of the adjusting and closing process as well as the preparation of the basic financial statements. The worksheet, then, is a tool which is useful in both a practical and a conceptual sense.

AN ILLUSTRATION

In order to illustrate the preparation of a worksheet we will return again to the Kilmer Contractors example used in the previous chapters. Note that a trial balance before adjustment as of May 31, 19x1, appears in the first two columns of the worksheet in Illustration 1.[1] This trial balance before adjustment is the starting point in the preparation of a worksheet. The steps which are involved in the preparation of a worksheet are described below and depicted in Illustrations 1 through 7.

Step 1. As indicated above, the initial step in the preparation of the worksheet is to insert the trial balance before adjustment in the first two columns of the worksheet. This has been done in Illustration 1. Note that the worksheet includes six pairs of columns with each set divided into a debit and credit column.

Step 2. This step involves recording the adjusting journal entries in the second set of columns of the worksheet, the adjustment columns. Recall that the adjusting entries which were required for Kilmer Contractors included recording: (*a*) the revenue which was earned from painting one of the two houses contracted for on May 10; and (*b*) the painting supplies

---

[1] This trial balance is the one that appeared in Chapter 3.

Illustration 1

Kilmer Contractors
Worksheet
For the Month Ended May 31, 19x1

	Trial Balance Before Adjustments		Adjustments		Trial Balance After Adjustments		Income Statement		Statement of Capital		Balance Sheet	
Cash...............	10,000											
Accounts receivable...	900											
Supplies............	3,000											
Note payable........		1,500										
Unearned fees.......		2,200										
Capital, 5/1/x1......		10,000										
Withdrawals.........	1,000											
Painting fees........		1,600										
Salaries.............	400											
	15,300	15,300										

which were used during the month of May. The Company received an advance payment of $2,200 from one of its customers on May 10 for the painting of two houses at some future date. At the end of May, Kilmer had painted one of the two houses and therefore half of the $2,200 had been earned but not recorded in the accounts as earned revenue. On May 2, Kilmer had purchased painting supplies at a cost of $3,000. At May 31, the unused painting supplies on hand had an original cost of $2,000 indicating that supplies with a cost of $1,000 (supplies costing $3,000 originally purchased less the supplies still on hand with an original cost of $2,000) had been used during the month of May and should therefore be charged to expense. The adjusting entries required in order to record these events have been made and recorded in the second set of columns of Illustration 2. Accounts which are affected by the adjusting entries but which do not appear in the trial balance before adjustment must be added below the original listing of accounts in the worksheet. For example, in adjustment (b) there was no account for supplies used in the trial balance before adjustment. Therefore, the account title "supplies used" was entered on the worksheet below the original trial balance accounts.

For purposes of reference, the debit and the credit amounts of each entry have been associated with an identifying letter to the left of each amount. For example, note that the debit to unearned fees and the related credit to painting fees recorded in the adjustments columns are labeled with the identifying letter (a). This notation indicates that this particular debit and credit represents a single journal entry. Also observe that each adjusting journal entry is explained at the bottom of the worksheet with the same notation used as a reference.

Step 3. The third step in the worksheet process is the preparation of an adjusted trial balance. The preparation of an adjusted trial balance indicates how the adjusting entries affect the various accounts which are included in the trial balance before adjustment. The adjusted trial balance is completed by combining the trial balance before adjustment (in the first two columns of the worksheet) with the related adjustments which were made in the second set of columns. This has been done in Illustration 3 and the resulting adjusted trial balance appears in the third set of columns of the worksheet. Note that the debit and credit columns of the trial balance after adjustment columns have been totaled in order to check the arithmetic accuracy of this step.

Step 4. The next step involves the distribution of each amount which appears in the adjusted trial balance to the appropriate columns of the income statement, statement of capital, or the balance sheet columns of the worksheet. Note that the balances in the cash, accounts receivable, supplies, notes payable, and unearned fees accounts were transferred directly to the balance sheet columns of the worksheet. The balances in the capital account and the withdrawals account were transferred to the state-

Illustration 2

Kilmer Contractors
Worksheet
For the Month Ended May 31, 19x1

	Trial Balance Before Adjustments		Adjustments		Trial Balance After Adjustments		Income Statement		Statement of Capital		Balance Sheet	
Cash................	10,000											
Accounts receivable....	900											
Supplies............	3,000			(b)1,000								
Note payable........		1,500										
Unearned fees.......		2,200	(a)1,100									
Capital, 5/1/x1......		10,000										
Withdrawals.........	1,000											
Painting fees........		1,600		(a)1,100								
Salaries............	400											
Supplies used........			(b)1,000									
	15,300	15,300	2,100	2,100								

Key to Adjustments:

(a) To record revenue from one of the two houses contracted for on May 10.
(b) To record the cost of the supplies used during the month of May.

Illustration 3

Kilmer Contractors
Worksheet
For the Month Ended May 31, 19x1

	Trial Balance Before Adjustments		Adjustments		Trial Balance After Adjustments		Income Statement		Statement of Capital		Balance Sheet	
Cash	10,000				10,000							
Accounts receivable	900				900							
Supplies	3,000			(b)1,000	2,000							
Note payable		1,500				1,500						
Unearned fees		2,200	(a)1,100			1,100						
Capital, 5/1/x1		10,000				10,000						
Withdrawals	1,000				1,000							
Painting fees		1,600		(a)1,100		2,700						
Salaries	400				400							
Supplies used			(b)1,000		1,000							
	15,300	15,300	2,100	2,100	15,300	15,300						

Key to Adjustments:
(a) To record revenue from one of the two houses contracted for on May 10.
(b) To record the cost of the supplies used during the month of May.

ment of capital columns. The remaining accounts—painting fees, salaries, and supplies—were transferred to the income statement columns. All asset and liability accounts are transferred to the balance sheet columns; equity accounts (including withdrawals) are transferred to the statement of capital columns; and all revenue and expense accounts are transferred to the income statement columns. The worksheet after the transfer of each of the items which were included in the adjusted trial balance is shown in Illustration 4. Observe that each amount in the adjusted trial balance is transferred to only one of the six remaining columns, as indicated above. above.

Step 5. The fifth step in the preparation of the worksheet involves the "balancing" of the income statement columns of the worksheet. Note that an amount which is equal to the difference between the credit (revenue) column and the debit (expense) column ($2,700 − $1,400 = $1,300) is entered in both the debit column of the income statement (as a balancing figure) and the credit column of the statement of capital set of columns. This amount is the net income for the period. The purpose of entering net income as a credit in the capital set of columns is that the excess of the revenues over the related expenses for the period is income and results in an increase in owner's equity. Of course, an increase in capital is recorded by a credit. If the balance in the debit (expense) column exceeds the balance in the credit (revenue) column of the income statement set of columns, the difference between the two totals would represent a net loss for the period. This amount would be entered as a credit in the income statement columns as the balancing figure and in the debit column of the statement of capital set of columns as a reduction of the owner's equity. It is also important to note that the income statement columns of the worksheet are identical to: (1) the income summary account used in the closing process; (2) the summary entry which may be used in order to close out revenues and expenses for the period; and (3) the income statement for the period. Step 5 of the worksheet process is presented in Illustration 5.

Step 6. This step involves the determination of the ending balance in the capital account for the period by adjusting the capital balance for the income (or loss) of the business and for any investments or withdrawals which were made by the owner. This ending balance in the capital account is entered in both the credit column of the balance sheet set of columns and the debit column of the statement of capital columns (as a balancing figure). The latter set of columns is, of course, identical to the formal Statement of Capital. Illustration 6 presents this step.

Step 7. The final step in the process of preparing a worksheet is the balancing of the final two columns, the balance sheet, as a test of the arithmetic accuracy of the process. These two columns are now identical to the balance sheet of the firm. The step is shown in Illustration 7.

Illustration 4

Kilmer Contractors
Worksheet
For the Month Ended May 31, 19x1

	Trial Balance Before Adjustments		Adjustments		Trial Balance After Adjustments		Income Statement		Statement of Capital		Balance Sheet	
Cash................	10,000				10,000						10,000	
Accounts receivable.....	900				900						900	
Supplies.............	3,000			(b)1,000	2,000						2,000	
Note payable........		1,500				1,500						1,500
Unearned fees.......		2,200	(a)1,100			1,100						1,100
Capital, 5/1/x1......		10,000				10,000				10,000		
Withdrawals.........	1,000				1,000				1,000			
Painting fees........		1,600		(a)1,100		2,700		2,700				
Salaries.............	400				400		400					
Supplies used........			(b)1,000		1,000		1,000					
	15,300	15,300	2,100	2,100	15,300	15,300						

Key to Adjustments:

(a) To record revenue from one of the two houses contracted for on May 10.
(b) To record the cost of the supplies used during the month of May.

Illustration 5

Kilmer Contractors
Worksheet
For the Month Ended May 31, 19x1

	Trial Balance Before Adjustments		Adjustments		Trial Balance After Adjustments		Income Statement		Statement of Capital		Balance Sheet	
Cash..............	10,000				10,000						10,000	
Accounts receivable.....	900				900						900	
Supplies...........	3,000			(b)1,000	2,000						2,000	
Note payable........		1,500				1,500						1,500
Unearned fees.......		2,200	(a)1,100			1,100						1,100
Capital, 5/1/x1......		10,000				10,000				10,000		
Withdrawals.........	1,000				1,000				1,000			
Painting fees........		1,600		(a)1,100		2,700		2,700				
Salaries............	400				400		400					
Supplies used........			(b)1,000		1,000		1,000					
	15,300	15,300	2,100	2,100	15,300	15,300	1,400	2,700				
Net income for May...							1,300			1,300		
							2,700	2,700				

Key to Adjustments:

(a) To record revenue from one of the two houses contracted for on May 10.
(b) To record the cost of the supplies used during the month of May.

Illustration 6

Kilmer Contractors
Worksheet
For the Month Ended May 31, 19x1

	Trial Balance Before Adjustments		Adjustments		Trial Balance After Adjustments		Income Statement		Statement of Capital		Balance Sheet	
Cash............	10,000				10,000						10,000	
Accounts receivable......	900				900						900	
Supplies........	3,000			(b)1,000	2,000						2,000	
Note payable........		1,500				1,500						1,500
Unearned fees.........		2,200	(a)1,100			1,100						1,100
Capital, 5/1/x1......		10,000				10,000				10,000		
Withdrawals........	1,000				1,000				1,000			
Painting fees........		1,600		(a)1,100		2,700		2,700				
Salaries........	400				400		400					
Supplies used.......			(b)1,000		1,000		1,000					
	15,300	15,300	2,100	2,100	15,300	15,300	1,400	2,700				
Net income for May......							1,300			1,300		
							2,700	2,700				
Capital, 5/31/x1......									11,300			10,300
									11,300	11,300	10,300	11,300

Key to Adjustments:
 (a) To record revenue from one of the two houses contracted for on May 10.
 (b) To record the cost of the supplies used during the month of May.

Illustration 7

Kilmer Contractors
Worksheet
For the Month Ended May 31, 19x1

	Trial Balance Before Adjustments		Adjustments		Trial Balance After Adjustments		Income Statement		Statement of Capital		Balance Sheet	
Cash	10,000				10,000						10,000	
Accounts receivable	900				900						900	
Supplies	3,000			(b)1,000	2,000						2,000	
Note payable		1,500				1,500						1,500
Unearned fees		2,200	(a)1,100			1,100						1,100
Capital, 5/1/x1		10,000				10,000				10,000		
Withdrawals	1,000				1,000				1,000			
Painting fees		1,600		(a)1,100		2,700		2,700				
Salaries	400				400		400					
Supplies used			(b)1,000		1,000		1,000					
	15,300	15,300	2,100	2,100	15,300	15,300	1,400	2,700				
Net income for May							1,300			1,300		
							2,700	2,700		11,300		
Capital, 5/31/x1									1,000			11,300
									10,300			
									11,300	11,300	12,900	12,900

Key to Adjustments:

(a) To record revenue from one of the two houses contracted for on May 10.
(b) To record the cost of the supplies used during the month of May.

As previously indicated, the completed worksheet is a one-page summary of the adjusting and closing procedures. A critical review of Illustration 7 will provide the reader with an excellent overview of this process. Observe that preparing the financial statements from the completed worksheet would be a simple process since all of the necessary information has already been sorted into the appropriate worksheet columns.

When the worksheet is used at the end of the period, it permits the preparation of financial statements before adjusting and closing entries are recorded in the accounts. At year-end, after the statements are prepared, the adjusting entries indicated on the worksheet and the normal closing entries must still be entered into the journal and then posted to the ledger. When a worksheet is used in the preparation of financial statements at the end of the period, the steps involved in the accounting process described in Chapter 3 will be modified as follows:

1. Record the transactions with journal entries.
2. Post journal entries to the ledger.
3. Prepare the worksheet.
4. Prepare the financial statements.
5. Record the adjusting entries in the journal and post to the ledger.
6. Record the closing entries in the journal and post to the ledger.

In addition to the end-of-period financial statements, many companies prepare interim financial statements which cover shorter periods of time such as a month or a quarter. The worksheet is a valuable aid to the accountant in preparing these interim statements since the adjustments made on the worksheet need not be journalized and posted to the accounts. If a worksheet is used, the journalizing and posting of the adjustments will usually be done only at the end of the accounting period.

ADJUSTING ENTRIES

As previously indicated, the accrual basis of accounting requires that all revenues be recorded as they are earned and that expenses be recorded as they are incurred. That is, there is a proper matching of revenues and expenses only if the income statement for the period includes all of the revenues and expenses which are applicable to the accounting period without regard to the timing of either the receipt or the disbursement of cash. At the end of any accounting period, then, there will usually be certain transactions which are still in the process of completion or which have occurred but which have not been recorded in the accounts. These transactions require adjusting entries to record revenues and expenses and to allocate them to the proper period or periods. In the case of Kilmer Contractors, adjustments were required to record for the revenue which was earned by painting one of the two houses for which payment had been received in advance and to record the cost of the painting supplies which were used during the month of May. In general, the types of transactions which require end-of-period adjusting entries fall into the following groups:

1. Allocation of prepaid expenses to the proper periods.
2. Recognition of unrecorded (accrued) expenses.
3. Allocation of a portion of the recorded cost of a fixed asset to the accounting periods which benefit from its use (depreciation).
4. Allocation of recorded revenue to the proper periods.
5. Recognition of unrecorded (accrued) revenues.

The remainder of this chapter will discuss these types of adjusting journal entries. In order to illustrate the different types of adjusting entries, the trial balance before adjustment of Brown Company as of December 31, 19x1, will be used. This trial balance appears in Illustration 8.

Illustration 8

Brown Company
Trial Balance Before Adjustment
December 31, 19x1

	Debit	Credit
Cash	$ 2,760	
Accounts receivable	4,000	
Supplies	3,000	
Office furniture	3,600	
Accumulated depreciation—office furniture		$ 360
Accounts payable		2,000
Unearned rent		3,000
Capital		5,000
Withdrawals	1,000	
Service revenues		20,000
Rent expense	9,000	
Salaries	6,000	
Other expense	1,000	
	$30,360	$30,360

Prepaid Expenses

Certain goods and services, such as insurance, rent, and supplies, are purchased prior to their use by the business. If these goods have been used or the services have expired during the accounting period, these costs should be classified as expenses. However, the portion of the goods which is unused or the services which have not expired should be included in the balance sheet and classified as an asset. These assets are referred to as prepaid expenses. A prepaid expense will be reclassified as an expense in a subsequent accounting period (or periods) as it is used or as it expired. Adjusting entries are necessary in order to allocate the cost of each item between the asset account and the expense account.

To illustrate, assume that Brown Company purchased supplies at a cost of $3,000 on June 30. This transaction was recorded by the following journal entry:

```
Supplies ....................................... 3,000
     Cash ...................................... 	      3,000
```

This entry indicates that an asset has been acquired by the company. Supplies will be carried in the accounts as an asset until they are used, at which time they will become an expense and be reclassified as such. Note that the trial balance before adjustment reflects the $3,000 balance in the supplies account as an asset.

At the end of December the supplies which were still on hand had a cost of $2,000. Subtracting the cost of the supplies on hand at December 31 ($2,000, as indicated above) from the cost of the supplies which were available for use during the year ($3,000 of supplies purchased on June 30) indicates that it is necessary to record the difference of $1,000, the cost of the supplies used during the year, as an expense. This would be accomplished by means of the following entry:

```
Supplies Used .................................. 1,000
     Supplies .................................. 	      1,000
```

Alternatively, a prepaid expense may be initially recorded as an expense. For example, Brown Company could have recorded the purchase of the supplies on June 30 with the following journal entry:

```
Supplies Used .................................. 3,000
     Cash ...................................... 	      3,000
```

Since only $1,000 of the supplies were actually used and should be considered as an expense, the following entry would be necessary at the end of the accounting period in order to reclassify the $2,000 of supplies which were still on hand as an asset.

```
Supplies ....................................... 2,000
     Supplies Used ............................. 	      2,000
```

Note that this alternative method results in identical balances at the end of the period in both the Supplies account ($2,000) and the Supplies Used account ($1,000). Thus, either method is acceptable as long as the appropriate adjusting entries are made at the end of the period.

In some instances, companies will purchase supplies or prepay expenses which will be entirely used or consumed prior to the preparation of financial statements. In these instances, the amounts paid may be charged directly to expense when the outlay is made, simply as a matter of convenience. For example, assume that Brown Company pays the monthly rent on its office space in advance on the first day of each month. This outlay could be recorded on December 1 as follows:

Prepaid Rent.	750	
Cash		750

If the transaction is recorded in this manner, the following adjusting entry would be required at the end of December in order to reclassify a part of the outlay which was made for two months' rent as an expense:

Rent Expense.	750	
Prepaid Rent		750

Alternatively, it might be expedient to record the expenditure as follows, since the rent is paid and the benefit is received during the month:

Rent Expense	750	
Cash		750

Assuming that Brown Company recorded the transaction in this manner, an adjusting entry would not be required at the end of the month since the expense has been fully incurred and the "prepayment" has been fully used by December 31.

Accrued Expenses

At the end of an accounting period there are usually expenses which have been incurred but which have not been paid because payment is not due until a subsequent period. Many expenses, such as wages and salaries or interest on loans, may be incurred during a period but not recorded in the accounts because they have not been paid. These expenses are referred to as accrued expenses. Adjusting entries are necessary at the end of an accounting period in order to record all accrued expenses. For example, assume that Brown Company placed a newspaper advertisement which appeared during the month of December, but was not billed for the ad until some time in January. Since Brown Company did not pay for the advertisement during December, this amount does not appear on the trial balance before adjustment. Therefore, the following adjusting entry would be required at the end of December:

Advertising Expense 75
    Accounts Payable.................................. 75

This adjusting entry records the expense which was incurred but not paid during December and the corresponding liability which exists at the end of the month.

When the bill is received in January and is paid, the payment would be recorded by the following journal entry:

Accounts Payable................................... 75
    Cash.. 75

This entry records the fact that the liability has been satisfied (and assets reduced) by the cash payment. The timing of the recognition of the expense is not determined by the date of the payment; the expense was recorded during the previous month when it was incurred.

Depreciation

Businesses normally acquire assets which are used in their operations over a number of years. Buildings and equipment are examples of this type of asset. A business may purchase equipment and use it for a number of years. For example, assume that Brown Company acquired office furniture on January 1, 19x0, and expects to use this furniture for ten years before it will be replaced. Assuming that the cost of this furniture was $3,600, the purchase would have been recorded as follows:

Office Furniture.................................... 3,600
    Cash.. 3,600

The office furniture is an asset of the business and is recorded as such. Its cost should be charged to expense over the period that it is used, in this case ten years. The process of allocating the cost of an asset to expense over its useful life is referred to as depreciation. Depreciation is the systematic allocation of the cost of an asset to the periods which benefit from its use. The primary difference between allocating the cost of a fixed asset to expense (i.e., depreciation) and the allocation of the cost of a prepaid item, such as supplies or insurance, to expense is that it is normally much more difficult to measure the portion of the cost of a fixed asset which has been used during an accounting period. Therefore, the allocation of the cost of a fixed asset to expense during an accounting period is only an *estimate* of the part of the usefulness of the asset which has expired or been used during the year. Since the cost of the furniture was $3,600 and the expected useful life of this asset was 10 years or 120 months, depreciation in the amount of $360 ($3,600 divided by 10) should be recorded annually. Assuming that Brown Company did not make monthly entries to record the depreciation, the adjusting entry which should be made on December 31, 19x0 and 19x1 in order to record depreciation expense would be as follows:

```
Depreciation Expense ............................ 360
    Accumulated Depreciation ........................    360
```

The debit to depreciation expense records the portion of the cost of the asset which is recorded as an expense of the year. The credit is to accumulated depreciation, a contra account which would appear as an offset or deduction from the related asset account in the balance sheet. As the title accumulated depreciation implies, the depreciation taken over the useful life of the asset is accumulated in this account. Usually a reduction in an asset account is recorded with a credit made directly to the account. However, a contra account is used for fixed assets in order to provide additional information concerning the asset—that is, both the original cost and the depreciation expense which has been taken to date may be recorded and reported in the balance sheet. The asset and the related accumulated depreciation account would appear in the balance sheet as follows at the end of 19x1:

```
Office Furniture................... $3,600
Less: Accumulated Depreciation ........    720   $2,880
```

A more complete discussion of the procedures which are involved in determining depreciation expense is presented in Chapter 10.

Unearned Revenues   Revenue which is collected before a business actually performs a service or delivers goods to a customer is referred to as unearned revenue. Since cash is received prior to the performance of the service or delivery of the goods, the amount received represents a liability to the firm. Unearned revenues are not a liability in the sense that the company will be required to repay the money. Rather, they represent an obligation of the company to perform a service or deliver goods at some future date (i.e., revenues that have been received but not earned). Examples of unearned revenues include rent collected in advance and subscription fees received prior to delivery of a magazine or newspaper.

To illustrate, assume that Brown Company subleased a portion of its office space to Smith for a rental of $3,000 per year. Terms of the lease agreement specify that Smith will pay the yearly rental in advance on July 1. The entry to record the receipt of the $3,000 advance payment on July 1, 19x1 would be as follows:

```
Cash ............................................. 3,000
    Unearned Rent ...............................    3,000
```

Note that the trial balance before adjustment includes the $3,000 balance in the unearned rent account. Since no service had been performed at the time the cash was received, the entire amount was initially recorded in a liability account, unearned rent. Since rent is earned over the 12 month period that Brown Company provides office space to Smith, exactly one-half of the service will be rendered during the period July 1 to December 31, 19x1. Thus $1,500 (½ × $3,000) of the rent has been earned and would be recorded by the following adjusting entry on December 31:

Unearned Rent	1,500	
Rental Income		1,500

The liability account, unearned rent, has been reduced by $1,500 and revenue for the period has been increased by this amount. The remaining balance in the unearned rent account represents an obligation to provide office space to Smith during the first six months of 19x2. This adjusting entry made on December 31 emphasizes the fact that income is recorded as it is earned, not as cash is received.

Accrued Revenues

Accrued revenues are revenues that have been earned but not recorded in the accounts during an accounting period because cash has not yet been received. As such, accrued revenues are the opposite, so to speak, of unearned revenues. Therefore, adjusting entries are necessary in order to record any revenue which has been earned but not recorded in the accounts as of the end of the accounting period. To illustrate, assume that Brown Company entered into an agreement with the Fooler Brush Company on December 1, 19x1. Brown Company agreed to display a line of brushes at their offices in return for a commission of 10 percent on any sales made by Fooler if the initial contact with the customer was made by Brown Company. The commissions are payable on a quarterly basis. Assume that Brown Company earned commissions of $100 during the month of December. The following adjusting journal entry would be made on December 31:

Commissions Receivable	100	
Commissions Earned		100

This entry increases the assets (commissions receivable) of Brown Company by the $100 due from Fooler Brush Company and records the revenue which has been earned to date by providing the agreed-upon service. When payment is received from the Fooler Brush Company, the following journal entry would be made:

Cash	100	
Commissions Receivable		100

It is important to note that this second entry simply records the fact that one asset, cash, was received in exchange for another, commissions receivable; revenues were not affected. The revenues were recorded at the time the service was performed, which was when they were earned by Brown Company.

ACCRUAL BASIS OF ACCOUNTING

When a company records revenues as they are earned and records its expenses as they are incurred, the company is using the *accrual* basis of accounting. Under the accrual basis, revenues must be recorded as they are earned and expenses recorded as they are incurred without regard to the timing of either the receipt or disbursement of cash. Thus, the purpose of end-of-period adjusting entries is to update the accounting records of a business so that they are on the accrual basis.

Preparation of the Worksheet

In order to illustrate the different types of adjustments which typically are made in the preparation of a worksheet, we will prepare the worksheet for Brown Company at December 31, 19x1. The trial balance before adjustment as of December 31, 19x1 (see Illustration 8), appears in the first two columns of the worksheet in Illustration 9.

The procedures followed in preparing the worksheet for Brown Company included the following:

1. The adjustments were entered in the adjustments columns.
2. Each amount in the trial balance was combined with the adjustment to that account, if any, and was entered in the trial balance after adjustment columns.
3. Each amount in the trial balance after adjustment columns was transferred to either the income statement columns, the statement of capital columns, or the balance sheet columns. The revenue and expense accounts were extended to the income statement columns; the capital and withdrawal accounts were extended to the statement of capital columns; and the asset and liability accounts were extended to the balance sheet columns.
4. The income statement columns were totaled, and the difference between the debit and credit totals was entered as a balancing figure in the income statement debit column and in the credit column of the statement of capital columns. This difference is, of course, equal to the net income for the year.
5. The statement of capital columns were totaled, and the difference between the debit and credit totals was entered as a balancing figure in the statement of capital debit column and in the credit column of the balance sheet columns. This difference is equal to the owners' equity at the end of the year.

Illustration 9

Brown Company
Worksheet
For the Month Ended December 31, 19x1

	Trial Balance Before Adjustments		Adjustments		Trial Balance After Adjustments		Income Statement		Statement of Capital		Balance Sheet	
Cash..................	2,760				2,760						2,760	
Accounts receivable......	4,000				4,000						4,000	
Supplies................	3,000			(a) 1,000	2,000						2,000	
Office furniture........	3,600				3,600						3,600	
Accumulated depreciation—office furniture..		360		(c) 360		720						720
Accounts payable........		2,000		(b) 75		2,075						2,075
Unearned rent...........		3,000	(d) 1,500			1,500						1,500
Capital, 1/1/x1.........		5,000				5,000				5,000		
Withdrawals............	1,000				1,000				1,000			
Service revenues........		20,000				20,000		20,000				
Rent expense...........	9,000				9,000		9,000					
Salaries................	6,000				6,000		6,000					
Other expense..........	1,000				1,000		1,000					
Supplies used...........			(a) 1,000		1,000		1,000					
Advertising expense.....			(b) 75		75		75					
Depreciation expense....			(c) 360		360		360					
Rental income..........				(d) 1,500		1,500		1,500				
Commissions earned.....				(e) 100		100		100				
Commissions receivable..			(e) 100		100						100	
	30,360	30,360	3,035	3,035	30,895	30,895	17,435	21,600				
Net income.............							4,165			4,165		
							21,600	21,600	1,000	9,165	12,460	8,165
Capital, 12/31/x1.......									8,165			4,165
									9,165	9,165	12,460	12,460

Key to Adjustments:

(a) To adjust for supplies used.
(b) To adjust for accrued advertising expense.
(c) To adjust for depreciation on office furniture.
(d) To adjust for portion of rent collected in advancee which was earned.
(e) To adjust for accrued commissions earned.

6. The balance sheet columns were totaled as a test of the arithmetic accuracy of the process. If the debit and credit balance sheet columns had not been equal, this would have indicated that the worksheet was prepared inaccurately.

At this point, the completed worksheet would be used in preparing the formal financial statements for Brown Company. All necessary information is included in the income statement, statement of capital, and the balance sheet columns of the worksheet.

After the preparation of financial statements, all adjustments appearing in the adjustments columns of the worksheet would be entered in the journal and then posted to the ledger accounts. Then, the entries to close the revenue and expense accounts would be journalized and posted to the ledger.

SUMMARY

The worksheet is a tool used by the accountant to facilitate the adjusting and closing procedures employed in the recording process and to simplify the preparation of financial statements. The worksheet in essence summarizes the trial balance, adjusting entries, and closing entries in one simple document. Although the worksheet is of particular assistance in the preparation of interim financial statements, since adjusting entries are usually not entered in the records at such times, it may also be used in conjunction with the regular closing process to prepare year-end statements.

The general format of the worksheet includes a listing of all journal accounts and six pairs of columns. The initial step in the preparation of the worksheet is to insert the trial balance before adjustment in the first two columns. Any necessary adjustments are then entered in the adjustment columns (columns three and four). Adjusting entries are usually required under the accrual system of accounting to insure that there is a proper matching of revenues and expenses for the period, without regard to the timing of either the receipt or disbursement of cash. Such entries generally fall into the following groups: (1) allocation of prepaid expenses, (2) recognition of unrecorded expenses, (3) recognition of depreciation, (4) allocation of recorded revenue, and (5) recognition of unrecorded revenue. Adjusting entries are generally coded in some manner and a key to the adjustments is included as a footnote to the worksheet.

The next step is to combine each amount in the trial balance before adjustment to that account, if any, and to enter the resulting amount in the trial balance after adjustment columns (columns five and six). Each amount in the trial balance after adjustment columns is then transferred to either the income statement columns (columns seven and eight), the statement of capital columns (columns nine and ten), or the balance sheet columns

(columns eleven and twelve). Specifically, the revenue and expense accounts are extended to the income statement columns, the capital and withdrawal accounts are extended to the statement of capital columns, and the asset and liability accounts are extended to the balance sheet columns.

The income statement columns are then "balanced" by entering a debit in the amount of net income for the period or a credit in the amount of net loss for the period. At the same time a credit in the amount of net income or a debit in the amount of net loss is entered in the appropriate statement of capital column.

The statement of capital columns are similarly "balanced" by entering an amount equal to the difference between the debit and credit totals in the statement of capital debit column and in the balance sheet credit column. This difference represents the owners' equity at the end of the period.

As a final step in the worksheet preparation, the balance sheet columns are totaled as a test of the arithmetic accuracy of the process. At this point all necessary information for preparing the formal financial statements is included in the income statement columns, the statement of capital columns, and the balance sheet columns. If the worksheet were being used as part of a year-end closing, the adjusting entries included on the worksheet as well as the normal closing entries would be entered in the general journal and posted to the ledger.

KEY DEFINITIONS

Accrual basis of accounting The accrual basis of accounting is the process of recording revenues in the period in which they are earned and recording expenses in the period in which they are incurred.

Accrued expenses Accrued expenses are expenses, such as wages and salaries or interest on loans, which have been incurred during a period but not yet recorded in the accounts because they have not yet been paid.

Accrued revenues Accrued revenues are revenues which have been earned but not yet recorded in the accounts during the accounting period because cash has not yet been received.

Accumulated depreciation Accumulated depreciation is a contra account which appears as an offset or deduction from the related asset account in the balance sheet. The depreciation taken over the useful life of the asset is accumulated in this account.

Adjusted trial balance The adjusted trial balance is prepared by combining the trial balance before adjustments with the related adjusting entries.

Adjusting entries At the end of any accounting period there will usually be certain transactions which are still in the process of completion or which have occurred but which have not yet been recorded in the accounts. These transactions require adjusting entries in order to record revenues and expenses and to allocate them to the proper period.

Closing entries Closing entries are entries which are prepared in order to close out or transfer the balances in temporary accounts to the capital account.

Contra account A contra account is an account which is offset against or deducted from another account in the financial statements.

Depreciation Depreciation is the systematic allocation of the cost of an asset to the periods which benefit from its use.

Interim financial statements These are financial statements which cover periods of less than a year such as a month or a quarter.

Prepaid expenses Certain goods and services, such as insurance, rent, and supplies, are often paid for prior to their use by the business. The portion of the goods which has not been used up or the services which have not expired should be included in the balance sheet and classified as an asset.

Unearned revenues Unearned revenues are revenues which are collected before a business actually performs a service or delivers goods to a customer.

Worksheet A worksheet summarizes the trial balance, adjusting entries, and closing entries in one simple document. It also permits the preparation of interim financial statements without recording the adjusting entries in the accounts. The worksheet may also be prepared and used in conjunction with the regular year-end closing process. Even if the accountant intends to record the adjusting and closing entries in the accounts, such as would be the case at year-end, the worksheet may still be used as a valuable check on the recording process.

QUESTIONS

1. What is the purpose of the worksheet?

2. How is the adjusted trial balance prepared?

3. Which accounts are closed at the end of the period?

4. Explain how the net income for the period is calculated and presented on the worksheet.

5. How are the adjusting entries for the period included in the worksheet?

6. Explain the relationship of the worksheet to the financial statements.

7. Are prepaid expenses reclassified as expenses in future periods? Why?

8. How is revenue which is collected before a business actually performs a service classified in the financial statements?

9. Explain the accrual basis of accounting. How does it differ from the cash basis?

10. What check may be used in order to determine if the worksheet was prepared accurately?

EXERCISES

11. Boyd Company purchased a two-year insurance policy on June 30 for $900 and recorded the transaction with a debit to the Prepaid Insurance account. Give the adjusting journal entry necessary to record the insurance that has expired as of December 31.

12. Below are the 19x1 adjusting entries for Branson Shoe Repairs.

a.	Supplies expense	275	
	Supplies		275
b.	Rent expense	500	
	Prepaid rent		500
c.	Interest receivable	150	
	Interest income		150
d.	Wage expense	75	
	Wages payable		75
e.	Repair fees	25	
	Unearned fees		25
f.	Fees receivable	33	
	Repair fees		33

Give a possible explanation for each of the above adjusting entries.

13. Gardner Company leases a building to a client at a rental of $2,400 per year on June 1, 19x1. Give the required December 31, 19x1, adjusting entry on the books of Gardner Company under each of the following assumptions.

    a. The rent is paid in advance on June 1, 19x1, and is recorded by crediting Unearned Rent.
    b. The rent is paid in advance on June 1, 19x1, and is recorded by crediting Rental Income.
    c. The rent for the period of June 1, 19x1, to May 31, 19x2, is to be paid on May 30, 19x2.

14. Prepare the adjusting entries required at December 31, 19x1, in each of the following cases:

    a. Herman Company was assessed property taxes of $350 for 19x1. The taxes were due April 15, 19x2.
    b. Norton Company's payroll was $6,000 per month and wages were paid on the 15th of the following month. The company closes its books on December 31.
    c. Frazier Company has $3,000 of savings bonds. Interest receivable on these bonds was $180 at December 31.
    d. Foreman Company owns a building costing $30,000. $1,000 of the cost is to be allocated to expense in 19x1.

15. The income statement for 19x2 for the Lang Company reflected wage expense of $80,000. The year-end balances in the wages payable account were $10,000 at December 31, 19x1, and $12,000 at December 31, 19x2. Determine the amount of cash paid for salaries during 19x2.

16. Yestramski, Inc. signed a contract on June 30, 19x1 to rent a building for three years. The total contract price of $9,000 was paid on June 30, 19x1. Give the journal entry to record payment and the adjusting entries made on December 31, 19x1 and 19x2.

17. On March 30, 19x1 the Dandridge Company purchased a truck for $8,000 cash. The company planned an annual depreciation of $2,000. Give the journal entries to record the purchase of the truck and depreciation on December 31, 19x1 and December 31, 19x2.

18. Hayes Company made a loan to Cane Company of $10,000 at 6 percent interest on January 1. Interest is payable on March 31 and September 30. Make the entries on the books of Cane Company to:

    a. Record the liability on January 1.
    b. Record the March 31 interest payment.
    c. Record the September 30 interest payment.
    d. Record the December 31 adjusting entry.

19. Henderson Incorporated purchased $7,800 of office supplies on August 1. On December 31, it was determined that 35 percent of these supplies had been used. Prepare the journal entries for the initial purchase and the later adjustment. Prepare one set of entries assuming supplies are initially recorded as an asset and another assuming they are recorded as an expense.

20. The Kupchak Company is adjusting its accounts as of December 31. Make the adjusting entries for the following accounts:

   a. Depreciation on equipment is $2,000 for the year.
   b. Two years' rent was paid on January 1. The amount paid ($36,000) was debited to prepaid rent.
   c. Unpaid salaries as of December 31 were $9,000.
   d. Interest not yet received on an investment was $1,700.
   e. Unearned revenues were reduced by $4,500.

PROBLEMS

21. The following information for adjustments was available at December 31, the end of the accounting period. Prepare the necessary adjusting entry for each item of information.

   a. Annual office rent of $1,200 was paid on July 1, when the lease was signed. This amount was recorded as prepaid rent.
   b. The office supplies account had a $100 balance at the beginning of the year and $600 of office supplies were purchased during the year. An inventory of unused supplies at the end of the year indicated that $150 of supplies were still on hand.
   c. Wages earned by employees during December but not yet paid amounted to $700 on December 31.
   d. The company subleased part of its office space at a rental of $50 per month. The tenant occupied the space on September 1 and paid six months rent in advance. This amount paid was credited to the unearned rent account.
   e. Equipment was purchased on January 1 for $5,000. The useful life was estimated to be ten years with no salvage value.
   f. Services provided for clients which were not chargeable until January amounted to $800. No entries had yet been made to record these earned revenues.

22. From the information given below concerning the College Inn Ski Resort, prepare the adjusting entries required at December 31, 19x1.

   a. Accrued property taxes at December 31, 19x1, were $500.
   b. Accrued wages payable at December 31, 19x1, were $2,400.
   c. Interest receivable on United States government bonds owned at December 31, 19x1, was $75.
   d. A tractor had been obtained on October 31 from Equipment Rentals, Inc., at a daily rate of $4. No rental payment had yet been made. Continued use of the tractor was expected through the month of January.

e. A portion of the land owned by the resort had been leased to a riding stable at a yearly rental of $3,600. One year's rent was collected in advance at the date of the lease (November 1) and credited to Unearned Rental Revenue.
f. Another portion of the land owned had also been rented on October 1 to a service station operator at an annual rate of $1,200. No rent had as yet been collected from this tenant.
g. On December 31, the College Inn Ski Resort signed an agreement to lease a truck from Gray Drive Ur-Self Company for the next calendar year at a rate of 10 cents for each mile of use. The Resort estimates that they will drive this truck for about 1,000 miles per month.
h. On September 1, the Company purchased a three-year fire insurance policy for $360. At the time the policy was acquired, the Company debited insurance expense and credited cash.

23. Below is given the September 30, 19x1, trial balance *before* adjustment of the Cavilier Company.

Cavilier Company
Trial Balance
September 30, 19x1

Cash	$ 2,700	
Supplies	1,250	
Prepaid rent	1,800	
Land	10,000	
Accounts payable		$ 3,500
Fees received in advance		2,500
Capital		7,250
Drawings	500	
Commissions earned		5,800
Fees earned		2,200
Wages and salaries expense	4,000	
Utilities expense	550	
Miscellaneous expense	450	
	$21,250	$21,250

Other data:
1. Supplies on hand at the end of September totaled $750.
2. In accordance with the terms of the lease, the annual rental of $1,800 was paid in advance on April 1, 19x1.
3. Wages and salaries earned by employees but unpaid at September 30, 19x1, amounted to $450.
4. Of the balance in the Fees Received in Advance account, $1,500 had not been earned as of September 30, 19x1.
5. On September 1, 19x1, Cavilier Company rented certain equipment to the Alpha Fraternity under the following terms: $50 per month payable on the first day of each month following the start of the rental arrangement.

Required:

Prepare all journal entries necessary to: (1) adjust the accounts and (2) close the books as of September 30, 19x1.

24. Given below is the trial balance before adjustment and the adjusted trial balance for Doak Company at December 31, 19x1.

Doak Company
Trial Balance and Adjusted Trial Balance
December 31, 19x1

	Trial Balance		Adjusted Trial Balance	
Cash.....................	$ 3,000		$ 3,000	
Accounts receivable...........	2,500		2,500	
Rent receivable...............	0		200	
Prepaid insurance.............	1,000		600	
Supplies	1,200		400	
Office furniture...............	3,000		3,000	
Accumulated depreciation—office furniture............		$ 900		$ 1,200
Land.......................	7,000		7,000	
Accounts payable.............		1,500		1,500
Notes payable................		2,000		2,000
Interest payable...............		0		100
Unearned fees................		800		300
Wages payable................		0		600
Withdrawals..................	500		500	
Capital.....................		9,000		9,000
Service fees...................		10,000		10,500
Rental income................		600		800
Wage expense.................	6,000		6,600	
Insurance expense.............	0		400	
Depreciation expense..........	0		300	
Interest expense...............	100		200	
Supplies expense..............	0		800	
Other expenses................	500		500	
	$24,800	$24,800	$26,000	$26,000

Prepare the adjusting and closing journal entries made by Doak Company on December 31, 19x1.

25. Below is the trial balance for the Martin Company:

Martin Company
Trial Balance
December 31, 19x1

Cash	$ 800	
Notes receivable...................................	2,500	
Prepaid insurance.................................	750	
Land..	21,000	
Service revenue received in advance....................		$ 3,500
Mortgage payable...................................		5,000
Capital		14,700
Commissions earned.................................		9,000
Salaries expense.....................................	6,500	
Miscellaneous expense...............................	650	
	$32,200	$32,200

Data for adjustments:

a. Accrued salaries at December 31, 19x1, were $220.
b. Accrued interest on the mortgage at December 31, 19x1, was $250.
c. At year-end, one-half of the service revenue received in advance had been earned.
d. Insurance expense for 19x1 was $375.
e. Accrued interest on the notes receivable at December 31, 19x1, was $20.

Required:

1. Prepare a worksheet for Martin Company at December 31, 19x1.
2. Prepare an income statement for the year and the balance sheet as of December 31, 19x1.

26. As chief accountant for Ford Company, it is your job to prepare end-of-period financial statements for the firm. You had an assistant prepare the following unadjusted trial balance from the books of the company.

Ford Company
Trial Balance
December 31, 19x1

Cash	$ 1,100	
Accounts receivable	800	
Prepaid insurance	900	
Office furniture	4,000	
Accumulated depreciation— office furniture		$ 400
Land	8,000	
Accounts payable		900
Unearned revenues		1,500
Note payable		2,500
Capital		9,600
Withdrawals	400	
Service revenues		4,100
Rent expense	600	
Salaries expense	1,000	
Supplies expense	2,000	
Other expenses	200	
	$19,000	$19,000

The following information was also gathered from the books of the Ford Company:

a. The company paid $900 for a three-year insurance policy on June 30, 19x1.
b. The office furniture was purchased January 1, 19x0, and is expected to have a 10-year life and no salvage value. Depreciation for 19x1 has not been recorded.
c. The unearned revenues account was created when Ford Company was paid $1,500 for services to be rendered. One-third of these services were rendered on December 1, 19x1.

d. Interest of $20 has accrued on the note payable at December 31.
e. Ford Company paid $600 on August 1 as annual rent for its warehouse. This amount was debited to rent expense.
f. $100 of salaries have been earned by employees but not yet paid or recorded on the books.
g. Supplies on hand at December 31 had a cost of $500.

Required:

1. Prepare a worksheet for Ford Company at December 31, 19x1.
2. Prepare the company's balance sheet, income statement, and statement of capital.

27. Given below is a trial balance before adjustment for Unseld Company.

Unseld Company
Trial Balance Before Adjustment
December 31, 19x3

Cash	$ 2,500	
Accounts receivable	1,600	
Notes receivable	2,100	
Office furniture	3,000	
Accumulated depreciation—office furniture		$ 300
Accounts payable		1,800
Unearned fees		425
Capital		5,900
Withdrawals	360	
Service fees		2,050
Rent income		350
Supplies expense	800	
Insurance expense	115	
Wage expense	350	
	$10,825	$10,825

On December 31, the accountant for Unseld Company found several items which he thought needed adjustment in the preparation of the worksheet. Below are listed these items which may or may not need adjustment.

a. The office furniture which was purchased on January 1, 19x1 is being depreciated over a 20-year life with no salvage value.
b. Wages for the last week of the year amounted to $50 which would not be paid until January 6, 19x4.
c. Unearned fees worth $200 will be earned as of December 31, and the rest will be earned in January.
d. Insurance of $100 was unexpired as of December 31.
e. Supplies worth $500 were on hand at the end of the year.
f. Accrued interest on notes receivable amounts to 6 percent of the ending notes receivable balance.
g. Rental income earned but not yet received included $200 for the month of November and $100 for December.

Required:

Prepare a worksheet as of December 31, 19x3 for Unseld Company using 14-column worksheet paper.

28. Given below is a trial balance before adjustment for Holmes Company.

Holmes Company
Trial Balance Before Adjustment
December 31, 19x1

Cash	$1,100	
Accounts receivable	800	
Notes receivable	1,500	
Office furniture	2,000	
Accumulated depreciation—		
office furniture		$ 400
Accounts payable		1,250
Unearned fees		500
Capital		4,350
Withdrawals	400	
Service fees		2,000
Rent income		300
Supplies expense	1,500	
Insurance expense	900	
Wage expense	600	
	$8,800	$8,800

After preparing the worksheet, the accountant for Holmes Company produces the following balance sheet for the year.

Holmes Company
Balance Sheet
As of December 31, 19x1

ASSETS

Cash		$1,100
Accounts receivable		800
Interest receivable		20
Supplies		250
Prepaid insurance		600
Notes receivable		1,500
Office furniture	$2,000	
Less: Accumulated depreciation	600	1,400
Total Assets		$5,670

LIABILITIES AND OWNERS' EQUITY

Accounts payable	$1,250
Unearned fees	300
Unearned rent	100
Total Liabilities	$1,650
Capital	4,020
Total Liabilities and Owners' Equity	$5,670

Required:

Reproduce the worksheet generated by the accountant for Holmes Company.

29. The trial balance of the Aggie Company as of September 30, 19x1, was as follows:

Aggie Company
Trial Balance
September 30, 19x1

Cash	$ 6,000	
Supplies	500	
Prepaid rent	900	
Land	8,500	
Accounts payable		$ 4,000
Unearned revenues		1,050
Capital		10,000
Withdrawals	1,000	
Commissions earned		10,100
Salaries expense	7,500	
Miscellaneous expense	750	
	$25,150	$25,150

Other financial data:

a. The cost of supplies on hand at the end of September was $100.
b. In accordance with the terms of its lease, the company paid its annual rent of $900 on September 1.
c. Salaries earned by employees but not paid as of September 30, 19x1 totaled $500.
d. Of the balance in the unearned revenues account, $450 had not been earned as of September 30, 19x1.
e. Included in the miscellaneous expense account was the cost of a fire insurance policy purchased on August 31, 19x1, at a cost of $180. The policy expires on August 31, 19x3.

Required:

Prepare adjusting journal entries for the above data. Prepare closing entries.

30. Given the worksheet on the next page for the CMB Construction Company, fill in the necessary amounts and prepare an income statement, a balance sheet, and a statement of capital as of December 31, 19x2.

CMB Construction Company
Worksheet
For the Year Ended December 31, 19x2

	Trial Balance Before Adjustments		Adjustments		Trial Balance After Adjustments		Income Statement		Statement of Capital		Balance Sheet	
Cash	$ 3,750				$ 3,750						$ 3,750	
Accounts receivable	2,000				2,000						2,000	
Supplies	500			$200	300						300	
Equipment	15,900				15,900						15,900	
Accumulated depreciation—equipment		$ 900		500		$ 1,400						$1,400
Accounts payable		400				400							400
Unearned fees		6,700				6,700							6,700
Capital (1/1/x2)		10,000				10,000				$10,000			
Revenues		6,625				6,625		$6,625					
Salaries	2,475				2,475		$2,475					
Depreciation expense			$500		500		500					
Supplies used			200		200		200					
	$24,625	$24,625	$700	$700	$25,125	$25,125	$3,175	$6,625				
Net income							(a)			(a)		
							(b)	(b)		(d)		
							$6,625	$6,625	(h)			(e)
Capital, 12/31/x2									(e)		(g)	(g)
									(f)	(f)		

31. Below is given a trial balance before and after adjustment for Bonham Company at December 31, 19x1.

Bonham Company
Trial Balance Before Adjustment
December 31, 19x1

Cash	$ 800	
Accounts receivable	1,100	
Prepaid insurance	600	
Supplies	2,250	
Office furniture	2,500	
Accumulated depreciation—office furniture		$ 500
Land	4,000	
Accounts payable		700
Unearned fees		750
Note payable		2,000
Capital		5,450
Withdrawals	150	
Service fees		3,750
Rent income		200
Salaries expense	1,200	
Other expenses	750	
	$13,350	$13,350

Bonham Company
Trial Balance After Adjustment
December 31, 19x1

Cash	$ 800	
Accounts receivable	1,100	
Rent receivable	200	
Prepaid insurance	300	
Supplies	750	
Office furniture	2,500	
Accumulated depreciation—office furniture		$ 1,000
Land	4,000	
Accounts payable		775
Interest payable		20
Unearned fees		500
Unearned rent		50
Note payable		2,000
Capital		5,450
Withdrawals	150	
Service fees		4,000
Rent income		350
Salaries expense	1,200	
Advertising expense	75	
Insurance expense	300	
Depreciation expense	500	
Interest expense	20	
Supplies expense	1,500	
Other expenses	750	
	$14,145	$14,145

Required:

Prepare the adjusting entries for Bonham Company for 19x1. Also, prepare closing entries.

32. The trial balance of the Blanchard Company as of September 30, 19x1, was as follows:

Blanchard Company
Trial Balance
September 30, 19x1

Cash	$ 8,450	
Supplies	900	
Prepaid rent	1,800	
Land	16,450	
Accounts payable		$ 9,750
Unearned revenues		900
Capital		21,850
Withdrawals	500	
Commissions earned		5,500
Salaries expense	9,000	
Miscellaneous expense	900	
	$38,000	$38,000

Other financial data:

a. The cost of supplies on hand at the end of September was $150.
b. In accordance with the terms of its lease, the company paid its annual rent of $1,800 on September 1.
c. Salaries earned by employees but not paid as of September 30, 19x1, totaled $725.
d. Of the balance in the unearned revenues account, $250 had not been earned as of September 30, 19x1.
e. Included in the miscellaneous expense account was the cost of a fire insurance policy purchased on August 31, 19x1, at a cost of $360. The policy expires on August 31, 19x3.

Required:

1. Prepare a worksheet for Blanchard Company at September 30, 19x1.
2. Prepare an income statement and a balance sheet from the above information.

33. Below is given the September 30, 19x1, trial balance *before* adjustment of the Duren Company.

Duren Company
Trial Balance
September 30, 19x1

Cash	$ 2,571.07	
Supplies	1,410.60	
Prepaid rent	1,200.00	
Land	15,000.00	
Accounts payable		$ 7,325.25
Fees received in advance		2,600.00
Capital		10,175.03
Drawings	120.00	
Commissions earned		4,925.00
Fees earned		1,110.00
Wages and salaries expense	5,315.75	
Utilities expense	200.00	
Miscellaneous expense	317.86	
	$26,135.28	$26,135.28

Other data:

a. Supplies on hand at the end of September totaled $840.
b. In accordance with the terms of the lease, the annual rental of $1,200 was paid in advance on April 1, 19x1.
c. Wages and salaries earned by employees but unpaid at September 30, 19x1, amounted to $211.
d. Of the balance in the Fees Received in Advance account, $2,100 had not been earned as of September 30.
e. On September 1, 19x1, Duren Company rented certain equipment to the Alpha Fraternity under the following terms: $75 per month payable on the first day of each month following the start of the rental arrangement.

Required:

Prepare a worksheet for Duren Company at September 30, 19x1.

34. Some of the files of Motta Company were burned in a fire and all that could be salvaged was the trial balance before adjustment and the statement of financial position as of December 31, 19x1. Both of these are listed below.

Motta Company
Trial Balance Before Adjustment
December 31, 19x1

Cash	$ 1,500	
Accounts receivable	2,600	
Buildings	50,000	
Accumulated depreciation—buildings		$18,750
Land	25,000	
Accounts payable		3,000
Unearned revenue		1,250
Capital		58,830
Withdrawals	1,600	
Revenue		2,560
Rent expense	1,220	
Insurance expense	650	
Salaries expense	1,270	
Taxes expense	550	
	$84,390	$84,390

Motta Company
Statement of Financial Position
As of December 31, 19x1

ASSETS

Cash		$ 1,500
Accounts receivable		2,600
Prepaid insurance		520
Buildings	$50,000	
Less: Accumulated depreciation—buildings	20,000	30,000
Land		25,000
Total Assets		$59,620

LIABILITIES AND OWNER'S EQUITY

Accounts payable	$ 3,000
Unearned revenue	350
Accrued salaries payable	210
Accrued taxes payable	50
Total Liabilities	$ 3,610
Capital	56,010
Total Liabilities and Owner's Equity	$59,620

Required:

Reproduce the worksheet for the records of Motta Company by comparing these two statements.

35. The trial balance of the Grevy Company as of June 30, 19x1 was as follows:

Grevy Company
Trial Balance
June 30, 19x1

Cash	$ 1,280	
Accounts receivable	1,160	
Inventory of supplies	800	
Prepaid insurance	240	
Buildings (net)	6,160	
Accounts payable		$ 6,100
Unearned service fees		550
Capital		7,600
Withdrawals	500	
Service fees earned		2,000
Salaries expense	3,600	
Taxes expense	2,510	
	$16,250	$16,250

Other financial data includes:

a. Salaries earned but not yet paid as of year-end were $250.
b. Taxes which related to the current year but were not yet recorded amounted to $60.
c. One-half of unearned service fees were earned as of June 30.
d. The prepaid insurance was bought on May 1, 19x1, at a cost of $240. It is a three-month policy.
e. Supplies used during the year totaled $200.
f. Depreciation on the buildings which were purchased on July 1, 19x0 is 10 percent of their original cost per year.

Required:

Prepare adjusting and closing journal entries for Grevy Company as of June 30, 19x1.

36. Complete the following worksheet and prepare a balance sheet, an income statement, and a statement of capital as of December 31, 19x1 for the Grow-It Company.

Grow-It Company
Worksheet
For the Year Ended December 31, 19x1

	Trial Balance Before Adjustments		Adjustments		Trial Balance After Adjustments		Income Statement		Statement of Capital		Balance Sheet	
Cash	$ 5,170				$ 5,170						$ 5,170	
Accounts receivable	1,300				1,300						1,300	
Supplies	2,675			$400	2,275						2,275	
Office furniture	12,000				12,000						12,000	
Accumulated depreciation—office furniture		$ 400		100		$ 500						$ 500
Accounts payable		900		1,000		1,900						1,900
Capital (1/1/x1)		17,845				17,845				$17,845		
Revenues		7,000				7,000		$7,000				
Rent expense	1,000				1,000		$1,000					
Salaries	4,000				4,000		4,000					
Depreciation expense			$ 100		100		100					
Supplies used			400		400		400					
Advertising expense			1,000		1,000		1,000					
	$26,145	$26,145	$1,500	$1,500	$27,245	$27,245	$6,500					
Net income							(e)	(f)	(h) (c)	(e) (d) (c)	(a)	(b) (a)
							$6,500	$7,000	(b)			
							(f)					
								$7,000				

Learning Objectives

Chapter 5 discusses the accounting for a company that sells a product. This chapter also discusses alternative methods of revenue and cost recognition. Studying this chapter should enable you to:

1. Illustrate the accounting for a retailing firm.

2. Discuss the components of inventory cost, including purchase discounts, freight-in, returns and allowances.

3. Distinguish between periodic and perpetual inventory methods.

4. Explain the concept of cost allocation.

5. Distinguish between product and period costs.

6. Discuss both the concept of revenue recognition and the commonly used methods of revenue recognition.

5
Accounting for a Merchandising Firm and Income Determination

INTRODUCTION

The preceding chapters have illustrated the basic steps of the complete accounting cycle for Kilmer Contractors, a firm rendering personal services. The income of a service business is equal to the excess of its revenues (i.e., its fees, commissions, etc.) earned for the services it provides over the expenses which were incurred by the company in rendering these services. Service companies, such as travel agencies, hotels and airlines, are responsible for a significant dollar volume of business in our economy. However, the majority of businesses in the United States are engaged in selling products. Businesses which earn revenues by selling products may be either merchandising firms or manufacturing companies. Merchandising companies, both wholesalers and retailers, acquire merchandise in ready-to-sell condition, whereas manufacturing companies acquire input materials and produce a product for sale. In contrast to a service type business, the net income of a merchandising or manufacturing company results when the revenues earned from selling products exceed the total of the cost of goods sold and the operating expenses.

While many of the accounting concepts discussed previously are also applicable to product oriented companies, there are certain additional techniques required to account for the purchase and sale of products.

ACCOUNTING FOR MERCHANDISING OPERATIONS

Accounting for Cost of Goods Sold

The cost of merchandise sold during the period is included in the income statement as an expense referred to as the cost of goods sold. The merchandise which was available for sale but which was not sold during the period is referred to as inventory on hand at the end of the year. The cost of this inventory is included in the balance sheet as an asset.

There are two general methods of recordkeeping which are used in accounting for inventories: the periodic and the perpetual inventory methods. The basic difference between these two methods is in the timing of the recording of the cost of goods sold for the period.

Under the periodic method the cost of goods sold is determined at the end of the period by making a physical count of the goods on hand and subtracting the cost of the goods which are still on hand from the total cost of goods which were available for sale. Using the perpetual method, an entry recording the cost of goods sold is usually made at the time a sale is made. A physical inventory is still taken, either at the end of the year or periodically during the year, and the inventory amounts on the books are then adjusted, if necessary, in order to reflect the cost of the actual goods which are on hand. The perpetual inventory method is most appropriate for a business which has only a limited number of sales each day. In such a case, it would not be difficult to determine the cost of each item sold and to record the specific cost of goods sold expense at the time of the sales transaction. However, in a business with a high volume of sales and/or a variety of merchandise items, it may not be practical to record the cost of each item sold at the time the sale is made. Instead, the periodic method could be used by taking a physical count of goods on hand at the end of the period to determine the cost of goods sold. To illustrate the application of accounting for merchandising operations, assume that Kilmer Contractors decided to expand its decorating operations by selling carpet to its customers in addition to its painting activities. Recall that its balance sheet at May 31, 19x1, was as follows:

Kilmer Contractors
Balance Sheet
May 31, 19x1

ASSETS		LIABILITIES AND OWNER'S EQUITY	
Cash	$10,000	Note payable	$ 1,500
Accounts receivable	900	Unearned fees	1,100
Supplies	2,000	Capital	10,300
	$12,900		$12,900

Cost of Merchandise Purchased

The cost of items purchased for resale is debited to a Purchases account. This Purchases account is used to accumulate the cost of all merchandise acquired for resale during an accounting period. To illustrate, assume that on June 1, the company purchased 1,000 square yards of carpet, paying $5 per yard in cash. The journal entry to record the purchase of this carpet would be as follows:

    Purchases................................ 5,000
        Cash   5,000

This transaction represents an exchange of one asset for another, i.e., cash for inventory. The debit to the Purchases account records the acquisition of the carpet, and the credit to cash indicates the Cash expenditure. Because the carpet has not been sold, its cost is considered an asset and not reclassified as an expense until the period the carpet is sold. Under the periodic inventory system, the Purchases account accumulates the total cost of merchandise purchased during the period. Therefore, the balance in the Purchases account during the period does not normally indicate whether the goods purchased during the period are still on hand or were sold.

Sales of Merchandise

When a business sells merchandise to its customers, it either receives immediate payment in cash or acquires a receivable from its customer which will be collected in cash at a future date. In this illustration, assume that during the month of June, Kilmer sold 800 square yards of this carpet at a selling price of $9 per yard. These sales would be recorded as follows, assuming that they were made for cash:

```
    Cash ................................ 7,200
        Sales ..............................        7,200
```

This transaction was a sale of a product for cash. The debit to the cash account records the increase in cash, and the credit to sales records the total amount of revenue generated from the sale of the carpet. If this sale had been made on a credit basis, the entry would have been a debit to accounts receivable and a credit to sales.

Determination of Cost of Goods Sold and Net Income

To continue our illustration, we will assume that the only expense (other than the cost of the carpet itself) incurred by Kilmer Contractors during the month of June was the payment of salaries to the crew which was hired to install carpet. This outlay of $1,500 would be recorded as follows:

```
    Salaries expense...................... 1,500
        Cash ..............................        1,500
```

This journal entry reflects the fact that period expenses of $1,500 were incurred and paid in cash. This cost is a period cost since it cannot be associated with the purchase or manufacture of a product and since the benefits were obtained by the firm from this outlay (that is, installation of the carpet sold) during the current accounting period.

The next step in the recording process would be to post the journal entries to appropriate ledger accounts in order to summarize the transactions which have occurred. This process would be identical to that described in Chapter 3 and will not be repeated here.

After the posting process is completed, the trial balance would appear as follows:

Kilmer Contractors
Trial Balance Before Adjustment
June 30, 19x1

Cash.............................	$10,700	
Accounts receivable................	900	
Supplies..........................	2,000	
Note payable......................		$ 1,500
Unearned fees.....................		1,100
Capital...........................		10,300
Sales.............................		7,200
Purchases	5,000	
Salaries expense...................	1,500	
	$20,100	$20,100

At the end of the accounting period, the balance accumulated in the Purchases account represents the total cost of the merchandise purchased during the period. An adjusting journal entry would now be required to determine the product cost for the month. Note that the balance in the Purchases account is $5,000, representing the cost of the 1,000 square yards of carpet which were purchased during the month of June. It is necessary to allocate this balance to record the cost of carpet which was still on hand as of June 30 and the cost of the carpet which was sold during the month of June. The cost of the items still on hand at the end of the period represents an asset referred to as *inventory*. The cost of the items sold during the period is an expense called *cost of goods sold*. The adjusting entry necessary to record the cost of the 800 square yards of carpet sold during June and the cost of the 200 square yards of carpet still on hand at June 30, 19x1, would be as follows:

```
Inventory ................................. 1,000
Cost of Goods Sold.......................... 4,000
    Purchases .............................         5,000
```

The debit to Cost of Goods Sold records the cost of the carpet which was sold during June (800 yards × $5) and the debit to Inventory records the cost of the carpet still on hand at June 30 (200 yards × $5). Since the Purchases account is closed out, it has a zero balance at the beginning of the next accounting period, July 1. The balance in the Inventory account at June 30 is also the inventory at the beginning of the next period. Thus, the cost of goods available for sale during the next accounting period will include the beginning inventory plus any purchases made during July. Note that cost of goods available for sale is divided into two components at the end of the period—the cost of goods sold and the inventory on hand. This is done by means of an adjusting entry which would then be posted to the ledger accounts. The next step in the recording process would be the preparation of a trial balance *after* adjustment. This trial balance is presented below:

Kilmer Contractors
Trial Balance After Adjustment
June 30, 19x1

Cash	$10,700	
Accounts receivable	900	
Supplies	2,000	
Inventory	1,000	
Note payable		$ 1,500
Unearned fees		1,100
Capital		10,300
Sales		7,200
Salaries expense	1,500	
Cost of goods sold	4,000	
	$20,100	$20,100

Again, the only difference between the trial balance above and the one presented previously is the inclusion of the effect of the adjusting entry which was made to record the cost of goods sold for June.

The next step in the recording process would be to prepare closing entries. The journal entries required to close out the revenue and expense accounts of Kilmer Contractors are as follows:

Sales	7,200	
Income Summary		7,200
Income Summary	5,500	
Salaries Expense		1,500
Cost of Goods Sold		4,000

The balance in the income summary account is then transferred to Kilmer's capital account by the following entry:

Income Summary	1,700	
Capital		1,700

The closing entries would then be posted to the general ledger. The reader should note that the closing entries for a retailing concern are almost identical to those for a service organization.

After the closing entries have been made and posted to the ledger, the financial statements would then be prepared as follows:

Kilmer Contractors
Balance Sheet
June 30, 19x1

ASSETS		LIABILITIES AND OWNER'S EQUITY	
Cash	$10,700	Note payable	$ 1,500
Accounts receivable	900	Unearned fees	1,100
Supplies	2,000		
Inventory	1,000	Capital	12,000
	$14,600		$14,600

Kilmer Contractors
Income Statement
For the Month Ending June 30, 19x1

Sales			$7,200
Less: Cost of goods sold:			
Beginning inventory		$ -0-	
Purchases		5,000	
Goods available for sale		$5,000	
Ending inventory		1,000	4,000
Gross profit			$3,200
Salaries			1,500
Income			$1,700

Note that the difference between the balance sheet for a service business and that of a retailing firm is that the latter includes inventory as an asset. The primary difference between the financial statements of the two types of organizations is in the income statement. The income statement for a service business (see Chapter 3) usually includes a revenue account for each major source of revenue followed by a grouping of expenses which are deducted, in total, from the total revenues for the period in order to determine income. The income statement for a retailing firm includes two major segments or sections. The revenue from the sale of goods is shown first. The determination of the cost of the goods sold (product cost) is then made and is deducted from sales in order to disclose the gross profit from sales for the period (sales less cost of goods sold). The other expenses (period costs) are then subtracted from the gross profit figure in order to determine the net income for the period.

Kilmer Contractors
Statement of Capital
For the Month Ending June 30, 19x1

Capital at June 1, 19x1..........................	$10,300
Add: Income for the month of June...............	1,700
Capital at June 30, 19x1..........................	$12,000

OBJECTIVE OF INVENTORY ACCOUNTING

The objective of inventory accounting is two-fold. First, it is concerned with valuation of the asset inventory. Valuation of the asset account is important because the funds invested by a firm in its inventories are usually quite significant; the inventory of a business is often the largest of its current assets. Second, and at least of equal importance, is the proper determination of net income of the business for the period by matching the appropriate costs (the cost of the inventory sold) against the related revenue (the revenue received from the sale of the inventory). In other words, the matching process requires that costs be assigned: (1) to those goods which were sold during the period and (2) to those goods which are still on hand and available for sale at the end of a period. It should be noted that this is really a single process; the procedures which are employed in the valuation of inventories also simultaneously determine the cost of goods sold. In order to illustrate this general process, consider the following activities of Art's Wholesalers for the month of June:

1. Purchased 100 cases of coca-cola at a cost of $3 per case.
2. Sold 80 cases of coca-cola at a price of $5 per case.
3. Selling expenses for June totaled $25.
4. On June 1, Art had 10 cases of coke which had also cost him $3 per

case on hand. At June 30, Art's inventory consisted of 30 cases of coke.

If Art were to prepare an income statement for the month of June, it would appear as follows:

Art's Wholesalers
Income Statement
For the Month of June

Sales (80 cases @ $5)		$400
Less: Cost of goods sold		
Beginning inventory, June 1 (10 cases @ $3)	$ 30	
Add: Purchases (100 cases @ $3)	300	
Goods available for sale	$330	
Deduct: Ending inventory, June 30 (30 cases @ $3)	90	
Cost of goods sold		240
Gross profit from sales		$160
Selling expenses		25
Income		$135

Several points should be noted from the analysis of the above income statement. The total inventory of coke which was available for sale, identified in the income statement as the *goods available for sale*, was accumulated by combining the cost of goods which were on hand at the start of the period (*beginning inventory*) with the cost of coke purchased during the period (*purchases*).

Goods available for sales was then divided into its two components: (1) the cost of coke which was still on hand and available for sale at the close of the period (*ending inventory*) and (2) the cost of coke which was sold during the period (*cost of goods sold*). *Cost of goods sold* was subtracted from the sales revenue for the period (*sales*) in order to determine *gross profit from sales*. Note that the gross profit from sales is determined and presented before the other costs and expenses incurred during the period are considered. The next step in the preparation of the income statement is the deduction of these expenses, in this example *selling expenses*, in order to arrive at the income for the period.

Of course, the example used above was very simple for purposes of illustration. All coke was assumed to be acquired at a single price and no discounts, returns, or losses were encountered. Our purpose was to illustrate the general concepts of inventory accounting; we will now consider some of the detailed procedures which are normally involved in this process.

INVENTORY COSTS

Inventory values should reflect all costs that are required in order to obtain merchandise (retailer or wholesaler) in the desired condition and location. If any costs of obtaining inventory (in addition to the purchase price) are not included as product costs and instead are considered to be costs of the period, inventory values on the balance sheet would be understated and expenses on the income statement would be overstated. When these goods are sold in a later period, expenses on the income statement of that period would be understated.

All indirect costs that were incurred by the business in obtaining and placing the goods in a marketable condition should be included as a part of inventory cost if it is possible and practical to identify these costs with inventory purchases. Examples of these costs would include such items as sales taxes, duties, freight-in, and insurance. The cost of merchandise is also reduced by any discounts, returns and allowances.

PERIODIC AND PERPETUAL INVENTORIES

There are two general methods of recordkeeping which are used in accounting for inventories: the periodic and the perpetual inventory methods. The basic difference between these two methods is in the timing of the recording of the cost of sales.

Under the periodic method the cost of goods sold is determined at the end of the period by making a physical count of the goods on hand and subtracting the cost of the goods which are still on hand from the total cost of goods which were available for sale. Using the perpetual method, an entry recording the cost of goods sold is usually made at the time a sale is made. A physical inventory is still taken, either at the end of the year or periodically during the year, and the inventory amounts on the books are then adjusted, if necessary, in order to reflect the cost of the actual goods which are on hand.

The above procedures describe periodic and perpetual systems in terms of dollar amounts. Either of these inventory systems can also be maintained on a quantity basis. For example, with a perpetual system on a quantity basis, a "running count" of each class or category of inventory item may be maintained, either manually or by the use of electronic data processing equipment, in order to provide information with regard to the quantity of a particular inventory item on hand at any particular point in time.

The basic difference between the two methods is illustrated by the following example:

1. Purchased 10 cases of beer @ $3 per case (assume that the firm had no inventory at the beginning of the period).

Perpetual			*Periodic*		
Inventory	30		Purchases.	30	
Cash		30	Cash		30

2. Sold 7 cases of beer for $5 per case.

Perpetual			*Periodic*		
Cash	35		Cash	35	
Sales		35	Sales		35
Cost of Goods Sold	21				
Inventory		21			

3. Ending inventory is 2 cases of beer.

Perpetual			*Periodic*		
Loss	3		Cost of Goods Sold	24	
Inventory		3	Inventory	6	
			Purchases		30

An analysis of the entries presented above indicates that using the perpetual system the cost of goods sold is $21 and a loss of $3 is shown for the missing case of beer (10 cases purchased minus 7 cases sold minus 2 cases in the ending inventory indicates that 1 case was "missing"). Using the periodic method, the $3 cost of the missing case would be included in the cost of goods sold since the cost of goods sold under this method was determined by subtracting the $6 cost of ending inventory from goods available for sale of $30 and assuming that the difference represented inventory that was sold. This is a disadvantage of the periodic method, because the cost of sales under this method will include not only the cost of the goods actually sold, but also the cost of any merchandise lost or stolen as well. More effective control over inventories may be established by using the perpetual method, either on a dollar or a quantity basis.

INVENTORY LOSSES   Under a periodic inventory system, it is assumed that all Cost of Goods Available for sale during the period are either sold or are on hand at the end of the period. Based upon this assumption, the cost of any merchandise lost through shrinkage, spoilage, or theft by shoplifting, etc. is automatically included in Cost of Goods Sold for the period. To illustrate, assume that a firm purchased ten cases of coke at $3 per case during a period, and the firm had no inventory at the beginning of the period. Further assume that the business sold seven cases of coke during the period, and that one case of coke was stolen by shoplifters. Thus, the ending inventory as determined by a physical count would be two cases of coke. Under the periodic method, the following entry would be made at the end of the period:

Cost of goods sold......................	24	
Inventory............................	6	
Purchases...........................		30

In this circumstance, the $3 cost of the stolen merchandise is included in Cost of Goods Sold because the Cost of Goods Sold was determined by subtracting the ending inventory ($6) from the Cost of Goods Available ($30). If the theft had not occurred, the ending inventory would have been $3 greater. In reality, the Cost of Goods Sold was $21 and the Cost of Goods Stolen was $3.

More effective control over inventories and inventory losses may be established by using the perpetual inventory method which was discussed earlier. However, because the perpetual method is impractical for many types of businesses, a means of estimating inventory losses have been developed. This estimation technique is discussed in Chapter 9.

The above procedures describe periodic and perpetual systems in terms of dollar amounts. Either of these inventory systems can also be maintained on a quantity basis. For example, with a perpetual system on a quantity basis, a "running count" of each class or category of inventory item may be maintained, either manually or by the use of electronic data processing equipment, in order to provide information with regard to the quantity of a particular inventory item on hand at any particular point in time.

BASIS OF ACCOUNTING

Historical cost is the primary basis used in accounting for inventories. This cost includes not only the price of the asset itself, but also any direct or indirect outlays which were made or incurred in order to bring the inventory to the firm's location in the desired form and condition. For example, shipping costs would be considered a part of the cost of the inventory if they were paid by the purchaser.

PURCHASE DISCOUNTS

Sellers of goods frequently offer discounts to their customers to recognize quantity purchases and to encourage prompt payment for goods sold on account. Quantity discounts, often referred to as trade discounts, usually represent an adjustment of a catalog or list price which is made to arrive at the selling price of merchandise to a particular customer. For this reason, trade discounts are not usually reflected in the accounts. For example, assume that the distributor offered coke at a list price of $4 per case and allowed Art's Wholesalers a trade discount of 25 percent. From an accounting viewpoint, Art would determine the cost to be employed in his accounts as follows:

List price per case.	$4
Less: Trade discount (25% of $4)	1
Cost per case	$3

Transaction	Coca-Cola Distributor	Art Net Method	Art Gross Method
Sale of 100 cases of Coca-Cola; terms: 2/10; n/30	Accounts receivable.... 300 Sales................. 300	Purchases............ 294 Accounts payable.... 294	Purchases............ 300 Accounts payable.... 300
Payment made *during* the discount period.	Cash................. 294 Sales discounts....... 6 Accounts receivable... 300	Accounts payable.... 294 Cash................. 294	Accounts payable.... 300 Cash................. 294 Purchase discount.... 6
Payment made *after* the discount period.	Cash................. 300 Accounts receivable... 300	Accounts payable.... 294 Discount lost......... 6 Cash................. 300	Accounts payable.... 300 Cash................. 300

Art would use the $3 figure as his cost; the $4 list price and the $1 discount would not appear anywhere in the accounts.

Discounts which are offered to encourage the prompt payment of purchases made on a credit basis are another matter. These discounts usually are reflected in the accounts. Such discounts, often referred to as purchase discounts, are usually stated in terms such as 2/10; n/30. This notation means that a 2 percent discount is offered to the customer if his account is settled within 10 days of the date of sale, the full amount is due at the end of the 30 day period. Two methods may be used in accounting for these discounts, the *net* method and the *gross* method. In order to illustrate these two methods, we will return to the transactions of Art's Wholesalers for the month of June and record the purchase of the 100 cases of coke at $3 per case in Art's books and in the distributor's accounts using both the net and gross methods. We will assume that the terms offered were 2/10; n/30.

Note that the seller of merchandise normally records the sale at the gross amount. One reason for this procedure lies in the fact that the seller has no control over whether or not the purchaser will make payment during or after the discount period. If payment is made by the purchaser during the discount period, the difference between the cash payment and the amount of the receivable (which was set up for the gross amount of the sale) is recorded by the seller as a *sales discount*. Of course, if payment is made after the expiration of the discount period there is no problem since the purchaser will be required to pay the gross amount in full. If this is the case, the seller will simply debit cash and credit accounts receivable for the amount of cash received.

In the purchaser's accounts, the sales price *less* the purchase discount will be recorded at the time of the purchase if the net method is used. If payment for the goods is made during the discount period, there is no problem. The purchaser will simply debit accounts payable and credit cash for the amount paid. On the other hand, if payment is made after the discount period has passed, the purchaser will be required to pay the full or gross price. Since the payable was originally recorded at the net amount, the entry for payment will require a debit to accounts payable for the net amount and a credit to cash for the amount paid (gross price); the difference between the gross and the net price will be debited to a *Discounts Lost* account. Discounts Lost is considered to be an expense of the period and is included as such in the income statement.

Under the gross method of recording purchases, the initial entry will be for the buyer to debit purchases and credit accounts payable for the full (gross) price. If payment is made during the discount period, the entry will consist of a debit to accounts payable for the original amount recorded as a liability (gross price), a credit to cash for the amount actually paid (net price), and the difference will be credited to a Purchase Discounts account. Purchase Discounts is reported as a deduction from the purchases made during the period. If the payment is made after the discount period has passed or expired, the entry will simply consist of a debit to accounts payable and a credit to cash for the full or gross price.

Note that the difference between the two methods lies in the information which is provided by each. The net method provides information as to the discounts which were lost but gives no data as to those which were taken. The gross method indicates the amount of discounts taken but gives no information as to the discounts which were lost. Because of the significance[1] of discounts lost to the business, the authors feel that information regarding the discounts not taken is critical and for this reason believe that the net method should be used by purchasers. We feel that any discounts lost are, in fact, interest costs and should be disclosed as such and not included as a part of the cost of inventories.

FREIGHT-IN, RETURNS, AND ALLOWANCES

The purchase of merchandise often involves payment of shipping costs necessary to bring the goods to the purchaser's place of business. The cost of the merchandise logically includes these transportation costs.

Frequently purchasers of goods will also find it necessary to return goods to their suppliers because the goods are damaged or unacceptable. In other instances, such goods will be retained by the purchaser and the supplier will allow him an adjustment of the purchase price, known as an allowance. To illustrate these occurrences, we will assume the following facts:

1. Art ordered 100 cases of Coke, 50 cases of Pepsi, and 50 cases of Dr. Pepper, all at a price of $3 per case. The terms were F.O.B. shipping point,[2] 2/10; n/30, and Art uses the net method for recording purchases. Art pays the freight of $10.
2. Art's distributor ships him 100 cases of Coke, 50 cases of Pepsi, and, by mistake, 50 cases of Orange Crush instead of the Dr. Pepper.
3. Art returns 50 cases of the Coke, agrees to keep the Orange Crush in lieu of the Dr. Pepper since the distributor gave him a $5 allowance, and pays the balance in full within the discount period.

---

[1] Failure to take a discount when the terms are 2/10; n/30 represents an interest cost in excess of 36 percent per annum. ($294 × R × $20/360$ = $6; solving for R, the interest rate is 36.7 percent.)

[2] The initials F.O.B. stand for free on board. F.O.B. shipping point means that the seller pays the costs *to* the shipping point only; the buyer pays the cost of transit from the shipping point to the destination. Alternatively, F.O.B. destination terms would require the seller to pay all shipping costs.

The entries to record these transactions would be as follows:

Art			*Distributor*		
Purchases	588		Accounts Receivable	600	
Freight-in	10		Sales		600
Accounts Payable		588			
Cash		10			
Accounts Payable	588		Cash	436	
Purchase Returns		147	Sales Returns	150	
Purchase Allowance		5	Sales Allowance	5	
Cash		436	Sales Discount	9	
			Accounts Receivable		600

Art debits Purchases and credits Accounts Payable for the net amount of the purchase ($600 less 2 percent of $600 or a net amount of $588). He debits Freight-in and credits Cash for the $10 freight charge that he paid in cash, since according to the terms of the purchase (F.O.B. shipping point) this is his responsibility. The seller, using the gross method, simply debits Accounts Receivable and credits Sales for the full price of the sale (200 cases @ $3).

At the time payment is made, Art would debit Accounts Payable for the amount of the liability originally recorded (net price). He would credit Purchase Returns for the net cost of the 50 cases of Coke that he returned to the seller (50 cases @ $3 or $150, less 2 percent of $150, or a net of $147) and credit Purchase Allowances for the $5 adjustment made to Art for keeping the Orange Crush, rather than the Dr. Pepper that he ordered. The credit to Cash would be for the net cash paid ($588 less the $147 return, less the $5 allowance, or a net amount of $436).

When the seller receives Art's payment, he would debit Cash for the $436 received, debit Sales Returns for $150 (the 50 cases of Coke returned @ $3), debit Sales Allowance for the $5 adjustment, and debit Sales Discounts for $9 (150 cases @ $3 or $450 multiplied by 2%). The distributor would credit Accounts Receivable for the amount he originally recorded, the gross amount of $600.

The partial income statement presented on the following page indicates how these items would be disclosed in the statements.

The reader should note that the account Purchase Discounts does not appear in the statements since we assumed that Art is using the net method of recording purchases. If the gross method were used, purchases would be included at their gross rather than net amount and purchase discounts would appear along with purchase returns and purchase allowances as a deduction in arriving at the net purchases for the period. Discounts lost would not appear in the statements when using the gross method.

Art's Wholesalers
(Partial) Income Statement
For the Year Ending December 31, 19x1

Sales			$102,800
Less: Sales returns		$ 500	
Sales allowances		300	
Sales discounts		2,000	2,800
Net sales			$100,000
Less: Cost of goods sold			
Beginning inventory		$10,000	
Purchases	$70,000		
Less: Purchase returns	$1,000		
Purchase allowances	100	1,100	
Net purchases		$68,900	
Add: Freight-in		600	$69,500
Goods available for sale			$79,500
Ending inventory			15,500
Cost of goods sold			64,000
Gross profit on sales			$ 36,000
Discounts lost		$ 100	
All other expenses		20,000	20,100
Income			$ 15,900

WORKSHEET FOR A MERCHANDISING FIRM

Like the service company discussed earlier, a merchandising firm may use a worksheet at the end of an accounting period to organize the financial information needed to adjust and close the accounts and to prepare financial statements. The following worksheet for Art's Wholesalers presents certain new elements; beginning inventory, ending inventory, and other merchandising accounts (including sales, sales returns, sales allowances, sales discounts, purchases, purchase returns, purchase allowances and freight-in).

The trial balance column is the listing of the ledger account balances at December 31, 19x1. The debit balance of $10,000 in the inventory account represents the cost of the inventory on hand at the beginning of the current year, (which, of course, is the ending balance of the prior year). This inventory would not be affected by the various purchases and sales of merchandise made during the current year. Art's Wholesalers' uses the periodic inventory technique and all purchases appear in the purchases account. The cost of goods sold for the period is calculated after the ending inventory is determined. This is done by the following adjusting **journal entry.**

Cost of goods sold	$64,000	
Inventory (at 12/31/x1)	15,500	
Purchase returns	1,000	
Purchase allowances	100	
Inventory (at 1/1/x1)		$10,000
Purchases		70,000
Freight-in		600

The credit of $10,000 to the inventory account removes the beginning inventory from the books by closing it to the Cost of Goods Sold account. Likewise, the purchases of $70,000 and the freight-in of $600 are closed to cost of goods sold. The debit to the Inventory account of $15,500 records the cost of the inventory on hand at December 31, 19x1. The debits to Purchase Returns of $1,000 and to Purchase Allowances of $100 close these balances to cost of goods sold. The amount required to balance this entry, a debit of $64,000, is the cost of goods sold for the period, determined as follows:

Beginning inventory		$10,000
Add: Purchases	$70,000	
Freight-in	600	
Purchase returns	(1,000)	
Purchase allowances	(100)	
Net purchases		69,500
Goods available for sale		79,500
Less: Ending inventory		15,500
Cost of goods sold		$64,000

Comparing the above computation to the adjusting journal entry reveals that identical procedures are used in each to determine the Cost of Goods Sold for the period (beginning inventory + net purchases[3] − ending inventory = cost of goods sold).

In this example, the only other adjustment necessary at December 31 was to record accrued Advertising Expense at year-end. The two adjusting entries appear in the adjustments columns of the worksheet. The adjustments columns are combined with the Trial Balance before adjustment to arrive at the Trial Balance after adjustments. All account balances which appear in the Trial Balance after adjustments columns are then distributed to the remaining columns of the worksheet: asset and liability accounts to the Balance Sheet columns; revenues and expenses to the Income Statement columns; and the capital (beginning capital) to the Statement of Capital columns.

---

[3] Net purchases are equal to purchases plus freight-in minus purchase returns and purchase allowances.

Art's Wholesalers
Worksheet
For the Year Ended December 31, 19x1

	Trial Balance Before Adjustments		Adjustments		Trial Balance After Adjustments		Income Statement		Statement of Capital		Balance Sheet	
Cash............................	15,000				15,000						15,000	
Accounts receivable.........	10,500				10,500						10,500	
Inventory at 1/1/x1.........	10,000		(a) 10,000									
Accounts payable............		5,100		(b) 100		5,200						5,200
Capital.........................		20,000				20,000				20,000		
Sales............................		102,800				102,800		102,800				
Sales returns..................	500				500		500					
Sales allowances.............	300				300		300					
Sales discounts...............	2,000				2,000		2,000					
Purchases (net)..............	70,000			(a) 70,000								
Purchase returns.............		1,000	(a) 1,000									
Purchase allowances........		100	(a) 100									
Freight-in......................	600			(a) 600								
Discounts lost................	100				100		100					
Other expenses..............	20,000		(b) 100		20,100		20,100					
	129,000	129,000										
Inventory at 12/31/x1......			(a) 15,500		15,500						15,500	
Cost of goods sold.........			(a) 64,000		64,000		64,000					
			80,700	80,700	128,000	128,000	87,000	102,800				
Net income for 19x1.......							15,800			15,800		
							102,800	102,800		35,800		
Capital, 12/31/x1............									35,800	0		35,800
									35,800	35,800	41,000	41,000

Key to Adjustments:
(a) To determine cost of goods sold.
(b) To adjust for accrued advertising expense.

The accounts which will appear in the company's income statement are carried from the Adjusted Trial Balance columns to the Income Statement columns of the worksheet. These are the revenue, cost of goods sold, and expense accounts.

The revenue accounts used are Sales, Sales Returns and Allowances, and Sales Discounts. The Sales account was credited throughout the period for both cash and credit sales of merchandise. At year-end, it has a credit balance which is transferred from the Adjusted Trial Balance credit column of the worksheet to the Income Statement credit column.

Both the Sales Returns and Allowances account and the Sales Discounts account have debit balances which are transferred to the Income Statement debit column, as offsets against or deductions from Sales. Since Sales Returns and Allowances and Sales Discounts are contra-revenue accounts (or negative sales), it is logical that they should be offset against Sales, the primary revenue account.

When all of the accounts on the worksheet have been extended into the Income Statement or Balance Sheet columns, the final four columns should be totaled. The net income is computed and the worksheet completed in the same manner as illustrated in Chapter 4 for a service business.

Time Period of Revenue and Expense Recognition

Although all firms earn revenue from activities such as selling a product or providing a service, the point in time at which these revenues are recognized may differ among businesses. In general, most businesses recognize revenue at the time a sale is made. There are exceptions to this rule, however. Many types of agricultural products are sold on the market in the form of "futures" even before the crops are planted. In the case of futures, the farmer makes a promise of future delivery at a specified price. Therefore, when the crop is harvested, revenues are recognized at that point in time since the sale of the crops at a fixed price is known with certainty. Similarly, the recognition of costs as expenses may also vary according to the nature of the cost incurred. A brief discussion of the timing of revenue and expense recognition is provided in the following sections of this chapter.

REVENUE RECOGNITION

Revenues are defined as inflows or other enhancements of assets of an entity or settlements of its liabilities (or a combination of both) during a period from delivering or producing goods, rendering services, or other activities that constitute the entity's ongoing major or cental operations.[4] It is the inflow of assets (cash or other resources) into a business which is obtained from the sale of goods or the rendering of services. Normally, the earning of

---

[4] "Elements of Financial Statements of Business Enterprises," FASB Statement of Financial Accounting Concepts No. 3 (Stamford, Conn. FASB, 1980), p. xii.

revenues through sales and services is a continuous process which takes place over a period of time. For example, the earning process of a manufacturer includes the acquisition of inputs, such as materials and labor, the use of these inputs in the completion of the product, selling effort, and the collection of cash. However, because financial statements are prepared for specific periods of time (i.e., one year), some point during the earning process must be selected for use in objectively measuring the revenue earned. The accounting principle underlying revenue recognition holds that revenue should be recognized (i.e., recorded in the accounting system) in the accounting period in which it is earned or realized, which may not be the period in which the cash proceeds are received. From an accounting standpoint, revenue is considered to be realized when two criteria are satisfied:

1. Objective evidence exists as to the amount of the revenue.
2. All necessary costs of generating the revenue have been incurred or can be reasonably estimated.

In the application of these criteria, revenue is generally considered to be earned when goods are sold or services have been performed and are billable. While revenue is theoretically earned throughout the entire process of performing a service or the process of acquiring and reselling merchandise, the total amount of revenue is measured and recognized at the point in time when cash or the right to receive cash in the future is received in exchange for goods sold or for services rendered. The fact that this approach results in recognizing revenue at a specific point in time even though the earning process occurs over a period of time is generally justified on the basis of the objectivity principle. That is, revenue is generally not recorded until objective evidence is available as to the existence and the amount of the revenue. However, under certain circumstnces, it is acceptable to record revenue at stages of the earning process rather than at the point of sale. These exceptions to the general rule of recognition at the time of sale are discussed below.

Revenue Recognition at Completed Production

When the production process is the final revenue-generating activity, a production-based revenue recognition point may be appropriate. This situation occurs when a business sells a product for which an objective market price may be determined as soon as it is produced. For example, if the Deep Coal Mines Company entered into a contract to sell to the Valley Power Generating Company all of the coal produced for the next five years at a price of $40 per ton, with Valley paying all transportation costs, recognition of revenue at the time of production may be appropriate.

If Deep Coal Mines produced 110,000 tons of coal at a production cost of $1,100,000 in 19x1 but only delivered 100,000 tons to Valley, the revenue recognized on a point-of-sale basis would be $4,000,000 (100,000 tons at

$40 per ton). The revenues associated with the remaining 10,000 tons ($400,000 or 10,000 tons at $40 per ton) would be recognized with next year's sales during the next accounting period. The production cost of this 10,000 tons would appear on the balance sheet prepared at the end of the current period as inventory. If production costs of $10 per ton ($1,100,000/110,000 = $10) remained constant throughout the year, the gross margin, calculated on a point-of-sale revenue recognition basis and the inventory included on the end-of-year balance sheet, would be as follows:

Deep Coal Mines
Partial Income Statement
For the Year Ending December 31, 19x1

Sales........................	$4,000,000
Less: Cost of goods sold.......	1,000,000
Gross margin................	$3,000,000

Deep Coal Mines
Partial Balance Sheet
December 31, 19x1

Coal inventory.............. $100,000

On a completed-production basis, the revenue recognized would reflect revenues from all of the coal produced during the period (110,000 tons) and not just that coal which was delivered or sold (100,000 tons). In this example, 110,000 tons of coal were produced so the revenue recognized on a completed-production basis would be $4,400,000 (110,000 tons at $40 per ton). Under the completed-production method, the income statement would include the total revenues on a production basis and the total production costs which were incurred in 19x1, as follows:

Deep Coal Mines
Partial Income Statement
For the Year Ending December 31, 19x1

Sales	$4,400,000
Less: Cost of goods sold.....................	1,100,000
Gross margin................................	$3,300,000

It is important to note that, using the point-of-completed-production basis for revenue recognition, the gross margin for 19x1 is $300,000 greater than it would be under the point-of-sale method. Under the completed-production method, the revenues that are associated with the 10,000 tons produced but not delivered, less the related costs of this production, account for the additional $300,000 of gross margin (10,000 × $40 less 10,000 × $10).

Revenue Recognition During Production

In some circumstances, the output of a business consists of a limited number of major jobs or projects under contract which require a long period of time to complete. If the general guidelines were applied, the total revenue for each project would be recognized only at the point of the final sale. This approach, which is referred to as the completed-contract method, might not result in a meaningful measure of income for various accounting periods. An alternative, the percentage-of-completion method, allows the recognition of revenue in each period as progress on the project is made.

A percentage-of-completion basis is applicable in those instances where long-term projects covering more than a single accounting period are a significant revenue generating function. Using the percentage-of-completion method, during each period, revenues are recognized in proportion to the stage of the project's completion in that accounting period. For example, if the project was 40 percent complete at the beginning of the accounting period and 60 percent complete at the end of the accounting period, 20 percent (60 percent less 40 percent) of the total revenues on the project and 20 percent of the total costs should be recognized. In actual practice, measuring the percentage-of-completion is often a problem. Ideally, the percentage should be measured on the basis of the actual amount of progress made on the project; however, in certain circumstances this estimate may be difficult to ascertain.

A comparison of the costs, incurred during a given accounting period, to the estimated total costs for the entire project may be used as a substitute for progress measurements. To illustrate the cost incurrence approach to revenue recognition on a percentage-of-completion basis, assume that the Building Construction Company signed a road building contract with the City of College Station to build ten miles of highway for a total price of $12,000,000. Building Construction Company's estimate of the total cost for the project is $10,000,000. If $2,000,000 in costs were incurred in 19x1, the initial year of the contract, Building Construction Company would recognize 20 percent of the revenues applicable to the contract ($2,000,000/$10,000,000). Building Construction Company's income statement for this contract would report a gross margin of $400,000 for 19x1.

Building Construction Company
Partial Income Statement
For the Year Ending December 31, 19x1

Revenues from road contract (.2 × $12,000,000)	$2,400,000
Less: Cost of construction to date	2,000,000
Gross margin on road contract	$ 400,000

The gross margin of $400,000 would represent 20 percent of the gross margin of $2,000,000 that is expected to result from the entire contract.

Total revenues on road contract	$12,000,000
Less: Estimated costs to complete	10,000,000
Estimated gross margin on road contract	$ 2,000,000

If at any time during the work on the contract it becomes apparent that a substantial cost overrun will be incurred or that a reduction in costs will be achieved, estimates of revenue recognized on a percentage-of-completion basis should be adjusted to reflect the anticipated change in the gross margin that will ultimately be realized from the contract.

Revenue Recognition When Cash is Received

An installment sale is a sale where the customer makes a down payment of a portion of the purchase price and the balance by making periodic payments to the seller under an installment contract. When the amount which will ultimately prove to be collectible from installment sales contracts is not reasonably predictable, the installment sales basis of revenue recognition may be appropriate. Alternatively, if the amount of uncollectible sales are reasonably predictable, the point-of-sale basis for revenue recognition should be used, even for installment sales.

Under the installment sales method for revenue recognition, all collections are considered to be comprised of two components, (1) a partial return of cost and (2) gross profit. To illustrate the use of this technique, assume that the Small Appliance Store sells direct to its customers and uses the installment sales basis for revenue recognition. On February 1, 19x1 the firm sold a washer and dryer that had a cost of $600 for a selling price of $800. The terms of the sale were no down payment and $50 per month for 16 months, beginning March 1, 19x1. Since cost represents 75 percent of the selling price ($600 divided by $800) the gross profit percentage on this sale is 25 percent (100 percent minus 75 percent). All collections from this sale will be considered to consist of a return of cost of 75 percent and gross profit of 25 percent. Revenue, cost, and gross margin will be recognized as each payment is received.

	19x1 (10 Payments)	19x2 (6 Payments)
Sales (100%)	$500	$300
Cost of goods sold (75%)	375	225
Gross margin (25%)	$125	$ 75

The Small Appliance Store would recognize $500 in revenue from this sale in 19x1 and $300 in 19x2. The gross margin and cost of goods sold would be recognized on a pro rata basis as cash is collected in installment payments.

The cash basis of revenue recognition, like the installment basis described above, avoids the problem of estimating the amount of a sale that will ultimately prove to be collectible. Revenue is recognized in the accounting period in which the cash proceeds of the sale are received, and expenses are recognized only as cash is paid. This method is often used by closely-held firms providing professional services such as attorneys, physicians, and dentists. There is little theoretical justification for the cash basis of revenue recognition, but it is simple and minimizes recordkeeping.

The cash and installment methods are widely used for income tax purposes since these methods generally postpone the recognition of income and, therefore, also postpone the payment of taxes until future periods. However, the use of these methods for tax purposes does not provide a basis or justification from the standpoint of theory for their use for financial accounting purposes.

RECOGNITION OF EXPENSES

Expenses are outflows or other using up of assets or incurrences of liabilities (or a combination of both) during a period from delivering or producing goods, rendering services, or carrying out other activities that constitute the entity's ongoing major or central operations.[5] Expenses are incurred to acquire goods and services which are used to generate or earn revenues. Under the matching concept (which was discussed in Chapter 1), the cost of the goods and services acquired are considered to be expenses of the accounting period or periods which benefit from their use in generating revenue. In other words, costs become expenses of the periods in which they are used or consumed in the process of generating revenues. It should be noted that the determination of the portion of the cost of an asset which should be considered an expense of a particular period is usually somewhat subjective. This subjectivity is caused primarily by the concept of the accounting period or periodicity of accounting, that is, the concept of determining the income earned during a specified period of time. For example, assume that a firm purchases an asset which is used in its operations for a period of ten years. Obviously, the cost of that asset represents an expense to the firm over ten years since the business will benefit from the use of the asset during this time. However, a subjective estimate is required in order to determine the expense during each separate year of that period.

In absolute terms, the earnings of a business can only be determined with certainty over its entire lifespan—from the date of inception of the business to its termination at the time of its liquidation. It is important, however, to measure income and financial position at various points in time throughout the life of the business in order to provide interested users

---

[5] *Ibid.*

such as managers, investors, creditors, and the public with relevant economic information for decision making. Therefore, the accountant has divided the life of the business into accounting periods which are usually defined as one year for reporting purposes. This aids the accountant in matching the revenues earned and the expenses incurred during a particular accounting period, even though the actual receipt of cash relating to revenues or the payment of cash relating to expenses may take place over a number of accounting periods.

Accountants have developed procedures which may be used in order to determine the portion of the cost of an asset which should be considered as an expense during a particular accounting period. For example, assume that a company paid cash for a building. At the time of its purchase, it was estimated that the building had a useful life of 25 years and would have no value at the end of its useful life. Since the building is expected to be of benefit to the company for more than one period, a portion of its cost should be recognized as an expense during each accounting period that the building is used by the firm. The total expense recognized by the firm during the useful life of the building should equal the cost of the asset since it was assumed that it would have no value at the end of 25 years. The net book value of the building included in the balance sheet (the original cost of the building less that portion of the cost of the building which has been recognized as an expense) will decrease each year since a portion of the cost is charged to expense during each period. There are certain expenditures for which the estimation of future benefit is so subjective that accountants usually make no attempt to allocate these costs to future accounting periods. Instead, costs are recognized as expenses in the period in which they are incurred because the measurement of a future benefit with any degree of accuracy is either impossible or impractical. For example, assume that Chevrolet purchased a 60-second advertising spot during the Redskins vs. Dolphins football game at a cost of $25,000. It would be extremely difficult, if not impossible, to determine the periods which would benefit from this advertising expenditure. Therefore, the usual accounting treatment would be to consider the outlay for advertising as an expense of the period in which the advertising was broadcast since the benefits to future periods usually are not measurable with a reasonable degree of accuracy.

Two general classifications of cost are used for purposes of matching revenues and expenses: *product cost* and *period cost*. A product cost is a cost that can be directly identified with the purchase or production of goods that are available for sale. These costs are carried as assets until the goods are sold. For example, merchandise purchased by a retailer would be considered to be an asset until it is sold. This cost, referred to as cost of goods sold, is included as an expense in the income statement in the period which the inventory is actually sold.

Period costs, on the other hand, cannot be easily identified with the purchase or manufacture of a product. Generally, the benefits associated with period costs expire with the passage of time. Examples of typical period costs include interest expense, rent expense, administrative employee salaries, and certain types of insurance expense. For a manufacturing company, period costs include all costs which would continue to be incurred if the company abandoned all of its manufacturing activities and instead purchased a product for resale to its customers. Period costs are recognized as expenses in the period(s) in which the benefits associated with the cost expire or are used up in the process of generating revenues.

SUMMARY

This chapter has discussed certain of the operational differences in companies, with special emphasis placed on the differences in retailing and service organizations.

For accounting purposes, inventories include all goods which are held for sale to customers, those in the process of being produced for sale, and those to be used in the production of goods for sale. The objective of inventory accounting is to provide a proper valuation of inventory, both for balance sheet reporting purposes and for the proper determination of income.

Inventories are normally accounted for at historical cost, with any savings due to trade and purchase discounts and expenses due to freight charges considered in the determination of historical cost. In addition, inventory costs must be adjusted for any returns or allowances on inventory items. When the market price falls below cost, inventories may be written down to their current replacement cost using the lower of cost or market concept.

The periodic and perpetual inventory methods are the two general methods of determining inventory amounts. The perpetual method requires recording the cost of goods sold as inventory items are sold. The periodic method involves making a physical count of goods on hand and subtracting this amount from the total goods available for sale to determine the cost of goods sold. Each inventory system can be maintained on either a dollar or unit basis or both.

Two basic general classifications of cost used for purposes of income determination are product costs and period costs. A product cost is a cost which can be directly identified with the purchase or manufacture of goods that are available for sale. A period cost, which is usually associated with the passage of time, is recognized on the income statement as an expense of the period in which it is incurred.

The matching concept requires that the accountant match the revenues earned during the accounting period with the expenses incurred to generate those revenues. Although revenues are usually recognized at the time the sale is made, other revenue recognition points may be used under certain circumstances. These alternative methods include recognition at the point of completed production, on a percentage-of-completion basis, on an installment basis, and on a cash basis.

KEY DEFINITIONS

Beginning inventory Beginning inventory includes the goods which are on hand and available for sale at the beginning of the period.

Cash basis A method of revenue recognition whereby revenues are recognized as the cash proceeds of sales are received.

Completed production method A method of revenue recognition whereby revenue is recognized at the time the production process is completed.

Cost of goods sold Cost of goods sold is the cost of the inventory sold during the period. Beginning inventory plus purchases minus the ending inventory equals the cost of goods sold.

Cost of inventory Cost of inventory is the price of the inventory itself plus all direct and indirect outlays incurred in order to bring it to the firm's location in the desired form.

Discounts lost Discounts lost is an account used under the net method of recording purchases to record the amount of the discounts which were not taken.

Ending inventory Ending inventory is goods which are still on hand and available for sale at the end of the period.

Expenses Expenses are outflows or other using up of assets or incurrences of liabilities (or a combination of both) during a period from delivering or producing goods, rendering services, or carrying out other activities that constitute the entity's ongoing major or central operations.

F.O.B. F.O.B. means "free on board."

F.O.B. destination F.O.B. destination terms would require the seller to pay all shipping costs.

F.O.B. shipping point F.O.B. shipping point means that the seller pays the costs to the shipping point only. The buyer pays the cost of transit from the shipping point to the destination.

Freight-in Freight-in is the shipping costs incurred for goods purchased.

Goods available for sale Goods available for sale includes the beginning inventory plus the net purchases for the period.

Gross profit from sales Gross profit from sales is the difference between the revenue from sales and the cost of the goods sold.

Installment sales method A method of revenue recognition whereby revenue is recognized as collections are made. Collections are considered to be comprised of two components (1) a partial return of cost and (2) gross profit.

Inventories Inventories include those assets which are acquired and/or produced for sale in the continuing operations of a business.

Net method The net method is a method of recording purchases whereby purchases are recorded at the net price—that is, the gross price less the purchase discount.

Operating cycle   The operating cycle includes the steps that take place from the purchase of inventory or raw materials to its sale and conversion into cash.

Percentage-of-completion method   A method of revenue recognition whereby revenues are recognized in proportion to the completion of the project.

Period cost   A period cost is a cost which cannot be directly identified with the production of a specific product or products. It is usually more closely associated with the passage of time.

Periodic inventories   Under the periodic method, the cost of goods sold is determined at the end of the period by making a physical count of the goods on hand and subtracting the cost of the goods which are still on hand from the total cost of goods available for sale. This inventory system may also be maintained on a quantity basis.

Perpetual inventories   Under the perpetual method, an entry recording the cost of goods sold is usually made at the time a sale is made. This inventory system may also be maintained on a quantity basis.

Product cost   A product cost is a cost which is directly associated with the production or purchase of goods that are available for sale.

Purchases   Purchases include all inventory acquired by purchase during the period.

Purchase allowances   Purchase allowances is an adjustment of the purchase price allowed the buyer by the seller. See sales allowances.

Purchase discounts   Purchase discounts are discounts which are offered to encourage the prompt payment of purchases made on account. Purchase discounts are reflected in the accounts. It is also an account used under the gross method to record purchase discounts taken. See sales discounts.

Purchase returns   Purchase returns is the account used by the buyer to record the cost of goods returned to the seller. See sales returns.

Revenues   Revenues are inflows or other enhancements of assets of an entity or settlements of its liabilities (or a combination of both) during a period from delivering or producing goods, rendering services, or other activities that constitute the entity's ongoing major or central operations.

Sales allowances   Sales allowances are adjustments of the purchase price allowed the buyer by the seller. See purchase allowances.

Sales discount   This is a discount offered by the seller to the purchaser. See purchase discounts.

Sales returns   Sales returns is the account used by the seller to record the goods returned by the buyer. See purchase returns.

Trade discount   A trade discount is a quantity discount that represents an adjustment of a catalog or list price which is made in order to arrive at the selling price to a particular customer. Trade discounts are not reflected in the accounts.

5 | Accounting for a Merchandising Firm and Income Determination   163

QUESTIONS

1. Describe the operating cycle for a retailer.

2. Explain the difference between product costs and period costs. Give examples of each type of cost.

3. The determination of the portion of the cost of an asset which should be allocated to expense during a period may be somewhat subjective. Explain.

4. When is revenue considered to be realized?

5. When is revenue recognition based upon production appropriate?

6. What is meant by the percentage-of-completion method?

7. What are the major differences between the income statements of a service organization and that of a retailer?

8. Why do businesses offer discounts and how are they recorded in the accounts?

9. Explain how the gross price method and the net price method each provide an evaluation of management. Which method is preferred?

10. Explain F.O.B. shipping point and F.O.B. destination. What effect do these have on the valuation of inventory?

11. What are two methods of inventory recordkeeping? Describe these methods.

12. How is the cost of goods sold figure arrived at under the periodic inventory method?

13. How does the perpetual inventory method act as a control?

EXERCISES

14. Using the following information, calculate the total sales for the period.

Inventory purchases	$ 50,200
Beginning inventory	10,350
Wage expense	9,300
Rent expense	1,500
Interest expense	700
Ending inventory	9,350
Net income	12,000

15. The following balances were taken from the accounts of Norris Company. Using this information, calculate the amount of the beginning inventory.

Sales	$510,000
Ending inventory	84,000
Purchases	300,000
Net income	162,000
Other expenses	108,000

16. Fill in the blanks:

Beginning inventory	$ 20,000
Purchases	(a)
Ending inventory	22,000
Cost of goods sold	54,000
Expenses	(d)
Net income	(c)
Beginning owners' equity	200,000
Owners' additional investments	12,000
Owners' withdrawals	8,000
Ending owners' equity	230,000
Gross margin	(b)
Net sales	108,000

17. Determine and fill in the missing amounts in the following situations. Each column of figures is a separate situation.

	A	B	C	D
Sales	$100,000	$100,000	$200,000	?
Beginning inventory	10,000	?	30,000	$15,000
Purchases	?	70,000	100,000	75,000
Ending inventory	20,000	10,000	?	10,000
Cost of goods sold	50,000	?	110,000	?
Gross profit	?	25,000	?	40,000
Expenses	?	?	60,000	25,000
Net income	20,000	10,000	?	?

18. Bryan Builders are in the process of constructing a new business building for Aggie University. At the beginning of 19x1, the building was 10 percent complete. At the end of the year, it was 70 percent complete. The total contract price is $1 million, and the total cost to Bryan Builders is $800,000. Prepare a partial income statement, assuming revenue is recognized on a percentage-of-completion basis, if costs incurred for 19x1 are $480,000.

19. Ivy Furniture Store recognizes revenue under the installment sales method. Recently, it sold a complete set of living room furniture for $3,000. The cost of this furniture was only $2,000. If the sale was made on March 1, compute the gross margin for the first and second year. The terms of sale were no down payment and 15 monthly payments of $200 each. The initial payment is made on April 1.

20. Prepare journal entries to record the following transactions under both a perpetual and a periodic inventory system.

    a. Purchased 15 dozen apples @ $2 per dozen (assume that the firm had a beginning inventory of 3 dozen apples which were purchased at $2 per dozen).
    b. Sold 14 dozen apples @ $3 per dozen.
    c. Counted the remaining apples and discovered that 3 dozen were on hand.

21. Scott ordered 50 cases of Swan soap, 90 cases of Sweet Breath mouthwash, 70 cases of Brush-It toothpaste, and 40 cases of Talc deodorant. Each case cost $15 regardless of the item. Carbo Distributor, the seller, extended credit terms of 2/10; n/30; however, Scott must pay the freight of $50. Carbo made an error in shipping the merchandise. Instead of the Swan soap, they shipped Rose soap. Scott agreed to keep this soap in return for a $20 allowance. Scott also returned 30 cases of Sweet Breath. Scott uses the net method for recording the purchases, and pays the balance within the discount period.

Required:

1. Make the journal entries for Scott.
2. Make the journal entries for Carbo.

PROBLEMS

22. The following transactions took place during October, 19x1. Prepare the journal entries to record these transactions.

    Oct. 1 Purchased merchandise from supplier A on account, $5,000.
    2 Merchandise was sold on account to R.P. Jones for $1,000.
    3 A $1,500 credit sale was made to J.R. Lowry.
    6 Purchased merchandise from supplier B on account, $3,000.
    9 Received payment from R.P. Jones.
    15 Sales on account of $2,000 and $2,500 were made to K.L. Putnam and A.R. Hardy, respectively.
    17 Paid supplier A in full.
    18 Received payment from J.R. Lowry.
    23 Sold merchandise on account to M.S. Fletcher for $2,500.
    24 Received payment of half of K.L. Putnam's account.
    25 Paid supplier B half of the amount owed to him.
    26 Received full payment from A.R. Hardy.
    30 Received balance of payment from K.L. Putnam.
    31 Paid supplier B the balance of the account.

23. A trial balance of the Sport Shop at the end of the first year of its operations is:

Sport Shop
Trial Balance
December 31, 19x1

Cash	$ 7,000	
Accounts receivable	9,000	
Supplies	3,000	
Inventory, January 1	0	
Accounts payable		$ 1,000
Notes payable		4,000
Capital		15,000
Sales		20,000
Purchases	15,000	
Wage expense	4,000	
Other expense	2,000	
	$40,000	$40,000

The inventory on hand at December 31, 19x1 was determined to be $3,000.

Required:

Prepare the income statement for the year ended December 31, 19x1.

24. Paul Peach opened a small office supply store on January 1, 19x1. The following trial balance was taken from the ledger at the end of the first year of operation.

Peach Office Supply
Trial Balance
December 31, 19x1

Cash	$ 3,500	
Accounts receivable	13,500	
Inventory	0	
Prepaid insurance	1,000	
Equipment	20,000	
Accounts payable		$ 5,000
Unearned revenue		15,000
Peach, capital		13,000
Sales		75,000
Purchases	40,000	
Wage expense	10,000	
Rent expense	12,000	
Other expense	8,000	
	$108,000	$108,000

A physical count taken on December 31, 19x1, showed merchandise on hand in the amount of $7,000. Other information available on December 31 included the following:

a. The equipment was purchased on January 1, 19x1, and had an estimated useful life of 10 years and no salvage value.
b. The amount of insurance that expired during the year was $400.
c. Certain customers paid in advance for regular deliveries of supplies. The amounts collected were credited to Unearned Revenue. As of December 31, $5,000 of the supplies purchased had been delivered.
d. Accrued wages payable amounted to $500.

Required:

1. Prepare the necessary adjusting journal entries at December 31, 19x1.
2. Prepare the entries required to close the books.
3. Prepare an income statement for the year ended December 31, 19x1.

25. Scott Appliance Store recognizes income on the installment basis. It sells the following items over a period of three years. Compute the gross margin on these sales for 19x1, 19x2, and 19x3. In each case, the first installment is to be paid one month following the date of the sale.

a. A dishwasher was sold on February 1, 19x3 for $400. No down payment was made. The customer must remit $40 per month for 10 months (cost was $250).
b. On May 30, 19x1, a washer and dryer were purchased for $935. The credit terms were $100 down and 20 months of equal payments for the balance (cost was $700).
c. A vacuum cleaner was sold on January 15, 19x2 for $145. There was no down payment and monthly remittances of $29 (cost was $85).
d. A refrigerator was purchased on August 15, 19x2. The purchase price was $1,075 with a $200 down payment. The balance is due in equal monthly installments of $35 (cost was $820).
e. On August 1, 19x1 a freezer was sold with no down payment for $1,210. Monthly payments of $48.40 will be made for 25 months (cost was $915).

26. The following transactions took place between Flintstone's Friendly Fish Market and Barney's Beanery during June of 19x1.

June 1 Barney buys the following items from Flintstone:

10 cases of Charlie the Tuna Fish @ $10 per case
1 Fishing submarine @ $2,000,000

Terms of the sale are 2/10; n/30. The purchase was made on account.

9 Barney notifies Flintstone that the shipment included eight cases as ordered, one case of horse meat, and one case of caviar. The submarine was O.K. Barney proposes that he keep the caviar and deduct 50¢ from the net amount which would otherwise be due. He plans to return the horse meat. Flintstone agrees and Barney mails him a check for the net amount after making the agreed-on deductions.

15 Barney pays for the submarine.

Required:

1. Record the above transactions on Flintstone's books assuming that he records sales using the gross method.
2. Record the above transactions on Barney's books assuming he uses:

    a. The net method of recording purchases.
    b. The gross method of recording purchases.

Learning Objectives

Chapter 6 introduces a model of an accounting system and discusses the basic components of such a system. Studying this chapter should enable you to:

1. Discuss the functions and requirements of a financial accounting system.

2. Identify and discuss the basic components of a financial accounting system.

3. Discuss the concept of internal control.

4. Define an audit trail and discuss its purpose.

5. Describe the effect of introducing automated equipment into the accounting system.

6

Accounting Systems and Internal Control

INTRODUCTION

A primary function of accounting is to accumulate the information which is required by decision makers and communicate this data to them. The accounting system used for communicating information consists of business documents (such as invoices or checks) and records the procedures that are used in recording transactions and preparing reports. A financial accounting system must communicate data to users in such a way that the operating performance and current financial position of a company is reported in a manner that is both meaningful and useful. All pertinent information which is required for decision making and planning and control purposes must be made available to the user on a timely basis. There are also certain other basic housekeeping functions that the system should accomplish. For example, detailed information must be made available in order to identify the specific accounts receivable balance of each customer, detailed information regarding payroll and deductions is required in order to pay employees and satisfy government regulations, and inventory balances must be available on a current basis for purposes of inventory planning and control. The accounting system of an organization should be designed to handle all of the many facets of accounting and the system must operate in a manner which is efficient, effective, accurate, and timely.

Model of a Financial Accounting System

A model of a basic financial accounting system is presented in tabular form and in the form of a diagram below. The financial accounting system shown in these illustrations indicates the procedures which are followed during the accounting cycle. Presentation of the system in these illustrations is intended to provide a comprehensive picture or overview of the information flows that are required in a typical organization. Note that this example is a summarization of the steps in the recording process which was discussed in Chapters 3 and 4. The next illustration diagrams the same general data flows in a financial accounting system. Certain features, which will be discussed in this chapter, have been added to the system which provide for more efficient means of processing the accounting data.

The basic components of the system are as follows:

1. A Chart of Accounts
2. A Coding System
3. A General Journal
4. A General Ledger
5. Subsidiary Ledgers
6. Special Journals
7. Internal Control
8. An Audit Trail

These components of the financial accounting system are discussed in the following paragraphs.

The Financial Accounting System

Inputs

- External Transactions Entered through Original Documents

Processing

- Journalize Transactions
  a. General Journal
  b. Special Journal
- Post to Ledger Accounts
  a. General Ledger
  b. Subsidiary Ledgers
- Preparation of Unadjusted Trial Balance
- Preparation of Adjusting Entries
  a. General Journal
- Post Adjusting Entries
  a. General Ledger
- Prepare Adjusted Trial Balance
- Prepare Closing Entries
  a. General Journal
- Post Closing Entries
  a. General Ledger
- Prepare Post–Closing Trial Balance (optional)
- Prepare Financial Reports

Outputs

- General Housekeeping Reports and Financial Reports for Interested and Required Users

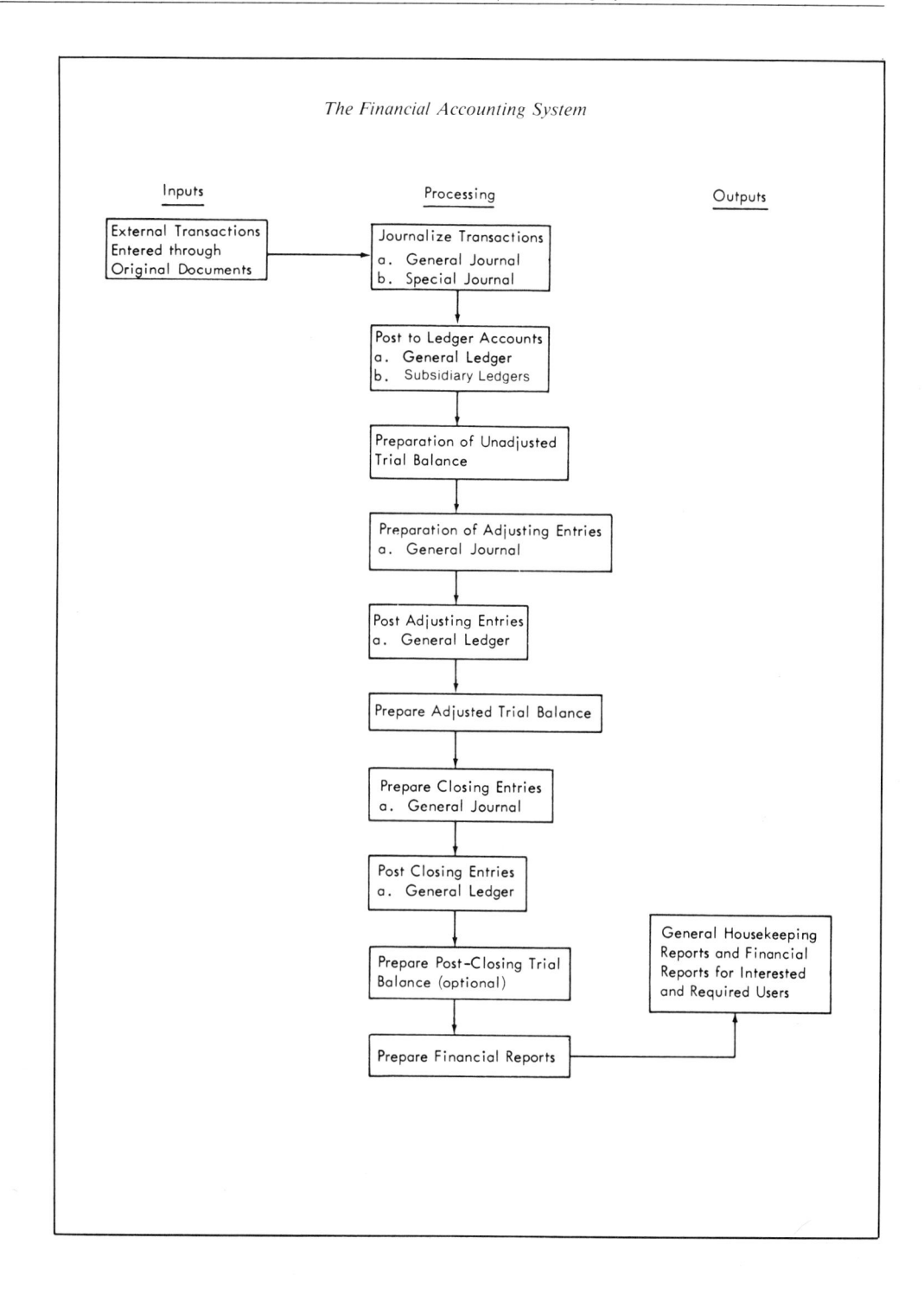

Information Flows in the Financial Accounting System

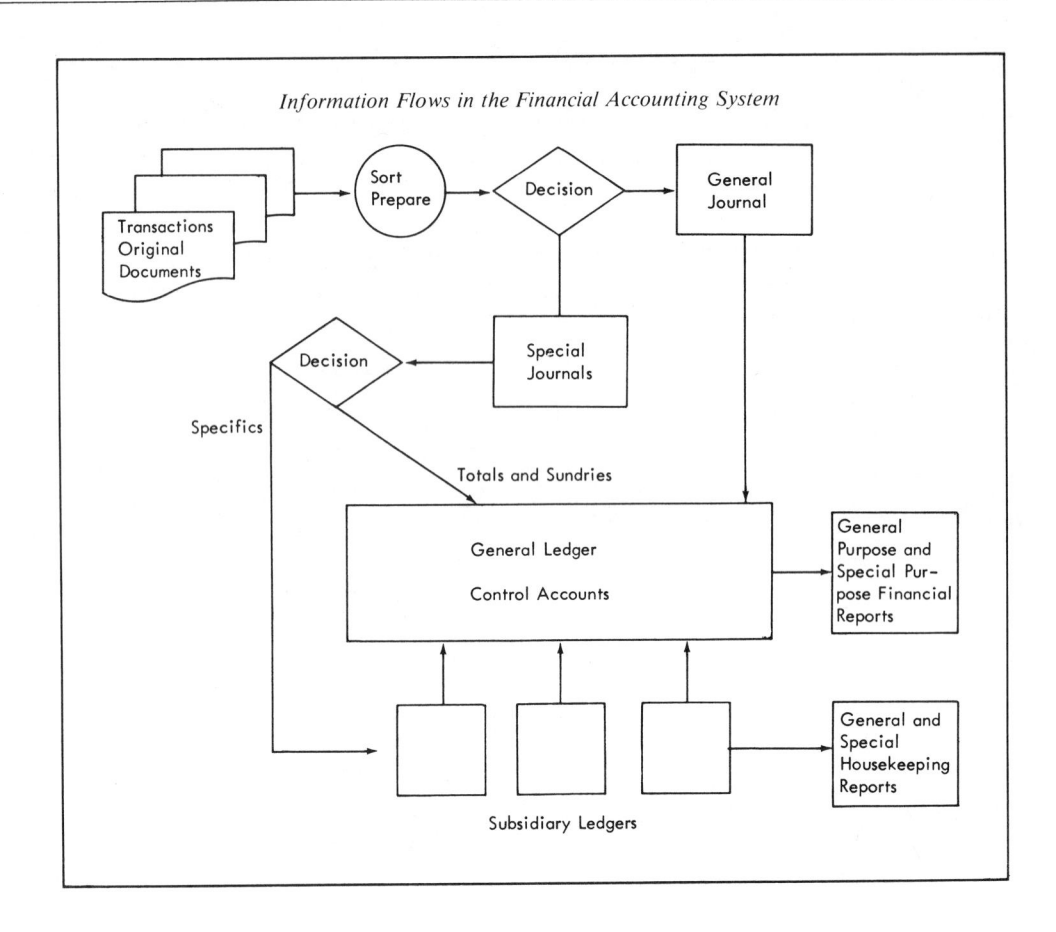

[Flowchart: Transactions Original Documents → Sort Prepare → Decision → General Journal; Special Journals → Decision (Specifics / Totals and Sundries) → General Ledger Control Accounts → General Purpose and Special Purpose Financial Reports; Subsidiary Ledgers → General and Special Housekeeping Reports]

The Chart of Accounts

A chart of accounts is a listing of all of the accounts that an organization may use in its accounting system. The scope of the chart of accounts and the ability to adapt new account titles to the existing listing is a very important factor to be considered in the process of designing and installing an accounting system. The design of the chart of accounts will affect the manner in which accounting information will be accumulated, summarized, and used by the organization.

At a minimum, the chart of accounts should include all of the accounts that appear on the balance sheet, income statement, and statement of capital or retained earnings. In most cases, however, limiting the chart to only these accounts would be inadequate since management often requires information which is more detailed than that which is included in the basic financial statements. This detailed information is required in order to manage the day-to-day operations of the business. Also, external users such as governmental agencies frequently require information not included in the financial statements, often in detailed and specified formats. In addition to the basic functional classifications, management normally requires:

1. Accounting information which is based on cost behavior patterns for purposes of planning and control.
2. Accounting information which is based on areas of responsibility for purposes of performance measurement and control. For example, information regarding divisions or geographical regions may be used in order to measure the performance of these segments.

Many of the accounts used by the organization will be utilized for multiple purposes in the management and operations of the business. For example, production cost data is required in the process of inventory valuation, but it is also necessary for evaluating the performance of the specific departments which are involved in the production process.

Coding the Chart of Accounts

In order to facilitate the use of data and to provide a unique identity for each account, the chart of accounts is normally coded numerically. A normal pattern of arrangement and coding of the chart of accounts is in the format and the order of the financial statements and the accounts included in these statements. A simplified example of the broad categories of accounts which might be included in a typical chart of accounts is presented below.

1000–1999	Asset Accounts
2000–2999	Liability Accounts
3000–3999	Owners' Equity Accounts
4000–4999	Revenue Accounts
5000–5999	Manufacturing Cost Accounts
6000–6999	Distribution Expense Accounts
7000–7999	Administrative Expense Accounts
8000–8999	Other Income Accounts
9000–9999	Other Expense Accounts

To illustrate the usefulness of coding and the means of identifying specific items using numerical codes, a code for asset accounts will be expanded and explained. The first digit in the code may be used to identify the general account classification. Any search of the accounts is then limited to one thousand possible accounts in that category. The second digit could be used to identify an asset's location; that is, for example, whether the asset is located at the home office or at a division. The third digit could be used to identify the classification of the asset; that is, whether the asset is a current asset, a long-term asset, an intangible asset, etc. The fourth digit might be used to identify the specific asset itself.

Obviously, in a large organization the coding structure may be very complex. In order to deal with the complexity of the coding structure, a code dictionary, identifying the specific account and its code, is often employed. In situations where automated equipment with sensing or scanning capability is used, numerical characters are usually considered necessary for reasons of both economy and efficiency.

The General Journal and General Ledger

Until this point, the mechanics of recording and handling transactions described in this text has been limited to the general journal and the general ledger. As previously indicated, each transaction is recorded in the general journal chronologically, and then the debits and credits from the general journal are posted individually to the appropriate accounts in the general ledger.

In the accounting procedures illustrated to this point, the general journal was used as the book of original entry while the general ledger served as the book of final entry. Financial statements were usually prepared from an adjusted trial balance or worksheet. The mechanics of this system would make it almost impossible for all but the smallest business to operate effectively or, at least, efficiently. This type of system is simply unable to process large volumes of transactions on a timely basis, primarily because no effective division of labor is possible since each and every journal entry must be written out on an individual basis.

In addition, this system might not provide the detailed information necessary to operate a business efficiently. For example, the system previously described did not always identify the specific individual who purchased goods on account. Likewise, it did not provide information as to the identity of individual creditors. Division of labor and necessary detail may be accomplished in this basic system by the addition and use of special journals and subsidiary ledgers in addition to the general journal and general ledger.

Subsidiary Ledgers

Subsidiary ledgers are supplemental detailed records which provide underlying support for the amounts recorded in control accounts included in the general ledger. An example of a subsidiary ledger is the accounts receivable subsidiary ledger. An individual record must be maintained on a current basis for every customer for purposes of control, billing, and for handling any inquiries.

The use of individual customer records eliminates the problem of including large numbers of detailed accounts receivable accounts in the general ledger. There are also many other obvious advantages to the use of subsidiary ledgers other than the accumulation of necessary detail. Subsidiary ledgers permit a division of duties among employees by allowing a number of different individuals to assist in the preparation of the records. In addition, personnel with less experience may be used to post to subsidiary ledgers. Also, an error in a trial balance may be localized in a subsidiary ledger, thus reducing the effort necessary to locate the error.

Subsidiary ledgers are necessary to permit the classification of a large group of accounts under a single control account in the general ledger. The subsidiary ledgers found in most systems include: accounts receivable, accounts payable, inventories, employee pay records, property records, and the stockholders' register.

When a company maintains a subsidiary ledger, the corresponding general ledger account is referred to as a control account. If no recording errors are made, the total of the balances in a subsidiary ledger should be equal to the total in the corresponding control account which is included in the general ledger.

Special Journals

The initial step in the flow of information through the financial accounting system is identifying the transactions that will be processed. One means of reducing the amount of individual recording and posting is to separate the transactions into groups that have common elements and to provide special journals for recording the transactions in each group. A decision is then made as to whether the transaction falls into a class that should be entered in a special journal or is an infrequently occurring transaction that should be entered directly in the general journal. A special journal is useful in those instances where there is a large volume of transactions which result in debits and credits to the same accounts. For such transactions, the recording process is facilitated by entering the amounts in the columns of a special journal and posting the totals periodically to the general ledger. The types of transactions which normally occur with sufficient frequency to justify the use of special journals include receipts of cash, disbursements of cash, sales of merchandise on credit, and the purchase of merchandise on account. Of course, transactions not recorded in any of the special journals are recorded in the general journal. That is, every transaction must be recorded in some type of journal, and the effects of all transactions are still posted, either individually or by cumulative totals, to the ledger.

The accounts receivable example which was employed to illustrate the use of subsidiary ledgers is also applicable to special journals. When goods are sold on account, the sale is made and should be recorded at that time. The relevant aspects of credit sales from a data gathering standpoint include: identity of the customer; amount of the sale; nature of any credit terms;[1] date of the sale; and, for any future inquiries, the invoice number. This is repetitive data which will be accumulated for each and every sale.

---

[1] Credit terms include the time allowed for payment and any discounts allowed. Payment required within 30 days would be shown by the notation N/30 indicating that the full amount is due in 30 days.

Special journals permit a division of labor, allow the use of less experienced personnel, employ preprinted account columns or summaries which reduce the incidence of error, and allow special transactions of like kind to be easily analyzed since the original data was accumulated by category rather than on an individual basis.

If a specific type of transaction occurs frequently in the business, a special journal should be designed and used for these transactions. As previously indicated, the types of special journals most frequently used by a business normally include: sales, cash receipts, cash disbursements, and purchases.

An Example—Special Journals and Subsidiary Ledgers

Before considering the following example, the reader should review the two examples given to make certain that the general steps included and the information flows illustrated are understood.

The credit sales and cash collections for the Yello Brewery for January are presented below to illustrate the interrelationships of special journals, subsidiary ledgers, and the general ledger.

Jan.	2	Sold 200 cases at $4 per case to Harry the Hat's Bar & Grill (on account)—Invoice #101.
	5	Sold 50 cases at $4 per case to Big Brother's Place (on account)—Invoice #102.
	7	Received a check from Harry the Hat's Bar & Grill for $800.
	11	Sold 200 cases at $4 per case to Harry the Hat's Bar & Grill (on account)—Invoice #103.
	13	Sold 10 cases at $4.50 per case to the Bachelor's Club (on account)—Invoice #104.
	15	Sold 20 cases at $4.10 per case to Dink's Place (on account)—Invoice #105.
	25	Received a check from Big Brother's Place for $200.
	31	Received a check from the Bachelor's Club for $45.
	31	Received a dividend check of $50 on marketable securities.

Sales Journal. The transactions for the Yello Brewery are journalized and posted in the special journals, subsidiary ledgers, and general ledger in Illustration 1.

Note that each individual credit sale is recorded in the sales journal. Any merchandise sold for cash would be recorded directly in the cash receipts journal. The amount of each credit sale is posted daily to the individual customer account in the accounts receivable subsidiary ledger. This procedure assures that each customer's account will be kept up-to-date for purposes of responding to inquiries from customers and for making decisions regarding future extensions of credit to individual customers. The check mark (√) in the sales journal indicates that the posting

6 | Accounting Systems and Internal Control 177

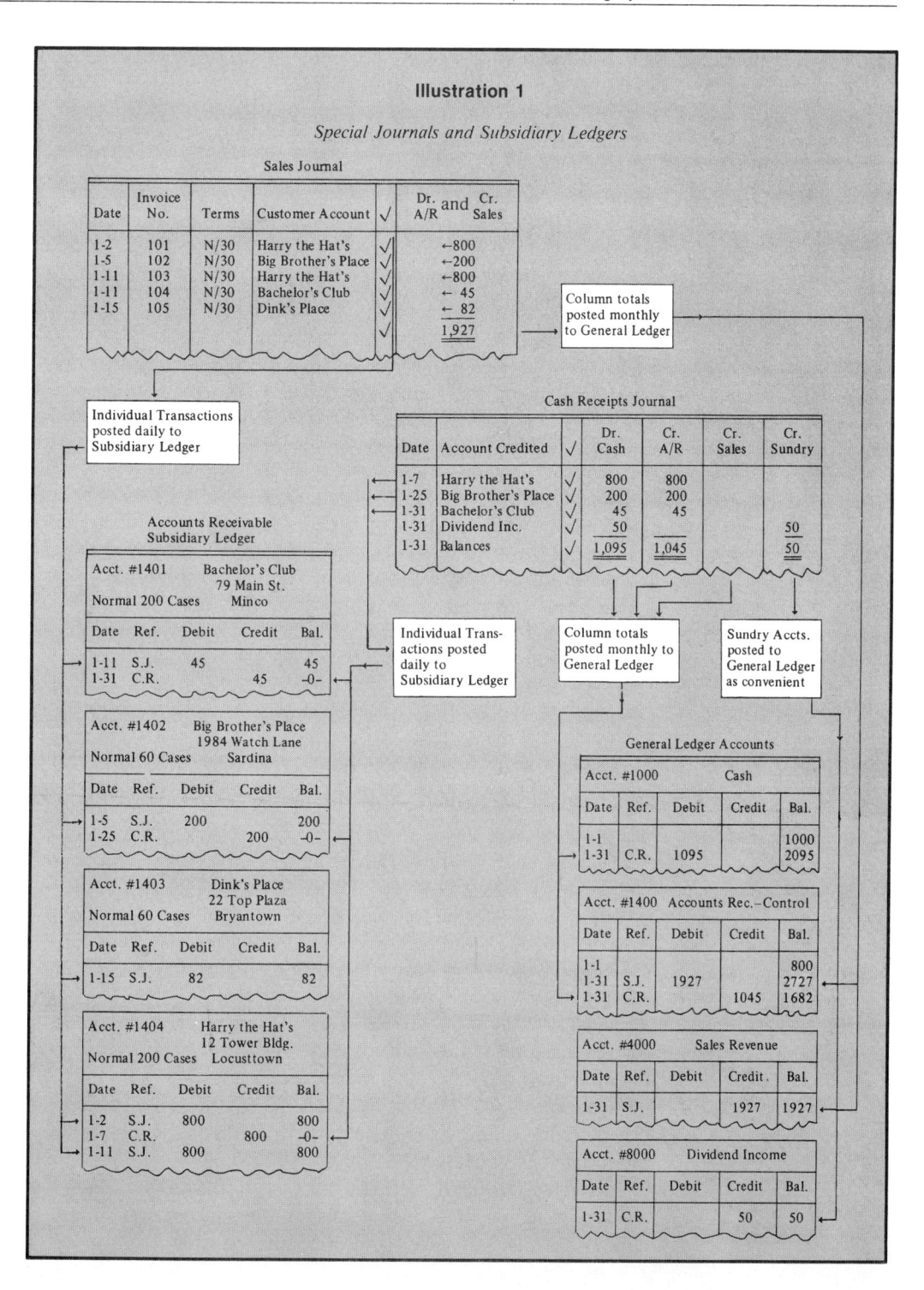

Illustration 1

Special Journals and Subsidiary Ledgers

Sales Journal

Date	Invoice No.	Terms	Customer Account	✓	Dr. A/R and Cr. Sales
1-2	101	N/30	Harry the Hat's	✓	←800
1-5	102	N/30	Big Brother's Place	✓	←200
1-11	103	N/30	Harry the Hat's	✓	←800
1-11	104	N/30	Bachelor's Club	✓	← 45
1-15	105	N/30	Dink's Place	✓	← 82
				✓	1,927

Column totals posted monthly to General Ledger

Individual Transactions posted daily to Subsidiary Ledger

Cash Receipts Journal

Date	Account Credited	✓	Dr. Cash	Cr. A/R	Cr. Sales	Cr. Sundry
1-7	Harry the Hat's	✓	800	800		
1-25	Big Brother's Place	✓	200	200		
1-31	Bachelor's Club	✓	45	45		
1-31	Dividend Inc.	✓	50			50
1-31	Balances	✓	1,095	1,045		50

Individual Transactions posted daily to Subsidiary Ledger

Column totals posted monthly to General Ledger

Sundry Accts. posted to General Ledger as convenient

Accounts Receivable Subsidiary Ledger

Acct. #1401   Bachelor's Club
79 Main St.
Normal 200 Cases   Minco

Date	Ref.	Debit	Credit	Bal.
1-11	S.J.	45		45
1-31	C.R.		45	-0-

Acct. #1402   Big Brother's Place
1984 Watch Lane
Normal 60 Cases   Sardina

Date	Ref.	Debit	Credit	Bal.
1-5	S.J.	200		200
1-25	C.R.		200	-0-

Acct. #1403   Dink's Place
22 Top Plaza
Normal 60 Cases   Bryantown

Date	Ref.	Debit	Credit	Bal.
1-15	S.J.	82		82

Acct. #1404   Harry the Hat's
12 Tower Bldg.
Normal 200 Cases   Locusttown

Date	Ref.	Debit	Credit	Bal.
1-2	S.J.	800		800
1-7	C.R.		800	-0-
1-11	S.J.	800		800

General Ledger Accounts

Acct. #1000   Cash

Date	Ref.	Debit	Credit	Bal.
1-1				1000
1-31	C.R.	1095		2095

Acct. #1400   Accounts Rec.–Control

Date	Ref.	Debit	Credit	Bal.
1-1				800
1-31	S.J.	1927		2727
1-31	C.R.		1045	1682

Acct. #4000   Sales Revenue

Date	Ref.	Debit	Credit	Bal.
1-31	S.J.		1927	1927

Acct. #8000   Dividend Income

Date	Ref.	Debit	Credit	Bal.
1-31	C.R.		50	50

to the subsidiary ledger has been made. Then, at the end of the month, the total of the sales journal column ($1,927) is debited to Accounts Receivable-Control and credited to Sales Revenue in the general ledger.

Cash Receipts Journal. Similarly, a cash receipts journal is used to record all transactions involving the receipt of cash. The cash receipts journal must include several columns for recording transactions since the source of the receipts may differ. For example, note that the cash receipts journal in Illustration 1 includes credit columns for collections on accounts receivable, sales of merchandise for cash, and all other (sundry) transactions. Thus, a receipt of cash is recorded by entering the amount received in the debit column for cash and in the appropriate column to record the credit.

As in the case of the sales journal, the individual credits in the accounts receivable credit column are posted daily to the customer accounts in the accounts receivable subsidiary ledger. The check mark (✓) in the cash receipts journal indicates that the posting has been made to the subsidiary ledger.

The various sales of merchandise in the business which are made for cash are typically recorded in total by the means of an entry in the cash receipts journal made at the end of the day. This entry is recorded in the cash debit column and the sales credit column of the journal. Cash received from sources other than collections of receivables on cash sales are recorded in the sundry credit column.

At the end of the month, the column totals in the cash receipts journal are posted to the appropriate general ledger accounts. Prior to this posting, it is necessary to prove that the total of the debit columns is equal to the total of the credit columns. After the totals in the cash receipts journal have been checked, the total in the cash column is posted as a debit to the cash account and the total of the accounts receivable column is posted as a credit to the accounts receivable-control account. Similarly, the total of the credits in the column for cash sales would be posted to the sales account in the general ledger. The individual items in the sundry account column are posted separately to the appropriate general ledger accounts.

Cash Disbursements Journal. A cash disbursements journal may be used to record all expenditures of cash made by the business. Normally, a journal of this type will include individual credit columns for cash and for purchase discounts and a sundry or other credit column. The total of the credits to cash and to purchase discounts would be posted directly to these accounts on a monthly basis while the amounts included in the other credit-column would be posted to the individual accounts at any time that it is convenient to do so. Debit columns are normally included for accounts frequently affected by cash disbursements such as purchases and accounts payable. The totals of these account columns are posted directly to the purchases and accounts payable control accounts on a monthly basis. The individual debits in the accounts payable debit column must be posted daily to the accounts payable subsidiary ledger. There will be a sundry or other debit column where debits to accounts other than purchases and accounts payable may be recorded. These entries would be posted to the appropriate general ledger accounts as it is convenient to do so.

The mechanics of the cash disbursements journal are almost identical to those of the cash receipts journal. Like any other special journal, the cash disbursements journal should be designed in a manner that meets the specific requirements of its user. It should include debit and credit columns for the accounts most often affected by the payment of cash. The columns suggested above are typical of those included in the cash disbursements journals of many businesses, but others may be required in particular circumstances. An example of a cash disbursements journal is included below.

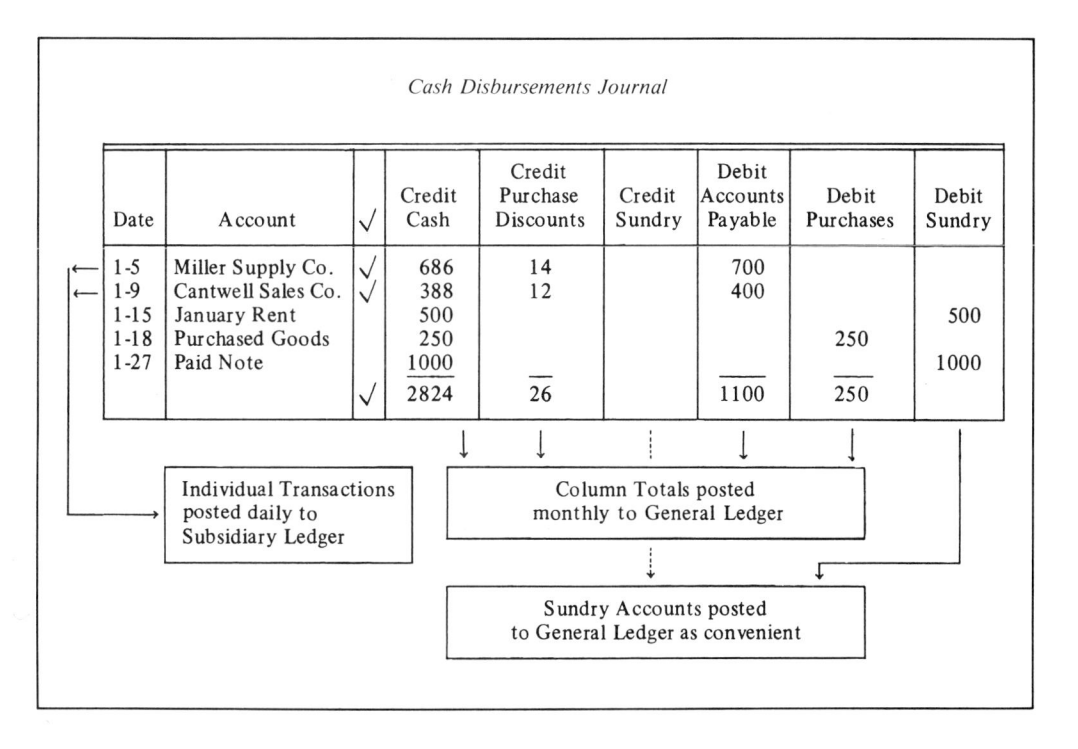

Cash Disbursements Journal

Date	Account	✓	Credit Cash	Credit Purchase Discounts	Credit Sundry	Debit Accounts Payable	Debit Purchases	Debit Sundry
1-5	Miller Supply Co.	✓	686	14		700		
1-9	Cantwell Sales Co.	✓	388	12		400		
1-15	January Rent		500					500
1-18	Purchased Goods		250				250	
1-27	Paid Note		1000					1000
		✓	2824	26		1100	250	

Individual Transactions posted daily to Subsidiary Ledger

Column Totals posted monthly to General Ledger

Sundry Accounts posted to General Ledger as convenient

Payroll Journal. A payroll journal is a specialized form of a cash disbursements journal. As its name implies, it is used exclusively to record the payment of salaries and wages to employees. A payroll journal will normally include credit columns for cash, federal income taxes withheld, state income taxes withheld, social security taxes withheld (employees' share), and other deductions such as union dues, employee hospitalization, etc. A debit column will be included for payroll expense, gross salaries, and the employer's share of social security taxes and federal and state unemployment taxes. Summary entries are made to record total payroll expense, payment of the salaries and wages, and the incurring of the liabilities related to the payroll. Information for individual employees is posted to the separate payroll records maintained for each employee. These records are, in effect, subsidiary records for payroll from which various reports and tax returns are prepared and filed.

Purchases Journal. A purchases journal is very similar to the sales journal. Credit purchases are entered in the journal, with a notation made of such information as the date of purchase, the name of the vendor, date of the invoice, terms of the purchase, and the purchase amount. As individual purchases are made, they are recorded in the accounts payable subsidiary ledger which would include a separate account for each of the suppliers of the business. Periodically, the total amount of the purchases is posted as a debit to the purchases account and a credit to the accounts payable control account. At this time, the balance in the control account should be equal to the total of the balances in the accounts payable subsidiary ledger. This information included in the accounts payable subsidiary ledger is used for making decisions regarding future purchases from particular suppliers, for checking prices, for testing the accuracy of billings made by suppliers, etc.

An example of a purchases journal is shown below. This journal includes an entry for each credit purchase of merchandise made during the month.

Form of Special Journals. There is no specified format for special journals nor is there any limit as to the number of types of special journals and subsidiary ledgers that are necessary. As mentioned previously, special journals and subsidiary ledgers should be designed so as to meet the individual needs of the particular company that will use them.

The check marks found in the special journals are made for purposes of control. The bookkeeper will check the transactions as he posts them to the appropriate ledger accounts.

PROVING THE CONTROL ACCOUNTS

After all posting is completed for a period, the general ledger control accounts should be checked (often referred to as proved) against the balances in the corresponding subsidiary ledger accounts. This proof is usually made by preparing a schedule of the individual balances in the subsidiary ledger. The total of the individual balances must be equal to the balance in the corresponding control account; otherwise, an error has occurred in the accounting process.

Purchases Journal

Date	Invoice Date	Account	√	Amount
1/3	1/2	Miller Supply Co.	√	700
1/7	1/6	Cantwell Sales Co.	√	400
1/15	1/15	Harwell Co.	√	600
1/20	1/17	Walter & Son	√	300
1/27	1/26	Burton Inc.	√	900
			√	2900

General Ledger

Purchases
1/31 2900

Accounts Payable
        1/31 2900

Accounts Payable Subsidiary Ledger

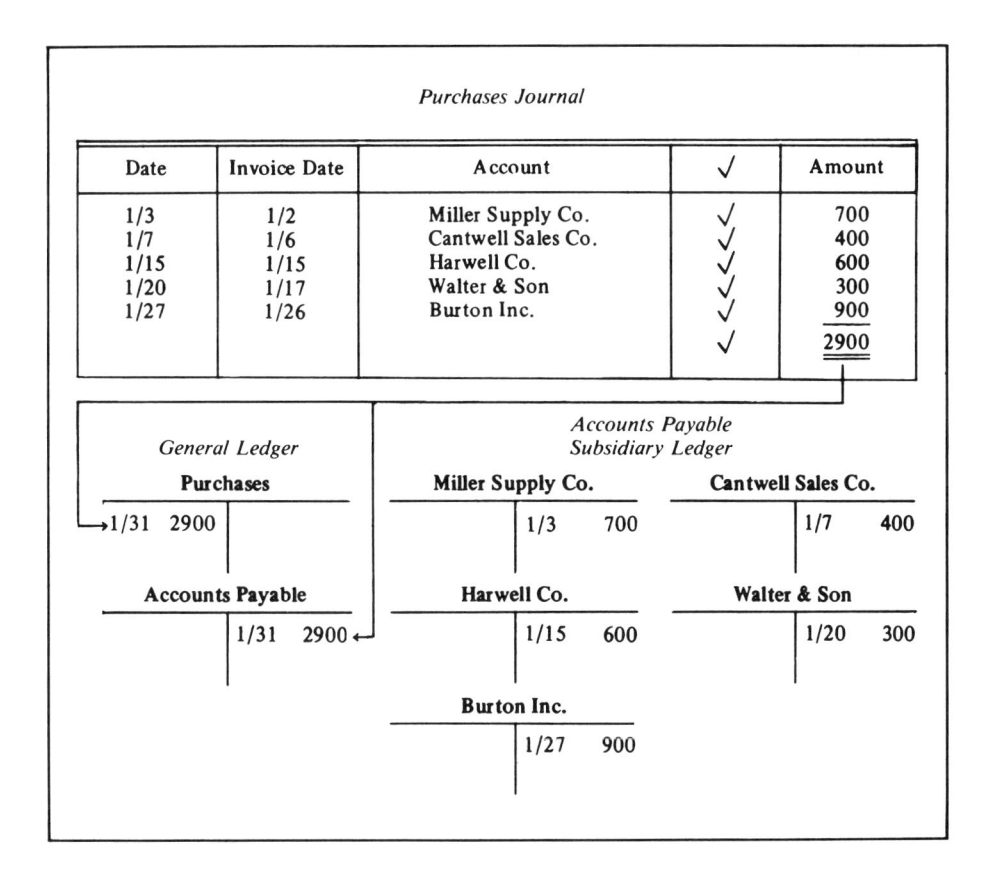

Miller Supply Co.
        1/3   700

Harwell Co.
        1/15 600

Burton Inc.
        1/27 900

Cantwell Sales Co.
        1/7   400

Walter & Son
        1/20 300

INTERNAL ACCOUNTING CONTROL

Certain accounting controls are necessary within a business to safeguard the assets from waste, fraud, and inefficiency and to ensure the accuracy and reliability of the accounting data. Ideally, the system of internal control should provide assurance regarding the dependability of the accounting data relied upon in making business decisions. Generally, these accounting controls include a specified system of authorization and approval of transactions, separation of the recordkeeping and reporting functions from the duties concerned with asset custody and operations, physical control over assets, and internal auditing.

A subdivision of responsibility in a financial accounting system is necessary to provide adequate checks on the work of company personnel. When one transaction is handled from beginning to end by a single individual and that person makes an error, the mistake will probably be carried through in the mechanics of recording the transaction and will be very difficult to locate. On the other hand, if different aspects of a transaction are processed by different people, each acting on an independent basis, an error will be much more readily identifiable. Many of the errors that would have affected the accounts will never occur because the mistake may be identified and corrected on a timely basis.

A division of responsibility among employees is also necessary for control purposes. In a properly designed accounting system that has adequate division of duties, fraud and embezzlement should be very difficult and require the collusion of two or more people. However, even in a properly designed system, the possibility of errors and embezzlement cannot be completely eliminated.

The division of duties should, of course, be logically based on the desired purposes of the system. For example, the person who maintains the subsidiary ledger of accounts receivable should not have access to cash. This will prevent him from being able to manipulate the accounts receivable and retain the cash. Likewise, a single individual should not be given the responsibility of both approving purchases and then signing the checks that are used to pay for them. Payments made to nonexistent companies for fictitious purchases would be difficult to prevent if one person is able to approve both the purchase and the payment.

A system of internal control is frequently justified because it assists the business in the detection of errors and the prevention of embezzlement. Another major benefit of a system of internal control is that it provides an atmosphere and system which are deterrents to inefficient utilization of the company's resources, fraudulent conversion of assets, and inefficient and inaccurate handling of the company's accounts.

The Audit Trail

An audit trail is the traceability factor that is built into an accounting system. It permits a person, normally an independent certified public accountant (referred to as an auditor), to follow the processing of a specific transaction from the beginning of the system described to the final output of the system. This procedure should also be reversible, that is, the final output of the system should be traceable back to the original source documentation that represents the transactions which caused the final output. An audit trail provides a path that can be followed in order to verify the accuracy with which transactions were handled as well as their legitimacy. The audit trail relies on a good system of internal control and documentation of transactions.

A flowchart of the purchase, receipt, payment, and use of office supplies for the Brown Grass Seed Company is presented below. This flowchart describes both the internal control and audit trail for these types of transactions. Note that only three sets of forms are used: a purchase requisition, the invoice prepared by purchasing (which is the first of a series of invoices in this case), and the bill of lading and the invoice received from the vendor.

Multiple copies of these documents are used by the business for internal control purposes. The entire transaction may be traced from the financial statements to any point in the accounting system.

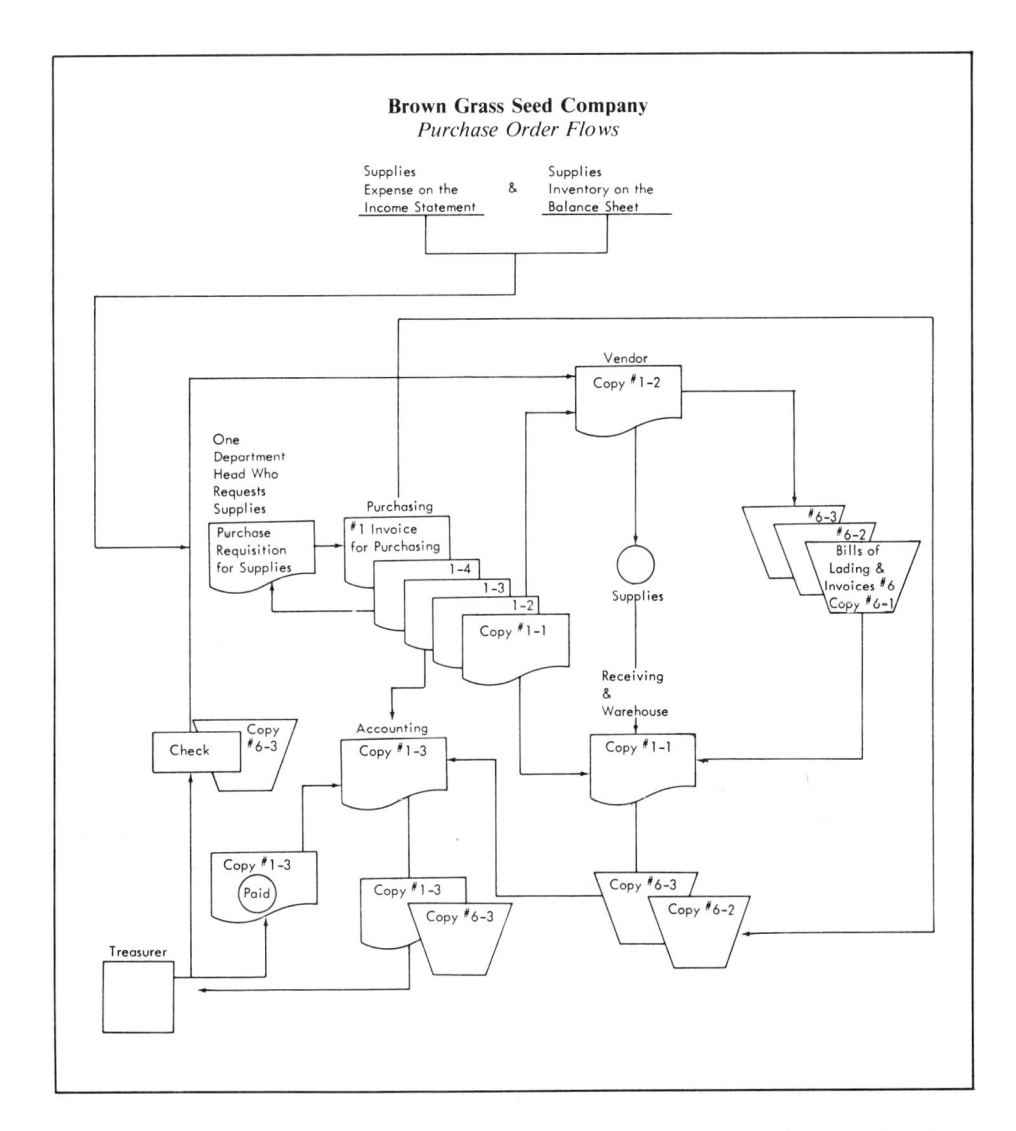

Brown Grass Seed Company
Purchase Order Flows

AUTOMATED ACCOUNTING SYSTEMS

The introduction of a computer system into the accounting function does not alter the data flow, but instead parallels the manual processing system. The computer system simply performs many functions that would be performed by people in a manual system. Any automated system will, however, affect the form of transaction documentation and other factors such as:

1. Methods of establishing source documents
2. Methods of transmitting data
3. Techniques of data preparation
4. Amount of data handled
5. Speed and accuracy
6. Processing of the data
7. Methods of data storage
8. Methods of information retrieval
9. Number of accounting reports used
10. Types of controls necessary for adequate internal control

The objective of any accounting information system (whether manual or automated) is to produce the financial information required by internal and external users. The basic components of any computer system are the "hardware" and appropriate "software."

Computer Hardware

Computer hardware is the equipment used to process the accounting information. Hardware can change from the very sophisticated and expensive system which possesses tremendous computing capability to the relatively simple and inexpensive system such as a personal computer which costs less than two thousand dollars. In general, the equipment can be classified into three categories; mainframe computers, minicomputers, and microcomputers.

Mainframe computers are large-scale systems that would be used when a large volume of data needs to be processed rapidly. Minicomputers are much cheaper and, obviously, much less powerful. Minicomputers provide the computing capacity needed by many small to medium size companies which need the capability to process many transactions but do not necessarily need the power and efficiency of a mainframe computer.

A microcomputer is a system which is smaller than a minicomputer and could be used by a small business that does not have a large number of transactions to process. The "home computer" is a microcomputer as are word processors. The microcomputer has been referred to as the "computer on a chip." Any transaction processing is not as fast nor can the system be as sophisticated as the mainframe or minicomputers.

Computer Software

Computer software are the instructions that are developed to make the hardware perform the functions that are necessary to process transactions. The software controls the computer activities by instructing the hardware, in a step-by-step program, to perform a specific function. For example, in a payroll program (software) all the deductions from each person's paycheck (such as taxes and other payroll deductions) would have to be programmed and "read" into or made available to the computer. When each employee's hours and pay rate are entered, the program could calculate payroll deductions and, with the proper hardware, print the employees' checks. When a program is written to handle a specific application such as payroll or order handling or inventory, the programs for that application are usually called a software package. Software packages are available from most computer vendors to perform the usual accounting functions. In addition, a company can have a program "tailored" or written to their specifications when they have unique processing and/or control requirements.

SUMMARY

A financial accounting system must communicate economic information efficiently, effectively, accurately, and on a timely basis. Basic components of the system include: (1) a chart of accounts, (2) a coding system, (3) a general journal, (4) a general ledger, (5) special journals, (6) subsidiary ledgers, (7) a system of internal control, and (8) an audit trail.

A chart of accounts is a listing of all the accounts that may be used by a company. The basic design of the chart of accounts determines how accounting information will be accumulated, summarized, and used. A coding system is necessary for the chart of accounts to provide a unique identity for each account included in the chart of accounts. A general journal is used to record those transactions which occur on an infrequent basis. A general ledger contains the control accounts for the system. Special journals will be used for recording transactions which occur frequently. Subsidiary ledgers are supplemental detailed records which provide underlying support for the control accounts included in the general ledger. An effective system of internal control serves as a deterrent to the inefficient utilization of a company's resources; it discourages the fraudulent conversion of assets and the inefficient and inaccurate handling of a company's accounts. An audit trail is necessary to allow traceability of transactions after the fact.

The use of automated equipment in the financial accounting system does not alter the data flows in the system per se; but the equipment may cause significant changes in: (1) the source documents, (2) methods of transmitting data, (3) techniques of data preparation, (4) amount of data handled, (5) speed and accuracy, (6) processing of data, (7) methods of data storage, (8) methods of information retrieval, (9) the number of accounting reports used, and (10) the controls necessary for adequate internal control.

KEY DEFINITIONS

Audit trail The audit trail is the traceable sequence of steps through which a transaction is processed from the beginning of the accounting system to the final output. The procedures and documentation should be clear so as to provide traceability from the output back to the original documents.

Cash disbursements journal A cash disbursements journal is a special journal which may be used to record all expenditures of cash made by the business.

Cash receipts journal A cash receipts journal is a special journal which may be used to record all transactions involving the receipt of cash.

Chart of accounts The chart of accounts is the list of all accounts that a company will use in conducting its business. It includes all accounts used in the preparation of the balance sheet, income statement, and statement of capital, and in addition, all accounts that management needs for planning and control purposes. The design of the chart of accounts will determine how the information will be gathered, summarized, and used in its accounting system.

Coding Coding is the process of assigning a system of numbers to the various accounts included in the chart of accounts.

Coding dictionary The coding dictionary identifies an account with its coding number to simplify use of the coding system and the accounts.

Control account A control account is a general ledger account which is supported by detailed information included in subsidiary accounts.

Internal control Internal control comprises the plan of organization and all of the coordinate methods and measures adopted within a business to safeguard its assets, check the accuracy and reliability of its accounting data, promote operational efficiency, and encourage adherence to prescribed managerial policies.

Payroll journal A payroll journal is a specialized form of a cash disbursements journal used exclusively to record the payment of salaries and wages to employees.

Purchases journal A purchases journal is a special journal which may be used to record credit purchases.

Special journals Special journals are designed to record the type of transactions where there is a large volume of transactions that occur on a frequent basis. Special journals are often used for accounts receivable, accounts payable, and cash receipts and disbursements.

Subsidiary ledgers A subsidiary ledger is a supplementary record which provides underlying support for control accounts which are included in the general ledger. A subsidiary ledger will include more detail than the related general ledger account, and the total of all subsidiary accounts will equal the balance of the applicable control account.

QUESTIONS

1. What are the functions of a financial accounting system?

2. Explain the importance of the chart of accounts.

3. What does coding accomplish?

4. List some shortcomings of the general journal and ledger.

5. What are some advantages of subsidiary ledgers?

6. Explain how a special journal and subsidiary ledger can be used with accounts receivable.

7. What are some important components of internal control?

8. What is the test for the clarity of an audit trail?

9. Why are automated systems introduced?

EXERCISES

10. Arrange the following activities in the order in which they normally occur.

    a. Prepare adjusting entries
    b. Prepare journal entries
    c. Prepare financial statements
    d. Transactions
    e. Prepare adjusted trial balance
    f. Post to ledger accounts
    g. Prepare closing entries
    h. Prepare post-closing trial balance
    i. Prepare unadjusted trial balance
    j. Post closing entries
    k. Post adjusting entries

11. The Huffman Company uses 5 special journals: sales (S), cash receipts (CR), cash disbursements (CD), purchases (PU), and payroll (P).

    The following transactions occurred during November, 19x1. Classify each account according to the special journal in which it would be entered.

    a. Purchased $1,000 of merchandise from Q.R. Trucker on account.
    b. Sold land for $10,500.
    c. Sold $50 of merchandise to Anne Rutledge on account.
    d. Purchased $300 insurance to cover the next 3 years.
    e. Paid $1,500 rent in advance.
    f. Paid back wages of $2,200.
    g. Purchased $3,000 of merchandise from K.O. Snyder on credit.
    h. Sold $300 of merchandise to Harry Benson, cash.
    i. Received payment in full from Anne Rutledge.

j. Paid Q.R. Trucker the full amount due.
k. Sold merchandise on account to Jane Donner, $450.
l. Paid $38 shipping charges on merchandise purchased from K.O. Snyder.
m. Paid Best, Blake and Bader $500 in legal fees.
n. Received payment in full from Harry Benson.
o. Paid $4,000 in wages.

12. Bond Company had the following credit sales during the month of March:

Mar. 1	Walter Manning	$ 600
5	Carl Stolle	900
9	Larry Pointer	400
16	Phil Youngdahl	700
25	Earl Bennett	300
29	Dan Lowe	1,100
		$4,000

The company records these transactions in a sales journal.

Required:

1. Prepare an accounts receivable ledger and post the above amounts to the subsidiary ledger.
2. Prepare an accounts receivable control account and a sales account and post the sales for the month to these accounts.
3. Prove the accounts receivable subsidiary ledger to the accounts receivable control account.

13. The following credit sales were made by the White Lightning Distillery in January:

Jan. 5   Sold 15 cases at $50 per case to the Tip-Top Saloon (on account)—Invoice #10.
  16   Sold 20 cases at $50 per case to Sam's Alley Cat (on account)—Invoice #11.
  20   Sold 5 cases at $52 per case to Ferguson A-Go-Go (on account)—Invoice #12.
  22   Sold 17 cases at $50 per case to the Tip-Top Saloon (on account)—Invoice #13.
  25   Sold 1 case at $55 per case to Mabel Tucker (on account)—Invoice #14.

Collection terms are n/30. Indicate the effects of these transactions on the sales journal, accounts receivable subsidiary ledger, and the general ledger.

14. Prepare a cash receipts journal for the Jackson Company to reflect the following events for the month of March. Then indicate the postings which would be made to the general journal at the end of March.

Mar. 5 Received $200 of interest revenue from an investment.
9 John Jacob paid his account balance of $75.
10 Cash sale of $110 was made.
13 Alice Adams made a $100 payment on her account.
15 Dividend income of $1,470 was received.
17 Cash sale of $55 was made.
20 Morris Martin paid $309 on his account.
24 Pat Partin sent his remittance of $80.
29 Cash sale of $103 was made.
30 Sam Smith made a $30 payment on his account.

15. The sales journal and the cash receipts journal of the Martin Paper Company are shown below. Make the necessary daily postings to the accounts receivable subsidiary ledger and determine the ending balance of each account for the month of August. Then post the necessary items to the general ledger.

Sales Journal

Date	Invoice No.	Terms	Customer Account	Dr. A/R Cr. Sales
8/1	801	N/30	Adam Alfred	97
8/6	802	N/30	Connie Carr	44
8/10	803	N/30	Elaine Ellis	123
8/11	804	N/30	Gary Gardner	85
8/13	805	N/30	Ivan Ingot	31
8/16	806	N/30	Karl Kernel	58
8/21	807	N/30	Norman Norton	200
8/23	808	N/30	Rita Reed	29
				667

Cash Receipts Journal

Date	Account Credited	Dr. Cash	Cr. A/R	Cr. Sales	Cr. Sundry
8/8	Adam Alfred	97	97		
8/13	Connie Carr	44	44		
8/19	Gary Gardner	85	85		
8/19	Interest Income	476			476
8/20	Karl Kernel	58	58		
8/23	Ivan Ingot	31	31		
8/28	Elaine Ellis	123	123		
8/30	Rita Reed	29	29		
8/30	Norman Norton	200	200		
8/30	Sales	75		75	
8/31	Balances	1,218	667	75	476

16. The Munson Company, a clothing manufacturer, maintains a purchases journal. Make the necessary journal entries for the following transactions. Then post the entries in the general ledger and the accounts payable subsidiary ledger.

   a. Purchased cotton fabric on June 15 for $547 on credit from Cotco Company.
   b. Buttons were bought on credit from the Spark Company for $163 on June 10.
   c. Zip-It sold Munson $89 worth of zippers on credit on June 4.
   d. On June 20 wool was purchased from Wooly Company for $846 on credit.
   e. Thread was bought from The Thread Factory on June 1 for $39 on credit.

17. Reconstruct the cash disbursements journal for the Randolph Corporation for the month of October from the following information.

Postings to Accounts Payable Subsidiary Ledger	*October Postings to General Ledger*
10/9 Cook's Cutlery... $146 debit	Purchases............ $ 374 debit
10/19 Donna's Dishes... 789 debit	Cash................ 1,762 credit
10/29 Glenda's Glasses.. 453 debit	Accounts payable..... 1,388 debit

18. Prepare a cash disbursements journal for the Dent Company for the month of April. Then make the required postings to the necessary ledgers.

   April 2 Paid the balance of $222 owed to the Adams Company.
          4 Dividends of $3,000 were paid.
          7 The account payable to Reed Store of $400 was paid, but the amount was reduced by a purchase discount of $40.
         11 Raw materials were purchased for $642 in cash.
         16 Paid salaries of $1,000.
         22 Paid $101 to Supply Company to reduce the balance due.
         29 A purchase discount of $14 reduced the amount paid the Static Company to $186.

19. The Needles Company uses five special journals: Sales (S), Cash Receipts (CR), Cash Disbursements (CD), Purchases (PU), and Payroll (P). They also use four subsidiary ledgers: Accounts Receivable (AR), Accounts Payable (AP), Inventories (I), and Employee Pay Records (EPR). The following transactions occurred during October 19x1. Classify each transaction according to the special journals and/or subsidiary ledgers where it would be entered.

   a. Sold merchandise to Lion Company on credit.
   b. Received dividends from Monkey Company stock.
   c. Bought office supplies for cash from the Bat Store.
   d. Sold merchandise to The Bear Factory for cash.
   e. Paid for annual audit by CPA firm.
   f. Paid October rent.

g. Received check for insurance claim.
h. Purchased raw materials on account from Deer Company.
i. Sold goods on account to Llama Company.
j. Collected amount owed from Lion Company.
k. Collected amount due from Cat Customer.
l. Bought raw materials for cash from Elephant Company.
m. Paid amount owed to Deer Company.
n. Paid salaries for October.
o. Paid interest due on note.

PROBLEMS

20. Below are listed certain transactions of Sorrenson Sales Company for the month of June, 19x1.

June 1 Sold goods on credit to J.P. Nelson, $1,500, Invoice #328, terms n/30.
3 Sold merchandise on credit to Joe's Bar and Grill, $2,300, Invoice #329, terms n/30.
4 Cash sales of merchandise, $900.
5 Sold merchandise to J.A. Baker, $1,300, Invoice #330, terms n/30.
7 Received payment in full on J.P. Nelson account.
11 Received dividend of $35 on marketable securities.
14 Received a check from Joe's Bar and Grill in full payment of account.
17 Sold merchandise to T.W. Stark, $1,700, Invoice #331, terms n/30.
19 Received full payment from J.A. Baker.
20 Sold merchandise to B.A. Spendler, $1,900, Invoice #332, terms n/30.
25 Cash sales of merchandise, $600.
26 Received payment in full from B.A. Spendler.
28 Received payment in full from T.W. Stark.
30 Cash sales of merchandise, $3,200.

Required:

1. Prepare a sales journal and a cash receipts journal.
2. Open general ledger accounts for accounts receivable, cash, and sales.
3. Open subsidiary accounts receivable ledger accounts for the credit customers.
4. Enter the above transactions in the sales and cash receipts journals and post to the appropriate ledger accounts.

21. During the month of May, 19x1, the Williamson Company purchased merchandise from the following suppliers on account for the respective amounts.

Date		Creditor	Amount
May	1	G & S Electronics	$ 3,000
	3	T.R. Lowry	2,500
	7	Western Enterprises	5,300
	8	Barnard and Ralph, Inc.	7,200
	10	Dobson and Heath Associates	1,500
	13	W.R. Blakely	4,700
	16	T.W. Barlett and Company	10,250
	18	J. Presser Richards	1,100
	22	Karen Prichard	500
	25	Shippers National Company	350
	27	Time Tickers Corporation	2,100
	30	J.W. Redford	750

Cash disbursements to creditors during the month were as follows:

Date	Creditor	Amount
May 10	G & S Electronics	$3,000
12	Western Enterprises	2,300
15	Barnard and Ralph, Inc.	7,200
21	W.R. Blakely	4,700
23	T.W. Barlett and Company	5,000
27	Karen Prichard	500
28	Dobson and Heath Associates	1,500
30	Western Enterprises	3,000

The company had the following cash purchases of merchandise during May:

Date	Amount
May 5	$600
13	800

Required:

1. Prepare a purchases journal and a cash disbursements journal.
2. Prepare general ledger accounts for accounts payable, cash, and purchases.
3. Open subsidiary accounts payable ledger accounts for the suppliers listed above.
4. Enter the above transactions in the purchases and cash disbursements journal and post to the appropriate ledger accounts.
5. Prove the balance in the accounts payable control account with a schedule of accounts payable.

22. Condor Company uses a cash receipts journal and a cash disbursements journal. Selected transactions during the month of April are listed below.

Apr. 1 Purchased merchandise on account from S. Klein, $600.
    2 Paid April rent, $500.
    3 Sold merchandise on credit to D. Gilman, $375.
    4 Sold merchandise on credit to W. Cox, $280.
    4 Received $200 rent for subleased office space.
    5 Paid $180 for advertisement in local newspaper.
    6 Received $105 dividend on marketable securities.
    8 Paid S. Klein $600 on account.
    9 Received payment in full from D. Gilman.
   10 Cash sales of merchandise, $6,250.
   11 Purchased merchandise on account from Main Supply Company, $7,100.
   12 Received payment in full from W. Cox.
   13 Paid $100 interest on loan from City National Bank.
   14 Sold merchandise on account to K. Telg, $625.
   15 Purchased equipment from Barton Brothers, $3,250 cash.
   17 Purchased merchandise for cash, $1,150.
   18 Cash sales of merchandise, $6,100
   19 Sold a plot of land for $15,000 cash.

Apr. 24 Paid Main Supply Company $7,100 on account.
27 Received payment in full from K. Telg.
28 Cash sales of merchandise, $4,300.
29 Paid salaries and wages, $6,750.

Required:

Prepare a cash receipts journal and a cash disbursements journal. Enter the above transactions in these journals as appropriate.

23. The special journals for a merchandising business are listed below.

Sales Journal

Date	Account	Amount
1/1	E.R. Smith	400
1/7	J.B. Conn	600
1/13	Robert Jones	300
1/17	Bart Banner	480
1/25	Pete Zapie	120

Purchases Journal

Date	Account	Amount
1/1	Smith Co.	200
1/12	Payne Brothers	350
1/19	Donnely & Sons	420
1/24	Barton Co.	175

Cash Receipts Journal

		Debits		Credits		
Date	Account	Cash	Sales Discounts	Sales	Accounts Receivable	Sundry Accounts
1/5	Cash Sales	1,000		1,000		
1/8	E.R. Smith	380	20		400	
1/11	Notes Payable	2,000				2,000
1/16	J.B. Conn	600			600	
1/21	Cash Sales	200		200		
1/27	Robert Jones	300			300	

Cash Disbursements Journal

		Credit	Debits		
Date	Account	Cash	Accounts Payable	Purchases	Sundry Accounts
1/1	Cash Purchases	700		700	
1/9	Prepaid Insurance	300			300
1/10	Smith Co.	200	200		
1/16	Payne Brothers	600	600		
1/25	Cash Purchases	250		250	

Required:

1. Prepare T-accounts for the following general ledger accounts with the indicated balances on January 1: Cash, $3,000; Accounts Receivable, $800; Sales, 0; Purchases, 0; Accounts Payable, $400; Notes Payable, $1,000; Prepaid Insurance, $100; Sales Discounts, 0.

2. Prepare the necessary subsidiary accounts receivable ledger accounts. Balances at January 1 were: E.R. Smith, $500 and Bart Banner, $300.
3. Prepare the necessary subsidiary accounts payable ledger accounts. Balances at January 1 were: Payne Brothers, $250 and Donnely & Sons, $150.
4. Post the entries from the journals listed above to the proper T-accounts.
5. Prove the balances in accounts receivable and accounts payable with the subsidiary ledgers at January 31.

24. During the month of August, Harcourt Company completed the following transactions.

Aug.	2	Purchased merchandise on account from Sands Company, $1,800.
	3	Sold merchandise on credit to Tom Beams, $350 (Invoice #101).
	5	Sold merchandise for cash, $2,200.
	6	Purchased merchandise on account from Bryan Supply Company, $1,400.
	7	Purchased office equipment on account from Town Supply Company, $300.
	9	Received payment from Tom Beams for Invoice #101.
	10	Sold merchandise on credit to Gene Seago, $225 (Invoice #102).
	11	Paid the Sands Company Invoice dated August 2.
	12	Sold merchandise for cash, $1,600.
	13	Paid cash for a two-year fire insurance policy, $800.
	14	Sold merchandise on credit to Wayne Lenner, $600 (Invoice #103).
	15	Purchased merchandise on account from Hardy Company, $2,100.
	16	Received payment from Gene Seago for Invoice #102.
	17	Sold merchandise for cash, $1,300.
	18	Sold merchandise on credit to Al Sheppard, $200 (Invoice #104).
	19	Borrowed $3,000 by giving the City National Bank a six-month note payable.
	20	Paid the Bryan Supply Company invoice dated August 6.
	21	Received payment from Wayne Lenner for Invoice #103.
	22	Paid August rent in cash, $350.
	23	Sold merchandise on credit to Jerry Connors, $400 (Invoice #105).
	24	Purchased merchandise on account from Eastside Supply Company, $1,600.
	25	Paid Town Supply Company invoice dated August 7.
	26	Purchased merchandise on account from Martin Company, $700.
	27	Sold merchandise for cash, $900.
	28	Sold merchandise on credit to Sam Lynch, $350 (Invoice #106).
	29	Purchased merchandise on account from Winters Company, $1,000.
	30	Paid monthly salaries, $1,500.
	31	Purchased merchandise for cash, $900.

Required:

1. Prepare a sales journal, a purchases journal, a cash receipts journal, a cash disbursements journal, and a general journal.
2. Enter the above transactions in the appropriate journals.
3. Open the necessary general ledger and subsidiary ledger accounts. Post the amounts from the journals to the appropriate ledger accounts.

25. Below are listed certain transactions of White Manufacturing Company for the month of March, 19x1.

Mar. 1 Purchased raw materials from Lily Company, $750, invoice dated March 1, on credit.
2 Bought raw materials on credit from Daisy Company, $310, invoice dated March 1.
4 Cash purchase of office supplies, $120.
5 Purchased raw materials on credit from Poppy corporation, $70, invoice dated March 2.
7 Paid Lily Company account in full.
10 Paid interest of $40 on note.
11 Paid Daisy Company account in full.
13 Bought raw materials from Aster Corporation, $430, invoice dated March 10, on credit.
16 Paid Poppy Corporation account in full.
20 Purchased raw materials from Acacia Company on credit, $240, invoice dated March 18.
22 Cash purchases of raw materials, $85.
28 Paid Acacia Company account in full.
29 Paid Aster Corporation account in full.
31 Cash purchases of raw materials, $45.

Required:

1. Prepare a purchases journal and a cash disbursement journal.
2. Open general ledger accounts for accounts payable, cash and purchases.
3. Open subsidiary accounts payable ledger accounts for the credit purchases.

26. The Lyle Fish Hatcheries made sales on credit for the month of May as follows:

May 1 Sold 2 tanks of bass to Lake Resorts at $70 a tank.
2 Sold 25 tanks of trout to Gulf Coast Resorts at $50 a tank.
4 Sold 5 tanks of catfish to Lake Resorts at $65 a tank.
6 Sold 13 tanks of cod to Fish Haven at $75 a tank.
7 Sold 8 tanks of catfish to River Resorts at $65 a tank.
9 Sold 30 tanks of whiting to Smith's Point Stocking Company at $45 a tank.
11 Sold 6 tanks of mackerel to Padre Resort at $55 a tank.
13 Sold 15 tanks of bass to Fish Haven at $60 a tank.
16 Sold 40 tanks of trout to Smith's Point Stocking Company at $40 a tank.
19 Sold 20 tanks of redfish to Gulf Coast Resorts at $75 a tank.
23 Sold 5 tanks of catfish to River Resorts at $65 a tank.
27 Sold 25 tanks of redfish to Smith's Point Stocking Company at $70 a tank.

Required:

1. Prepare a sales journal reflecting May's sales.
2. Prepare an accounts receivable subsidiary ledger.
3. Post the necessary amounts to the general ledger for May.

27. Referring back to Problem 26, prepare a cash receipts journal for the Lyle Fish Hatcheries assuming each credit sale is collected 30 days after the date of sale. Then make any necessary postings to the accounts receivable subsidiary ledger.

28. The special journals kept for the Martin Manufacturing Company are listed below.

Sales Journal

Date	Account	Amount
8/1	Robert Ryan	375
8/4	Mark Martin	440
8/8	Bob Bart	210
8/13	Tom Tyler	195
8/25	Hal Hall	550

Purchases Journal

Date	Account	Amount
8/2	Sawyer Company	75
8/5	Kart, Incorporated	110
8/10	West Industries	265
8/17	Tex Company	120

Cash Receipts Journal

		Debits		Credits		
Date	Account	Cash	Sales Discounts	Sales	Accounts Receivable	Sundry Accounts
8/3	Robert Ryan	360	15		375	
8/6	Cash Sales	215		215		
8/11	Interest Income	100				100
8/20	Tom Tyler	190	5		195	
8/26	Cash Sales	400		400		
8/30	Hal Hall	525	25		550	

Cash Disbursements Journal

		Credit		Debits	
Date	Account	Cash	Accounts Payable	Purchases	Sundry Accounts
8/1	Rent	1,000			1,000
8/7	Cash Purchases	150		150	
8/12	Sawyer Company	75	75		
8/16	Kart, Incorporated	110	110		
8/28	West Industries	265	265		

Required:

1. Post the necessary entries to the general ledger. The balances on August 1 were: Cash, $1,500; Accounts Receivable, $360; Sales, $8,000; Purchases, $3,075; Accounts Payable, $540; Rent Expense, $7,000; Sales Discounts, $500; Interest Income, $4,000.

2. Make the necessary entries to the accounts receivable subsidiary ledger. The balances on August 1 were: Mark Martin, $250 and Tom Tyler, $110.
3. Make the necessary entries to the accounts payable subsidiary ledger. The August 1 balances were: Kart, Incorporated, $240 and West Industries, $300.

29. The ledgers which are kept for the Hunter Company are listed below.

General Ledger Accounts

#1000	Cash		
Date	Debit	Credit	Balance
10/1			4,000
10/31	4,100	2,500	5,600

#1400	Accounts Receivable		
Date	Debit	Credit	Balance
10/1			3,700
10/31	2,500	3,000	3,200

#4000	Sales		
Date	Debit	Credit	Balance
10/1			12,000
10/31		2,500	14,500

#5000	Purchases		
Date	Debit	Credit	Balance
10/1			9,000
10/31	1,450		10,450

#2000	Accounts Payable		
Date	Debit	Credit	Balance
10/1			2,900
10/31	2,500	1,450	1,800

#9000	Sales Discounts		
Date	Debit	Credit	Balance
10/1			500
10/31			500

#4001	Dividend Income		
Date	Debit	Credit	Balance
10/1			2,000
10/31		1,100	3,100

Accounts Receivable Subsidiary Ledger

#1401	Alice Adams		
Date	Debit	Credit	Balance
10/1			200
10/8	200		400
10/25		200	200

#1401	Carl Carpenter		
Date	Debit	Credit	Balance
10/9	400		400

#1403	George Gem		
Date	Debit	Credit	Balance
10/1			300
10/15		300	0

#1404	Lance Little		
Date	Debit	Credit	Balance
10/1			800
10/29		800	0
10/30	450		450

#1405	Marvin Mott		
Date	Debit	Credit	Balance
10/1			900
10/12	400		1,300
10/20		1,000	300

#1406	Tom Toll		
Date	Debit	Credit	Balance
10/1			100
10/21	1,050		1,150
10/30		700	450

Accounts Payable Subsidiary Ledger

#2001	Barney Barton		
Date	Debit	Credit	Balance
10/8		600	600

#2002	Horace Horton		
Date	Debit	Credit	Balance
10/1			500
10/17	500		0

#2003	Nan Nance		
Date	Debit	Credit	Balance
10/1			300
10/5	100		200
10/27		400	600

#2004	Steve Schietze		
Date	Debit	Credit	Balance
10/1			300
10/17		450	750
10/31	750		0

#2005	Dan Doggett		
Date	Debit	Credit	Balance
10/1			1,150
10/24	1,150		0

Required:

Prepare a sales, purchases, cash receipts, and cash disbursements journal.

30. Blake and Hoss Company completed the following transactions during September, 19x1.

Sept.	2	Purchased merchandise for $3,000 on credit from Thompson Suppliers.
	3	Purchased office equipment for $75 on credit from Franklin Office Supply.
	4	Sold merchandise on credit to J.K. Allred, $350, Invoice #1, terms n/30.
	5	Sold merchandise on credit to N.M. Snyder, $175, Invoice #2, terms n/30.
	6	Purchased merchandise for $1,200 on credit from Jackson, Inc.
	7	Borrowed $2,000 by giving the University National Bank a 60-day note payable.
	8	Sold merchandise on credit to T.S. Wheelwright, $230, Invoice #3, terms n/30.
	9	Paid $1,500 on account to Thompson Suppliers.
	10	Received payment in full from J.K. Allred.
	11	Paid cash for a two-year fire insurance policy, $300.
	12	Sold merchandise on account to M.W. Scavely, $450, Invoice #4, terms n/30.
	13	Received payment in full from N.M. Snyder.
	14	Sold merchandise on credit to C.R. Anderson, $780, Invoice #5, terms n/30.
	15	Paid Franklin Office Supply in full.
	16	Received payment in full from T.S. Wheelright.
	17	Purchased merchandise for $3,300 on credit from Thompson Suppliers.
	18	Sold merchandise on credit to D.W. Landale, $1,000, Invoice #6, terms n/30.
	19	Sold merchandise on credit to J.K. Allred, $475, Invoice #7, terms n/30.
	20	Paid $1,500 to Thompson Suppliers.
	21	Received payment in full from M.W. Scavely.
	22	Received $400 on C.R. Anderson's account.
	23	Paid Jackson, Inc., total on account.
	24	Sold merchandise on credit to N.M. Snyder, $250, Invoice #8, terms n/30.
	26	Received payment in full from D.W. Landale.
	28	Purchased office supplies from Franklin Office Supply, $75 on credit.

Required:

1. Prepare a sales journal, a purchases journal, a cash receipts journal, a cash disbursements journal, and a general journal.
2. Enter the above transactions in the appropriate journals.
3. Open the necessary general ledger and subsidiary ledger accounts. Post the amounts from the journals to the appropriate ledger accounts.

Learning Objectives

Chapter 7 discusses the accounting procedures used to record and control cash. Studying this chapter should enable you to:

1. Describe the basic procedures for controlling cash receipts and disbursements.

2. Discuss the steps involved in preparing a bank statement reconciliation.

3. Describe the procedures used to control and account for imprest funds.

4. Describe the procedures used to operate a voucher system.

7 Cash

INTRODUCTION

Cash includes currency, coins, checks, money orders and monies on deposit with banks. On the balance sheet, cash is classified as a current asset. Usually, the total of all cash on hand and cash on deposit in multiple bank accounts will be shown as a single amount in the balance sheet.

Almost every transaction of any business organization will eventually result in either the receipt or disbursement of cash. The accounting procedures which enable a business to establish effective control over its cash transactions are among the most important, if not *the* most important, "controls" necessary for the operation of a business. While it is certainly true that cash is no more important than any of the other individual assets of the business, cash is more susceptible to misappropriation or theft because it can easily be concealed and because it is not readily identifiable. It is essential, therefore, that the company institute procedures or controls throughout every phase of its operations in order to safeguard cash from the time of its receipt until the time it is deposited in the company's bank account.

A good system of internal control over cash transactions should provide adequate procedures for protecting both cash receipts and cash disbursements. Such procedures should include the following elements:

1. Responsibilities for handling cash receipts, making cash payments, and recording cash transactions should be clearly defined.
2. Employees who handle cash transactions should not maintain the accounting records for cash.
3. All cash receipts should be deposited daily in a bank account and all significant cash payments should be made by check.
4. The validity and amount of cash payments should be verified, and different employees should be responsible for approving the disbursement and for signing the check.

The application of these procedures in developing an adequate system of internal control over cash transactions varies from company to company depending upon such factors as the size of the company, the number of its employees, its sources of cash, etc. However, the following discussion illustrates typical procedures which may be used effectively in the control of cash receipts and cash disbursements.

CASH RECEIPTS

The effective control of cash transactions begins at the moment cash is received by the business. Among the basic principles to be followed in controlling cash receipts are the following:

1. A complete record of all cash receipts should be prepared as soon as cash is received. This involves the listing of all cash items received by mail (often accomplished by the use of EDP equipment) and the use of

devices such as cash registers to record "over-the-counter" sales. The immediate recording of each cash transaction is important because the likelihood of misappropriations of cash receipts occurring is usually greatest before a record of the receipt has been prepared. Once the receipt of cash has been properly recorded, misappropriation or theft is much more difficult to accomplish and conceal.

2. Each day's cash receipts should be deposited intact in the company's bank account as soon as possible. Disbursements should never be made directly from cash receipts; each and every cash item received should be promptly deposited in the bank. All major disbursements should be made by check, while outlays of smaller amounts may be made from controlled petty cash funds (described in a later section of this chapter). Adherence to these procedures will provide the firm with a valuable test of the accuracy of its cash records since every major cash transaction will be recorded twice: by the firm in its accounting records and by the bank. The periodic comparison or reconciliation of the accounting records of the business with those maintained by an independent, external source (the bank) is an important control feature in itself and will be discussed in detail in a later section of this chapter.

3. The employees charged with the responsibility of handling cash receipts should not be involved in making cash disbursements. This is a normal procedure employed by most firms of any size. Insofar as possible, the internal functions of receiving and disbursing cash should be kept separate in order to prevent the possible misappropriation or theft of cash. The employees handling cash receipts should not have access to the other accounting records of the firm for the same reasons.

"Over-The-Counter Sales." The cash proceeds received at the time a sale is made should be recorded by means of a cash register. In larger firms, it may be preferable to have all sales recorded by a cashier at a centrally located cash register. One employee may "make the sale" and prepare a pre-numbered sales slip which is given to the cashier who then records the sale on the cash register and accepts the customer's payment. Involving two (or more) employees in each sales transaction, rather than permitting a single employee to handle a transaction in its entirety, increases the control over cash. The use of a cash register also provides certain other benefits. Customers will observe that their purchases are recorded at the proper amount (another form of control). You may recall making a purchase where your money was refunded "if a star appears on your receipt" or where your drink was free if the waiter failed to give you a receipt. These are simple, yet effective examples of control procedures which are intended to encourage customers to note whether the sale has been properly recorded at the correct amount. The cash register may

also be used as a means of classifying the sources of receipts, such as sales by departments.

At the end of each day, or more often if necessary (for example at the end of each cashier's shift), the cash in the register should be counted and recorded on a cash register summary or other report by an employee who does not have access to the sales slips. A second employee should total the sales slips and reconcile the total of the sales slips to the cash register total. As previously indicated, all cash received should be deposited intact in the bank and the receipts recorded in the accounting records.

In certain circumstances, it may not be feasible to use prenumbered sales slips. If this is the case and a cash register is used, the above procedures should still be followed to the extent applicable. The major difference will be that the cash in the register will be reconciled to the totals contained in the register rather than to totals obtained from sales slips.

Receipts from Charge Sales. Remittances from customers for sales which were made on account may be received either by mail or by payment in person. In either case, procedures should be employed so that the receipt and the recording of the cash is performed by different employees whenever it is possible and practical to do so. If this separation of duties can be effectively maintained, the misappropriation of cash would require the collusion of two or more employees, thus diminishing the likelihood of the occurrence of any irregularity.

The employee who opens the mail should immediately prepare a listing of all cash items received. Of course this can be done "automatically," such as by the use of punched cards as remittance forms and EDP equipment. This listing, along with a summary of over-the-counter receipts described previously, may be used to record each day's receipts in the cash receipts summary. Mail remittances are then combined with over-the-counter receipts, and the daily bank deposit is prepared and made. The amount deposited will be equal to the total cash receipts for the day. The employee making the bank deposit should obtain a duplicate deposit slip or other receipt from the bank for subsequent comparison to the cash receipts book.

The advantages of the procedures described above are many. The most important of these benefits may be summarized as follows:

1. The possibility of irregularities with respect to cash transactions are reduced, since any misappropriation will generally require the collusion of two or more employees.
2. The prompt deposit of each day's receipts intact (along with the disbursement procedures described in a later section of this chapter) provides the basis for an independent, external check on the internal records of the firm by reconciliation with bank statements.

3. Frequent deposits of receipts minimizes the idle cash and thereby reduces interest or other carrying charges which might otherwise be incurred by the business.

Several sections of this chapter have discussed the possible misappropriations of cash and outlined certain procedures which are intended to minimize these occurrences. It is obvious that the owners and/or management of any organization are naturally concerned with establishing effective controls that will prevent irregularities, but it may not be as apparent that every employee of the business also has a definite interest in these safeguards. If, for example, cash is misappropriated in an instance where the control procedures are ineffective or not in existence, any employee who might possibly be involved will be under suspicion. Although it may not be possible to identify the guilty person, no employee will be able to prove his (or her) innocence. Employee morale and efficiency will be adversely effected. An effective system of internal control avoids this situation; responsibilities are well-defined, definite, and fixed. Internal control is often an excellent preventive measure, as it often removes the temptation which might cause an otherwise good employee to succumb.

Cash Over and Short. Regardless of the care exercised in handling cash transactions, employees may make errors which cause cash overages or shortages. These differences will normally be detected when the cash on hand is counted and reconciled to the beginning cash balance plus any inflows of cash less any cash outlays.

Assume, for example, that total "over the counter" cash sales for the day are shown as $1,500 on the cash register while cash on hand after deducting the $100 beginning balance, is counted and found to be $1,505. The following journal entry would be made to record the cash sales for the day:

Cash	1,505	
Sales		1,500
Cash over and short		5

The cash over and short account is credited for any cash overages and debited for any cash shortages. At the end of the accounting period, the net balance in the cash over and short account is treated as miscellaneous revenues if there is a net credit balance or as a miscellaneous expense if there is a net debit balance.

CASH DISBURSEMENTS

As previously indicated, one of the basic rules of effective internal control over cash transactions is that each day's receipts should be deposited intact in the bank and that all disbursements should be made by check. The functions of handling cash receipts and cash disbursements should be separated or divided among employees to the greatest extent practical. Other procedures which may be used to establish effective control over cash disbursements include the following:

1. All checks should be prenumbered consecutively and should be controlled and accounted for on a regular basis. Checks which are voided or spoiled should be retained and mutilated to prevent any possible unauthorized use.
2. Each disbursement should be supported or evidenced by an invoice and/or voucher which has been properly approved. The procedures which identify that obligations for which checks are prepared are proper obligations and in the appropriate amount are often referred to as a voucher system. The details of a voucher system will be discussed later in this chapter.
3. Invoices and vouchers should be indelibly marked as "paid" or otherwise cancelled in order to prevent duplicate payments.
4. The bank statement and returned checks should be routed to the employee charged with the preparation of the bank reconciliation statement (described below). This employee should be someone other than the person who is responsible for making cash disbursements.

THE BANK RECONCILIATION STATEMENT

As indicated earlier, if all receipts are deposited intact in the bank and all major disbursements are made by check, each cash transaction will be recorded twice: by the business in its accounting records, and in the records of the bank. It might seem logical, then, that at any given time the cash balance obtained from the accounting records of the firm should be identical to (i.e., equal to) the balance in the business's checking account at the bank. This is very seldom the case, however. Comparison of the balance shown in the firm's records with the balance shown at the same date by the bank statement usually reveals a difference in the two amounts. One reason for the difference could, of course, be erroneous entries made either by the firm or by the bank. A more frequent cause for the difference is, however, attributable to the difference in the timing of the recording of the transactions by the firm and the bank. If all transactions were recorded simultaneously by the business and by the bank no differences would result (except in the case of errors), but this is almost never the case. The firm, for example, will write a check and immediately deduct the amount of the expenditure from the cash balance in its checkbook. The bank will not deduct this same disbursement from the firm's account until the check is presented to the bank for payment, perhaps several days later. Until the disbursement is deducted by the bank, the balance in the firm's account at the bank will exceed the firm's cash balance in its checkbook by the amount of the check. Similarly, the bank may levy a service charge against the firm's bank account from time to time. The business is usually unaware of the amount of this charge until it receives its monthly statement from the bank. Until the bank statement is received and the service charge is deducted, the balance on the firm's records will exceed the bank statement balance by the amount of the service charge.

The above examples are but two of the many items which may cause a difference between the bank statement balance and the cash balance as shown on the accounting records of the business. Other items which are often reflected in the bank statement but which have not yet been recorded by the depositor include:

1. N.S.F checks—checks that were received from the depositor's customers and which were deposited in the bank, but for which the bank on which the check was written refuses payment (usually because of insufficient funds in the customer's account).
2. Deductions for bank service charges, printing of checks, safe deposit box rentals, etc.
3. Collections by the bank in acting as a collecting agent for the depositor.

A bank reconciliation is prepared to identify and account for all items which cause a difference between the cash balance as shown on the bank statement and the balance as it appears in the firm's accounting records. One format of this statement which is often used is such that both the book and bank balances are adjusted to the actual amount of cash which is available to the business. This amount is often referred to as the "adjusted cash balance" or "true cash." This is the amount which should appear on the balance sheet. A typical bank reconciliation statement is presented in Illustration 1.

The initial step in preparing a bank reconciliation statement is to examine the bank statement and any debit and credit memoranda accompanying it. A debit memorandum is evidence of a deduction made by the bank from a depositor's account which arises from a transaction other than the normal payment of a check by the bank. Likewise, a credit memorandum is an addition to the depositor's account which arises from a transaction other than a normal deposit. These documents should be compared with the firm's accounting records in order to determine whether or not they have been previously (and properly) recorded by the business. If these transactions have not been recorded, they will be included as additions or deductions in the bank reconciliation statement and then recorded at a subsequent time. Examples of these types of reconciling items which were included in Illustration 1 are as follows:

Illustration 1

Carol's Bakery
Bank Reconciliation Statement
June 30, 19x1

Balance per the bank statement, June 30, 19x1	$4,590
Add: Deposit in transit	500
Bank error, check drawn by Carrol's Tavern charged to the account of Carol's Bakery	10
Less: Outstanding checks:	
Number 95—$50	
Number 101— 15	
Number 106— 30	
Number 110— 5	(100)
"True" cash balance, June 30, 19x1	$5,000
Balance per the books, June 30, 19x1	$4,000
Add: Note collected by the bank	1,000
Error made by the accountant in recording check #100	45
Less: Bank charges	(5)
N.S.F. check	(40)
"True" cash balance, June 30, 19x1	$5,000

1. The $1,000 addition to the book balance represents the proceeds from a note payable to Carol's Bakery which was collected by the bank and added to Carol's bank account.
2. The bank charges of $5 for the month of June were deducted from Carol's account by the bank.
3. The N.S.F. (Not Sufficient Funds) check of $40 represents a check received from a customer and deposited by Carol. The check was returned unpaid by the customer's bank.

The second step in preparing the reconciliation is to arrange the paid checks returned with the bank statement in numerical sequence. The checks returned by the bank are then compared with the checks issued as listed in the business checkbook or cash disbursements journal. Distinctive "tick marks" or symbols (such as a ✓) may be used in the checkbook in order to indicate those checks which have been returned by the bank. The amount of each check should be compared to the amount listed in the checkbook during this process. The outstanding checks are those which have been issued but not yet returned by the bank.

Checks which were outstanding at the beginning of the month and which cleared the bank during the month may be traced to the bank reconciliation statement prepared at the end of the previous month. Any checks which were outstanding at the beginning of the month and which did not clear the bank will, of course, still be included as outstanding in the current month's reconciliation. In the example, the $100 total of outstanding checks included in the bank reconciliation statement was determined by comparing the cancelled checks returned with the bank statement with the checkbook and the listing of outstanding checks included in the previous month's bank reconciliation.

In our example, examination of the cancelled checks returned with the bank statement disclosed the fact that the bank had deducted a check of Carrol's Tavern in the amount of $10 from the Carol's Bakery account. This item is shown as an addition to the balance per bank in the reconciliation and would be called to the attention of the bank for correction.

The next step in the reconciliation process is to ascertain whether or not there are any deposits in transit. A deposit in transit is a receipt which has been included in the cash balance per books and deposited in the bank (for example, in a night depository or by mail) but which has not yet been processed by the bank and credited to the depositor's account. In the illustration, the total receipts of $500 for June 30th were deposited in the bank's night depository on that date. The bank, however, did not credit the firm's account until the next day, July 1st. The $500 amount is therefore shown as a deposit in transit in the June 30, 19x1, bank reconciliation statement.

An excellent test of the accuracy of the firm's cash receipts records is to reconcile the total receipts for the month (or other period) to the total deposits credited to the bank account in the bank statement. In order to perform this test, the following information would be required:

1. The total deposits which are included in the bank statement for the month of June [including a deposit in transit at the beginning of the month (May 31, 19x1) of $700] $15,000
2. The total cash receipts shown in the firm's accounting records for the month of June (including the receipts of June 30th of $500) $14,800

The receipts as per the books for the month of June would be reconciled with the deposits as per the June 30, 19x1, bank statement as follows:

Deposits per bank statement.................	$15,000
Less: Deposit in transit at the end of the prior month......................	700
	$14,300
Add: Deposit in transit at the end of the current month	500
Cash receipts per the books	$14,800

In many instances, deposits in transit, outstanding checks, service charges, and errors will be the only reconciling items between the book and the bank balances. Omissions from, or errors in, the accounting records of the firm should, of course, be corrected immediately. If errors made by the bank are discovered in the reconciliation process (such as a check charged to the wrong account), they should be called to the attention of the bank for immediate correction.

In the example, several adjusting or correcting entries would be required. These are as follows:

Note collected by the bank

Cash	1,000	
Notes Receivable		1,000

Error

Cash	45	
Accounts Receivable		45*

Bank service charges

Service charge expense	5	
Cash		5

N.S.F. check

Accounts Receivable	40	
Cash		40

* The receipt of a payment on account of $572 was erroneously recorded as $527 by the firm. This entry reduces the customer's account in order to reflect the actual amount which was paid and increases cash to the proper amount.

The effect of these three entries will be to adjust the balance per books as of June 30, 19x1, to the "true cash" balance as of that date. This adjustment procedure may be illustrated as follows:

Cash

4,000	
1,000	5
45	40
5,000	

It should be noted that only those items which are adjustments of the "balance per books" in the bank reconciliation statement will require adjusting or correcting entries. This is because these items have either not been previously recorded on the books of the firm (in the example, the note collected by the bank, the bank charges, and the check which was returned N.S.F.) or have been recorded erroneously (in the example, the receipt of $572 which was recorded by the firm as $527[1]). Items which

---

[1] Transposition errors (i.e. $572 − $527) are always divisible by nine. This fact may be helpful in locating differences, errors, etc.

are included as adjustments of the "balance per the bank statement" do not require adjustment on the firm's books since these items are either transactions which have been already recorded by the firm but not by the bank (in the example, the deposit in transit and the outstanding checks) or errors which were made by the bank (in the example, the check of Carrol's Tavern which was erroneously charged to the account of Carol's Bakery).

The bank reconciliation procedure may be summarized as follows:

Balance per the bank statement—Adjust for:

1. Transactions recorded by the firm but not by the bank (deposits in transit, outstanding checks, etc.).
2. Errors made by the bank.

Balance per the books—Adjust for:

1. Transactions recorded by the bank but not by the firm (collections made for the firm by the bank, service charges, N.S.F. checks, etc.).
2. Errors made by the firm.

PETTY CASH FUNDS

A basic principle of control over cash is that all cash disbursements should be made by check. This is not practicable, however, in instances where small expenditures are required for items such as postage, freight, carfare, employees' "supper money," etc. In circumstances such as these, it is usually more convenient and cost effective to make payments in currency and/or coin. This can be accomplished and effective control over cash still maintained by the use of an imprest fund called petty cash.

A petty cash fund is established by drawing a check on the regular checking account, cashing it, and placing the proceeds in a fund. The amount of the fund depends upon the extent to which petty cash will be used and how often it will be reimbursed. As a practical matter it should be large enough to cover petty cash disbursements for a reasonable period of time—for example, a week. A single employee should be placed in charge of the fund and made responsible for its operation.

A major difference between making disbursements from a petty cash fund and from a regular checking account is that disbursements from petty cash funds are recorded in the accounting records not as they are made, but when the fund is reimbursed. At the time each expenditure is made from the fund, a petty cash voucher, such as the one illustrated below is prepared. If an invoice or other receipt is available in support of the

```
                        Petty Cash Voucher #53

       TO    Vince Brenner         DATE    May 1        19x1

       EXPLANATION     ACCOUNT              AMOUNT
            Postage      119                 $5.00


       APPROVED                     RECEIVED
       BY         P D               PAYMENT     V. B.
```

disbursement, it should be attached to the voucher. In any event, the person receiving the cash should always be required to sign the petty cash voucher as evidence of his or her receipt of the disbursement. If this procedure is followed, at any given time the total of the cash on hand in the petty cash fund plus the total of the unreimbursed receipts should be exactly equal to the original amount of the fund.

The fund would be reimbursed on a periodic basis or whenever necessary. In order to obtain reimbursement of the fund, the employee acting as petty cashier would bring the paid petty cash vouchers to the person who is authorized to write checks on the firm's bank account and exchange them for a check equal to the total of the vouchers. At this point, the petty cash vouchers would be separated and summarized according to the appropriate expense category for recording in the firm's accounting records. Before the check is issued, the vouchers would be reviewed in order to ascertain that all the expenditures made were for valid business purposes. After the petty cash vouchers are approved and the fund replenished, the vouchers and the underlying support should be marked as "paid" or otherwise mutilated in order to prevent their reuse, either intentionally or unintentionally.

To illustrate the operation of a petty cash fund, assume that Barney Company establishes a $100 petty cash fund on January 1, 19x1, by cashing a check in the amount of $100 and placing the proceeds in the fund. The entry to record this transaction would be as follows:

```
January 1   Petty Cash . . . . . . . . . . . . . . . . . . . . . . . . . . . 100
                Cash . . . . . . . . . . . . . . . . . . . . . . . . . . . . .      100
```

Assume further that during the month of January, disbursements from the fund (supported by vouchers) totaled $85. In order to replenish the fund on January 31, the employee responsible for the fund would exchange the vouchers for a check drawn on the regular cash account for $85. This check would be cashed and the $85 proceeds would be used to restore the fund to its original cash balance of $100. This transaction would be recorded by the following entry:

January 31 Various Expenses 85
                Cash   85

Note that no entry is made to the "petty cash" account after the fund is established (unless the firm wishes to increase or decrease the fund balance).

Effective control over petty cash operations is accomplished in two ways: at any time the cash on hand in the fund plus the unreimbursed petty cash vouchers must be equal to the fund balance, and the expense vouchers must be examined and approved upon reimbursement by a person other than the employee who made the disbursement. If considered necessary or desirable, surprise counts of the petty cash fund also may be made in order to insure that the fund is operating according to its intended purpose.

THE VOUCHER SYSTEM

A voucher system may be used to enhance the internal control over cash transactions. The installation and use of a voucher system is relatively simple, yet effective, and is described in the paragraphs which follow.

Effective control over cash disbursements requires:

1. *Authorization.* All expenditures for goods and services must be properly authorized in accordance with company policies.
2. *Receipt.* All goods and services must be inspected upon receipt in order to ascertain that the acquisition was properly approved and the goods or services received were indeed those which were ordered.
3. *Vouching.* Bills and invoices received from the suppliers of goods and services must be reviewed and compared to purchase orders and receiving reports. Credit terms, prices, discounts, extensions and shipping costs should be checked and verified.
4. *Payment.* When all of the procedures noted above have been completed, a check must be issued to the vendor in payment for the goods or services.

The implementation of these procedures may be effected by the use of voucher system.

A voucher is a standard form created by a company to its own specifications to assist its personnel in processing bills and invoices for payment. When a voucher system is in use, it requires that every liability be recorded at the time it is incurred. This is accomplished by the preparation of a separate voucher for every transaction that will ultimately result in a cash disbursement by the business. While the specific format of the voucher may vary from company to company, the following features are normally included on or with the voucher:

1. *Voucher number.* All vouchers should be numbered consecutively and, as indicated above, a separate voucher should be prepared for each liability as it is incurred.
2. *Vendor data.* Vouchers would include information as to the name and address of the supplier of the goods or services, the vendor's invoice number, the date of the invoice and payment terms.
3. *Description of the goods or services.*
4. *Price information.* This would include the gross amount of the transaction, any discounts available, the net amount which will be paid and the due date of the payment.
5. *Other information.* The other information on or with a voucher would include the identification of the purchase order and receiving report used by the company, the number and the date of the check issued in payment of the voucher and the distribution of the expenditure to the accounts.
6. *Approvals.* The voucher would have spaces where various employees would indicate that specific internal control procedures had been performed with regard to the expenditure. These procedures would include notations concerning the:

    a. Authorization for the acquisition, including prices and credit terms.
    b. Receipt of the goods and services, verified by comparison of the invoice with receiving documents.
    c. Arithmetic accuracy of the invoice.
    d. Correctness of the accounting distribution.
    e. Recording of the voucher.
    f. Approval of the payment.
    g. Issuance of the check.

The above information may be noted on the voucher itself or by attaching available documentation to the voucher.

A voucher is normally prepared by the company immediately upon the receipt of an invoice from the supplier of goods or services. The appropriate information from the invoice is entered on the voucher and the vendor's in-

```
Voucher No. _____          Date _____
Payment due on _____


Vendor _____
Street address _____
City _____        State _____  Zip _____


Invoice number _____       Gross amount $ _____
Invoice date _____         Less: Discount(s) _____
Terms _____
Check number _____ Date _____  Net amount $ _____


Purchase order number _____    Date _____
Receiving report number _____  Date _____

                                    Date        By
    Agreed to purchase order       _____    _____
    Agreed to shipping report      _____    _____
    Verified arithmetical accuracy _____    _____
    Verified account distribution  _____    _____
    Approved for payment           _____    _____
    Entered in voucher register    _____    _____

Account(s) debited                              amount(s)


Account(s) credited                             amount(s)
```

voice is attached to it along with the company's purchase order and receiving report. This documentation is then used by the company to verify approval of the purchase, receipt of the goods or services, correctness of the invoice and the accounting distribution of the transaction (i.e., which accounts are to be debited and credited).

To illustrate the effect of the operation of a voucher system, assume that the Carter Company received an invoice in the amount of $1,000 for advertising from the Houston Post. The following entry would be required at the time the invoice was received.

$$\text{Advertising expense} \dots \dots 1{,}000$$
$$\text{Vouchers payable} \dots \dots \qquad 1{,}000$$

Carter Company would follow the procedures outlined above in processing and recording the voucher and invoice. At the time payment is made, the following entry would be recorded:

$$\text{Vouchers payable} \dots \dots 1{,}000$$
$$\text{Cash} \dots \dots \qquad 1{,}000$$

When the voucher has been completely assembled (voucher, invoice, purchase order and receiving report) and the appropriate comparisons and verifications have been completed, the document is approved and entered in a voucher register. The voucher register is one type of special journal, similar to the purchases journal described in Chapter 6. The basic difference between these two journals is that the purchases journal is used only for the purchase of merchandise for resale while the voucher register is used to

Voucher Date Month	Day	Voucher Number	Vendor	Date Paid Month	Day	Check Number	Vouchers Payable Cr.	Purchases Dr.	Freight-in Dr.
June	2	106	R. D. Irvin	June	12	609	496	490	6
	3	107	Southeastern		13	610	989	980	9
	5	108	Porter's Ads		14	611	1,000		
	5	109	CNB		14	612	525		
	6	110	Jeff Strawser		15	613	50		
	6	111	Billy Strawser		15	614	65		
	26	136	Fran Cia		26	639	150		
	27	137	Ben Jamin, CPA		27	640	75		
	30	138	Central Freight		30	641	12		12
	30	139	Pam Porter		30	642	125		
							27,650	11,350	95
							(201)	(510)	(511)

record all types of expenditures. The voucher register contains a listing of all vouchers, in numerical (and chronological) order and includes columns for:

1. Date of voucher
2. Voucher number
3. Vendor
4. Date of payment
5. Check number
6. Credits to vouchers payable
7. Credits to other accounts
8. Debits to accounts

Like other special journals, a voucher register is useful in those instances where there is a large volume of transactions which result in debits and credits to the same accounts. For such transactions, the recording process is facilitated by entering the amounts in the columns of a voucher register and posting the totals periodically to the general ledger. The types of transactions which normally occur with sufficient frequency to justify the use of

Discounts lost Dr.	Advertising Dr.	Salaries Dr.	Selling Dr.	Office Dr.	General Ledger Account			
					Account	Acct. No.	Amount Dr.	Cr.
	1,000							
					Notes Payable	210	500	
					Interest Exp.	615	25	
				50				
				65				
~~	~~~	~~~	~~~	~~~	~~~	~~~	~~~	~~~
~~	~~~	~~~	~~~	~~~	~~~	~~~	~~~	~~~
		150						
					Professional Fees	636	75	
			125					
	1,000	4,500	3,655	2,750			4,300	
(520)	(521)	(522)	(525)				(x)	(x)

special columns in the voucher register would, of course, depend on the nature of the business. When a company establishes its voucher system, it will include columns in the voucher register for those accounts which are frequently debited and credited. For example, Carter Company operates a bookstore in a location which is adjacent to a large urban university and sells college textbooks and supplies. Carter Company's voucher register might include columns for: vouchers payable (cr.), purchases (dr.), freight-in (dr.), discounts lost (dr.), advertising (dr.), salaries (dr.), selling expenses (dr.) and office expenses (dr.). These columns would be totaled periodically and the totals posted to the appropriate general ledger accounts. Miscellaneous debit and credit columns would be used to record entries to any account which did not have its own individual column. These items would, of course, be posted to the appropriate general ledger accounts on an individual basis.

The use of a voucher system not only simplifies the recording and processing of accounting information, but provides assurance that each and every disbursement made by the company is systematically reviewed, verified, and approved prior to payment.

SUMMARY

The proper recording and controlling of cash receipts and disbursements is a concern common to all firms. Certain basic control procedures must be followed to eliminate the probability that cash will be lost or misappropriated. Control procedures applicable to the receipt of cash include preparing a complete record immediately upon the receipt of cash, depositing the cash intact in the company's bank on a daily basis, and involving more than one employee in the handling and recording of cash transactions. In addition, employees involved in handling cash receipts should not also be authorized to make cash disbursements. Cash disbursement control measures include using pre-numbered checks to make payments for all items not paid for from petty cash, supporting each disbursement with an invoice or voucher, and having an employee that does not make cash disbursements reconcile the bank statement at frequent intervals.

A voucher system is a commonly used method of establishing control over cash disbursements. It provides a system that forces verification and approval for any transaction requiring a cash (check) payment.

This chapter has discussed the basic aspects of accounting for and controlling cash.

Comprehensive Illustration—Bank Reconciliation

A bank statement for Kilbourne, Inc., shows a balance as of December 31, 19x1, of $3,691.18. The cash account for the company as of this date shows an overdraft of $611.48. In reconciling the bank statement with the book balance, the following items are discovered:

a. The balance in the cash account includes $400 representing a change fund on hand. When this change fund is counted, only $374.70 is found to be on hand.
b. The cash balance includes $500 representing a petty cash fund. An inspection of this fund reveals cash of $420 on hand and a replenishing check drawn on December 31, 19x1 for $80.
c. Proceeds from cash sales of December 27, 19x1 were stolen. The company expects to recover the full amount stolen ($690) from its insurance company and has made no entry for the loss.
d. The bank statement shows that the company was charged with a customer's N.S.F. check for $125.84, bank services charges of $39.50, and a check drawn by another firm for $136 which was incorrectly charged to Kilbourne's account.
e. The bank statement does not show receipts of December 31, 19x1, totaling $1,837, which were mailed to the bank on that date but not received by the bank and credited to Kilbourne's account until January 2, 19x2.
f. Checks outstanding were found to be $8,031. This includes the check transferred to the petty cash fund and also two checks, each for $182 and payable to I.M. Acrook. Acrook had notified Kilbourne that he had lost the original check and had been sent a second one; Kilbourne stopped payment on the first check. Also, among the checks outstanding was one for $120 which has been outstanding for 17 years. This check was originally issued as final payment for the company's African Puma, which is still being used to guard the company's shop at nights. It is decided to cancel this item since the payee, P.U. Maroper, cannot be found and payment will never be claimed.

Required:

1. Prepare a bank reconciliation using the format where both bank and book balances are adjusted to a corrected cash balance.
2. Give any correcting or adjusting entries required by the foregoing information.
3. List the cash items as they should appear on the Balance Sheet on December 31.

(AICPA adapted)

Solution for Comprehensive Illustration

Balance per bank statement		$3,691.18
Add: Deposit in transit		1,837.00
Bank error		136.00
		$5,664.18
Less: Outstanding checks		7,729.00
		($2,064.82)
Balance per books		($ 611.48)
Add: Stop payment		182.00
Check canceled		120.00
		($ 309.48)
Less: Change fund	$400.00	
Petty cash fund	500.00	
Loss from theft	690.00	
N.S.F. check	125.84	
Service charges	39.50	1,755.34
		($2,064.82)

Correcting entry:
Cash change fund	$374.70	
Petty cash	500.00	
Cash shortage	25.30	
Receivable from insurance company	690.00	
Accounts receivable	125.84	
Expense	39.50	
Accounts payable		$ 182.00
Puma		120.00
Cash		1,453.34

Statement presentation:
Current assets:	
Cash on hand	$ 874.70
Current liabilities:	
Cash overdraft	$2,064.82

KEY DEFINITIONS

Balance per bank statement This balance is the amount in the cash account of the business according to the bank's records.

Balance per books This amount is the balance in the cash account according to the firm's records.

Bank reconciliation A bank reconciliation is an analysis made to identify and account for all items which cause differences between the cash balance as shown on the bank statement and the cash balance as it appears in the firm's accounting records.

Cash Cash consists of currency, coins, checks and certain other forms of negotiable paper.

Cash disbursement A cash disbursement is an outlay of cash made by the firm.

Cash over and short The cash over and short account is an account which is credited for any cash overages and debited for any cash shortages. The net balance in this account at the end of a period is treated as miscellaneous revenue or expense.

Cash receipt A cash receipt is an inflow of cash into the firm.

Cash transaction A cash transaction is an accounting transaction that involves either a cash receipt or a cash disbursement.

Charge sales Charge sales are sales in which the firm provides a customer with goods or services in exchange for the customer's promise to pay at a later date.

Credit memorandum This memorandum is an addition which is made by the bank to a depositor's account. The addition arises from a transaction other than a normal deposit.

Debit memorandum This memorandum is a deduction which is made by the bank from a depositor's account. The deduction arises from a transaction other than the normal payment of a check by the bank.

Deposit in transit This deposit is a receipt which has been included in the cash balance per books and deposited in the bank, but not yet processed by the bank and credited to the depositor's account.

Outstanding check This is a check which has been issued by the business but not yet presented to the bank for payment.

Over-the-counter sales These sales are consummated by the immediate payment of cash for the goods or services purchased.

Petty cash fund The petty cash fund is a fund established to make cash disbursements for small expenditures.

Petty cash voucher This voucher is an authorization to disburse cash from the petty cash fund and is usually retained as a receipt for the expenditure.

True cash True cash is the amount of cash that is actually available to the entity. One format for the bank reconciliation statement adjusts both the book and bank balances to true cash.

Voucher A voucher is a standard form created by a company to its own specifications to assist its personnel in processing bills and invoices for payment.

Voucher system A voucher system is a system used to enhance the internal control over cash transactions and to simplify the recording and processing of accounting information.

QUESTIONS

1. Why is control over cash transactions considered to be more important than other assets of a business?

2. List a few basic principles in connection with cash control. You may wish to organize your discussion along the line of the normal cash flow.

3. What are the principal advantages of maintaining a separation of duties involving cash transactions?

4. In order to establish control over the cash receipts from over the counter sales, a small firm installs a cash register with each sales clerk responsible for ringing up his or her own sales. Discuss.

5. List some procedures other than separation of duties which may be employed in order to establish effective control over cash disbursements.

6. What is the purpose of a bank reconciliation statement?

7. What are the necessary adjustments in the bank reconciliation statement to the balance per the bank statement? To the balance per the books?

8. The petty cash account has a debit balance of $300. At the end of the accounting period there is $35 in the petty cash fund along with petty cash vouchers totaling $265. Should the fund be replenished as of the last day of the period? Discuss.

9. What are some of the steps necessary to achieve effective control over cash disbursements?

10. What is a voucher? How and why is it used?

11. Describe a voucher register.

12. When is a voucher normally prepared?

13. How might a particular company decide upon the design of its voucher register? What factors might be taken into consideration in this process?

14. Briefly summarize the benefits which may be obtained by the use of a voucher system.

EXERCISES

15. State whether the following bank reconciliation items would need an adjusting or correcting entry on the *depositor's* books:

    a. Checks totaling $1,850 were issued by the depositor but not paid by the bank.
    b. A $1,000 note was collected for the depositor by the bank and was deposited in his account. Notice was sent to the depositor with the bank statement.

c. The last day's receipts ($1,750) for the month were not recorded as a deposit by the bank until the following month.
d. The depositor issued a check for $180 but entered it in his records as $810.
e. The bank paid a check for $150 but entered it as $510 on their records.
f. The bank charged a bad check that it received in a deposit back against the depositor's account. Notice to the depositor was made by the bank with the bank statement.
g. The bank charged $21 for service charges and notified the depositor with the bank statement.
h. The bank had erroneously charged a check, drawn by another depositor with a similar name, to the depositor's account.

16. Prepare the journal entries that are necessary to adjust the cash account on the depositor's books, based on the information included in Exercise 15 above.

17. The following information is taken from the books and records of the Terp Company.

Balance per the cash account (before adjustment)...	$2,860
Outstanding checks..........................	820
Deposit in transit............................	208
Bank service charges.........................	18
Cash on hand—unrecorded on the books and not yet deposited in the bank.................	180
Balance per the bank statement................	unavailable

Required:

Prepare a bank reconciliation showing the "true" cash balance.

18. Prepare, in general journal form, the entries that Terp Company should make to adjust its cash balance as a result of the bank reconciliation in Exercise 17 above.

19. Test the accuracy of Willard Company's cash receipts records for August given the following information:

Total cash receipts as shown in the firm's records were $14,910.
Payment of $1,110 was received on August 31 but the deposit was not yet recorded by the bank.
Total deposits included in the August bank statement were $14,700.
Deposit in transit at end of July was $900.

20. The Gibbons Company reconciles its one bank account on a monthly basis. The company follows the procedure of reconciling the balance as reported on the bank statement and the balance per books *to a corrected balance*. The corrected balance appears on the balance sheet.

The facts stated in items 1 through 10 below are involved in a reconciliation for the month of December. Decide which of the five answer choices best indicates how each fact should be handled in the December 31 bank reconciliation.

Answer choices for items 1 through 9:

(1) An addition to the balance per books.
(2) A deduction from the balance per books.
(3) An addition to the balance per bank.
(4) A deduction from the balance per bank.
(5) Should not appear in the reconciliation.

1. A deposit of $100 made on December 31 did not appear in the December bank statement.................... ( )
2. A deposit of $130 made on November 30 was recorded by the bank on December 1............................. ( )
3. Three checks totalling $180 drawn in December did not clear the bank.. ( )
4. A check from customer Kay for $75 was returned by the bank marked N.S.F................................... ( )
5. The bank statement was accompanied by a credit memo dated December 30 for the proceeds of a note ($198) which Gibbons Company had left with the bank for collection..................................... ( )
6. Gibbons Company discovered that a December check recorded in the check register as $150 was actually drawn for $105. This check was cleared by the bank in December..................................... ( )
7. Two checks totalling $120 drawn in November had cleared the bank in December........................... ( )
8. Accompanying the December bank statement was a cancelled check for $60 of Gibson Company................ ( )
9. The bookkeeper of Gibbons Company had recorded a $90 check received from customer Fay on December 29 as $190.. ( )
10. Which of the facts disclosed in items 1 through 9 above require adjusting entries on the books of the Gibbons Company?

    (1)   1, 3, 8   (2)   6, 8, 9
    (3)   1, 2, 3, 7   (4)   4, 5, 6, 9
    (5)   Some other group

21. Show in general journal form all entries that should be made to reflect the operation of the Eljon Corporation's petty cash fund.

May 10   The company established a petty cash fund of $225.
     12   Paid miscellaneous office expenses amounting to $52.
     14   Paid $15 to messengers for cab fares.
     19   Paid telephone bill of $63.
     25   Paid $21 in postage.
     30   The petty cash fund was reimbursed for the first time.
     31   Eljon Corporation increased its petty cash fund to $300.

22. Determine the "true cash" balance after the following adjustments or corrections have been made to the Cash account. The cash balance per books was $3,650. (Use a T-account to do this.)

   a. A deposit in transit at the end of the period was $350.
   b. Check #501 for $89 was still outstanding at the end of the period.
   c. An account receivable of $110 was collected by the bank.
   d. The service charge for the period was $47.
   e. Check #101 for $680 which had been outstanding for 10 years was cancelled.
   f. The bank paid $20 more on Check #509 than was written on the face of the check.
   g. Check #513 was incorrectly entered in the books by the bookkeeper for $315 instead of $513.
   h. A stop payment was placed on Check #507 for $265.

PROBLEMS

23. Red, Inc.'s bank statement for the month ending June 30 shows a balance of $231. The cash account as of the close of business on June 30 indicates a credit balance or overdraft of $123. In reconciling the balances, the auditor discovers the following:

   Receipts on June 30 of $1,860 were not deposited until July 1.
   Checks outstanding on June 30 were $2,215.
   The bank has charged the depositor $10 for service charges.
   A check payable to S.S. Dohr for $56 was entered in Red's cash payments journal in error as $65.

   Required:

   Prepare a bank reconciliation.

24. The following refers to Ginger's Floral Shop:

   a. Prepare a bank reconciliation showing the "true" cash balance for July 31 given the following information:

      1. Balance per bank statement at July 31, $4,610.
      2. Balance per books at July 31, $3,900.
      3. Deposits in transit not recorded by banks, $445.
      4. Bank error, check drawn by the Ginger Bread Shop debited to account of Ginger's Floral Shop, $20.
      5. Note collected by bank for Ginger's, $1,025.
      6. Debit memorandum for bank charges, $10.
      7. N.S.F. check returned by bank, $35.
      8. Ginger's accountant credited cash account for $175 rather than the correct figure of $100 in recording her check #55.
      9. Outstanding checks of $120 on July 31.

   b. Prepare the adjusting or correcting entries required.

25. You have been engaged to audit the Able Company. In the course of your examination, you gather the following information:

a. Balance per cash account, July 31, 19x1, $2,750.
b. Bank service charges for the month included as a debit memo with the bank statement, $22.
c. Outstanding checks at June 30, $195.
d. Deposits received on July 31 and sent to bank but not yet recorded by bank, $216.
e. Checks written in month of June and returned with July statement, $135.
f. Checks written in July but not returned with July 31 bank statement, $535.

Required:

Compute the balance reported on July 31, 19x1 bank statement.

26. In connection with an examination of the cash account you are given the following worksheet:

Bank Reconciliation
December 31, 19x1

Balance per books at December 31, 19x1.............		$17,174.86
Add: Collections received on the last day of December and charged to "cash in bank" on books but not deposited..........		2,662.25
Debit memo for customer's check returned unpaid (check is on hand but no entry has been made on the books).......		200.00
Debit memo for bank service charge for December............................		5.50
		$20,142.61
Less: Checks drawn but not paid by bank (see detailed list below)....................	$2,267.75	
Credit memo for proceeds of a note receivable which had been left at the bank for collection but which has not been recorded as collected................	400.00	
Check for an account payable entered on books as $240.90 but drawn and paid by bank as $419.....................	178.10	2,945.85
Computed balance.............................		$17,196.76
Unlocated difference............................		200.00
Balance per bank.................................		$16,996.76

Checks Drawn but Not Paid by Bank

No.	Amount
573	$ 67.27
724	9.90
903	456.67
907	305.50
911	482.75
913	550.00
914	366.76
916	10.00
917	218.90
	$2,267.75

Required:

1. Prepare a corrected reconciliation.
2. Prepare journal entries for items which should be adjusted prior to closing the books.

(AICPA adapted)

27. The Backward Company decided to create a petty cash fund because of the increase in small cash disbursements such as supplies and postage. The following transactions took place in the month of May.

Postage	$13
Delivery costs	9
Supplies	25
Tapes for recorder	3

The petty cash fund was established at $300 on May 1. It was replenished on May 30 and then increased by $50 on May 31.

Required:

Prepare all journal entries related to the petty cash fund for the month of May.

28. The Medich Company's petty cash fund for the first month of operations was as follows:

   a. $1,000 was placed in the fund on April 1.
   b. Petty cash record for April:

	April 1-15	April 16-30
Postage	$ 50	$ 60
Supplies	400	600
Miscellaneous expenses	90	70
Total	$540	$730

c. On April 16 the fund was replenished.
d. On April 30 the fund was replenished and decreased by $100.

Required:

Prepare all entries.

29. The Ellis Company's bank reconciliation at March 31 was as follows:

Balance per bank statement.................	$7,000
Deposits outstanding......................	400
Checks outstanding........................	(75)
	$7,325
Balance per books.........................	$7,332
Unrecorded service charge.................	(7)
	$7,325

April data are as follows:

	Bank	Books
Checks recorded........................	$5,750	$5,900
Deposits recorded......................	5,050	5,500
Service charges recorded................	6	7
Collection by bank.....................	410	0
N.S.F. check returned..................	25	0
Balances April 30......................	6,679	6,925

Required:

1. What are the amounts of the unrecorded deposits and outstanding checks at April 30?
2. Prepare a bank reconciliation for April.
3. Prepare the needed entries at April 30.

30. The balance reported on the bank statement of Harrah Corporation on April 30, 19x1 was $65,978.40. The bookkeeper found the following by comparing the bank and the book balances:

a. Checks totaling $10,798.50 had not cleared the bank.
b. A check was recorded in the books at $730 when the correct amount was $370. The check was for the purchase of office supplies.
c. No entry was made in the books for an N.S.F. check of $210.
d. The bank had not recorded a deposit of $2,432.
e. $3 was charged for printing checks.

Required:

1. Determine the balance per books before any corrections or adjustments are made.
2. Prepare a bank reconciliation and any necessary journal entries.

31. Prepare a bank reconciliation for the May Company for September 30, 19x1.

a. Book cash balance on September 30 was $230.80.
b. On August 31 outstanding checks totaled $1,394.80. By September 30, only two of these checks had not cleared. Because of the amount of time it had been outstanding, one of the checks for $100 had a stop payment put on it. The other outstanding check was for $57.10.
c. Checks drawn and still outstanding in September amount to $1,733.48 (assume this figure is correct).
d. A check was written for $472, but was recorded as $652. It is among the outstanding checks at the end of September.
e. The September service charge of $6.80 has not been recorded by the company.
f. Receipts of $236.30 were deposited by mail on September 30.
g. The bank statement showed the collection of a note by the bank in the amount of $406.
h. Included in the checks accompanying the September bank statement was a check drawn by Moy Company but charged to May Company for $114.32.

32. Use the following data concerning King Company to prepare a bank reconciliation statement.

Balance per bank	$10,500
Balance per books	9,250
Deposit in transit	1,015
Refund of cash to King Co. for damaged material (not yet deposited)	35
Outstanding checks	175
Bank service charge	3
N.S.F. check received by bank from the Goodman Company (a customer)	62
Interest collected by the bank for King Company on a note receivable	1,111
$400 deposit from King Company recorded as $410 by King's bookkeeper.	

Hint: Watch for cash overage or shortage.

33. On December 31, 19x1, the accounting records of the Cavilier Sales Company showed a cash balance of $6,600. A review of its bank reconciliation as of that date disclosed that a deposit of $7,200 was in transit and that checks of $6,350 were outstanding. Cavilier's books showed cash receipts of $108,700 and cash disbursements of $115,250 during the year. The company's bank paid checks totaling $121,000 during 19x1. A deposit of $9,000 was in transit at the beginning of the year.

Required:

Reconstruct the December 31, 19x0 bank reconcilation of the Cavilier Sales Company.

34. The Patrick Company had poor internal control over its cash transactions. Information about its cash position at November 30, 19x1 was as follows:

The cash books showed a balance of $18,901.62, which included undeposited receipts. A credit of $100 on the bank's records did not appear on the books of the company. The balance per bank statement was $15,550. Outstanding checks were: No. 62 for $116.25, No. 183 for $150, No. 284 for $253.25, No. 8621 for $190.71, No. 8623 for $206.80, and No. 8632 for $145.28.

The cashier embezzled all undeposited receipts in excess of $3,794.41 and prepared the following reconciliation:

Balance, per books, November 30, 19x1..		$18,901.62
Add: Outstanding checks:		
8621........................	$190.71	
8623........................	206.80	
8632........................	145.28	442.79
		$19,344.41
Less: Undeposited receipts............		3,794.41
Balance per bank, November 30, 19x1...		$15,550.00
Deduct: Unrecorded credit...........		100.00
True cash, November 30, 19x1..........		$15,450.00

(AICPA adapted)

Required:

1. Prepare a supporting schedule showing how much the cashier embezzled.
2. How did he attempt to conceal his theft?
3. Taking only the information given, name two specific features of internal control which were apparently missing.

Learning Objectives

Chapter 8 discusses the accounting procedures used for recording receivables and payables. Studying this chapter should enable you to:

1. Explain the basic procedures used for controlling receivables.

2. Illustrate the use of control and subsidiary accounts for recording receivables.

3. Discuss the purposes and mechanics of estimating bad debt expense.

4. Make the entries necessary to record the issuance and payment of a note and the related interest on the books of both the borrower and the lender.

5. Describe the process of discounting a note and the effect it has on a firm's accounts.

6. Calculate and prepare the entry to record the payroll taxes levied on an employer.

8

Receivables and Payables

INTRODUCTION

The extension of credit is a significant factor in the operation of many businesses. Most businesses are both grantors of credit (creating receivables) and receivers of credit (creating payables). Receivables are assets representing the claims that a business has against others. While receivables may be generated by various types of transactions, the most common sources of receivables are the sale of merchandise or services on a credit basis. Normally these assets will be realized or converted into cash by the business. Payables are obligations of a firm which arise from past transactions and which are to be discharged at a future date by payment of cash, transfer of other assets, or performance of a service.

Typically claims against a firm originate from transactions such as purchases of merchandise or services on credit, purchases of equipment on credit, and loans from banks. In an economic system such as ours, which is based so extensively on credit, almost all business concerns incur liabilities. The purpose of this chapter is to describe and discuss the procedures which are necessary to establish effective control over receivables and payables, and to illustrate the accounting practices and procedures which are employed with regard to these assets and liabilities.

CLASSIFICATION OF RECEIVABLES AND PAYABLES

Receivables are classified according to the timing of their expected realization (i.e.—as current assets if realization is anticipated within a year, or as noncurrent assets if collection is expected subsequent to the current period). Receivables are also classified according to their form. Notes receivable are claims against others which are supported by "formal" or written promises to pay. These may or may not be negotiable instruments, depending on such factors as the terms, form, and content of the note. An example of a note receivable would be the written promise by a borrower to repay a loan with interest, at a stated date. Accounts receivable, on the other hand, are not supported by "formal" or written promises to pay. An example of an account receivable would be the claim of a business against a customer who makes a purchase on account.

Creditors of a business have claims against the assets of the firm. Depending upon the nature of the particular liability, a claim may either be against specific assets or against assets in general. In any case, claims of creditors have priority over the claims of owners. Thus, in the event of the liquidation of a business, all debts must be satisfied before any payments are made to owners.

Amounts shown in the balance sheet as liabilities may be classified as either current or noncurrent liabilities. A proper distinction between current and noncurrent liabilities is essential because comparison of current assets with current liabilities is an important means of evaluating the short-run liquidity or debt-paying ability of the firm.

Current liabilities are those debts or obligations of a firm that must either be paid in cash or settled by providing goods or services within the operating cycle of the firm or one year, whichever is longer. The operating cycle of a business is the average period of time that elapses between purchase of an inventory item and conversion of the inventory into cash. This cycle includes the initial purchase of the inventory, the sale of the item on credit, and the collection of the receivable. The most common current liabilities include accounts payable, notes payable, and accrued liabilities.

CONTROL OVER RECEIVABLES

At the time an over-the-counter sale is made, it should be recorded by means of a cash register whether it is a cash sale or a charge sale. The controls described in Chapter 7 apply to both charge or credit sales as well as to cash sales. If a sale is made on account, a prenumbered sales ticket should be prepared and signed by the customer making the purchase. As a minimum, this charge ticket should include the following information:

1. The date.
2. The customer's name and account number.
3. A description of the item(s) purchased by the customer.
4. The total amount of the sale.
5. The customer's signature.

Effective control procedures require that the sales slip be prepared in triplicate: one copy would be given to the customer; a second copy would be placed in the cash register; and a third copy would be retained by the salesperson. An invoice dispenser which automatically retains a copy in a locked container is an ideal control device for this purpose.

At the end of each day, or more often if necessary, the charge slips accumulated in the register would be used in the reconciliation of the cash register receipts as previously described in Chapter 7.

The charge slips will serve as the basis for recording credit purchases in customers' accounts. A "control" account, trade accounts receivable for example, would be used to record the total charge sales and the total payments which are received from customers. Individual ledger accounts, referred to as "subsidiary" accounts, would be maintained for each customer. The amount of each charge sale would be recorded individually in the particular customer's account, and the total sales would be recorded in the control account. Bills would be prepared from the individual customers' ledger accounts and mailed out periodically, usually on a monthly basis.

As payments are received from customers, the remittances would be recorded individually in the customer's account and in total in the "control" account. Cash receipts, received either by mail or "over-the-counter," would be controlled according to the procedures outlined in Chapter 7. At any point in time, the balance in the "control" account should be equal[1] to the total of the balances in the individual customers' accounts. Therefore, a periodic reconciliation should be made of the control and the subsidiary accounts.

ACCOUNTS RECEIVABLE

As credit sales are made, entries are recorded in both the "control" and the "subsidiary" accounts. For purposes of illustration, assume that a department store makes the following sales during the month of June:

To Larry Killough.	$ 100
To Gene Seago	150
To Pat Kemp.	200
To all other charge customers	10,000
	$10,450

These sales would be recorded in the "control" account, trade accounts receivable, by the following entry:

Accounts Receivable	10,450	
Sales		10,450

At the same time, these sales would also be recorded in the individual customers' accounts, so that at all times the balance in the "control" account (accounts receivable) would be equal to the total of all the balances in the "subsidiary" accounts (individual customers' accounts). Using T-accounts, this process is illustrated as follows:

---

[1] If a special journal is used, they may be equal only at the end of the period.

Control Accounts		Subsidiary Accounts	
Accounts Receivable	=	**Killough**	**Seago**
100		100	150
150			
200			
10,000		**Kemp**	**All Others**
Bal. 10,450		200	10,000

Sales
100
150
200
10,000
10,450 Bal.

Now assume that the collections received from customers are as follows:

From Killough.	$ 100
From Seago	100
From other customers	8,000
	$8,200

These collections would also be recorded in the control account by the following entry:

Cash	8,200	
Accounts Receivable		8,200

At the same time, the collections would also be recorded in the subsidiary accounts, thereby maintaining a balance with the control account. This procedure is illustrated as follows:

Control Account		Subsidiary Accounts			
Accounts Receivable		**Killough**		**Seago**	
Bal. 10,450	8,200	100	100	150	100
2,250		0		50	

	Kemp		**All Others**	
	200		10,000	8,000
			2,000	

BAD DEBT EXPENSE

One of the costs of making sales on a credit basis is the expense that results from the fact that some of the customers who make purchases on account may never pay the amounts which are owed to the firm. This is to be expected and should be considered a normal cost of doing business. Obviously, if a firm were able to identify the particular customers who would ultimately fail to pay their accounts, it would not sell to them on a credit basis. Unfortunately, although credit investigations of varying degrees of effectiveness are made by firms, some bad debts will still result. In fact, if a firm had no bad debts whatsoever, this might be an indication that its credit department was performing unsatisfactorily. If credit standards were set so high as to eliminate *all* those potential customers whose credit rating was judged to be marginal, the revenue lost from refusing credit to these customers would no doubt exceed the potential losses, thus decreasing the firm's net income. From a theoretical viewpoint, the firm should grant credit to its customers up to that point where the marginal revenue from the granting of credit sales is exactly equal to the marginal expense, including the cost of bad debts. Of course this goal is impossible to attain in actual practice, but a firm's credit policy should attempt to approximate this objective to the extent possible and/or practical.

Bad debt expense, then, is a normal business expense which should be expected by those firms selling goods or services on a credit basis. The proper determination of income for a period requires that the revenue earned during that period be matched with the expenses which were incurred in generating that revenue. For firms that make sales or render services on a credit basis, this requires that bad debt expense be matched against revenue in the period in which the revenue is earned. Most accountants agree that this is the period in which the sale was originally made, and not the period in which a particular account is determined to be uncollectible. For example, assume that a credit sale made during the month of June is determined to be uncollectible during July, due to the bankruptcy of the customer. This would represent an expense of the month of June (when the sale was made and the revenue recognized) *not* the month of July (when the account was found to be uncollectible).

Since the particular accounts which will ultimately prove to be uncollectible are unknown, bad debt expense must be estimated using the past experience of the firm modified as necessary according to any changes in the firm's credit policies, current business conditions, etc. Two general approaches are often used to estimate bad debts: (1) an income statement approach which involves the use of a percentage of credit sales with the percentage determined by the firm's past credit experience; and (2) a balance sheet approach which is determined by an analysis of the receivable account at the end of the period. Under either method, the calculation of bad debts is necessarily an estimate, the distinction between the two methods normally is not a critical matter in practice. The important point is that a company make a good faith estimate of its probable bad debt losses for the period. The two methods of meeting this objective are explained below.

Income Statement Approach

Even though a firm makes credit sales during a period, it will normally record the estimated bad debt expense which is related to these sales on a periodic basis. Using the income statement approach, the estimate of bad debts for the period is associated directly with the current period's credit sales. Assume, for purposes of illustration, that the credit experience of a small firm has been as follows:

Year	Credit Sales	Losses from Bad Debts
19x1	$120,000	$2,300
19x2	130,000	2,650
19x3	150,000	3,050
	$400,000	$8,000

For 19x4, it might be reasonable for the firm to estimate that its losses from uncollectible accounts would be similar to its experience in prior-years. A percentage which could be used in estimating bad debts would be $8,000 divided by $400,000 or 2 percent of credit sales. In practice, of course, this percentage would be adjusted for any expected changes in general economic conditions, credit policies, etc.

Returning to the example used earlier in the chapter, recall that credit sales for the period were $10,450. Using the income statement or percentage of sales method, the estimated bad debts from these sales would be calculated by multiplying $10,450 by 2 percent or $209. This estimated bad debt expense would be recorded in the accounts by the following journal entry:

```
Bad debt expense.......................   209
    Allowance for bad debts...............        209
```

Note that the credit portion of this entry is to an Allowance for Bad Debts account and not to Accounts Receivable. While the firm's best estimate of its bad debt expense, based on its past experience, indicates that approximately $209 of the receivables arising from sales made during the month of June will not be collectible, it is unable to identify the individual accounts that may not be paid at this time. Since the particular individual(s) whose account(s) may ultimately prove to be uncollectible cannot be identified at this time, a direct credit to accounts receivable is inappropriate since such a procedure would eliminate the equality of the control and the subsidiary accounts. The effect of the entry to record bad debt expense on the control and subsidiary accounts is as follows:

Control Accounts			*Subsidiary Accounts*			
Accounts Receivable		**Killough**		**Seago**		
10,450	8,200	100	100	150	100	
2,250		0		50		

Allowance for Bad Debts		**Kemp**		**All Others**	
	209	200		10,000	8,000
				2,000	

Bad Debt Expense	
209	

The allowance for bad debts account has a credit balance after this end-of-period entry. This credit balance is deducted from the asset account, accounts receivable, to produce the proper balance sheet value for this asset.

The income statement or percentage of sales method matches the revenue (sales) earned during the period with the expenses (bad debts) which were incurred in generating that revenue. Thus, when this method is used, the amount of the debit to bad debt expense and the credit to the allowance for bad debts is determined directly by the application of the percentage to credit sales and is not affected by the balance in the allowance account prior to the recording of bad debt expense. The income statement approach emphasizes the relationship between the credit sales and potential bad debts which arise from these sales, and does not consider any existing balance in the allowance account.

Balance Sheet Approach

An alternative approach to the estimation of bad debts is the analysis of the receivable balance at the end of a period in order to make a judgment as to which accounts are likely to prove to be uncollectible. This approach is often referred to as the balance sheet approach since it focuses on determining the proper balance in the allowance for bad debts account so that the net receivable balance is stated at its realizable value. An "aging" of the accounts is usually a part of this procedure. Aging involves the classifying or grouping of accounts according to the period of time that the accounts have been outstanding. The basic assumption is that, all other factors being equal, the collectibility of receivables decreases as the account remains outstanding. An example of the "aging" process is presented below:

		Number of Days Outstanding			
Account	Balance	0-30	31-60	61-90	91 and Older
Killough	$ 0	$ 0	$ 0	$ 0	$ 0
Seago	50	50	0	0	0
Kemp	200	200	0	0	0
All others	2,000	1,350	400	50	200
	$2,250	$1,600	$400	$50	$200

Based on the experience of the firm, different percentages may be applied to the different classifications of accounts to estimate the amount of uncollectible receivables. For example, the following calculation might be appropriate:

Number of Days Outstanding	Amount	Percentage*	Estimated to be Uncollectible
0-30	$1,600	1%	$ 16
31-60	400	10	40
61-90	50	50	25
91 and older	200	75	150
	$2,250		$231

* The percentage used would be determined by the credit experience of the firm, adjusted as considered necessary for such factors as changes in economic conditions, credit policies, etc.

The older accounts, as well as those which are known to be in financial difficulty, should also be reviewed on an individual basis as an additional test of the amount which is estimated to be uncollectible. Assume that, after this review, the firm decided that the calculation of the amount estimated to be uncollectible using the analysis of receivables by age was appropriate. The balance in the allowance for bad debts account should be increased to $231, the amount estimated to be uncollectible at the end of June. Since this approach is based on the question of how large of an allowance account is needed to reduce the net receivables balance to the amount which is expected to be collected, it is necessary to consider any balance in the allowance account before making the adjusting entry. The allowance account will have a debit or credit balance at the end of the period, prior to the adjustment if the receivables which were actually determined to be uncollectible during the period were not exactly equal to the balance in the allowance account at the beginning of the period. The procedure for writing-off an uncollectible receivable will be discussed in the next section. Assuming that the allowance for bad debts account had a debit balance of $20 prior to this determination, the following journal entry would be required:

Bad debt expense....................	251	
Allowance for bad debts...............		251

After this entry has been posted to the allowance account, the balance in the account would be $231.

Allowance for Bad Debts

20	251
	231

Note that when the balance sheet analysis of the receivable balance method is used, the total amount which is estimated to be uncollectible is determined. This amount is then compared to the existing balance in the allowance for bad debts account and the journal entry required to adjust the allowance for bad debts account to the appropriate amount is made.

The income statement or percentage of sales method focuses upon the determination of income by emphasizing the matching of revenue (sales) with the expenses (bad debts) which were incurred in generating this revenue. The balance sheet or analysis of the receivable balance method emphasizes the valuation of the receivable balance at the net realizable amount. Again, since the allowance for bad debts is necessarily an estimate, a firm may decide to use one or the other or may choose to employ both in combination. For example, the percentage of sales method might be used in preparing interim financial statements on a monthly or quarterly basis and the analysis or aging of the receivable balance method in preparing annual or year-end financial statements.

Balance Sheet Presentation

In the balance sheet, the allowance for bad debts would appear as an offset to, or deduction from, accounts receivable. For example, the receivables of the firm would be shown as follows:

ASSETS

Cash		$ 5,000
Accounts receivable...............	$2,250	
Less: Allowance for bad debts.........	231	2,019
Other assets		10,000
Total Assets..................		$17,019

Writing-off an Uncollectible Account

When a particular account balance is determined to be uncollectible, an entry is made in the accounts to recognize this fact. Returning to the example used earlier in the chapter, assume that the $50 balance owed by Seago proves to be uncollectible. The following entry would be required:

```
Allowance for Bad Debts .......................... 50
    Accounts Receivable............................     50
```

After this entry has been posted to the accounts, the control[2] account would appear as follows:

Accounts Receivable		Allowance for Bad Debts	
2,250	50	50	231
2,200			181

In the balance sheet, the receivables would appear as follows:

```
Accounts receivable .............. $2,200
Less: Allowance for bad debts........   181    $2,019
```

It is important to note that the entry for the write-off of the uncollectible receivable affects neither expense nor total assets. The net receivable balance (accounts receivable less the allowance for bad debts) remains the same since both accounts receivable and the allowance for bad debts are reduced by the same amount. The expense related to bad debts is recorded when the estimated bad debts are recorded (i.e., when the provision for bad debts is made). The entry to record bad debts expense is normally made during the year-end adjustment process.

Even though a company writes off an account as uncollectible, it will still attempt to collect the balance due. In some instances, it may continue its own efforts to collect the account; in others, it may turn the account over to a collection agency. In any event, if the collection efforts prove to be successful, the company will receive cash; two entries are required in order to record this receipt. The first entry reinstates the balance which has been written off by reversing the original entry made at the time of the write-off. The second entry records the collection of the account balance.

To illustrate the recovery of an account which had previously been written off, we will return to the example used above. Assume now that the $50 balance owed by Seago which was written off as uncollectible is subsequently collected. The collection would be recorded by the following entries:

---

[2] The effect on the subsidiary accounts would be to reduce the balance in Seago's account from $50 to zero, thus maintaining the equality between the control and the subsidiary accounts.

Accounts receivable................	50	
Allowance for bad debts............		50
Cash.............................	50	
Accounts receivable...............		50

Again, note that the first entry simply reverses the previous write-off. The second entry records the collection of the balance.

Direct Write-off Method

In circumstances where receivables are not material in amount, a company may choose not to record its estimated bad debt expense. In this approach, the company debits bad debt expense and credits accounts receivables in the period in which the individual receivable is determined to be uncollectible. The total accounts receivable will be listed in the balance sheet at its gross amount; no allowance account is used. This method does not state accounts receivable at their expected collectible amount; it makes no attempt to match the costs of bad debts with the related sales. Theoretically, the allowance method is superior, but the direct write-off approach is acceptable if receivables are not significant in amount.

ACCOUNTS PAYABLE

The major source of accounts payable are debts to trade creditors for goods or services purchased on a credit basis by the business. Other accounts payable may consist of various debts, such as advances from officers, employees, or stockholders, or refundable deposits which were made by customers. Accounts payable are normally classified in terms of their origin in the balance sheet. An account payable does not usually involve the payment of interest, and there is no formal written promise to pay signed by the debtor.

NOTES RECEIVABLE AND PAYABLE

As previously indicated, notes receivable are claims against others which, unlike accounts receivable, are supported by formal or written promises to pay. A typical note is shown below.

```
$ 1000.00                                    May 1         19x1
Two (2) months               after date
promise(s) to pay to the order of    Willie Davis
the sum of $  1000.00    with interest at   18   percent.
                                 Don Sutton
```

The note shown above is an interest-bearing note: Don Sutton (the maker of the note) agrees to pay Willie Davis (the payee) $1,000 (the principal amount of the note) plus interest at eighteen percent on July 1, 19x1 (the maturity date). The eighteen percent annual interest is the charge that Sutton pays for the use of Davis' funds. Interest, which is an expense for Sutton and income for Davis, is calculated by the following formula:

$$\text{Principal} \times \text{Rate} \times \text{Time} = \text{Interest}$$
$$\$1,000 \times .18 \times \tfrac{2}{12} = \$30$$

The maturity value of this note is $1,030 (the principal amount of $1,000 plus interest at $30); this is the amount that Sutton must pay Davis on July 1, 19x1, when the note becomes due and payable (matures).

Note that for ease of calculation, the eighteen percent interest rate was expressed as a decimal, .18. Alternatively, a fraction ($\tfrac{18}{100}$) could have been used in the computation. The interest rate stated in a note is usually expressed in terms of an annual or yearly rate. Since the note used in the illustration was for a duration of two months, time was expressed as a fraction of year, $\tfrac{2}{12}$. In some instances, time may be stated in days. If this is the case, a year is usually considered to have 360 days in order to simplify the computation of interest. For example, if the note in the illustration was for a period of 30 days, the calculation of interest would be as follows:

$$\$1,000 \times .18 \times \tfrac{30}{360} = \$15$$

To illustrate the accounting for notes receivable, the entries necessary to record the transactions regarding the Sutton-Davis note will be presented in the sections which follow.

Issuance of the Note

On May 1, 19x1, when Sutton borrowed the $1,000 from Davis, the following entry would be made on Davis' books to record the loan:

Notes receivable......................	1,000	
Cash		1,000

This entry indicates that Davis has exchanged one asset (cash of $1,000) for another asset of equal value (a note receivable of $1,000).[3]

The following entry would be made by Sutton:

Cash	1,000	
Notes payable.....................		1,000

---

[3] In some instances, a note may be taken in settlement of an open account receivable (dr. note receivable, cr. accounts receivable) or at the time of sale (dr. notes receivable, cr. sales). Except for the initial entry, these circumstances do not change the accounting or recording considerations illustrated and discussed.

This entry indicates that Sutton has incurred a liability (a note payable of $1,000) in order to obtain an asset (cash of $1,000).

Accrual of Interest

Interest is the cost of borrowing to the maker of the note or, from the payee's (lender's) viewpoint, the income which is earned. In the example, Davis' earnings during the month of May would be calculated as follows:

$$\$1,000 \times .18 \times 1/12 = \$15$$

If Davis wished to accrue the interest earned during the month of May, (i.e., record it on his books) the following entry would be necessary:

Interest receivable...................... 15
Interest earned........................ 15

This entry recognizes the fact that Davis' assets have increased by $15 because of the interest earned during the month of May. This entry would be necessary only if Davis prepares financial statements as of the end of May.

If Sutton wished to record the interest expense incurred during May, the following entry would be required:

Interest expense........................ 15
Interest payable...................... 15

This entry recognizes that Sutton has incurred an expense of $15 for the use of the money borrowed from Davis for the month of May. Again, an entry is necessary only if financial statements are prepared as of the end of May.

Payment of the Note

On July 1, 19x1, the maturity date of the note, it becomes due and payable. As previously indicated, the interest for the two-month period was:

$$\$1,000 \times .18 \times 2/12 = \$30$$

The maturity value, (i.e., the total amount that Sutton should pay to Davis), is $1,000 plus $30 or $1,030. Since we have assumed that Davis had previously recorded or accrued the $15 of interest earned during the month of May, the entry which would be required on Davis' books in order to record the receipt of the $1,030 from Sutton at the maturity date of the note would be as follows:

Cash................................. 1,030
    Notes receivable...................... 1,000
    Interest receivable.................... 15
    Interest earned....................... 15

Analyzing this entry, the debit to cash of $1,030 records the total proceeds of the note (i.e., its maturity value). This maturity value includes both the principal amount and the total interest earned by Davis during the two-month period that he held the note. The credit to notes receivable removes the note balance from Davis' books since it has been paid at maturity. The credit of $15 to interest receivable eliminates the receivable which had been set up at the end of May when Davis accrued the interest earned for that month. The $15 credit to interest earned is made in order to record the interest income on the note for the month of June.

The entry that would be required on Sutton's books to record the payment by Sutton to Davis would be:

```
Notes payable.......................... 1,000
Interest payable.......................    15
Interest expense.......................    15
    Cash ..............................         1,030
```

The debit to notes payable of $1,000 removes the note balance from Sutton's books since it has been paid at maturity. The debit to interest payable of $15 eliminates the payable which had been recorded at the end of May when Sutton accrued the interest expense for the month. The $15 debit to interest expense is made to record the interest expense for June. The credit to cash of $1,030 records the payment of the maturity value of the note (i.e., principal and interest) by Sutton.

Dishonored Note

If Sutton had not paid the note at maturity, the note would be said to be dishonored. Of course, Davis would continue his efforts to collect the amount due him and Sutton would still be liable for his obligation. In the event that the note was not paid at maturity, Davis would make an entry to remove the note from the notes receivable account as follows:

```
Receivable from dishonored note.......... 1,030
    Notes receivable......................         1,000
    Interest receivable...................            15
    Interest earned.......................            15
```

This entry would remove the note from the notes receivable account and place it in a separate receivable classification—receivable from dishonored notes. If Sutton subsequently pays the note, Davis would record the receipt by debiting cash and crediting "receivable from dishonored note." If Davis is unable to collect the $1,030 from Sutton, he would eventually write off the receivable as an uncollectible account against the allowance for bad debts account.

Notes Issued at a Discount

In some circumstances, the interest on notes is deducted in advance (i.e., at the time the note is issued). The difference between the amount due at maturity and the amount loaned is classified as unearned interest at the date of issuance on the books of the lender. As the note matures, this unearned interest is earned and is reclassified as interest income. For example, assume that on November 1, 19x1, Wynn Company borrows $1,000 from Osteen Company on a three-month note with an eighteen percent rate of interest. The entry made on November 1, 19x1, by Osteen Company to record the loan of $955 [$1,000 − ($1,000 × .18 × 3/12)] would be as follows:

Notes receivable	1,000	
Unearned interest		45
Cash		955

Wynn Company would record the transaction with the following entry:

Cash	955	
Discount on notes payable	45	
Notes payable		1,000

Since interest accrues over time, the $45 which is shown as a discount on notes payable at the date the note is issued is not interest expense at that point in time. The actual net liability to Osteen at the date of the loan is equal to the amount of cash received, or $955. Therefore, a balance sheet prepared at the time of the loan would include discount on notes payable as a contra-liability deducted from notes payable as follows:

Notes payable	$1,000
Less: Discount on notes payable	(45)
	$ 955

At December 31, the following adjusting entry is necessary in order for Osteen to record the interest earned of $30 ($1,000 × .18 × 2/12) for the months of November and December:

Unearned interest	30	
Interest income		30

Wynn Company would record its interest expense for the two-month period with the following adjusting entry:

Interest expense	30	
Discount on notes payable		30

At December 31, Wynn Company's liability would appear in its balance sheet as follows:

```
Notes payable.......................... $1,000
Less:  Discount on notes payable..........   (15)
                                           $  985
```

Note that the original amount of $45 in the discount on notes payable has been reduced by $30 (interest expense for the months of November and December) to $15 (which represents the amount to be charged to interest expense in January).

When the note matures and is paid, the entry to record the receipt is as follows:

```
Cash................................  1,000
Unearned interest.....................     15
    Notes receivable.....................         1,000
    Interest income......................             15
```

The total interest income earned on the note and recorded in the accounts is $45 ($30 in 19x1 and $15 in 19x2). Although a rate of 18 percent was used in determining the original discount on the note, the effective interest rate is actually 18.8 percent since the borrower paid $45 for the use of $955 (not $1,000) for a period of three months.

Wynn Company would make the following entry to record its payment:

```
Notes payable.......................  1,000
Interest expense.......................     15
    Cash................................          1,000
    Discount on notes payable.............             15
```

This entry records the payment of the note at maturity by Wynn and the interest expense for the month of January.

Discounting Notes Receivable

Notes receivable are sometimes sold by the payee to a third party in order to obtain funds prior to the maturity date of a note. The process of selling a note in this manner is referred to as discounting a note. The payee endorses the note, delivers it to the purchaser (usually a bank) and receives his funds. The payee discounting the note is usually contingently liable on the note, i.e., he must pay the note at the maturity if the maker fails to do so.

The calculation of the discount charged by the purchaser is somewhat similar to the calculation of interest:

$$\text{Maturity Value} \times \text{Discount Period} \times \text{Discount Rate} = \text{Discount}$$

As previously indicated, the maturity value is the total amount, both principal and interest, due at the maturity of a note. The discount period is the period of time from the date a note is discounted to the maturity date of the note. The discount rate is the rate charged by the purchaser to discount a note. The amount received by the payee, referred to as the proceeds of the note, is calculated as follows:

$$\text{Maturity Value} - \text{Discount} = \text{Proceeds}$$

To illustrate the procedures which are involved in discounting a note, we will assume that *before* recording the interest earned for the month of May, Davis sold or discounted the Sutton note on May 31 and was charged a discount rate of twenty percent. The calculation of the amount of the discount and the net proceeds to Davis from the note would be as follows:

$$\$1{,}000 \times .18 \times \tfrac{2}{12} = \$30 \text{ (interest)}$$
$$\$1{,}000 + \$30 = \$1{,}030 \text{ (maturity value)}$$
$$\$1{,}030 \times .20 \times \tfrac{1}{12} = \$17.17 \text{ (discount)}$$
$$\$1{,}030 - \$17.17 = \$1{,}012.83 \text{ (proceeds)}$$

The discounting of the note will be recorded in the accounts by Davis as follows:

Cash	1,012.83	
Interest expense	2.17	
Interest revenue		15.00
Notes receivable discounted		1,000.00

The debit of $1,012.83 to cash records the proceeds received from the sale of the note. The charge to interest expense of $2.17 was calculated as follows:

Principal		$1,000.00
Interest earned during May		15.00
Book value of the note at the date of sale		$1,015.00
Principal	$1,000.00	
Total interest for the note to maturity	30.00	
Maturity value of the note	$1,030.00	
Discount	17.17	
Net proceeds		1,012.83
Interest expense		$ 2.17

As the above calculation indicates, interest expense represents the difference between the cash proceeds and the total of the: (1) face or principal amount of the note; and (2) interest earned up to the date the note was discounted.[4] The credit to interest receivable removes the interest which had been previously accrued at the end of May from the accounts. It should be noted that the credit in the entry is to notes receivable *discounted,* rather than to notes receivable. The credit to notes receivable discounted indicates that Davis is contingently liable for the note—i.e., in the event that Sutton fails to pay the note at maturity, Davis must pay it. On Davis' balance sheet the notes receivable would appear as follows:

Cash		$10,000
Notes receivable	$1,000	
Less: Notes receivable discounted	1,000	0
Other assets		50,000
Total Assets		$60,000

Offsetting the notes receivable discounted account against the notes receivable account discloses the contingent liability of Davis with regard to the Sutton note. An alternative to this presentation would be to disclose the contingent liability by means of a footnote to the balance sheet. Such a footnote might be worded as follows: "Davis is contingently liable for notes receivable discounted in the amount of $1,000."

If Sutton pays the note at its maturity, Davis would be notified of this payment and the following entry would be made on Davis' books:

Notes receivable discounted	1,000	
Notes receivable		1,000

By removing both the notes receivable discounted and the notes receivable balances from the accounts, the effect of this entry is to recognize the fact that the contingent liability for the note no longer exists.

If Sutton fails to pay the note at maturity, Davis' *contingent* liability becomes a *real* liability that he must now pay. He would recognize this fact by the same entry as that which was made above:

Notes receivable discounted	1,000	
Notes receivable		1,000

---

[4] Had the discount rate been ten percent, the entry would have been as follows:

Cash	1,021.42	
Notes receivable discounted		1,000.00
Interest revenue		21.42

In this instance the credit of $21.42 to interest income represents the excess of the proceeds over the principal amount of the note including the interest of $15.00 earned in May.

It should be noted that both the contingent liability and the notes receivable balance are removed from the books at the maturity date of the note whether or not it is paid by the maker. If it is paid, that is all that is required—no further action on the part of Davis is necessary. If it is not paid, Davis must pay the full amount due (principal plus interest, or full maturity value) to the holder of the note. This payment would be recorded as follows:

>   Receivable from dishonored note.......... 1,030
>   Cash   1,030

Davis would then attempt to recover the $1,030 from Sutton.

STATEMENT PRESENTATION OF RECEIVABLES

Receivables are classified first according to their form: notes receivable and accounts receivable. Generally, those which are expected to be converted into cash within a year are classified as current assets while those which will be realized in subsequent periods are included in a noncurrent category. Any interest receivable from interest-bearing notes will also be classified according to the timing of its expected collection. The income from interest appears on the income statement, usually as an addition to net income from operations, as follows:

Davis Company
Income Statement
For the Year Ended December 31, 19x1

Sales	$100,000
Cost of sales	60,000
Gross profit on sales	$ 40,000
Expenses.	25,000
Income from operations	$ 15,000
Other income:	
Interest income	100
Net income	$ 15,100

If there are receivables from sources other than normal operations, such as from officers, employees, affiliated companies, etc., these would be shown as separate items rather than included as a part of regular accounts or notes receivable in the balance sheet.

PAYROLL ACCOUNTING

An employer incurs certain liabilities to the Federal and state governments for taxes related to its payroll—both for the taxes levied on the business itself and for taxes withheld from the earnings of its employees.

The employer may also deduct from employees' salaries and wages amounts withheld for such items as union dues, insurance premiums, pension plans, and investment plans.

An employer incurs a number of liabilities relating to state and Federal payroll taxes. These include the following taxes:

1. Federal old-age, survivors, disability, and hospital insurance (Social Security)
2. Federal unemployment insurance
3. State unemployment insurance
4. Income taxes withheld

Social Security Taxes. The Federal Insurance Contributions Act (FICA) imposes equal taxes on both employers and employees. This Act provides for old age, disability, hospitalization, and survivors' benefits for qualified employees and members of their families. The tax rate is applied to the employee's gross wages up to a designated maximum. Both the rate and the maximum earnings to which the tax is applied have been increased frequently over the years. The rate for 1983 was 6.70 percent of the initial $35,700 of salaries and wages paid to each employee. The employee's share of this tax is withheld from the wage payment, and employers periodically remit the amounts withheld together with the amounts matched by the employer.

Federal Unemployment Tax. The Federal Unemployment Tax Act (FUTA) provides for a system of unemployment insurance with joint participation of the Federal and state governments. Employers are also required to pay state and Federal unemployment taxes for their employees. No tax is levied on the employee. Under current provisions, the Federal rate is currently 3.4 percent of the initial $6,000 in salaries and wages paid to each employee during the year. However, the employer is allowed a credit against the Federal unemployment tax for state unemployment tax payments.

State Unemployment Tax. The provisions of the unemployment programs of the various states differ in certain respects. All states levy a payroll tax on employers and a few states levy a tax on employees as well. The basic rate in most states is 2.7% of the first $6,000 in salaries and wages paid to each employee.

Income Tax Withholding. Employers of one or more persons are required to withhold income taxes from their employees and remit these withholdings to the Federal government. A number of states and cities also levy income taxes which are required to be withheld by the employer from the earnings of the employees. The amounts to be withheld by the employer may be computed by formulas provided by the law or from tax withholding tables made available by the government. The Federal income tax withheld and the FICA taxes (both employer's and employee's shares) are remitted to the Federal government at regular intervals.

Recording the Payroll. To illustrate the accounting for wages and salaries and the related taxes, assume that the gross salaries of a small business total $10,000 for the month of January. Assume that the FICA rate is 6.70 percent for the employer and employee, and that the State unemployment tax is 2.7 percent of gross salaries. The Federal unemployment tax (net of the credit for state unemployment taxes) is .7 percent, and Federal income taxes withheld for the month total $710. The employer's taxes would be computed as follows:

FICA (.067 × $10,000)	$ 670
State unemployment (.027 × $10,000)	270
FUTA (.007 × $10,000)	70
Total employer's taxes	$ 1,010

The cash paid to employees would be:

Salaries earned		$10,000
Withholding		
FICA	$670	
Income taxes	710	1,380
Net amount paid to employees		$ 8,620

The journal entries to record the payroll and the employer's payroll taxes follow:

Payroll tax expense	1,010	
FICA taxes payable		670
State unemployment taxes payable		270
Federal unemployment taxes payable		70
Salaries expense	10,000	
FICA taxes payable		670
Income taxes payable		710
Cash		8,620

The liabilities recorded in the above entries are eliminated when the employer remits the taxes to the appropriate governmental units.

SUMMARY

Receivables are assets representing the claims that a business has against others. The two principal forms of receivables are accounts receivable and notes receivable. Accounts receivable generally arise from a company's normal course of trade or business and are normally not supported by formal written promises to pay. Notes receivable, on the other hand, are claims that are supported by formal written promises to pay.

Liabilities are claims against the business by its creditors. As such, they represent obligations which must be discharged at some future date.

Current liabilities are those obligations which must be discharged within the operating cycle of the firm or one year, whichever is longer. The two major types of current liabilities are accounts payable that arise from transactions with trade creditors and short-term notes payable. A note payable is supported by a written promise to pay and requires the accrual and payment of interest.

Accounting for receivables requires the use of both a control account and individual subsidiary accounts. At the end of a period, the total of the subsidiary balances should equal the balance in the control account. In addition, bad debt expense must be estimated for each period to match this cost of selling on a credit basis with the appropriate revenues. Two common methods of estimating the bad debt expense (often used in combination) are (1) the use of a percentage based on the firm's past credit sales and (2) the analysis of the receivables balance at the end of the period. An allowance for bad debts account is used to record and report the resulting offset to accounts receivable.

Accounting procedures for notes receivable include recording the initial issuance of the note at either face or discounted value, accruing the interest income earned on the note, and recording the collection of the principal and interest. In addition, firms may wish to sell notes receivable to a third party to obtain funds prior to the maturity dates of the notes. This process is referred to as discounting the notes. Generally the firm discounting the note is contingently liable if the maker fails to pay it at maturity.

Receivables are classified on the balance sheet as accounts receivable or notes receivable and according to their status as current or noncurrent assets. Current receivables are those that are expected to be converted into cash within a year.

Comprehensive Illustration

Listed below are certain transactions of A Company during 19x1:

January 10	Sold merchandise on account to B Company for $10,000. The terms of the sale required payment within 10 days.
January 15	Sold merchandise on account to C Company for $5,000. The terms of the sale required payment within 10 days.
January 25	Accepted a $10,000, 10%, 3-month note from B Company in settlement of the past due account.
February 25	Discounted the B Company note at City National Bank at 12%.
March 1	The account receivable from C Company was written off as uncollectible.
April 25	The Bank notified A Company that B Company's note was dishonored. A Company paid the bank the maturity value of the note plus a protest fee of $25.
May 1	Received $5,000 payment from C Company on account previously written off.
May 5	Collected maturity value of dishonored note plus the protest fee from B Company.
December 31	Determined that the allowance for bad debts account should have a $12,000 balance. The account had a $700 debit balance prior to adjustment.

Required:

Prepare all the journal entries to record the above transactions on the books of A Company.

Solution to Comprehensive Illustration

Jan.	10	Accounts receivable................	10,000	
		Sales...........................		10,000
	15	Accounts receivable................	5,000	
		Sales...........................		5,000
	25	Note receivable....................	10,000	
		Accounts receivable...............		10,000
Feb.	25	Cash...........................	10,045	
		Notes receivable discounted.........		10,000
		Interest income..................		45
Mar.	1	Allowance for bad debts..............	5,000	
		Accounts receivable...............		5,000
Apr.	25	Notes receivable discounted...........	10,000	
		Notes receivable..................		10,000
		Receivable from dishonored note.......	10,275	
		Cash...........................		10,275
May	1	Accounts receivable................	5,000	
		Allowance for bad debts.............		5,000
		Cash...........................	5,000	
		Accounts receivable...............		5,000
	5	Cash...........................	10,275	
		Receivable from Dishonored note.....		10,275
Dec.	31	Bad debt expense....................	12,700	
		Allowance for bad debts............		12,700

KEY DEFINITIONS

Accounts receivable Accounts receivable are receivables not supported by formal or written promises to pay.

Accrued interest expense Accrued interest expense is interest that has been incurred on a note payable but not paid.

Aging of accounts receivable Aging of accounts receivable is the process of classifying accounts according to the period of time that the accounts have been outstanding.

Allowance for bad debts Allowance for bad debts is a contra account to accounts receivable that reflects the portion of the total dollar amount of accounts receivable that is expected to be uncollectible.

Bad debt expense Bad debt expense is the expense that occurs from customers' failure to pay debts to the firm.

Contingent liability A contingent liability is an amount which may become a liability at some future date, depending on the occurrence of some future event. For example, the payee who discounts a note is contingently liable if the maker of the note fails to pay it at maturity.

Contra account A contra account is an account which is offset against or deducted from another account in the financial statements.

"Control" account A "control" account is used to record the total charge sales and the total payments which are received from customers.

Current liability Current debts of a firm which must be paid within the operating cycle of the firm or one year, whichever is longer.

Discount (D) Discount is the charge made by the purchaser of a note prior to its maturity. (MV × DR × DP = D)

Discount period (DP) The discount period is the period from the date a note is discounted until its maturity.

Discount rate (DR) The discount rate is the rate charged to discount a note. This percentage is expressed in an annual rate and is used to calculate a discount.

Discounting Discounting is the sale of a note by the payee prior to its maturity date.

Discounted note On discounted notes payable, the interest is deducted from the maturity value of the note at the time the note is issued.

Dishonored notes receivable Dishonored notes receivable are notes which are not paid at their maturity.

Effective interest rate The effective interest rate is the actual rate of interest that the issuing corporation pays on the bond as evidenced by the relationship between the periodic interest payment and the issue price of the bonds.

Interest expense (I) Interest expense is the cost to the borrower of borrowing funds. (P × R × T = I)

Interest income Interest income is the income to the lender from the lending of funds. (P × R × T = I)

Interest receivable Interest receivable is interest earned but not yet received.

Liability A liability is an obligation which arises from a past transaction and which is to be discharged at a future date by the transfer of assets or the performance of services.

Maker A maker is the borrower of funds on a note receivable.

Maturity date The maturity date is the date a note becomes due and payable.

Maturity value (MV) Maturity value is the value of a note at its maturity, i.e., principal plus interest.

Note payable A note payable represents a written promise to pay a definite amount of money on demand or at some specified future date to the holder of the note.

Note receivable A note receivable is a receivable supported by a formal or written promise to pay.

Payee The payee is the lender of funds on a note receivable.

Principal (P) The principal is the face amount of a note receivable.

Proceeds Proceeds are the net amount received by a payee selling or discounting a note prior to its maturity. Maturity value less discount equals proceeds.

Rate (R) Rate is the percentage usually expressed as an annual rate used to calculate interest.

Receivable A receivable is an asset representing the claim that a firm has against others.

Receivable from dishonored note This receivable is equal to the maturity value of a note arising from the failure of the maker to pay it at maturity.

Time (T) Time is the period usually expressed in years or a fraction thereof used to calculate interest. It is normal to assume a 360-day year when calculating simple interest.

QUESTIONS

1. Compare and contrast accounts receivable and notes receivable.

2. Distinguish between current and long-term liabilities.

3. Why is control over receivables important? How can control be achieved?

4. Explain how the control account, accounts receivable, is related to the individual subsidiary ledger accounts. What could make the two be out of balance?

5. Theoretically, when should a firm cease to grant credit to its customers?

6. Another method for handling bad debt expense—called the direct write-off method—is to wait until the account is known to be uncollectible. The journal entry then is a debit to bad debt expense and a credit to accounts receivable. Compare and contrast this with the allowance method. Which method is theoretically correct? Why?

7. What accounting principle does the allowance method rest upon?

8. What are the two methods for estimating bad debts?

9. Could an allowance method be used with notes receivable? Would it be feasible?

10. What is the entry to increase Allowance for Bad Debts? To decrease it?

11. Suppose an account is written off as uncollectible, but later the customer remits payment. What would the entry be?

12. Calculate the interest on a $10,000, 6-month note, with interest at 6 percent.

13. What adjusting entries may be required with regard to notes receivable at the end of the period?

14. Smith Co. borrowed $5,000 from the bank and signed a 60-day, 6 percent note dated June 1. (1) What is the face amount of the note? (2) What is the amount of interest on the note? (3) What is the maturity value of the note?

15. What is the nature of the notes receivable discounted account?

16. Why is an entry on the books of the payee necessary whether or not a discounted note is paid by the maker at maturity?

17. Explain how the proceeds from the discounting of a note receivable are calculated.

EXERCISES

18. By reviewing their past credit experience, Brown Company estimated that its losses from uncollectible accounts would be three percent of credit sales for 19x1. Sales for 19x1 amounted to $360,000, of which $100,000 were in cash. Make the entry recording bad debt expense for the year in the books of the Brown Company.

19. Based on an aging of receivables, Blue Company estimated doubtful accounts to be a total of $5,000. Give the adjusting entry for bad debts under each of the following independent situations:

    a. The Allowance for Bad Debts has a zero balance.
    b. The Allowance for Bad Debts has a debit balance of $400.
    c. The Allowance for Bad Debts has a credit balance of $700.

20. Bobby Mitchell's 6%, 60-day note for $600 (principal amount) was discounted by the Washington Deadskunks to the Second National Bank after it was held for 30 days. The Deadskunks received $603.96 as proceeds from the sale.

Required:

1. Calculate the discount rate on the sale.
2. Prepare the journal entry to record the sale of the note on the books of the Washington Deadskunks.
3. Prepare the entry necessary if Mitchell fails to pay the note at maturity.

21. On February 1, 19x1, Alex Grammas borrowed $700 from Vic Wertz and signed a note in evidence of the loan. Grammas agreed to pay Wertz $700 plus 10 percent interest on August 31, 19x1. Wertz's accounting period ends June 30. Make all entries related to the note on the books of Wertz (assume Grammas does not default on payment).

22. Dallas Company discounted three separate notes receivable at a bank on August 1, 19x1. Each note is in the amount of $1,000. The bank charged a discount rate of 10 percent. Compute the proceeds of each note from the following data.

	Date Note Received	Interest Rate	Life of Note
1.	July 1	8%	3 months
2.	June 1	6%	6 months
3.	July 15	9%	1 month

23. Give the journal entries to record the following transactions:

Mar. 15   Accepted a $2,000, 3-month, 10% note from Bob Hanson in settlement of a past due account.
Apr. 15   Discounted the Hanson note at the bank at a discount rate of 12%.
June 15   Received notice from the bank that the Hanson note was in default. Paid the bank the maturity value of the note.
July 15   Received a check from Hanson for the maturity value of the note plus 10% interest on the maturity value of the note for the 30-day period subsequent to maturity.

24. Determine the maturity value of the following notes receivable held by Staubach Company.

    a. $1,000 principal, 4 percent interest, matures in 6 months.
    b. $ 800 principal, 7 percent interest, matures in 60 days.
    c. $ 600 principal, 3 percent interest, matures in 100 days.
    d. $ 500 principal, 5 percent interest, matures in 1 month.
    e. $ 900 principal, 6 percent interest, matures in 3 months.
    f. $ 200 principal, 7 percent interest, matures in 30 days.
    g. $ 400 principal, 4 percent interest, matures in 10 days.

25. The Dorsett Company borrowed $500 from the Pearson Company and issued a note at an 8 percent rate of interest. The interest was deducted in advance and the note was issued on October 1, 19x1 and matures February 1, 19x2. Make the necessary journal entries on Pearson Company's books for the date of issuance, December 31, 19x1, and the maturity date.

26. Prepare the necessary journal entries in Henderson's books for the following events.

    a. On March 1, Sam Donaldson agreed to pay David Henderson $2,000 plus 7 percent interest on August 1.
    b. Henderson accrued interest earned on June 30 for the months of March, April, May, and June.
    c. Donaldson did not pay the note at maturity.

27. Prepare the necessary journal entries in Martin's books for the following events.

    a. Mike Mason purchased merchandise on credit from Martin's Retail Outlet for $150.
    b. Mason's account proves to be uncollectible. (Assume an allowance for bad debts account already exists.)
    c. Mason's account was subsequently collected.

28. Determine the interest on each of the following notes:

	Face Amount	Interest Rate	Days to Maturity
a.	$1,000	6%	60
b.	$5,000	8%	90
c.	$4,000	4%	180
d.	$2,500	5%	36

29. On December 1, King, Inc. issued a 90-day, 6 percent note for $3,000 to Miller Co. to replace an account payable. Give the journal entries necessary to record the following on the books of King, Inc.

a. Issuance of the note by King, Inc.
b. Adjusting entry on December 31.
c. Payment of the note at maturity.

30. Assume that Richardson Company borrows $1,500 on a 6-month note bearing a 9 percent rate of discount. Three months later, the company closes its books. In the next accounting period, the note matures and is paid by Richardson Company. Prepare the necessary journal entries for Richardson Company related to this note.

31. Thompson Co. issues a 180-day, non-interest-bearing note for $10,000 to First National Bank on May 1. The bank discounts the note at 8 percent. Give the necessary journal entries for Thompson Co. to record the issuance of the note and the payment of the note at maturity.

32. On May 1, 19x1, the Bucks Company borrowed $600 on a 120-day note payable bearing an interest rate of 7 percent. This note was used to purchase equipment costing $1,000; the balance of which was paid in cash. On June 15, the company borrowed $800 on a non-interest-bearing 90-day note with a discount rate of 7 percent. The proceeds from the note were used entirely to pay for office supplies. The Bucks Company closes its year on June 30.

Required:

Give journal entries to record the issuance of the loans, adjusting entries on June 30, 19x1, and entries to record their payments when due.

PROBLEMS

33. When aging their accounts receivable, the Wingfoot Company drew up the following schedule:

Accounts Receivable Balance	Number of Days Outstanding			
	0-30	31-60	61-90	91 and older
$5,250	$3,450	$900	$650	$250
	Estimated % Uncollectible			
	1%	5%	15%	50%

Required:

Prepare a table calculating the estimated bad debt expense for the period and make the appropriate journal entry on the books of the Wingfoot Company, assuming that there is a credit balance of $100 in the Allowance for Bad Debts before adjustment.

34. During 19x1, Squeeze, Inc. had $800,000 of sales on credit. Also, during 19x1 the company wrote off $14,000 of accounts receivable as definitely uncollectible and collected $700 from individuals whose accounts had been written off during previous years. The company estimates its bad debts each year to be 2% of credit sales. On January 1, 19x1, the accounts receivable balance was $60,000. Collections on account for 19x1 totaled $775,000 and customers returned goods for credit in the amount of $20,000. The company offers no cash discounts. On December 31, 19x1, after all adjustments and accruals, accounts receivable net of the allowance for uncollectible accounts amounted to $45,400.

Required:

1. Prepare journal entries for *all* transactions during 19x1 involving accounts receivable and the related allowance account.
2. The balance in the allowance account at:

    a. January 1, 19x1.
    b. December 31, 19x1 (after all adjustments).

35. Charlie Tuna, owner of Tuna's Fish Wholesalers, has instructed his accountant, Jack D. Ripper, to make sure the Allowance for Bad Debts account is at least 10 percent of total accounts receivable at the end of each calendar year. The January 1, 19x1, balance in Allowance for Bad Debts is $10,000.

    During 19x1, the following transactions took place:

    Jan. 13   Notice was received that I.M. Acrook, who owed the company $4,000, was in bankruptcy and no payment could be expected.
    May 13   Wheel & Deal, Inc. paid $14,000 applicable to its account which totaled $20,000. Its treasurer was last seen boarding a steamer for South America (with all the company's funds), so no other payments would be forthcoming.
    July 10   Received a check for $2,000 from A. Lincoln whose account had been written off as uncollectible in 19x0.
    Oct. 13   H.E. Asucker, a customer, notified Charlie that his partner had absconded with all the company funds. Asucker stated that their business had folded and he was unable to pay Charlie the $8,000 he owed him.
    Dec. 31   The balance of accounts receivable, as of the close of today's business, was $200,000.

    Required:

    Prepare general journal entries to record the above transactions.

36. On January 1, 19x1, H.E. Asucker made a loan of $1,000 to S.H. Esacrook. Asucker accepted a one (1)-year, 6 percent note as evidence of this transaction. On July 1, 19x1, Asucker, in need of funds, sold (discounted) Esacrook's note to the Piggy Bank. Piggy charged a discount rate of 10 percent. On January 1, 19x2, Piggy notified Asucker that the note had not been paid by Esacrook. Asucker paid the note.

Required:

Prepare journal entries for H.E. Asucker to record all of the above information.

37. The Marrion Company purchases and sells merchandise on account. The following transactions occurred in 19x1.

Apr.	1	Sold $2,000 worth of merchandise to Jack Palmer on account.
May	17	Purchased $275 of merchandise from the Colonial Company on account.
June	1	Jack Palmer signed a 12 percent two-month note in payment on his account.
	15	Paid for merchandise purchased from Colonial Company.
July	15	Discounted Palmer's note at the Republic Bank. The discount rate was 18 percent.
Aug.	1	Palmer dishonors his note. Marrion Company pays the bank the required amount.

Required:

Prepare journal entries to record the above transactions on the books of Marrion Company.

38. Listed below are selected transactions of Eastern Company for a six-month period ending March 31, 19x1. Eastern's accounting period ends on December 31.

Oct.	1	Sold merchandise on account to Ed Jackson for $1,600. The terms of the sale were n/30.
Nov.	1	Loaned $4,000 to Roger Herman on a three-month, 10 percent note.
	5	Accepted a $1,600, 90-day, 10 percent note from Ed Jackson in settlement of his past due account.
Dec.	5	Discounted the Jackson note at 12 percent at the bank.
	15	Sold merchandise on account to Bill Martin for $400; the terms of the sale were n/30.
	31	Determined by aging of accounts receivable that a $6,500 credit balance in the allowance for bad debts is required. There was a $300 debit balance in the allowance account prior to an adjusting entry.
	31	Made an adjusting entry to record the accrued interest on the note receivable from Roger Herman.
Jan.	24	Determined that the account receivable from Bill Martin was uncollectible, and it was then written off.
Feb.	5	Received notice from the bank that the Jackson note was in default. Paid the bank the maturity value of the note plus a $10 protest fee.
Mar.	5	Collected from Jackson the maturity value of the dishonored note plus 10 percent interest on that amount since the date of default and the protest fee.
	20	Full payment of $400 was received from Bill Martin on an account previously written off.

Required:

Prepare general journal entries to record the transactions and adjustments listed above.

39. Calculate the proceeds and the interest expense from discounting the notes described below.

   a. A two-month, 8 percent, $1,500 note discounted one month before maturity at a 10 percent discount rate. One month of interest income had been recorded.

   b. A four-month, 9 percent, $2,500 note discounted two months before maturity at a 12 percent discount rate. Two months of interest income had been recorded.

40. The Laguna Company's sales on account and the related losses from bad debts for previous years were as follows:

Year	Sales on Account	Losses from Bad Debts
19x1	$100,000	$ 9,000
19x2	200,000	21,000
19x3	300,000	30,000

Sales for the current year are $600,000.

Required:

Use the percentage of credit sales method to estimate the losses from bad debts for the current year and make the journal entry to record bad debt expense for the year.

41. The following balances relate to the Grub Company:

	(all balances are credits)
Allowance for bad debts (*before* the provision for bad debts), 12/31/x1	$ 700
Allowance for bad debts (*after* the provision for bad debts), 12/31/x2	2,950
Credit sales, 19x2	152,450

The Grub Company estimates its annual bad debts to be 2 percent of credit sales. During 19x2, various customers' accounts were adjudged uncollectible and were written off. The total of such write-offs was $3,300. Also, in 19x2, money totaling $500 was received from several customers whose accounts had previously been written off; some of these had been written off as far back as 19x0.

Required:

1. What was the balance in the Allowance for Bad Debts account at December 31, 19x1, *after* the provision for bad debts?
2. What was the 19x1 provision for bad debts?
3. What was the balance in the Allowance for Bad Debts account at December 31, 19x2, before the 19x2 provision for bad debts?

42. The Neely Company has been aging their accounts receivable for several years now and has found that bad debts have occurred at the following rates:

   2 percent of accounts 1-30 days old
   4 percent of accounts 31-60 days old
   20 percent of accounts 61-90 days old
   40 percent of accounts over 90 days old

Below is a listing of customers' credit accounts outstanding as of 12/31/x2 and the dates on which they purchased the items.

Account Number	Date	Customer	Amount
1	3/ 5/x1	John Nogood	$ 250
2	1/10/x2	Oscar Good	325
3	10/18/x2	Joan Walker	210
4	11/19/x2	George Dope	140
5	12/10/x2	Cindy Haines	95
6	6/20/x2	Chuck Welster	615
7	12/14/x2	Bob Barker	295
8	12/31/x2	Joe Mantle	150
9	10/12/x2	Susan Lane	80
10	11/16/x2	Danny Findlen	25
11	11/21/x2	Joanne Beaulieu	190
12	7/ 2/x2	Micky Driscall	530
			$2,905

Required:

Prepare an aging of accounts receivable for Neely Company as of December 31, 19x2. Assume a current balance in the allowance for doubtful accounts of $0 and make the appropriate journal entry to record the bad debt expense for the year.

43. The following balances relate to the Lewis Company:

   Allowance for bad debts, January 1, 19x1............ $ 700
   Accounts receivable, January 1, 19x1................ 21,000
   Credit sales, 19x1................................ 320,000

The Lewis Company estimates its annual bad debts to be 2 percent of credit sales. During 19x1, $215,000 was collected on accounts receivable, $340 of which included accounts which had been previously written off in 19x0. Accounts considered uncollectible and written off in 19x1 totaled $960.

Required:

1. What are the balances in the (a) Allowance for Bad Debts, and the (b) Accounts Receivable accounts as of December 31, 19x1?
2. Record journal entries for all transactions related to Accounts Receivable and the Allowance for Bad Debts accounts for the year 19x1.

44. Dixie, Inc. had the following transactions with regard to notes payable during the year ended December 31, 19x1.

Sept.	1	Purchased merchandise from Silver Co. in the amount of $2,000. Signed a 60-day, 6 percent interest-bearing note.
Oct.	1	Borrowed $5,000 from the City Bank, signing a 120-day non-interest-bearing note with an 8 percent discount.
	15	Purchase a machine at a cost of $10,000 from Olson Corp. Signed a 6 percent, two-month note in payment.
	30	Paid the note to Silver Co.
Dec.	14	Paid the interest on the note payable to Olson Corp. and issued a new 60-day, 6 percent note.

Required:

1. Prepare the necessary journal entries to record the above transactions.
2. Give the necessary adjusting entries required at December 31.

Refer to the Annual Report included in the Appendix at the end of the text:

45. What were the total collections from accounts receivable during the most recent year, assuming that all sales were made on account?

46. Comparing the two years presented, what was the increase in current liabilities?

47. What are the total current liabilities in the most recent year?

Learning Objectives

Chapter 9 discusses alternative methods of accounting for inventory. Studying this chapter should enable you to:

1. Describe basic inventory control procedures.

2. Discuss the objective of inventory accounting.

3. Identify the primary cost basis used in accounting for inventories and describe the elements of this cost.

4. Discuss inventory cost flow methods and the basic assumption each makes.

5. Explain the concept of lower of cost or market as it relates to inventories.

6. Apply the retail and gross profit methods of estimating inventory costs.

9 Inventories

INTRODUCTION

The inventories of a firm include those assets which are held for sale in the continuing operations of a business and goods which are in the process of production or materials which are held for the future production of goods to be produced and sold. With the exception of relatively small inventories of materials and supplies which are used in the operations of the business, the inventories of a merchandising company consist of all goods that are held for resale to customers of the firm. The inventories of a manufacturing business include all goods which are held for sale to customers (finished goods inventory), goods which are in the process of being produced for sale (work-in-process inventory), and goods which are to be used in the production of inventories for sale (raw materials, manufacturing supplies, etc.).

In this chapter we will discuss the objectives of inventory accounting, the basis for recording inventories in the accounting records, the procedures which are required to establish control over inventories, and the procedures and techniques which may be employed in the valuation of these assets as well as in the determination of the expenses which are related to their use.

CONTROL OVER INVENTORIES

An important function in maintaining effective control over a company's inventories is establishing physical control over its raw materials, purchased parts, work-in-process, finished goods, and supplies. Each category of inventory should be placed under the responsibility of a designated stores keeper who should notify the accounting department of all receipts of merchandise by means of receiving or production reports. Issues of goods should be made only against signed requisitions or shipping orders. Every item included in the inventory should be counted at least once a year, either periodically during the year or at the end of the year.

Accounting control is also an effective means of establishing internal control over inventories. These controls, such as the use of the net method of recording inventories and the perpetual inventory method, were described in Chapter 5.

OBJECTIVE OF INVENTORY ACCOUNTING

The objective of inventory accounting is two-fold. First, it is concerned with valuation of the asset inventory. Valuation of the asset accounts is important because the funds invested by a firm in its inventories are usually quite significant; the inventory of a business is often the largest of its current assets. Second, and at least of equal importance, is the proper determination of net income of the business for the period by matching the appropriate costs (the cost of the inventory sold) against the related revenue (the revenue received from the sale of the inventory). In other words, the matching process requires that costs be assigned: (1) to those goods which were sold during the period, and (2) to those goods which are still on hand

and available for sale at the end of a period. It should be noted that this is really a single process; the procedures which are employed in the valuation of inventories also simultaneously determine the cost of goods sold. Recall that this general process was illustrated and discussed in Chapter 5.

BASIS OF ACCOUNTING

Cost is the primary basis used in accounting for inventories. This cost includes not only the price of the asset itself, but also any direct or indirect outlays which were made or incurred to bring the inventory to the firm's location in the desired form and condition. For example, shipping costs and customs duties would be considered a part of the cost of the inventory if they were paid by the purchaser.

Under the periodic inventory method (which was discussed in Chapter 5), the balance in the ledger account for inventory represents the amount of the beginning inventory. All purchases of merchandise made during the period are recorded in a purchases account. Thus, the inventory on hand at the end of the accounting period must be determined by a physical count of merchandise. While the specific procedures for determining the amount of inventory on hand vary among companies, the end result must be a detailed listing of the description and quality of each type of merchandise on hand and owned by the business.

The physical count of inventory should include all goods owned by the business at the end of the period. Thus, the inventory would include goods purchased from a supplier with terms of F.O.B. shipping point which were in transit at the end of the period. These goods would be included in the physical count and they should also be recorded in the accounting records by a debit to the purchases account and a credit to accounts payable as of the end of the period.

INVENTORY COST FLOW METHODS

Once the quantities of goods on hand at the end of the period and the quantity of goods sold during the period are determined, the next step is to decide how costs should be allocated between cost of goods sold and ending inventory. If all purchases of inventory were made at the same unit price, this allocation does not create any problems. However, if the inventory items were acquired at different unit costs, it is necessary to determine which costs should be assigned to each inventory item. One method of determining the cost of the inventory on hand would be to maintain records of the exact cost of each item sold during the period and each item on hand at the end of the period. In many cases, this specific identification procedure would require excessive recordkeeping costs, while in other instances it would be impossible to do so. Consequently, some arbitrary method for assigning costs to inventory must be used. The three most common methods used in pricing inventories (and therefore determining cost of goods sold for the period) are the average method; the first-in, first-out (Fifo) method; and the last-in, first-out (Lifo) method. The application of these methods result in a different amount of ending inventory and cost of goods sold for each period because they are based upon different arbitrary assumptions as to the flow of costs of merchandise through the business.

These methods are assumptions regarding the flow of inventory *costs* and not about the actual *physical* flow of goods. The following data relating to a special brand of foreign beer, again taken from the inventory records of Art's Wholesalers, will be used to illustrate these methods:

January 1 – Beginning inventory (100 cases @ $2)	$200
February 7 – Purchase (150 cases @ $3)	450
March 25 – Purchase (200 cases @ $4)	800
October 6 – Purchase (150 cases @ $5)	750
November 10 – Purchase (100 cases @ $6)	600

Thus, the goods available for sale during the year were 700 cases at a total cost of $2,800. Art's records indicate that 500 cases were sold during the year. The accounting problem is in assigning or allocating the $2,800 cost of goods available for sale between the ending inventory and the cost of goods sold. The valuation of the ending inventory (and therefore the determination of the cost of goods sold) under each of the alternative methods of inventory valuation is illustrated in the paragraphs which follow.

Average Method

The average cost method assumes that no definite relationship exists between the receipt and the usage of quantities of inventory. This method averages costs on the assumption that one unit cannot be distinguished from another. One feature of the average method is the assignment of cost on an equal unit basis to both the ending inventory and cost of goods sold. The average cost is computed by dividing the total cost of the beginning inventory plus purchases by the total number of units included in the inventory.

In the example stated above, the average cost would be calculated as follows:

January 1 – Inventory (100 cases @ $2)	$ 200
February 7 – Purchase (150 cases @ $3)	450
March 25 – Purchase (200 cases @ $4)	800
October 6 – Purchase (150 cases @ $5)	750
November 10 – Purchase (100 cases @ $6)	600
Total 700 cases	$2,800

The total cost of the goods available for sale ($2,800) would be divided by the number of cases (700) and the result of $4 would be the average cost of the inventory. This average cost figure would be used both in valuing the ending inventory (200 × $4 = $800) and in determining the cost of goods sold for the period (500 × $4 = $2,000).

First-in, First-out (Fifo) Method

The Fifo method assumes that the cost of the first item acquired or produced is the cost of the first item used or sold. Its use is advantageous because it assigns a current cost to inventories on the balance sheet and is relatively easy to apply. In many cases, the assumption is also consistent with the actual flow of goods. (Fifo inventories are priced by using the actual invoice costs or production costs for the latest quantities purchased or produced which are still on hand.) It is a good method to use in those instances where the inventory turnover is rapid or where changes in the composition of the inventory are frequent since the costs associated with the oldest inventory are always transferred to cost of goods sold first.

Its disadvantage is that it does not match the most recent costs with current revenues. On the other hand, it does give a fairly current valuation of the ending inventory balance. The Fifo inventory and the related cost of goods sold for Art's Wholesalers would be calculated as follows:

Fifo Cost of Goods Sold—the First 500 Units

January 1—Inventory (100 cases @ $2)	$ 200
February 7—Purchase (150 cases @ $3)	450
March 25—Purchase (200 cases @ $4)	800
October 6—Purchase (50 cases @ $5)	250
Fifo Cost of Goods Sold	$1,700

Fifo Ending Inventory—the Last 200 Units

October 6—Purchase (100 cases @ $5)	$ 500
November 10—Purchase (100 cases @ $6)	600
Fifo Cost of Ending Inventory	$1,100

Last-in, First-out (Lifo) Method

This method assumes that the cost of the last item received or produced is the cost of the first item used or sold. A principal advantage of the Lifo method is that it matches current costs more nearly with current revenues. Another advantage of Lifo is the fact that in periods of price increases, net income computed using Lifo is less than the amount that would result from using Fifo or the average cost method. Therefore, it reduces federal income taxes. Providing that prices do not decline below the prices of the year in which Lifo was adopted, the method results in a postponement of income taxes. Unlike many other instances where alternative accounting procedures exist, Federal income tax laws require the use of the Lifo inventory method for financial reporting purposes whenever it is used for income tax purposes.

Its disadvantages are that it gives a "noncurrent" value to inventories in the balance sheet and it reduces reported income in periods of rising prices.

When there is an increase in the quantity of inventory, the year-end Lifo inventory consists of the prior year-end inventory plus the earliest additions at cost in the current year. The cost of the Lifo inventory and the related cost of goods sold would be calculated as follows:

Lifo Ending Inventory – the First 200 Units

January 1 – Inventory (100 cases @ $2)	$200
February 7 – Purchase (100 cases @ $3)	300
Lifo Cost of Ending Inventory	$500

Lifo Cost of Goods Sold – the Last 500 Units

February 7 – Purchase (50 cases @ $3)	$ 150
March 25 – Purchase (200 cases @ $4)	800
October 6 – Purchase (150 cases @ $5)	750
November 10 – Purchase (100 cases @ $6)	600
Lifo Cost of Goods Sold	$2,300

Differences in Methods

The effect of the differences in the three methods which we described above are illustrated by the following summary.

	Average	Fifo	Lifo
Sales (500 cases @ $10)	$5,000	$5,000	$5,000
Less: Cost of goods sold			
Beginning inventory (100 cases)	$ 200	$ 200	$ 200
Purchases (600 cases)	2,600	2,600	2,600
Goods available for sale (700 cases)	$2,800	$2,800	$2,800
Ending inventory (200 cases)	800	1,100	500
Cost of goods sold (500 cases)	$2,000	$1,700	$2,300
Gross profit on sales	$3,000	$3,300	$2,700

The total cost of goods available for sale ($2,800) was allocated either to cost of goods sold or ending inventory in every case. The sales, beginning inventory, and purchases included in the example are identical irrespective of the inventory method chosen. An inventory method is only used to cost the ending inventory and determine the cost of goods sold. It does not necessarily reflect the actual physical flow of goods. That is, a bakery could use the Lifo method for accounting purposes although obviously the physical flow would be Fifo—who wants a ten-year-old cake!

Although a firm may select any one of several acceptable methods, the consistency principle requires that a firm use the same method over time. The selection of the method to be used should depend upon such factors as the potential effect upon the balance sheet and the income statement, and the effect on taxable income.

LOWER OF COST OR MARKET

As previously indicated, the primary basis for accounting for inventories is cost. Therefore, if the value of the item increases or decreases prior to its sale, no record of this fact is normally entered in the books. However, an exception to this rule may occur when the market price, which is defined as the current replacement cost of the goods, is less than their historical cost. In this case, the inventory may be carried at its replacement cost. In other words, inventories may be carried at the lower of their cost or their market value. If the market price for a firm's inventory falls below its original cost, an entry is made recognizing the difference between cost and market as a loss and reducing the carrying value of the inventory to market. The reduced figure becomes the new "cost" of the inventory for accounting purposes. However, if the market price exceeds the original cost, no entry is made in the accounts. The recognition of losses but not gains prior to sale is based on the principle of conservatism. To illustrate the lower of cost or market method, assume the same facts as presented above—that a firm had 700 cases of beer available for sale and that this beer had been purchased at an average price of $4 per case. Sales for the period were 500 cases at a selling price of $10 per case. If the business used the "average" inventory method, the gross profit on sales would be calculated as follows:

Sales (500 cases @ $10)	$5,000
Less: Cost of goods sold	
Beginning inventory (100 cases)	$ 200
Purchases (600 cases)	2,600
Goods available for sale (700 cases)	$2,800
Ending inventory (200 cases)	800
Cost of goods sold	$2,000
Gross profit on sales	$3,000

If the replacement cost of the ending inventory had declined to $750 as of the end of the period, the ending inventory might be written down from its original cost of $800 to its current replacement cost of $750 by the following entry:

Loss on Inventory Decline	50	
Inventory		50

The effect of the write-down of inventory would be to reduce income for the period by $50 by recognizing the reduction in the replacement cost of the inventory below its original cost. In subsequent periods, inventory would be carried at a "cost" of $750 in the balance sheet and this amount would be used in determining the cost of goods sold when the inventory was sold. The lower of cost or market method may be applied: (1) to each individual type of inventory item; (2) to major classes of inventory; or (3) to the inventory as a whole. Although the application of lower of cost or market valuation is optional, once the method is adopted it should be followed consistently from year to year.

GROSS PROFIT METHOD

In many instances, such as in the case of the preparation of interim financial statements, it may be desirable simply to estimate the amount of the ending inventory rather than go to the time and trouble of taking a physical inventory. One method which is often used in estimating inventories is the gross profit method.

This method assumes that the relationship between sales, the cost of goods sold, and gross profit will remain relatively constant from one accounting period to the next. This relationship is normally based upon actual amounts from the preceding year, adjusted for any changes which occurred in the current year. To illustrate, consider the following example for Art's Wholesalers for the month of January, 19x1.

Sales	$10,500
Sales returns	500
Purchases	5,500
Purchase returns	100
Purchase allowances	50
Freight	150
Inventory, January 1, 19x1	15,500

In addition to the data summarized above, information concerning the gross profit percentage (gross profit of $36,000 divided by net sales of $100,000 or 36%)[1] and the inventory at the beginning of the year ($15,500) was obtained from the 19x0 income statement. This information would be used to estimate the cost of the ending inventory on hand at January 31, 19x1 as follows:

1. Determine the cost of goods available for sale to date, using the ledger accounts.
2. Estimate the cost of goods sold by multiplying the net sales by the reciprocal of the estimated gross profit rate (1.0 − .36 = .64).

---

[1] Information from the 19x0 income statement was as follows:

Sales	$100,000	(100%)
Cost of goods sold	64,000	(64%)
Gross profit on sales	$ 36,000	(36%)

3. Subtract the estimated cost of goods sold from the cost of goods available for sale to determine the estimated inventory on hand.

The calculation of the estimated inventory at January 31, 19x1 for Art's Wholesalers is as follows:

Beginning inventory			$15,500
Purchases		$ 5,500	
Less: Purchase returns	$100		
Purchase allowances	50	150	
Net purchases		$ 5,350	
Freight-in		150	5,500
Goods available for sale			$21,000
Less: Estimated cost of goods sold			
Sales		$10,500	
Less: Sales returns		500	
Net sales		$10,000	
Multiply by the cost of goods sold percentage (100% − 36%)		× 64%	
Estimated cost of goods sold			6,400
Estimated cost of January 31, 19x1 inventory			$14,600

The reader should keep in mind that the gross profit method is a method of *estimating* inventories, not *costing* inventories. The gross profit method can be used in order to estimate inventories for interim statement purposes; to test the accuracy of inventories determined by physical count; and to estimate inventory destroyed by fire, lost by theft, etc.

RETAIL INVENTORY METHOD

The retail inventory method is commonly used by retail businesses to simplify their accounting for inventories. An advantage of the use of this method is that the physical inventory is computed on the basis of selling prices, which are readily available. The physical inventory at selling prices is then converted to its estimated cost by applying the average ratio of costs to selling prices of goods that were on hand during the period. Thus, it is an averaging method which assumes that the cost of merchandise on hand at any time bears the same relationship to total retail prices as the total cost of all goods handled during the period bears to original selling prices. In using this method, when sales are subtracted from goods available for sale at retail selling prices, the result is the estimated ending inventory at retail prices. Then, this amount is multiplied by the average ratio of cost to selling prices to give an estimate of ending inventory at cost. Its principal advantages are: it provides a clerically feasible means of determining inventories on hand; it provides a measure of control over inventories and a means of computing the cost of merchandise sold at any time, even though the store handles a large number of items and has a very high volume of sales transactions; it simplifies the taking and pricing of physical inventories; it provides information for a monthly determination of gross profit for each department and store; and it helps control inventory by disclosing shortages which may indicate either thefts or sales made at unauthorized prices.

As goods are purchased, information regarding the goods is accumulated on both a cost and a selling price basis. The determination of the estimated cost of inventory using the retail method is illustrated with the following example:

	Cost	Selling Price
Beginning inventory	$ 1,500	$ 2,000
Add: Purchases	10,000	18,000
Freight	500	
	$12,000	$20,000
Deduct: Sales		16,000
Ending inventory, at retail		$ 4,000

Cost percentage: $\dfrac{\$12,000}{\$20,000} = 60\%$

Ending inventory, at cost: $\$4,000 \times 60\% = \underline{\underline{\$2,400}}$

SUMMARY

Where inventory items are purchased at different prices, certain assumptions regarding cost flows must be made to allocate costs between cost of goods sold and ending inventory. The average cost method assumes that all units should carry the same cost. The first-in, first-out (Fifo) method assumes that the cost of the first item acquired or produced is the cost of the first item used or sold. The last-in, first-out (Lifo) method assumes that the cost of the last item received or produced is the cost of the first item used or sold. Currently, the Fifo method results in balance sheet valuations that reflect current cost more appropriately than Lifo, but the Lifo method results in a better matching of current costs with current revenues.

For a variety of reasons, firms may wish to estimate ending inventory amounts instead of taking an actual physical count. Two methods for such estimation are the retail method and the gross profit method. Neither of these should be considered costing methods; they are basically methods of estimating cost.

This chapter has discussed inventory accounting primarily from the standpoint of merchandising firms.

KEY DEFINITIONS

Average inventory method The average inventory method is a method based on the theory that one unit cannot be distinguished from another. The average cost is computed by dividing the total cost of the beginning inventory plus purchases by the total number of units.

Cost percentage Cost percentage is the percentage obtained from the ratio of the goods available for sale at cost to the goods available for sale at selling price. This percentage is used in the retail method in order to calculate the estimated cost of the ending inventory.

Finished goods inventory Finished goods inventory includes completed goods which are held for resale.

First-in, first-out (Fifo) Fifo is an inventory method which assumes that the cost of the first item acquired or produced is the cost of the first item used or sold.

Gross method Gross method is a method of recording purchases (sales) whereby purchases (sales) are recorded at the gross price.

Gross profit method This is a method which estimates the cost of the ending inventory by assuming that the relationship between sales, cost of goods sold, and gross profit remains constant.

Gross profit percentage Gross profit percentage is the gross profit or gross margin (sales minus cost of goods sold) divided by sales.

Last-in, first-out (Lifo) Lifo is an inventory method which assumes that the cost of the last item received or produced is the cost of the first item used or sold.

Lower of cost or market Lower of cost or market is a method of pricing inventory whereby the original cost or the market value, whichever is lower, is used to value inventory for financial statement purposes.

Materials Materials are goods which are to be used in the production of inventories for sale.

Retail method This is a method of estimating inventories which assumes that the cost of merchandise on hand at any time bears the same relationship to total retail prices as the total cost of all goods handled during the period bears to the original selling prices.

Work-in-process inventory Work-in-process inventory represents goods which are in the process of being produced for resale.

QUESTIONS

1. Why should a company have accounting control over its inventory?

2. What are "goods available for sale"?

3. Explain the term "cost" with respect to accounting for inventories.

4. Briefly discuss three inventory cost flow methods.

5. Give examples of some kinds of inventories in which average cost, Fifo, and Lifo would actually match the flow of goods.

6. What problems of valuation occur with Fifo? With Lifo?

7. What is the main advantage of Lifo?

8. Explain the exception to the general cost rule for inventories.

9. What are some reasons why a company would want to estimate its inventory?

10. What is the basic assumption of the retail method of estimating inventory? What are some advantages of this method?

11. What is the gross profit method? When is it especially useful?

EXERCISES

12. Given below are the pertinent data for Griswold's Bookkeeping Services for August.

    a. Purchased 100 cartons of ledger tablets @ $5 per carton during August.
    b. Sold 90 cartons of tablets at $7.50 per carton during the month.
    c. Incurred selling expenses of $35 during August.
    d. On August 1, Griswold had 15 cartons of tablets on hand which had cost $5 per carton.

    From the above information, prepare an income statment for Griswold's Services for the month of August.

13. Determine the missing figures in each of the following independent cases.

	Sales	Beginning Inventory	Ending Inventory	Gross Profit	Expenses	Net Income	Purchases	Cost of Goods Sold
1.	$1,000	$300	a	b	$100	c	$500	$600
2.	a	100	$200	$400	b	$200	700	c
3.	800	a	150	100	100	b	400	c

14. Grasso, Inc. began its operations on January 1, 19x1. It purchased goods for resale during the month as follows:

    January 3.......................... 3 units @ $3
    January 11......................... 2 units @ $4
    January 20......................... 3 units @ $5
    January 30......................... 2 units @ $6

    Sales for the month totaled 6 units. The selling price per unit was $10. A count of the units as of January 31, 19x1, shows four (4) units on hand.

    Required:

    The inventory at January 31, 19x1 would be carried at the following amounts (for each method listed below):

    Fifo .... _____
    Lifo .... _____
    Weighted Average..................... _____

    All computations should be shown.

15. On December 31, 19x1, the end of its first year of operations, the management of the Busby Company is trying to decide whether to use the Fifo or Lifo method of measuring inventory. It determines that the Lifo method would produce the lower asset amount.

    Required:

    1. Which method would produce the higher cost of goods sold?
    2. Which method would produce the higher net income for 19x1?
    3. Which method would produce the higher cost of goods available for sale for 19x1?
    4. In what direction do you think prices have been moving during the year?

16. The following information was available from the records of a merchandising company at the end of an accounting period.

	At Cost	At Retail
Beginning inventory...............	$10,000	$ 20,000
Net purchases.....................	69,000	100,000
Freight-in	1,000	(n/a)
Sales	(n/a)	90,000

    Required:

    Estimate the cost of the ending merchandise inventory using the retail inventory method.

17. Bando Company determines its ending inventory by taking a physical inventory at the end of each accounting period. On June 15, the merchandise inventory was completely destroyed by a fire. In the past, the normal gross profit rate was 20 percent. The following data were salvaged from the accounting records:

Inventory, January 1	$ 20,000
Purchases, January 1 to June 15	90,000
Sales, January 1 to June 15	100,000

Required:

Estimate the cost of the merchandise destroyed by the fire.

18. For the month of March, Lynn Distributors had the following transactions:

Sales	$ 50,000
Sales returns	6,000
Purchases	24,000
Purchase returns	900
Purchase allowances	200
Freight	575

Inventory at the beginning of March was $32,700. This amount, as well as the gross profit percentage of 34 percent, was obtained from the February financial statements.

Required:

Use the gross profit method to estimate the ending inventory for March.

19. For each of the following five inventory cases, give the necessary journal entry to reflect the lower of cost or market rule.

	1	2	3	4	5
Cost	900	750	400	1,000	620
Market (replacement cost)	950	600	300	1,200	590

PROBLEMS

20. Peterson Company sells a single product. The company began 19x1 with 20 units of the product on hand with a cost of $4 each. During 19x1 Peterson made the following purchases:

February 3, 19x1	10 units @ $5
April 16, 19x1	25 units @ $6
October 6, 19x1	10 units @ $7
December 7, 19x1	10 units @ $8

During the year, 50 units of the product were sold. The periodic inventory method is used.

Required:

Compute the ending inventory balance and the cost of goods sold under each of the following methods:

1. Fifo.
2. Lifo.
3. Weighted Average.

21. Dente Company began business on January 1, 19x1. Purchases of merchandise for resale during 19x1 were as follows:

January 1.....................	300 units @ $3.00	$ 900.00
February 7....................	600 units @ $3.50	2,100.00
March 25.....................	400 units @ $3.00	1,200.00
October 6.....................	800 units @ $2.50	2,000.00
November 10..................	300 units @ $2.50	750.00
November 16..................	300 units @ $2.25	675.00
	2,700 units	$7,625.00

A total of 2,200 units were sold during 19x1.

Required:

1. Compute the ending inventory at December 31, 19x1, under each of the following methods: (1) Fifo; (2) Lifo; (3) Average.
2. Considering the information given above and your computations for Dente Company, answer the following:

   a. Would the net income for 19x1 have been greater if the company had used (a) Fifo or (b) Lifo in computing its inventory?
   b. Assume that the market cost of the merchandise sold by Dente Company was $2.15 per unit at December 31, 19x1. Assuming the Fifo method of inventory valuation, what would the *total* carrying value of the inventory be if the lower of cost or market method is used?
   c. Give the journal entry necessary to reduce the inventory to market in (b) above.

22. On February 1, 19x1, the Sporting Goods Department of the Most Store had an inventory of $11,000 at retail selling price; the cost of this merchandise was $8,000.

During the three months ended April 30, purchases of $18,000 were made for that department and were marked to sell for $25,000. Freight-in on this merchandise was $1,000. Sales for the period amounted to $25,000. Sales returns and allowances were $900.

The physical inventory at retail amounted to $2,500.

Required:

Estimate the cost of theft or shrinkage.

23. The McDermott Company had a fire on June 30, 19x2, which completely destroyed its inventory. No physical inventory count had been taken since December 31, 19x1. The company's books showed the following balances at the date of the fire:

Sales		$180,000
Sales returns and allowances	$ 1,400	
Inventory, December 31, 19x1	40,000	
Purchases	130,000	
Purchases returns and allowances		2,000
Transportation-in	1,600	
Selling expenses	50,000	
Administrative expenses	30,000	

Assume that the company's records show that in prior years it made a gross profit of approximately 25 percent of net sales, and there is no indication that this percentage cannot be considered to have continued during the first six months of this year.

Required:

Determine the cost of inventory destroyed by fire on June 30, 19x2.

24. A condensed income statement for the year ended December 31, 19x1 for Murcer Products shows the following:

Sales	$80,000
Cost of goods sold	50,000
Gross profit on sales	$30,000
Expenses	20,000
Net income	$10,000

An investigation of the records discloses the following errors in summarizing transactions for 19x1.

a. Ending inventory was overstated by $3,100.
b. Accrued expenses of $400 and prepaid expenses of $900 were not given accounting recognition at the end of 19x1.
c. Sales of $250 were not recorded although the goods were shipped and excluded from the inventory.
d. Purchases of $3,000 were made at the end of 19x1 but were not recorded although the goods were received and included in the ending inventory.

Required:

1. Prepare a corrected income statement for 19x1.
2. Prepare the entries necessary to correct the accounts in 19x1, assuming the books have not been closed.

25. The Yost Company began business on January 1, 19x1. Its reported net losses for the calendar years 19x1 and 19x2 were as follows:

19x1	$95,000 loss
19x2	$40,000 loss

Selected information from its accounting records is presented below:

Purchases of Goods for Resale

Date	Units		Price
February 1, 19x1	10,000	@	$10
May 1, 19x1	10,000	@	12
September 1, 19x1	10,000	@	15
December 1, 19x1	10,000	@	18
January 1, 19x2	10,000	@	20
March 1, 19x2	10,000	@	24
June 1, 19x2	10,000	@	25
November 1, 19x2	10,000	@	26

Sales

19x1	25,000 units
19x2	40,000 units

Other data:

The company uses the last-in, first-out (Lifo) method of inventory valuation.

Required:

1. Using the company's present inventory method (Lifo) compute:

    a. Ending inventory for the calendar years 19x1 and 19x2.
    b. Cost of goods sold for the calendar years 19x1 and 19x2.

2. Determine what the net income or net loss for each year would have been if the company had used the first-in, first-out (Fifo) method of inventory valuation.

26. Selected data for the Vernon Co., is as follows:

	Sales	Purchases
October	$10,000	$ 8,000
November	12,000	8,000
December	13,000	10,000

The inventory on hand at October 1st had a cost of $4,000. Goods are sold at a gross profit of 20 percent on sales.

Required:

Estimate the cost of the inventory on hand at October 31, November 30, and December 31.

27. Purchases and sales for the Yastrzemski Company are as follows:

Date		Event	Units	Unit Cost	Total Value
June	1	Balance	300	$1.00	$300.00
	8	Sale	150		
			150		
	15	Purchase	330	2.00	660.00
			480		
	23	Sale	300		
			180		
	29	Purchase	400	2.10	840.00
	30	Balance	580		

Required: (Assume a periodic inventory.)

1. What is ending inventory under Fifo?
2. Determine ending inventory under Lifo.
3. Under Fifo, what is the cost of goods that were sold on June 23?
4. Using the average price, what is ending inventory?
5. Determine gross profit on sales of $4,000 for June, assuming the average, Fifo, and Lifo methods of inventory accounting.

28. Tiant Company began business on January 1, 19x1. During 19x1, it reported a loss of $104,000; during 19x2, it had a loss of $60,000.

Selected information from its accounting records is presented below.

Purchases of Goods for Resale

Date	Units		Price
January 1, 19x1	10,000	@	$11
April 1, 19x1	10,000	@	13
August 1, 19x1	10,000	@	14
November 1, 19x1	10,000	@	16
February 1, 19x2	10,000	@	17
May 1, 19x2	10,000	@	20
August 1, 19x2	10,000	@	22
October 1, 19x2	10,000	@	23

Sales

19x1	27,000 units
19x2	42,000 units

Other data:

The company uses Lifo in valuing its inventory.

Required:

1. Using the company's present inventory method (Lifo) compute:

    a. Ending inventory for 19x1 and 19x2.
    b. Cost of goods sold for 19x1 and 19x2.

2. Determine what the net income or net loss for each year would have been if the company had used first-in, first-out (Fifo) method of inventory valuation.

Refer to the Annual Report included in the Appendix at the end of the text:

29. Comparing the two years presented, was there an increase or decrease in inventories?

30. What was the average inventory maintained during the most recent year?

31. During the most recent year, what percentage profit was earned in relation to sales?

32. During the most recent year, what were net sales?

33. What inventory method is used?

Learning Objectives

Chapter 10 discusses the accounting procedures used for recording and allocating the cost of plant and equipment. Studying this chapter should enable you to:

1. Identify the purpose of and information included on a fixed asset ledger card.

2. Recognize the three basic factors that must be considered in recording periodic depreciation.

3. Discuss and apply the depreciation methods discussed in the chapter.

4. Differentiate between capital expenditures and revenue expenditures.

10

Long-Term Assets Plant and Equipment: Depreciation

INTRODUCTION

The term plant and equipment refers to long-lived tangible assets which are used in the continuing operations of a business over a number of years. They are assets which are acquired for *use* in the firm's operations as contrasted to those assets which are purchased for *resale* to the customers of a business. Examples of plant and equipment include land, buildings, equipment, furniture, and fixtures. Plant and equipment may be regarded as a "bundle" of services that are used over the life of the asset in the process of generating revenue. In accordance with the matching principle, as these services expire through use in generating revenue, a portion of the cost of the asset should be allocated to expense. The costs which are to be allocated to expense in future periods may be considered deferred costs and are shown as assets on the balance sheet. This process of periodically allocating the cost of tangible plant and equipment to expense is referred to as *depreciation*.

In this chapter we will discuss the accounting procedures used to record the acquisition and use of long-lived assets including intangibles and material resources, and those procedures used to determine the depreciation expense for the period.

CONTROL OVER TANGIBLE LONG-TERM ASSETS

A fixed asset ledger card should be prepared and maintained for each individual asset purchased. This card should include all of the pertinent information relating to the asset and its use. This data will enable the management of the firm to establish and maintain control over each individual asset (for example, by providing the basis for taking a physical inventory of all fixed assets owned by the firm). It will also assist in accounting for all transactions relating to plant assets. For example, the fixed asset ledger card will provide the information which is required in order to calculate the periodic depreciation expense for the asset and the data required to adjust the accounts as assets are sold or retired.

Using a ledger card for an automobile as an illustration, the following information should ordinarily be provided:

Asset Ledger Account

Description	*Cost*	*Depreciation*	*Other Information*
Name of asset	Date acquired	Estimated life	Repairs
Account number	Invoice cost	Estimated salvage	Date
Asset number	Other costs	value	Amount
Manufacturer's serial number		Depreciation to date	Actual life
Horsepower			Data on disposal:
Insurance carried			Date
Property tax valuation			Sales price (if any)
			Gain or loss
			To whom sold

TYPES OF PLANT AND EQUIPMENT

Plant and equipment may be classified into two categories for accounting purposes: land and depreciable assets. Since the assumption is made that land is not used up over time, the cost of land is not subject to depreciation. All other items of plant and equipment are assumed to have a limited useful life and, therefore, the cost of these items is allocated to expense through periodic depreciation charges.

ACCOUNTING FOR TANGIBLE FIXED ASSETS

All costs incurred in acquiring an asset and preparing the asset for productive use are capitalized as the cost of the asset by debiting them to the asset account. The costs include the net invoice price, transportation costs and installation costs. All costs that are incurred before the asset becomes productive, such as demolition of old buildings on a building site or repairs of or to used equipment acquired for production, is considered to be a cost of the acquired asset. A proper determination of the total cost of a plant asset is important because the cost of an asset (less any salvage value, i.e., the amount the firm can recover when the firm has finished using it) becomes an expense which should be charged against the income of the business during the periods the asset is used by the firm.[1]. This process of allocating the cost of an asset to expense is known as depreciation.

Plant assets are normally acquired either by cash purchase or by incurring a liability (or by a combination of a cash down payment and incurring a liability for future payments). If a liability is incurred, the interest cost associated with the liability should be recorded as interest expense and not as a cost of the asset acquired. Plant assets may also be acquired in exchange for other assets owned by the firm. The procedures used in accounting for assets acquired by exchange are discussed in the following chapter.

In certain cases, more than a single asset may be acquired for a lump sum purchase price. Because the assets acquired may have different useful lives (or, in the case of land, an unlimited life), it is necessary to allocate the total purchase price among the assets acquired. Normally, this allocation is based upon the relative appraisal values of the assets involved. For example, assume that a company acquired land, building, and equipment for a total cost of $200,000. Assume that the company making the acquisition determined the following appraisal values for the individual items:

Land	$ 75,000
Building	150,000
Equipment	25,000
Total appraised value	$250,000

---

[1] The cost of land, which is not used up in the generation of revenue, is not allocated to expense. Instead, the original cost of the asset is maintained in the accounts until the asset is disposed of.

The apportionment of the $200,000 purchase price is made on the basis of the relative values of the assets and would be as follows:

Asset	Appraisal Value	Fraction of Total Appraisal Value	Allocation of Cost
Land	$ 75,000	$ 75,000/$250,000 = .3	$ 60,000
Building	150,000	$150,000/$250,000 = .6	120,000
Equipment	25,000	$ 25,000/$250,000 = .1	20,000
	$250,000		$200,000

The cost of an asset includes all expenditures which are necessary to acquire the asset and place it in use. For example, a company buys a delivery truck with a list price of $10,000. The company received a 10% reduction in price from the dealer and also a 2% cash discount. The company pays a 5% sales tax and in addition, purchases a stereo for the truck paying $300 including installation. The cost of the new truck is computed as follows:

List price....................	$10,000
Less 10% reduction............	1,000
	$ 9,000
Less 2% cash discount..........	180
	$ 8,820
Sales taxes...................	441
Stereo.......................	300
Cost of the truck..............	$ 9,561

The $9,561 cost is the balance in the asset account and is the basis for computing depreciation. To charge the sales tax and the stereo to the expenses in the year the truck is acquired would overstate expenses for that period and understate expenses for the following periods.

Land. The cost of land includes the purchase price, commissions, any taxes due, and other similar costs. Any cost incurred to grade, level and demolish old buildings are added to the cost of the land but any proceeds from the sale of scrap reduces the cost. Land is not subject to depreciation and its cost is retained in the land account until it is sold.

Buildings. The cost of constructing a building includes excavation, building materials, labor, and all other costs necessary to place the building in use. Costs such as interest on borrowed construction funds and real estate taxes incurred during the construction are also part of the total building cost.

Machinery and equipment. In addition to the normal costs of acquiring machinery and equipment, such costs as supports, wiring, inspection and testing are charged to the machinery and equipment account.

DEPRECIATION

Depreciation is the process of allocating the cost of an asset to the periods in which services are received from the asset. The basic nature of and the problems involved in depreciation accounting may be illustrated by the use of a simple example. Assume that you decide to purchase a Chevrolet Impala for use as a taxi cab. The cost of the auto is $9,000. You feel that you will be able to earn approximately $12,000 each year in fares, and the estimated operating costs (gas, oil, repairs, insurance, etc.) will be approximately $4,000 per year. You further estimate that the auto will last for four years at which time it will probably have to be replaced. At the end of the four-year period you estimate that your used Chevrolet may be sold for about $1,000. What would your earnings be over the four years if your estimates prove to be accurate? Total income for the four-year period might be calculated as follows:

Your Taxi Company
Income Statement
For Four Years

Revenues ($12,000 per year for 4 years)...............		$48,000
Operating costs ($4,000 per year for 4 years)............	$16,000	
Cost of the taxi ($9,000 cost less $1,000 received from its sale at the end of the four-year period)...............................	8,000	
Total costs.......................................		24,000
Net income......................................		$24,000

Assume now that you wished to prepare separate income statements for each of the four years. You could do the following:

Your Taxi Company
Income Statements

For the Year

	1	2	3	4	Total
Revnues.............	$12,000	$12,000	$12,000	$12,000	$48,000
Operating costs......	$ 4,000	$ 4,000	$ 4,000	$ 4,000	$16,000
Cost of the taxi.......	9,000	0	0	(1,000)*	8,000
	$13,000	$ 4,000	$ 4,000	$ 3,000	$24,000
Net income (loss).....	($1,000)	$ 8,000	$ 8,000	$ 9,000	$24,000

*The negative thousand dollars shown as "cost of the taxi" represents the proceeds received from its sale at the end of the fourth year—i.e., its salvage value.

But do these statements really reflect the actual facts of the situation? Is it reasonable to report that your income increased significantly during year 2, remained constant during the third year and then increased slightly in year 4? Of course not. The total for the four years seems to be reasonable, but the problem lies in attempting to measure the income for *each* individual year. This difficulty arises because you purchased the car and paid for it at the beginning of year 1, used it for four years and sold it at the end of the fourth year. In order to measure the income for each year properly, it is necessary to allocate, in a rational and systematic manner, the net cost of owning the auto (i.e., the purchase price of the car less its estimated salvage value) over the periods which benefit from its use.

As previously indicated, the process of amortizing or charging the cost of a fixed asset to expense over the period of its useful life is referred to as depreciation. A more formal definition of depreciation is ". . . the systematic allocation of the cost of an asset, less salvage value (if any) over its estimated useful life."

From a theoretical viewpoint, depreciation expense for a particular period represents an estimate of the portion of the cost of an asset which is used up or which otherwise expires during that period. A precise determination of the depreciation expense related to an individual asset for any given year is difficult because it is almost impossible to accurately predict the exact useful life of an asset. The life of an asset, and therefore its depreciation, is affected by a combination of factors such as the passage of time, normal wear and tear, physical deterioration, and obsolescence. Even though the various techniques which can be employed in determining the depreciation may appear to be precise, and from a mathematical viewpoint they are, it should be noted that because of the estimating of useful life, salvage value, etc., depreciation is always an estimate or approximation. However, periodic measurement of that portion of the cost of an asset which has been used up or has expired during a period is a necessary element in determining the income of the firm for that period. Depreciation accounting is a method of allocation by which an attempt is made to "match" the cost of an asset against the revenue which has been generated or produced from using the asset.

ELEMENTS AFFECTING THE DETERMINATION OF PERIODIC DEPRECIATION

The depreciation process represents the allocation of the costs (less any estimated residual or salvage value) of property, plant and equipment over the expected useful life of the asset. As discussed previously, the cost of a long-lived asset includes all of the expenditures associated with its acquisition and preparation for use. The additional factors which must be considered in the estimate of periodic depreciation for an asset include:

1. Estimated Useful Life
2. Estimated Salvage (Residual) Value
3. Methods of Allocation

USEFUL LIFE

The useful life of an asset is that period of time during which it is of economic use to the business. The estimation of the useful life of an asset should consider such factors as economic analysis, engineering studies, previous experience with similar assets, and any other available information concerning the characteristics of the asset. However, regardless of the quantity of information available, the determination of the useful life of an asset is a judgment process which requires the prediction of future events.

The period of economic usefulness of an asset to a business is a function of both physical and functional factors. Physical factors include normal wear, deterioration and decay, and damage or destruction. These physical factors limit the economic useful life of an asset by rendering the asset incapable of effectively performing its intended function. Thus, the physical factors limit the maximum potential economic life of the asset.

Functional factors may also cause the useful life of an asset to be less than its physical life. The primary functional factors which may limit the service life of an asset are obsolescence and inadequacy. Obsolescence is caused by changes in technology or changes in demand for the output product or services which cause the asset to be inefficient or uneconomical before the end of its physical life. Inadequacy may result from changes in the size or volume of activity which cause an asset to be economically incapable of handling or processing the required output. In a high technology, growth-oriented economy such as that of the United States, functional factors generally impact significantly upon the determination of the useful life of an asset.

SALVAGE VALUE

Salvage value is the estimated realizable value of an asset at the end of its expected life. Depending upon the expectations regarding the disposition of an asset, this amount may be based on such factors as scrap value, second-hand market value or anticipated trade-in value. The depreciation base used for an asset normally is equal to the difference between the acquisition cost of the asset and its salvage value.

This depreciation base is the amount of the cost of an asset which is allocated to expense over the expected useful life of the asset.

The relationship between salvage value and the cost of an asset varies considerably. In some cases, particularly when the estimated useful life of an asset is significantly less than its physical life, salvage value may be substantial. On the other hand, in certain instances, the estimated residual value of an asset may be so small that the salvage value is assumed to be zero in computing the depreciation base. Of course, the validity of the periodic depreciation expense is dependent upon a reasonably accurate estimate of both the salvage value of an asset and its useful life.

DEPRECIATION METHODS

Theoretically, the selection of a depreciation method should be based on the expectations regarding the pattern of decline in the service potential of the asset under consideration. Because both the nature and the characteristics of various assets may vary significantly, alternative depreciation patterns may be justified. Accordingly, there are a number of acceptable depreciation methods which mathematically approximate the possible pattern of use expected from an asset. However, in practice, the criteria for selecting a particular depreciation method are often not determinable. It has been suggested by some that depreciation accounting is used by management as a factor in implementing its financial policy. That is, management may select the method(s) which contribute to the desired financial results that it hopes to achieve over time. The consistency principle does require that once a method has been adopted for a particular type of asset, the firm must continue to use that method over time. Because of the number of alternative methods which are available, the depreciation expense for each period may vary significantly depending upon the method selected. Each of the methods, however, results in the identical total depreciation expense over the useful life of the asset(s).

In recording the periodic depreciation for fixed costs, three basic factors must be considered:

1. The cost of the asset—the invoice cost plus all costs which are necessary to place it in use.
2. The estimated useful life of the asset.
3. The estimated salvage or scrap value of the asset—the amount which will be recovered when the asset is retired.

This section of the chapter will discuss four of the methods which are used in accounting for the use of long-term tangible assets in the operations of businesses: the straight-line method, the declining-balance method, the sum-of-the-years'-digits method and the accelerated cost recovery system. Each of these methods results in identical total depreciation over the life of a fixed asset—an amount equal to the original cost of the asset or, when appropriate, the original cost less its estimated salvage value. The methods differ, however, in the amount of cost which is allocated to expense during each year of the life of the asset. To illustrate these techniques, the following data will be used:

Type of asset............................... Chevrolet Impala
Date acquired.............................. January 1, 19x1
Cost (including delivery, sales tax, etc.)............ $9,000
Estimated useful life........................... 4 years
Estimated salvage value........................ $1,000

Straight-Line Depreciation. One of the simplest and most commonly used methods of computing depreciation is the straight-line method. This method considers the passage of time to be the most important single factor or limitation on the useful life of an asset. It assumes that other factors such as wear and tear and obsolescence are somewhat proportional to the elapsed time; this may or may not be the case in fact. The straight-line method allocates the cost of an asset, less its salvage value, to expense equally over its useful life. A formula which may be employed in calculating depreciation using the straight-line method is as follows:

$$\frac{\left(\begin{array}{c}\text{Cost of} \\ \text{the Asset}\end{array} - \begin{array}{c}\text{Estimated} \\ \text{Salvage} \\ \text{Value}\end{array}\right)}{\text{Estimated Useful Life}} = \text{Depreciation for the Period}$$

Substituting the illustrative data presented above in the formula, we obtain the following calculation of depreciation for 19x1:

$$\frac{(\$9,000 - \$1,000)}{4 \text{ years}} = \$2,000 \text{ Per Year}$$

Since the straight-line method of depreciation allocates an identical dollar amount of depreciation expense to each period, depreciation for the years 19x2, 19x3 and 19x4 (the remaining useful life of the automobile) would also be $2,000 each year.

Accelerated Methods of Depreciation. Businessmen recognize that the benefits obtained from the use of a fixed asset frequently may not be uniform over its useful life. Both the revenue-producing ability of an asset and its value may decline at a faster rate during the early years of its life. Also, the costs of repairing and maintaining the asset may increase during the later years of its life. Furthermore, one accelerated depreciation method, Accelerated Cost Recovery System (ACRS) is permitted for income tax purposes and may benefit the taxpayer by postponing or deferring the payment of taxes to a later year. Although a business may use different methods of computing depreciation for accounting and tax purposes, firms often wish to simplify their recordkeeping by using the same method for both purposes. For these reasons, many businesses will adopt ACRS. In general, accelerated methods of calculating depreciation allow the recording of larger amounts of depreciation in the early periods of an asset's life than in later years. As indicated above, a business may choose to employ the ACRS method for computing the expense relating to the use of its fixed assets for tax purposes because the increased depreciation charges (which do not require the outlay of cash, since the cash expenditure was made at the time the asset was acquired) reduce taxable income and therefore reduce the amount of income tax currently payable. By postponing or deferring the payment of income taxes from an earlier to a later year of an asset's life, the business has obtained, in effect, an interest-free loan from the taxing authority.[2]

Three commonly-used methods of accelerated depreciation will be illustrated: the double-declining balance method, the sum-of-the-years'-digits method and ACRS.

The Double-Declining Balance Method. The procedures used in applying the double-declining balance method arbitrarily double the depreciation rate which would be used in calculating depreciation under the straight-line method.[3] This increased rate is then applied to the book value (i.e., the cost of the asset less the total depreciation taken to date) of the assets. The formula used in calculating double-declining balance depreciation is as follows:

$$(2 \times \text{Straight-Line Rate}) \times (\text{Cost} - \text{Depreciation Taken in Prior Periods})$$
$$= \text{Depreciation for the Period}$$

Salvage value is ignored in the computation of depreciation under the double-declining balance method with the exception of the final year. In the final year of the asset's life, the formula is ignored and the depreciation taken is simply whatever amount is necessary to reduce the book value of the asset to its salvage value.

Using the same data as in the previous example, the calculation of double-declining balance depreciation may be illustrated as follows:

$$(2 \times 25\%) \times (\$9,000 - \$0) = \$4,500 \text{ Depreciation for 19x1}$$

The straight-line rate is 25 percent; since the asset has a useful life of four years, one-fourth (or 25 percent) of the cost is expensed each year using the straight-line method. The doubled rate (2 × 25 percent) is applied to the full cost of $9,000 since the salvage value is ignored in the initial years of the asset's life and there is, of course, no depreciation from prior years.

The depreciation charge for 19x2 would be calculated as follows:

---

[2] See Chapter 20 for a detailed discussion of income tax allocation.
[3] The straight-line rate may be calculated by dividing the useful life of the asset (in years) into 100%. For the example used, the straight-line rate would be 100% divided by 4 or 25%.

$$(2 \times 25\%) \times (\$9,000 - \$4,500) = \$2,250 \text{ Depreciation for 19x2}$$

The only change from the previous year is that $4,500, the depreciation taken in 19x1, is substituted for $0 in the first calculation.

Depreciation for 19x3 would be:

$$(2 \times 25\%) \times (\$9,000 - \$6,750) = \$1,125 \text{ Depreciation for 19x3}$$

Again, the only change in the formula is in the depreciation taken in prior years. The $6,750 amount used in the computation of depreciation for 19x3 is the 19x1 depreciation of $4,500 plus the 19x2 depreciation of $2,250.

The formula would not be used to calculate the depreciation expense for 19x4, since this is the final year of the asset's useful life. Depreciation for 19x4 would be computed as follows:

Cost of the asset..............................		$9,000
Less: Depreciation taken in prior years:		
19x1...................................	$4,500	
19x2...................................	2,250	
19x3...................................	1,125	7,875
Net book value of the asset at January 1, 19x4.....		$1,125
Less: Estimated salvage value...............		1,000
Depreciation for 19x4........................		$ 125

The Sum-of-the-Years'-Digits Method. The use of the sum-of-the-years'-digits method also produces greater charges for depreciation in the early years of an asset's useful life. The life-years of an asset are totaled[4] and utilized as the denominator of a fraction that uses the number of years of life remaining from the beginning of the year (i.e., the years in reverse order) as the numerator. This fraction is then applied to the cost of the asset less its estimated salvage value in order to compute the depreciation for the period.

Again, using the same data as in the previous illustrations, the depreciation expense for each of the four years, 19x1 through 19x4, using the sum-of-the-years'-digits method, would be calculated as follows:

Sum-of-the-years'-digits:

$$1 + 2 + 3 + 4 = 10$$

---

[4] The sum of the numbers from one to the estimated life of an asset in years. For example, the life-years of an asset with a 3-year estimated life would be $1 + 2 + 3 = 6$. [Sum of arithmetic progression of n consecutive numbers $= n \left(\dfrac{n+1}{2}\right)$.]

Depreciation for each period:

$$
\begin{aligned}
&19x1: && 4/10 \times (\$9{,}000 - \$1{,}000) = \$3{,}200 \\
&19x2: && 3/10 \times (\$9{,}000 - \$1{,}000) = \$2{,}400 \\
&19x3: && 2/10 \times (\$9{,}000 - \$1{,}000) = \$1{,}600 \\
&19x4: && 1/10 \times (\$9{,}000 - \$1{,}000) = \$800
\end{aligned}
$$

Accelerated Cost Recovery System

Effective January 1, 1981, the Accelerated Cost Recovery System (ACRS) was implemented, introducing significant changes in the manner in which depreciation expense is computed for federal income tax purposes. While the straight-line, sum-of-the-years'-digits and double-declining balance methods may still be used for financial accounting and reporting purposes, ACRS methods are the only accelerated methods which may be used for federal income tax purposes.[5] Essentially, ACRS places all depreciable assets into recovery periods of 3, 5, 10 or 15 years as summarized below:

ACRS Classes

ACRS Property Class	*Includes*
3-year	Automobiles, light-trucks, research and development equipment, special tools.
5-year	All items of machinery and equipment (other than those in 3-year property class).
10-year	Public utility property (18 to 25 years useful life) and limited real property.
15-year	All depreciable real business property and all public utility property (other than that in 10-year property class).

Although the property classes described above are identified by years, the concept of useful life for the calculation of depreciation expense has been discontinued under the ACRS rules. Rather, depreciation expense for each class of property is determined by the use of a table, which is based upon the application of a stated percentage to the original cost of the asset. Salvage value is not considered in computing depreciation deductions under ACRS rules.

---

[5] As a general statement for plant and equipment acquired prior to 1981, the depreciation methods that are permissable for tax purposes are: straight-line, double-declining balance, and sum-of-the-years'-digits. For years after 1980, the Economic Recovery Tax Act of 1981 provides an Accelerated Cost Recovery System (ACRS) that uses lives shorter than the economic lives and accelerated rates, changing to straight-line rates when it becomes advantageous. The Act does provide for the election of straight-line rates and longer recovery periods.

The ACRS tables were prepared based upon a 150 percent declining-balance method for those classes which include machinery and equipment and a 175 percent declining-balance method for classes which include real property. It may be noted that the percentages included in the tables switch to a straight-line approach in the year that the depreciation expense using the straight-line method exceeds declining-balance depreciation.

Using the same data as in the previous examples, the depreciation expense using ACRS would be calculated as follows:

Year 1: 25% × $9,000 = $2,250
Year 2: 38% × $9,000 = $3,420
Year 3: 37% × $9,000 = $3,330
Year 4: No depreciation, since the 3-year ACRS property tax is used for automobiles.

Under ACRS rules, a taxpayer may elect to use the straight-line method of depreciation rather than the ACRS percentages. If this election is made, the taxpayer must use useful lives which are equal to or greater than those included in the ACRS classes: 3-year (3, 5 or 12 years); 5-year (5, 12 or 25 years); 10-year (10, 25 or 35 years); and 15-year (15, 35 or 45 years). Also, the taxpayer electing straight-line depreciation, rather than the ACRS percentages, must use the half-year convention which requires that the taxpayer take one-half year's depreciation expense in the year an asset is acquired, irregardless of the actual date the asset was acquired. Salvage value may be ignored in calculating depreciation under this optional straight-line method.

As is now apparent, except for ACRS (which ignores salvage value), the *total* amount of depreciation taken for a fixed asset over its useful life will be identical regardless of the method used, although the timing and pattern of the depreciation charges vary widely according to the particular method chosen. The effects of the various methods on the example data are illustrated below:

Year	Straight-line	Double-Declining Balance	Sum-of-the-years'-digits	ACRS
19x1	$2,000	$4,500	$3,200	$2,250
19x2	2,000	2,250	2,400	3,420
19x3	2,000	1,125	1,600	3,330
19x4	2,000	125	800	0
Total	$8,000	$8,000	$8,000	$9,000

The differences in the depreciation expense depending on the method chosen are illustrated graphically below.

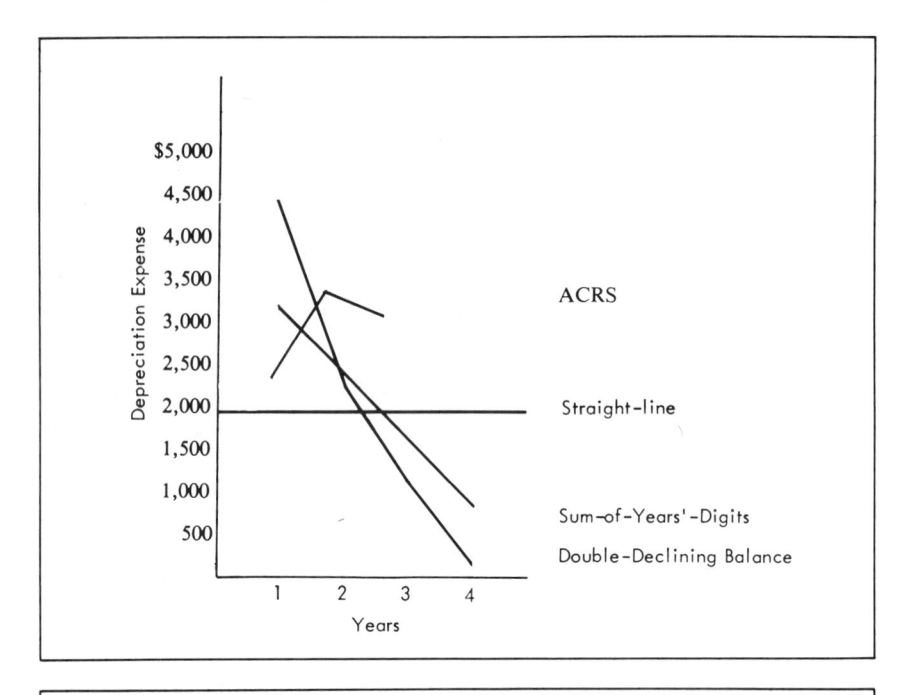

ACRS Table 1981-1984

ACRS Property Class

Year	3-Year	5-Year	10-Year	15-Year Real Business	Utility
1	25	15	8	12 *	5
2	38	22	14	10	10
3	37	21	12	9	9
4		21	10	8	8
5		21	10	7	7
6			10	6	7
7			9	6	6
8			9	6	6
9			9	6	6
10			9	5	6
11				5	6
12				5	6
13				5	6
14				5	6
15				5	6

*Assumes acquisition on January 1. Real property is depreciated according to the number of months in the year of acquisition.

Because depreciation expense is an important factor which enters into the determination of the income of a firm for a period, the reported income will also vary according to the depreciation method selected. The effect of depreciation on the reported income of the firm (and therefore its income taxes) is an important factor in the selection of the depreciation method(s) a firm will use.

RECORDING LONG-TERM ASSETS

Using the Chevrolet Impala acquired by Your Taxi Company as an example, the accounting procedures for recording the acquisition and use of plant assets will be illustrated.

On January 1, 19x1, the acquisition of the automobile would be recorded as follows:

    Automobile........................... 9,000
        Cash.............................   9,000

It should be noted that the debit to the asset account was for the total cost of the Chevrolet including delivery charges, sales tax, etc. In this instance the car was paid for in cash. Had a liability been incurred, it would have been recorded by a credit. The procedures required when an old asset is traded in on a new asset are discussed later in this chapter.

At the end of 19x1, it would be necessary to record depreciation on the asset in order to charge to expense the portion of the cost of the asset which had been "used up" during the period. For purposes of illustration, we will assume that the straight-line method of depreciation was used. On December 31, 19x1, depreciation would be recorded in the books of Your Taxi Company by the following entry:

    Depreciation expense................... 2,000
        Accumulated depreciation..............   2,000

The debit to depreciation expense records the portion of the cost of the asset which is to be charged as an expense of the period. The credit to the accumulated depreciation account adds the current period's depreciation to that which was taken in prior years (in this case zero since this is the initial year of the asset's useful life); the total of this account indicates the total amount of depreciation taken to date at any given point in time. The depreciation expense of $2,000 would appear in the income statement along with the other expenses of the period and would be deducted from revenue in the determination of income. Accumulated depreciation would appear as an offset (called a contra account) against the related asset account in the balance sheet as follows:

Current assets.........................		$10,000
Automobile............................	$9,000	
Less: Accumulated depreciation..........	2,000	7,000
Total assets...........................		$17,000

Since the straight-line method of depreciation was used, the entries which are required in order to record depreciation expense for the years 19x2, 19x3 and 19x4 will be the same as the one which was made on December 31, 19x1, shown above. The automobile and accumulated depreciation accounts would appear as follows:

Automobile		Accumulated Depreciation	
(a) 9,000		(b)	2,000
		(c)	2,000
		(d)	2,000
		(e)	2,000
		(f)	8,000

Key:
(a) Cost of the automobile on January 1, 19x1.
(b) Depreciation for 19x1.
(c) Depreciation for 19x2.
(d) Depreciation for 19x3.
(e) Depreciation for 19x4.
(f) Balance in the account at December 31, 19x5.

Occasionally, plant assets are used for periods of time beyond their originally estimated lives. Since the purpose or objective of depreciation accounting is to allocate the cost of a plant asset to expense over its useful life, no additional depreciation should be recorded for an asset which has already been fully depreciated. The cost of the asset, along with the associated accumulated depreciation, should remain in the accounts until the asset is disposed of.

Assets Acquired During the Period

In the example used in the previous section, the automobile was acquired at the beginning of the period. In practice, assets will be acquired throughout the accounting period and this will require that depreciation be recorded for a part of a period in the year of acquisition. For example, the purchase of the automobile on June 1, 19x1, would be recorded as follows:

Automobile...........................	9,000	
Cash................................		9,000

At the end of 19x1, it would be necessary to record depreciation on the asset for the seven-month period that it was used during the year (June 1, 19x1 to December 31, 19x1). Again, we will assume the same facts as before (4-year life, $1,000 salvage value) and that the straight-line method of depreciation was used, so the calculation would be as follows:

$$\frac{(\$9{,}000 - \$1{,}000)}{4 \text{ years}} = \$2{,}000 \text{ per year}$$

$$\frac{\$2{,}000}{12 \text{ months}} = \$166.67 \text{ per month}$$

Depreciation for the period June 1, 19x1 to December 31, 19x1 would be 7 months × $166.67 per month or a total of $1,167 (rounded). At December 31, 19x1, depreciation for the period would be recorded by the following entry:

```
Depreciation expense.................... 1,167
    Accumulated depreciation..............        1,167
```

The entries to record depreciation expense for the years 19x2, 19x3, and 19x4 would each cover a full year and each would be as follows:

```
Depreciation expense.................... 2,000
    Accumulated depreciation..............        2,000
```

In 19x5, depreciation would be recorded for the final five months of the life of the asset (5 months × $166.67 per month or $833) by the following entry:

```
Depreciation expense....................  833
    Accumulated depreciation..............         833
```

The automobile and accumulated depreciation accounts would appear as follows:

Automobile		Accumulated Depreciation	
(a) 9,000		(b)	1,167
		(c)	2,000
		(d)	2,000
		(e)	2,000
		(f)	833
		(g)	8,000

Key:
(a) Cost of the automobile on June 1, 19x1.
(b) Depreciation for 19x1 (7 months).
(c) Depreciation for 19x2 (12 months).
(d) Depreciation for 19x3 (12 months).
(e) Depreciation for 19x4 (12 months).
(f) Depreciation for 19x5 (5 months).
(g) Balance in the account at May 31, 19x5.

In the above example, depreciation was calculated from the exact date of acquisition until the end of the useful life of the asset. In practice, as a matter of convenience, a business may establish a procedure whereby it will always take six months' depreciation in the year an asset is acquired and six months' depreciation in the year it is disposed of (see next section) irrespective of the exact dates of acquisition or disposal. Alternatively, a firm might take a full year's depreciation in the year of acquisition and no depreciation in the year of disposal, or vice-versa. The use of procedures such as those described above do not change the entries illustrated and are generally acceptable as long as there is no significant distortion of depreciation expense or income.

Interest Costs

Frequently, firms borrow substantial sums for the purpose of constructing or acquiring property, plant, and equipment. A basic accounting issue which exists with regard to the interest costs relating to these borrowings is whether the interest should be considered an expense of the period or included (capitalized) as a part of the cost of the asset acquired or constructed. The charging of interest to expense has been defended on the grounds that interest represents the cost of financing and is not a cost which should be associated with a specific asset. Capitalizing interest costs, on the other hand, has been justified on the basis that an asset should be charged with all of the costs necessary to place it in its intended use. It may be argued that the interest incurred is as much a cost of acquiring an asset as is the cost of any other resources used or expended.

Until recently, the proper accounting for interest costs had been an unresolved issue. In 1979, however, the FASB issued its *Statement No. 34*, "Capitalization of Interest Costs," which *requires* capitalizing interest as a part of the cost of acquiring *certain* assets. In this pronouncement, the FASB concluded:

> On the premise that the historical cost of acquiring an asset should include all costs necessarily incurred to bring it to the condition and location necessary for its intended use,... in principle, the cost incurred in financing expenditures for an asset during a required construction or development period is itself a part of the asset's historical acquisition cost.

The assets which qualify for interest capitalization generally are those assets that require a period of time to place them in their intended use. Examples of these qualifying assets include those constructed for an entity's own use (e.g., a manufacturing facility) or those intended for sale or lease that are constructed as discrete projects (e.g., ships or real estate projects). Interest should not be capitalized as a part of the cost of inventories that are routinely manufactured or otherwise produced in large quantities on a repetitive basis even if these inventories require lengthy maturation periods, such as is the case with whiskey or tobacco. Interest cost eligible for capitalization is limited to amounts incurred on borrowings and other obligations. The amount to be capitalized is determined by applying an interest rate to the average amount of accumulated expenditures for the asset during the construction or development period.

Disclosure in the Financial Statements

Because the amount of periodic depreciation depends on the method or methods of depreciation in use, it is necessary that information on the depreciation method(s) be disclosed in the financial statements. Such information is necessary for a meaningful comparison of the depreciation charges of different companies or for prediction of future depreciation charges of a company. Consequently, the Accounting Principles Board in Opinion No. 12 indicated that the following disclosures should be made in the financial statements or accompanying notes:

1. Depreciation expense for the period.
2. Balances of major classes of depreciable assets, by nature or function, at the balance sheet date.
3. Accumulated depreciation, either by major classes of depreciable assets or in total, at the balance sheet date.
4. A general description of the method or methods used in computing depreciation with respect to major classes of depreciable assets.[6]

COSTS INCURRED AFTER ACQUISITION

It is often necessary to make additional expenditures relating to plant assets subsequent to the date of acquisition. Such expenditures are classified into one of two groups:

1. *Capital Expenditures*—Expenditures which extend the useful life or the quality of services of plant assets.
2. *Revenue Expenditures*—Expenditures for ordinary maintenance, repairs, and other items necessary for the operation and use of plant and equipment.

Since capital expenditures increase the future economic benefits of an asset, the costs incurred are recorded in an asset account. On the other hand, revenue expenditures benefit only the current operations, and these costs are recorded by debits to expense accounts.

Capital expenditures for existing assets are often classified as additions or improvements. An addition represents an increase in the physical substance

---

[6] Opinions of the Accounting Principles Board No. 12, "Omnibus Opinion - 1967" (New York: AICPA, 1967), Par. 5.

of an asset, such as a new wing on a building. Improvements (or replacements) involve the substitution of new parts on an existing asset. Examples of improvements include the installation of elevators in a building or an air conditioner in a delivery truck. If the addition or improvement has the same economic life as the existing asset, the cost should be capitalized directly to the asset account. When the expenditure extends the economic life of the asset, the depreciable life of the asset should be extended accordingly. If the item has a different economic life than the existing asset, the cost should be capitalized in a separate asset account and expensed over the period of expected benefit.

Revenue expenditures are routine and recurring expenditures which are incurred to maintain an asset in operating condition and which do not increase the economic benefits associated with the asset. Examples of typical revenue expenditures are routine maintenance (i.e., oil change and lubrication) and ordinary repairs (i.e., replacing a worn out tire).

Theoretically, if an expenditure increases the economic benefits originally expected from an asset, then the cost should be capitalized. In practice, however, it is often difficult to make a distinction between a capital expenditure and a revenue expenditure. In many companies, arbitrary policies are established for defining capital and revenue expenditures. For example, an expenditure might be capitalized only if it (1) clearly increases the economic benefits associated with an existing asset and (2) exceeds a minimum cost (such as $50). The use of a minimum cost for capitalization eliminates the need to recompute depreciation schedules for minor improvements or additions.

To illustrate the accounting for a capital expenditure, assume that in January, 19x5 a company spent $3,000 to recondition an existing delivery truck. The truck had been acquired on January 1, 19x1 for $16,000, and at that time had an estimated useful life of 5 years and a salvage value of $1,000. The truck was depreciated using the straight-line method. Therefore, as of December 31, 19x4, the balance in accumulated depreciation was $12,000 [($15,000 ÷ 5) × 4]. The company estimated that the reconditioning process would both significantly improve the gas mileage of the truck and extend the useful life to a total of 7 years (with no change in salvage value). The journal entry to record the improvement is:

Delivery truck.......................... 3,000
Cash................................ 3,000

The new balance in the asset account is $19,000 (the original cost plus the improvement). The remaining book value of $7,000 ($19,000 − $12,000) less the estimated salvage value is divided equally over the three remaining years of the estimated life. Thus, the depreciation expense for 19x5, 19x6, and 19x7 would be recorded as follows:

```
Depreciation expense................... 2,000
    Accumulated depreciation.............       2,000
```

Plant and Equipment in the Financial Statements

Plant assets are carried in the balance sheet at their acquisition cost, less any accumulated depreciation. The depreciation on long-term assets is included in the income statement as an expense and is deducted in determining income from operations. Gains or losses on the disposal of long-term assets would appear on the income statement in a special section after income from operations, since they are normally not considered to be a part of the normal operations of the firm.

SUMMARY

The resources of a firm which are used in the continuing operations of a business over a number of years are referred to as plant and equipment or fixed assets. Such assets are generally classified as tangible fixed assets if they have physical substance and are depreciable or non-depreciable assets (land).

Control over tangible fixed assets is usually achieved by the use of a ledger card that includes all data related to the asset item. This card will reflect the cost of the item, which includes all expenditures necessary to place the asset in use as well as the actual invoice price.

Since long-term assets benefit a firm over an extended period of time, the cost of the asset must be allocated in some manner to the periods which benefit from its use. This is achieved through the process of depreciation. In the case of most tangible fixed assets, the depreciation process will result in either a uniform charge for each year (under the straight-line depreciation method) or larger charges in the early years of operation (under the accelerated depreciation methods). In either case, the consistency principle requires that the same method of depreciation be used in all periods. Fixed tangible assets are presented on the balance sheet at their acquisition cost along with an offset or deduction for accumulated depreciation.

Costs incurred for existing assets subsequent to acquisition are classified as either capital expenditures or revenue expenditures. Capital expenditures increase the economic benefits of the existing asset and the cost is debited to an asset account. Revenue expenditures are routine expenditures incurred to maintain an asset in operating condition and such costs are debited to expense.

KEY DEFINITIONS

Accelerated Cost Recovery System (ACRS) ACRS is an accelerated method of depreciation permitted for federal income tax purposes and may also be used for financial accounting purposes.

Accelerated methods of depreciation Accelerated methods of depreciation are techniques for computing depreciation that assume the rate of depreciation decreases with the passage of time.

Capital Expenditures Expenditures which extend the useful life or quality of services provided by plant assets.

Contra account A contra account is an account which is offset against or deducted from another account in the financial statements.

Declining balance method The declining balance method is an accelerated method of depreciation that assumes the rate of depreciation to be some multiple of the rate which would have been used in the case of the straight-line method.

Depreciation Depreciation is the systematic allocation of the cost of an asset, less the salvage value (if any), over its estimated useful life.

Fixed asset ledger card A fixed asset ledger card is prepared for each individual asset purchased. It includes all of the important information relating to the asset and its use.

Plant and equipment Long-term or fixed assets are those resources of a firm which are used in the continuing operations of a business over a number of years.

Revenue Expenditures Expenditures for ordinary maintenance, repairs, and other items necessary for the operation and use of plant and equipment.

Salvage value Salvage value is the residual amount of a long-term tangible asset that the firm expects to recover at the end of the useful life of the asset.

Straight-line depreciation This method of depreciation assumes that factors such as wear and tear and obsolescence are somewhat uniform over time. The method allocates the cost of an asset, less its salvage value, to expenses equally over its useful life.

Sum-of-the-years'-digits method This is an accelerated method of depreciation where the life-years of an asset are totaled and utilized as the denominator of a fraction that uses the number of years of life remaining from the beginning of the year as the numerator.

Tangible fixed asset A tangible fixed asset is a long-term asset that has physical substance.

QUESTIONS

1. Which expenditures are included in the total cost of a fixed asset?

2. What is the purpose of depreciation accounting?

3. What factors should be considered when determining periodic depreciation?

4. Explain the equations used in calculating straight-line, double-declining balance, and sum-of-the-years'-digits depreciation.

5. Four basic depreciation methods are straight-line, sum-of-the-years'-digits, double-declining balance and ACRS. In what ways are the four depreciation methods similar? In what ways are they different?

6. What is the purpose of the accumulated depreciation account?

7. What does the balance in the accumulated depreciation account indicate at any given point in time?

8. What is the difference between a capital expenditure and a revenue expenditure?

9. Why is periodic depreciation not recorded for land?

10. What factors must be known to compute depreciation on a plant asset?

11. How is accumulated depreciation reported in the balance sheet?

EXERCISES

12. A machine was purchased for an invoice price of $10,000, F.O.B. destination. The freight charges were $200. Costs of installation amounted to $500. At what cost should the machine be recorded?

13. Determine which of the following accounts is to be debited for each of the transactions below.

    A. Buildings
    B. Accumulated Depreciation
    C. Land
    D. Furniture
    E. Depreciation Expense
    F. Machinery
    G. Insurance Expense
    H. Freight Expense
    I. General Repairs
    J. Legal Fees

    _____ 1. Purchased land and unusable building.
    _____ 2. Paid legal fees for above purchase.
    _____ 3. Constructed new building on site.
    _____ 4. Purchased machinery for building.
    _____ 5. Paid freight on machinery.
    _____ 6. Paid cost of installing machinery.
    _____ 7. Paid minor repairs on building.
    _____ 8. Recorded depreciation of equipment.
    _____ 9. Paid insurance for year on building.
    _____ 10. Purchased office furniture.

14. A machine was installed at a total cost of $8,000, assumed to have an estimated useful life of 5 years and a salvage value of $2,000. Calculate the initial year's depreciation assuming (a) the straight-line method is used, (b) the sum-of-the-years'-digits method is used, (c) the double-declining balance method is used, and (d) ACRS depreciation is used.

15. In each of the following cases, make the journal entry for the initial year of depreciation, assuming the straight-line method is used by Pat Kelly. (Round to the nearest dollar.) The company's accounting period ends on December 31.

   a. Original cost, $9,000; salvage value, $500; useful life, 4 years; purchased on April 1.
   b. Original cost, $25,000; salvage value, $5,000; useful life, 5 years; purchased on October 1.
   c. Original cost, $16,000; salvage value, $0; useful life, 8 years; purchased on December 1.
   d. Original cost $5,000; salvage value, $1,000; useful life, 2 years; purchased on July 31.
   e. Original cost, $30,000; salvage value, $2,000; useful life, 7 years; purchased on May 31.

16. Smith Company paid $100,000 to acquire land, building, and equipment. At the time of acquisition, appraisal values for the individual assets were determined as: land, $30,000; building, $60,000; and equipment, $30,000. What cost should be allocated to the land, building, and equipment, respectively?

17. Putnam Company purchased a new machine on January 1, 19x1 for a $1,000 down payment and a liability for six monthly payments of $2,000 beginning on February 1, 19x1. The machine could have been purchased for a cash price of $8,600. The company paid delivery and installation costs of $400. Prepare the journal entry to record the acquisition of the machine.

18. Which of the following items are capital expenditures and which are revenue expenditures?

   a. Cost of a major overhaul of a machine.
   b. Routine maintenance of a delivery truck.
   c. Replacement of an oil furnace with a gas furnace.
   d. Replacement of stairs with an escalator.
   e. Annual repainting of the administrative offices.
   f. Lubricating, inspecting, and cleaning factory machinery.
   g. Addition to a new wing on the factory building.

PROBLEMS

19. The Carson Carton Company purchased a new cutting machine at an invoice price of $13,000. It paid the seller in time to take advantage of a 3 percent discount. Carson Carton then paid $400 shipping charges and $550 installation costs. However, after the machine was installed, it was discovered that

the electrical wiring in the plant was not adequate to carry the additional current needed by the new asset. The company rewired that section of the building at a cost of $875. At what amount should Carson Carton Company value the new cutting machine on its books?

20. Cutler Cutlery Company purchased a large storage cabinet on January 1, 19x1, at a cost of $7,500. It was assigned an estimated useful life of 5 years and a salvage value of $500. Prepare a depreciation schedule for the cabinet under the straight-line, double-declining balance, sum-of-the-years'-digits and ACRS methods.

21. For each of the depreciation methods listed, complete the following schedule of depreciation over the first two years of the life of equipment costing $8,800 and having a salvage value of $800. The equipment has an estimated life of 5 years.

Method	Year	Depreciation Expense	Accumulated Depreciation	Book Value
Straight-line	1	$ _____	$ _____	$ _____
Straight-line	2	_____	_____	_____
Sum-of-the-years'-digits	1	_____	_____	_____
Sum-of-the-years'-digits	2	_____	_____	_____
Double-declining balance	1	_____	_____	_____
Double-declining balance	2	_____	_____	_____
ACRS	1	_____	_____	_____
ACRS	2	_____	_____	_____

22. During the course of your audit of Confused, Inc. for the year ended December 31, 19x2, you find the following account:

Equipment

(a) 20,000	(c) 3,400
(b) 14,000	(d) 6,600

Key:
(a) Cost of machine A purchased on January 1, 19x1.
(b) Cost of machine B purchased on January 1, 19x1.
(c) Credit resulting from the recording of depreciation expense for 19x1. (Debit was to "depreciation expense.")
(d) Credit resulting from the recording of the sale of machine B on April 1, 19x2. (Debit was to cash.)

Each machine had an estimated life of ten years with no salvage value anticipated. The company uses the straight-line method of recording depreciation.

Required:

Give all the adjusting and correcting entries (or entry) required on April 1, 19x2.

23. Snowden Manufacturing Company decided to construct a new plant in 19x1 rather than continue to rent its present plant. On January 1, 19x1, the company purchased 10 acres of land with two old buildings standing on it. The old

buildings were demolished and construction of the new plant was begun. The company set up a Land and Buildings account to which all expenditures relating to the new plant were charged.

The balance in the Land and Buildings account after completion of the plant was $740,450. Entries in the account during the construction period were:

a.	Cost of land and old buildings (old buildings appraised at $17,000).....................	$137,000
b.	Legal fees involved in securing title to property.............	250
c.	Cost of demolishing old buildings.......................	9,500
d.	Surveying costs..	1,200
e.	Price paid for construction of new building................	425,000
f.	Salary paid to Jim Seales, engineer, supervisor of construction of new plant............................	12,500
g.	Fencing of plant property...............................	3,000
h.	Machinery for new plant................................	113,000
i.	Installation costs of new machinery......................	9,500
j.	Landscaping of grounds................................	6,250
k.	Office equipment.......................................	12,000
l.	Payment to architect for designing plans and for services during construction.........................	13,000
m.	Paneling and finishing work done on executive offices...	2,250
	Total Debits...	$744,450
n.	Proceeds from sale of scrap from old buildings.............	4,000
	Total Credit...	$ 4,000
	Balance..	$740,450

Required:

Reclassify the items presently in the Land and Buildings account to the proper general ledger accounts.

24. Blintz, Inc. has followed the practice of depreciating its building on a straight-line basis. The building has an estimated useful life of 20 years and a salvage value of $20,000. The company's depreciation expense for 19x3 was $20,000 on the building. The building was purchased on January 1, 19x1.

Required:

1. The original cost of the building.
2. Depreciation expense for 19x2 assuming:

   a. The company has used the double-declining balance method.
   b. The company has used the sum-of-the-years'-digits method.

25. The Silver Fox Company purchased a parcel of land on which was located a large home and a riding stable on January 7, 19x2, for $87,500. Additional expenditures made at the time of settlement were as follows:

Attorney's fees in connection with the purchase	$ 500
Cost of property transfer taxes	1,000
Real estate taxes for 19x1 (the seller was to repay Silver Fox for these taxes)	2,000
Title insurance	500
Broker's commission	500
Gardening equipment	1,000
	$5,500

Silver Fox had the property appraised by a professional appraiser on the purchase date. His appraisal showed the following valuations:

Land	$ 55,000
Home	45,000
Stable	10,000
Total appraised value of property	$110,000

Extensive remodeling and redecorating was undertaken immediately to ready the property for rental. The following outlays were made during the month of January:

Cost of tearing down the stable	$ 10,000
Cost of removing fourth story of home	35,000
Architect's fee	15,000
Replacement of plumbing	11,000
New electrical wiring	14,000
Landscaping	25,000
Payment of hospital bill of passer-by injured by falling debris	5,000
	$115,000
Less: Sale of materials salvaged from stable	1
	$114,999

Required:

Indicate the accounts which would be charged with the cost of each of the items listed below. If an item is to be allocated to more than one account, simply list each account that would be charged.

In indicating your answers, use the following code:

Land....................	L	Any expense or loss account......	E
Home...................	H	Any revenue or gain account.....	R
Stable...................	S	Any other account.............	X
Any other asset account......	A		

Purchase price of $87,500................. ( )
Attorney's fees.......................... ( )
Property transfer taxes................... ( )
Real estate taxes for 19x1................ ( )
Title insurance.......................... ( )
Broker's commission..................... ( )
Gardening equipment.................... ( )
Cost of tearing down stable.............. ( )
Cost of tearing down fourth
   floor of home....................... ( )
Architect's fee.......................... ( )
Plumbing............................... ( )
Electrical wiring......................... ( )
Landscaping............................ ( )
Hospital bill............................ ( )
Sale of materials salvaged
   from stable.......................... ( )

26. On October 30, 19x1, Thomas Brothers, Inc. purchased a used machine for $7,800 from a company in a neighboring state. The machine could not be shipped until November 15 so Thomas Brothers were forced to pay $150 storage costs and $35 insurance fees. After the asset was received and $250 shipping costs had been paid, it was overhauled and installed at a cost of $320, including parts costing $130. On December 21, additional repair work was performed at a cost of $180 in order to put the asset in working condition. At what value should this machine be recorded on the balance sheet on December 31?

27. For each of the depreciation methods listed, complete the following schedule of depreciation over the first two years of the life of equipment costing $57,500. The equipment is expected to have a salvage value of $7,500 at the end of 5 years.

Method	Year	Depreciation Expense	Accumulated Depreciation	Book Value
Straight-line	1	$ _____	$ _____	$ _____
Straight-line	2	_____	_____	_____
Sum-of-the-years'-digits	1	_____	_____	_____
Sum-of-the-years'-digits	2	_____	_____	_____
Double-declining balance	1	_____	_____	_____
Double-declining balance	2	_____	_____	_____
ACRS	1	_____	_____	_____
ACRS	2	_____	_____	_____

10 | Long-Term Assets Plant and Equipment: Depreciation

28. Crowley Company decided to construct a new plant in order to meet the rising demand for its product. On January 1, 19x1, the company purchased five acres which adjoin their present plant site. The land had an old barn on it and a number of trees which had to be cleared before construction could begin. A Land & Buildings account was charged with all expenditures relating to the new plant. Entries in the account included:

a.	Cost of land...................................	$ 50,000
b.	Survey costs..................................	750
c.	Legal fees involved in securing title to property.....	500
d.	Cost of clearing trees and removing barn..........	1,600
e.	Proceeds from sale of trees for lumber............	(2,000)
f.	Construction costs for new plant................	375,000
g.	Cost of parking lot at new plant................	87,000
h.	Machinery for new plant.......................	167,500
i.	Shipping costs for machinery....................	875
j.	Installation cost of machinery..................	980
k.	Office equipment..............................	7,800
l.	Office supplies................................	690
m.	Raw materials to be used in production of product..	10,750
	Balance......................................	$701,445

Required:

Reclassify the items presently in the Land & Buildings account to the proper general ledger accounts.

Refer to the Annual Report included in the Appendix at the end of the text:

29. Comparing the two years, what is the change in gross investment in real estate and plant and equipment?

30. What causes the difference in the change in net investment and in the change in gross investment mentioned above?

31. Which account included in the asset sections always carries a credit balance?

32. What is the balance in the accumulated depreciation account at the end of the most recent year?

33. Why does an asset account carry a credit balance?

34. What is the amount of the intangible assets at the end of the most recent year?

35. Where else in the financial statements does the change in accumulated depreciation appear?

36. Referring to the above question, how is this shown?

37. What is the total of net fixed assets for GM at the end of the most recent year?

Learning Objectives

Chapter 11 discusses the accounting procedures used for the disposition of plant and equipment, and the accounting for intangible assets and natural resources. Studying this chapter should enable you to:

1. Record the disposition of plant and equipment.

2. Discuss the nature of intangible assets and the computation of amortization.

3. Explain the concept of depletion of natural resources.

11
Plant and Equipment
Intangible Assets
and Natural Resources

INTRODUCTION

At some point in time, the cost of continuing to use a particular asset will exceed the benefits derived from its use and it will be to the advantage of the firm to dispose of it. Upon disposal of an asset, the cost of the asset must be removed from the asset account and the accumulated depreciation at the date of disposal also must be removed from the accumulated depreciation account.

For example, assume that after using the Chevrolet as a taxi for four years, it was sold for $1,000, its book value at that time. (Recall that the auto had an original cost of $9,000, an estimated life of four years, and an anticipated salvage value of $1,000.) The entry to record the sale of the Chevrolet would be as follows:

Cash	1,000	
Accumulated depreciation	8,000	
Automobile		9,000

The debit to cash records the amount of cash received while the debit to accumulated depreciation and the credit to automobile remove the automobile and its related accumulated depreciation account from the books of Your Taxi Company. In this example, the estimate of useful life and salvage value were precise. This would occur only infrequently in actual practice.

At the time of the disposal of an asset, if the book value of the asset (cost less accumulated depreciation) is not exactly equal to the amount received from the sale, the difference is a gain or loss on disposal. If the selling price exceeds the book value there is a gain, while if the sales price is less than book value there is a loss. Such gains or losses are included in the income statement in the determination of income from operations.

For example, if the same Chevrolet were sold at the end of the fourth year for $1,100, the entry to record this transaction would be as follows:

Cash	1,100	
Accumulated depreciation	8,000	
Automobile		9,000
Gain		100

The only difference between this entry and the preceding entry is that the amount of cash received increased from $1,000 to $1,100. This amount exceeds the book value of the asset (original cost of $9,000 less accumulated depreciation of $8,000 or $1,000) and therefore a gain ($1,100 minus $1,000 or $100) is realized. On the other hand, if the car had been sold for $350, a loss would have been incurred. The calculation of the gain and/or loss on the disposal of the automobile in all three cases mentioned above may be summarized as follows:

	A	B	C
Selling price.............................		$1,000	$1,100	$350
Cost of automobile..................... $9,000			
Accumulated depreciation............... (8,000)			
Book value...........................	(1,000)	(1,000)	(1,000)
Gain (loss) on the sale of the automobile.....	$ 0	$ 100	($650)

The entries for the disposal of the asset under Cases A and B have been presented above. The entry for Case C, the loss situation, is as follows:

Cash...................................	350	
Accumulated depreciation..................	8,000	
Loss...................................	650	
Automobile............................		9,000

Again, the only difference between this entry and the two preceding entries is the amount of cash received, $350. Since the cash received was less than the book value of the automobile ($9,000 less $8,000 or $1,000) a loss equal to the difference ($1,000 less $350 or $650) occurred and should be recorded in the accounts.

In some instances, an asset may be discarded prior to the end of its useful life. For example, assume that the automobile was involved in an accident at the end of its third year of use and was damaged to the extent that repairs were not considered to be feasible. The entry to record the loss from the accident would be as follows:

Loss...................................	3,000	
Accumulated depreciation..................	6,000*	
Automobile............................		9,000

*For purposes of the example, it was assumed that the straight-line method of depreciation was used.

Of course, the taxi would probably be insured. If this was the case and $1,000 was received from an insurance policy on the automobile, the entry would be as follows:

Cash...................................	1,000	
Accumulated depreciation..................	6,000*	
Loss...................................	2,000	
Automobile............................		9,000

*For purposes of the example, it was assumed that the straight-line method of depreciation had been used.

In any case, cash is debited for the amount received (if any), accumulated depreciation is debited for the depreciation taken to the date of disposal, and the asset is credited for its original cost in order to remove these accounts from the books. A loss (or gain) is recorded for the difference between the book value of the asset and the cash received (if any).

In each of the illustrations included above, it was assumed that the disposal of the asset took place at the end of the period. If the disposal is made during the period, the only difference would be that an entry would be required to record the depreciation for the period from the end of the preceding year up to the date of the disposal. The entry to record the disposal itself would be exactly the same as those illustrated above.

In the above examples it was assumed that cash was received in the disposition of the asset. In some cases, however, a plant asset may be simply retired from productive service. When this occurs, the asset's cost and accumulated depreciation are removed from the accounts, and any difference is recorded as a loss on retirement.

Trade-Ins

In acquiring assets, a firm will frequently trade in an old asset in purchasing the new asset. In these cases, a trade-in allowance is given on the old asset and the balance of the purchase price is paid in cash or by a combination of cash and debt. The accounting procedures used in recording a trade-in depend on whether the assets exchanged are *similar* (an automobile traded in on another automobile) or *dissimilar* (an automobile traded in on a printing press). When items of property, plant, and equipment are acquired by trading in a *dissimilar* asset, the transaction should be accounted for using the fair market values of the assets involved as the base. Thus, the cost of the acquired asset is the fair market value of the assets given up (old asset and cash) or the fair market value of the asset acquired, if its fair value is more clearly determinable. Any difference between the fair value of the asset surrendered and the book value of the old asset should be recognized as a gain or a loss on the disposition of the old asset. Caution must be used in determining and recording the fair values of the assets involved, as the quoted list prices of new assets and trade-in allowances are often not good or accurate indicators of actual or true market values. Dealers often establish list prices that are in excess of the actual cash price to allow them to offer inflated trade-in allowances to their customers.

When *similar* assets are exchanged, a loss may be recognized based upon the fair market value of the asset traded in but not a gain. If the terms of the exchange of similar assets indicates that there is a gain, this "gain" is not recognized. Rather, the new asset is recorded at an amount equal to the total of the book value of the old asset traded in and the cash paid. The logic supporting the nonrecognition of gains is that the income of a firm should not be increased by the act of substituting a new productive asset for an old one. The "gain" is recognized in future years because the recorded cost of the new asset will be less than if the gain was recognized in the current period. Thus, depreciation expense will be less in future years (and income greater) because of the reduced recorded cost of the new asset.

Assume that Your Taxi Company traded in its Chevrolet on a new asset on January 1, 19x5. The following data will be used in the example:

List-price of the new asset	$10,000
Cost of the Chevrolet (at January 1, 19x1)	9,000
Accumulated depreciation on the Chevrolet (at December 31, 19x4)	8,000
Trade-in allowance	500
Fair market value of the Chevrolet (at January 1, 19x5)	200
Cash difference paid	9,500

The entry to record the acquisition of the new asset would be as follows:

New asset	9,700	
Accumulated depreciation	8,000	
Loss	800	
Automobile		9,000
Cash		9,500

The debit to new asset records the $9,700 "cost" of the new asset as the $9,500 cash paid plus the $200 fair market value of the Chevrolet traded-in. The debit to accumulated depreciation of $8,000 and the credit to automobile of $9,000 remove the original cost of the Chevrolet and its related accumulated depreciation from the accounts. The debit to loss of $800 records the loss on the disposal of the Chevrolet and was calculated as follows:

Original cost of the Chevrolet	$9,000
Less: Accumulated depreciation as of the date of trade-in	8,000
Book value of the Chevrolet at the date of trade-in	$1,000
Less: Fair market value of the Chevrolet at the date of the trade-in	200
Loss	$ 800

The credit to cash of $9,500 records the cash outlay which was made in order to acquire the new asset.

If, in the above example, the fair market value of the old car was not available, but it was known that the new asset could have been acquired for a cash price of $9,800, this value would have been used in recording the acquisition of the new asset. In this situation, the apparent value of the old asset is $300 ($9,800 − $9,500) even though the trade-in allowance is stated at $500. Thus, the loss on this exchange is $700, the difference between the actual or apparent trade-in value ($300) and the book value ($1,000) of the old asset. The entry required to record this transaction would be as follows:

New asset	9,800	
Accumulated depreciation	8,000	
Loss	700	
Automobile		9,000
Cash		9,500

In the above example, there was a loss on the trade, so the entries would be the same whether the assets were similar or dissimilar.

We will now modify the example as follows:

Trade-in allowance....................................	$1,500
Fair market value of the Chevrolet (at January 1, 19x5).......	1,500
Cash difference paid..................................	8,300

These facts indicate a gain on the disposal of the Chevrolet, calculated as follows:

Fair market value of the Chevrolet at the date of the trade-in..................		$1,500
Original cost of the Chevrolet..............	$9,000	
Less: Accumulated depreciation as of the date of trade-in.................	8,000	
Book value of the Chevrolet at the date of the trade-in..........................		1,000
Gain		$ 500

If the assets are dissimilar, the entry to record the acquisition of the new asset would be as follows:

New asset...............................	9,800	
Accumulated depreciation...................	8,000	
Automobile		9,000
Cash		8,300
Gain		500

If the assets are assumed to be similar, the entry required to record the trade would be as follows:

New asset...............................	9,300	
Accumulated depreciation...................	8,000	
Automobile		9,000
Cash		8,300

Note that the debit of $9,300 to the new asset is the total of the cash paid and the book value of the asset traded in ($8,300 + $1,000).

In the preceding examples, the trade-in took place at the beginning of the period. If a trade-in is made during the period, depreciation should be recognized on the old asset for the period up to the time of the trade-in, and the entry to record the exchange should recognize the book value of the old asset as of the date of exchange.

In APB, *Opinion No. 29*, "Accounting for Nonmonetary Transactions" (1973), the Accounting Principles Board recognized several exceptions to the general requirement of using market values to determine the gain or loss on the exchange of nonmonetary assets. The circumstances which require exceptions to the general rule include:

1. If market values are not determinable within reasonable limits.
2. If the general rule indicates a gain, and the exchange is:

   a. An exchange of inventory between dealers to facilitate sales to customers other than the parties involved in the exchange.
   b. An exchange of *similar* productive assets not held for sale.

3. If nonmonetary assets are transferred to owners in a spin-off, or other forms of reorganization.

The details of the accounting procedures required to record the other exceptions are beyond the scope of this text.

For federal income tax purposes, a gain or loss is never recognized on the exchange of similar productive assets. Rather, the cost of the new asset is considered to be the book value (cost less accumulated depreciation) of the old asset plus the additional cash paid (or cash and debt incurred) in the exchange.

Natural Resources

In addition to plant assets such as property, plant, and equipment described in the earlier sections of this chapter, a firm may also own assets in the form of natural resources. These resources include such items as oil deposits, tracts of timber, and coal deposits. Like the other long-term assets of the firm, the basis for accounting for these resources is primarily cost. As these resources are converted into salable inventory by drilling, cutting, and mining operations, the cost of these operations along with the original cost of the resources themselves are transferred to expense.

The process of writing off or amortizing the cost of these natual resources is generally referred to as depletion. Since the natural resource provides a salable product, the depletion charges are included in inventory costs as production occurs and cost of goods sold as the natural resource is sold. The primary difference between depreciation and depletion is that depreciation represents the allocation of the cost of a productive asset in relation to the decline in service potential, while depletion represents the allocation of cost of a natural resource in relation to the quantitative physical exhaustion of the resource.

Depletion Base and Amortization

The depletion base of any wasting asset is the total cost of acquiring and developing the property less the estimated residual value of the land after the natural resource has been economically exhausted. The total cost of the natural resource may be classified in three categories: (1) acquisition cost of the property, (2) exploration costs, and (3) development costs.

Generally, depletion for the period is determined on the basis of the relationship between actual production for the period and total estimated production during the economic life of the resource. To apply this approach, the quantity of economically recoverable units of the natural resource must be estimated. Then the total cost of the natural resource less any estimated residual value is divided by the estimated number of recoverable units to obtain a cost per unit of output. This cost per unit is multiplied by the number of units extracted during the period to determine the depletion charge.

To illustrate this process, consider the following example:

1. An oil field is acquired at a cost of $1,000,000. Geological surveys indicate that a total of approximately 400,000 barrels of oil will ultimately be taken from the field.
2. The estimated residual value of the field after the oil has been extracted is approximately $200,000 (net of restoration costs).
3. During the first year of operations, the drilling costs total $75,000. A total of 25,000 barrels of oil are extracted and sold at a price of $40 per barrel.

These transactions would be recorded as follows:

Acquisition of the Field

Oil field	1,000,000	
Cash		1,000,000

Drilling during the First Year

Inventory of oil	75,000	
Cash		75,000
Inventory of oil	50,000	
Accumulated depletion—oil field		50,000

The $75,000 cost of drilling was assumed to be entirely applicable to the oil taken during the year and was therefore assigned to the inventory of oil as a part of its costs. The depletion of $50,000 was calculated as follows:

Cost of the field	$1,000,000
Estimated residual value of the field	200,000
Cost of the 400,000 barrels of oil	$ 800,000
Divide by 400,000 in order to obtain the cost per barrel	$2
$2 × 25,000 barrels extracted	$50,000

The total cost per barrel would be the cost of the oil, that is the depletion per barrel, of $2 plus the drilling cost of $3 per barrel[1] or $5.

Sale of the 25,000 Barrels of Oil

Cash.	1,000,000	
Sales.		1,000,000
Cost of goods sold.	125,000	
Inventory of oil.		125,000

Frequently, additional development costs may be incurred after the production begins or estimates of recoverable units are revised based on production data. In either case, a revision in the unit depletion charge is necessary. In the revision process, a new rate is determined by dividing the unamortized total cost less the estimated residual value by the estimate of the remaining recoverable units.

The procedures described above are known as cost depletion and are required for accounting and financial reporting purposes. For income tax purposes, firms use either depletion based on cost or percentage depletion. Further, if cost depletion is used for tax purposes, the amount of periodic tax depletion need not be equal to the cost depletion determined for financial reporting purposes. It is often advantageous from a tax standpoint to use the percentage depletion method, since depletion calculated by this method frequently exceeds depletion on a cost basis. Furthermore, in many cases it allows the taxpayer to deduct more than the cost of the property over its useful life. The percentage depletion method allows the firm to deduct from revenues a given percentage of gross income depletion without regard to the number of units produced or the cost of the property. In this method, the amount of depletion for tax purposes may exceed the total cost of the natural resource. Percentage depletion is not acceptable for financial accounting purposes.

Accounting for Oil and Gas Producers

Normally the exploration costs of oil and gas companies are substantial. There have been two methods which have long been used by oil and gas companies to account for costs incurred in the exploration, development and production of crude oil and natural gas—the successful efforts method and the full cost method. The larger oil and gas companies have tended to use the successful efforts method; the smaller companies have tended to use the full cost method.

Under the successful efforts method, only the costs of successful drilling

---

[1] Drilling costs of $75,000 divided by the 25,000 barrels extracted, or $3 per barrel.

efforts are capitalized and subsequently charged against the revenue of the producing wells. Costs in connection with nonproducing wells are written off as expenses in the period incurred. Under the full cost method, the costs of both successful and unsuccessful drilling efforts are capitalized and amortized against subsequent petroleum production in the same relatively large cost center (e.g., a country or a continent).

There has been considerable pressure on the accounting profession to eliminate the alternatives available for accounting for exploratory costs in the oil and gas industry. In December 1977, the FASB issued Statement No. 19, "Financial Accounting and Reporting by Oil and Gas Producers," which essentially required the adoption of a form of the successful efforts method by all oil and gas producers. However, in Accounting Series Release No. 253 issued in August 1978, the SEC rejected the FASB's attempt to eliminate use of the full cost method, asserting that both cost-based methods were so inadequate that it did not matter which method was employed.

In 1982, the FASB issued Statement No. 69, "Disclosures about Oil and Gas Producing Activities," which superceded the disclosure requirements of all previous FASB statements concerned with oil and gas producing activities. In applying Statement No. 69, companies are required to disclose information about quantities of reserves, capitalized costs, costs incurred, and a standardized measure of discounted cash flows related to proved reserves.

Intangible Assets

Intangible assets are resources such as organization costs, trademarks, patents, copyrights, and goodwill which have value but do not have physical substance. An intangible asset derives its value from certain special rights and privileges which accrue to the firm which owns it. For example, the ownership of a patent has value because it gives the owner of the patent exclusive right to the manufacture, sale, or other use of an invention or process for a period of 17 years.

A firm may obtain an intangible asset by purchase or by development within the firm. The objectives of accounting for intangible assets are similar to those for tangible assets which were described earlier in the chapter—the cost of the asset is recorded upon acquisition and this cost is allocated to expense over the useful life of the intangible. The cost of an intangible asset includes all expenditures which are incurred in the acquisition of the rights or privileges. The cost of an intangible asset acquired by purchase can usually be measured with little difficulty. The cost of internally developed intangibles is often more difficult to determine. For example, it may be quite difficult to estimate how much of the total research and development cost for a particular period should be allocated to the development of a single patent. For this reason the cost of internally developed patents includes only legal fees. Any other costs incurred in developing the patent are expenses as they are incurred. This treatment is consistent with the handling of research and development costs in general.

The costs of intangible assets are written off to expense over their estimated useful lives in a manner similar to the depreciation of tangible fixed assets. This is referred to as amortization. Amortization is recorded by a debit to amortization expense and a credit to the intangible asset account. Like tangible fixed assets, the cost of intangibles should be amortized over their estimated useful lives. However, according to Accounting Principles Board *Opinion No. 17,* the period of amortization should not exceed a maximum of 40 years. The Board also concluded that the straight-line method of amortization should be used unless the firm shows evidence that some other systematic method is more appropriate in the circumstances.

To illustrate the accounting for intangible assets, assume that Landry Company purchased a patent from Allen Company for $10,000 on January 1, 19x1. The purchase would be recorded as follows:

```
Patents ..................................... 10,000
    Cash ....................................          10,000
```

If the remaining useful or economic life of the patent was ten years, the adjusting entry required to record the amortization of the patent at the end of each year of its useful life would be as follows:

```
Amortization expense ......................... 1,000
    Patents ...................................          1,000
```

Note that the amortization is credited directly to the asset account rather than to an accumulated amortization account as in the case of tangible fixed assets. There appears to be no logical reason for this procedure other than tradition.

Certain intangibles, such as patents, copyrights, and franchises, may be identified with a specific right or privilege. The costs of these intangibles when purchased can be measured and amortized or allocated to expense over their useful lives. Other intangibles, however, cannot be specifically identified. This type of intangible is usually referred to as goodwill. The intangible asset goodwill represents the sum of all the special advantages which are not identifiable and which relate to the business as a whole. It encompasses such items as a favorable location, good customer relations, and superior ability of management. The existence of such factors enables the firm to earn an above normal rate of return.

Unlike tangible assets or identifiable intangible assets, goodwill cannot be sold or acquired separately from the business as a whole. Because of the uncertainty involved in estimating the goodwill of a business enterprise, goodwill is normally recorded only when a business is acquired by purchase. In a purchase transaction, goodwill may be measured as the excess of the purchase price of an entity over the sum of the fair values of all its identifiable assets less its liabilities. The source of this excess is the potential of the firm to earn an above average rate of return.

To illustrate, assume that Richard Smith purchased the Campus Book Store on January 1, 19x1, for $100,000 cash. Further assume that the identifiable assets were determined to have a total fair value of $90,000 at the date of purchase (including inventory, $10,000; equipment, $20,000; building, $40,000; and land, $20,000). The liabilities assumed by the purchaser were accounts payable of $20,000. The $30,000 excess of the purchase price over the value of all the identifiable assets less the liabilities represents the value of the goodwill. The purchase would be recorded as follows:

Inventory	10,000	
Equipment	20,000	
Building	40,000	
Land	20,000	
Goodwill	30,000	
Accounts Payable		20,000
Cash		100,000

Once goodwill is recorded in a purchase transaction, it is amortized like all other intangible assets—the recorded cost is allocated to expense over its estimated life with a maximum of 40 years.

Many businesses engage in research and development (R&D) activities in order to develop new products or processes, or to improve present products. A problem in accounting for R&D expenditures lies in determining the amount and timing of the future benefits which are associated with such activities. Prior to 1974, there was considerable diversity in the procedures used in accounting for R&D costs. In 1974, however, the FASB issued its *Statement No. 2* which simplified the accounting for R&D expenditures by requiring that most research and development costs should be charged to expense as they are incurred. This treatment eliminated the need to assess the uncertain future benefits associated with R&D costs and to measure the cause and effect relationship of these costs for accounting purposes.

FASB *Statement No. 2* stated that R&D costs include the costs of materials, personnel, purchased intangibles, contract services, and a reasonable allocation of indirect costs which are specifically related to R&D activities and have no alternative future uses. Disclosure should be made in the financial statements of the total R&D costs charged to expense for each period for which an income statement is presented.

SUMMARY

Eventually, the economic usefulness of an item of plant and equipment expires and the asset must be sold, scrapped, retired or traded-in on a new asset. When an asset is disposed of, the cost of the asset is removed from the asset account and the accumulated depreciation balance is eliminated. When a plant asset is sold, there is a gain or loss equal to the difference between the asset's book value (cost less accumulated depreciation) and its sales price.

When an old asset is traded in on a new asset, the accounting treatment depends upon the nature of the assets involved. If the assets are dissimilar, the cost of the new asset is equal to the fair market value of the old asset plus the cash paid, and a gain or loss on the disposition of the old asset is recognized for the difference between the book value and the fair market value at the date of exchange. If the assets are similar, the accounting treatment is the same as for dissimilar assets if a loss is indicated. However, if the fair market value is greater than the book value of the old asset, no gain is recognized and the new asset is recorded at the book value of the old asset plus the cash paid.

Identifiable intangible assets, which generally involve property rights rather than physical property, are written off in a similar manner referred to as amortization. Goodwill differs from tangible assets and identifiable intangible assets in that it cannot be sold or acquired separate from the business. Therefore, due to the uncertainty of measuring goodwill, it is only recorded and amortized if purchased with a business already in existence. A similar uncertainty exists in matching expenses incurred by research and development efforts with possible future revenues resulting from these efforts. Therefore, R&D expenditures are considered expenses of the period in which they are incurred.

Allocation of the cost of natural resources is referred to as depletion. For financial accounting purposes, depletion must be calculated on a cost basis over the estimated units to be produced. However, for tax purposes, firms must take the higher of cost depletion or a specified percentage of gross income (referred to as percentage depletion).

KEY DEFINITIONS

Accumulated depreciation Accumulated depreciation is a contra account which appears as an offset or deduction from the related asset account in the balance sheet. The depreciation taken over the useful life of the asset is accumulated in this account.

Book value of an asset The book value of an asset is the cost of an asset less accumulated depreciation. The book value of an asset is the remaining undepreciated cost.

Depletion Depletion is the process of writing-off or amortizing the cost of natural resources over the periods which benefit from their use.

Goodwill Goodwill may be measured as the excess of the purchase price of an entity over the sum of the fair values of all its identifiable assets less its liabilities.

Intangible fixed asset An intangible fixed asset is one that does not have physical substance, usually a property right.

QUESTIONS

1. When a plant asset is disposed of for cash, how is the gain or loss on the sale determined?

2. If an old asset is traded in on a dissimilar new asset, how should the cost basis of the new asset be measured?

3. Explain the rules for recognizing gains or losses on the exchange of similar productive assets.

4. Over what period should the cost of an intangible asset be amortized?

5. When should goodwill be recorded in the accounts?

6. Discuss the appropriate accounting treatment of research and development costs.

7. List some possible causes of goodwill.

8. What is the basis for accounting for natural resources? Is this basis the same as that for other long-term assets?

9. What is depletion? Is it similar to depreciation, and if so, in what way?

10. What is the difference in the accounting for intangible assets and the accounting for tangible assets?

EXERCISES

11. A truck with an original cost of $10,000 and accumulated depreciation to date of $8,000 was traded in on a new truck with a list price of $20,000. The dealer allowed a trade-in allowance of $3,000 on the old truck (which was equal to the fair market value). Give the journal entry to record the exchange.

12. Assume the same facts as in 11, except that the trade-in allowance and the fair market value of the old truck were $1,000. Give the journal entry to record the exchange.

13. A company had a plant asset with an original cost of $15,000 and accumulated depreciation to date of $12,000. Give the journal entry to record the disposition of the asset under the following circumstances:

    a. Sold the asset for $5,000.
    b. Sold the asset for $2,000.
    c. The asset was destroyed by fire; insurance proceeds of $1,500 were received.
    d. Abandoned the asset.

14. The Get Rich Quick Mining Company obtained a uranium mine for $1,350,000 on February 1, 19x1. It is estimated that approximately 335,000 pounds of uranium can be extracted from the mine. The residual value of the property after uranium has been removed is approximately $10,000. In 19x1, 74,000 pounds of uranium were extracted from the mine and in 19x2, 90,000 pounds were extracted. Mining costs were $14,800 for 19x1 and $22,500 for 19x2. The uranium is sold for $10 per pound.

    Required:

    Record the above transactions on the books of the Mining Company.

15. The Bratton Company purchased a patent for $56,000 on January 1, 19x1. Additional legal costs of $4,000 were incurred in obtaining the patent. The patent was estimated to have a useful life of 10 years. (Its legal life is 17 years.) What will be the patent amortization expense for 19x1?

16. From the following information make the necessary journal entries for the trade-in of an asset by the Singleton Company. Assume that the old and new assets were dissimilar.

List-price of new machine	$20,795
Original cost of old machine	18,560
Accumulated depreciation on old machine at trade-in date	10,560
Trade-in allowance	2,000
Fair market value of old machine at trade-in date	1,000
Cash difference paid	18,795

17. Al Bumbry bought Billy's Grocery on March 27 for $250,000 cash. On the date of purchase, the following fair values were determined: inventory, $50,000; equipment, $18,000; building, $68,000; land, $45,000; and accounts payable, $7,000. Make the entry required on the date of purchase.

18. For each of the following items owned by Mark Belanger, determine what the gain or loss will be upon the disposition of the asset and make the necessary journal entries.

    a. Original outlay, $7,900; sales price, $1,750; accumulated depreciation, $6,450.

    b. Original outlay, $13,050; sales price, $5,110; accumulated depreciation, $10,250.

    c. Original outlay, $21,400; sales price, $9,790; accumulated depreciation, $8,330.

    d. Original outlay, $91,625; sales price, $40,000; accumulated depreciation, $40,580.

    e. Original outlay, $47,985; sales price, $25,470; accumulated depreciation, $29,645.

PROBLEMS

19. Anderson Aerospace Company traded in its Boeing 707 for a new Boeing 747 on January 1, 19x5. The following is the pertinent data for the transaction:

Cost of the 707 (at January 1, 19x1)	$785,000
Accumulated depreciation on the 707 (at December 31, 19x4)	300,000
Fair market value of the 707 (at January 1, 19x5)	325,000
List price of the 747	925,000
Trade-in allowance	350,000
Note payable given for difference	575,000

Required:

Record the acquisition of the Boeing 747. Discuss the theoretical validity of this accounting treatment.

20. Marshall Furniture Manufacturers purchased a new lathe on January 1, 19x1, for $1,600. It has an estimated salvage value of $100 and an estimated useful life of 3 years. The company uses the sum-of-the-years'-digits depreciation method and maintains records on a calendar year basis. Prepare the journal entries to record the disposal of the lathe under each of the following independent conditions:

a. Sold for $725 cash on October 1, 19x2.
b. Destroyed by flood on July 1, 19x3. Insurance proceeds were $200.
c. Traded in on purchase of new lathe on January 1, 19x2. List price of new lathe was $2,000, market value of old lathe was $1,200, and $700 cash was paid on the transaction.

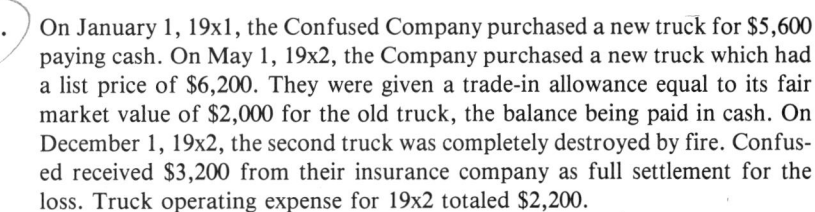

21. On January 1, 19x1, the Confused Company purchased a new truck for $5,600 paying cash. On May 1, 19x2, the Company purchased a new truck which had a list price of $6,200. They were given a trade-in allowance equal to its fair market value of $2,000 for the old truck, the balance being paid in cash. On December 1, 19x2, the second truck was completely destroyed by fire. Confused received $3,200 from their insurance company as full settlement for the loss. Truck operating expense for 19x2 totaled $2,200.

You are called in by the company's accountant who states that in preparing the December 31, 19x2, trial balance he noted that the truck account had a balance of $8,800 although the company does not own any trucks. He also tells you that he failed to record depreciation on either truck during 19x2, although the company's accounting manual requires straight-line depreciation, two-year life, and $800 salvage value for all automotive equipment.

You obtain a copy of the company's ledger account "Trucks," which shows the following:

Trucks	
5,600	2,000
6,200	3,200
2,200	
8,800	

Required:

1. Prepare all journal entries regarding the trucks as they *should* have been made originally.
2. Prepare an entry to correct the accounts as of December 31, 19x2. You may assume that the books have not yet been closed for 19x2.

22. During an audit of Lee May Company for the year ended December 31, 19x2, you find the following account:

Machinery	
(a) 42,000	(b) 7,273
(c) 200	(d) 6,545
	(e) 5,600

Key:

(a) Cost of machinery purchased on January 1, 19x0.
(b) Credit to record the depreciation expense for 19x0. (Debit was to Depreciation Expense.)
(c) Cost of minor repairs which will not lengthen the life of the machine.
(d) Credit to record depreciation expense for 19x1. (Debit was to Depreciation Expense.)
(e) Credit to record sale of machinery on March 31, 19x2.

The machinery had an estimated life of ten years with a salvage value of $2,000. The company uses the sum-of-the-years'-digits method of recording depreciation.

Required:

Give all of the adjusting and correcting entries (or entry) required.

23. King Company purchased a truck on January 1, 19x1, at a cost of $4,200. The truck was depreciated using the straight-line method with an estimated useful life of four years and a salvage value of $200. On January 1, 19x3, the truck was traded in on a new truck with a list price of $6,000. The fair market value of the old truck was $1,500 and the truck dealer gave a trade-in allowance of $2,400 on the old truck. King Company gave a note payable for the balance of the purchase price.

Required:

Record the acquisition of the new truck.

24. A truck was purchased on October 1, 19x1, at a cost of $29,400. The expected life of this truck was 4 years with an expected salvage value of $600. The company used the straight-line depreciation method and the accounting records are maintained on a calendar year basis.

Required:

Prepare journal entries to record the disposal of the truck on *May 1, 19x3* under *each* of the following *separate* conditions:

a. Sold for $18,000 cash.
b. Completely destroyed by fire, and the insurance company paid $6,000 as full settlement of the loss.
c. Traded in on the purchase of another truck which had a cash price of $34,000; trade-in allowance granted on the old truck was equal to its fair market value of $20,000 and the balance was paid in cash.

25. Kelly Company acquired a mine for $2,500,000. It was estimated that the land would have a value of $400,000 after completion of the mining operations, and that 1,000,000 tons of ore could be extracted from the mine. During the first year of operations, 100,000 tons of ore were extracted and additional production costs of $200,000 were incurred.

Required:

Prepare the journal entries to record the acquisition of the property and the cost of production for the year.

Learning Objectives

Chapter 12 discusses the issues related to the accounting for sole proprietorships and partnerships. Studying this chapter should enable you to:

1. Discuss the advantages and disadvantages of the sole proprietorship and partnership forms of business organization.

2. Explain how the owners' equity accounts are affected by investments, withdrawals, and earnings.

3. Identify the purpose of the partnership agreement and the information it normally includes.

4. Summarize the significant characteristics of a partnership.

5. Describe the procedures for recording the formation of a partnership, division of profits and losses, admission and withdrawal of partners, and liquidation of a partnership.

12

**Unincorporated
Business
Organizations**

INTRODUCTION

There are three basic types of business organizations: (1) the sole proprietorship; (2) the partnership; and (3) the corporation. This chapter considers the accounting for unincorporated business organizations—sole proprietorships and partnerships. The following two chapters concentrate on the accounting issues related to corporations.

THE SOLE PROPRIETORSHIP

The simplest form of business organization is the sole-proprietorship, a business owned by a single individual. In terms of the absolute number of business firms, the sole proprietorship greatly outnumbers all other forms of business organizations in the United States. Because of their size, however, corporations account for the greatest dollar amount of both assets and sales. Sole proprietorships are the dominant form of business organization among smaller firms, particularly among businesses engaged in retail trade and in the rendering of services.

One of the principal advantages of the sole proprietorship is the ease of establishing this type of business. Other than local and possibly state licensing requirements, an owner need only have the necessary capital and begin operations in order to establish his firm. Legal contracts are not necessary and the proprietor is not required to comply with provisions of certain regulations or laws which apply to corporations. A proprietor owns, controls, and usually manages the firm's assets and receives the profits (or losses) from its operations. All earnings of the business are taxable to the owner whether he withdraws them from the firm or not. A sole proprietorship is not considered to be a separate entity for income tax purposes.

Usually, the primary disadvantage of a sole proprietorship as a form of business organization is its unlimited liability feature. If the assets of the business are insufficient to meet its obligations, a sole proprietor will be required to satisfy business creditors from his own personal resources. Other principal disadvantages of the sole proprietorship form of business organization include limitations on the availability of funds to the business and difficulties involved in the transferability of ownership. Funds or resources available to a sole proprietorship are limited to the personal assets of the owner and what he is able to borrow. Ownership may be transferred only by selling the entire business or by changing to another form of business organization.

Accounting for a Proprietorship

It is primarily in the accounting for owner's equity that the accounts of an unincorporated business differ significantly from those of a corporation. The owner's equity accounts of a sole proprietorship normally include only a capital account and a drawing account.

The capital account reflects the proprietor's equity in the assets of the business as of a specific point in time. Capital is credited for the investments made by the owner in the business and for the earnings of the period, and it is debited for a net loss during the period.

A separate drawing or withdrawals account may be maintained which is debited for the withdrawals of cash or other business assets made by the owner, or for any payments which are made from business funds in order to satisfy personal debts of the owner. The balance in the drawing account is closed or transferred to the capital account during the preparation of closing entries which are made at the end of the period. As an alternative, the drawing account may be omitted with all changes in the owner's equity recorded directly in the capital account. Either procedure accomplishes the same end result.

THE PARTNERSHIP

A somewhat more complicated form of business organization is the partnership. A major difference between the sole proprietorship and the partnership is that the partnership has more than a single owner. The partnership form of business organization is often used as a means of combining the resources and special skills or talents of two or more persons. In addition, state laws sometimes prevent the incorporation of certain businesses which provide professional services such as certified public accounting firms or associations of physicians. Although only two persons are required to form a partnership, there is no limit as to the number of partners. For example, in some CPA firms there are more than 800 partners.

The Uniform Partnership Act defines a partnership as "an association of two or more persons to carry on, as co-owners, a business for profit." Even though two or more persons may, in fact, operate a business as a partnership without a formal agreement, it is important that a written contract, known as the articles of co-partnership, be drawn up in order to clearly delineate the rights and duties of all partners and thereby avoid possible misunderstandings and disagreements. The partnership agreement serves as the basis for the formation and operation of the partnership. At a minimum, the partnership contract should usually include the following points:

1. Names of all partners.
2. Rights and duties of each partner.
3. Name of the partnership.
4. Nature and location of the business.
5. Effective date and the duration of the agreement.
6. Capital contribution of each partner.
7. Procedures for dividing profits and losses.
8. Any rights or limitations of withdrawals by partners.
9. Accounting period to be used.

10. Provisions for dissolution.
11. Procedures for arbitrating disputes.

Characteristics of a Partnership

The significant characteristics of the partnership form of organization are summarized briefly in the following paragraphs.

Ease of Formation. Partnerships may be formed with little difficulty. As was the case with a sole proprietorship, there are few legal formalities or regulations (aside from local and possibly state licensing requirements) to be complied with.

Mutual Agency. Normally, all partners act as agents of the partnership and as such have the power to enter into contracts in the ordinary course of business. These contracts bind the remaining partners. The concept of mutual agency provides an important reason for the careful selection of partners.

Unlimited Liability. Usually each partner may be held personally liable to partnership creditors for all the debts of the partnership in the event that the partnership assets are insufficient to meet its obligations. If one partner is unable to meet his obligations under the partnership agreement, the remaining partners are liable for these debts.

If a new partner is admitted to a partnership, the partnership agreement should indicate whether he assumes a liability for debts which were incurred prior to his admission into the partnership. When a partner withdraws from a partnership, he is not liable for partnership debts incurred *after* his withdrawal if proper notice has been given to the public, for example, by a legal notice in a newspaper. He is, however, liable for all debts which were incurred prior to his withdrawal unless he is released from these obligations by the creditors of the partnership.

Since any partner may bind the entire partnership when making contracts in the normal scope of business, a lack of good judgment on the part of a single partner could jeopardize both partnership assets and the personal resources of the individual partners. The mutual agency and unlimited liability features may discourage certain individuals with substantial personal resources from entering into a partnership agreement.

Limited Life. Since a partnership is based on a contract, a partnership is legally ended by the withdrawal, death, incapacity, or bankruptcy of any of its partners. Addition of a new partner also terminates the old partnership. Although the entry of a new partner or the exit of an old partner legally dissolves the partnership, the business may be continued without interruption by the formation of a new partnership. This is done on a continual basis by firms of attorneys, doctors, and CPAs.

Co-ownership by Partners. Partners are the co-owners of both the assets and the earnings of a partnership. The assets invested by each partner in the partnership are owned by all of the partners collectively. The income or loss of a partnership is divided among the partners according to the terms which are specified in the partnership agreement. If the partnership agreement specifies a method of dividing profits among the partners but is silent as to the division of losses, losses will be shared in the same manner as profits. If the manner of dividing profits or losses is not specified in the partnership agreement, partners will share profits and losses equally.

Evaluation of the Partnership Form of Organization

The primary disadvantages of organizing a business as a partnership include the unlimited liability of the owners, the mutual agency of all partners, and the limited life of the partnership. However, a partnership has certain advantages over both the sole proprietorship and the incorporated forms of business organization. In comparison to a sole proprietorship, a partnership has the advantage of being able to combine the individual skills or talents of partners and of pooling the capital of several individuals, both of which may be required to carry on a successful business. A partnership is much easier to form than a corporation and is subject to much less governmental regulation. In addition, a partnership may provide certain tax advantages. Like the sole proprietorship, the partnership itself is not subject to taxes. Individual partners are, however, required to pay income taxes on their share of the income of the partnership, whether or not these earnings are withdrawn from the business.

Accounting for a Partnership

The accounting for a partnership is very similar to that of a proprietorship except with regard to specific transactions involving the accounting for owners' equity. Since a partnership is owned by two or more persons, a separate capital account must be maintained for each owner and a separate drawing account may also be used for each partner. Further, the net income or loss for a period must be divided among the partners as specified by the terms of the partnership agreement. Additional accounting problems which are unique to partnerships may occur with the formation of a partnership, admission of a partner, withdrawal or death of a partner, and liquidation of a partnership.

Formation of a Partnership

Upon the formation of a partnership, resources invested by the partners are recorded in the accounts. A capital account for each partner is credited for the amount of net assets invested (assets contributed less liabilities assumed by the partnership). Individual asset accounts are debited for the assets contributed and liability accounts are credited for any debts assumed by the partnership.

If the investments made by the partners are entirely in the form of cash, the entry required would be a debit to cash and a credit to the partner's capital account for the amount of cash invested. When noncash assets such as land, equipment, or merchandise are invested, these assets should be recorded at their fair market values as of the date of investment. The valuations assigned to these assets may differ from the cost or book value of the assets on the books of the contributing partner prior to the formation of the partnership. Of course, the amounts recorded by the partnership must be agreed upon by all partners. Amounts agreed upon represent the acquisition cost of the assets to the newly formed partnership. The recording of assets at their current market value as of the date they were contributed to the partnership is necessary in order to provide a fair presentation in the partnership financial statements, and to assure a fair distribution of the property among partners in the event a dissolution of the partnership occurs.

To illustrate the entries which are required at the formation of a partnership, assume that Mantle and Maris, who operate separate sporting goods stores as sole proprietorships, agree to form a partnership by combining their two businesses. It is agreed that each partner will contribute $10,000 in cash and all of his individual business assets, and that the partnership will assume the liabilities of each of their separate businesses. Assuming that the partners have agreed upon the amounts at which noncash assets are to be recorded, the following journal entries on the books of the partnership would be necessary in order to record the formation of the M & M partnership:

Cash	10,000	
Accounts receivable	15,000	
Merchandise inventory	30,000	
Accounts payable		5,000
Mantle, Capital		50,000
Cash	10,000	
Merchandise inventory	35,000	
Building	50,000	
Land	15,000	
Notes payable		10,000
Maris, Capital		100,000

Division of Profits and Losses

The net income or loss of a partnership is divided among the partners according to the terms or procedures specified in the partnership agreement. As previously indicated, if provisions are made only for dividing profits, any losses are divided in the same manner as profits. In the absence of any provisions for sharing profits and losses in the partnership agreement, the law provides that they must be shared equally among the partners.

The specific method of dividing profits and losses selected in a partnership situation may be designed to recognize and compensate the partners for differences in their investments in the partnership, for differences in their personal services rendered, for special abilities or reputations of individual partners, or for some combination of these and other factors. The following are examples of some of the methods which may be given consideration in the division of partnership profits or losses:

1. A fixed ratio base.
2. A capital ratio base.
3. Interest on capital.
4. Salaries to partners.

The specific method chosen by the partners may incorporate one or more of the methods of dividing partnership profits and losses which are mentioned above and illustrated in the following paragraphs. As a basis for these illustrations, assume that the M & M partnership had net income of $30,000 for the year ended December 31, 19x1. The following capital accounts reflect the investments made by Mantle and Maris during 19x1.

Mantle, Capital	Maris, Capital
1/1/x1 50,000	1/1/x1 100,000
7/1/x1 20,000	5/1/x1 60,000

Fixed Fractional Basis. Partners may agree on any fractional or percentage basis as a means of dividing partnership profits and losses. For example, assume that in order to reflect differences in their initial capital contributions, services provided, and abilities, Mantle and Maris agreed to allocate one-fourth of any profits or losses to Mantle and three-fourths to Maris. Consequently, at the end of 19x1 the $30,000 net income would be allocated $7,500 to Mantle (¼ × $30,000) and $22,500 to Maris (¾ × $30,000). The division of net income is recorded with a closing entry—the income summary account is closed to each partner's individual capital account according to the terms of the partnership agreement. The entry required in order to divide the net income among the two partners is as follows:

```
Income summary ............................. 30,000
    Mantle, Capital ...........................        7,500
    Maris, Capital ............................       22,500
```

Additional closing entries are also necessary in order to transfer any balances in the partners' drawing accounts to their respective capital accounts.

Capital Ratio. When the invested capital of a partnership is a major factor in the generation of income, net income is often divided on the basis of the relative capital balances of the partners. If a capital ratio is used, the partners must agree whether the beginning capital balances or average capital balances should be used.

For example, the partners may agree to distribute net income on the basis of capital balances at the beginning of the period. Division of the $30,000 net income of the M & M partnership on the basis of the ratio of the partners' beginning capital balances would be as follows:

Partner	Capital Balance 1/1/x1	Fraction of Total Capital	Division of Income
Mantle	$ 50,000	$50/$150 or 1/3	$10,000
Maris	100,000	$100/$150 or 2/3	20,000
Total	$150,000		$30,000

Thus, the income summary account would be closed to the partners' capital accounts at the end of the year by the following journal entry.

```
Income summary ............................. 30,000
    Mantle, Capital .............................        10,000
    Maris, Capital ..............................        20,000
```

In order to reflect any significant changes in the capital accounts which may occur during a period in the division of income, the partners may agree to use the average capital balance ratio as a means of sharing partnership income. The average capital balance for each partner is equal to the weighted average of the different balances in their capital account during a period. In order to compute the weighted average, each balance in a partner's capital account is multiplied by the number of months until the next transaction affected the balance or to the end of the period. The sum of these amounts is divided by 12 in order to yield the partner's average capital balance during the period.

For purposes of illustration we will assume that Mantle's capital balance at the beginning of the year was $50,000 and that Maris's was $100,000. Maris invested an additional $60,000 on May 1 and Mantle invested an additional $20,000 on July 1. The computation of the average capital balance for Mantle and Maris is as follows:

Partner	Date	Balance × Time	Total			Weighted Average
Mantle	1/1/x1	$ 50,000 × 6	= $ 300,000			
	7/1/x1	70,000 × 6	= 420,000			
			$ 720,000	÷ 12	=	$ 60,000

Partner	Date	Balance × Time	Total			Weighted Average
Maris	1/1/x1	$100,000 × 4	= $ 400,000			
	5/1/x1	160,000 × 8	= 1,280,000			
			$1,680,000	÷ 12	=	$140,000

After the average capital balances have been computed, the division of net income is based on the ratios of average capital per partner to total average capital. In the case of the M & M partnership, the calculation would be as follows:

Partner	Average Capital	Fraction of Total Average Capital	Division of Income
Mantle	$ 60,000	$60/$200 or 3/10	$ 9,000
Maris	140,000	$140/$200 or 7/10	21,000
Total	$200,000		$30,000

Interest on Capital. In some instances, only partial recognition may be given to unequal investments made by the partners in determining the division of income. This may be accomplished by allowing some fixed rate of interest on the capital balances and dividing remaining profits on some other basis. As in the use of capital ratios, interest may be based on beginning or on average capital balances during the period.

To illustrate, assume that Mantle and Maris agreed to allow each partner interest at the rate of 8 percent on his beginning capital balance, with any remaining profit to be divided equally. Under this agreement, the $30,000 net income for 19x1 would be divided as follows:

	Mantle	Maris	
Income			$30,000
Interest:			
8% × $50,000	$ 4,000		$ 4,000
8% × $100,000		$ 8,000	8,000
			$12,000
Remainder:			$18,000
$18,000 × ½	$ 9,000		$ 9,000
$18,000 × ½		$ 9,000	9,000
Total	$13,000	$17,000	$30,000

Salaries to Partners. As a means of recognizing differences in the value of personal services contributed to the partnership by individual partners, the partnership agreement may provide for "salary" allowances in the division of income. For this purpose, the agreed-upon salaries are used in the allocation of income but need not actually be paid to the partners. The partnership agreement may also allow for withdrawals of cash by the partners described as salaries. These withdrawals are treated like all withdrawals made by partners and debited to the drawing accounts; they are *not* salary expenses similar to those paid to employees. Salary allowances may be used in the division of partnership income whether or not the partners make any cash withdrawals.

To illustrate, assume that Mantle and Maris are allowed annual salaries of $6,000 and $8,000 respectively, with any remaining profits divided equally. The following division of the $30,000 profit for 19x1 would be made:

	Mantle	Maris	Total
Salaries............	$ 6,000	$ 8,000	$14,000
Remainder..........	8,000	8,000	16,000
Total............	$14,000	$16,000	$30,000

Salaries and Interest on Capital. Sometimes both the investments of the individual partners and the value of personal services contributed by each may be quite different. In these situations, partners may agree to take into consideration both salaries and interest on capital investments in determining the division of income. Any remaining profit or loss may then be allocated on any agreed-upon fractional basis.

For example, assume that Mantle and Maris agree on the following division of income:

1. Annual salaries of $6,000 to Mantle and $8,000 to Maris.
2. Eight percent interest on beginning capital balances.
3. Any remainder to be divided equally.

Under this agreement, the $30,000 net income for 19x1 would be divided as follows:

	Mantle	Maris	Total
Salaries (per agreement)	$ 6,000	$ 8,000	$14,000
Interest:			
8% × $50,000.............	4,000		4,000
8% × $100,000............		8,000	8,000
Remainder.................	2,000	2,000	4,000
Total..................	$12,000	$18,000	$30,000

Allowing salaries or interest on capital is simply a procedure or step in the process of dividing partnership profits. Since partners are owners, their contributions of capital and personal services are made in an attempt to earn profits. Therefore, these amounts are not considered to be expenses and do not reduce the income of the business.

Salaries And/Or Interest in Excess of Income. In the previous illustrations, partnership net income exceeded the total salary and interest allowances to the partners, and the balance was divided between the partners according to the agreed-upon percentage. If net income is less than the sum of the allowable salaries and interest, or if there is a net loss for the period, the residual after the deduction of salaries and interest will be negative in amount. This negative amount must then be divided between the partners according to the agreed-upon fractional basis.

To illustrate this situation, assume the same salary and interest allowances as in the previous example. Further, assume that the M & M partnership had net income of only $20,000 for 19x1. The salary and interest allowances total $10,000 for Mantle and $16,000 for Maris. The total interest and salary allowances of $26,000 exceed the net income of the partnership for the period by $6,000. This excess must be deducted in determining the partners' share of the income as follows:

	Mantle	Maris	Total
Salaries	$ 6,000	$ 8,000	$14,000
Interest	4,000	8,000	12,000
Remainder (divided equally)	(3,000)	(3,000)	(6,000)
Total	$ 7,000	$13,000	$20,000

Partnership Financial Statements

The income statement of a partnership is very similar to that of either a sole proprietorship or a corporation. The statement does not reflect income tax expense, however, because the partnership is not subject to an income tax on its earnings. (Partners are taxed as individuals on their share of the partnership income.) In addition, the allocation of the net income among the partners is often included in the income statement as a final item below the net income figure.

The balance sheet of a partnership differs from that of a sole proprietorship or a corporation primarily in the owners' equity section. The equity section of a partnership reflects the end-of-period capital balances of each individual partner.

A statement disclosing the nature and amount of changes in the partners' capital balances during a period is often prepared for a partnership. For example, the Statement of Partners' Capital for the M & M partnership might appear as follows:

M & M
Statement of Partners' Capital
For the Year Ended December 31, 19x1

	Mantle	Maris	Total
Balances, January 1, 19x1	$50,000	$100,000	$150,000
Add: Additional investments	20,000	60,000	80,000
Net income	15,000	15,000	30,000
Total	$85,000	$175,000	$260,000
Less: Withdrawals	(5,000)	(15,000)	(20,000)
Balances, December 31, 19x1	$80,000	$160,000	$240,000

Thus, the December 31, 19x1 balance sheet for M & M would include capital balances of $80,000 for Mantle and $160,000 for Maris.

Admission of a Partner

Although the admission of a new partner to a partnership legally dissolves the existing partnership, a new agreement may be created without disruption of business activities. An additional person may be admitted by purchasing an interest directly from one or more of the current partners or by making an investment in the partnership. When a new partner purchases his share of the partnership from a current partner, the payment is made directly to the selling partner(s). Therefore, there is no change in either the total assets or the total capital of the partnership. When a new partner invests in the partnership by contributing assets to the partnership, however, both the total assets and total capital of the partnership are increased.

Purchase of an Interest from Current Partner(s). When a new partner acquires his interest by purchasing all or part of the interest of one or more of the existing partners, the purchase price is paid directly to the selling partner(s). Therefore, the amount paid is not recorded in the partnership records. The only entry which is required in the accounts of the partnership is to transfer the interest sold from the selling partner's capital account(s) to a capital account for the new partner.

For example, assume that Mantle and Maris have capital balances of $80,000 and $160,000, respectively. Mantle agrees to sell one-half of his $80,000 interest in the partnership directly to Berra for $50,000. The entry to record this transaction on the partnership books is as follows:

Mantle, Capital	40,000	
Berra, Capital		40,000

The effect of this transaction is to transfer one half of Mantle's current capital balance ($½ \times \$80,000$) to the new capital account created for Berra. The total capital of the partnership, $240,000, is not affected by the transaction. The entry which was made was not affected by the amount paid by the incoming partner to the selling partner. The $50,000 payment made by Berra to Mantle reflects a bargained transaction between the two men acting as individuals, and as such does not affect the assets of the partnership.

Purchase of Interest by Investment in the Partnership. When the incoming partner contributes assets *to* the partnership for his interest, both the assets and the capital of the partnership are increased. To illustrate, again assume that Mantle and Maris are partners in the M & M Partnership with capital accounts of $80,000 and $160,000 respectively. They agree to admit Berra as a new partner with a one-fourth interest in the partnership for an investment of $80,000. The admission of Berra would be recorded by the following journal entry:

```
Cash ....................................... 80,000
     Berra, Capital ....................................  80,000
```

After the admission of Berra, the total capital of the new partnership is as follows:

Maris, Capital.	$160,000
Mantle, Capital	80,000
Berra, Capital.	80,000
Total Capital	$320,000

Berra's capital balance of $80,000 represents a one-fourth interest in the total partnership capital of $320,000. It does not necessarily follow, however, that the new partner is entitled to a one-fourth share in the division of partnership income. Instead, the division of income or loss must be specified in the new partnership agrement.

Because balances in the asset accounts usually are not equal to their current values, the investment of the new partner may be more or less than the proportion of total assets represented by his agreed-upon capital interest. However, since the agreement concerning the new partner's relative capital interest should be reflected in the capital accounts, adjustments to the capital accounts will be necessary if the amount invested is not equal to the book value of the capital interest acquired. The adjustment required in recording the investment of the new partner is accomplished by using either the bonus method or the goodwill method.

When a new partner invests more than book value for his relative capital interest, a bonus or goodwill may be allocated to the old partners. To illustrate these two different methods, assume that Mantle and Maris, who share profits equally and have capital balances of $80,000 and $160,000 respectively, agree to admit Berra to a one-fourth interest in the new partnership for $120,000.

Bonus to Old Partners. The total net assets of the partnership after the $120,000 investment by Berra will be $360,000 ($240,000 + $120,000). In order to acquire a one-fourth interest in the net assets of the partnership, or $90,000 (¼ × $360,000), Berra was required to invest $120,000. The excess of the investment over the amount of capital allocated to Berra may be regarded as a bonus to the old partners. The old partners share the bonus in their agreed-upon profit and loss ratio. Each partner's share of the bonus is credited to his capital account. The entry to record Berra's investment in the partnership (assuming an equal distribution of profits and losses between Mantle and Maris) is:

Cash	120,000	
Berra, Capital		90,000
Mantle, Capital		15,000
Maris, Capital		15,000

Thus, after the investment, Berra has a capital balance of $90,000 which represents one fourth of the total capital of $360,000.

Goodwill to Old Partners. Alternatively, if the new partner's investment exceeds his relative share of the net assets of the new partnership, it may be assumed that the old partnership had goodwill. The amount of goodwill is determined by the initial investment of the new partner. To illustrate, the $120,000 investment made by Berra represented a one-fourth interest in the partnership. The fact that a one-fourth interest required an investment of $120,000 implies that the business is worth $480,000 ($120,000 ÷ ¼). The amount of goodwill is computed as follows:

Investment by Berra for a ¼ interest		$120,000
Implied value of Business ($120,000 ÷ ¼)		$480,000
Net asset value exclusive of goodwill:		
Capital of old partners	$240,000	
Investment by Berra	120,000	360,000
Goodwill		$120,000

As was the case with the bonus, the goodwill is divided between the old partners in the same proportion as their profit and loss ratios unless a specific agreement is made to the contrary. The entries which are required in order to record the admission of the new partner (again assuming an equal distribution of profits and losses) are as follows:

Cash	120,000	
Berra, Capital		120,000
Goodwill	120,000	
Mantle, Capital		60,000
Maris, Capital		60,000

The capital balances of the partners after the admission of Berra are as follows:

Mantle, Capital	$140,000
Maris, Capital	220,000
Berra, Capital	120,000
	$480,000

It can be seen that Berra's share of the total capital is the agreed-upon one-fourth interest in the partnership ($120,000/$480,000).

Note that the choice between the bonus and goodwill methods results in different account balances (but the same relative capital interests). The goodwill method causes the total capital of the partners to be larger by the amount of the goodwill recorded. Thus, the choice between methods results in different financial statements.

When the new partner invests less than the book value of his relative capital interest, a bonus or goodwill may be allocated to the incoming partner. To illustrate, assume that Mantle and Maris agree to admit Berra with a one fourth interest in the partnership for an investment of only $60,000.

Bonus to New Partner. Based on this method, the excess of the new partner's share of total capital over his investment is allocated as a bonus to the new partner. The amount of the bonus is calculated as follows:

Total capital prior to admission:		
Mantle, Capital	$ 80,000	
Maris, Capital	160,000	$240,000
Investment by Berra		60,000
Total capital		$300,000
Berra's one-fourth interest		$ 75,000
Investment by Berra		60,000
Bonus to Berra		$ 15,000

The bonus may be treated as a reduction of the old partners' capital accounts on the basis of their profit and loss ratio and as a credit to the new partner's capital. The entry to record the admission of the new partner assuming an equal distribution of profits and losses between Mantle and Maris is:

Cash	60,000	
Mantle, Capital	7,500	
Maris, Capital	7,500	
Berra, Capital		75,000

Goodwill to New Partner. If the new partner's investment is less than his agreed-upon capital interest, the difference may be due to goodwill brought to the partnership by the incoming partner. This goodwill may be attributable to the reputation or special skills of the new partner which might be imparted to increase the earning power of the partnership entity. The goodwill is recorded as an asset with a corresponding credit to the new partner's capital account in order to allow him the agreed-upon capital interest in the partnership. There is no change in the capital accounts of the old partners.

To illustrate, assume that Mantle and Maris had capital balances of $80,000 and $160,000 respectively prior to the admission of Berra with a one-fourth interest in the partnership. Since the total capital of Mantle and Maris, $240,000, represents a three-fourths interest in the total capital of the partnership after Berra is admitted, the implied value of the partnership is $320,000 ($240,000 ÷ ¾). However, the actual tangible assets of the firm after Berra's investment are $300,000, consisting of net assets of $240,000 prior to the admission of Berra plus the $60,000 investment. Therefore, the implied goodwill is $20,000 ($320,000 − $300,000). The entry required to record the admission of the new partner under the goodwill method is as follows:

```
Cash . . . . . . . . . . . . . . . . . . . . . . . . . . . . . . . . . . . . . .   60,000
Goodwill . . . . . . . . . . . . . . . . . . . . . . . . . . . . . . . . . . . .   20,000
    Berra, Capital . . . . . . . . . . . . . . . . . . . . . . . . . . . .            80,000
```

After his admission, Berra has the agreed-upon one-fourth interest in total capital ($80,000/$320,000).

Withdrawal of a Partner

When one partner withdraws from a partnership, he may dispose of his partnership interest in any one of several ways:

1. Sell his interest to a new partner.
2. Sell his interest to one or more of the remaining partners with the payment coming from the personal resources of the purchasing partner(s).
3. Sell his interest to the partnership with the payment from partnership funds.

In the first two cases, the sale and purchase is made among the partners themselves acting as individuals. Therefore, the accounting treatment is the same as for the admission of a new partner through the purchase of an interest from the existing partners. The journal entry required on the partnership books is simply to transfer the capital account balance by debiting the capital account of the retiring partner and crediting the capital account(s) of the purchasing partner(s). There is no effect on either the assets or the total capital of the partnership.

If the withdrawing partner is paid from partnership assets, both the total assets and total capital of the firm are decreased. Because the current value and the recorded book values of the partnership assets probably differ, the withdrawing partner may be paid either more or less than the amount of his capital balance. The difference may be attributable, for example, to the change in value of certain specific assets or alternatively to the existence of goodwill or to a combination of both factors. The change in the asset values or goodwill may be recorded in the accounts and shared by the partners in their profit and loss ratios.

For example, assume that Mantle, Berra, and Maris have capital balances of $100,000, $120,000, and $180,000 respectively, and share profits and losses on a one-fourth, one-fourth, and one-half basis. Further, assume that it is agreed to pay Mantle $120,000 from partnership funds upon his withdrawal from the partnership, and that the fair value of the partnership at that time is $480,000. Assuming that specific assets cannot be identified to account for the increase in value, the entries required in order to record the goodwill and the withdrawal of Mantle are as follows:

Goodwill.	80,000	
Mantle, Capital		20,000
Berra, Capital.		20,000
Maris, Capital		40,000
Mantle, Capital	120,000	
Cash		120,000

Instead of an increase in the value of specific assets or the existence of goodwill, the difference between the payment to the withdrawing partner and his capital balance may be regarded as a bonus paid to the withdrawing partner by the remaining partners. This bonus is charged to the capital accounts of the old partners in the relative profit and loss ratios of the remaining partners. Under this assumption, the withdrawal of Mantle would be recorded as follows:

Mantle, Capital	100,000	
Maris, Capital	13,333	
Berra, Capital	6,667	
Cash		120,000

The $20,000 bonus to the retiring partner was deducted from the remaining partners' capital balances on the basis of their relative profit and loss ratios of ⅔ for Maris (50%/75%) and ⅓ for Berra (25%/75%).

If the payment made to the withdrawing partner is less than his capital balance, the difference may be attributable either to specific assets that have fair values which are less than their recorded book values or to a bonus paid by the retiring partner to the remaining partners in order to retire from the partnership without undergoing a liquidation of the business. Again, the revaluation of the assets of the partnership or the bonus is divided among the partners according to their profit and loss sharing ratio.

For example, if Mantle agrees to retire for a payment of $85,000, and it is agreed that the assets of the partnership are not overvalued, the entry to record the withdrawal would be as follows:

Mantle, Capital	100,000	
Maris, Capital		10,000
Berra, Capital		5,000
Cash		85,000

Again, Maris and Berra would share the $15,000 difference ($100,000 — $85,000) on the basis of their relative profit and loss ratios of ⅔ and ⅓ (as above).

LIQUIDATION OF THE PARTNERSHIP

When a partnership goes out of business, its assets are sold, its liabilities are paid, and any remaining cash is distributed to the partners. This process is referred to as a liquidation.

As a basis for illustration, assume that Mantle, Maris, and Berra agree to liquidate their partnership. Profits and losses are allocated one-fourth to Mantle, one-fourth to Berra, and one-half to Maris. The balance sheet of the partnership just prior to the liquidation process appeared as follows:

M, M & B
Balance Sheet
As of December 31, 19x1

Cash	$ 20,000	Liabilities	$ 50,000
Noncash assets.......	430,000	Mantle, Capital	100,000
		Maris, Capital.......	180,000
		Berra, Capital.......	120,000
	$450,000		$450,000

Assume that all of the noncash assets of the partnership are sold for $330,000, a loss of $100,000 ($430,000 — $330,000).

Any gain or loss on the sale of the partnership assets must be divided among the partners according to their agreed-upon profit and loss ratios before any cash is distributed to the partners. Thus, the $100,000 loss on the sale of the noncash assets of the partnership would be distributed among the partners as follows:

	Total	Mantle	Maris	Berra
Capital balance	$400,000	$100,000	$180,000	$120,000
Distribution of loss	(100,000)	(25,000)	(50,000)	(25,000)
Capital balance after sale.........	$300,000	$ 75,000	$130,000	$ 95,000

The entries required in order to record the sale of the assets and the distribution of the loss would be as follows:

Cash	330,000	
Loss on sale	100,000	
Noncash assets		430,000
Mantle, Capital	25,000	
Maris, Capital	50,000	
Berra, Capital	25,000	
Loss on sale		100,000

After the noncash assets of the partnership have been sold and the gain or loss has been divided among the partners, the cash will be distributed first to creditors and then to the partners. The amount of cash to be distributed to each partner is reflected in the capital balances after all gains or losses on the sale of noncash assets have been recorded. The balance sheet prior to the distribution of cash appears as follows:

M, M & B
Balance Sheet
January 10, 19x2

Cash	$350,000	Liabilities	$ 50,000
		Mantle, Capital	75,000
		Maris, Capital	130,000
		Berra, Capital	95,000
	$350,000		$350,000

The distribution of the cash, first to the creditors of the partnership and then to the partners, is recorded by the following entries:

Liabilities	50,000	
Cash		50,000
Mantle, Capital	75,000	
Maris, Capital	130,000	
Berra, Capital	95,000	
Cash		300,000

In the previous example, the capital account of each partner had a credit balance after the loss on the sale of noncash assets was distributed. In some instances, one or more of the partners may have a debit balance in his capital account as a result of losses on the disposal of the assets. This debit balance is referred to as a capital deficit since the partnership has a legal claim against the partner. If this claim cannot be collected by the partnership, the deficit must be divided among the remaining partners' capital balances according to their profit and loss ratios.

To illustrate, assume that the M, M & B partnership has the same assets and liabilities as in the preceding example. Further assume that the capital balances prior to liquidation are Mantle, $40,000; Maris, $210,000; and Berra, $150,000; and that the noncash assets are sold for $230,000 (a loss of $200,000). The capital accounts after the distribution of the loss would be as follows:

	Total	Mantle	Maris	Berra
Capital balances	$400,000	$40,000	$210,000	$150,000
Loss on sale of noncash assets	(200,000)	(50,000)	(100,000)	(50,000)
Capital balance	$200,000	($10,000)	$110,000	$100,000

After payment of the $50,000 of liabilities, the balance sheet of M, M & B would appear as follows:

M, M & B
Balance Sheet
January 10, 19x2

Cash	$200,000	Mantle, Capital	$ (10,000)
		Maris, Capital	110,000
		Berra, Capital	100,000
	$200,000		$200,000

If Mantle is able to pay his capital deficiency to the partnership, the following entry would be made:

Cash	10,000	
Mantle, Capital		10,000

At this point Mantle would have a zero capital balance, and the $210,000 cash on hand would be distributed to Maris and Berra in amounts equal to the balances in their capital accounts.

If the partnership is unable to collect the capital deficiency from Mantle, this loss would be absorbed by the remaining partners. Since the partnership agreement provides that Maris had a one-half share and Berra a one-fourth share of profits and losses, their current interest in profits and losses is Maris's two-thirds (50%/75%) and Berra's one-third (25%/75%). The loss should be written off against the capital accounts of the remaining partners as follows:

Maris, Capital	6,667	
Berra, Capital	3,333	
Mantle, Capital		10,000

Accordingly, the distribution of the $200,000 cash would be based on the amount of the partners' capital balances after allowances for the loss on the noncollection of the capital deficiency. These amounts are as follows:

	Mantle	Maris	Berra
Capital balances	($10,000)	$110,000	$100,000
Capital deficiency	10,000	(6,667)	(3,333)
	-0-	$103,333	$ 96,667

The entry to record the distribution of the cash would be:

```
Maris, Capital . . . . . . . . . . . . . . . . . . . . . . . . . . . 103,333
Berra, Capital . . . . . . . . . . . . . . . . . . . . . . . . . . .  96,667
    Cash . . . . . . . . . . . . . . . . . . . . . . . . . . . . . . . . .        200,000
```

In the event that any cash is subsequently received from the deficient partner, it would be divided between the remaining partners in their profit and loss sharing ratio, since that is how they shared the deficiency.

SUMMARY

The simplest and most common form of business organization is the sole proprietorship. A single individual owns, controls, and usually manages the firm's assets and receives the profits from its operations. The sole proprietorship is not considered a separate entity for income tax purposes and the owner is taxed on all earnings of the business, whether or not the owner withdraws them. Investments and earnings are generally recorded in the capital account and withdrawals in the drawing account. The drawing account, if used, is then closed to the capital account at the end of the period.

Accounting for the partnership form of business organization is considerably more complex in that more than a single owner is involved. A partnership is an association of two or more persons organized to carry on, as co-owners, a business for profit. The partnership agreement serves as the basis for the formation and operation of the partnership and should include all essential data. Significant characteristics of a partnership include the ease of formation, the applicability of the mutual agency concept, the existence of unlimited liability of each partner and limited life of the enterprise, and the co-ownership of the assets and earnings. The partnership has certain advantages, such as the ability to combine the skills and capital of several individuals, and certain disadvantages, such as unlimited liability of the partners. Of course, these (and other relevant) factors should be evaluated and weighed in each case.

A separate individual capital and drawing account is maintained for each partner. Upon the formation of the partnership, each capital account is credited for that individual's cash contibution or an agreed-upon value of property contributions. At the end of each period, profits or losses are divided among the partners according to the terms of the partnership agreement. When a new partner is admitted to an existing partnership, either by the purchase of an interest from a current partner or by a direct investment in the partnership, the old partners may receive a bonus which is credited to their capital accounts. In addition, if the new partner's investment differs from his relative share of the net assets of the new partnership, goodwill may need to be allocated to either the old partners or the new partner. When an existing partner withdraws from the partnership, the exact nature of the necessary entries to record the withdrawal will depend on whether it is accomplished by a sale to a new partner, by a sale to existing partners as individuals, or by a sale to existing partners with payment from partnership funds. When and if the partnership is liquidated, its assets are sold, its liabilities are paid, and any remaining cash is distributed to the partners.

This chapter has discussed the basic accounting procedures applicable to unincorporated business organizations. The next two chapters will discuss the accounting for corporations.

KEY DEFINITIONS

Capital account The capital account of a partnership consists of a separate account for each partner which reflects the investments by the partners plus each partner's share of the earnings or losses from the operations of the business less any withdrawals made by the partners.

Division of profits and losses The agreement determines the method of dividing partnership profits or losses among the partners. In the absence of such an agreement, the law provides that profits or losses shall be divided equally among the partners.

Drawing account Cash or other assets withdrawn by a partner during the period are reflected in the partner's drawing account. The drawing accounts are closed to the partners' capital accounts at the end of the period.

Interest on capital This is a method which provides for partners' capital interests as a factor in the distribution of the partnership earnings.

Limited life A partnership is legally dissolved upon the withdrawals, death, incapacity, or bankruptcy of any of its partners.

Liquidation The process of terminating a business in which its assets are sold, its liabilities are paid, and any remaining cash or other assets are distributed to its owners.

Mutual agency Each partner may act as an agent of the partnership, with the power to enter into contracts within the scope of the normal business operations.

Partnership An association of two or more persons to carry on a business under a contractual arrangement.

Partnership agreement This written contract of partnership sets forth the agreement between the partners as to the conditions for the formation and operation of the partnership.

Salaries to partners A method which provides for the division of a portion of the partnership income by allocating specified salaries to the partners.

Sole proprietorship A business owned by one person.

Statement of partners' capital This statement shows the nature and amount of changes in the partners' capital accounts during a period.

Uniform Partnership Act This act, which has been adopted in most states, governs the formation, operation, and liquidation of partnerships.

Unlimited liability Each partner is personally liable to the creditors of the partnership in the event that the partnership assets are insufficient to meet its obligations.

QUESTIONS

1. List the three basic types of business organizations.

2. What are the primary advantages of the partnership form of organization?

3. List and describe three important disadvantages of organizing a business as a partnership.

4. Explain the difference between admittance of a new partner to a partnership by making an investment in the partnership and admittance by purchasing an interest from a partner.

5. Smith is a partner in the Smith and Jones Partnership. At the end of the year, Smith's share of the partnership income is $20,000. During the year, Smith had withdrawals of $10,000. What amount of income should be included in Smith's taxable income for the year?

6. Upon the formation of a partnership, at what amount should the investments of noncash assets be recorded? Why is this necessary?

7. What factors are usually considered in determining the method for dividing partnership income?

8. In the absence of a specific agreement, how should the profit or loss of a partnership be allocated among the partners? If there is a specific method for allocating profits in the partnership agreement but no mention of losses, how should a net loss be divided among the partners?

9. Why does the agreement for division of partnership earnings often allow for salaries and interest on partners' capital balances?

10. When a new partner is admitted to a partnership and goodwill or a bonus is attributed to the old partners, how is the goodwill or bonus distributed to the capital accounts?

11. What is the effect of gains or losses resulting from the liquidation of a partnership on the partners' capital balances? How are the gains or losses divided among the partners?

12. After the distribution of a loss on liquidation, assume that one partner has a debit balance in his capital account. If the partner is unable to contribute any personal assets, how is the loss divided among the remaining partners?

EXERCISES

13. Bibby and Rowe formed a partnership on January 1, 19x1. Bibby contributed $75,000 capital while Rowe contributed $50,000 capital. No additions to capital were made during the year. For the year ended December 31, 19x1, the partnership had net income of $25,000. Prepare a schedule showing the division of income in each of the following cases:

a. Partners agree to allocate ⅓ of profits or losses to Rowe and ⅔ to Bibby.
b. Partners agree to distribute net income on the basis of their capital balances in the partnership.
c. Bibby and Rowe agree to allow each partner 8 percent interest on his beginning capital balance and divide the remaining profits equally.

14. Assume that Bibby and Rowe made withdrawals of $5,000 and $7,000, respectively, during 19x1. Give the entries to record the division of income in 13(a) above and the entries to record the closing of the withdrawals account.

15. Assume that Erickson and Goodrich, who have capital balances of $160,000 and $320,000, respectively, and who divide profits equally, agree to admit Hazard to a ¼ interest in the new partnership for $200,000. Make the entry to record Hazard's investment in the partnership under both the bonus method and the goodwill method.

16. Martin is withdrawing from the partnership of Martin, Water, and Osmond. The capital accounts of partnership are as follows: Martin, $10,000; Water, $10,000; and Osmond, $20,000. The partners share profits and losses equally. The partners agree that Martin will be paid $12,000 cash for his interest in the partnership. Give the entries to record the retirement of Martin using the bonus method.

17. The partnership of Jones, Clare, and Jackson is being liquidated on December 31, 19x1. The balances in the capital accounts prior to liquidation of the assets were as follows: Jones, $25,000; Clare, $20,000; and Jackson, $5,000. The partners share profits and losses equally. On December 31, partnership assets with a book value of $60,000 were sold for $39,000, and liabilities of $10,000 were paid.

Required:

How should the remaining $29,000 available cash be distributed if Jackson is unable to pay the amount he owes to the firm?

18. Bob Billy and Thomas Sloan decided to form a partnership. Bob said he would contribute a building which he purchased three years ago for $15,000. The book value of the building now is $10,000. A real estate dealer said the building could be sold presently for $18,000. Thomas said he would contribute land worth $50,000 to the partnership. The land had a mortgage of $35,000 which was to be paid over the next 10 years.

Required:

1. What will be the balance in Bob and Thomas' capital accounts when the partnership is formed?
2. Make entries to record the formation of the partnership.

19. In the Bell and Grubb Partnership, Bell had a capital balance on January 1, 19x1 of $26,000 and Grubb, $32,000. On June 1, Bell made a contribution of $6,000 to the partnership and on October 1, Grubb made a $3,000 contribution. The partners both receive 6 percent interest a year on their average capital balances and also divide net income based on the capital ratio of their average capital balances. If net income for 19x1 is $12,000, calculate each partner's share of the profits.

20. The capital balances for the partners of the Kingston Company as of December 31, 19x1 are as follows: Joe Kingston, $12,000; Bill Kingston, $15,000; and Paul Kingston, $13,000. The following transactions affecting their capital accounts occurred during the year.

    a. Joe and Bill Kingston withdrew $1,000 a month from the business and Paul withdrew $1,500 a month.
    b. Bill and Paul contributed $3,000 and $5,000 to the partnership, respectively.
    c. Net income for the year ending 12/31/x2 is $35,600. The profits are divided in the following manner: Joe, 50 percent; Bill, 20 percent; Paul, 30 percent.

    Required:

    Write a statement of partners' capital for the year December 31, 19x2.

21. Assume that in the Torberg and Haddix Partnership, Torberg has a capital balance of $75,000 and Haddix has a capital balance of $60,000. Make journal entries under each of the following unrelated assumptions.

    a. Haddix sells one-half of his $60,000 interest in the partnership to Carty for $40,000.
    b. Carty is admitted with a one-third interest in the partnership for an investment of $67,500. Total capital is to be $202,500.
    c. Carty is admitted with a one-third interest in the partnership for an investment of $70,500. Bonus is allowed old partners.
    d. Carty is admitted with a one-third interest in the partnership for an investment of $66,000. Bonus to Carty is recognized.

22. Lowenstein, Manning, and Norris have decided to liquidate their partnership. The balance sheet just prior to liquidation appears as follows:

LM&N
Balance Sheet
As of September 30, 19x1

Cash................	$ 40,000	Liabilities.............	$100,000
Noncash assets........	860,000	Lowenstein, Capital.....	360,000
		Manning, Capital.......	200,000
		Norris, Capital.........	240,000
	$900,000		$900,000

The noncash assets were sold for $980,000. Make the journal entries to record the gain or loss on the sale of the assets, payment of liabilities, and distribution of remaining cash to the partners. The profits and losses are shared equally.

PROBLEMS

23. Vallely and Patterson form a partnership with Vallely investing capital of $70,000 and Patterson investing capital of $30,000. The partners agree to allow 8 percent interest on each partner's beginning capital balance. Also, due to differences in services rendered, Patterson is to receive a salary of $8,000 while Vallely receives a salary of $4,500. Any remaining profits or losses are to be divided equally. Make a schedule showing the division of partnership net income assuming the partnership earned $16,000 for the first year of its operations.

24. Johnson and Kennedy formed a partnership on January 1, 19x1, with investments of $40,000 each. Kennedy made an additional investment of $20,000 on June 30, 19x1. Given each of the following assumptions, determine the division of partnership net income of $27,000 for the year:

    a. No method for division of income specified in the partnership agreement.
    b. Divided in the ratio of the ending capital balance.
    c. Divided in the ratio of the average capital balances.
    d. Interest at a rate of 10 percent on the ending capital balance and the remainder divided equally.
    e. Salary allowances of $10,000 to Johnson and $5,000 to Kennedy and any remainder divided ⅓ to Johnson and ⅔ to Kennedy.
    f. Interest at a rate of 10 percent on the ending capital balances, salary allowance of $12,000 to Johnson and $8,000 to Kennedy, and any remainder divided equally.

25. Taylor, Smith, and Jones are partners in the TSJ Partnership. The partnership agreement provides for the following procedures for division of income:

    a. Each partner is allowed 5 percent interest on the average capital balance.
    b. Salary allowances of $10,000 to Taylor and $12,000 to Smith.
    c. Remainder divided 50 percent to Taylor, 30 percent to Smith, and 20 percent to Jones.

During the current year, the average capital balances were $60,000, Taylor; $40,000, Smith; and $20,000, Jones.

Calculate the division of income among the partners in each of the following cases:

a. Net income, $38,000.
b. Net income, $18,000.
c. Net loss, $2,000.

26. Able and Baker agree to admit Comer into their partnership with a one-fourth interest. Currently, Able has capital of $20,000 and Baker has capital of $10,000. They share profits and losses equally. Give the journal entries necessary to record the admission of Comer for each of the following investments by Comer:

a. $10,000.
b. $20,000 using the bonus method.
c. $20,000 using the goodwill method.
d. $ 6,000 using the bonus method.
e. $ 6,000 using the goodwill method.

27. Wilkes, Lee, and Curtis have capital balances of $60,000, $80,000, and $100,000, respectively, in their partnership. They share profits on a ¼, ¼, and ½ basis, respectively. Wilkes withdraws from the partnership, and it is agreed that he will be paid $70,000 for his share of the partnership. At the time of Wilkes's withdrawal, the fair value of the partnership is $280,000.

Required:

Make the entries to record the withdrawal of Wilkes under the goodwill and bonus methods.

28. Kemp, Killough, and Kubin agree to liquidate their partnership on January 1, 19x1. The balance sheet of the firm as of that date is as follows:

Cash		$10,000
Accounts receivable		15,000
Inventory		30,000
Equipment	$60,000	
Less: Accumulated depreciation	(30,000)	30,000
Total Assets		$85,000
Accounts payable		$ 5,000
Kemp, capital		40,000
Killough, capital		30,000
Kubin, capital		10,000
Total Liabilities and Capital		$85,000

Profits and losses are distributed 50 percent to Kemp, 30 percent to Killough, and 20 percent to Kubin. On January 1, 19x1, the noncash assets were sold as follows: Accounts Receivable, $10,000; Inventory, $20,000; and Equipment, $15,000.

Required:

Prepare a schedule showing the distribution of cash to the partners upon liquidation.

29. Brown, Gray, and White agree to liquidate their partnership. Prior to beginning the liquidation process, they have cash, $15,000; other assets, $90,000; liabilities, $20,000; and capital balances of $50,000, $25,000, and $10,000, respectively. Profits and losses are divided among the partners in the ratio of 4:4:2, respectively. None of the partners had any personal assets outside of the firm. The realization and liquidation proceeded as follows:

   a. $50,000 of other assets were sold for $30,000.
   b. The liabilities were paid.
   c. The remaining other assets were sold for $10,000.
   d. The cash was distributed to the partners.

Required:

Prepare a schedule showing the effects of the liquidation process on the partners' capital accounts and the amounts distributed to the partners upon liquidation.

30. Hawk and Dove formed a partnership on January 1, 19x1, combining their separate businesses that they had operated as sole proprietorships. The account balances of the noncash assets contributed, and their agreed-upon fair values are shown below:

Hawk	Book Value	Fair Value
Accounts receivable	$20,000	$20,000
Inventory	10,000	15,000
Equipment	20,000	25,000
Accounts payable	10,000	10,000
Dove		
Inventory	5,000	6,000
Building	25,000	32,000
Land	10,000	12,000

In addition, Hawk invested $5,000 in cash and Dove contributed $25,000 in cash. They agreed to share profits and losses equally.

Required:

1. Prepare the journal entries required on the books of the partnership to record the investments in the partnerships on January 1, 19x1.
2. Prepare a balance sheet for the partnership on January 1, 19x1.
3. On December 31, 19x1, the partnership income was calculated as $20,000. Hawk and Dove had $5,000 and $8,000 debit balances, respectively, in their drawing accounts. Prepare the entries to close the Income Summary and Drawing accounts on December 31, 19x1.

31. The Lord & Davis partnership began business on January 1, 19x1, Lord and Davis were to share profits in a 2:1 ratio. Below is a list of transactions affecting the partner's capital accounts which occurred during their first year of business. Journalize these transactions in chronological order, including closing entries.

   a. Initially, Lord contributed a building with a fair market value of $55,000. The building held an unpaid mortgage of $15,000. Davis contributed cash of $35,000.
   b. On February 10, July 16, and November 12, Lord withdrew $7,000 and Davis withdrew $6,500 (i.e., Lord withdrew a total of $21,000 during the year).
   c. On June 15, Lord contributed stock to the partnership worth $25,000.
   d. On September 30, the partnership admitted a new partner, Gagnon, for a one-fourth interest. Gagnon invested $15,000 in cash and his capital balance was to equal $17,000. A bonus was recognized to Gagnon because of his knowledge and expertise in the business.
   e. Net income for the year ended December 31, 19x1 was $96,000. Since Gagnon entered the partnership on September 30, he was to receive one-fourth of his pro rata share of the profits and losses.
   f. Due to severe illness, Davis decided to withdraw from the partnership as of the end of the year. It is agreed upon by the other partners that the assets of the partnership are not overvalued, and that Davis should receive a payment of $40,000 with a bonus recognized to the remaining partners.

32. Below is the trial balance for the A&M Partnership.

A&M
Trial Balance
For the Year Ended December 31, 19x1

	Dr.(Cr.)
Current assets	$307,100
Fixed assets, net	844,180
Current liabilities	(157,000)
8 percent mortgage note payable	(290,000)
Anthony, Capital	(515,000)
Martini, Capital	(150,000)
Anthony, Drawing	24,000
Martini, Drawing	16,000
Sales	(827,000)
Cost of sales	695,000
Administrative expenses	16,900
Other miscellaneous expenses	11,120
Interest expense	11,700
Depreciation expense	13,000

Anthony and Martini share profits and losses in 3:1 ratio. Anthony has a tax rate of 35 percent and Martini has a tax rate of 20 percent.

Required:

1. What is the net income for the A&M Partnership for the year ended December 31, 19x1?
2. After allocation of net income and closing entries, what is the balance in each partner's capital account?
3. What income taxes must be paid by the partnership? The partners? (Disregard any other possible deductions by the partners).

33. On July 1, 19x1, Alford and Billy combined their two potato chip businesses into a partnership. Below are the balances in their accounts at that date:

	Book Value	Fair Market Value
Alford:		
Accounts receivable	$ 30,000	$30,000
Inventory	12,000	9,000
Equipment	45,000	50,000
Accounts payable	18,000	18,000

	Book Value	Fair Market Value
Billy:		
Accounts receivable	$ 22,000	$22,000
Marketable securities	35,000	42,000
Buildings and land	100,000	90,000
Accounts payable	23,000	23,000

The fair-market value has been agreed upon by the two partners on each item. Also, Alford and Billy each contributed $5,000 in cash. During the year, Alford withdrew $20,000 in cash and Billy, $25,000 in cash. The net profit for the year was $65,000.

Required:

Prepare journal entries to record:

1. Initial investment in the partnership on July 1, 19x1.
2. Closing entries as of June 30, 19x2, the end of the partnership's fiscal year along with a statement of Partner's Capital for the year then ended.

34. The 3C's Partnership began operations on July 1, 19x1. Each partner, Coon, Cassidy, and Candon, was to receive a one-third interest in the partnership. The following transactions occurred during the fiscal year which affected their capital accounts:

a. On July 1, each partner contributed $25,000 in cash to the partnership. In addition to the cash, Coon contributed a building with a fair market value of $33,000 and a book value of $37,000.
b. Each partner decided to withdraw their yearly salary at different dates. Therefore, Coon withdrew $15,000 on October 1; Cassidy withdrew $13,500 on December 15; and Candon withdrew $14,000 on February 1, 19x2.
c. On December 30, Cassidy decided he wanted to sell his partnership interest and join the Peace Corps. Candon's brother-in-law, Casey, said he would pay Cassidy $12,000 for his one-third interest. It was decided at this time that Casey would receive Cassidy's share of the profit or loss up to December 30.
d. On January 31, Candon contributed land to the partnership with a fair market value of $80,000. However, the land still had an outstanding mortgage of $60,000.
e. On March 19, Casey contributed an additional $15,000 in cash.
f. The first year ending June 30, 19x2 turned out to be rather unsuccessful, netting a loss of $27,000.
g. Also on June 30, Coon decided to withdraw from the partnership and join Vista. The remaining partners agreed to pay Coon $36,500, and that the fair value of the partnership at this time is $81,000. The partners could not identify specific assets which had increased in values. Therefore, goodwill was recognized.

Required:

Record these transactions in journal form, including closing entries as of June 30, 19x2.

Learning Objectives

Chapter 13 considers issues relating to the formation of a corporation and the issuance of capital stock. Studying this chapter should enable you to:

1. Identify the significant characteristics of the corporate form of business organization.

2. Discuss the steps required to form a corporation and the accounting treatment of any related expenditures incurred in so doing.

3. Distinguish between capital stock authorized, issued, and outstanding.

4. Compare the rights and privileges associated with common versus preferred stock.

5. Describe the accounting entries necessary to record issuance of or subscriptions to capital stock.

13

The Corporation:
Organization and
Capital Stock

INTRODUCTION

A corporation is an artificial "legal" person that is both separate and distinct from its owners and, as such, is permitted to engage in any acts which could be performed by a natural person. It may hold property, enter into contracts, and engage in other activities not prohibited by law. The classic definition of a corporation was given by Chief Justice Marshall in 1819 as " . . . an artificial being, invisible, intangible, and existing only in contemplation of the law."

Although there are fewer businesses organized as corporations than as either sole proprietorships or partnerships, corporations are by far the dominant form of business organization in terms of both total assets and dollar value of output of goods and services. Because of the dominance of the corporate form of business organization and the widespread ownership interests in corporations, accounting for corporations is a very important topic.

CHARACTERISTICS OF THE CORPORATION

Because it is a separate legal entity, a corporation has several characteristics which differentiate it from both partnerships and sole proprietorships. The most important of these characteristics are described in the following paragraphs.

Separate Legal Existence. A corporation, unlike both sole proprietorships and partnerships, is a legal entity which is separate and distinct from its owners. Accordingly, a corporate entity may acquire and dispose of property, enter into contracts, and incur liabilities as an individual entity separate from its owners.

Transferable Units of Ownership. Ownership of a corporation is usually evidenced by shares of capital stock. These shares permit the subdivision of ownership into numerous units which may be readily transferred from one person to another without disrupting business operations and without prior approval of the other owners.

Continuity of Life. Status as a separate legal entity provides the corporation with a continuity of life. Unlike a partnership, the life or existence of a corporation is not affected by factors such as the death, incapacity, or withdrawal of an individual owner. A corporation may have a perpetual life or in some instances, its existence may be limited by the terms specified in its charter.

Limited Liability of Owners. As a separate legal entity, a corporation is legally liable for any debts which it incurs. Usually, the creditors of a corporation may not look to the personal property of the corporate stockholders for payment of any debts which are incurred by the corporation. Thus, the maximum loss which may be incurred by an individual stockholder is normally limited to the amount of his investment in the capital stock he owns. This limited liability feature is a primary advantage of the corporate form of business organization from the viewpoint of the owners.

In addition, the absence of stockholder liability and the transferability of ownership usually increase the ability of a corporate entity to raise substantial capital by means of individual investments made by many owners. On the other hand, the limited liability feature may limit the ability of a corporation to obtain funds from creditors in those instances where solvency of the corporate entity may be questionable.

Separation of Ownership and Management. Although a corporation is owned by the individuals who hold its shares of capital stock, their control over the general management of the business is generally limited to their right to elect a board of directors. The board of directors, as representatives of individual owners or stockholders of the corporation, establishes corporate policies and appoints corporate officers who are responsible for the day-to-day management of the business and its operations. Officers of a corporation usually include a president, one or more vice presidents responsible for various functions within the business, a treasurer, a secretary, and a controller. The controller is the officer responsible for the accounting function of the business. A summary organization chart indicating the normal structure of a corporation is presented below.

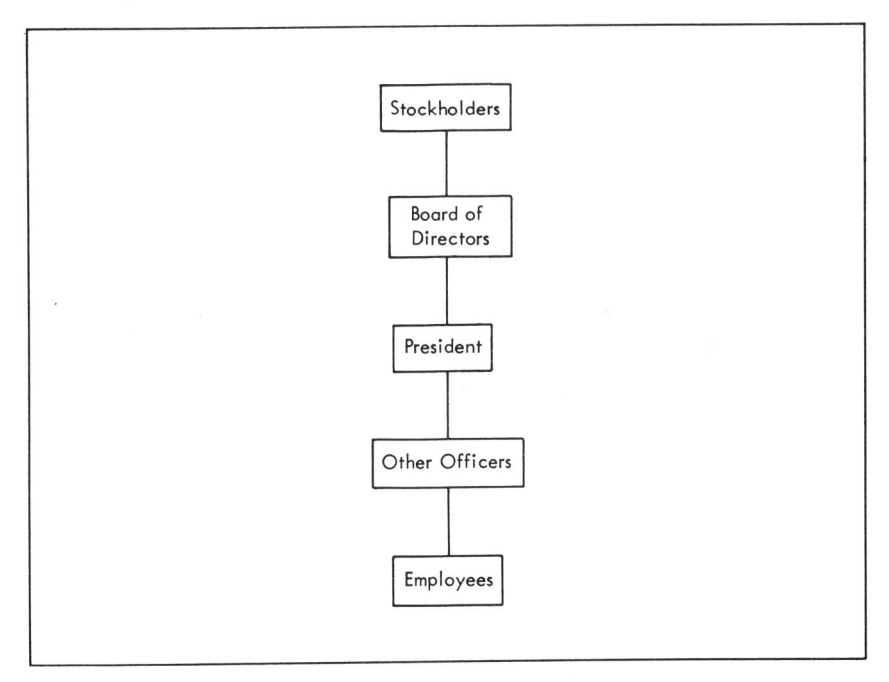

```
          ┌──────────────┐
          │ Stockholders │
          └──────┬───────┘
                 │
          ┌──────┴───────┐
          │   Board of   │
          │  Directors   │
          └──────┬───────┘
                 │
          ┌──────┴───────┐
          │  President   │
          └──────┬───────┘
                 │
          ┌──────┴───────┐
          │Other Officers│
          └──────┬───────┘
                 │
          ┌──────┴───────┐
          │  Employees   │
          └──────────────┘
```

Corporate Taxation. As a separate legal entity, corporations are required to file and pay local, state, and federal income taxes on corporate earnings. In addition, when corporate earnings are distributed to shareholders as dividends, these distributions are included in the taxable income of individuals receiving the dividend. Thus, "double taxation" occurs because earnings of a corporation are taxed twice—initially as corporate income and subsequently as dividend income when distributed to stockholders.

Certain businesses may elect to operate as corporations without filing and paying corporate income taxes. In order to qualify for such an election, a corporation must meet certain requirements—for example, it must have only a single class of stock and ten or fewer stockholders. If this election is made, corporate income is taxed directly to the shareholders as it is earned by the corporation, just as would be the case if the business were organized as a partnership.

Government Regulation. Corporations are subject to numerous state and federal regulations and restrictions which are not imposed on either partnerships or sole proprietorships. This occurs primarily because corporations are separate legal entities and shareholders normally have limited liability for actions of the corporation.

FORMING A CORPORATION

A business corporation may be created by obtaining a charter from the state in which the business is to be incorporated. Although requirements for establishing a corporation vary, most states require a minimum of three natural persons to act as incorporators. An application for a corporate charter is usually made by filing articles of incorporation with the appropriate state official. Some of the more important information usually included in the articles of incorporation are:

1. Name of the corporation.
2. Location of its principal offices.
3. Nature of the business to be conducted by the corporation.
4. Identity and addresses of incorporators.
5. A detailed description of the capital stock authorized to be issued.
6. Identity of, and the amounts paid by, the original subscribers for the corporation's capital stock.
7. Names of the initial directors.

If the articles of incorporation are approved, the state issues a corporate charter which includes the general corporation laws of the state as well as any specific provisions of the articles of incorporation. The state usually charges a fee or organization tax for the privilege of incorporation.

Upon approval of the corporate charter, a corporation is authorized to begin its operations. Incorporators are required to hold a meeting in order to elect a board of directors and to adopt a set of bylaws which provide detailed operating regulations for the corporation. Directors of the corporation then elect appropriate corporate officers and authorize the issuance of capital stock certificates to the original stockholders.

Various expenditures such as those for state taxes and charter fees, legal costs, and other organizational costs are necessary in order to establish a corporation. These costs are normally accumulated in an intangible asset account referred to as organization costs. Since organization costs are expenditures which are necessary in order to provide for the creation and continued existence of a business, benefits obtained from these costs extend over the entire life of a corporation. Therefore, from a theoretical viewpoint, organization costs should be amortized over the life of the business. However, except when otherwise specified in the corporate charter, the life of a corporation is considered to be indefinite. Consequently, two different methods have evolved for accounting for organization costs. One is to simply retain organization costs as an intangible asset for an indefinite period of time without any amortization or charge to expense. The other alternative is to amortize these costs over a selected reasonable, but somewhat arbitrary, period of time. Although this alternative is certainly not justified in theory, it is usually acceptable in practice since organization costs are normally immaterial in amount and since this procedure is acceptable for income tax purposes.

CAPITAL OF A CORPORATION

Owners' equity of a corporation is commonly referred to as stockholders' equity and is accounted for in separate classifications according to the source of capital. Two primary sources of equity capital are: (1) contributed capital—amounts invested directly by shareholders; and (2) earned capital—amounts which are provided by profitable operations and retained in the business. A third major source of corporate capital, amounts obtained from creditors through borrowing, is discussed in Chapter 15.

Corporate capital provided by operations of the corporation is referred to as Retained Earnings. At the end of each period, any income or loss from operations of the corporation is transferred from the income summary account to retained earnings. The dividends account, which is used to record the dividends declared during the period, is also closed out to retained earnings during the closing process. Therefore, the balance in retained earnings at any point in time is equal to the total accumulated earnings of the business (net of any losses) less the total distributions which were paid to the stockholders in the form of dividends since the corporation's inception. If losses and dividends paid to stockholders exceed the cumulative earnings of the corporation, the resulting debit balance in retained earnings is referred to as a deficit. This deficit is deducted from invested capital in order to determine total stockholders' equity of the corporation.

NATURE OF CAPITAL STOCK

The investments made by stockholders in a corporation are represented by shares of ownership referred to as Capital Stock. Ownership of corporate stock is evidenced by a stock certificate. This certificate usually includes such information as the name of the corporation, rights of the shareholders, and the number of shares owned by each individual shareholder.

The maximum number of shares of stock *authorized* for issuance by the corporation is specified in the corporate charter. The number of shares *issued* refers to the total number of shares of stock which have been issued to stockholders since the formation of the corporation. Under certain circumstances, a corporation may reacquire shares of stock which were originally issued to its stockholders. Therefore, the remaining shares held by stockholders are referred to as *outstanding* shares. A current listing of the stockholders who own outstanding shares is maintained by the corporation's registrar or by the firm itself in a stockholders' ledger.

A corporation with a large number of shares outstanding which are traded regularly on an organized stock exchange must assign the function of transferring stocks and maintaining stock records to a stock transfer agent and a registrar. Banks or trust companies usually fulfill these functions for corporations. When a stockholder wishes to sell his stock, he endorses the stock certificate and forwards it to the transfer agent. The transfer agent cancels the certificate which was sold and prepares a new certificate which he sends to the registrar. The registrar records the stock transfer and issues a new stock certificate to the purchaser(s). Independent records maintained by the independent transfer agent and registrar provide additional controls which are intended to decrease the possibility of error or fraud in a corporation's ownership records.

RIGHTS OF STOCKHOLDERS

Many corporations issue only a single class of stock. In this instance, each shareholder possesses identical ownership rights and privileges. For an individual stockholder, these rights are proportionate to the number of shares of stock owned. Among these basic rights are:

1. The right to vote in stockholders' meetings. This includes the right to vote for directors and on decisions requiring stockholder approval as specified by the terms of the corporate charter. A stockholder has one vote for each share of stock that he owns. For example, if a stockholder owns 1,000 shares of stock, he is entitled to 1,000 votes. If a shareowner does not wish to attend a stockholders' meeting, he may assign his votes to a specified representative through a proxy statement.

2. The right to share in corporate earnings through dividends declared by the board of directors.

3. The right to maintain a proportionate interest in the ownership of

the corporation whenever any additional shares of stock are issued by the corporation. This right, referred to as the preemptive right, provides that each stockholder may purchase a percentage of the number of new shares to be issued which is equal to his ownership percentage in the number of shares outstanding prior to the new issuance. To illustrate, assume that Aaron owns 100 (10 percent) of the 1,000 outstanding shares of stock of Matthews Co. If Matthews Co. decides to issue an additional 100 shares of stock, Aaron has a right to purchase 10 percent (100/1,000), or 10 of the new shares issued. Therefore, Aaron will be permitted to maintain his 10 percent interest (110/1,100) in the corporation. Thus, by exercising his preemptive right, a stockholder is able to maintain his relative interest or ownership in the corporation. However, a shareholder is not required to exercise his preemptive right; he may elect to do so at his option.

4. The right to a proportionate share in assets upon the liquidation of the corporation. Shareholders, however, are entitled only to those assets which remain after all corporate creditors have been paid in full.

When a corporation issues only a single class of stock, its shares are referred to as common stock and the four basic rights described above apply to all shares issued and outstanding. In certain circumstances, a corporation may issue additional types of capital stock in order to satisfy management objectives and to appeal to investors who may have various investment objectives. These additional classes of stock usually grant certain preferential rights to the holders of these shares. Accordingly, such shares are usually referred to as preferred stock. Ordinarily, preferred stockholders either have no voting rights or only limited voting rights under certain conditions specified by the corporate charter. Preferred stock usually has one or more of the following preferences or privileges:

1. *Dividend preference.* Stock which is preferred as to dividends entitles its owner to receive a stated dividend *before* any distributions are made to owners of common stock. Dividends on preferred stock are normally limited to a fixed amount per share. However, this dividend preference does not assure the stockholder that he will receive a dividend. Thus, if the board of directors of a corporation chooses not to declare a dividend, neither common nor preferred shareholders will receive any distribution from the corporation.

2. *Cumulative preference.* Cumulative preferred stock provides that if all or part of the required dividend on preferred stock is not paid during a given year, the unpaid dividend accumulates and carries forward to succeeding years. The accumulated amount of unpaid dividends as well as current dividends must be paid before any dividends can be paid on common stock. Unpaid dividends on cumulative preferred stock are referred

to as dividends in arrears. To illustrate, assume that a corporation has 10,000 shares of cumulative preferred stock outstanding and a $5 stated dividend per share was not paid in the preceding year. In the current year, no dividends may be paid on the common stock until preferred dividends of $50,000 ($5 × 10,000) from the preceding year and the dividend of $50,000 for the current year are paid. Dividends in arrears are not considered to be a liability of the corporation until they are declared by the board of directors. However, because this information is important to the users of financial statements, any dividends in arrears on preferred stock should be disclosed, usually by means of a footnote to the balance sheet.

Preferred stock not having cumulative rights is referred to as noncumulative. Dividends omitted in any one year on noncumulative preferred stock do not carry forward. Therefore, dividends may be paid on common stock if preferred stock dividends are paid for the current year. Since a dividend preference is usually one of the most important rights or features of preferred stock, noncumulative preferred stock is normally not considered to be a very desirable investment under most circumstances. Consequently, most preferred stock issues provide for cumulative dividends.

3. *Participating preference.* Preferred stock is usually entitled to receive a dividend of a specified amount each year. Preferred stock is nonparticipating when preferred stockholders receive only this amount regardless of the dividends paid to common stockholders. In some cases, however, certain types of preferred stock also provide for the possibility of dividends in excess of the normal amount. This preferred stock, referred to as participating, has the right to participate with common stockholders in dividends in excess of a specified amount paid to common shareholders. The preferred stock contract must indicate the extent to which preferred shares will participate with common shares. Fully participating preferred stock is entitled to dividends at an amount which is equal to the excess of the common dividend over the regular amount for preferred. Partially participating preferred stock is entitled to participate with common stock, but it is limited to a maximum rate or amount. Issues of preferred stock normally do not include participation rights.

4. *Liquidation preference.* Preferred stock is normally preferred as to assets upon liquidation of the corporation. That is, owners of such preferred stock are entitled to receive the stated liquidation value for their shares before any payments may be made to common stockholders.

5. *Convertible preferred stock.* Preferred stock is convertible when it includes a privilege which allows stockholders to exchange their preferred shares for a specified number of common shares of the corporation at the shareholders' option. A conversion privilege allows the owner of preferred stock the option of obtaining common stock on which there is no dividend limitation in exchange for his preferred stock.

6. *Callable preferred stock.* Preferred stock contracts frequently allow corporations to repurchase outstanding shares from preferred stockholders at a fixed price in excess of the issue price of the stock. When a corporation has this option, the preferred stock is referred to as callable.

PAR VALUE AND NO-PAR VALUE

The par value of a share of capital stock is an arbitrary value established by the corporate charter. It is usually printed on the stock certificate and may be any amount decided upon by the corporation. The par value specified has no relationship whatsoever to the actual market value of the stock. Market value, which is the price at which a share of stock can be bought or sold, is dependent upon factors such as expected earnings and dividends, financial condition of the corporation, and general economic conditions. It is not unusual for a stock with a par value of $5 per share to be traded at a market value of $50, $100 or more.

The primary significance of par value is that it is used in many states in order to establish the corporation's "legal capital." The concept of legal capital was used by state laws to protect corporate creditors from possible dishonest actions of stockholders or corporate directors. In the absence of such a provision, corporate assets could be distributed to stockholders prior to the final liquidation of a corporation. Since stockholders have no liability for corporate debts, creditors would be unable to obtain satisfaction of their claims. Therefore, the concept of legal capital limits the assets that may be distributed to stockholders prior to the liquidation of the corporation and the settlement of its debts. Consequently, dividends cannot be declared by a corporation if such payments would decrease the owners' equity to an amount which is below the specified minimum legal capital—that is, the par value of the outstanding shares or, in some instances, par value plus a certain additional amount. Most state laws also provide that if the amount invested by individual stockholders is less than the established par value of the stock purchased, the stockholders may be held liable to the corporation's creditors for any difference between the amount paid and par value in the event the corporation is unable to meet its debts.

Laws requiring that stock have a par value were originally intended to protect the creditors of a corporation by restricting the distribution of a portion of corporate capital. However, the existence of a par value for capital stock has also caused certain problems. In some instances, investors have confused an arbitrary par value with the actual value of the ownership interest in the corporation. Also, if the market value of the stock falls below the par value established by the corporate charter, a potential liability to the investor may prevent the sale of additional[1] shares of stock by

---
[1] This liability applies only to the original issue of stock, not to stock purchased and then resold by investors.

the corporation unless or until the corporate charter is amended to change the par value of the stock. Consequently, some states have enacted legislation permitting the issuance of stock without par value, referred to as no-par stock. In these states, the legal capital of the corporation may be the total amount paid for the shares by the stockholders, or a stated value per share may be established by the board of directors.

ISSUANCE OF PAR VALUE STOCK

The primary significance of par value from an accounting viewpoint is that the capital stock account is credited with the par value of shares issued regardless of the amount received when the stock is sold. For example, if 1,000 shares of $10 par value common stock are sold at par value for cash, the entry would be as follows:

```
Cash ............................................. 10,000
    Common stock ............................           10,000
```

When stock is sold for more than its par value, the amount received in excess of the par value is recorded as "additional paid-in capital." To illustrate, assume that 1,000 shares of $10 par value common stock were sold for $12 per share. The entry to record the issuance is as follows:

```
Cash ............................................. 12,000
    Common stock ............................           10,000
    Additional paid-in capital in excess of par value    2,000
```

The additional paid-in capital account is added to the capital stock account in reporting the total invested or contributed capital of the corporation. Contributed capital of the corporation in the above example would be shown in the stockholders' equity section of the balance sheet as shown below:

STOCKHOLDERS' EQUITY:

Common stock, $10 par value, 5,000 shares authorized, 1,000 shares issued and outstanding	$10,000
Additional paid-in capital on common stock	2,000
Total Contributed Capital	$12,000

If capital stock is issued for an amount less than its par value, the difference is charged or debited to a "discount on capital stock" account. This account would be shown as a deduction from the capital stock account in the balance sheet. Since selling stock at a discount is illegal in many states and usually represents a contingent liability to the creditors of the corporation in the remaining states, it is seldom encountered in practice.

The par value of stock will normally be set at an amount which is less than its anticipated selling price, thus avoiding this problem.

ISSUANCE OF STOCK FOR NONCASH ASSETS

Sometimes a corporation may issue shares of its capital stock in exchange for assets such as land, buildings, or equipment. In such a case, the transaction may be recorded at the market value of the shares issued or at the market value of the assets acquired, whichever is a better indicator of market value. The market value of stock may be determined by reference to recent cash purchases and sales of the same class of stock by investors. Often, many shares of a large, publicly held corporation are traded daily through stock exchanges. Alternatively, if the market value of the shares issued cannot be determined, recent cash sales of similar assets or an independent appraisal of the asset may be used in order to record the transaction. Usually, the board of directors is given the responsibility by law for establishing a proper valuation for the issuance of stock for assets other than cash. To illustrate, assume that a corporation acquired land in exchange for five hundred shares of its $10 par value common stock. If the stock is traded on an established stock exchange and the current market price was $20, the transaction would be recorded as follows:

```
Land ..................................... 10,000
    Common stock ..........................         5,000
    Additional paid-in capital ............         5,000
```

If there is no established market for the stock, the market value of the asset acquired may be used in recording the exchange. For example, if similar acreage had recently sold for $11,000, the entry to record the transaction would be:

```
Land ..................................... 11,000
    Common stock ..........................         5,000
    Additional paid-in capital ............         6,000
```

ISSUANCE OF NO-PAR STOCK

At one time, all states required that stocks have a specified par value. However, to eliminate problems such as the liability for issuance discount and potential confusion over the meaning of par value, many states now permit the issuance of stock without par value.

The accounting entries which are necessary in order to record the issuance of no-par capital stock depend upon the specific laws of the state in which the shares are sold. Some states require that the entire issue price of no-par stock be regarded as legal capital. In these states, the capital account is credited for the entire amount received when the stock is issued.

To illustrate, assume that a corporation issues 1,000 shares of its no-par common stock for $12 per share. This transaction would be recorded as follows:

```
Cash ....................................... 12,000
    Common stock ............................    12,000
```

Other states allow the corporation to specify a stated value for no-par shares. When a stated value has been established, that amount is credited to Capital Stock and any excess is credited to Additional Paid-in Capital in Excess of Stated Value. For example, assume that the board of directors established a stated value of $10 per share for its stock. Issuance of 1,000 shares at a price of $12 would be recorded as follows:

```
Cash ....................................... 12,000
    Common stock ............................    10,000
    Additional paid-in capital ..............     2,000
```

The additional paid-in capital in excess of stated value account is reported as a part of contributed capital in the stockholders' equity section of the balance sheet.

SUBSCRIPTIONS FOR CAPITAL STOCK

In some instances, a corporation may make an agreement with an investor to sell a number of shares of stock to him at a stipulated price. If the purchaser agrees to pay for the stock at some future date or with installment payments over a period of time, the sale of stock is referred to as a subscription. Subscriptions are an asset to the corporation since they represent cash or other assets to be received from the investor at some future date. Therefore, an account entitled subscriptions receivable is debited when subscriptions are accepted. Although shares are not actually issued until they are paid for, a corporation accepting stock subscriptions is committed to issue the shares upon receipt of the total specified purchase price. Accordingly, a common stock subscribed account is credited for the par value of the stock subscribed. The difference between the specified subscription price and par value is credited to additional paid-in capital (or discount). For example, assume that a corporation accepts subscriptions for 1,000 shares of its $10 par value common stock at a price of $18 per share. The subscription contract requires payment in two equal installments due in 60 and 90 days. This transaction would be recorded as follows:

```
Subscriptions receivable ........................ 18,000
    Common stock subscribed .....................    10,000
    Additional paid-in capital ..................     8,000
```

When subscribers make payments on their subscriptions, the amount collected by the corporation is credited to the subscriptions receivable account. For example, upon receipt of the first installment of the subscription illustrated above, the following entry would be made:

```
Cash ..................................... 9,000
    Subscriptions receivable  ...................     9,000
```

When the subscription price has been collected in full, shares of stock are issued to the investor by the corporation. For example, when the second installment is collected, stock certificates for 1,000 shares of stock will be issued. Collection of the installment payment and issuance of the shares would be recorded as follows:

```
Cash ..................................... 9,000
    Subscriptions receivable  ...................     9,000
Common stock subscribed  ................... 10,000
    Common stock  ...........................    10,000
```

During the period in which subscriptions are outstanding, subscriptions receivable from investors are reported as an asset on the balance sheet and common stock subscribed is shown as a part of contributed capital in the stockholders' equity section of the balance sheet.

STOCKHOLDERS' EQUITY IN THE BALANCE SHEET

The stockholders' equity section of the balance sheet should report adequate information concerning each class of corporate stock outstanding. If more than a single class of stock is issued, the nature, special rights, and dollar amounts outstanding should be shown for each. Presentation of stockholders' equity in the balance sheet might appear as follows:

STOCKHOLDERS' EQUITY:

6% preferred stock, $100 par value, 10,000 shares authorized, 6,000 shares issued and outstanding		$ 600,000
Common stock, $10 par value, 100,000 shares authorized, 50,000 shares issued and outstanding		500,000
Common stock subscribed, 1,000 shares		10,000
Additional paid-in capital:		
Common stock issued and subscribed	$130,000	
Preferred stock	60,000	190,000
Total Contributed Capital		$1,300,000
Retained earnings		450,000
Total Stockholders' Equity		$1,750,000

SUMMARY

A corporation is a separate legal entity permitted to engage in activities in a manner similar to those performed by a natural person. Other important characteristics of a corporation include the transferability of ownership, continuity of life, limited liability of owners, separation of ownership and management, corporate taxation, and government regulation.

Forming a corporation includes obtaining a state corporate charter, electing a board of directors, adopting bylaws, and issuing capital stock to shareholders. The expenses incurred in this process are referred to as organization costs and are accumulated in an intangible asset account and either retained as an asset indefinitely or amortized over a reasonable but arbitrarily selected period of time.

The two primary sources of the equity capital of a corporation are contributions by shareholders and earnings retained in the business. In exchange for their contributions, the shareholders receive stock certificates and certain basic rights. Common stock usually entitles its owners to vote in stockholders' meetings, to share in corporate earnings through dividends, to maintain a proportionate interest in the firm when additional shares are issued, and to share in the distribution of remaining assets upon liquidation. Preferred stock usually has limited or no voting rights but does have preference in dividend and liquidation distributions. In addition, preferred stock may be cumulative, participating, convertible, and/or callable.

Capital stock may have an arbitrary value established by the corporate charter (referred to as par value) or established by the corporate directors (referred to as stated value). This value generally has no relationship to the selling price of the stock, but a firm may be required to retain a corresponding amount in the business to protect corporate creditors. Upon issuance of stock, the corporation credits the Capital Stock account for the par or stated value and credits Additional Paid-in Capital for any excess. If the stock has no par or stated value, the entire proceeds of the sale are usually credited to Capital Stock.

When common stock subscriptions are taken by a corporation, receivables are created and a Common Stock Subscribed account is credited. The actual stock is not issued until the payment is received, at which time Common Stock Subscribed is debited and Common Stock is credited.

This chapter has discussed issues relating to the contributed capital segment of the stockholders' equity section of the balance sheet. The next chapter will discuss issues relating to the other major stockholders' equity segment, retained earnings.

KEY DEFINITIONS

Additional paid-in capital   Additional paid-in capital is the amount received on the issuance of capital stock in excess of its par or stated value.

Articles of incorporation   Articles of incorporation are included in the application made to the state for a corporate charter and include information concerning the corporation.

Capital stock   Capital stock is transferable shares of stock which evidence ownership in a corporation.

Charter   A charter is a contract between the state and the corporation which includes the general corporation laws of the state and the specific provisions of the articles of incorporation.

Common stock   Common stock is stock which has the basic rights of ownership and represents the residual ownership in the corporation.

Continuity of life   Status as a separate legal entity gives the corporation a perpetual existence.

Contributed capital   Contributed capital is capital invested directly by the shareholders of the corporation.

Controller   The controller is an officer who is responsible for the accounting function of the business.

Convertible preferred stock   Convertible preferred stock is stock which includes the privilege of allowing the shareholder to exchange preferred shares for a specified number of common shares at his option.

Corporation   A corporation is an association of persons joined together for some common purpose, organized in accordance with state laws as a legal entity, separate and distinct from its owners.

Cumulative preferred stock   Cumulative preferred stock is backed by a provision that if all or part of the specified dividend on preferred stock is not paid during a given year, the amount of the unpaid dividends accumulates and must be paid in a subsequent year before any dividends can be paid on common stock.

Deficit   A deficit is a debit balance in the retained earnings account.

Earned capital   Earned capital includes amounts provided by profitable operations and retained by the business.

Incorporators   Incorporators are the persons who legally form a corporation.

Legal capital   Legal capital is a limit on the amount of assets that can be distributed to the stockholders of a corporation prior to liquidation and settlement of the corporate debts.

Limited liability   The creditors of the corporation have a claim against the assets of the corporation and not against the personal property of the stockholders.

No-par stock   No-par stock is stock without a par value.

Organization costs   Organization costs are the costs which are necessary to form the corporation.

Par value   Par value is an arbitrary value which is established in the corporate charter and printed on the stock certificate. It establishes the legal capital of the corporation in many states.

Participating preferred stock Participating preferred stock is preferred stock which has the right to participate in some specified manner with common stockholders in dividends in excess of a stipulated amount paid to the common shareholders.

Preferred as to dividends Stock which is preferred as to dividends is entitled to receive a stated dividend each year before any dividend is paid on the common stock.

Preferred stock Preferred stock is a class of stock which has different rights from those associated with common stock.

Retained earnings Retained earnings represent the accumulated earnings of the corporation, increased by net income and reduced by net losses and distributions to shareholders.

Stock subscriptions Stock subscriptions involve an agreement by the corporation to sell a certain number of shares at a specified price to an investor with the payment at some future date(s). Upon full payment, the purchaser gains control of the stock.

QUESTIONS

1. What are some of the main advantages of organizing a business as a corporation rather than as a sole proprietorship or partnership?

2. Describe the following characteristics of a corporation:

    a. separate legal entity
    b. limited liability
    c. transferability of ownership interest
    d. continuity of existence

3. Explain the meaning of the term "double taxation" as it applies to a corporation.

4. Explain what is meant by the number of shares of stock authorized, issued, and outstanding.

5. What are four basic rights of a stockholder?

6. Describe the following features which may be applied to an issuance of preferred stock:

    a. cumulative
    b. participating
    c. preferred as to assets
    d. callable
    e. convertible

7. Explain the meaning of par value. Describe the accounting treatment of stock issued for more or less than par value.

8. Distinguish between par value and no-par stock.

9. What is the primary disadvantage of issuing stock for an amount less than par value?

10. What are organization costs? Describe two alternative accounting treatments for such costs.

11. Indicate the nature and balance sheet classification of the subscriptions receivable and common stock subscribed accounts.

12. What information regarding preferred stock should be disclosed in the balance sheet?

13. How should preferred dividends in arrears be reported in the balance sheet?

EXERCISES

14. Give the journal entries required to record each of the following stock transactions:

    a. Issuance of 1,000 shares of $10 par value common stock at $14 per share.
    b. Issuance of 100 shares of $100 par value preferred stock for a total of $12,000.
    c. Issuance of 500 shares of no-par common stock for $20 per share.
    d. Issuance of 2,000 shares of $10 par value common stock for land. Recent sales and purchases of the stock have been made at a price of $20 per share. The value of the land is not readily determinable.

15. Make the journal entries necessary to record the issuance of stock in each of the following independent cases.

    a. One hundred shares of $25 par value stock are sold at par for cash.
    b. Eighty shares of $15 par value stock are sold at $17 each for cash.
    c. One thousand shares of no-par capital stock are issued at $14 per share.
    d. Five hundred shares of no-par capital stock with a stated value of $10 per share are sold for $11 per share.

16. Jeffry Company was organized on March 1, 19x1. The authorized capital was 20,000 shares of $50 par value, 6 percent, cumulative preferred stock and 50,000 shares of $10 par value common stock. At the date of organization, all the common stock was issued at $20 per share and 10,000 shares of the preferred stock were sold at par.

Required:

Prepare the stockholders' equity section of the balance sheet for Jeffry Co. on March 1, after the issuance of the stock.

17. Niblet Corporation was organized on January 1, 19x1. On that date, the corporation issued 1,000 shares of $100 par value, 6 percent preferred stock and 20,000 shares of $10 par value common stock. During the first five years of its life, the corporation paid the following total dividends to its stockholders.

19x1	$ 0
19x2	6,000
19x3	20,000
19x4	15,000
19x5	18,000

Determine the total dividends paid to each class of stockholders assuming that the preferred stock is:

    a. cumulative and nonparticipating.
    b. noncumulative and nonparticipating.

18. Loggins Music Stores, Inc. accepted subscriptions for 250 shares of its no-par, $10 stated value capital stock on January 1, 19x1, at a price of $13 per share. On March 1, the firm collected $1,625 as a partial payment on the subscriptions. Then, on April 1, the balance in the subscriptions account was paid and all the shares were issued.

Required:

Prepare the journal entries necessary to record the above transactions on the books of Loggins Music Stores, Inc.

19. Monte Carter owns 300 of the 30,000 outstanding shares of stock in the MNX Company, which allows preemptive rights to all its existing stockholders. If MNX Company decides to issue an additional 6,000 shares of stock, how many of the new shares may Carter purchase? What would be his percent interest in the company?

20. The Drinkwater Corporation, still in its preliminary stages of organization, is trying to decide in which state they should incorporate. They have selected two possible states (fictitious names) in which to incorporate: Atokad and Odaroloc. Atokad requires that the entire issue price of no-par stock be regarded as legal capital. Odaroloc allows the corporation to specify a stated value for no-par shares. If Drinkwater Corporation issues 3,000 shares of no-par capital stock for a price of $40 and a stated value of $35, what would be the entries for this transaction in each of these two states?

21. Gung-Hoe contributed land to the Howdy-Handy Corporation in exchange for 3,600 shares of its $12 par value stock. Journalize this transaction under each of the following assumptions:

  a. For the past 2 weeks, Howdy-Handy's stock has traded for about $33 a share on the American Stock Exchange.
  b. Howdy-Handy's stock is not traded on any stock exchange and therefore has no established market. However, Gung-Hoe did receive an offer from a broker a week ago to buy the land for $130,000.

22. Hoagland, Inc. accepted subscriptions for 3,000 shares of its $20 par value common stock at a price of $21 a share. However, because of the large quantity of stock being issued, Hoagland required the subscriber to pay a downpayment of 20 percent and the remainder in two months.

Required:

Prepare the journal entries to record these transactions assuming the downpayment was made on June 30, 19x1 and the remainder was paid when due.

23. A junior accountant for the Fetters Company is unsure as to how to complete the following stockholders' equity section of the balance sheet.

Stockholders' Equity:

5 percent preferred stock *(1)* par value, 15,000 shares authorized, 9,000 shares issued and outstanding................................	$ 810,000
Common stock, $20 par value, 200,000 shares authorized, *(2)* shares issued and outstanding........	3,000,000
Common stock subscribed, 1,500 shares..............	*(3)*
Additional paid-in capital:	
Common stock issued and subscribed..............	*(4)*
Preferred stock................................	80,000
Total Contributed Capital.....................	*(5)*
Retained earnings................................	*(6)*
Total Stockholders' Equity...................	$4,099,000

Additional information:

Earnings for the corporation over its three year life were $18,000 a year. No dividends had ever been paid.

Required:

Complete this stockholders' equity section by filling in the numbers 1-6.

PROBLEMS

24. The Fabian Co. is organized on January 1, 19x1, with authorized stock of 30,000 shares of $5 par value common and 5,000 shares of $100 par value preferred. Give the entries required to record each of the following transactions:

   a. Assets are accepted as payment for 10,000 shares of common stock. The assets are valued as follows: land, $50,000; buildings, $130,000; and equipment, $20,000.
   b. The 5,000 preferred shares are sold at $105 per share.
   c. Subscriptions are received for 5,000 shares of common stock at $25.
   d. A payment of $50,000 is received on the subscribed stock.
   e. Subscriptions receivable of $75,000 are collected and the stock is issued.
   f. The remaining common stock is sold for $30 per share.

25. Consider each of the following independent cases.

   a. Kanoch, Inc. issues 50 shares of $25 par value stock in exchange for land appraised at $1,500. The shares are not actively traded. Record the issuance of the stock on the books of Kanoch, Inc.
   b. Red Rider Stables, Inc. acquired 100 acres of prime grazing land in exchange for 200 shares of no-par capital stock. It was found that a similar

13 | The Corporation: Organization and Capital Stock   395

100-acre tract had sold the previous year for $11,000. The company's stock has not been registered with a major exchange but the company's balance sheet reveals a book value of $50 per share. Record the issuance of the stock on the books of Red Rider Stables, Inc.

c. Monzingo Grocers, Inc. obtained a new store site in exchange for 400 shares of its $15 par value capital stock. The store site is in a recently developed area. Ten years ago wooded lots of similar size sold for $8,000. The latest New York Stock Exchange quotation for the stock was $30 per share. Record the issuance of the stock on the books of Monzingo Grocers, Inc.

26. Jones Co. had the following stock outstanding from January 1, 19x0, to December 31, 19x5.

   a. Common stock, $10 par value, 20,000 shares authorized and outstanding.
   b. Preferred stock, $100 par value with a $6 stated dividend, 10,000 shares authorized, 5,000 shares issued and outstanding.

During that period, Jones Co. paid the following dividends:

19x0	$ 0
19x1	80,000
19x2	0
19x3	30,000
19x4	70,000
19x5	20,000

Compute the amount of preferred dividends and common stock dividends in each year assuming that:

1. The preferred stock is noncumulative.
2. The preferred stock is cumulative.

27. Smith Corporation was organized on January 1, 19x1, with 100,000 shares of $10 par value common stock and 10,000 shares of $50 par value preferred stock authorized. During 19x1, Smith Corporation had the following stock transactions:

Jan. 1   Issued 5,000 shares of preferred stock for $60 per share.
Jan. 1   Issued 5,000 shares of common stock for $60 per share.
Oct. 1   Accepted subscriptions for 1,000 shares of common stock at a price of $16 per share. Payment is to be made in two equal installments payable in 60 and 120 days.
Nov. 30 Collected the first installment on the subscribed stock but issued no stock at this time.

Required:

a. Prepare the journal entries to record the stock transactions.
b. Prepare the stockholders' equity section of the balance sheet for Smith Corporation as of December 31, 19x1. (Assume that retained earnings are $64,000 on December 31, 19x1.)

28. Akens Co. was organized on January 1, 19x1. A portion of the December 31, 19x2, balance sheet of Akens Co. appeared as follows:

Stockholders' Equity:

6 percent preferred stock, $100 par value, 20,000 shares authorized............		$ 500,000
Preferred stock subscribed..................		100,000
Common stock, $10 par value, 100,000 shares authorized.................		400,000
Common stock subscribed..................		50,000
Additional paid-in capital:		
On common stock issued..................	$200,000	
On common stock subscribed.............	50,000	
On preferred stock issued.................	25,000	
On preferred stock subscribed............	10,000	285,000
Retained earnings...........................		$ 330,000
Total Stockholders' Equity..............		$1,665,000

Required:

1. How many shares of preferred stock are outstanding?
2. How many shares of common stock are outstanding?
3. How many shares of preferred stock are subscribed?
4. How many shares of common stock are subscribed?
5. What were the average issue prices of the common and the preferred shares outstanding?
6. What were the average subscription prices of the common stock and the preferred stock?
7. What is the total contributed capital of Akens Co.?

29. In examining the accounts of Longhorn Steel Company, you discover the following information pertaining to the stockholders' equity of the company at December 31, 19x1.

    a. 3,000 shares of $100 par value preferred stock issued, 9,000 shares authorized.
    b. The preferred dividend requirement for the year was met by paying dividends of $18,000.
    c. 16,000 shares of $10 par value common stock issued and outstanding.
    d. 20,000 shares of $10 par value common stock authorized.
    e. 2,000 shares of common stock subscribed.
    f. The average issue price of the common stock was $17.
    g. The average issue price of the preferred stock was $106.
    h. The average subscription price of the common stock was $19.
    i. Retained earnings were $219,000.

Required:

Prepare the stockholders' equity section of Longhorn Steel Company's balance sheet at December 31, 19x1.

13 | The Corporation: Organization and Capital Stock 397

30. The Babson Corporation began business on January 1, 19x1. During the first year of operations, the following transactions were completed that affected stockholders' equity.

   a. Sold for cash 300,000 shares of capital stock for $13 per share. The charter for the corporation authorized 1,000,000 shares of capital stock.
   b. Sold 5,000 shares of capital stock to the president of the company for $14 per share. Collected 35 percent of the subscription immediately and the balance is due at the end of 11 months.
   c. Exchanged 30,000 shares for a plant site. The seller had recently had an offer to sell the plant site for $380,000 and the site was carried on the seller's books at $420,000.
   d. Collected 25 percent on the subscription contract in (b).

   Required:

   Give entries for the above transactions using each of the following assumptions:

   1. The stock has a par value of $8 per share.
   2. The stock has no par value and no stated value.
   3. The stock has no par value but has a stated value of $10 per share. State any necessary assumptions of your own.

31. The Auburn Corporation earned income of $33,000, $25,000, $15,000, $12,000 and $55,000 during the last five years. The common stock consisted of 200,000 shares outstanding for the first three years and 250,000 shares for the last two years. Common stock has a par value of $1 per share. The preferred stock is 7 percent cumulative and nonparticipating. There were 50,000 shares of preferred stock issued and outstanding for the first two years and 75,000 shares the last three years. Preferred stock has a par value of $5 per share.

   Required:

   Calculate the dividends which each class of stock would receive over each of the last five years assuming (1) the entire net income was distributed each year, and (2) only 80 percent of the reported net income was distributed in the first three years, 90 percent in the last two years.

32. Record the following transactions on the books of the El Paso Corporation.

   a. The El Paso Corporation accepted subscriptions for 2,500 shares of its $15 par value common stock at a price of $23 per share. The subscription contract requires three installments, ½ now, ¼ in 60 days and the remainder in 90 days.
   b. The second installment was made on time.

c. The subscriber didn't pay for the third installment when it became due. It is the policy of the corporation to issue to a forfeiting subscriber the number of shares actually paid for rather than the total number contracted.

33. The Charles Brothers Company has decided to dissolve their partnership on January 1, 19x2, and incorporate their company in order to obtain additional capital. The new company will be called Charles Manufacturing Corporation. There were three brothers in the partnership, Joe, Jim, and Dick. Joe had an adjusted capital balance on December 31, 19x1 of $135,000, Jim's balance was $129,000, and Dick's balance was $141,000. Record the following transactions dealing with the incorporation of the Charles Manufacturing Corporation and prepare the stockholders' equity portion of the balance sheet for the newly-formed company.

   a. 100,000 shares of common stock with a par value of $5 per share were authorized and 20,000 shares were issued to the public for cash at $8 per share on January 1, 19x2.
   b. Each partner received 20,000 shares of stock in exchange for his share of the partnership's total capital. Goodwill was recognized.
   c. Dick Charles also contributed 500 shares of Lakeview Company stock to the corporation in exchange for 300 shares of the new corporation's stock. Dick had purchased the stock several years earlier for $10 a share.

34. Below is the stockholders' equity portion of Corpos Company's balance sheet.

    Stockholders' Equity:

6 percent preferred stock, $200 par value, 25,000 shares authorized	$1,000,000
Class A common stock, $12 par value 200,000 shares authorized	1,800,000
Class B common stock, $15 stated value, 150,000 shares authorized	1,500,000
Class B common stock subscribed	45,000
Paid-in capital:	
Preferred stock issued	210,000
Class A common stock issued	865,000
Class B common stock issued	125,000
Class B common stock subscribed	12,000
Retained earnings	$ 216,000
Total Stockholders' Equity	$5,773,000

    a. What is the total contributed capital of Corpos Company?
    b. How many shares of preferred stock are outstanding?
    c. How many shares of Class A common stock are outstanding?
    d. How many shares of Class B common stock are outstanding?
    e. How many shares of Class B common stock are subscribed?

f. What are the average prices for which the common stock, Classes A and B, were issued?
g. What is the average subscription price for the Class B common stock subscribed?

35. In order to obtain additional capital and limited liability, the Star Street Partnership decided to dissolve on January 1, 19x1, in order to form the Star Street Corporation. The newly-formed corporation was issued a charter from the state which authorized them to issue 60,000 shares of $8 par value common stock. The adjusted balances in the four partners' capital accounts before incorporation was Ott, $65,000; Sinclair, $45,000; Hanscom, $96,000; and Shute, $21,000. Each partner received one share of the new corporation's stock for every $10 in their capital account. Goodwill was recognized. In addition, 30,000 shares of the corporation's stock was issued to the public for $12 a share. Also, a building with a book value of $58,715 was contributed in exchange for 4,900 shares of capital stock.

Required:

Record the above transactions in journal form and prepare the stockholders' equity portion of the balance sheet for the newly-formed corporation.

Refer to the Annual Report included in the Appendix at the end of the text:

36. At the end of the most recent year, what is the total equity?

37. At the end of the most recent year, which account(s) represent(s) the major portion of equity?

38. At the end of the most recent year, where is net income reflected in the stockholders' equity section of the balance sheet?

39. Comparing the two years, what is the increase/decrease in the common stock account?

40. What factors cause an increase in the common stock account? What factors cause a decrease?

Learning Objectives

Chapter 14 discusses matters relating to the retained earnings and dividends of a corporation. Studying this chapter should enable you to:

1. Discuss the concept of retained earnings and how it is accounted for.

2. Provide examples of extraordinary items and discuss the two essential characteristics of an extraordinary item.

3. Describe the situation in which prior period adjustments are appropriate.

4. List and give examples of three types of accounting changes.

5. Compute earnings per share and book value per share and explain the significance of each.

6. Recognize the accounting entries required to record the declaration and payment of both cash and stock dividends.

7. Discuss the purpose of and accounting procedures for treasury stock.

14

The Corporation: Earnings and Dividends

INTRODUCTION

The stockholders' equity section of a corporation is divided into two major segments, contributed capital and retained earnings. Retained earnings represent accumulated earnings which were retained in the business. The retained earnings account is increased by the net income of the business and reduced by net losses and distributions to shareholders in the form of dividends. In the end-of-period closing entries, revenue and expense accounts are closed to the income summary account. When revenues exceed expenses, the credit balance which remains in the income summary account is equal to the firm's net income for the period. Conversely, a debit balance in the income summary account indicates a net loss for the accounting period. The balance in the income summary account is closed to retained earnings. Similarly, the debit balance in the dividends account is transferred or closed out as a reduction in retained earnings. This chapter considers the accounting for transactions affecting retained earnings and discusses various issues which are related to both corporate earnings and dividends.

NATURE OF EARNINGS

A primary purpose of reporting corporate earnings is to provide useful information to stockholders, potential investors, creditors, and other interested users of financial statements. The net income or loss of a corporation is determined in basically the same manner as that of a partnership or sole proprietorship.

There are several special problems which are related to the preparation of the income statement that have not been discussed previously. These include (1) accounting for transactions which are not related to the normal business activities and which occur infrequently; (2) accounting for discontinued operations; (3) prior period adjustments; (4) recording the effects of accounting changes; and (5) determination of earnings on a per share basis.

EXTRAORDINARY ITEMS

The net income of a corporation as reported in its income statement includes earnings from normal operations of the business as well as certain infrequently occurring transactions which are not related to the ordinary activities of the business. As a result of *Opinions No. 9* and *No. 30* of the Accounting Principles Board, transactions which occur infrequently and which do not result from the normal operations of the business, referred to as extraordinary items, are reported as a separate amount in the income statement.

To be classified as an extraordinary item in the income statement, an item must be both unusual in nature and not reasonably expected to recur in the foreseeable future. Determining the degree of abnormality and the probability of recurrence of a particular transaction should take into account the environment in which the business operates. Examples of potential extraordinary items include the effects of major casualties (e.g., an earthquake, if rare in the area, and an expropriation of assets by a foreign government). In addition, the effect of an extraordinary event should be classified separately only if it is considered to be material in amount in relation to income from normal operations. To illustrate, assume that in 19x1 the Dolphin Company had income after taxes from normal operations of $100,000 and a $20,000 gain (net of taxes)[1] which meets the criteria for classification as an extraordinary item. A simplified income statement for the Dolphin Company might appear as follows:

Dolphin Co.
Income Statement
For the Year Ended December 31, 19x1

Net sales	$400,000
Cost of goods sold	100,000
Gross margin	$300,000
Expenses	200,000
Income before extraordinary items	$100,000
Extraordinary gain, net of tax	20,000
Net Income	$120,000

As indicated above, special consideration is given to the reporting of gains and losses. The FASB has defined gains and losses as follows:

> Gains are increases in equity (net assets) from peripheral or incidental transactions of an entity and from all other transactions and other events and circumstances affecting the entity during a period except those that result from revenues or investments by owners.
> Losses are decreases in equity (net assets) from peripheral or incidental transactions of an entity and from all other transactions and other events and circumstances affecting the entity during a period except those that result from expenses or distributions to owners.[2]

Certain gains or losses should not be classified as extraordinary items, even if material in amount, because they could be expected to occur in the normal or ordinary operations of the business. For example, a loss resulting from a write-down made to recognize a decline in the value of inventory due to obsolescence should not be reported as an extraordinary item. Such an item should be included in the computation of income before extraordinary items. Other examples of items that would not normally be considered extraordinary items regardless of their amount include:

---

[1] See Chapter 20 for a discussion of the allocation of income tax within a period.

[2] "Elements of Financial Statements of Business Enterprises," FASB Statement No. 3 (Stamford, Conn. FASB, 1980), p. xii.

1. The write-down or write-off of receivables, inventories, equipment leased to others, or intangible assets.
2. The gains or losses from exchanges or translation of foreign currencies, including those relating to major devaluation or revaluations.
3. The gains or losses on the disposal of a segment of a business.
4. Other gains or losses from the sale or abandonment of property, plant, or equipment used in the business.
5. The effects of a strike.
6. The adjustments or accruals on long-term contracts.

Items which are either unusual in nature or occur infrequently, but do not meet both criteria, should not be classified as extraordinary items. However, if such items are material in amount, they should be separately disclosed by reporting them as separate components in income before extraordinary items or by including a description of the item and its effect as a footnote to the income statement.

DISCONTINUED OPERATIONS

The term "discontinued operations" refers to the operation of any subsidiary, division, or department of a business that has been or will be sold, abandoned, or otherwise disposed of. In APB *Opinion No. 30,* the Board concluded that the results of continuing normal operations should be reported separately from discontinued operations. Any gain or loss from the disposal of a segment of a business along with the results of operations of the segment should be reported in a separate section of the income statement. The purpose of reporting on the continuing operations of a business separately from the discontinued operations is that it allows financial statement users to make better judgments about the future earnings prospects of the business. Accordingly, an income statement of a firm that has discontinued operations would appear as follows:

Kingsberry Company
Income Statement
For the Year Ended December 31, 19x1

Sales		$10,000
Less: Cost of goods sold		4,000
Gross profit		$ 6,000
Operating expenses		4,000
Income from continuing operations before income taxes		$ 2,000
Provision for income taxes		800
Income from continuing operations		$ 1,200
Discontinued operations (Footnote):		
Income from operations of discontinued division (less taxes of $300)	$500	
Loss on disposal of division (less tax effect of $200)	(300)	200
Net Income		$ 1,400

PRIOR PERIOD ADJUSTMENTS

The provisions of FASB *Statement No. 16* indicate that, with two exceptions, all items of profit or loss recognized in a given year should be included in the determination of net income for that year. The only exceptions are corrections of errors in previous financial statements and adjustments that result from realization of income tax benefits of preacquisition loss carry forwards on purchased subsidiaries. Errors may result from computational mistakes, omission of data, incorrect application of accounting principles, or the use of unacceptable accounting principles. Corrections of errors of prior periods are not included in the income statement of the year in which the error is discovered. Instead, these items are shown as direct adjustments to beginning retained earnings.[3]

ACCOUNTING CHANGES

Changes in accounting occur because of the uncertainty involved in the preparation of periodic financial reports. Subsequent to the preparation of financial statements, additional information may be obtained which necessitates an adjustment of the accounting records. Prior to the issuance of APB *Opinion No. 20* on accounting changes, there were various practices and procedures for reporting the effects of accounting changes on financial statements. In *Opinion No. 20*, the Board clarified the different types of changes and provided guidelines for the reporting procedures to be employed. Three types of changes may be involved: (1) a change in accounting principle; (2) a change in accounting estimate; and (3) a correction of an error of a prior period.[4] These three types of changes will be illustrated and discussed in the paragraphs that follow.

Change in Accounting Principle. As previously indicated, the consistency principle requires that the same accounting methods be used from one accounting period to the next. However, as an exception to this principle, a change in accounting methods is allowed if the new method used can be justified as being preferable to the previously used method, and the effects of the change are adequately disclosed in financial statements. Thus, a change in accounting principle results from the adoption of a generally accepted accounting method which differs from the one that was previously used. An example would be a change from the sum-of-the-years'-digits method of depreciation to the straight-line method. For most types of changes in accounting methods, the cumulative effect which the use of the new method would have had on income in all prior periods that the old method was used must be included in the income statement in the year in which the accounting change is made.[5]

---

[3] *Statement on Financial Accounting Standards No. 16*, "Prior Period Adjustments" (Stamford, Conn.: Financial Accounting Standards Board, 1977).

[4] A fourth type of accounting change, a change in reporting entity, is not applicable to this discussion.

[5] Certain specific types of accounting changes are disclosed by revising the financial statements of prior periods to reflect the effects of the use of the new method.

To illustrate, assume that a company acquired a truck on January 1, 19x1, at a cost of $4,000. The useful life of the truck was estimated to be 4 years with a salvage value of $400. At the date of acquisition, the company decided to use the sum-of-the-years'-digits depreciation method. Further assume that the company decided to switch to the straight-line method at the end of 19x3. At the time of the change in methods, the cumulative difference between the old and the new methods of depreciation must be determined. The amount of this difference would be computed as follows:

Year	Sum-of-the-Years' Digits	Straight-Line	Difference to December 31, 19x2
19x1	$1,440	$ 900	$540
19x2	1,080	900	180
	$2,520	$1,800	$720

The $720 difference in depreciation between the two methods would be adjusted during 19x3 as follows:

Accumulated Depreciation 720
    Depreciation Adjustment, Change in Accounting Principle   720

This entry reduces the balance in the accumulated depreciation account to what it would have been had the straight-line method been used from the time the asset was purchased. The depreciation adjustment would appear in the income statement in the year of the change. After the adjustment is made, the depreciation expense for 19x3 and 19x4 would be recorded at $900 per year on the straight-line method.

The effect of this change on the current and prior years' income should be explained by a footnote to the financial statements. A change in accounting principle is appropriate only when it can be demonstrated that the new method is preferable.

Change in Accounting Estimate. Changes in the estimates used in accounting may occur as additional information regarding the original estimate is obtained. An example of such a change would be a change in the estimated salvage value or service life of an asset. The procedure used in adjusting for this change is to spread the remaining undepreciated cost of the asset over its remaining useful life. This procedure will allocate the remaining book value of the asset, less the new estimated salvage value, to expense over the revised estimated remaining useful life of the asset.

To illustrate, assume the company in the previous example decided in 19x4 that while the straight-line method should be used, the useful life of the asset should have been six (rather than four) years and the salvage value should have been $100 (instead of $400). The amount of depreciation expense for 19x4 would be computed as follows:

Original cost		$4,000
Less: Accumulated depreciation to December 31, 19x3		2,700
Book value at December 31, 19x3		1,300
Less: Estimated salvage value		100
Amount to be depreciated		$1,200
Divide by: Estimated remaining useful life		3 years
Depreciation per year		$ 400

At the end of 19x4, 19x5, 19x6, the following entry would be made to record the depreciation expense:

Depreciation expense	400	
Accumulated depreciation		400

Errors. Accounting errors may result from mistakes in the application of accounting principles, oversights, misuse of facts, or mistakes in mathematics. To illustrate, assume that the truck acquired on January 1, 19x1, had been incorrectly recorded as an expense rather than as an asset. This error was discovered on December 31, 19x2, at which time it was decided that the asset should have been assigned an estimated useful life of four years and a $400 salvage value. The company uses the straight-line method of depreciation. The entry at December 31, 19x2, to record the correction of the error would be:

Asset	4,000	
Accumulated depreciation		900
Prior period adjustment		3,100

This entry records the asset at its cost of $4,000, the accumulated depreciation of $900 that should have been recorded in 19x1, and an adjustment of the prior year's earnings of $3,100 ($4,000 asset expenditure erroneously recorded as an expense less $900 depreciation expense which should have been recorded in 19x1). The prior period adjustment would be a correction of retained earnings and would not appear in the income statement. Depreciation for 19x2 would be recorded in the normal manner:

Depreciation expense	900	
Accumulated depreciation		900

EARNINGS PER SHARE

An amount referred to as earnings per share is basically the net income of a company per share of common stock outstanding for a given period. Data on earnings per share of a corporation probably receive more attention than any other single item of financial information. Earnings per share ratios are included in annual reports issued by corporations and receive extensive coverage in the financial press and the investment services. Earnings per share is often considered to be an important indicator of the market price of common stock and, in some cases, an indication of expected dividends per share.

Because of the widespread attention given to earnings per share data, it was recognized that such information should be computed on a consistent and meaningful basis by all companies. Accordingly, *Opinion No. 15* of the Accounting Principles Board provided detailed procedures for the computation and presentation of earnings per share figures under different circumstances.[6] Further, the APB concluded that earnings per share data should be disclosed in income statements for all periods covered by the statement. If extraordinary items and gains or losses from discontinued operations are included in net income for the period, separate earnings per share figures would normally be provided for: (1) income from continuing operations; (2) discontinued operations; (3) extraordinary items; and (4) net income. This data is usually presented in the income statement following the net income figure.

The computation of earnings per share is relatively simple when the capital structure of the corporation includes only common stock and the number of shares outstanding have not changed during the period. In this case, earnings per share of common stock is computed by dividing net income by the number of shares of common stock outstanding. To illustrate, assume that Dolphin Co. had 40,000 shares of common stock outstanding during 19x1 and earnings as shown below. Its earnings per share information would be computed as follows:

$$\text{Ordinary income} \quad \frac{\$100,000}{40,000} = \$2.50$$

$$\text{Extraordinary gain} \quad \frac{\$20,000}{40,000} = \$.50$$

$$\text{Net income} \quad \frac{\$120,000}{40,000} = \$3.00$$

When there are both common and preferred stock outstanding, the net income must be reduced by the preferred dividend requirements to determine the net income available to common stockholders. If the firm issues or acquires shares of stock during the period, the divisor in the calculation is the average number of shares outstanding during the year. In such circumstances, the earnings per share is computed as follows:

---

[6] *Opinions of the Accounting Principles Board, No. 15*, "Earnings Per Share" (New York: American Institute of Certified Public Accountants, 1969).

$$\frac{\text{Earnings}}{\text{Per Share}} = \frac{\text{Net Income} - \text{Preferred Dividends}}{\text{Average Number of Common Shares Outstanding}}$$

The capital structures of many corporations include convertible securities, stock options, and other securities which may include rights that can be converted into shares of common stock at the option of the holder. A capital structure is considered to be complex when it includes securities and rights that could potentially decrease earnings per share by increasing the number of common shares outstanding. The existence of a complex capital structure results in significant complications in computations of earnings per share data. Essentially, they involve the calculation of hypothetical earnings per share figures which assume conversion of certain securities into common stock. The details of these considerations, however, are beyond the scope of this text.

DIVIDENDS

Dividends are distributions made by a corporation to its shareholders. Such distributions are paid in proportion to the number of shares owned by each stockholder. Dividends may be in the form of cash, other assets, or shares of the corporation's own stock. Unless otherwise specified, a dividend represents a distribution of cash. Payment of dividends is provided by action of the board of directors. The board has complete control of the type, amount, and timing of any and all dividend payments. However, once dividends are declared, they become a legal liability of the corporation to its stockholders.

In most cases, dividends represent a distribution of accumulated corporate earnings. It is ordinarily illegal to declare dividends in excess of the balance in the retained earnings account. In other words, an ordinary dividend usually may not be paid from any amounts which were invested by stockholders. The existence of a credit balance in the retained earnings account, however, does not necessarily indicate that there is cash available for the payment of dividends. Retained earnings is unrelated to the balance in the cash account because funds obtained from the accumulated income of the business may have been used to increase noncash assets or to decrease liabilities. Thus, a corporation with a large retained earnings balance may be unable to distribute cash dividends to its stockholders. On the other hand, a corporation with a substantial amount of cash may decide to pay little or no dividends to its stockholders so that the cash may be retained and used for other corporate objectives.

Because dividends are important to investors and therefore have an effect on the market price of the stock, most corporations attempt to adhere to a well formulated or established dividend policy. Although the percentage of earnings paid out in dividends varies widely according to the objectives of the firm, most corporations usually attempt to maintain a stable or increasing record of dividend payments.

While ordinary dividends are usually limited to the amount of retained earnings, a corporation may pay a liquidating dividend in order to return to the stockholders a portion of their original investment. Such a dividend is normally paid in conjunction with a permanent reduction in the size of a business or, alternatively, upon liquidation of a firm. Accordingly, such distributions are recorded by reducing capital stock and additional paid-in capital accounts.

Important Dates Related to Dividends

There are three important dates related to dividends:

1. Date of declaration.
2. Date of record.
3. Date of payment.

On the date of declaration, the board of directors of a corporation formally establishes a liability of a specified amount to its stockholders. The dividend and related liability, dividends payable, are recorded at that time. If financial statements are prepared after dividends are declared but before they are paid, dividends payable are classified as a current liability in the balance sheet. Following the declaration date, the corporation prepares a list of the stockholders as of the date of record—these are the stockholders who are entitled to receive the dividends. No entry is required by the corporation on the record date.

A period of time is usually necessary between the record date and the date of payment to allow the corporation sufficient time to identify those stockholders who will receive dividends and to process the dividend checks. An entry is made on the date of payment to record the distribution of cash and to remove the liability for dividends payable.

Cash Dividends

Dividends are usually paid in cash. Such dividends result in a reduction of both the cash and retained earnings of a corporation. Dividends on common stock are usually stated as a specific amount per share, while preferred stock dividends may be stated at either a specific dollar amount or a percentage of the par value per share. For example, a dividend on $100 par value preferred stock might be specified as either $5 or as 5 percent of par value. In either case, dividends paid to each stockholder are in proportion to the number of shares owned.

To illustrate, assume that the Jet Co. has 10,000 shares of common stock and 5,000 shares of 6 percent, $100 par value preferred stock outstanding. Further assume that on December 15 the company declares the preferred dividend and a $5 per share dividend on common stock. The

$30,000 preferred dividend (.06 × $100 × 5,000 shares) and the $50,000 common dividend ($5 × 10,000 shares) are payable on January 15 to its stockholders of record on December 20. The entries which are required to record the declaration of the dividend on December 15 and its payment on January 15 are as follows:

Dec.	15	Preferred dividends..................	30,000	
		Common dividends..................	50,000	
		Dividends payable.................		80,000
	20	No entry		
Jan.	15	Dividends payable...................	80,000	
		Cash............................		80,000

The dividend accounts are closed to retained earnings during the normal year-end closing process. Assuming that the accounting period for the Jet Co. ends on December 31, the following entry would be made on that date:

Dec.	31	Retained earnings....................	80,000	
		Preferred dividends................		30,000
		Common dividends.................		50,000

In some instances, the corporation may debit retained earnings directly, rather than a dividend account. In these instances, a closing entry would not be required.

Stock Dividends

A distribution made to stockholders in the form of additional shares of a company's own stock is referred to as a stock dividend. Usually, such a distribution consists of additional common stock given to common stockholders. A stock dividend results in a proportionate increase in the number of shares owned by each stockholder. For example, a ten percent stock dividend entitles a stockholder to receive one additional share for each ten shares of stock he owns.

Since a stock dividend is paid on a pro rata basis, each stockholder retains the identical percentage interest in the firm after the dividend as he owned prior to the distribution. For example, assume that a stockholder owned 100 of 1,000 outstanding shares of a corporation. Thus, the stockholder owned 10 percent (100/1,000) of the corporation's outstanding stock. Further assume that the corporation declared a 5 percent stock dividend. The stockholder would receive 5 (.05 × 100) of the 50 (.05 × 1,000) additional shares of stock issued. Consequently, the stockholder's percentage interest in the corporation remains at 10 percent (105/1,050) after the stock dividend. A stockholder, however, may benefit from a stock dividend if there is less than a proportionate decrease in the market price of the stock associated with the distribution. In this case, the market value of the total shares owned by the stockholder would increase.

Unlike a cash dividend, a stock dividend does not result in a decrease in either the corporation's assets or its total stockholders' equity. If a stock dividend has no effect on either the assets or the equity of the corporation, or in the relative ownership interests of the shareholders, why do corporations distribute such dividends? A primary purpose of issuing stock dividends is to enable the corporation to give its stockholders some evidence of increased retained earnings without actually distributing cash. Thus, although a stock dividend does not affect corporate assets or increase the individual stockholder's relative interest in the corporation, it is perceived to be a distribution of earnings by many shareholders.

Another reason for distributing a stock dividend is to reduce the selling price of the corporation's stock. Because a stock dividend of a sizable amount increases the number of shares outstanding with no change in corporate assets, the market price of the stock normally decreases. A corporation may desire to reduce the market price of its stock so that it will be more readily marketable among investors.

Since a stock dividend increases the number of shares outstanding, many states require an associated increase in the legal capital of the corporation. Therefore, even though such a dividend has no effect on total stockholders' equity, an entry is required in order to transfer a portion of retained earnings to contributed capital if such capitalization is required by the state. This is referred to as "capitalizing" a part of retained earnings. Consequently, the retained earnings "capitalized" is no longer available for distribution to stockholders in the form of cash dividends.

In many states, the minimum amount which must be transferred from retained earnings to contributed capital is an amount equal to the par or stated value of the shares issued. In other states, there is no such requirement. However, because it is generally believed that most shareholders regard a stock dividend as something of value, the American Institute of CPAs has recommended that in certain circumstances an amount equal to the fair market value of the shares to be issued as a stock dividend should be capitalized. This reasoning was explained by the Committee on Accounting Procedure of the AICPA as follows:

> ... many recipients of stock dividends look upon them as distributions of corporate earnings and usually in an amount equivalent to the fair value of the additional shares received. Furthermore, it is presumed that such views of recipients are materially strengthened in those instances, which are by far the most numerous, where the issuances are so small in comparison with the shares previously outstanding that they do not have any apparent effect upon the share market price and,

consequently, the market value of the shares previously held remains substantially unchanged.[7]

The Committee further suggested that these circumstances exist with the issuance of a small stock dividend. A small stock dividend is defined as an increase of less than 20 percent to 25 percent of the number of shares previously outstanding.

To illustrate the entries for the issuance of a small stock dividend, assume that the stockholders' equity of a corporation on May 1 was as follows:

Common stock, $5 par value, 20,000 shares outstanding	$100,000
Additional paid-in capital	20,000
Total Contributed Capital	$120,000
Retained earnings	80,000
Total Stockholders' Equity	$200,000

Assume further that on May 2 the company declares a 10 percent stock dividend, or a dividend of 2,000 shares (.10 × 20,000), which is to be distributed on June 1. Assuming that the shares are selling in the market on the declaration date at a price of $20 per share, an amount equal to the fair value of the shares to be issued, or $40,000 (2,000 × $20), would be transferred from retained earnings to the appropriate contributed capital accounts. The capital stock account is credited for the par value of the shares issued and the remainder is added to additional paid-in capital. The following entries would be made to record the declaration and distribution of the stock dividend:

May 2	Retained Earnings	40,000	
	Stock Dividend Distributable		10,000
	Additional Paid-in Capital		30,000
June 1	Stock Dividend Distributable	10,000	
	Common Stock		10,000

If financial statements are prepared between the date of declaration and the date of distribution of a stock dividend, the stock dividend distributable account should be included in the stockholders' equity section of the balance sheet. It is not classified as a liability because the corporation has no obligation to distribute cash or any other asset.

As previously indicated, the distribution of a stock dividend has no

---

[7] *Accounting Research Bulletin No. 43*, "Restatement and Revision of Accounting Research Bulletins" (New York: American Institute of Certified Public Accountants, 1953), Ch. 7, par. 10.

effect on either the assets or the total stockholders' equity of a corporation. In the illustration above, the only effect on the corporation was a transfer of $40,000 from retained earnings to contributed capital. The stockholders' equity after payment of the stock dividend on June 1 would appear as follows:

Common stock, $5 par value, 22,000 shares outstanding	$110,000
Additional paid-in capital	50,000
Total Contributed Capital	$160,000
Retained earnings	40,000
Total Stockholders' Equity	$200,000

The Committee on Accounting Procedure further indicated that stock dividends in excess of 20% to 25% would be expected to materially reduce the market value per share of stock. Accordingly, the Committee recommended that if capitalization is required by the state, such stock dividends should be recorded by capitalizing retained earnings only to the extent of the par or stated value of the shares issued. Under these circumstances, the entry to record the stock dividend would be a debit to retained earnings and a credit to capital stock for the par value of the shares issued. Again, there is no effect on the total stockholders' equity of the corporation.

STOCK SPLITS

A corporation may desire to reduce the selling price of its stock in order to facilitate purchases and sales of its shares by investors. Reducing the price of shares to a reasonable amount normally increases the number of investors who are willing to purchase a corporation's stock. This may be accomplished by increasing the number of shares outstanding and decreasing the par or stated value of the stock by a proportionate amount. This procedure is referred to as a stock split.

For example, assume that a corporation has 20,000 shares of $10 par value common stock outstanding with a current market price of $200 per share. The company might declare a two-for-one stock split in which each current stockholder receives two new shares with a $5 par value for each share of $10 par stock he owned prior to the split. This action would tend to cause the market price to decrease to approximately $100 per share because there would be twice as many shares outstanding after the split with no change in the value of the corporation.

In a stock split there is a significant increase in the number of shares outstanding without a change in total stockholders' equity. A basic difference between a stock split and a stock dividend is the magnitude of the increase in the number of shares outstanding. Also, a stock split never requires any capitalization of retained earnings. Consequently, only a memorandum entry to the common stock account to indicate the change in par value and the new number of shares outstanding is required upon a stock split.

TREASURY STOCK

Corporations often acquire shares of their own stock from its stockholders. If the corporation does not cancel these shares but instead holds the stock, it is referred to as treasury stock. A corporation may desire to reacquire shares of its stock which have been previously issued in order to have stock available for employee stock purchase plans, for stock options, for bonuses, or for some other legitimate reason. Unissued stock may not be used for these purposes because of the preemptive right of the existing stockholders. Purchases of treasury stock are limited to the amount of retained earnings if the corporation is to maintain its legal capital. This occurs because the purchase of treasury stock results in the distribution of cash to certain stockholders. If assets are distributed to stockholders in excess of the retained earnings, the corporation is returning a portion of the invested capital. Therefore, the purchase of treasury stock reduces the amount available for subsequent distributions to the stockholders.

Although the stock of another corporation is an asset of the firm which owns it, treasury stock is generally not considered to be an asset because a corporation cannot have an ownership interest in itself. Instead, the purchase of a corporation's own shares represents a return of capital to the selling shareholder and, thus, a reduction in the stockholders' equity of the corporation. Consequently, treasury stock is shown as a deduction in the stockholders' equity section of the balance sheet.

There are several different methods for recording treasury stock transactions. However, one approach, referred to as the cost method, is a method commonly used in practice for recording the acquisition of treasury stock. For this reason, the cost method will be discussed in the paragraphs which follow.

When a corporation acquires its own shares, treasury stock is debited for the cost of the shares purchased. Note that neither the par (or stated) value of the stock nor the amount originally received for the shares when they were issued is used to record the acquisition of treasury stock. If treasury shares are subsequently reissued, the difference between the cost of the shares and their selling price does not represent a gain or a loss to the corporation. Instead, the corporation has simply changed the amount of invested capital by acquiring and reissuing treasury shares. Consequently, any difference between the acquisition cost and the resale price of treasury stock is credited to additional paid-in capital if the selling price exceeds cost. If the shares are sold below cost, additional paid-in capital is reduced. If this account is not sufficient to absorb the excess of the cost over the selling price, any remainder may be charged or debited to retained earnings. To illustrate, assume that the stockholders' equity of a corporation appeared as follows on January 1:

Common stock, $10 par value, 10,000 shares authorized, issued, and outstanding	$100,000
Additional paid-in capital	20,000
Total Contributed Capital	$120,000
Retained earnings	30,000
Total Stockholders' Equity	$150,000

Further assume that the corporation purchased 300 of its outstanding shares on January 15 at a price of $20 per share. The following entry would be necessary to record the purchase:

Treasury Stock	6,000	
Cash		6,000

To illustrate the reissuance of treasury stock, assume that the corporation subsequently sold 100 of the treasury shares on March 15 for $25 per share and another 100 shares on April 15 for $18 per share. The entries to record these transactions are as follows:

March 15	Cash	2,500	
	Treasury Stock		2,000
	Additional Paid-in Capital from Treasury Stock Transactions		500
April 15	Cash	1,800	
	Additional Paid-in Capital from Treasury Stock Transactions	200	
	Treasury Stock		2,000

When the treasury shares were sold, the treasury stock account was credited for the acquisition cost and carrying value of the shares, or $20 per share. Further, note that the $200 excess of cost over the resale price in the April 15 sale was debited to an "additional paid-in capital from treasury stock transactions" account. If the balance in the "additional paid in capital from treasury stock transactions" account is not sufficient to absorb the difference between cost and resale price, any remaining amount is normally charged against retained earnings.

If a company holds treasury shares at the time financial statements are prepared, any balance in the treasury stock account should be shown as a deduction from total stockholders' equity. In addition, any restriction on the amount of retained earnings available for dividends should be disclosed. Additional paid-in capital from treasury stock transactions is reported in the contributed capital section of stockholders' equity. For example, the stockholders' equity of the corporation on April 15 would appear as follows:

Common stock, $10 par value, 10,000 shares authorized and issued of which 100 shares are in the treasury.............		$100,000
Additional paid-in capital:		
From stock issuances.........................	$20,000	
From treasury stock transactions...................	300	20,300
Total Contributed Capital.....................		$120,300
Retained earnings (of which $2,000 is not available for dividends because of the purchase of treasury stock).........		30,000
Total..		$150,300
Less: Treasury stock at cost (100 shares)................		2,000
Total Stockholders' Equity		$148,300

For various reasons, stockholders may donate shares of stock to the corporation. Since there is no cost to the corporation, no entry is required for the receipt of the donated stock. When these shares are resold, the entire proceeds would be credited to the additional paid-in capital from treasury stock transactions account. An alternative treatment is to record donated treasury stock at its fair market value as of the date of donation with a corresponding credit to a donated capital account. If this procedure is followed, subsequent entries affecting treasury stock would be recorded in the same manner as if the treasury stock had been purchased.

RETAINED EARNINGS

Retained earnings is that portion of stockholders' equity which results from the total net earnings of the firm less any dividends paid to stockholders since its inception. Accumulated earnings include income from normal operations and discontinued operations, extraordinary gains or losses, and prior period adjustments. Thus, the following types of transactions all affect retained earnings, either directly or indirectly.

1. Transfer of the net income or loss for the period to retained earnings (including discontinued operations and extraordinary gains or losses).
2. Reduction in retained earnings for dividends declared during the period.
3. Increase or decrease in retained earnings for prior period adjustments.
4. Transfer from or to appropriation accounts.

The first three types of entries have been discussed previously. The appropriation of retained earnings is discussed below.

Appropriation of Retained Earnings

In general, the balance in the retained earnings account of a corporation is the amount which is legally available for dividend distribution to stockholders. However, in some cases the board of directors may restrict the amount of retained earnings that can be used to pay dividends. Such restrictions may be required either by law or by contract, or they may be made at the discretion of the board of directors. For example, retained earnings available for dividends are often legally limited by the cost of any treasury stock held by the company. In addition, contractual agreements with creditors or certain classes of stockholders may also impose limitations on the amount of retained earnings which is available for dividends. On the other hand, the board of directors may desire to voluntarily restrict dividends in order to provide for a future use of the assets represented by accumulated earnings. For example, a firm may wish to retain assets generated from profitable operations for future expansion of the business.

There are several methods which may be used for disclosing such restrictions on the amount of the retained earnings available for distribution to shareholders. The simplest, and probably the most logical method, is to indicate the amount and nature of the restriction by footnote or parenthetical disclosure in the financial statements. However, because many stockholders may not readily understand such disclosures, an alternative is to reclassify a portion of the retained earnings in order to indicate the amount of earnings which is unavailable for dividends. This reclassification, referred to as an appropriation, is accomplished by transferring the desired amount of retained earnings to an appropriation account.

To illustrate an appropriation of retained earnings, assume that the directors of a corporation with retained earnings of $300,000 decide that $100,000 of retained earnings should be restricted for future plant expansion. The following entry is necessary to record this appropriation:

Retained Earnings	100,000	
Appropriation for Plant Expansion		100,000

This appropriation does not affect either the assets or liabilities of the corporation. The appropriation account is not an asset to be used for expansion nor does it guarantee that cash or other assets will actually be available for this purpose. Instead, it merely restricts the assets that may be distributed to shareholders. Further, the appropriation does not change the total retained earnings; it simply divides it into appropriated and unappropriated segments. The retained earnings of the corporation in the example would appear as follows after the appropriation was made:

Retained earnings:	
Appropriated for plant expansion	$100,000
Unappropriated	200,000
Total Retained Earnings	$300,000

When the purpose for the appropriation ceases to exist, the amount of the appropriated retained earnings account should be transferred back to unappropriated retained earnings. Since an appropriation represents a segregation of retained earnings, no other entry may be made to this account. For example, assume that the corporation in the previous illustration completed the desired expansion of the business. The appropriation would be restored to unappropriated retained earnings by means of the following entry:

Appropriation for Plant Expansion	100,000	
Retained Earnings		100,000

In recent years, the formal appropriation of retained earnings has been recognized as potentially confusing or misleading to the users of financial statements. Consequently, there has been a trend to disclose both voluntary and required restriction of retained earnings in the notes accompanying the financial statements.

Statement of Retained Earnings

Normally, the periodic financial statements issued by a corporation include a statement of retained earnings as well as a balance sheet, income statement, and statement of changes in financial position. The retained earnings statement indicates all changes which have occurred in that account during the period. The format of the statement varies considerably; sometimes the changes in retained earnings are included with income data in a combined statement of income and retained earnings. The general form of the statement is illustrated below.

Redskins Company
Statement of Retained Earnings
For the Year Ended December 31, 19x1

Balance at beginning of the year:		
As originally reported		$200,000
Prior period adjustment—correction of an error applicable to 19x0		(50,000)
As Restated		$150,000
Add: Net income for the year		90,000
		$240,000
Less: Cash dividends:		
$6 per share on preferred	$30,000	
$5 per share on common	50,000	(80,000)
Balance at end of the year		$160,000

BOOK VALUE PER SHARE OF COMMON STOCK

The book value of a share of stock is the amount of stockholders' equity which is applicable to a single share of stock. Since the stockholders' equity is equal to total assets minus total liabilities, book value also represents the net assets per share of stock. Data on book value per share of a corporation's common stock is often included in corporate annual reports and in the financial press.

If a corporation has only common stock outstanding, book value per share is computed by dividing total stockholders' equity by the number of shares outstanding. When a corporation has both preferred and common stock outstanding, the stockholders' equity must be divided between or among the various classes of stock. This allocation depends on the nature of the preferred stock. Generally, if preferred stock is nonparticipating, the equity allocated to the preferred shares is an amount equal to the liquidation or redemption value of the preferred stock plus any cumulative dividends in arrears. To illustrate, assume that a corporation has the following stockholders' equity:

5% cumulative preferred stock, $100 par value, 1,000 shares authorized and outstanding, (callable at $106)		$100,000
Common stock, $10 par value, 20,000 shares authorized, issued, and outstanding		200,000
Additional paid-in capital:		
On preferred stock	$40,000	
On common stock	10,000	50,000
Total Contributed Capital		$350,000
Retained earnings		56,000
Total Stockholders' Equity		$406,000

If there are no unpaid dividends on the preferred stock, equity equal to the call price or redemption value of the preferred stock ($106 per share) is allocated to the preferred shares, and the remainder applies to the common stock. Thus, the book value per share of common stock is computed as follows:

Total stockholders' equity	$406,000
Less: Amount allocated to preferred	106,000
Equity to common stock	$300,000

$$\text{Book value per share of common stock} = \frac{\$300,000}{20,000} = \$15$$

If there are unpaid preferred dividends, an additional amount equal to the arrearage is allocated to the preferred stock. For example, assume that the preferred stock mentioned in the previous illustration had one year of dividends in arrears. In that situation, the unpaid preferred dividends of $5,000 would also be allocated to the preferred stock, and the book value per share of common stock would be computed as follows:

Total stockholders' equity		$406,000
Less: Amount allocated to preferred:		
Redemption value	$106,000	
Dividends in arrears	5,000	111,000
Equity to common stock		$295,000

$$\text{Book value per share of common stock} = \frac{\$295{,}000}{20{,}000} = \$14.75$$

Because the market value of the assets may differ from book values based on generally accepted accounting principles, the book value per share does not indicate the amount that would be distributed to the owner of each share of stock if the assets of the corporation were sold and its liabilities were paid. That is, any gains or losses from the disposal of assets or the settlement of liabilities, and any expenses involved in the liquidation process, would affect the shareholders' equity. As noted above, book value per share is not necessarily equal to the market price of the stock. Although book value per share may have some effect on the market price, market price is much more likely to be influenced by factors such as current and expected future earnings, dividend prospects, and general economic conditions. Depending upon the specific circumstances, book value per share may be more or less than market price per share. Therefore, book value data should be used with extreme caution in making decisions concerning the value of a corporation's stock.

SUMMARY

The retained earnings of a corporation reflect the accumulated net income and losses of the firm less all dividend distributions to shareholders. The net income of the firm is usually presented on the income statement in a manner that separates earnings related to the normal operations of the business from other income-related items. Such other items include extraordinary items and discontinued operations. Prior period adjustments are direct adjustments to the beginning balance of Retained Earnings resulting from error correction and other adjustments stipulated in FASB *Statement No. 16*.

The income statement will also include information regarding the earnings per share of the firm. This amount is basically the net income per share of common stock outstanding for a given period. Where preferred stock or convertible securities are outstanding, certain adjustments must be made to either the net income or number of shares of common stock outstanding to compute the earnings per share of the firm. In addition, if there are extraordinary items or gains or losses from discontinued operations it will be necessary to compute several earnings per share figures.

Certain accounting changes may necessitate an adjustment of the accounting records and/or mention in the corporation's financial statements. Included in this category are changes in accounting principles, changes in accounting estimates, and corrections of errors made in prior periods.

A corporation may distribute a portion or all of its accumulated earnings to the stockholders in the form of ordinary dividends. Additionally, the firm may return a portion of the original investment in the form of a liquidating dividend. The important dates to be noted in relation to a dividend distribution are the dates of declaration, record, and payment. Although dividends are usually paid in cash, the corporation may choose to issue a stock dividend. A stock dividend has no effect on the amount of stockholders' equity, but does require a transfer of an appropriate amount from the retained earnings account to the capital accounts. Stockholders may also be issued additional shares in a stock split. In this case, no capitalization of retained earnings is required although a memorandum is made to indicate the change in the number of shares outstanding and in the par value of the stock.

A firm may wish to purchase its own stock from shareholders and retain the shares for future reissuance or cancellation. The purchase and resale of such stock is referred to as treasury stock transactions. Treasury stock held by a corporation when financial statements are prepared is shown on the balance sheet as a deduction from total stockholders' equity.

In reporting financial position to its stockholders, a firm may wish to indicate that the entire balance of retained earnings is not available for distribution as dividends, because certain amounts have been appropriated for special purposes. This is commonly accomplished by segregating the unappropriated retained earnings from the appropriated amount on the balance sheet. Additional detail regarding the retained earnings account is provided by the statement of retained earnings, which is normally included as one of the periodic financial statements issued by a corporation.

The book value per share of common stock represents the amount of stockholders' equity or net assets applicable to a single share of common stock. If preferred stock is outstanding, an appropriate amount of equity must first be allocated to those shares before computing book value.

This chapter concludes the discussion of the stockholders' equity section of the balance sheet.

KEY DEFINITIONS

Appropriation of retained earnings An appropriation of retained earnings is the reclassification of a portion of retained earnings by transfer to an appropriation account.

Book value per share Book value per share is the amount of stockholders' equity (i.e., net assets) applicable to each share of common stock outstanding.

Capitalization of retained earnings The capitalization of retained earnings is an amount which is transferred from retained earnings to contributed capital at the time a stock dividend is declared.

Cash dividend A cash dividend is a distribution of cash to stockholders in the form of a dividend.

Change due to accounting errors Changes due to accounting errors may result from errors in the application of accounting principles, oversights, misuse of facts, or mistakes in mathematics.

Change in accounting estimate A change in accounting estimate occurs as additional information modifying an original estimate is obtained.

Change in accounting principle A change in accounting principle results from the adoption of a generally accepted accounting principle which differs from one that was previously used.

Date of declaration The date of declaration is the date on which the board of directors formally establishes a liability for a dividend of a specified amount to the stockholders.

Date of payment The date of payment of a dividend is the date on which the dividends are paid to the stockholders of record.

Date of record The date of record of a dividend is the date on which the corporation prepares a list of stockholders who are to receive the dividends.

Deficit A deficit is a debit balance in the retained earnings account.

Discontinued operations Discontinued operations refers to the operations of any subsidiary, division, or department of a business that has been, or will be sold, abandoned, or disposed of.

Dividends Dividends are distributions which are made by a corporation to its shareholders.

Earnings per share The earnings per share is the amount of net income per share of the common stock outstanding during a period.

Extraordinary item An extraordinary item is a gain or loss which is both unusual in nature and not reasonably expected to recur in the foreseeable future. As a result of *Opinions No. 9* and *No. 30* of the Accounting Principles Board, these items are reported as separate amounts in the income statement.

Gains Gains are increases in equity (net assets) from peripheral or incidental transactions of an entity and from all other transactions and other events and circumstances affecting the entity during a period except those that result from revenues or investments by owners.

Losses Losses are decreases in equity (net assets) from peripheral or incidental transactions of an entity and from all other transactions and other events and circumstances affecting the entity during a period except those that result from expenses or distributions to owners.

Prior period adjustment Prior period adjustments are items of gain or loss which represent material corrections of reported earnings of prior periods and are shown as direct adjustments of retained earnings.

Retained earnings Retained earnings represent the accumulated earnings of the corporation, increased by net income and reduced by net losses and distributions to shareholders.

Stock dividend A stock dividend is a distribution of additional shares to the stockholders in proportion to their existing holdings.

Stock split A stock split is a proportionate increase in the number of shares outstanding, usually intended to effect a decrease in the market value of the stock.

Treasury stock Treasury stock consists of shares of stock which have been previously issued and are reacquired by the corporation but not formally retired.

QUESTIONS

1. Distinguish between an ordinary item and an extraordinary item on an income statement. How is an extraordinary item presented in the income statement?

2. What is a prior period adjustment? Where is a prior period adjustment shown in the financial statements?

3. Define earnings per share of common stock. Where is this information shown in the financial statements?

4. What is the effect on earnings per share presentation when a company has extraordinary gains or losses?

5. Describe the nature of the following three dates related to dividends: (a) date of declaration, (b) date of record, and (c) date of payment. What is the accounting significance of each of these dates?

6. Distinguish between a cash dividend and a stock dividend.

7. Why does a corporation normally declare (a) a stock dividend and (b) a stock split?

8. Why is a portion of retained earnings capitalized upon the issuance of a stock dividend?

9. What is the difference between a stock dividend and a stock split? How does the accounting for a large stock dividend and a stock split differ?

10. For what purposes might a company purchase shares of its own stock?

11. What is treasury stock? How does it affect the ability of the corporation to pay dividends? How does it differ from authorized but unissued stock?

12. What is the effect on stockholders' equity when treasury stock is reissued for (a) more than the original cost, (b) less than its cost to the corporation?

13. What is the purpose of an appropriation of retained earnings? How does a company provide for and eliminate an appropriation of retained earnings?

14. What is the significance of the book value per share of common stock? Does the book value equal the amount of assets which would be distributed to each share of stock upon liquidation? Explain.

15. How is the book value per share of common stock computed when there is preferred stock outstanding?

EXERCISES

16. Assume that Ham Farm Supplies, Inc. had income after taxes from normal operations for 19x1 of $200,000. Also, the firm had an extraordinary loss of $40,000 (net of tax). The firm had 25,000 shares of stock outstanding throughout 19x1. Compute the earnings per share figures required by APB *Opinion No. 15*.

17. Make the journal entries necessary to record the declaration and payment of dividends in each of the following situations:

   a. Bruin Company has 8,000 shares of common stock and 3,000 shares of 7 percent, $100 par value preferred stock outstanding. On June 15 the company declares a preferred dividend and a $3.50 per share dividend on the common stock. The dividends are payable on July 15 to the stockholders of record on June 30.
   b. Wolfpack Company has 10,000 shares of $15 par value common stock outstanding. On May 1, the company declares a 10 percent stock dividend to be distributed on May 15. At the time, the market price of a share is $19.

18. On March 15, the board of directors of Gunsmith Corporation declared a cash dividend of $1 per share to the stockholders of record on March 20. The dividend is payable on April 1. The corporation had 10,000 shares of common stock outstanding.

   Required:

   Prepare the journal entries required on the date of declaration, the date of record, and the payment date.

19. The Robinson Corporation was organized in 19x0. The company was authorized to issue 5,000 shares of $50 par value common and 1,000 shares of $100 par value, cumulative preferred stock. All of the preferred and 4,000 shares of common were issued at par. The preferred shares were entitled to dividends of 6 percent before any dividends were paid to common. During the first 5 years of its existence, the corporation earned a total of $120,000 and paid dividends of 50 cents per share each year on common stock.

   Required:

   Prepare *in good form* the stockholders' equity section as of December 31, 19x4.

20. Shown below is the stockholders' equity section of the balance sheet of Falcon Company at December 31, 19x1.

Common stock, 10,000 shares issued and outstanding, $10 par value......................	$100,000
Additional paid-in capital........................	50,000
Retained earnings...............................	75,000
Total Stockholders' Equity.....................	$225,000

   On January 1, 19x2 the company reacquired 500 shares of its stock at $15 per share.

Required:

1. Prepare the entry to record the purchase of the stock.
2. Prepare the entry to record the reissuance of the treasury stock at $18 per share.
3. Prepare the entry to record the reissuance of the stock at $13 per share.

21. Arnold Company had a $100,000 balance in its retained earnings account on January 1, 19x1. On January 2, 19x1, by action of the Board of Directors, $25,000 of retained earnings was appropriated for future plant expansion. The plant expansion was completed on December 31, 19x2, and the appropriation of retained earnings was released.

Required:

1. Give the journal entry necessary to record the appropriation.
2. Give the entry necessary to release the appropriation.

22. The stockholders' equity section of the balance sheet of Park Company on December 31, 19x1, is shown below:

6% preferred stock, $100 par value (callable at $105) 5,000 shares authorized, issued, and outstanding............................	$ 500,000
Common stock, $5 par value, 60,000 shares, authorized and 50,000 shares issued and outstanding....	250,000
Additional paid-in capital............................	400,000
Retained earnings..................................	75,000
Total Stockholders' Equity........................	$1,225,000

Required:

Compute the book value per share of common stock.

23. Williams Company purchased a machine for $22,000 on January 1, 19x0. At the time, it was estimated to have a useful life of 10 years and a salvage value of $2,000. Depreciation was recorded for five years on the straight-line basis. During 19x5, it was determined that the total estimated life of the machine should be 15 years with the same estimated salvage value.

Required:

Prepare the entry to record the depreciation expense for 19x5.

24. Walters Company purchased a machine for $15,000 on January 1, 19x1. At that time, it was estimated to have a useful life of 5 years and no salvage value. Depreciation was recorded for 19x1 and 19x2 using the sum-of-the-years'-digits method. During 19x3, the company decided to change to the straight-line method of depreciation.

Required:

1. Give the adjusting entry required to record the change in depreciation method.
2. Give the journal entry to record depreciation expense for 19x3.

25. By using the following code, indicate each transaction's effect on the respective columns.

+	= increases	0	= no effect
−	= decreases	?	= cannot be determined

The market value of the company's common stock exceeds par value.

		Common Stock	Retained Earnings	Stockholders' Equity	Book Value Per Share of Common Stock
a.	Company declared a cash dividend payable in the next fiscal year to persons holding shares of preferred stock.				
b.	Company received shares of its own common stock, donated by a wealthy shareholder.				
c.	Company purchased shares of its own common stock through a broker at the New York Stock Exchange.				
d.	Company declared and issued a stock dividend on the common stock.				
e.	A cash dividend was declared and paid.				
f.	Retained Earnings were appropriated for plant expansion.				
g.	Treasury shares of common stock were sold at an amount in excess of the purchase price to the corporation.				

PROBLEMS

26. Certain account balances of the Gobbler Company as of December 31, 19x2, are shown below:

Sales	$1,000,000
Cost of goods sold	500,000
Gain on sale of Meat Packing Division (net of tax)	100,000
Loss from earthquake (net of tax)	50,000
Operating expenses	350,000
Cash dividends:	
Common stock	250,000
Preferred stock	100,000
Correction of an error—prior period (income overstated)	100,000
Taxes on income from normal operations	75,000

The retained earnings balance on December 31, 19x1, was $850,000. The sale of the Division should be treated as a discontinued operation.

Required:

1. Prepare an income statement for 19x2.
2. Prepare a statement of retained earnings for the year ended December 31, 19x2.

27. The income statement for Bonko Company for the year ending December 31, 19x1, is shown below:

Bonko Company
Income Statement
For the Year Ended December 31, 19x1

Sales	$200,000
Cost of goods sold	100,000
Gross profit	$100,000
Operating expenses	80,000
Income before extraordinary items	$ 20,000
Extraordinary gain (net of tax)	10,000
Net income	$ 30,000

Bonko Company had 60,000 shares of common stock outstanding during 19x1.

Required:

Compute earnings per share for 19x1.

28. The stockholders' equity of Billy, Inc. appears as follows on its December 31, 19x1 balance sheet.

Common stock, $9 par value, 25,000 shares outstanding	$225,000
Additional paid-in capital	125,000
Total contributed capital	$350,000
Retained earnings	195,000
Total Stockholders' Equity	$545,000

Required:

Make the journal entries necessary to record the transactions in the following independent cases:

1. Billy, Inc. declares and distributes a 60 percent stock dividend on July 1 when the stock is selling for $30 per share.
2. Billy, Inc. declares a 3-for-1 stock split on July 1 when the market price of its stock is $60 per share.
3. Billy, Inc. declares and distributes a 5 percent stock dividend on July 1 when the market price of the stock is $15 per share.

29. The stockholders' equity section of the Buckeye Company appeared as follows on January 1:

Common stock, $15 par value, 20,000 shares authorized, issued, and outstanding	$300,000
Additional paid-in capital	75,000
Total contributed capital	$375,000
Retained earnings	80,000
Total Stockholders' Equity	$455,000

On February 1, the company purchased 800 of its outstanding shares at $25 per share. On June 15, the company reissued 500 of these shares at $29 per share. Then, on July 15, the company resold the other 300 shares for $24 per share.

Required:

Prepare the journal entries necessary to record the above transactions on the books of the Buckeye Company. Also, prepare the stockholders' equity section of their balance sheet as of July 15.

30. The stockholders' equity section of the X Corporation as of December 31, 19x1 shows:

6% preferred, cumulative capital stock, $100 par value, 50,000 shares authorized, 20,000 shares issued and outstanding..........................		$2,000,000
Common stock, no par, $10 stated value, 400,000 shares authorized, 260,000 shares issued and outstanding.......		2,600,000
Additional paid-in capital:		
On preferred stock.....................	$ 80,000	
On common stock.....................	1,560,000	1,640,000
Retained earnings..........................		1,200,000
Total Stockholders' Equity................		$7,440,000

Note: Dividends on preferred stock are three years in arrears.

Required:

Compute the book value per share of the common stock at December 31, 19x1.

31. The Texan Co. had the following stockholders' equity on January 1, 19x1.

Common stock, $5 par value, 100,000 shares authorized, 50,000 shares issued and outstanding................................	$250,000
Additional paid-in capital..........................	150,000
Total Contributed Capital........................	$400,000
Retained earnings................................	100,000
Total Stockholders' Equity......................	$500,000

During 19x1, the company had the following transactions related to the stockholders' equity.

Jan.	20	Issued 5,000 shares of stock for $10 per share.
Feb.	15	Purchased 3,000 shares of Texan Co. common stock for $11 per share.
May	10	Declared a $.20 per share cash dividend to the stockholders of record on May 15. The dividend is payable on June 1.
June	1	Paid the cash dividend.
	15	Sold 1,000 shares of treasury stock for $13 per share.
Aug.	15	Sold 1,000 shares of treasury stock for $10 per share.
Sept.	10	Declared a 10 percent stock dividend for the stockholders of record on September 15 to be distributed on October 1. The market price of the stock was $11 per share on September 15.
Oct.	1	Distributed the stock dividend.
Nov.	1	The Board of Directors decided to appropriate $20,000 of retained earnings for future plant expansion.
Dec.	31	Net income for the year was $35,000. The income summary and dividend accounts were closed to retained earnings.

Required:

1. Give the necessary journal entries to record the transactions.
2. Prepare a statement of retained earnings at December 31, 19x1.

32. The stockholders' equity of the National Company at December 31, 19x1, was as follows:

6% noncumulative preferred stock, $100 par value, call price per share $110, authorized 70,000 shares, issued 10,000 shares.............................	$1,000,000
$5 noncumulative preferred stock, $100 par value, call price per share $105, authorized 100,000 shares, issued 5,000 shares.............................	500,000
Common stock, $50 par value, authorized 100,000 shares, issued 40,000 shares, of which 1,000 shares are held in the treasury......................	2,000,000
Additional paid-in capital:	
On 6% preferred stock...........................	100,000
On common stock...............................	255,000
Total Contributed Capital......................	$3,855,000
Retained earnings (of which $60,000, an amount equal to the cost of the treasury stock purchased, is unavailable for dividends).......................	1,500,000
	$5,355,000
Deduct: Cost of treasury stock (1,000 shares)...........	60,000
Total Stockholders' Equity......................	$5,295,000

Note: Preferred dividends for 19x0 and 19x1 have not been paid.

During 19x2, National Company had the following transactions affecting the stockholders' equity:

Jan.	5	Sold 11,000 shares of the common stock at $55 per share.
Feb.	1	Declared a 10 percent stock dividend on the common stock; the market value of the stock on that date was $60 per share.
	28	Paid the stock dividend declared on February 1.
May	1	Purchased 500 shares of the common stock for the treasury at a cost of $65 per share.
	5	Sold all of the treasury stock held for $70 per share.
	9	Stockholders voted to reduce the par value of common stock to $25 per share and increase authorized shares to 200,000. The company issued the additional shares to effect this stock split.
June	30	The Board of Directors declared a $1 per share dividend on common stock and the regular annual dividend on both classes of preferred stock. All dividends are payable on July 20 to shareholders of record as of July 10.

Required:

1. Prepare the necessary journal entries to record the preceding transactions.
2. Prepare the stockholders' equity section of the balance sheet at June 30, 19x2.

33. Below is data relating to the income statement of the Benjamin Corporation:

a. Sales for the year ended September 30, 19x1 were $850,000. Cost of goods sold were $600,000 and expenses were $260,000.

b. In addition to the above, certain other revenue and expense items were incurred during the year:

1. Benjamin Corporation discontinued the operations of a segment of its firm. There was no income from that segment for the current year and the segment was sold at a gain of $30,000.
2. A write-down of inventory totaling $1,500 was recorded because of a decline in demand for the inventory due to obsolescence.
3. An earthquake occurred during the year which caused a total loss in corporate property valued at $75,000. Earthquakes are not a usual occurrence in the corporation's geographic area.
4. The average number of shares of common stock for the year was 80,000. The corporation does not have preferred stock.

Required:

Ignoring income taxes:

1. Calculate the total amount of extraordinary items.
2. Prepare an income statement in proper form including all appropriate earnings per share calculations.

34. On January 2, 19x0, the White Company purchased a building for $178,000. At that time, it was estimated that the building would have a useful life of 32 years and a salvage value of $18,000. The company decided to use the straight-line depreciation method. Calculate the effect in the financial statements of each of the following unrelated accounting changes and give journal entries to record current depreciation and any other necessary adjusting entries.

   a. On December 31, 19x3, before the depreciation adjustment for the year had been made, it was decided that the building should be depreciated by the sum-of-the-years'-digits method.
   b. On December 31, 19x3, the building was found to have a remaining useful life of only 22 years and a salvage value of $20,000.
   c. Depreciation was inappropriately calculated for three years because the asset was recorded on the books at an original cost of $78,000 (i.e., the building was debited for $78,000 and cash was credited for $78,000).

35. The accountant for the Sloan Manufacturing Corporation has provided you with the following data:

   a. Average common shares outstanding during 19x1, 60,000 shares, par $3; outstanding December 31, 19x1, 70,000 shares.
   b. 6 percent cumulative preferred stock outstanding December 31, 19x1, 10,000 shares; redemption value, $120 per share; par value, $100 per share.
   c. Cash dividends declared on December 31, 19x1—$420,000 to common stockholders and $60,000 to preferred stockholders. There are no dividends of preferred stock in arrears.

d. Net income for the year was $560,000.
e. Total stockholders' equity as of December 31, 19x1 was $2,600,000.

Required:

1. What is the earnings per share for common stock?
2. What is the dividend declared per share of common stock?
3. What is the dividend declared per share of preferred stock?
4. What is the book value of common stock?

36. The Peterson Company was organized on January 1, 19x0, with 10,000 shares of $10 par value common stock authorized, issued, and outstanding. Journalize the following transactions which took place in 19x4:

Jan. 1   The corporation purchased 100 shares of its common stock for $15 a share.
Feb. 1   The corporation sold the 100 shares purchased on January 1 for a total price of $1,750.
Mar. 1   Mrs. Moneybags, a stockholder, donated 100 shares of the X Corporation's common stock to the corporation.
     5   The corporation sold the 100 donated shares for a total price of $2,500.
Apr. 1   The corporation purchased 100 shares of its own stock for $9 a share.
May 1   The corporation sold the 100 shares purchased on April 1 for a total price of $500.
Dec. 15   A $.50 per share dividend on common stock was declared, to be paid on January 15, 19x5.

37. The Jones Co. was organized on January 1, 19x0, with 20,000 shares of $10 par value common stock and 5,000 shares of $100 par value, 6 percent preferred stock authorized. The balances in the stockholders' equity accounts on December 31, 19x3, were as follows:

Preferred stock	$100,000
Common stock	120,000
Additional paid-in capital:	
On preferred stock	5,000
On common stock	60,000
Retained earnings	$190,000

During 19x4, the company had the following transactions that affected the stockholders' equity:

		Number	*Amount*
a.	Issuance of common stock	5,000	$ 20 per share
b.	Purchase of its own shares of common stock	4,000	$ 22 per share
c.	Reissuance of treasury stock	1,000	$ 24 per share
d.	Issuance of preferred stock	1,000	$102 per share
e.	Payment of dividend on common stock		$ .50 per share
f.	Payment of dividend on preferred stock		$ 6 per share
g.	Appropriation of retained earnings for future plant expansion		$100,000
h.	Net income for the year		$ 60,000
i.	Stock split on common stock with par value reduced to $5 per share	2 for 1	

Required:

Prepare the stockholders' equity section of the balance sheet for Jones Co. on December 31, 19x4.

38. On July 1, 19x0, the Morehouse Company purchased two pieces of equipment: a tractor for $11,000 and a truck for $9,000. On that date it was estimated that the tractor would have a life of eight years with a salvage value of $300 and the truck would have a life of ten years with a salvage value of $500. The company decided to use the double-declining balance method to depreciate both assets. Calculate the effect on the financial statements of each of the following unrelated accounting changes. Also, give journal entries to record any necessary adjusting entries and current depreciation expense. The company's fiscal year ends on June 30.

   a. On June 30, 19x3, the company realized the truck only had a remaining life of four years. Salvage value was expected to remain at $500.
   b. On June 30, 19x4, the accountant found an error in the calculation of the tractor's depreciation expense. The bookkeeper had erroneously subtracted out the salvage value in the first year when calculating depreciation on the declining balance method.
   c. On June 30, 19x3, it was decided that the tractor should be depreciated using the straight-line method.

Refer to the Annual Report included in the Appendix at the end of the text:

39. What is the EPS for the most recent year?

40. On which financial statement can the EPS amount be located?

41. In which statement would a prior period adjustment be reflected?

42. What amount of stock was issued? What amount of common stock?

43. In either year, was there an accounting change? If so, what type of change was it and how did it affect net income?

Learning Objectives

Chapter 15 presents information relating to the determination and presentation of bonds payable and investments in corporate securities. Studying this chapter should enable you to:

1. Describe the various classes of bonds.

2. Explain the concepts of bond discount and bond premium and how they are handled for accounting purposes.

3. Record the early retirement of bonds, including either a gain or loss if applicable.

4. Identify the elements of cost of stocks and bonds purchased as investments.

5. Discuss the methods of accounting for long-term and temporary investments subsequent to acquisition.

15

Long-Term Liabilities and Investments

INTRODUCTION

When a corporation desires to raise additional capital for long-term purposes, it has several alternatives. It may borrow funds by issuing bonds, or it may obtain funds by issuing additional stock to shareholders. Each source of funds has its particular advantages and disadvantages to the issuing corporation. A bondholder is a creditor of a corporation while a stockholder is an owner. As creditors, bondholders normally do not participate in the management of the firm. Therefore, by issuing bonds, a corporation does not spread or dilute control of management over a larger number of owners. Interest expense is deductible for federal income tax purposes while dividends are not a tax deduction.

The interest expense on a bond is a fixed obligation to the borrower. If the interest is not paid on the dates specified by the contract, legal action may be brought by the bondholders. Dividends on stock, on the other hand, are declared at the discretion of the board of directors of the issuing corporation.

BOND OBLIGATIONS

Bonds are issued as a means of borrowing money for long-term purposes. The desired funds are obtained by issuing a number of bonds with a certain denomination (usually $1,000). Normally, a corporation sells all of its bonds to an investment firm, referred to as an underwriter. The underwriter then resells the bonds to investors. For accounting purposes, only the amount received from the underwriter is relevant to the issuing firm. Individual bonds are sold to investors with a promise to pay a definite sum of money to the holder at a fixed future date and periodic interest payments at a stated rate throughout the life of the liability. Since bonds usually do not name individual lenders, they may be bought and sold by investors until their maturity.

When funds are borrowed by issuing bonds, interest payments and the timing of the repayment of the principal of the debt to bondholders are obligations which are fixed in amount and must be paid at specified dates regardless of the amount of income earned by the firm. If the rate of earnings on invested funds exceeds the interest rate on the bonds, it is usually to the owners' advantage for the firm to issue bonds. However, if the expected rate of earnings is less than the interest rate, it would not be to the advantage of the owners to borrow funds. Furthermore, interest payments must be made when due regardless of whether or not sufficient income is earned. If interest payments are not made, the bondholders may bring action in order to foreclose against the assets of the corporation in the settlement of their claims. Bondholders are creditors and their claims for interest and the repayment of principal have priority over the claims of owners. Therefore, the feasibility of obtaining funds by issuing bonds depends upon factors such as the expected rate of interest and the stability of the earnings of the firm.

Bond interest payments are a deductible expense in the computation of taxable income, while dividends paid to owners are not deductible for tax purposes. Because of the magnitude of corporate income taxes, the effect of taxes is often an important factor in determining the source which will be used by the business to obtain its long-term funds.

Approval of the board of directors and stockholders of the corporation is normally required prior to issuance of bonds. In addition, the firm issuing bonds selects a trustee to represent the bondholders. The trustee acts to protect the bondholders' interests, and takes legal action if the pledged responsibilities of the corporation are not satisfied.

CLASSES OF BONDS

Bonds may be either secured by specific assets or unsecured. Unsecured bonds are referred to as debenture bonds. Debenture bonds have as "security" the general credit standing of the issuing corporation. Therefore, debenture bonds are usually issued successfully only by companies with a favorable financial position.

A secured bond gives the bondholder a prior claim against specific assets in the event that the issuing corporation is unable to make the required interest or principal payments as they become due. Secured bonds differ as to the type of assets pledged. Real estate mortgage bonds are secured by a mortgage on specific land or buildings. Equipment trust bonds are secured by mortgages on tangible personal property such as equipment. Collateral trust bonds are secured by stocks and bonds of other companies owned by the corporation issuing the bonds.

A bond issue that matures on a single date is referred to as a term bond. Bonds that mature on several different dates and are retired in installments over a period of time are called serial bonds. Bonds that may be retired before maturity at the option of the issuing corporation are referred to as callable bonds. Bonds which may be exchanged for a specified amount of stock at the option of the bondholder are termed convertible bonds.

Bonds may also differ as to the method of interest payment. Registered bonds require that the bondholders' names be registered with the issuing corporation. The corporation issuing bonds is required to maintain a record of the current owners; periodic interest payments are mailed directly to the registered owners. Other bonds, called coupon bonds, have interest coupons attached which call for the payment of the required amount of interest on specified dates. A bond coupon is similar to a note payable to the holder at the date specified on the coupon. At each interest date, the appropriate coupon may be detached by the bondholder and presented at a bank for payment.

Despite the wide variety of bonds offered, it should be noted that the value of bonds to the investor depends to a significant degree on the financial condition and long-term earning prospects of the issuing corporation. While the various optional provisions that may be included in a bond issue may affect the issue price of the bonds, it would be difficult for a company in poor financial condition to issue bonds regardless of the provisions.

When a corporation issues bonds, it is obligated to pay the principal or face amount of the bonds at a specified maturity date and to make periodic interest payments as well. The interest rate specified on the bonds is referred to as the coupon rate. The interest rate which investors are willing to accept on a bond at the time of its issue depends upon factors such as the market evaluation of the quality of the bond issue as evidenced by the financial strength of the business, the firm's earnings prospects and the particular provisions of the bond issue. This rate is referred to as the market or effective interest rate. If the effective interest rate exceeds the coupon rate, the issue price of the bonds will fall below the face amount of the bonds. When the issue price is less than face value, the difference is referred to as a discount. For example, if Pearson Co. offers bonds with an interest rate of 7 percent when the market rate is 8 percent for similar bonds, the selling price of the bonds will be less than their face value. Since annual interest payments on each $1,000 of bonds will be $70 (.07 × $1,000), the issue price of the bonds will fall to the point where the interest received will yield an effective rate of 8 percent. Similarly, if the coupon rate exceeds the market interest rate for comparable bonds at the time of the issue, the price of the bonds will exceed the face amount. That is, the bonds will be issued at a premium. The bonds will sell at their face amount only when the coupon rate is exactly equal to the market rate.[1]

Bonds Issued at Face Value

If the coupon rate offered on bonds is identical to the market rate, the bonds will be issued at their face value. To illustrate, assume that Dascher Co. had authorization to issue $100,000 of 25-year, 18 percent debenture bonds on January 1, 19x1, with interest payable semiannually on June 30 and December 31. If $50,000 of the bonds are issued at face value on January 1, 19x1, the entry for the issuance would be:

Cash	50,000	
Bonds payable		50,000

No journal entry is made for the authorization of the bonds. The balance sheet, however, should disclose all of the pertinent facts with respect to the bond issue. For example, a balance sheet for Dascher Co. on January 1, 19x1, would include the following information:

---

[1] The procedures for computing the selling price for a bond are presented in the appendix to this chapter.

Long-term liabilities:
    18% debenture bonds payable, due on December 31, 19x25....... $50,000

After the bonds are issued, Dascher Co. must make semiannual interest payments of $4,500 on each June 30 and December 31 that the bonds remain outstanding ($50,000 × $\frac{18}{100}$ × $\frac{1}{2}$). The entry to record each payment would be as follows:

    Interest expense........................ 4,500
        Cash................................   4,500

If the accounting period used by the firm ends between interest dates, an adjusting entry must be made to accrue the interest expense from the last interest date to the end of the period. For example, if the accounting period of Dascher Co. ended on September 30, the following adjusting entry would be necessary in order to record the accrued interest expense of $2,250 ($50,000 × $\frac{18}{100}$ × $\frac{3}{12}$) from June 30 to September 30.

    Interest expense........................ 2,250
        Interest payable.....................   2,250

Interest expense will be closed to the Income Summary account, and interest payable will remain as a liability until the next regular semiannual interest payment. The entry to record the interest payment on December 31 would be:

    Interest expense........................ 2,250
    Interest payable....................... 2,250
        Cash................................   4,500

Issuance Between Interest Dates

Once authorized, bonds may be issued at any time. Bonds are often issued at a time between the interest dates. Since the corporation will pay the full semiannual interest on all bonds outstanding at an interest date, the bondholder is usually required to purchase the interest that has accrued from the previous interest date to the date of sale. This interest paid by the bondholder is returned as part of the first interest payment after issuance. To illustrate, assume that the Dascher Co. bonds from the previous example were issued at face value plus accrued interest on March 1, 19x1. The issue price would be $50,000 plus two months' interest of $1,500 ($50,000 × $\frac{18}{100}$ × $\frac{2}{12}$). The entry to record the issuance is:

    Cash................................. 51,500
        Bonds payable.......................   50,000
        Interest payable.....................   1,500

On the first semiannual interest payment date, June 30, which occurs four months after issuance, a full six months' interest ($4,500) will be paid. Of this amount, $1,500 is a return to the investor of accrued interest paid at the time of the purchase of the bonds and the remaining $3,000 represents the interest expense for the four months since the issuance. Therefore, the entry for the interest payment on June 30, 19x1, would be as follows:

Interest payable.......................	1,500	
Interest expense.......................	3,000	
Cash..............................		4,500

Issuance of Bonds at a Discount

When the coupon rate on a bond issue is less than the prevailing market interest rate for similar bonds, the bonds will sell at a discount. For example, assume the prevailing market interest rate exceeds 18 percent when Dascher Co. offers $50,000 face value of 18 percent, 25-year debenture bonds. As a result, assume that the $50,000 of Dascher Co. bonds are issued at a price of $47,500 on January 1, 19x1. The $2,500 excess of the face value over the issue price represents a discount. Normally bonds are carried in the accounts at face value with the discount recorded in a separate contra account. The issuance of the bonds would be recorded by the following entry:

Cash................................	47,500	
Discount on bonds payable...............	2,500	
Bonds payable.......................		50,000

Although the issuing corporation receives less than the face amount of the issue when bonds are sold at a discount, the entire face amount must be repaid at maturity. Therefore, the total cost of borrowing includes the discount as well as the interest payments. To illustrate, the total interest cost to Dascher Co. for the bonds issued at a discount is computed as follows:

Amount to be repaid at maturity.........................	$ 50,000
Amount received at issuance............................	47,500
Excess of cash to be paid over cash received (discount).....	$ 2,500
Cash interest payments ($9,000 annually for 25 years)........	225,000
Total Interest Cost.................................	$227,500

The average yearly interest expense over the period until the maturity of the bonds is $9,100 ($227,500 ÷ 25). Therefore, in order to reflect the total interest cost of the bonds, bond discount should be allocated to expense over the 25-year life of the bonds as additional interest expense. The process of transferring a portion of bond discount to interest expense during each period is referred to as amortization. One common method of amortizing discount is to transfer or write off equal amounts at each interest payment date. This process is referred to as straight-line amortization.[2] In the illustration above, application of the straight-line method would yield amortization of $100 ($1/25 \times $2,500) each year, or $50 on each semiannual interest date. The following entry would be made at each interest payment date.

Interest expense............................	4,550	
Discount on bonds payable.............		50
Cash.................................		4,500

Because of the amortization of the discount, total interest expense recorded over the life of the bond issue will be equal to the cash interest payments plus the bond discount. Further, amortization reduces the balance in the Discount of Bonds Payable account to zero at the maturity date of the bonds.

Unamortized discount on bonds payable should be classified as a deduction from the related Bonds Payable account. To illustrate, the Dascher Co. bonds in the preceding example were issued at a discount of $2,500 on January 1, 19x1. After two years, on December 31, 19x2, a total of $200 ($2,500 $\times$ $2/25$) of the original discount would have been amortized, and the balance sheet would include the following amounts in the long-term liabilities section:

Long-term liabilities:		
18% debenture bonds payable, due on		
December 31, 19x25............................	$50,000	
Less: Unamortized discount on bonds payable........	2,300	$47,700

If the accounting period of the firm falls between interest dates, amortization of bond discount must be included in the adjusting entry which is made for the accrual of interest expense. For example, if the accounting period of Dascher Co. ends on September 30, the following adjusting entry would be required in order to record the interest expense for the period from June 30 (the last regular interest payment date) to September 30.

Interest expense........................	2,275	
Discount on bonds payable.............		25
Interest payable......................		2,250

The interest payable of $2,250 ($50,000 $\times$ $18/100$ $\times$ $3/12$) and the discount amortization of $25 ($1/4 \times $100) is the interest expense for the three-month period since the last interest payment was made.

---

[2] The interest method of discount amortization is discussed in the appendix to this chapter.

Issuance of Bonds at a Premium

If the coupon rate on a bond issue exceeds the prevailing market interest rate for comparable bonds, the bonds will sell at an amount above their face value. The excess of the issue price over the face value is referred to as premium. For example, assume that $50,000 of Brenner Co. 25-year, 18 percent debenture bonds are issued on January 1, 19x1, when the market rate is less than 18 percent. As a result, assume that the bonds are sold for $55,000. The entry to record the issuance of the bonds would be:

Cash	55,000	
Bonds payable		50,000
Premium on bonds payable		5,000

When a premium is received on the issuance of bonds, the total cost of borrowing funds is equal to the cash interest payments made reduced by the amount of the premium. The total interest cost for Brenner Co. over the life of the bonds is calculated as follows:

Amount received at issuance	$ 55,000
Amount to be repaid at maturity	50,000
Excess of cash received over cash paid (premium)	($ 5,000)
Cash interest payments ($9,000 × 25)	225,000
Total Interest Cost	$220,000

The average yearly interest cost over the life of the bond issue is $8,800 ($220,000/25). Consequently, in order to reflect the actual interest cost of the bond issue, the premium should be periodically written off or amortized as a reduction of the interest cost over the life of the issue. The procedures for the amortization of premium are similar to those used for bonds issued at a discount. In the Brenner Co. example, application of the straight-line method would result in premium amortization of $200 ($1/25$ × $5,000) each year and, therefore, $100 on each semiannual interest date. The entry to record each semiannual interest payment and premium amortization would be as follows:

Interest expense	4,400	
Premium on bonds payable	100	
Cash		4,500

The unamortized balance in the premium account would be reported as an addition to bonds payable on the balance sheet.

As indicated with respect to bond discount, if the firm's accounting period falls between interest payment dates, an adjusting entry is required in order to record the accrued interest expense and amortization of premium for the period since the last interest date.

Convertible Bonds

In certain circumstances, a company may issue bonds which are convertible at a specific rate into the common stock of the corporation at the option of the bondholder. This provision may be attached to a bond in order to enhance the marketability of the bond issue. The holder initially has the right of a creditor, but he may later convert to common stock and share in the earnings of the business.

The entries to record the issuance of convertible bonds are similar to those which were discussed previously. At the date of conversion, the carrying value of the bond (face value plus any premium or less any discount) is normally transferred to the stockholder equity accounts which are associated with the new shares of stock issued in the conversion. To illustrate, assume that a corporation had issued a $1,000, 10-year, convertible bond for $1,100 on January 1, 19x1. The bond is convertible into 20 shares of $10 par value common stock at the option of the holder. Further assume that the holder converted the bond into common stock on December 31, 19x5. At the time of the conversion, there is unamortized premium of $50. The entry to record the conversion would be as follows:

Bonds payable..........................	1,000	
Premium...............................	50	
Common stock.......................		200
Additional paid-in capital..............		850

RETIREMENT OF BONDS

Bonds may be retired by the issuing corporation at maturity or before the maturity date either by redeeming callable bonds or by repurchasing bonds in the open market. If bonds are retired at their maturity, any premium or discount will have been completely amortized and the entry to record the retirement of the bonds would be a debit to bonds payable and a credit to cash for an amount equal to the face or maturity value of the bonds.

Callable bonds may be redeemed at the option of the issuing corporation within a specified period and at a stated price referred to as the call price. The call price is usually an amount which is in excess of face value, with the excess referred to as call premium. In the absence of a call provision, the issuing corporation may retire its bonds by purchasing them in the open market at the prevailing market price.

If bonds are repurchased by the issuing corporation at a price less than their book value (i.e., maturity value less discount or plus premium), the corporation realizes a gain on the retirement of the bonds. The carrying value of the bonds is equal to the face value plus any unamortized premium or less any unamortized discount. Similarly, if the purchase price is greater than the carrying value, a loss is incurred on the retirement of the debt.[3]

To illustrate a redemption prior to maturity, assume that the Carpenter Co. has a $50,000 bond issue outstanding with $2,000 of unamortized premium. Further assume that the corporation has the option of calling the bonds at 105 (i.e., 105 percent of the face value) and that the company exercises its call provision. The entry to record the redemption of the bonds for $52,500 ($50,000 × 1.05) would be as follows:

Bonds payable	50,000	
Premium on bonds payable	2,000	
Loss on redemption	500	
Cash		52,500

If the bonds do not include a call provision, the corporation could purchase the bonds in the open market. For example, assume that Carpenter Co. purchased one fifth of the $50,000 face value bonds outstanding for $9,800. The carrying value of the bonds purchased is $10,400 (face value plus one fifth of the unamortized premium), while the purchase price is $9,800. Therefore, the company would realize a $600 gain on the retirement. The entry to record the retirement of the bonds would be as follows:

Bonds payable	10,000	
Premium on bonds payable	400	
Gain on retirement		600
Cash		9,800

BOND SINKING FUND

In order to offer additional security to the investor, a provision may be included in the bond indenture which requires the issuing corporation to set aside funds for repayment of the bond at maturity by periodic accumulations over the life of the issue. These funds may be accumulated by periodically depositing cash in a bond sinking fund. The cash deposited in the fund is usually invested in income producing assets. Therefore, the total deposits made by the issuing corporation over the life of the bond issue are normally less than the total maturity value of the bonds. At maturity, the securities in the fund are sold and the proceeds are used to retire the bonds.

Cash and securities included in a sinking fund are not available for the retirement of current liabilities; they are normally shown as a single total and included under the caption of investments. Similarly, earnings on the sinking fund assets are shown as a separate item in the income statement.

---

[3] According to FASB *Statement No. 4,* "Reporting Gains and Losses From Extinguishment of Debt," (1975), gains or losses from retirement of bonds should be aggregated and, if material in amount, classified in the income statement as an extraordinary item (net of the related income tax effect).

RESTRICTION ON DIVIDENDS

Another means of increasing the security of the bondholder is a provision whereby dividend payments by the issuing company will be restricted during the life of the bond issue. The actual restriction on dividends may vary. For example, a restriction may limit the payment of dividends during a given year to the excess of net income over the sinking fund requirements for the period. There are various methods for disclosing this restriction in the financial statements. Such a restriction could be shown by a footnote or parenthetically in the balance sheet. Alternatively, the restriction could be indicated by appropriating retained earnings each year. To illustrate, assume that the sinking fund requirement for the year is $20,000 and that net income is $35,000. If dividends are limited to the excess of net income over the sinking fund requirement, an appropriation of retained earnings could be made with the following entry:

Retained earnings.....................	20,000	
Appropriation for bonded debt..........		20,000

BALANCE SHEET PRESENTATION

The presentation of long-term liabilities in the balance sheet should disclose all information which is relevant to the debt including the maturity dates, interest rates, conversion privileges, etc. In addition, if a liability is secured by specific assets, or restricts the payment of dividends, such information should also be disclosed in the financial statements. To illustrate, the long-term liabilities section of the balance sheet might appear as follows:

Long-term liabilities:		
25-year, 16% mortgage bonds due on December 31, 19x9.............................	$100,000	
Less: Unamortized discount......................	4,000	$ 96,000
20-year, 18% debenture bonds, convertible into 15 shares of common stock, due on December 31, 19x4............................	$ 50,000	
Add: Unamortized premium.....................	1,000	51,000
Total Long-Term Liabilities.....................		$147,000

INVESTMENTS IN CORPORATE SECURITIES

Corporations frequently acquire the stocks and bonds of other corporations as investments. If the securities are readily marketable and if a firm intends to hold these securities for a relatively short period of time, the investments are normally classified as a current asset, Marketable Securities. On the other hand, investments in stocks and bonds which do not meet the criteria for temporary investments are classified as a noncurrent asset, long-term investments. The remainder of this chapter discusses the accounting for investments in stocks and bonds.

INVESTMENTS IN BONDS

Bonds may be purchased as a long-term investment or as a temporary investment. The purpose for acquiring bonds must be determined on the basis of management's intention. Bonds held as temporary investments are classified as current assets, and bonds acquired for long-term purposes are reported as noncurrent assets. The primary difference in the accounting for bonds classified as temporary versus long-term is in the treatment of the premium or discount on the purchase. Companies making long-term investments in bonds must amortize the difference between the cost of the investment and its maturity value over the life of the bonds. This parallels the treatment used for the issuance of bonds discussed earlier in the chapter. Companies acquiring bonds for temporary purposes, however, are not required to amortize premium or discount. Instead, a short-term investment in bonds is normally carried in the investor's accounts at the acquisition cost, and any gain or loss is recognized in the period the investment is sold. The logic for not amortizing premium or discount is that since it is a temporary investment, the company does not expect to hold the bond until it matures. The following discussion deals with the accounting treatment for long-term investments in bonds.

The cost of a bond includes the quoted price of the bond plus brokerage commissions, transfer taxes, etc. When bonds are purchased between interest dates, the purchase price of the bonds usually includes payment for the interest which has accrued since the previous interest payment date. To illustrate, assume that on June 1, 19x0, Edwards Co. purchases $10,000 face value of 12 percent bonds of the Bell Co. at 111½ plus accrued interest. The bonds pay interest on June 30 and December 31 and mature on December 31, 19x9. The entry to record the purchase would be:

Investment in bonds....................	11,150	
Bond interest receivable.................	500	
Cash		11,650

The debit to the Investment in Bonds account records the cost of the bond—the face value of $10,000 × 111.5 percent or $11,150. This indicates that the bonds were purchased at a premium. Note that this premium is not recorded in a separate account, but instead is included as a part of the Investment in Bonds account. The debit to bond interest receivable records the fact that Edwards Co. purchased five months accrued interest along with the bonds ($10,000 × .12 × $5/12$ = $500). The credit to cash is for the total amount paid by Edwards.

Amortization of Premium

On June 30, 19x0, Edwards Co. will receive its first interest payment which will be recorded as follows:

Cash	600	
Bond interest receivable		500
Investment in bonds		10
Interest income		90

This entry records the receipt of the $600 interest payment ($10,000 × .12 × 6/12 = $600). Of this amount, $500 is the return of the accrued interest that was purchased when the bonds were acquired. Recall that the bonds were purchased at a premium of $1,150 ($11,150 purchase − $10,000 face value). This premium is amortized as a reduction of interest income over the life of the bonds (June 1, 19x0 to December 31, 19x9 = 115 months). The amortization is $10 per month ($1,150 ÷ 115 months). Since Edwards Co. had held the bonds for one month (June 1 to June 30) when the first interest payment was received, $10 of the purchase premium was amortized at that time. Note that the amortization is recorded by a credit to the bond investment account. The income for June is $90, one month's interest of $100 ($10,000 × .12 × 1/12 = $100) minus $10 amortization of premium.

On December 31, 19x0, Edwards Co. will receive its second interest payment of $600. The entry to record the receipt of this interest and the amortization of premium is:

Cash	600	
Investment in bonds		60
Interest income		540

Again, the debit to cash records the receipt of six months' interest ($10,000 × .12 × 6/12 = $600). The credit to the bond investment account is for six months' amortization of premium ($1,150/115 months = $10 per month × 6 months = $60). The interest income is the receipt of $600 less the $60 amortization. The total interest income recognized over the life of the bonds will be equal to the total cash interest received minus the amount of the premium.

At December 31, 19x0, the bond investment account would appear in the balance sheet as follows:

Investment in bonds..................... $11,080

This represents the original cost of the bonds, $11,150 less $70 for seven months' amortization of premium.[4] The investment in bonds account will decrease each period by the amount of the premium amortized and, therefore, at maturity will be equal to the face amount of the bonds.

---

[4] Premium or discount on bonds held as long-term investments is amortized over the life of the bonds. If bonds are held as a temporary investment, no amortization is required.

Amortization of Discount

When bonds are purchased at less than their face value, the discount is not shown separately, but as a part of the investment in bonds account. Discount is amortized as an increase in the interest income earned over the life of the bonds. The interest income recognized on bonds that were acquired at a discount and held to maturity is equal to the total of the cash interest payments received plus the amount of the purchase discount. The carrying value of the investment will increase each period by the amount of the discount amortized and at maturity will equal the face amount of the bonds.

Sale of Bonds

If bonds are sold prior to maturity, accrued interest from the last interest payment date to the date of sale should be recorded. Any difference between this accrued interest plus the carrying value of the bond investment account and the net cash proceeds of the sale represents a gain or loss on the sale and is recorded as such. For example, assume that the bonds used in the above illustration were sold on January 1, 19x1, for $12,000. The entry to record the sale would be as follows:

Cash...............................	12,000	
Investment in bonds....................		11,080
Gain on the sale of bonds...............		920

Alternatively, had the selling price on January 1, 19x1, been $11,000, the entry would have been:

Cash...............................	11,000	
Loss on sale of bonds....................	80	
Investment in bonds....................		11,080

INVESTMENTS IN STOCK

Investments in stock are the temporary or long-term conversion of cash into productive use by the purchase of securities. Such investments are found among the assets of almost all businesses. In general, investments are classified as either temporary or long-term depending on the nature of the security and the intention of the investor firm.

It should be noted that when stock is purchased as an investment, the seller of the stock receives the money paid. Most investment transactions in stock are between two individual investors, one who already owned the stock and then sells it to the new investor who purchases it. The corporation whose stock is traded in the transaction becomes involved directly only if the shares exchanged are a part of a new issue of securities it sold to raise funds.

Temporary Investments

Temporary investments, usually referred to as marketable securities, normally arise from seasonal excesses of cash and represent its conversion to productive use (earning interest or dividends) on a short-term basis. In order to be classified as a temporary investment, a security must be readily salable and the volume of trading of the security should be such that the sale does not materially affect the market price. In addition, there is general agreement that there should be an intention on the part of the investor firm to sell the securities in the short run as the need for cash arises.

Control Over Investments

The effective control over marketable securities includes the physical safeguarding of the certificates. This usually means that the securities should be kept in a safe if they are retained by the firm, and access to the certificates controlled. In many instances, the firm will leave its investments in the custody of its broker. The authority to purchase and sell is usually vested in the Board of Directors of the firm or in a specifically designated investments committee. In either case, requiring written authorization in order to either acquire or dispose of investments is another important control feature. Finally, the accounting records themselves are important in establishing control over investments. The periodic reconciliation of the accounting records to the securities on hand or in the custody of the broker and the reconciliation of the recorded income to the income which should have been earned (as determined by calculation and reference to sources such as *Standard & Poor's Dividend Record*) help to provide effective control over investments.

Accounting for Acquisition of Temporary Investments

The basis for recording temporary investments in the accounts is the cost of the investment. Cost includes all outlays which are required to acquire the investment including the quoted price of the security, brokerage commissions, transfer taxes, etc. To illustrate the accounting for the acquisition of marketable securities, assume that Jones Company purchased 100 shares of the stock of IBM Corporation at a price of $200 per share on January 1, 19x1. The entry to record this purchase would be as follows:

Investment in stock......................	20,000	
Cash...............................		20,000

When a temporary investment is sold, the difference between the selling price and the cost of the investment is recorded as a gain or loss of the period in which the sale took place.

Valuation of Temporary Investments

Temporary investments are classified as either debt securities (government and corporate bonds) or equity securities (preferred and common stock). Prior to 1976 there was considerable diversity in the accounting for temporary investments. However, a significant degree of uniformity in practice resulted from the issuance of FASB *Statement No. 12* which was concerned with the accounting for certain marketable securities. This statement requires that marketable equity securities be accounted for at the lower of aggregate cost or market value. Other marketable securities may be valued either at cost or at lower of cost or market.

If a company owns more than a single kind of marketable equity security, the lower of cost or market procedure is applied to the securities as a group. In applying this method, the *total cost* of the group (often referred to as the portfolio) of securities is compared to the *total current market value* of the securities, and the *lower* of these two amounts is reported as the balance sheet valuation. A decline in value of the aggregate marketable equity securities is recorded as a debit to an unrealized loss account and a credit to a valuation allowance account. The unrealized loss is included in the income statement and the valuation allowance account is deducted from the original cost of the marketable securities in the balance sheet. The loss from decline in value is referred to as an *unrealized* loss to differentiate it from a loss which is realized upon the sale of the securities.

The balance in the valuation allowance account must be adjusted at the end of every period so that the portfolio of marketable equity securities will be reflected in the balance sheet at the *lower* of cost or current market value. Thus, if there are further declines in market value, the adjusting entry will recognize an additional unrealized loss. On the other hand, if the excess of aggregate cost over market value decreases (or is eliminated) in a subsequent period, a gain on recovery is recognized to the extent of previously recognized unrealized losses. The entry to record a recovery in value is a debit to the valuation allowance account and a credit to an unrealized gain account which is included in the income statement. The limitation on unrealized gains to the extent of unrealized losses previously recognized requires that the valuation allowance account must either have a credit or a zero balance. For income tax purposes, the lower of cost or market method is not acceptable, and taxable gain or loss is determined in the period of sale as the difference between original cost and the selling price.

To illustrate the use of the lower of cost or market method, assume that during 19x1 Carol Company acquires 100 shares of IBM stock for $20,000 and 100 shares of AT&T stock for $10,000. On December 31, 19x1, the company determined the carrying amount of its portfolio to be:

	Cost	Market
IBM stock	$20,000	$19,000
AT&T stock	10,000	10,500
	$30,000	$29,500

The following entry would be required in order to record the unrealized loss (i.e., $30,000 − $29,500):

```
Unrealized loss on marketable equity securities  . . . . . . . . . . . . . . .  500
     Allowance for decline in value . . . . . . . . . . . . . . . . . . . . . . . .     500
```

The $500 loss would be reported in the 19x1 income statement, and the allowance account would be deducted from marketable securities at cost in the December 31, 19x1 balance sheet.

An increase in aggregate market value in a subsequent period reduces or eliminates the allowance account. For example, assume that Carol Company had no transactions relating to marketable securities during 19x2, and that the aggregate market value of the securities held at December 31, 19x2 was $29,750. The adjustment to the valuation allowance account at December 31, 19x2, would be recorded as follows:

```
Allowance for decline in value. . . . . . . . . . . . . . . . . . . . .  250
     Unrealized gain on marketable equity securities . . . . .     250
```

The gain of $250 ($29,750 − $29,500) would be included in the income statement for 19x2. If the aggregate market value had increased to $30,000 or more, the amount of the unrealized gain would be limited to $500 (the amount required to eliminate the allowance account). If the market value of the temporary investments in marketable equity securities had decreased below $29,500 during 19x2, an unrealized loss account would have been debited and the allowance account credited in order to increase the balance in the allowance for decline in value account to the aggregate difference between the original cost and the current market value of the securities.

Because the allowance for decline in value is based on a comparison of the total portfolio cost and its market value, there is no effect upon the gain or loss recognized when an investment is sold. When a specific temporary investment in marketable equity securities is sold, the total difference between the net proceeds of the sale and the original cost is recorded as a realized gain or loss. For example, assume that Carol Company sold the 100 shares of IBM stock on June 30, 19x3 for $20,600 (net of commissions). This sale would be recorded as follows:

```
Cash . . . . . . . . . . . . . . . . . . . . . . . . . . . . . . . . . . . . . . . . . . . 20,600
     Investment in stock. . . . . . . . . . . . . . . . . . . . . . . . . . . . .           20,000
     Gain on sale of marketable equity securities . . . . . . . .              600
```

Note that the entry made at the time of sale makes no adjustment for previously recorded unrealized gains or losses or for the allowance account. These accounts are adjusted at the end of the period when the aggregate cost and market values of the securities held are compared.

Long-Term Investments in Stock

Investments in stocks which are not held as temporary investments are classified as long-term assets. Such investments are recorded at their cost as of the date of acquisition. This cost includes the purchase price of the shares plus all brokerage fees, transfer costs, and excise taxes paid by the purchaser. The accounting treatment for long-term investments subsequent to acquisition is generally a function of the degree of ownership interest one corporation (investor) acquires in the other corporation (investee). For purposes of determining the appropriate accounting treatment, long-term investments in common stock may be classified according to the percentage of stock owned by the investor: (1) more than 50 percent ownership; (2) ownership of between 20 percent and 50 percent; (3) ownership of less than 20 percent. When an investor corporation acquires more than 50 percent of the common stock of another corporation, *Consolidated Financial Statements* which treat the investor and investee corporations as a single business entity are normally prepared. The details involved in the preparation of such statements are presented and discussed in the next chapter. However, whether or not consolidated statements are prepared, the investment must still be accounted for in the investor corporation's books. Depending upon the particular circumstances of the investment, there are three methods which may be used in accounting for long-term investments in stock: (1) *the cost method*—the investment is valued at the original acquisition cost; (2) *the lower of cost or market method*—similar to the cost method except the investments are reflected in the balance sheet at the lower of the aggregate cost or market value of the securities; (3) *the equity method*—the investment is valued so as to reflect changes in the underlying net assets of the investee corporation.

The cost method is based on the fact that the two corporations are separate legal entities. Therefore, the carrying value of the investment included in the accounts of the investor remains at the original cost. Any changes in the underlying net assets of the investee corporation which may have occurred as a result of its operations are ignored under this method. The logic underlying the lower of cost or market method is similar to that of the cost method—that is, since both the investor and investee are viewed as separate entities, dividends are recorded as income when received and a gain or loss on the investment is not recognized until the time of disposition. The difference in the methods is that in the lower of cost or market method a year-end adjustment is used to reflect the investment at the lower of aggregate cost or aggregate market value. The equity method, on the other hand, is intended to reflect the economic relationship which exists between the two companies. This method recognizes that an investment in stock which allows the investor company to exercise significant control or influence over the operations of the investee company should be accounted for in such a way that changes in the underlying net assets of the investee company are reflected in the accounts of the investor company.

The choice between the methods was, for all practical purposes, optional prior to the issuance of *Opinion No. 18* of the Accounting Principles Board in 1971. However, the Board stated in this Opinion that the equity method should be used if the investment in stock enables the investor company to exercise significant influence over the operating and financial policies of an investee. The Board assumed that, in the absence of evidence to the contrary, ownership of 20 percent or more of the voting stock of an investee represented evidence of the ability of the investor company to exercise significant influence over the activities of the investee firm. Thus, the cost method or the lower of cost or market method would normally be used for an investment of less than 20 percent of the voting common stock and the equity method would be used for an investment of 20 percent or more of the voting stock of an investee. Most investments in preferred stocks (regardless of the percentage ownership) would also be accounted for by either the cost method or lower of cost or market method because preferred stock does not normally have voting rights. For investments of less than 20 percent of the common stock or investments in preferred stock, the lower of cost or market method must be used to account for investments in marketable equity securities. Generally, a security is classified as "marketable" if there is a currently available sales price in the securities market. The cost method is appropriate for investments in nonmarketable securities which are not required to be accounted for under the equity method. In summary, long-term investments in stock are accounted for as follows:

Investment	*Method*
Ownership of 20 percent or more of the common stock.........................	Equity
Ownership of less than 20 percent of the common stock and ownership of preferred stock in the form of marketable equity securities.................	Lower of Cost or Market
Ownership of less than 20 percent of the common stock and ownership of preferred stock in the form of non-marketable securities.........................	Cost

To illustrate the use of the lower of cost or market method, assume that Winston Company made the following long-term investments in marketable equity securities during 19x1:

1. Purchased 100 shares of IBM Common Stock at a price of $20,000 including commissions.
2. Purchased 100 shares of AT&T Common Stock at a price of $10,000 including commissions.

On December 31, 19x1, Winston Company determined the following information regarding its investments:

Investment	Cost	Market Value	Difference
IBM Stock	$20,000	$19,000	($1,000)
AT&T Stock	10,000	10,500	500
	$30,000	$29,500	($500)

As is the case with the application of the lower of cost or market rule to temporary investments in marketable equity securities, when market value is less than cost, this difference is recorded in an allowance account which is offset against the investment account on the balance sheet. However, unlike temporary investments, this decrease is not reflected as an "unrealized loss" in the income statement. Rather, a separate allowance account with a debit balance is used and this account is shown as a deduction from stockholders' equity in the balance sheet. The following journal entry would be required at December 31, 19x1:

Allowance for net unrealized loss on long-term investments......... 500
    Allowance for decline in value of long-term investments.......... 500

If the market value of the Winston Company portfolio of long-term investments in marketable equity securities increases in a subsequent period, the above entry would be reversed to the extent of the increase or to bring the allowance accounts to zero, whichever is less. That is, if market value should exceed cost in a future period, the allowance accounts are eliminated. The procedures which are employed in accounting for each of these two methods are summarized below.

Cost Method. Under the cost method, the investment account is carried at the original cost of the investment. Any increases or decreases in the net assets of the investee company resulting from earnings or losses do not affect the investor company's investment account. Dividends received by the investor company are recorded as dividend income.

Equity Method. Under the equity method, the investment is initially recorded at its original cost. After acquisition, the investment account is adjusted for any increases or decreases in the net assets of the investee company which have occurred since the stock was acquired. Net income of the investee results in an increase in its net assets. Therefore, the investor company increases the carrying value of its investment and recognizes investment income to the extent of its share (determined by the percentage of the investee's stock owned by the investor company) of the net income of the investee. For example, assume that an investor firm owned 20 percent of the outstanding voting stock of an investee. If the investee reported earnings of $50,000, the investor would increase the carrying value of its investment by $10,000 and simultaneously recognize investment income of $10,000. Similarly, a net loss incurred by the investee company would result in a reduction of the investment account and the recognition of a loss on investments by the investor firm. Since dividends also reduce the net assets of the investee, any dividend distributions made to the investor are recorded by a decrease in the investment account balance. The effect of the equity method is to value the investment at the original cost plus the investor's share of the undistributed retained earnings (net income less dividends) of the investee company since its acquisition of the stock.

To illustrate the difference between the cost and the equity methods, assume that Stolle Company purchases 1,000 of the 5,000 outstanding shares of Most Company stock on January 1, 19x1, at a cost of $10 per share. During 19x1, Most Company reports net income of $20,000 and pays dividends of $10,000, and during 19x2 Most Company reports a net loss of $5,000 and pays no dividends. The journal entries of Stolle Company under both the cost and the equity methods are shown on the following page.

These entries have the following effect on the financial statements of Stolle Company as of the end of 19x2.

	Cost Method	Equity Method
Investment in Most Company December 31, 19x2..................	$10,000	$11,000
Income Statement:		
19x1	2,000	4,000
19x2	0	(1,000)

Under the cost method, Stolle Company would report its investment in Most Company at December 31, 19x2, at its original cost of $10,000. Under the equity method the investment would be carried at $11,000. The $1,000 increase in the investment account under the equity method reflects Stolle Company's share (20 percent) of the $5,000 increase in the net assets of Most Company since the time the Most Company stock was acquired by Stolle.

Under the cost method, the investor recognizes income only to the extent of assets received from the investee (i.e., dividends). The equity method, on the other hand, recognizes income to the extent of the investor's share of the net income of the investee company, whether or not dividends were received.

Event	Cost Method	Equity Method

January 1, 19x1
Acquisition of 1,000 shares of the common stock of Most Company
	Investment in Most Company... 10,000
	    Cash................................. 10,000
		Investment in Most Company... 10,000
		    Cash................................. 10,000

December 31, 19x1 Net income of $20,000 reported by Most Company	No Entry	Investment in Most Company....... 4,000 Investment income.................... 4,000 To record Stolle Company's $4,000 share (20% × $20,000) of Most Company's net income.

June 30, 19x2
Stolle Company received dividends of $2,000. (20% of $10,000 dividend paid by Most Company.)
	Cash........................... 2,000
	    Dividend income............. 2,000
		Cash... 2,000
		    Investment in Most Company............ 2,000

December 31, 19x2 Net loss of $5,000 reported by Most Company	No Entry	Investment loss............................ 1,000 Investment in Most Company......... 1,000 To record Stolle Company's $1,000 share (20% × $5,000) of Most Company's net loss.

When the long-term investment is in the form of marketable equity securities and the use of the equity method is not appropriate, the lower of cost or market method must be used. The application of this method to the aggregate long-term equity securities is basically similar to the procedures used for short-term investments which were discussed previously. The major difference is that the changes in the valuation allowance account for the noncurrent investment in marketable equity securities is recorded as a contra account (reduction) in stockholders' equity rather than as an unrealized loss or gain to be reported in the income statement.

SUMMARY

To raise additional funds for long-term purposes, a firm may borrow by issuing bonds. Bonds require the firm to pay a definite amount (the face value) at a specified date (the maturity date) and may be traded by the investors until that date. In addition, the firm agrees to make periodic interest payments at a stated rate throughout the life of the liability. Bonds may either be secured by specific assets or, in the case of debenture bonds, by only the general credit rating of the issuing corporation.

Since bonds may be traded by investors, the actual selling price received by the issuing corporation may vary from face value. If the selling price is less than the face value of the bond, it is said to be selling at a discount and if the selling price is greater than face value, at a premium. This discount or premium is amortized over the life of the bond and results in either an increase or a decrease in the interest expense incurred on the bond issue.

Bonds may be retired prior to maturity, either by redeeming callable bonds or by repurchasing bonds on the open market. In either case it may be necessary for the firm to recognize either a gain or loss on the early retirement of the debt, depending on the repurchase price. A firm may be required to provide investors with a degree of security, either by periodically setting aside funds in a sinking fund or by making an appropriation of retained earnings.

Companies often make temporary investments in marketable securities to obtain productive use of seasonal excesses of cash. Temporary investments are considered current assets and include both stocks and bonds that are readily salable. Because of this liquidity, careful control should be exercised over the investment documents. Marketable securities are typically valued at cost, but FASB *Statement 12* requires that marketable equity securities be valued in the aggregate at the lower of cost or market for financial reporting purposes.

Corporations often make long-term investments in the stocks and bonds of other corporations. Since bonds may be purchased for an amount greater or lesser than face value, the acquiring company will amortize the resulting bond premium or discount. This amortization is recorded as an adjustment to the interest income earned on the bond. When bonds are purchased or sold between interest dates, the firm must calculate the amount of interest receivable being purchased or sold. In the case of a sale, the firm may also recognize a resulting gain or loss.

Investments in the securities of other corporations are recorded at the purchaser's cost. If there is no significant relationship between the investor and investee corporations, this acquisition cost will remain as the carrying value of the investment. However, if the investor company may exercise significant control or influence over the investee company (for example, as evidenced by an ownership of 20 percent or more of its voting stock) subsequent increases and decreases in the net assets of the investee must be reflected in the carrying value of the investment on the investor's books.

This chapter has discussed long-term liabilities and investments. The next chapter will consider and illustrate the use of consolidated financial statements.

KEY DEFINITIONS

Amortization of premium or discount Amortization is the process of allocating a portion of the discount or premium on bonds payable (investment in bonds) to interest expense (revenue).

Bond A bond is an issuance of debt used as a means of borrowing money for long-term purposes.

Bond discount The discount is the amount by which the face value of a bond payable exceeds the issue price. A discount occurs when the coupon rate on the bonds is less than the market interest rate at the time the bonds are issued.

Bond premium The premium is the amount by which the issue price of a bond payable exceeds the face value. A premium occurs when the coupon rate of interest on a bond is higher than the market interest rate at the time of issuance.

Bond sinking fund A sinking fund is accumulated by the issuing corporation specifically for the repayment of bonds at maturity. A sinking fund may be created voluntarily or required by provisions of the bond issue.

Callable bonds Callable bonds may be repurchased at the option of the issuing corporation within a specified period at a specified price.

Convertible bonds Convertible bonds may be exchanged for a specified amount of capital stock at the option of the bondholder.

Cost method The cost method of accounting is used for an investment in the stock of another company in which the investment account is carried at the original cost and income is recognized when dividends are received.

Coupon bonds Coupon bonds have interest coupons attached which call for the payment of a specified amount of interest on the interest dates.

Coupon rate The interest rate specified on the bond is the coupon rate. Periodic interest payments equal the coupon interest rate multiplied by the face amount of the bond.

Debenture bonds Debenture bonds are not secured by any specific assets of the corporation. Their security is dependent upon the general credit standing of the issuing corporation.

Equity method The equity method of accounting is used for an investment in the stock of another company in which the investment account is adjusted for changes in the net assets of the investee, and income is recognized by the investor company as the investee earns profits or incurs losses.

Long-term investment in stock This involves the acquisition of stock of other corporations as long-term, income-producing investments. Such purchases are often made for the purpose of obtaining a controlling interest in a company or for some other continuing business advantage.

Maturity value Maturity value constitutes the amount that the holder of a note is entitled to receive at the due date. This amount includes the principal plus any accrued interest.

Mortgage A mortgage is a conditional conveyance or transfer of property to a creditor as security for a loan.

Registered bonds Registered bonds have the name of the owner registered with the issuing corporation. Periodic interest payments are mailed directly to the registered owner.

Retirement of bonds Retiring bonds is the process of redeeming bonds or repurchasing bonds in the open market.

Secured bond Secured bonds are secured by prior claim against specific assets of the business in the event that the issuing corporation is unable to make the required interest or principal payments.

Serial bonds Serial bond issues are bonds which mature on several different dates.

Temporary investments A temporary investment is a security that is readily salable, and the volume of trading of the security should be such that the sale does not materially affect the market price. In addition, there should be an intention on the part of the investor firm to sell the security in the short run as the need for cash arises.

Term bonds A term bond is a bond issue that matures on a single date.

QUESTIONS

1. Define each of the following terms related to the issue of bonds: (a) debenture, (b) secured, (c) callable, (d) convertible, (e) serial bonds.

2. How are interest payments made to the holders of (a) coupon bonds, and (b) registered bonds?

3. How can bonds be sold when the market interest rate for comparable bonds is higher than the stated contract rate on the bond certificate?

4. How does a discount on the issuance of bonds affect the total cost of borrowing to the issuing corporation?

5. What is the effect of a premium on the interest expense of the company issuing bonds? Explain.

6. What is the effect of a discount on the interest expense of the company issuing bonds? Explain.

7. Give the journal entries required for the amortization of (a) Discount on Bonds Payable and (b) Premium on Bonds Payable.

8. How should Discount on Bonds Payable and Premium on Bonds Payable be classified and presented on the balance sheet?

9. If bonds are issued at a time between interest payment dates, why does the issuing company receive an amount of cash equal to the issue price of the bonds plus the accrued interest?

10. Differentiate between long-term (permanent) and short-term (temporary) investments in stocks.

11. Explain the essential characteristics of the cost method.

12. Explain the essential characteristics of the equity method.

13. Under what circumstances would each of the following methods of accounting for long-term investment in stocks be used: (a) cost method? (b) equity method?

EXERCISES

14. Stengel Company has authorization to issue $200,000 of 10-year, 7 percent bonds on January 1, 19x1, with semiannual interest payments on June 30 and December 31. Stengel Company issues $100,000 of the bonds on January 1 at face value. Another $100,000 of bonds are issued on August 1, 19x1, at face value plus accrued interest. Assume Stengel Company's accounting period ends March 31.

Required:

Give the firm's journal entries with respect to the bonds for 19x1.

15. Terry Tractors, Inc., has outstanding a $100,000, 10-year bond issue which was sold on January 1, 19x0, at a price of $110,000. The following liability, shown below, appeared on the balance sheet on December 31, 19x4.

        Bonds payable................. $100,000
        Premium......................   5,000 $105,000

Make the entry necessary to record the retirement of the bonds in each of the following two situations:

a. The firm calls the bonds at 106 on January 1, 19x5.
b. Terry Tractors, Inc., purchases half of the outstanding bonds in the open market for $51,000 on January 1, 19x5.

16. Boyer, Inc., issued 100, $1,000, 20-year convertible bonds at a price of $1,020 each on January 1, 19x1. Each of the bonds is convertible into 20 shares of $20 par value common stock. On December 31, 19x7, 50 of these bonds were converted into common stock. Make the journal entry necessary to record the conversion on the books of Boyer, Inc.

17. The Trail Blazers Company issued a $70,000, 7 percent, 15-year debenture bond on July 1, 19x1, at a price of $68,000. Interest is to be paid on December 31 and June 30 of each year.

Required:

1. Record the journal entries with respect to the bond up to and including December 31, 19x1.
2. What is the total interest cost to the Trail Blazers Company for this bond issue?
3. Assuming the Trail Blazers Company has only this bond issue in long-term debt outstanding, prepare the long-term liabilities section of the balance sheet as of December 31, 19x1.

18. Ames Company had the following transactions relating to marketable securities during the last three months of 19x1.

Sept. 1   Purchased 100 shares of Burden Company common stock for $27 per share plus commission of $100.
Nov. 1   Received a $1 per share dividend on the Burden Company stock.
Dec. 1   Sold 50 shares of Burden Company stock at $32 per share net of commissions.

Required:

1. Prepare the journal entries necessary to record the above transactions.
2. Determine the cost basis for marketable securities at December 31, 19x1.

19. On January 1, 19x1, Lang Company acquired 25 percent of the outstanding shares of stock of Brenner Company at a cost of $250,000. On that date, Brenner Company had common stock of $750,000 and retained earnings of $250,000. Brenner Company reported net income of $100,000 during 19x1, and paid a cash dividend of $20,000. Make the necessary journal entries on Lang's books during 19x1 using the equity method.

20. Assume that Lang Company (Exercise 19) acquired only 19 percent of the shares of Brenner Company at a cost of $100,000. Prepare the necessary journal entries on Lang's books during 19x1 using the cost methods.

PROBLEMS

21. Kubek Company is authorized to issue $50,000 of 10-year, 8 percent bonds with semiannual interest payments on June 30 and December 31. Record the journal entries necessary on January 1 and June 30, 19x1, on the books of Kubek Company in each of the following independent cases.

    a. The bonds are issued at a price of $45,000 on January 1, 19x1. Interest is paid on June 30 and December 31.
    b. The bonds are issued at a price of $53,000 on January 1, 19x1. Interest is paid on June 30 and December 31.

22. Dean Co. issued $100,000 of 6 percent, 20-year debenture bonds on January 1, 19x1. Interest is payable semiannually on June 30 and December 31. The following information is given on the bonds at December 31, 19x1:

    Carrying value of bonds........................ $103,800
    Interest expense for the year.................... 5,800

    a. Were the bonds issued at a premium or discount?
    b. What was the amount of premium or discount on the issuance of the bonds?
    c. How much of the discount or premium was amortized during the year?

23. On January 1, 19x1, the stockholders of Howard Company authorized the issuance of $8,000 (par value) of 3-year bonds paying interest (8 percent) semiannually on June 30 and December 31. The bonds were sold on April 1, 19x1, for $8,330 plus accrued interest. On April 1, 19x2, Howard Company retired half of the issue at 102 (plus accrued interest).

    Required:

    Prepare all general journal entries for:

    1. Issuance of the bonds.
    2. Interest payment on June 30, 19x1.
    3. Interest payment on December 31, 19x1.
    4. Retirement of portion of issue on April 1, 19x2.
    5. Interest payment on June 30, 19x2.

24. On October 1, 19x1, the Badger Company issued $10,000 (face value) of 3 percent bonds which will mature on September 30, 19x3. On December 31, 19x1, the company's accountant made the following adjusting journal entry relative to the bonds (Badger Company's accounting period is the calendar year):

Interest expense............................	90	
Interest payable...........................		75
Discount on bonds payable.................		15

Required:

Give the journal entry made to record the sale of the bonds on October 1, 19x1. Assume that interest is payable annually on September 30.

25. The following data related to long-term liabilities appeared on the books of Summer Co. on December 31, 19x1 (after the payment of interest on December 31, 19x1).

Bonds payable—6 percent, 20-year debenture bonds due on December 31, 19x15, $100,000 authorized, interest payable semiannually on June 30 and December 31................	$100,000	
Discount on bonds payable..............	3,000	$97,000

On January 1, 19x2, half of the bonds were purchased and retired at 102 percent of face value. Prepare the necessary journal entries to record the semiannual interest payment on December 31, 19x1, and the retirement of $50,000 of bonds on January 1, 19x2.

26. Cavalier Corporation issued a $10,000, 5-year, 6 percent convertible bond for $9,280 on September 1, 19x1. Interest is to be paid semiannually on March 1 and September 1 each year. The bond is convertible into 10 shares of $20 par value common stock for each $1,000 of the bond issue.

Required:

Make the required journal entries to record the:

1. Issuance of the bond.
2. Accrual of interest on December 31, 19x1, the end of the fiscal year.
3. Payment of interest on March 1, 19x2.
4. Conversion of $5,000 worth of bonds payable into common stock on November 30, 19x4.
5. Payment of interest on September 1, 19x5.
6. Payment on the remainder of the bond principle and interest on the due date.

27. The Knick Company decided to issue a 5-year, $20,000 bond on January 2, 19x1, at a price and interest rate which has not yet been determined. Interest payments are to be made annually on December 31.

Required:

Prepare a table showing the cash interest payments, amortization of premium or discount, interest expense, and carrying value of the bond (as shown on the end-of-year balance sheet) over the bond's life using each of the following assumptions:

1. The bond was issued at 6 percent interest for $19,520.
2. The bond was issued at 8 percent interest for $20,360.

28. Jason Company issued $100,000 of 6 percent, 10-year debenture bonds at face value plus accrued interest on April 1, 19x1. Interest is payable semiannually on January 1 and July 1.

Required:

Prepare the journal entries necessary to record the issuance of the bonds and to record interest expense for the first interest date subsequent to issuance.

29. Dorey Co. issued $500,000 of 20-year, 8 percent bonds on April 1, 19x1, with interest payable on June 30 and December 31. The bonds were callable after January 1, 19x8 at 105 percent of face value and mature on December 31, 19x20. The fiscal year of the company ends on September 30. Give the necessary journal entries for the following transactions:

19x1

Apr. 1 Issued the bonds for $529,750 including accrued interest.
June 30 Paid interest.
Sept. 30 Recorded adjusting entry for accrued interest.
Dec. 31 Paid interest.

19x8

Jan. 1 Called the bonds.

30. Hawk Company issued $150,000, 10-year, 8 percent convertible bonds for $155,392 including four months accrued interest on April 30, 19x0. Interest is to be paid semiannually on June 30 and December 31. The bonds are convertible into 5 shares of $50 par value common stock for each $1,000 of the bond issue. (Any premium or discount on the bonds should be amortized over 116 months, the remaining life of the bonds.)

Required:

Make the required journal entries to record the

1. Issuance of bonds.
2. Accrual of interest on September 30, 19x0, the end of the fiscal year.
3. Payment of interest on December 31, 19x0.
4. Conversion of a portion of the bonds into 375 shares of common stock on August 31, 19x2.
5. Payment of interest on June 30, 19x3.
6. Payment on the remainder of the bond principal and interest on the due date—December 31, 19x9.

31. The transactions of Sandy Company relating to marketable securities during 19x1 are listed below.

    Jan. 10   Purchased 500 shares of Smith Corporation common stock at a price of $21 per share plus a $200 commission.
    Feb. 5   Purchased 100 shares of Dade Corporation common stock at a price of $40 per share plus an $80 commission.
    Mar. 1   Received a cash dividend of $1 per share on Smith Corporation common stock.
    Apr. 16   Purchased 200 shares of Consolidated Company common stock at $80 per share plus $120 commission.
    June 1   Received a cash dividend of $2 per share on Dade Corporation common stock.
    Aug. 20   Sold 100 shares of Dade Corporation stock at $42 per share, net of sales commissions.
    Sept. 1   Received a $1 per share dividend on Consolidated Company common stock.

    Required:

    1. Prepare the journal entries necessary to record the above transactions.
    2. Prepare the necessary adjusting entry at December 31, 19x1, assuming that the aggregate market value of the portfolio is $11,000.

32. Handy Company had the following transactions relating to marketable securities during 19x1:

    Jan. 20   Purchased 100 shares of Bear Corporation common stock at $50 per share plus a $105 commission.
    Apr. 16   Purchased 400 shares of River Corporation common stock at $10 per share plus a commission of $95.
    May   1   Received a cash dividend of $1 per share on Bear Corporation common stock.
    June 5   Purchased 100 shares of Gunner Corporation common stock at $75 per share plus a $160 commission.
    Aug. 11   Received a cash dividend of $2 per share on River Corporation common stock.
    Nov. 1   Sold 100 shares of Bear Corporation common stock at $55 per share, net of commissions.
    Dec. 1   Received a $1 per share dividend on Gunner Corporation common stock.

Required:

1. Prepare the journal entries to record the above transactions.
2. Prepare the necessary adjusting entry at December 31, 19x1, assuming that the aggregate market value of the portfolio is $9,600.

Refer to the Annual Report included in the Appendix at the end of the text:

33. Comparing the two years, did long-term liabilities increase or decrease?

34. What factors might cause an increase in long-term liabilities?

35. What factors could cause a decrease in liabilities?

36. What is the total debt due in more than one year at the end of the most recent year?

37. Was the long-term debt issued at a premium or at a discount? Where can this information be located?

38. Are current liabilities greater than long-term liabilities at the end of the most recent year?

39. Can the amount of amortization be determined from the body of the financial statements?

40. What is the highest interest paid on long-term debt? Where can this information be found?

41. Was there amortization expense in either year?

APPENDIX INTEREST AND PRESENT VALUE CONCEPTS

The principles used in discounting cash flows due at certain future points in time by the use of compound interest concepts are discussed in this appendix. These concepts have a broad application in business decisions. For example, most business entities often make decisions to: (1) borrow funds in the current period in return for a promise to pay cash or other resources in future periods; and (2) invest resources at the current time with the expectation of receiving benefits at various future times. For both of these types of decisions, the timing of the various cash inflows and outflows has a significant effect on the desirability of the various possible investment and borrowing alternatives. Timing of the cash flows is important because of the following principle: *an amount of cash to be received in the future is not equivalent to the same amount of cash held at the present time.* This statement is true because money has a time value—it can be invested to earn a return (i.e., interest or dividends). For this reason, in both borrowing and investing decisions, consideration must be given to the time values of the various cash inflows and outflows.

In order to understand the implications of such decisions, the accountant must be able to determine the *present value* of future cash flows. Although there are a number of important applications of present value concepts in the financial accounting area, this appendix is limited to the application of these concepts to long-term liabilities.

INTEREST

Interest represents the amount received by the lender and paid by the borrower for the use of money for a given period of time. Thus, upon payment of a debt, interest is the excess of the cash repaid over the amount originally borrowed (referred to as the *principal*). Interest is normally stated as a rate for a one year period.

Simple interest is the amount of interest that is computed on the principal *only,* for a given period of time. Simple interest is computed as follows:

$$\text{Interest} = \text{Principal} \times \text{Rate} \times \text{Time}$$
$$\text{Interest} = P \times I \times T \quad (1)$$

To illustrate, interest on $1,000 for 6 months at an annual interest rate of 10 percent is:

$$\$50 = \$1,000 \times .10 \times \tfrac{6}{12}$$

Compound interest is interest that is computed for a period of time both on the principal and on the interest which has been earned but not paid. That is, interest is compounded when the interest earned in each period is added to the principal amount and both principal and interest earn interest in all subsequent periods. To illustrate, assume that $1,000 is deposited in a bank which pays interest at 10 percent annually. If the interest was withdrawn each year (simple interest), the depositor would collect $100 in interest each year (or $300 in interest over a three-year period):

$$\text{Interest Per Year} = \$1,000 \times .10 \times 1 = \$100$$
$$\text{Total Interest for 3 Years} = \$100 \times 3 = \$300$$

However, if the interest at the end of each period is added to the principal sum (compound interest), the amount earned over the three-year period is computed as follows:

Original investment			$1,000
Balance at the End of Year:	1.	$1,000 + (.10 × $1,000 × 1)	1,100
	2.	$1,100 + (.10 × $1,100 × 1)	1,210
	3.	$1,210 + (.10 × $1,210 × 1)	1,331

Compound interest for the three-year period is $331 ($1,331 − $1,000), the difference between the balance at the end of the three-year period and the original investment. This amount exceeds simple interest because interest was earned each year both on the principal and on the interest earned in previous years.

Since compounding occurs when interest is earned on previously accumulated interest, a formula can be developed for computing the compound amount at which the principal sum will increase over a given time period. To develop this formula, consider the compound interest on one dollar invested at an interest rate of I percent. The amount accumulated at the end of the first year would be [$1 + (1 × I)] or (1 + I). If this amount is allowed to accumulate and earn interest for the second year, the amount accumulated is (1 + I)(1 + I) which is equal to $(1 + I)^2$. Similarly, the amount at the end of T periods is $(1 + I)^T$. Consequently, the amount (A) that a principal amount (P) will accumulate over a time period (T) at an interest rate (I) is expressed as:

$$A = P(1 + I)^T \qquad (2)$$

For example, if $1,000 is invested for three years at 10 percent interest per year, the amount accumulated at the end of three years is computed as follows:

$$A = \$1,000 (1 + .10)^3$$
$$A = \$1,000 (1.331)$$
$$A = \$1,331$$

This computation of the sum for a single principal amount and the compound interest at a specified future time may be illustrated as follows:

```
$1,000  ────────────▶  $1,331
  0        1       2       3
              Time (years)
```

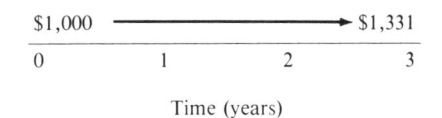

PRESENT VALUES OF A FUTURE SUM

The present value of a given amount at a specified future time is the sum that would have to be invested at the present time in order to equal that future value at a given rate of compound interest. For example, it was determined that $1,000 invested at 10 percent compound interest would accumulate to a total of $1,331 in three years. Therefore, $1,000 is the *present value* of $1,331 three years from the present time (given a 10 percent rate of interest). That is, if you could earn 10 percent on a bank deposit, you would be indifferent between receiving $1,000 now (which could be deposited to accumulate to $1,331 in three years) or $1,331 three years from now, all other factors being equal.

The present value of a future amount is determined by computing the amount that a principal sum will accumulate to over a specified period of time. Consequently, by dividing equation (2) by $(1 + I)^T$, we obtain the formula for computing the present value of a future amount (A):

$$P = \frac{A}{(1 + I)^T} \tag{3}$$

For example, the present value of $1,331 three years from now would be computed as follows:

$$P = \frac{\$1,331}{(1 + .10)^3}$$
$$P = \$1,000$$

Because of the number and variety of decisions which are based on the present value of future cash flows, tables have been developed from the formula which give the present value of $1 for various interest rates and for various periods of time. These values may be multiplied by any future amount to determine its present value. The factors for the present value of $1 are listed in Table A-1.

To illustrate the use of this table, let us compute the present value of $1,331 to be received three years from now at a compound interest rate of 10 percent. The value from the table for 3 years at 10 percent is .7513. This is the present value of $1. Accordingly, the present value of $1,331 is computed as $1,331 × .7513 = $999.80, (this amount is not exactly equal to $1,000 because of the rounding error in the present value factor included in the table). The computation of the present value of a simple payment due in the future may be illustrated as follows:

```
$1,000 ←─────────── $1,331
───┼────┼────┼────┼───
   0    1    2    3
```

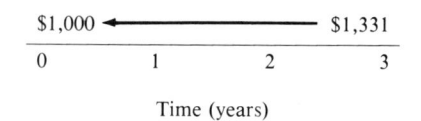

Time (years)

COMPOUND INTEREST AND PRESENT VALUE ON A SERIES OF EQUAL PAYMENTS

Business decisions involving a series of cash flows to be paid or received periodically are more common than decisions involving the accumulation of a single principal sum. It is possible to determine the present value of a series of payments (or receipts) by computing the present value of each payment or receipt and adding these values to obtain the present value for the entire series. However, if all the payments are equal, formulas or tables may be used to compute the present value of a series of payments. Such a series of equal periodic payments is normally referred to as an *annuity*. If the payments are made at the end of each period, the annuity is referred to as an *ordinary annuity*.

The accumulated amount (future value) of an ordinary annuity is the sum of the periodic payments and the compound interest on these payments. For example, the future value of an annuity of $1,000 per year (at the end of each year) for three years at 10 percent interest could be determined as follows:

The initial payment accumulates at 10 percent for two years to....................................	$1,210
The second payment accumulates at 10 percent for one year to.......................................	1,100
The third payment is due at the end of the third year.........	1,000
Amount of an ordinary annuity of $1,000 for three years at 10 percent..............................	$3,310

The computation of the future value of a series of payments may be expressed as follows:

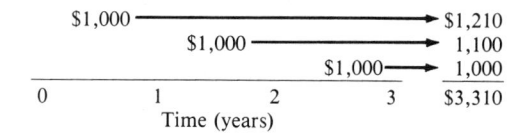

```
$1,000 ──────────────→ $1,210
       $1,000 ───────→   1,100
              $1,000 →   1,000
───┼────┼────┼────┼───   $3,310
   0    1    2    3
       Time (years)
```

The present value of an ordinary annuity is the amount which, if invested at the present time at a compound rate of interest, would provide for a series of equal withdrawals at the end of a certain number of periods. The present value of an ordinary annuity may be computed as the present values of each of the individual payments. For example, the present value of an ordinary annuity of $1,000 per year for three years at 10 percent could be computed as follows (see Table A-1):

Present value of $1,000 in one year........	.9091 × $1,000 =	$ 909.10
Present value of $1,000 in two years.......	.8264 × $1,000 =	826.40
Present value of $1,000 in three years......	.7513 × $1,000 =	751.30
Present value of an annuity of $1,000 for three periods at 10 percent...........		$2,486.80

This computation indicates that if $2,486.80 is invested at an interest rate of 10 percent, it would be possible to withdraw $1,000 at the end of each year for three years.

The formula for the present value of an ordinary annuity of $R per period for T periods at I rate of interest may be stated:

$$P = R \left[\frac{1 - \frac{1}{(1 + I)^T}}{I} \right]$$

Table A-2 gives the present value of an ordinary annuity of $1 per period for various periods at varying rates of interest. By multiplying the appropriate value from the table by the dollar amount of the periodic payment, the present value of the payments may be calculated. For example, the present value of three annual cash payments of $1,000 made at the end of the next three years at a 10 percent interest rate would be computed as follows:

$$\$1,000 \times 2.4869 = \$2,486.90^1$$

This amount may be interpreted as the present cash payment which would be exactly equivalent to the three future installments of $1,000 if money earns 10 percent compounded annually. The computation of the present value of a series of future payments may be illustrated as follows:

```
$ 909.10 ←——— $1,000
  826.40 ←——————— $1,000
  751.30 ←——————————— $1,000
$2,486.80
─────────────────────────────
0          1          2          3
              Time (years)
```

APPLICATION OF PRESENT VALUE CONCEPTS TO BONDS PAYABLE

A bond is a contract between an issuing company and the purchaser of the bond. There are two types of payments that a company will have to make to bondholders. One payment is a lump-sum payment made at

---
[1] Difference of $.10 due to rounding in tables.

the end of the life of the bond, which is the return of the *face value* or *maturity value* of the bond. The other payment is for interest, which will be made at specific intervals in fixed amounts over the life of the bond. Interest is usually paid semiannually by the issuing company. Bond contracts will state the *coupon* or *nominal rate* of interest on an annual basis.

To calculate the selling price of a bond (the amount the firm will receive upon issuance of the bond), consider a company that has sold a $1,000 face value bond with a nominal rate of interest of 8 percent. The bond will mature in 5 years and the interest is payable June 30 and December 31 of each year. The company has made two promises to the purchaser of the bond:

Promise 1: To pay $1,000 at the end of 5 years.
Promise 2: To pay $40 semiannually for 5 years.

The price that any investor would pay for a bond would depend upon the *effective rate*[2] of interest on the date that the investor decided to buy the bond. The effective rate will be dependent upon many factors such as the prime interest rate in money markets, the risks involved in buying the bond of that specific company, and the provisions of the bond that may make it more attractive for investment purposes. In general, the effective rate will be determined by supply and demand in the bond market.

There are three possible general cases that illustrate the potential selling price of the bond. These three cases are dependent upon the earnings expectations of buyers of bonds in the market place. In the prior example, where the nominal rate is eight percent, the three possible cases are:

1. The effective (market) rate of interest is equal to eight percent.
2. The effective (market) rate of interest is below eight percent.
3. The effective (market) rate of interest is greater than eight percent.

If the market is demanding an eight percent return on bonds of like kind, and the company enters the market with an eight percent coupon rate on its bond, the bond should sell at its face value of $1,000. The buyer is demanding eight percent and the seller is paying eight percent; therefore the bond would sell at *par*.

If the market is demanding a return that is less than eight percent and the company enters the market with an eight percent coupon rate on its bond, the company is paying a greater return than is demanded in the market. Therefore, the bond will sell for a price in excess of $1,000. This

---

[2] The effective rate is also referred to as the market rate or the yield.

excess is referred to as a *premium*. The investors will buy the bond at a price greater than $1,000 because the coupon rate exceeds the rate demanded by the market.

If the market is demanding a return that is greater than eight percent and the company enters the market with an eight percent coupon rate on its bond, the company is paying less than the return demanded by the market. Therefore, the bond will sell for less than $1,000. The difference between $1,000 and the selling price will be a *discount* on the bond.

To calculate the selling price of the bond, assume that the market rate of interest was either eight percent, six percent, or ten percent. Note that the bond contract provides for a lump-sum payment at maturity and semiannual interest payments over the life of the bond. Thus, in order to find the current value, or selling price, of the bond, it is necessary to determine the present value of the lump-sum payment at maturity and the present value of the periodic interest payments (an ordinary annuity). Illustration A-1 presents the calculations which are necessary to determine the selling price of the $1,000 bond at the three market rates of interest assumed above.

Illustration A-1

Selling Price of a Bond with 8% Coupon Rate, 5-Year Life, and Semiannual Payments

Present Value Factors for 10 Periods at 4% Semiannual Interest

	Table 1	Table 2	Totals

8% Coupon, 8% Market
Bond Sells at Par

Promise #1 = $1,000–lump sum	.6756		= $ 675.60
Promise #2 = $40–annuity		8.1109	= 324.44
		Selling price (rounded)	= $1,000.00

8% Coupon, 6% Market
Bond Sells at Premium

Promise #1 = $1,000–lump sum	.7441		= $ 744.10
Promise #2 = $40–annuity		8.5302	= 341.21
		Selling price (rounded)	= $1,085.31

8% Coupon, 10% Market
Bond Sells at Discount

Promise #1 = $1,000–lump sum	.6139		= $ 613.90
Promise #2 = $40–annuity		7.7217	= 308.87
		Selling price (rounded)	= $ 922.77

Even though the selling price of the bond will vary according to the three different market rate assumptions, it is important to remember that the bond is a fixed contract that will pay a return of $40 to the bondholder semiannually and $1,000 at its maturity date. These amounts are paid regardless of the initial selling price of the bond.

ACCOUNTING FOR PREMIUM OR DISCOUNT ON BONDS—THE INTEREST METHOD

The following example will be used to illustrate the accounting treatment of a bond issue sold at a premium or discount using the interest method. Assume that on July 1, 19x1, a company sold a $1,000,000 bond issue with a nominal interest rate of eight percent and a maturity date of July 1, 19x6. Interest will be paid on June 30 and December 31. The company's fiscal year ends on December 31.

The calculations necessary in order to compute the initial selling price of the bond are the same as the calculations in Illustration A-1, except that the entire issue, $1,000,000, is under consideration. If the market rate of interest demanded is eight percent, the bonds will sell for $1,000,000. If the market rate of interest is six percent, the bonds will sell at a premium. The selling price will be ($1,000,000 × .7441) + ($40,000 × 8.5302) = $1,085,308. If the market rate of interest demanded is ten percent, the bonds will sell at a discount. The selling price will be ($1,000,000 × .6139) + ($40,000 × 7.7217) = $922,768.

The face value of the bonds is paid to bondholders at the maturity date regardless of the original price of the bonds. The premium or discount on a bond is paid or received, respectively, to adjust the interest that will be paid on the bond to the return on the investment demanded by the market (market rate of interest) given the type of bond and the risk involved as perceived by investors.

There are two acceptable methods for amortizing bond premium or discount. One technique for amortization, the straight-line method, was discussed in the chapter. A second technique, referred to as the interest method, has been suggested by the Accounting Principles Board.[3] This method of amortization results in recognizing a constant rate of interest on the bond liability over the life of the bond. The interest expense for each period is computed by multiplying a constant rate of interest by the beginning liability for that period. The interest method is described in this appendix.

Bonds Sold at a Premium

If the market rate of interest in the prior example is six percent, the bonds will sell at a premium of $85,308 ($1,085,308 − $1,000,000). The interest method will yield a different interest expense for each interest period. To determine the interest expense, the carrying value of the liability (face value plus unamortized premium or minus unamortized discount) is multiplied by

---
[3] *APB Opinion No. 21* (New York, American Institute of Certified Public Accountants, 1972).

the semiannual effective rate of interest. Thus, the interest expense will be a constant percentage (equal to the effective semiannual interest rate on the issuance of the bonds) of six percent per year or three percent on the outstanding liability at the beginning of each semiannual interest period. The following journal entries would be made in 19x1 under the interest method:

June 30, 19x1	Cash.......................	1,085,308.00	
	Bond premium.............		85,308.00
	Bonds payable.............		1,000,000.00
December 31, 19x1	Interest expense.............	32,559.24	
	Bond premium..............	7,440.76	
	Cash....................		40,000.00

(Interest expense = $1,085,308.00 × .03 = $32,559.24)

At the end of 19x1, the balance sheet presentation of the liability will include both the bonds payable and bond premium accounts. The bond premium account is rounded in the example.

Bonds payable...................	$1,000,000	
Add: Bond premium............	77,867	
Total bonds payable............		$1,077,867

When bonds are issued at a premium, use of the *interest* method will cause the *interest* expense to decrease over the life of the bond because both the premium account and the carrying value of the liability will decrease over the life of the bonds. The bond premium amortization will increase because the cash payment to bondholders remains constant and the interest expense decreases each period. The total interest expense and premium amortization schedule is given in Illustration A-2.

Bonds Sold at a Discount

If the market rate of interest demanded by investors is ten percent, the bonds in the prior example will sell at a discount because the face rate of interest is eight percent. The discount will be the difference between the maturity value of $1,000,000 and the selling price of $922,768, or $77,232.

The concepts underlying the *interest* method for bond discount are the same as those discussed in the prior section on bonds sold at a premium. The journal entries for 19x1 for bonds sold at a discount are:

June 30, 19x1	Cash.......................	922,768.00	
	Bond discount..............	77,232.00	
	Bonds payable.............		1,000,000.00
December 31, 19x1	Interest expense.............	46,138.40	
	Bond discount............		6,138.40
	Cash....................		40,000.00

(Interest expense = $922,768 × .05 = $46,138.40)

Illustration A-2

Interest Expense and Premium Amortization Schedule

Date	Debit to Interest Expense*	Debit to Bond Premium	Credit to Cash	Bond Premium Balance	Total Liability
July 1, 19x1.........	0	0	0	$85,308.00	$1,085,308.00
December 31, 19x1....	$32,559.24	$ 7,440.76	$ 40,000	77,867.24	1,077,867.24
July 1, 19x2.........	32,336.02	7,663.98	40,000	70,203.26	1,070,203.26
December 31, 19x2....	32,106.10	7,893.90	40,000	62,309.36	1,062,309.36
July 1, 19x3.........	31,869.28	8,130.72	40,000	54,178.64	1,054,178.64
December 31, 19x3....	31,625.36	8,374.64	40,000	45,804.00	1,045,804.00
July 1, 19x4.........	31,374.12	8,625.88	40,000	37,178.12	1,037,178.12
December 31, 19x4....	31,115.34	8,884.66	40,000	28,293.46	1,028,293.46
July 1, 19x5.........	30,848.80	9,151.20	40,000	19,142.26	1,019,142.26
December 31, 19x5....	30,574.27	9,425.73	40,000	9,716.53	1,009,716.53
July 1, 19x6.........	30,291.47*	9,716.53	40,000	0	1,000,000.00
		$85,308.00	$400,000		

*To determine interest expense, the total liability at the beginning of the period was multiplied by the semiannual market interest rate of three percent. Any rounding errors are included in the July 1, 19x6 debit to interest expense.

At the end of 19x1, the balance sheet presentation of the liability will include both the bonds payable and the bond discount account. The bond discount account is rounded in the example.

Bonds payable..............	$1,000,000	
Less: Bond discount........	71,094	
Total bonds payable.......		$ 928,906

In the case of bonds sold at a discount, using the interest method, interest expense increases over the life of the bond because discount decreases and the carrying value of the bonds increases. The total interest expense and discount amortization schedule is given in Illustration A-3.

Illustration A-3

Interest Expense and Discount Amortization Schedule

Date	Debit to Interest Expense*	Credit to Bond Discount	Credit to Cash	Bond Discount Balance	Total Liability
July 1, 19x1.........	0	0	0	$77,232.00	$ 922,768.00
December 31, 19x1....	$46,138.40	$ 6,138.40	$ 40,000	71,093.60	928,906.40
July 1, 19x2.........	46,445.32	6,445.32	40,000	64,648.28	935,351.72
December 31, 19x2....	46,767.59	6,767.59	40,000	57,880.69	942,119.31
July 1, 19x3.........	47,105.97	7,105.97	40,000	50,774.72	949,225.28
December 31, 19x3....	47,461.26	7,461.26	40,000	43,313.46	956,686.54
July 1, 19x4.........	47,834.33	7,834.33	40,000	35,479.13	964,520.87
December 31, 19x4....	48,226.04	8,226.04	40,000	27,253.09	972,746.91
July 1, 19x5.........	48,637.35	8,637.35	40,000	18,615.74	981,384.26
December 31, 19x5....	49,069.21	9,069.21	40,000	9,546.53	990,453.47
July 1, 19x6.........	49,522.53*	9,546.53	40,000	0	1,000,000.00
		$77,232.00	$400,000		

*To determine interest expense, the total liability at the beginning of the period was multiplied by the semiannual market interest rate—in this case, five percent. Any rounding errors are included in the July 1, 19x6, debit to interest expense.

Table A-1
Present Value of $1.00

Periods (n)	1%	1½%	2%	2½%	3%	3½%	4%	4½%	5%	6%	7%	8%	10%
1	0.9901	0.9852	0.9804	0.9756	0.9709	0.9662	0.9615	0.9569	0.9524	0.9434	0.9346	0.9259	0.9091
2	0.9803	0.9707	0.9612	0.9518	0.9426	0.9335	0.9246	0.9157	0.9070	0.8900	0.8734	0.8573	0.8264
3	0.9706	0.9563	0.9423	0.9286	0.9151	0.9019	0.8890	0.8763	0.8638	0.8396	0.8163	0.7938	0.7513
4	0.9610	0.9422	0.9238	0.9060	0.8885	0.8714	0.8548	0.8386	0.8227	0.7921	0.7629	0.7350	0.6830
5	0.9515	0.9283	0.9057	0.8839	0.8626	0.8420	0.8219	0.8025	0.7835	0.7473	0.7130	0.6806	0.6209
6	0.9420	0.9145	0.8880	0.8623	0.8375	0.8135	0.7903	0.7679	0.7462	0.7050	0.6663	0.6302	0.5645
7	0.9327	0.9010	0.8706	0.8413	0.8131	0.7860	0.7599	0.7348	0.7107	0.6651	0.6227	0.5835	0.5132
8	0.9235	0.8877	0.8535	0.8207	0.7894	0.7594	0.7307	0.7032	0.6768	0.6274	0.5820	0.5403	0.4665
9	0.9143	0.8746	0.8368	0.8007	0.7664	0.7337	0.7026	0.6729	0.6446	0.5919	0.5439	0.5002	0.4241
10	0.9053	0.8617	0.8203	0.7812	0.7441	0.7089	0.6756	0.6439	0.6139	0.5584	0.5083	0.4632	0.3855
11	0.8963	0.8489	0.8043	0.7621	0.7224	0.6849	0.6496	0.6162	0.5847	0.5268	0.4751	0.4289	0.3505
12	0.8874	0.8364	0.7885	0.7436	0.7014	0.6618	0.6246	0.5897	0.5568	0.4970	0.4440	0.3971	0.3186
13	0.8787	0.8240	0.7730	0.7254	0.6810	0.6394	0.6006	0.5643	0.5303	0.4688	0.4150	0.3677	0.2897
14	0.8700	0.8118	0.7579	0.7077	0.6611	0.6178	0.5775	0.5400	0.5051	0.4423	0.3878	0.3405	0.2633
15	0.8613	0.7999	0.7430	0.6905	0.6419	0.5969	0.5553	0.5167	0.4810	0.4173	0.3624	0.3153	0.2394
16	0.8528	0.7880	0.7284	0.6736	0.6232	0.5767	0.5339	0.4945	0.4581	0.3936	0.3387	0.2919	0.2176
17	0.8444	0.7764	0.7142	0.6572	0.6050	0.5572	0.5134	0.4732	0.4363	0.3714	0.3166	0.2703	0.1978
18	0.8360	0.7649	0.7002	0.6412	0.5874	0.5384	0.4936	0.4528	0.4155	0.3503	0.2959	0.2502	0.1799
19	0.8277	0.7536	0.6864	0.6255	0.5703	0.5202	0.4746	0.4333	0.3957	0.3305	0.2765	0.2317	0.1635
20	0.8195	0.7425	0.6730	0.6103	0.5537	0.5026	0.4564	0.4146	0.3769	0.3118	0.2584	0.2145	0.1486
21	0.8114	0.7315	0.6598	0.5954	0.5375	0.4856	0.4388	0.3968	0.3589	0.2942	0.2415	0.1987	0.1351
22	0.8034	0.7207	0.6468	0.5809	0.5219	0.4692	0.4220	0.3797	0.3418	0.2775	0.2257	0.1839	0.1228
23	0.7954	0.7100	0.6342	0.5667	0.5067	0.4533	0.4057	0.3634	0.3256	0.2618	0.2109	0.1703	0.1117
24	0.7876	0.6995	0.6217	0.5529	0.4919	0.4380	0.3901	0.3477	0.3101	0.2470	0.1971	0.1577	0.1015
25	0.7798	0.6892	0.6095	0.5394	0.4776	0.4231	0.3751	0.3327	0.2953	0.2330	0.1842	0.1460	0.0923
26	0.7720	0.6790	0.5976	0.5262	0.4637	0.4088	0.3607	0.3184	0.2812	0.2198	0.1722	0.1352	0.0839
27	0.7644	0.6690	0.5859	0.5134	0.4502	0.3950	0.3468	0.3047	0.2678	0.2074	0.1609	0.1252	0.0763
28	0.7568	0.6591	0.5744	0.5009	0.4371	0.3817	0.3335	0.2916	0.2551	0.1956	0.1504	0.1159	0.0693
29	0.7493	0.6494	0.5631	0.4887	0.4243	0.3687	0.3207	0.2790	0.2429	0.1846	0.1406	0.1073	0.0630
30	0.7419	0.6398	0.5521	0.4767	0.4120	0.3563	0.3083	0.2670	0.2314	0.1741	0.1314	0.0994	0.0573
40	0.6717	0.5513	0.4529	0.3724	0.3066	0.2526	0.2083	0.1719	0.1420	0.0972	0.0668	0.0460	0.0221
50	0.6080	0.4750	0.3715	0.2909	0.2281	0.1791	0.1407	0.1107	0.0872	0.0543	0.0339	0.0213	0.0085

Table A-1 (Continued)
Present Value of $1.00

12%	14%	15%	16%	18%	20%	22%	24%	25%	26%	28%	30%	40%	50%
0.893	0.877	0.870	0.862	0.847	0.833	0.820	0.806	0.800	0.794	0.781	0.769	0.714	0.667
0.797	0.769	0.756	0.743	0.718	0.694	0.672	0.650	0.640	0.630	0.610	0.592	0.510	0.444
0.712	0.675	0.658	0.641	0.609	0.579	0.551	0.524	0.512	0.500	0.477	0.455	0.364	0.296
0.636	0.592	0.572	0.552	0.516	0.482	0.451	0.423	0.410	0.397	0.373	0.350	0.260	0.198
0.567	0.519	0.497	0.476	0.437	0.402	0.370	0.341	0.328	0.315	0.291	0.269	0.186	0.132
0.507	0.456	0.432	0.410	0.370	0.335	0.303	0.275	0.262	0.250	0.227	0.207	0.133	0.088
0.452	0.400	0.376	0.354	0.314	0.279	0.249	0.222	0.210	0.198	0.178	0.159	0.095	0.059
0.404	0.351	0.327	0.305	0.266	0.233	0.204	0.179	0.168	0.157	0.139	0.123	0.068	0.039
0.361	0.308	0.284	0.263	0.225	0.194	0.167	0.144	0.134	0.125	0.108	0.094	0.048	0.026
0.322	0.270	0.247	0.227	0.191	0.162	0.137	0.116	0.107	0.099	0.085	0.073	0.035	0.017
0.287	0.237	0.215	0.195	0.162	0.135	0.112	0.094	0.086	0.079	0.066	0.056	0.025	0.012
0.257	0.208	0.187	0.168	0.137	0.112	0.092	0.076	0.069	0.062	0.052	0.043	0.018	0.008
0.229	0.182	0.163	0.145	0.116	0.093	0.075	0.061	0.055	0.050	0.040	0.033	0.013	0.005
0.205	0.160	0.141	0.125	0.099	0.078	0.062	0.049	0.044	0.039	0.032	0.025	0.009	0.003
0.183	0.140	0.123	0.108	0.084	0.065	0.051	0.040	0.035	0.031	0.025	0.020	0.006	0.002
0.163	0.123	0.107	0.093	0.071	0.054	0.042	0.032	0.028	0.025	0.019	0.015	0.005	0.002
0.146	0.108	0.093	0.080	0.060	0.045	0.034	0.026	0.023	0.020	0.015	0.012	0.003	0.001
0.130	0.095	0.081	0.069	0.051	0.038	0.028	0.021	0.018	0.016	0.012	0.009	0.002	0.001
0.116	0.083	0.070	0.060	0.043	0.031	0.023	0.017	0.014	0.012	0.009	0.007	0.002	
0.104	0.073	0.061	0.051	0.037	0.026	0.019	0.014	0.012	0.010	0.007	0.005	0.001	
0.093	0.064	0.053	0.044	0.031	0.022	0.015	0.011	0.009	0.008	0.006	0.004	0.001	
0.083	0.056	0.046	0.038	0.026	0.018	0.013	0.009	0.007	0.006	0.004	0.003	0.001	
0.074	0.049	0.040	0.033	0.022	0.015	0.010	0.007	0.006	0.005	0.003	0.002		
0.066	0.043	0.035	0.028	0.019	0.013	0.008	0.006	0.005	0.004	0.003	0.002		
0.059	0.038	0.030	0.024	0.016	0.010	0.007	0.005	0.004	0.003	0.002	0.001		
0.053	0.033	0.026	0.021	0.014	0.009	0.006	0.004	0.003	0.002	0.002	0.001		
0.047	0.029	0.023	0.018	0.011	0.007	0.005	0.003	0.002	0.002	0.001	0.001		
0.042	0.026	0.020	0.016	0.010	0.006	0.004	0.002	0.002	0.002	0.001	0.001		
0.037	0.022	0.017	0.014	0.008	0.005	0.003	0.002	0.002	0.001	0.001	0.001		
0.033	0.020	0.015	0.012	0.007	0.004	0.003	0.002	0.001	0.001	0.001			
0.011	0.005	0.004	0.003	0.001	0.001								
0.003	0.001	0.001	0.001										

Table A-2
Present Value of Annuity of $1.00 Per Period

Periods (n)	1%	1½%	2%	2½%	3%	3½%	4%	4½%	5%	6%	7%
1	0.9901	0.9852	0.9804	0.9756	0.9709	0.9662	0.9615	0.9569	0.9524	0.9434	0.9346
2	1.9704	1.9559	1.9416	1.9274	1.9135	1.8997	1.8861	1.8727	1.8594	1.8334	1.8080
3	2.9410	2.9122	2.8839	2.8560	2.8286	2.8016	2.7751	2.7490	2.7232	2.6730	2.6243
4	3.9020	3.8544	3.8077	3.7620	3.7171	3.6731	3.6299	3.5875	3.5460	3.4651	3.3872
5	4.8534	4.7826	4.7135	4.6458	4.5797	4.5151	4.4518	4.3900	4.3295	4.2124	4.1002
6	5.7955	5.6972	5.6014	5.5081	5.4172	5.3286	5.2421	5.1579	5.0757	4.9173	4.7665
7	6.7282	6.5982	6.4720	6.3494	6.2303	6.1145	6.0021	5.8927	5.7864	5.5824	5.3893
8	7.6517	7.4859	7.3255	7.1701	7.0197	6.8740	6.7327	6.5959	6.4632	6.2098	5.9713
9	8.5660	8.3605	8.1622	7.9709	7.7861	7.6077	7.4353	7.2688	7.1078	6.8017	6.5152
10	9.4713	9.2222	8.9826	8.7521	8.5302	8.3166	8.1109	7.9127	7.7217	7.3601	7.0236
11	10.3676	10.0711	9.7868	9.5142	9.2526	9.0016	8.7605	8.5289	8.3064	7.8869	7.4987
12	11.2551	10.9075	10.5753	10.2578	9.9540	9.6633	9.3851	9.1186	8.8633	8.3838	7.9427
13	12.1337	11.7315	11.3484	10.9832	10.6350	10.3027	9.9856	9.6829	9.3936	8.8527	8.3577
14	13.0037	12.5434	12.1062	11.6909	11.2961	10.9205	10.5631	10.2228	9.8986	9.2950	8.7455
15	13.8651	13.3432	12.8493	12.3814	11.9379	11.5174	11.1184	10.7395	10.3797	9.7122	9.1079
16	14.7179	14.1313	13.5777	13.0550	12.5611	12.0941	11.6523	11.2340	10.8378	10.1059	9.4466
17	15.5623	14.9076	14.2919	13.7122	13.1661	12.6513	12.1657	11.7072	11.2741	10.4773	9.7632
18	16.3983	15.6726	14.9920	14.3534	13.7535	13.1897	12.6593	12.1600	11.6896	10.8276	10.0591
19	17.2260	16.4262	15.6785	14.9789	14.3238	13.7098	13.1339	12.5933	12.0853	11.1581	10.3356
20	18.0456	17.1686	16.3514	15.5892	14.8775	14.2124	13.5903	13.0079	12.4622	11.4699	10.5940
21	18.8570	17.9001	17.0112	16.1845	15.4150	14.6980	14.0292	13.4047	12.8212	11.7640	10.8355
22	19.6604	18.6208	17.6580	16.7654	15.9369	15.1671	14.4511	13.7844	13.1630	12.0416	11.0612
23	20.4558	19.3309	18.2922	17.3321	16.4436	15.6204	14.8568	14.1478	13.4886	12.3034	11.2722
24	21.2434	20.0304	18.9139	17.8850	16.9355	16.0584	15.2470	14.4955	13.7986	12.5504	11.4693
25	22.0232	20.7196	19.5235	18.4244	17.4131	16.4815	15.6221	14.8282	14.0939	12.7834	11.6536
26	22.7952	21.3986	20.1210	18.9506	17.8768	16.8904	15.9828	15.1466	14.3752	13.0032	11.8258
27	23.5596	22.0676	20.7069	19.4640	18.3270	17.2854	16.3296	15.4513	14.6430	13.2105	11.9867
28	24.3164	22.7267	21.2813	19.9649	18.7641	17.6670	15.6631	15.7429	14.8981	13.4062	12.1371
29	25.0658	23.3761	21.8444	20.4535	19.1885	18.0358	16.9837	16.0219	15.1411	13.5907	12.2777
30	25.8077	24.0158	22.3965	20.9303	19.6004	18.3920	17.2920	16.2889	15.3725	13.7648	12.4090
40	32.8347	29.9158	27.3555	25.1028	23.1148	21.3551	19.7928	18.4016	17.1591	15.0463	13.3317
50	39.1961	34.9997	31.4236	28.3623	25.7298	23.4556	21.4822	19.7620	18.2559	15.7619	13.8007

Table A-2 (continued)
Present Value of Annuity of $1.00 Per Period

8%	10%	12%	14%	15%	16%	18%	20%	22%	24%	25%	26%	28%	30%	40%	50%
0.9259	0.9091	0.893	0.877	0.870	0.862	0.847	0.833	0.820	0.806	0.800	0.794	0.781	0.769	0.714	0.667
1.7833	1.7355	1.690	1.647	1.626	1.605	1.566	1.528	1.492	1.457	1.440	1.424	1.392	1.361	1.224	1.111
2.5771	2.4869	2.402	2.322	2.283	2.246	2.174	2.106	2.042	1.981	1.952	1.923	1.868	1.816	1.589	1.407
3.3121	3.1699	3.037	2.914	2.855	2.798	2.690	2.589	2.494	2.404	2.362	2.320	2.241	2.166	1.849	1.605
3.9927	3.7908	3.605	3.433	3.352	3.274	3.127	2.991	2.864	2.745	2.689	2.635	2.532	2.436	2.035	1.737
4.6229	4.3553	4.111	3.889	3.784	3.685	3.498	3.326	3.167	3.020	2.951	2.885	2.759	2.643	2.168	1.824
5.2064	4.8684	4.564	4.288	4.160	4.039	3.812	3.605	3.416	3.242	3.161	3.083	2.937	2.802	2.263	1.883
5.7466	5.3349	4.968	4.639	4.487	4.344	4.078	3.837	3.619	3.421	3.329	3.241	3.076	2.925	2.331	1.922
6.2469	5.7590	5.328	4.946	4.772	4.607	4.303	4.031	3.786	3.566	3.463	3.366	3.184	3.019	2.379	1.948
6.7101	6.1446	5.650	5.216	5.019	4.833	4.494	4.192	3.923	3.682	3.571	3.465	3.269	3.092	2.414	1.965
7.1390	6.4951	5.988	5.453	5.234	5.029	4.656	4.327	4.035	3.776	3.656	3.544	3.335	3.147	2.438	1.977
7.5361	6.8137	6.194	5.660	5.421	5.197	4.793	4.439	4.127	3.851	3.725	3.606	3.387	3.190	2.456	1.985
7.9038	7.1034	6.424	5.842	5.583	5.342	4.910	4.533	4.203	3.912	3.780	3.656	3.427	3.223	2.468	1.990
8.2442	7.3667	6.628	6.002	5.724	5.468	5.008	4.611	4.265	3.962	3.824	3.695	3.459	3.249	2.477	1.993
8.5595	7.6061	6.811	6.142	5.847	5.575	5.092	4.675	4.315	4.001	3.859	3.726	3.483	3.268	2.484	1.995
8.8514	7.8237	6.974	6.265	5.954	5.669	5.162	4.730	4.357	4.033	3.887	3.751	3.503	3.283	2.489	1.997
9.1216	8.0216	7.120	6.373	6.047	5.749	5.222	4.775	4.391	4.059	3.910	3.771	3.518	3.295	2.492	1.998
9.3719	8.2014	7.250	6.467	6.128	5.818	5.273	4.812	4.419	4.080	3.928	3.786	3.529	3.304	2.494	1.999
9.6036	8.3649	7.366	6.550	6.198	5.877	5.316	4.844	4.442	4.097	3.942	3.799	3.539	3.311	2.496	1.999
9.8181	8.5136	7.469	6.623	6.259	5.929	5.353	4.870	4.460	4.110	3.954	3.808	3.546	3.316	2.497	1.999
10.0168	8.6487	7.562	6.687	6.312	5.973	5.384	4.891	4.476	4.121	3.963	3.816	3.551	3.320	2.498	2.000
10.2007	8.7715	7.645	6.743	6.359	6.011	5.410	4.909	4.488	4.130	3.970	3.822	3.556	3.323	2.498	2.000
10.3711	8.8832	7.718	6.792	6.399	6.044	5.432	4.925	4.499	4.137	3.976	3.827	3.559	3.325	2.499	2.000
10.5288	8.9847	7.784	6.835	6.434	6.073	5.451	4.937	4.507	4.143	3.981	3.831	3.562	3.327	2.499	2.000
10.6748	9.0770	7.843	6.873	6.464	6.097	5.467	4.948	4.514	4.147	3.985	3.834	3.564	3.329	2.499	2.000
10.8100	9.1609	7.896	6.906	6.491	6.118	5.480	4.956	4.520	4.151	3.988	3.837	3.566	3.330	2.500	2.000
10.9352	9.2372	7.943	6.935	6.514	6.136	5.492	4.964	4.524	4.154	3.990	3.839	3.567	3.331	2.500	2.000
11.0511	9.3066	7.984	6.961	6.534	6.152	5.502	4.970	4.528	4.157	3.992	3.840	3.568	3.331	2.500	2.000
11.1584	9.3696	8.022	6.983	6.551	6.166	5.510	4.975	4.531	4.159	3.994	3.841	3.569	3.332	2.500	2.000
11.2578	9.4269	8.055	7.003	6.566	6.177	5.517	4.979	4.534	4.160	3.995	3.842	3.569	3.332	2.500	2.000
11.9246	9.7791	8.244	7.105	6.642	6.234	5.548	4.997	4.544	4.166	3.999	3.846	3.571	3.333	2.500	2.000
12.2335	9.9148	8.304	7.133	6.661	6.246	5.554	4.999	4.545	4.167	4.000	3.846	3.571	3.333	2.500	2.000

NOTE: To convert this table to values of an annuity in advance, take one less period and add 1.0000.

EXERCISES—APPENDIX

1. Determine the amount that $1,000 will accumulate to in three years at an 8 percent annual interest rate.

2. Determine the present value of $1,000 due in five years at each of the following interest rates:

   a. 6 percent
   b. 8 percent
   c. 10 percent

3. An investor wishes to have $5,000 available at the end of five years. State the amount of money that must be invested at the present time if the interest rate is:

   a. 6 percent
   b. 8 percent
   c. 12 percent

4. Determine the present value of an ordinary annuity for a period of five years with annual payments of $2,000, assuming that the interest rate is:

   a. 7 percent
   b. 10 percent
   c. 12 percent

5. What is the maximum amount you would be willing to pay at the present time in order to receive 10 annual payments of $1,000 beginning one year from now? The current interest rate is 10 percent.

6. Hays Company leases a building at an annual rental of $2,000 paid at the end of each year. The company has been given the alternative of paying the remaining 10 years of the lease in advance on January 1, 19x0. Assuming an interest rate of 8 percent, what is the maximum amount that should be paid now for the advance rent?

7. Determine the selling price of the bonds in each of the following situations (assume that the bonds are dated and sold on the same date):

   a. A 10-year, $1,000 face value bond with annual interest of 9 percent (payable annually) sold to yield 8 percent effective interest.
   b. A 10-year, $1,000 face value bond with annual interest of 9 percent (payable annually) sold to yield 10 percent effective interest.
   c. A 10-year, $1,000 face value bond with annual interest of 9 percent (payable annually) sold to yield 9 percent effective interest.

8. Nancy Company issued $10,000 of bonds payable on January 1, 19x1 with an 8 percent coupon interest rate, payable annually on December 31. The bonds mature in 5 years and were sold at a 10 percent effective interest rate.

a. Determine the selling price of the bonds.
b. Prepare a schedule showing the amount of discount to be amortized each year for the life of the bonds, assuming the interest method of amortization.
c. Give the journal entry to record the interest payment on December 31, 19x1.

9. Joyce Company issued $10,000 of bond payable on January 1, 19x1, with an 8 percent coupon interest rate payable annually on December 31. The bonds mature in 5 years and were sold at a 7 percent effective interest rate.

Required:

1. Determine the selling price of the bonds.
2. Prepare a schedule showing the premium to be amortized each year for the life of the bonds, assuming the interest method of amortization.
3. Give the journal entry to record the interest payment on December 31, 19x1.

Learning Objectives

Chapter 16 discusses and illustrates the use of consolidated financial statements. Studying this chapter should enable you to:

1. Describe the criteria used to determine when to prepare consolidated financial statements.

2. Illustrate the procedures and necessary worksheet adjustments for preparing consolidated financial statements.

3. Differentiate between the purchase and pooling of interests methods in accounting for business combinations.

16 Consolidated Financial Statements

INTRODUCTION

In many instances, investments in stock are made to secure ownership of a controlling interest in the voting stock of another company. A firm owning a majority of the voting stock of another company is usually referred to as a *parent company*; the company whose stock is owned is called the *subsidiary company*. A parent company and one or more of its related subsidiary companies are usually referred to as *affiliated companies*. Since a parent and its subsidiary are separate legal entities, separate financial statements are prepared for the stockholders and creditors of each company.

The relationship between a parent and its subsidiary is disclosed in the parent company's financial statements in the investment in stock account. However, parent company statements do not reflect the complete economic effect of the parent's ownership of the subsidiary. Therefore, it is often useful to prepare financial statements based on the financial position and operating results of the combined affiliated companies as if they were a single economic entity. The combined financial statements of two or more affiliated companies are called *consolidated statements*. Consolidated statements provide the stockholders and creditors of the parent company with an overall view of the combined financial position and operating activities of the parent company and its subsidiaries.

There are a variety of economic, legal, and tax advantages which encourage large organizations to operate through a group of affiliated corporations, rather than a single legal entity. For example, the financial statements of General Motors Corporation, which are reproduced in Chapters 2 and 17, are consolidated financial statements.

Two basic criteria are used in deciding whether or not to prepare consolidated statements. The subsidiary company must be under the continuing control of the parent and the activities of the affiliated companies must be similar. There is no general agreement among accountants as to the percentage ownership which gives the parent company sufficient control to influence the activities of a subsidiary. In many cases, however, ownership of a majority of the voting stock of a subsidiary is considered to be adequate evidence of the ability to control a subsidiary for the purpose of deciding whether or not to prepare consolidated statements. If the operations of the parent and subsidiary companies are unrelated (for example, a bank owning a manufacturing concern), consolidated statements should not be prepared even if the parent owns a majority of the voting stock of the subsidiary. An evaluation of the relationship between the operations of the two firms is based primarily upon the nature of the business activities and the structure of their respective financial statements. For example, consolidated statements prepared for a retail firm that held a controlling interest in an insurance company would normally be of little value to the user of such statements.

From a legal standpoint, a subsidiary company is a separate entity. Accordingly, the subsidiary maintains its own accounting records and prepares separate financial statements. However, since the parent owns a majority of the voting stock of its subsidiary, the parent and subsidiary companies are a business entity under common control. Therefore, individual financial statements of the parent and subsidiary do not provide a comprehensive view of the financial position of the affiliated companies as a single economic unit. Consolidated financial statements, which ignore the legal distinction between the parent and its subsidiary, serve this purpose by reflecting the financial position and results of operations of the affiliated companies as a single economic entity.

Consolidated Balance Sheet at Date of Acquisition

In preparing a consolidated balance sheet, the accounts which are included in the individual parent and subsidiary company records are combined. In the process of this combination, however, certain adjustments must be made to avoid duplication or double-counting in determining the balances to be used. For example, the investment account of the parent company reflects its equity in the net assets of the subsidiary. Including both the parent company's investment account and the net assets of the subsidiary in a consolidated statement would result in double-counting the net assets of the subsidiary. Therefore, the parent's investment account should not be included in the consolidated statements. Since the stockholder's equity of the subsidiary is represented by the investment account, it should also be excluded from the consolidated financial statement. The investment of the parent company is referred to as the reciprocal of the stockholders' equity of the subsidiary. Therefore, these accounts and any other reciprocal accounts which may exist as a result of transactions between the parent and its subsidiaries must be eliminated in combining the accounts of the parent and subsidiary companies.

Separate financial records are not maintained for the consolidated entity. The amounts reported in consolidated financial statements are determined using a worksheet and combining the amounts of like items from the financial statements of the affiliated companies. Entries included on the consolidation worksheet are made for the sole purpose of preparing consolidated financial statements. Consequently, consolidating adjustments and eliminations are not posted to the books of either the parent or its subsidiary.

Preparation of consolidated balance sheets under varying circumstances is illustrated by the following examples. First, let us consider the process of consolidating two balance sheets at the time a parent company initially acquired the stock of a subsidiary company.

Complete Ownership Acquired at Book Value. Assume that the parent company, P, acquired 100 percent of the common stock of a subsidiary company, S, at a price of $20,000 on December 31, 19x1. Separate balance sheets of P Company and S Company immediately following the acquisition are presented in Illustration 1.

Illustration 1

P Company and S Company
Balance Sheets
At December 31, 19x1

	P Company	S Company
Cash	$ 10,000	$ 5,000
Accounts receivable	10,000	5,000
Fixed assets	60,000	20,000
Investment in S Company	20,000	-0-
Total Assets	$100,000	$30,000
Accounts payable	$ 10,000	$10,000
Capital stock	60,000	15,000
Retained earnings	30,000	5,000
Total Liabilities and Equities	$100,000	$30,000

P Company paid an amount equal to the stockholders' equity (common stock and retained earnings) of the subsidiary for 100 percent ownership of S. This indicates that the acquisition was made at the book value of the subsidiary's net assets. Since no transactions have occurred between the companies, the only adjustment required is to eliminate the investment account of the parent against the stockholders' equity accounts of the subsidiary, as shown in Illustration 2.

As previously indicated, the elimination entry is made on a worksheet which is used in order to facilitate the preparation of the consolidated balance sheet. No entries are made in the accounting records of either the parent or the subsidiary.

Complete Ownership Acquired at More than Net Asset Value. In most cases when the parent acquires stock in a subsidiary, the cost of the investment will differ from the recorded value of the net assets (assets less liabilities) of the subsidiary. From a consolidated standpoint, the purchase of subsidiary stock may be regarded as similar to the purchase of the subsidiary's net assets (i.e., its assets less liabilities). Consequently, subsidiary

Illustration 2

P Company and S Company
Consolidation Worksheet
At December 31, 19x1

	P Co.	S Co.	Eliminations Dr.	Eliminations Cr.	Consolidation
Cash	$ 10,000	$ 5,000			$ 15,000
Accounts receivable	10,000	5,000			15,000
Fixed assets	60,000	20,000			80,000
Investment in S Company	20,000			$20,000[a]	
Total Assets	$100,000	$30,000			$110,000
Accounts payable	$ 10,000	$10,000			$ 20,000
Capital stock	60,000	15,000	$15,000[a]		60,000
Retained earnings	30,000	5,000	5,000[a]		30,000
Total Liabilities and Equity	$100,000	$30,000			$110,000

[a] Elimination of the investment account against book value of the subsidiary's stock.

assets should be recorded at an amount equal to the price paid by the parent for its 100 percent interest in the subsidiary. To adjust the carrying values of subsidiary assets to reflect the price paid by the parent for the stock, information concerning the fair values of the subsidiary assets at the time of acquisition must be obtained.

The amount paid by the parent company for the subsidiary's stock may differ from the net asset value of the subsidiary for two primary reasons. First, subsidiary assets may have a fair market value which differs from their recorded book value. This may occur because the accounting methods used for recording assets are normally not intended to reflect the fair value of the assets of the firm. Thus, if the parent company pays an amount which is in excess of book value, this excess may exist because the net assets of the subsidiary are undervalued (that is, the book value of the assets determined on the basis of proper accounting methods is less than their fair market value). Also, the excess may be due to the existence of unrecorded intangible assets of the subsidiary or from anticipated advantages which are expected because of the affiliation. If the assets of the subsidiary are undervalued, any specific tangible or intangible assets with fair market values in excess of recorded book values should be restated at fair market value in the consolidation worksheet. Thus, identifiable assets will be reported in the consolidated balance sheet at an amount equal to their fair market values at the date of acquisition. If the cost of the subsidiary stock still exceeds the amount assigned to the net assets of the subsidiary in the consolidation worksheet, this excess is assigned to an intangible asset, Goodwill or "Excess of Cost Over Book Value." Therefore, the total excess of the cost of the subsidiary stock over the book value of the subsidiary's net assets is included among consolidated assets—either as increases in the value of specific assets or alternatively as goodwill. Again, it is important to note that these adjustments are made only in the consolidation worksheet.

To illustrate, assume the same facts as in the previous illustration except that P Company acquired all of the stock of S Company at a cost of $25,000. Thus, the cost of investment ($25,000) exceeds the stockholders' equity of the subsidiary ($20,000) by $5,000. Apparently the management of P Company believes that the fair value of specific assets of S Company is greater than their recorded book value or that there are advantages of affiliation, such as future earnings prospects, which justify payment of $5,000 in excess of book value for S Company's net assets. In this illustration, assume that the excess of cost over book value existed because the fair market value of S Company's land exceeded its recorded book value by $5,000. Therefore, this excess would be assigned to land (which is summarized in fixed assets in this example) in the consolidation worksheet. The consolidation worksheet would be as shown in Illustration 3. The eliminating entries on the consolidation worksheet would be:

(a)	Fixed Assets—S Company	5,000	
	Investment in S Company		5,000
(b)	Capital Stock—S Company	15,000	
	Retained Earnings—S Company	5,000	
	Investment in S Company		20,000

Again, it is important to note that these entries would not appear in the accounts of either P Company or S Company. These are worksheet entries that would be used to facilitate the consolidation of the financial reports of the parent and subsidiary company.

If the excess cannot be assigned to any specific assets (that is, the recorded book values of the subsidiary assets are equal to their fair values at acquisition), the $5,000 excess would have been reported in the consolidated balance sheet as Goodwill or "Excess of Cost Over Book Value." This is a new account which is introduced in the consolidated worksheet—it does not appear in the accounts of either P or S.

Complete Ownership Acquired for Less than Net Asset Value. If the cost of the stock acquired by the parent company is less than book value, a similar problem exists. When specific overvalued assets can be

Illustration 3

P Company and S Company
Consolidation Worksheet
At December 31, 19x1

	P Co.	S Co.	Eliminations Dr.	Eliminations Cr.	Consolidation
Cash	$ 5,000	$ 5,000			$ 10,000
Accounts receivable	10,000	5,000			15,000
Fixed assets	60,000	20,000	$ 5,000 (a)		85,000
Investment in S Company	25,000			$ 5,000 (a) 20,000 (b)	
Total Assets	$100,000	$30,000			$110,000
Accounts payable	$ 10,000	$10,000			$ 20,000
Capital stock	60,000	15,000	15,000 (b)		60,000
Retained earnings	30,000	5,000	5,000 (b)		30,000
Total Liabilities and Equity	$100,000	$30,000			$110,000

a Adjustment for undervaluation of Subsidiary's assets.
b Elimination of the investment against the book value of the Subsidiary's stock.

identified, the excess would be reflected on the balance sheet by reducing the value of specific assets of the subsidiary. Thus, subsidiary assets would be reported at their fair values in the consolidated balance sheet. When specific assets which are overvalued cannot be identified, the excess is used to reduce noncurrent assets. If the allocation reduces the noncurrent assets to zero, the remainder of the excess is credited to an account referred to as "Excess of Book Value of Subsidiary Interest Over Cost." This account is shown as a reduction of assets on the consolidated balance sheet. For example, assume P Company purchased 100 percent of the stock of S Company at a price of $18,000 on December 31, 19x1. At that date the stockholders' equity of S Company was $20,000, consisting of $15,000 capital stock and $5,000 retained earnings. Eliminating entries on the consolidation worksheet would be as follows:

(a) Investment in S Company 2,000
      Specific Assets of S Company.   2,000

(b) Capital Stock—S Company. 15,000
      Retained Earnings—S Company 5,000
          Investment in S Company (from P's books).   20,000

Less Than Complete Ownership. A parent company may obtain control of a subsidiary by acquiring less than 100 percent of the capital stock of the subsidiary. When a parent owns less than 100 percent of the stock, the remainder of the stock held by stockholders outside the affiliated companies is classified as a *minority interest* in the consolidated balance sheet. The existence of a minority interest does not affect the amount at which the assets and liabilities of the affiliated companies will ultimately appear on the consolidated balance sheet. However, only a portion of the equity in the net assets of the subsidiary company is owned by the parent since a portion of the owners' equity is held by minority stockholders. Equity held by minority stockholders, or minority interest, is a part of the stockholders' equity of the consolidated entity.

To illustrate, assume that P Company acquired only 90 percent of the capital stock of the subsidiary at a cost of $18,000. The remaining 10 percent of the subsidiary's stock represents the minority interest in S Company. The only change required in the elimination entries is that only 90 percent of the capital stock and retained earnings of S Company is eliminated. The remaining 10 percent of S Company stockholders' equity represents the minority interest in the subsidiary and is classified as such in the consolidated balance sheet. The consolidated worksheet used to prepare the consolidated balance sheet is shown in Illustration 4.

The initial consolidation entry (a) eliminated 90 percent of the capital stock and retained earnings of S Company against the investment account of the parent. The remaining 10 percent of the stockholders' equity of S Company was then reclassified as a minority interest in entry (b).

It should be noted that, in this example, the parent company paid an amount which was equal to book value for its interest in the subsidiary. Therefore, the investment account was exactly equal to 90 percent of the stockholders' equity of S Company at acquisition. The existence of a minority interest, however, would not affect the procedures which are required when the investment is acquired at either more or less than book value. Any difference between the cost of the investment and the amount representing the parent company's interest in the stockholders' equity of the subsidiary increases consolidated assets if cost exceeds book value, and reduces consolidated assets if cost is less than book value.

Consolidated Balance Sheet after the Date of Acquisition

Net assets of a subsidiary change subsequent to the date of affiliation as a result of the difference between the net income earned and the dividends paid by the subsidiary since the date the parent acquired its interest in the subsidiary. If the parent company carries its investment using the equity method, the parent's share of such changes in the net assets of a subsidiary is reflected in the investment account. This occurs because the parent company increases the investment account and records investment

Illustration 4

P Company and S Company
Consolidation Worksheet
At December 31, 19x1

	P Co.	S Co.	Eliminations Dr.	Eliminations Cr.	Consolidation
Cash	$ 12,000	$ 5,000			$ 17,000
Accounts receivable	10,000	5,000			15,000
Fixed assets	60,000	20,000			80,000
Investment in S Company	18,000			$18,000[a]	
Total Assets	$100,000	$30,000			$112,000
Accounts payable	$ 10,000	$10,000			$ 20,000
Capital stock	60,000	15,000	$ 1,500[b] 13,500[a]		60,000
Retained earnings	30,000	5,000	500[b] 4,500[a]		30,000
Minority interest	-0-	-0-		2,000[b]	2,000
Total Liabilities and Equity	$100,000	$30,000			$112,000

[a] Elimination of investment against 90 percent of the Subsidiary's stockholders' equity.
[b] Adjustment to reclassify 10 percent of the Subsidiary's stockholders' equity as minority interest.

---

income for its share of subsidiary earnings and reduces the investment account for any dividends which it receives from the subsidiary. Similarly, a loss incurred by the subsidiary is recorded by the parent as a decrease in the investment account and a corresponding decrease in the parent company's earnings. At any time subsequent to the date of affiliation, the change in the parent's investment account for each year must be equal to the parent company's share (that is, the parent company's percentage ownership of the voting stock of its subsidiary) of the change in the retained earnings of the subsidiary company. The eliminations which are required in order to prepare a consolidated balance sheet are basically the same as those which were required at the date of acquisition except that the amount eliminated from the investment account of the parent and the stockholders' equity of the subsidiary will change each year. Since the two entries which are made in the elimination of the parent's investment account against the stockholders' equity of the subsidiary will change by the same amount, the original difference between the cost of the investment and the book value of the subsidiary will be the same for each period.

To illustrate the procedures required for the preparation of a worksheet for a consolidated balance sheet, assume that P Company purchases 90 percent of the outstanding stock of S Company on December 31, 19x1, at a price of $21,000. At that time, S Company had capital stock of $15,000 and retained earnings of $5,000. Therefore, the cost of the investment exceeded the book value of the subsidiary stock by $3,000 (the book value of the net assets purchased was 90% × $20,000 or $18,000). It was determined that this excess of cost over book value was attributed to the excess of the market value of land owned by the subsidiary over the book value of the land. Further, assume that the subsidiary company had net income of $20,000 and paid dividends totaling $10,000 during 19x2. The effect of these transactions is to increase the retained earnings of the subsidiary by $10,000, from $5,000 to $15,000 (retained earnings on December 31, 19x1, of $5,000 plus 19x2, net income of $20,000 minus 19x2 dividends of $10,000). Similarly, net income and dividends paid by the subsidiary will cause a net increase of $9,000 in the parent company's investment account (90% of $20,000 net income minus 90% of the $10,000 dividends). The remaining 10 percent of the increase in the subsidiary's retained earnings represents an increase in the equity of the minority stockholders and would be classified as such. The worksheet (Illustration 5) for consolidation illustrates the procedures which are required in preparing a consolidated balance sheet (Illustration 6) one year after the date of acquisition of the subsidiary.

OTHER RECIPROCAL ACCOUNTS

In preparing a consolidated balance sheet, the investment account of the parent company must be eliminated against the stockholders' equity accounts of its subsidiary. If any transactions occurred between the parent and subsidiary companies, there might be additional reciprocal accounts which would also be eliminated in the consolidation worksheet in order to avoid the double counting of assets and liabilities.

One of the most common of these additional reciprocal accounts involves intercompany receivables and payables. If one affiliated company borrows from another, the debtor firm incurs a liability (payable) equal to an asset (receivable) of the creditor company. From a consolidated standpoint, the payable does not represent an amount owed to an entity outside the affiliated group, nor does the related asset represent a receivable from an outside group. Therefore, in the consolidation worksheet, both the reciprocal asset and liability should be eliminated.

To illustrate this point, assume that the parent company owes the subsidiary company $5,000 as of December 31, 19x2. The following entry would be made on the consolidation worksheet in order to eliminate the reciprocal accounts:

Accounts payable—P Company	5,000	
Accounts receivable—S Company		5,000

Illustration 5

P Company and S Company
Consolidation Worksheet
At December 31, 19x2

	P Co.	S Co.	Eliminations Dr.	Eliminations Cr.	Consolidations
Cash	$ 10,000	$ 7,000			$ 17,000
Accounts receivable	10,000	6,000			16,000
Fixed assets	70,000	20,000	$ 3,000[a]		93,000
Investment in S Company	30,000			$ 3,000[a] 27,000[b]	
Total Assets	$120,000	$33,000			$126,000
Accounts payable	$ 15,000	$ 3,000			$ 18,000
Capital stock	60,000	15,000	1,500[c] 13,500[b]		60,000
Retained earnings	45,000	15,000	1,500[c] 13,500[b]		45,000
Minority interest				3,000[c]	3,000
Total Liabilities and Equity	$120,000	$33,000			$126,000

[a] Adjustment for undervaluaton of Subsidiary's assets.
[b] Elimination of investment against 90% of the Subsidiary's Stockholders' equity.
[c] Adjustment to reclassify 10% of the Subsidiary's stockholders' equity as minority interest.

Illustration 6

P Company and S Company
Consolidated Balance Sheet
At December 31, 19x2

Current assets:		
Cash	$17,000	
Accounts receivable	16,000	
Total current assets		$ 33,000
Fixed assets		93,000
Total Assets		$126,000
Liabilities:		
Accounts payable		$ 18,000
Minority interest in S Co.		3,000
Stockholders' equity:		
Capital stock	$60,000	
Retained earnings	45,000	$105,000
Total Liabilities and Equities		$126,000

POOLING OF INTEREST

In the discussion of consolidated statements included in the preceeding section of this chapter, it was assumed that the parent company purchased the stock of the subsidiary with cash or other assets. The consolidated statements were prepared on the premise that the purchase of stock represented a purchase of the underlying net assets of the subsidiary. Therefore, in the consolidated statements, the cost of the acquisition was allocated to the individual assets of the subsidiary with any excess reported as "excess of cost over book value."

A subsidiary may also be acquired by the exchange of the parent's stock for the stock of the subsidiary. Under certain circumstances, this combination may be accounted for as a *pooling of interests*. Because the stockholders of the subsidiary become stockholders of the parent company, one group has not acquired the interests of the other. Rather, both have "pooled" their interests in a combined entity. A pooling of interests unites the ownership interests of two or more firms by the exchange of stock. A purchase transaction is not recognized because the combination is accomplished without disbursing the assets of either company. A key feature of a pooling is that the former ownership interests continue and the basis of accounting remains the same.

Since no purchase is recognized and basically the same ownership interests continue, there is no justification for revaluing assets in a pooling of interests. All assets and liabilities of the companies are carried forward to the consolidated statements at their recorded book value. The parent company records the acquisition by debiting the investment account for the par value of the stock issued. Since assets and liabilities are combined at their recorded amounts, there is no excess of cost over book value to be accounted for in the consolidated statements. In addition, retained earnings of the subsidiary at acquisition may be combined with the parent's retained earnings in determining consolidated retained earnings.

To illustrate, assume that P Company issued 1,000 shares of its $50 par value stock in exchange for all of the stock of S Company. Assume that S Company has 6,000 shares of $10 par value stock outstanding. The parent company records the acquisition at the par value of the stock issued as follows:

Investment in S Company	50,000	
Capital stock		50,000

Under the pooling of interests method, the fair values of the subsidiary's assets are not considered to be relevant for purposes of consolidation. Therefore, the entry required on the worksheet eliminates the investment account of the parent company against the capital stock of the subsidiary. The consolidation worksheet at the date of acquisition is shown in Illustration 7. Since the par value of the stock issued by the parent ($50,000)

Illustration 7

P Company and S Company
Consolidation Worksheet
At January 1, 19x2

	P Co.	S Co.	Eliminations Dr.	Eliminations Cr.	Consolidations
Other assets	$250,000	$120,000			$370,000
Investment in S Co..	50,000	-0-		$50,000(a)	-0-
Total	$300,000	$120,000			$370,000
Liabilities	$ 30,000	$ 20,000			$ 50,000
Capital stock—					
P Co. ($50 par value). . . .	150,000	-0-			150,000
S Co. ($10 par value). . . .	-0-	60,000	$60,000(a)		-0-
Capital in excess of					
par value	50,000	-0-		10,000(a)	60,000
Retained earnings	70,000	40,000			110,000
Total	$300,000	$120,000			$370,000

[a] Elimination of investment account against an equal amount of stockholders' equity.

is less than the par value of the shares acquired ($60,000), the difference was shown as an addition to capital in excess of par value in the consolidated balance sheet. If the par value of the stock issued exceeds the par value of the shares acquired, the difference may be charged or debited to capital in excess of par value. If capital in excess is insufficient to absorb the difference, the remainder may be charged against retained earnings.

Note that combining the parent and subsidiary retained earnings accounts is allowable under the pooling method. In the example, consolidated retained earnings at acquisition ($110,000) was equal to the sum of the parent's and subsidiary's retained earnings balances. Consolidated retained earnings may be less than the sum of the retained earnings balances if the par value of the stock issued by the parent is more than the par value of the shares acquired and if there is insufficient capital in excess of par value to absorb this difference.

Prior to 1970, accountants often considered the purchase and pooling of interests method to be acceptable alternatives for accounting for any given business combination. The pooling of interests method was popular because in circumstances where the fair value of the subsidiary assets exceeds the recorded book values, the pooling treatment results in higher future net income and earnings per share to be reported than does the purchase method. In addition, pooling normally causes higher retained earnings than the purchase method. The Accounting Principles Board, however, attempted to resolve this problem by issuing *Opinion No. 16*. With respect to the purchase versus pooling issue, the Board concluded that ". . . the purchase method and the pooling of interests method are both acceptable in accounting for business combinations, although not as alternatives in accounting for the same business combinations." The Board specified the conditions under which each of the two methods is applicable to a business combination.[2]

USEFULNESS OF CONSOLIDATED STATEMENTS

In a situation where one corporation owns a majority of the voting stock of one or more other corporations, financial statements which are prepared for the separate legal corporate entities may not provide the most useful information to management, stockholders, and potential investors of the parent company. Instead, these users are interested in the financial position and results of operations of the combined entity, i.e., the parent company and all other companies under the control of the parent.

On the other hand, minority stockholders of a subsidiary company ordinarily have little use for consolidated financial statements. Since minority stockholders are primarily concerned with their ownership in the subsidiary company, separate financial statements of the subsidiary are usually more useful to them. Similarly, creditors of either the parent or a subsidiary are primarily concerned with their individual legal claims. Therefore, separate financial statements based on the individual entities concerned are of primary interest to these creditors.

CONSOLIDATED INCOME STATEMENT

A consolidated income statement is prepared by combining the revenues and expenses of the parent and subsidiary companies. If the parent company owns 100 percent of the subsidiary stock and there have been no transactions between the parent and its subsidiary, consolidation is simply a combination of revenues and expenses resulting from the parent and subsidiary companies' operations. The only adjustment necessary is that which is required in order to eliminate the investment income of the parent company (the parent company's share of the subsidiary's net income). This amount must be eliminated in order to avoid duplication or double-counting of earnings in the consolidated income statement.

As in the case of the consolidated balance sheet, elimination of reciprocal accounts may be necessary in order to avoid duplication or double-counting of revenues and expenses resulting from transactions which have

---

[2] Discussion of the specific criteria for purchase vs. pooling is beyond the scope of this text.

MINORITY INTEREST

occurred between the parent and its subsidiary. For example, interest expense of one company and interest income of the other resulting from an intercompany loan are eliminated because they do not change the net assets of the total entity from a consolidated viewpoint.

If the parent owns less than 100 percent of the subsidiary stock, an additional adjustment is required in the consolidated worksheet in order to allocate the net income of the subsidiary between the parent company and the minority stockholders of the subsidiary. This division of the consolidated income is based on the percentage of the subsidiary stock owned by the parent company and the minority stockholders.

To illustrate the consolidation procedure for the income statement, again assume that P Company purchased 90 percent of the stock of S Company on December 31, 19x2. The 19x2 income statement for P Company is presented in Illustration 8. Also, assume that the parent rents a building to its subsidiary at a rental of $5,000 per year. The procedures which are necessary in order to prepare a consolidated income statement are illustrated in the consolidated worksheet in Illustration 9. It should be noted that the worksheet has a self-balancing format. That is, the net income figures have been included along with the expenses so that the revenues are equal to income plus expenses.

Elimination (a) removes the duplication or double-counting effect of the intercompany building rental. This entry has no effect on consolidated net income since it simply offsets rent revenue of P Company against an

Illustration 8

P Company and S Company
Income Statements
For the Year Ended December 31, 19x2

	P Company	S Company
Revenues:		
Sales	$195,000	$100,000
Rent revenue	5,000	0
Investment income	18,000	0
Total Revenues	$218,000	$100,000
Expenses:		
Cost of goods sold	$150,000	$ 70,000
Other expenses	20,000	10,000
Total Expenses	$170,000	$ 80,000
Net Income	$ 48,000	$ 20,000

> **Illustration 9**
>
> **P Company and S Company**
> *Consolidation Worksheet*
> *At December 31, 19x2*
>
> | | P Co. | S Co. | Eliminations Dr. | Eliminations Cr. | Consolidations |
> |---|---|---|---|---|---|
> | Sales | $195,000 | $100,000 | | | $295,000 |
> | Rent revenue | 5,000 | 0 | $ 5,000(a) | | |
> | Investment income | 18,000 | 0 | 18,000(b) | | |
> | Total revenues | $218,000 | $100,000 | | | $295,000 |
> | Cost of goods sold | $150,000 | $ 70,000 | | | $220,000 |
> | Other expenses | 20,000 | 10,000 | | $ 5,000(a) | 25,000 |
> | Net income–P Co. | 48,000 | | | | 48,000 |
> | Net income–S Co. | | 20,000 | | 2,000(c) 18,000(b) | |
> | Minority interest in net income | | | 2,000(c) | | 2,000 |
> | Total expenses and net income | $218,000 | $100,000 | | | $295,000 |
>
> a Elimination of intercompany rent revenue and rent expense.
> b Elimination of investment income against 90 percent of subsidiary net income.
> c Adjustment to reclassify 10 percent of the subsidiary's net income as minority interest.

equal amount of rent expense of S Company. Elimination (b) cancels the investment income which P Company records as its share of the net income of S Company under the equity method. This entry corrects the double-counting of S Company's net income. Elimination (c) allocates 10 percent of S Company's net income to the minority stockholders of the subsidiary company.

The amounts in the consolidation column of the worksheet are used in order to prepare the consolidated income statement in Illustration 10. Notice that the minority interest in net income is treated as a reduction of net income of the consolidated entity to arrive at consolidated net income.

PROFIT ON INTERCOMPANY SALES

An additional problem occurs if the assets which were transferred in intercompany sales were sold at a price which differed from the cost to the selling affiliate. If these assets were not resold by the end of the period, the gain or loss on the sale between the affiliates must be eliminated in

---

Illustration 10

P Company and Subsidiary
Consolidated Income Statement
For the Year 19x2

Sales	$295,000
Cost of goods sold	220,000
Gross profit	$ 75,000
Other expenses	25,000
Combined net income	$ 50,000
Less minority interest in net income	2,000
Consolidated Net Income	$ 48,000

---

the consolidation process. To illustrate this point, assume that the following transactions take place between a parent company (P) and its subsidiary (S):

1. P purchases two ten-speed bicycles for $100.
2. P sells the two bicycles to S for $120 on account.
3. S sells one of the bicycles to an outsider for $80 in cash.

These entries would be recorded on the books of P and S as follows:

"P" Books			"S" Books		
1. Inventory	100		No Entry		
Cash		100			
2. Accounts Receivable	120		Inventories	120	
Sales		120	Accounts Payable		120
Cost of Goods Sold	100				
Inventories		100			
3. No Entry			Cash	80	
			Sales		80
			Cost of Goods Sold	60	
			Inventories		60

As a result of these transactions, there is a receivable of $120 from S on P's books and a payable of $120 to P on S's books. Also, P's books show sales of $120 (to S) and a related cost of goods sold of $100, while S's books show the cost of the bicycle sold to the outsider as $60. The unsold bicycle is carried in S's inventory at a cost of $60.

The problem, in terms of preparing consolidated financial statements, is that the intercompany receivables and payables and the effects of the intercompany sales must be eliminated. Also, the cost of the bicycle remaining in S's inventory must be reduced from $60 to $50 (the cost to P) and the $10 profit on the "sale" of this bicycle by P to S must be eliminated from the net income of P Company. The worksheet entries required to accomplish these objectives are as follows:

Accounts payable....................	120	
Accounts receivable..................		120
Sales................................	120	
Cost of goods sold....................		120
Cost of goods sold....................	10	
Inventories..........................		10

The first entry eliminates the intercompany receivables and payables. The second entry eliminates the intercompany sale and the related cost of goods sold, while the final entry corrects the cost of goods sold (and therefore net income) by eliminating the intercompany profit in the ending inventory.

SUMMARY

If two firms are associated in such a manner that one owns a controlling interest in the other, the firms are referred to as affiliated companies. Since these firms remain separate legal entities, separate financial statements are prepared for each company. However, if the subsidiary company is under the continuing control of the parent company and their activities are similar, it may be desirable to prepare consolidated financial statements. When a consolidated balance sheet is prepared at the date of acquisition (unless the purchase price equals the book value of the subsidiary's stock) the subsidiary's assets must be adjusted prior to being combined with the value of the parent's assets. In addition, elimination entries must be made on the worksheet for the parent's investment account and the subsidiary's owners' equity accounts to avoid duplication of information. The elimination entries are varied slightly if the parent company acquires less than complete ownership of the subsidiary. In addition, such a situation will require adjustments to the entries recording changes in the net assets of the subsidiary after acquisition. Regardless of the percentage of ownership by the parent, certain elimination entries may be required on the consolidation worksheet if the affiliated companies engage in business transactions with each other.

A business combination may also be affected by one company exchanging its stock for the stock of another corporation. The former ownership interests continue and the basis for accounting remains the same. Such a situation is referred to as a pooling of interests and requires appropriate worksheet elimination entries prior to final preparation of consolidated statements.

KEY DEFINITIONS

Affiliated companies A parent company and one or more related subsidiary companies are said to be affiliated.

Consolidated statements Consolidated financial statements present the combined assets, equities, and results of operations of affiliated corporations.

Consolidation worksheet Consolidation working papers are used in the preparation of consolidated statements for two or more companies. The consolidating adjustments and eliminations are never posted to the books of the individual companies involved, only to the worksheet.

Minority interest Shares held by stockholders of a subsidiary company when the parent acquires less than 100 percent of the subsidiary stock are referred to as a minority interest.

Parent company A firm owning a majority of the voting stock of another company is called a parent company.

Pooling of interests Pooling of interests is a method used for recording a business acquisition where the assets and liabilities of the combining companies are combined at their existing book values.

Purchase The purchase method for recording a business acquisition is the use of the cost to the acquiring corporation in valuing the assets of the subsidiary.

Subsidiary company A subsidiary company is a firm which has a majority of its voting stock owned by a parent company.

QUESTIONS

1. Define: (a) parent company, (b) subsidiary company, and (c) affiliated companies.

2. Describe the two essential conditions for the preparation of consolidated financial statements.

3. A consolidated balance sheet prepared for a parent company that owns less than 100 percent of the common stock of the subsidiary shows an item called "minority interest." What is the nature of this balance sheet account, and where does it appear on the consolidated balance sheet?

4. How is the difference between the cost of the subsidiary stock and the book value of the stock at the date of acquisition reported on the consolidated balance sheet?

5. Explain why intercompany debts and receivables should be eliminated in preparing consolidated balance sheets.

6. Why is the investment account of the parent company eliminated in preparing a consolidated balance sheet?

7. What types of users of financial statements are primarily interested in consolidated financial statements?

8. If the parent owns less than 100 percent of the subsidiary stock, the consolidated income statement shows an item called "minority interest in subsidiary income." What does this item represent?

9. Where are the entries recorded for the eliminations that are made in the process of preparing consolidated statements?

EXERCISES

10. On December 31, 19x1, P Company acquired a controlling interest in S Company. The balance sheets prior to acquisition were as follows:

	P Company	S Company
Current assets	$100,000	$ 50,000
Fixed assets (net)	300,000	70,000
	$400,000	$120,000
Liabilities	$ 40,000	$ 20,000
Common stock	300,000	80,000
Retained earnings	60,000	20,000
	$400,000	$120,000

Prepare a consolidation worksheet at the date of acquisition assuming that P Company paid $100,000 cash for all the outstanding common stock of S Company.

11. Prepare a consolidation worksheet at the date of acquisition assuming that P Company (of Exercise 10) paid $90,000 cash for 90 percent of the outstanding common stock of S Company.

12. On December 31, 19x1, the account balances of a parent and its subsidiary included the following amounts:

	Parent	Subsidiary
Notes receivable	$ 10,000	$ 20,000
Notes payable	30,000	15,000
Sales	500,000	100,000
Purchases	300,000	70,000

All of the subsidiary sales were made to the parent company. All of the goods purchased from the subsidiary were sold by the parent company during the year. The parent company owed the subsidiary $10,000 as of December 31, 19x1.

   a. What amounts of notes receivable and notes payable should be reported on the consolidated balance sheet?
   b. What amount of sales and purchases should be reported on the consolidated income statement?

13. Walton, Inc. is a 100 percent owned subsidiary of Portland Company. The following transactions occurred in 19x1.

   a. Portland Company purchased two basketballs for $10.
   b. Portland Company sold the two basketballs to Walton, Inc. for $12 on account.
   c. Walton, Inc. sold one of the basketballs to an outsider for $8.

   Required:

   1. Prepare journal entries on the books of Portland Company and Walton, Inc., to reflect the above information.
   2. Prepare the necessary elimination entries for consolidation.

14. Prepare the following *worksheet* entries which would appear on the consolidation worksheet of the Samson and Golieth Company as of December 31, 19x1. Do not prepare a consolidation worksheet.

a. The Samson Company had purchased 90 percent of the common stock of the Golieth Company, for $38,000, on January 1, 19x1, when the stockholders' equity portion of Golieth Company's balance sheet appeared as follows:

Capital stock............................	$30,000
Retained earnings........................	10,000
	$40,000

The management of the Samson Company believes that the fair value of specific assets of Golieth Company is greater than their recorded assets.

b. During the year, Samson sold Golieth two chariots (the company's stock-in-trade) on account for a total of $2,000. Prior to this sale, Samson had purchased the chariots for $800 each. Neither of these chariots were sold by Golieth during the remainder of the year.

c. Golieth rented a building to Samson during the year at a rental of $300 per month.

15. On December 31, 19x1, the Brewer Company issued 2,000 shares of its $10 par value stock in exchange for all of the stock of the White Sox Company. White Sox Company has 3,000 shares of $5 par value stock outstanding. Below are their balance sheets prior to acquisition:

	Brewer Company	White Sox Company
Cash.......................................	$ 30,000	$ 12,000
Accounts receivable.........................	75,000	36,000
Fixed assets................................	110,000	78,000
	$215,000	$126,000

	Brewer Company	White Sox Company
Liabilities	$100,000	$ 45,000
Common stock.............................	65,000	15,000
Capital in excess of par value.................	35,000	0
Retained earnings...........................	15,000	66,000
	$215,000	$126,000

Required:

Prepare a consolidation worksheet at the date of acquisition assuming the pooling of interests method is used.

PROBLEMS

16. The balance sheets of Stevens Corporation and Thomas Corporation reflected the following on December 31, 19x1:

	Stevens Corporation	Thomas Corporation
Current assets	$100,000	$ 30,000
Other assets	500,000	100,000
Investment in Thomas	120,000	0
	$720,000	$130,000

	Stevens Corporation	Thomas Corporation
Current liabilities	$100,000	$ 10,000
Common stock	500,000	100,000
Retained earnings	120,000	20,000
	$720,000	$130,000

Stevens Corporation purchased 100 percent of the capital stock of Thomas Corporation on January 1, 19x1, for $111,000. The stockholders' equity of Thomas Corporation on that date included common stock of $100,000 and retained earnings of $11,000. Stevens Corporation had an account payable of $10,000 to Thomas Corporation at December 31, 19x1.

Required:

Prepare the December 31, 19x1, consolidated balance sheet.

17. The balances presented below were taken from the books of the Burns Co. and its subsidiary, the Gentry Co., as of December 31, 19x2. Burns Co. purchased 90 percent of the stock of Gentry Co. for $110,000 on December 31, 19x1. At the date of acquisition, Gentry Co. had common stock of $100,000 and retained earnings of $10,000. The difference between cost and book value was attributed to land owned by Gentry Co. Burns Co. uses the equity method for accounting for its investment in Gentry Co.

	Burns Co.	Gentry Co.
Cash	$ 20,000	$ 20,000
Accounts receivable	40,000	20,000
Inventories	60,000	25,000
Land	80,000	25,000
Buildings and equipment (net)	281,000	60,000
Investment in Gentry Co.	119,000	0
	$600,000	$150,000
Accounts payable	$120,000	$ 30,000
Capital stock	400,000	100,000
Retained earnings	80,000	20,000
	$600,000	$150,000

At the end of the year, Gentry Co. owed Burns Co. $10,000 on open account.

Required:

1. Prepare a worksheet for a consolidated balance sheet as of the end of 19x2.
2. Prepare a consolidated balance sheet in good form for the two companies.

18. Condensed balance sheet information of P Company and S Company at the end of 19x1 is shown below:

	P Company	S Company
Current assets	$300,000	$ 50,000
Other assets	500,000	100,000
	$800,000	$150,000
Liabilities	$100,000	$ 30,000
Capital stock ($100 par value)	500,000	100,000
Retained earnings	200,000	20,000
	$800,000	$150,000

Each of the cases described below involves a situation in which P Company acquires a controlling interest in the stock of S Company on December 31, 19x1.

Required:

Prepare a consolidated balance sheet at the date of acquisition for each of the following cases:

1. P Company purchased all of the outstanding shares of S Company for $140,000. There was evidence that the buildings and equipment of S Company were worth more than their book value.
2. P Company purchases all the outstanding shares of S Company for $110,000.
3. P Company purchases 80 percent of the outstanding shares of S Company for $105,000. The management of P Company paid more than book value because of anticipated advantages of affiliation.

19. On January 1, 19x1, Ace Co. purchased a 90 percent interest in Deuce Co. Income statement data for 19x1 are shown below:

	Ace Co.	Deuce Co.
Sales	$500,000	$ 88,000
Rental income	0	12,000
Interest income	1,000	0
Investment income	9,000	0
Total income	$510,000	$100,000
Cost of goods sold	$300,000	$ 55,000
Operating expenses (including rent)	180,000	30,000
Interest expense	10,000	5,000
Total expenses	$490,000	$ 90,000
Net income	$ 20,000	$ 10,000

Intercompany items were as follows:

a. Deuce Co. rented a building to Ace Co. for $1,000 a month during 19x1.
b. Deuce Co. paid Ace Co. $1,000 interest on intercompany notes during the year.
c. Ace Co. sold goods to Deuce Co. for $50,000 during the year. All the goods were resold by Deuce Co. to outsiders by the end of the year.

Required:

1. Prepare working papers for a consolidated income statement for 19x1.
2. Did the parent company use the cost method or equity method for accounting for its investment in the subsidiary?
3. If you had not been told that Ace Co. owned 90 percent of Deuce Co., how could you have determined this fact from the income statement data?

20. On January 1, 19x1, the Strock Co. acquired 90 percent of the common stock of the Bristow Co. for $145,000. The stockholders' equity of Bristow Co. on that date was as follows:

Common stock	$120,000
Retained earnings	30,000
	$150,000

During 19x1, the Bristow Co. earned $20,000 of net income and paid cash dividends of $12,000. The Strock Co. reported net income of $50,000 (including investment income) and paid dividends of $20,000. The Strock Co. uses the equity method for accounting for its investment in Bristow. The stockholders' equity of the Strock Co. on December 31, 19x1, was as follows:

Common stock	$400,000
Retained earnings	180,000
	$580,000

Required:

Determine the amounts at which the following items would be shown in the December 31, 19x1, consolidated statements.

    a.   Difference between cost and book value of subsidiary stock.
    b.   Consolidated net income.
    c.   Consolidated retained earnings.
    d.   Minority interest.

21. Income statement data for 19x1 for King Co. and its 100 percent owned subsidiary, Queen Co., are shown below.

	King Co.	Queen Co.
Sales	$200,000	$100,000
Investment income	20,000	0
	$220,000	$100,000
Cost of goods sold	$100,000	$ 60,000
Operating expenses	80,000	20,000
	$180,000	$ 80,000
Net income	$ 40,000	$ 20,000

During 19x1, Queen Co. sold all of its goods to King Co. An intercompany profit of $5,000 was recorded by Queen Co. on the sale of goods held in King Co.'s inventory at the end of 19x1.

Required:

Prepare the worksheet to develop a consolidated income statement at the end of 19x1.

22. Separate balance sheets for the Cat Company and Mouse Company for the years ended December 31, 19x1 and 19x2 are presented below:

	December 31, 19x1		December 31, 19x2	
	Cat Co.	Mouse Co.	Cat Co.	Mouse Co.
Cash	$ 24,000	$10,000	$ 20,000	$14,000
Accounts receivable	20,000	10,000	20,000	12,000
Fixed assets	120,000	40,000	140,000	44,000
Investment in Mouse Co.	36,000		60,000	
Total Assets	$200,000	$60,000	$240,000	$70,000
Accounts payable	$ 20,000	$20,000	$ 30,000	$ 6,000
Capital stock	120,000	30,000	120,000	30,000
Retained earnings	60,000	10,000	90,000	34,000
Total Liabilities and Equities	$200,000	$60,000	$240,000	$70,000

Cat Company had acquired a 100 percent interest in Mouse Company on December 31, 19x1. The difference in the cost of the company versus its book value is due to a difference between the book value and market value of fixed assets. During 19x2, Mouse Company earned $35,000 in net income and paid out $11,000 in cash dividends. As of December 31, 19x2, Cat Company owes Mouse Company $5,000 and Mouse Company owes Cat Company $3,000.

Required:

1. Prepare a consolidation worksheet for December 31, 19x1 and 19x2.
2. Does the Cat Company use the cost or equity method to record its investment in the Mouse Company?

23. Below is the adjusted trial balance for the Indian Company and Tiger Company for the year ended December 31, 19x1.

	Indian Company	Tiger Company
Cash	$ 10,000	$ 8,000
Accounts receivable	23,000	21,000
Accrued interest receivable	600	1,200
Accrued rent receivable	1,200	0
Fixed assets	168,100	123,600
Investment in Tiger Company	72,900	0
Accounts payable	(9,500)	(6,600)
Rent payable	0	(1,200)
Long-term debt	(126,000)	(65,000)
Capital stock	(84,000)	(41,500)
Retained earnings	(18,000)	(26,000)
Sales	(205,000)	(150,000)
Cost of goods sold	133,250	97,500
Other expenses	60,000	39,000
Rent revenue	(14,400)	0
Investment revenue	(12,150)	0

The Indian Company had purchased a 90 percent interest in the Tiger Company on December 31, 19x0 when Tiger Company had the following balances in its stockholders' equity accounts.

Capital stock	$41,500
Retained earnings	26,000
	$67,500

The Indian Company uses the equity method to record its investment in the subsidiary.

During 19x1, Tiger Company rented a building from Indian Company for $1,200 a month. Rent is paid on the first day of each month.

Required:

Prepare consolidation income statement worksheets and consolidation balance sheet worksheets for the Indian and Tiger Companies as of December 31, 19x1. Don't forget to add net income earned during the year to retained earnings for each company.

24. Jijo Co. purchased 80 percent of the outstanding stock of Eli Co. for $175,000 on January 1, 19x1. Balance sheet data for the two corporations immediately after the transaction are presented below.

	Jijo Co.	Eli Co.
Cash	$ 10,000	$ 5,000
Accounts receivable	30,000	15,000
Inventories	60,000	30,000
Fixed assets (net)	300,000	170,000
Investment in Eli Co.	175,000	0
	$575,000	$220,000

Assume that the difference between the cost of the investment and the book value of the subsidiary was attributed to advantages of affiliation.

Required:

Prepare a consolidated balance sheet for Jijo Co. and Eli Co. at January 1, 19x1.

25. Below are given the trial balances of Moore Company and its 90 percent owned subsidiary, Parker Company, as of December 31, 19x1:

	Moore Company		Parker Company	
Cash	$ 31,000		$ 12,750	
Accounts receivable	24,000		12,400	
Advances to Parker Company	10,000			
Investment in Parker Company	76,500			
Inventory	26,000		28,100	
Other assets	80,840		50,000	
Accounts payable		$ 31,960		$ 8,250
Advances from Moore Company				10,000
Capital stock		200,000		60,000
Retained earnings		16,380		25,000
	$248,340	$248,340	$103,250	$103,250

Additional data:

The advances are non-interest bearing. At the time of acquisition, Parker Company's equity section was as follows:

Capital stock	$60,000
Retained earnings	15,000

Required:

1. Elimination entries.
2. Consolidated balance sheet.

26. Below is shown the condensed balance sheets of the A's and Angel Companies at the end of 19x1, before the acquisition of the stock of Angel Company.

	A's Company	Angel Company
Current assets	$100,000	$ 25,000
Other assets	400,000	75,000
Total Assets	$500,000	$100,000

	A's Company	Angel Company
Liabilities	$ 50,000	$ 10,000
Capital stock ($50 par value)	150,000	35,000
Retained earnings	300,000	55,000
Total Liabilities and Equities	$500,000	$100,000

Required:

Prepare a consolidated balance sheet for the year 19x1, under each of the following unrelated assumptions. A's Company has acquired a controlling interest in the stock of Angel Company in each case.

1. A's Company purchased all of the outstanding shares of Angel Company for $80,000 in cash. An appraisal of land held by Angel Company determined the land to be worth less than its book value.
2. A's Company purchased all the outstanding shares of Angel Company for $100,000. They paid more for the shares than book value because the value of several assets had increased over their book value.
3. A's Company purchased 90 percent of the outstanding shares of Angel Company for $79,000. A's Company paid less than book value because the product manufactured by Angel Company was outdated.

27. On January 1, 19x1, Royals Company purchased an 80 percent interest in Twins Company. Their income statements for the year ended December 31, 19x1 are shown below.

	Royals Company	Twins Company
Sales..............................	$250,000	$28,000
Rental income......................	18,000	3,000
Interest income....................	1,500	500
Investment income..................	6,720	0
Total Revenues..................	$276,220	$31,500
Cost of goods sold.................	$100,000	$14,000
Operating expenses.................	50,500	7,900
Interest expense...................	300	1,200
Total Expenses..................	$150,800	$23,100
Net Income.........................	$125,420	$ 8,400

Additional data:

a. Royals Company rented a building from Twins Company for $250 a month during 19x1.
b. Royals Company sold $13,000 worth of goods to Twins Company and all these goods were later resold.
c. Royals Company paid $280 interest to Twins Company during the year and Twins Company paid $1,000 interest to Royals Company.

Required:

Prepare working papers for a consolidated income statement for 19x1.

28. On January 1, 19x2, the Ranger Company purchased 80 percent of the common stock of the Blue Jay Company for $310,000. The stockholders' equity of Blue Jay Company on that date was:

Common stock..........................	$100,000
Retained earnings.....................	260,000
	$360,000

The Ranger Company decided to use the equity method to account for its investment in Blue Jay Company. During 19x2, the Blue Jay Company earned $50,000 in net income and paid $30,000 in dividends. The Ranger Company reported $150,000 in net income (excluding investment income) and paid dividends of $90,000.

Required:

1. What amount would be shown on the consolidated balance sheet as "Excess of cost over book value of subsidiary," assuming the fair value of the assets of Blue Jay Company was $10,000 above the book value?

2. What is the amount of the consolidated net income as of December 31, 19x2?
3. What is the amount of Ranger Company's investment in Blue Jay Company which must be eliminated at year-end using the equity method?
4. What is the minority interest on December 31, 19x2 to be disclosed in the consolidated balance sheet?

29. Below are the income statements for Dodger and Red Companies. Red owns 100 percent of Dodger.

	Red Company	Dodger Company
Sales	$56,000	$25,000
Investment income	6,000	0
	$62,000	$25,000
Cost of goods sold	$29,000	$18,000
Operating expenses	6,000	1,000
	$35,000	$19,000
Net Income	$27,000	$ 6,000

During 19x1, Red Company sold $15,000 of its goods to Dodger Company at a mark-up of 30 percent (cost to Red Company being $15,000). At the end of the year, Dodger Company still had $3,900 (cost plus mark-up) in its ending inventory.

Required:

Prepare the worksheet to develop a consolidated income statement on December 31, 19x1.

Learning Objectives

Chapter 17 illustrates the procedures used in preparing the statement of changes in financial position. Studying this chapter should enable you to:

1. Understand and give examples of the types of information an analysis of funds flow will provide.

2. Identify the primary sources and uses of funds.

3. Describe the procedures involved in preparing the statement of changes in financial position.

4. Prepare a statement of changes in financial position using both the working capital and cash definitions of funds.

17

The Statement of Changes in Financial Position

INTRODUCTION

An important consideration in the decision process of many users of financial statements is the amount of, and the changes in, the resources of a business. Comparative balance sheets indicate the resources available at the beginning and the end of a period. These statements do not, however, explain the causes of any changes in the resources. While a part of the change in resources may result from the operations of the business, the net income as reported in the income statement may not be accompanied by an equivalent increase in resources. Consequently, the combination of the balance sheet and income statement may not provide an adequate indication of the flow of the various liquid resources which takes place during the business cycle. For this reason, a statement which discloses the analysis of the funds flows of a firm is now required along with the balance sheet and income statement as a part of a firm's basic report "package." The Accounting Principles Board concluded that:

> ... information concerning the financing and investing activities of a business enterprise and the changes in its financial position for a period is essential for financial statement users, particularly owners and creditors, in making economic decisions. When financial statements purporting to present both financial position (balance sheet) and results of operations (statement of income and retained earnings) are issued, a statement summarizing changes in financial position should also be presented as a basic financial statement for each period for which an income statement is presented.[1]

This statement, the statement of changes in financial position, is a significant measure of the effectiveness of the financing activities of a firm.

The analysis of funds flow is designed to provide answers to several questions of significance to the various users of financial statements such as the following:

1. If comparative income statements indicate an increase in net income as compared to the previous year, why did the current position deteriorate?
2. Where did the company obtain the funds used to finance its expansion?
3. If the company had a net loss for the previous year, where did it obtain the funds to pay dividends to the owners?

As indicated above, this analysis and the information that it provides is considered to be of sufficient importance that it is now included as a

---

[1] "Reporting Changes in Financial Position" *Opinions of the Accounting Principles Board, No. 19* (American Institute of Certified Public Accountants, 1971), p. 373.

formal statement in the published annual reports of firms. The Accounting Principles Board in its *Opinion No. 19* made the funds-flow statement, which is now to be titled "Statement of Changes in Financial Position," a required part of annual reports. The objectives of this statement are to summarize the financing and investing activities of a firm and to disclose the changes in financial position that occurred during the period.

DEFINITION OF FUNDS

A problem that has frequently arisen in the past with regard to funds flow reporting is the lack of a uniform definition of the term "funds." This is of the utmost importance since the definition of "funds" determines both the nature and format of the funds statement.

In everyday usage, the term funds usually means cash. Therefore, it might appear that a statement of changes in financial position would provide a summary of the firm's cash receipts and disbursements for the period. Using this definition of funds, the statement is essentially an analysis of cash flow.

In financial reporting, the term "funds" has usually been defined as working capital, or the excess of current assets over current liabilities. According to this concept, the statement reports financing and investing activities as a summary of the sources and uses of working capital for the period. Thus, the purpose of the statement is to indicate the sources of working capital inflow into the firm and the uses which were made of working capital during the period.

In recognition of the need for flexibility in the reporting practices of different firms, APB *Opinion No. 19* allows "funds" to be defined as either cash or working capital. The following section of this chapter will focus on the working capital definition of funds.

SOURCES AND USES OF WORKING CAPITAL

The statement of changes in financial position is divided into two major segments: funds that the firm has obtained during the period (sources of funds), and the outflow of funds which has occurred (uses of funds). The "sources of funds" section summarizes all transactions of the business that caused an increase in its working capital. Working capital may be increased by the operating activities of the firm as well as by its financing and other activities. The "uses of funds" section of the statement summarizes all transactions that caused a decrease in working capital during the period. Of course, a transaction that affects current assets and/or current liabilities but does not increase or decrease working capital is neither a source nor a use of funds. For example, the repayment of a short-term loan with cash decreases both current assets and current liabilities by an equal amount, and therefore does not affect working capital.

Sources of Funds

Transactions that increase working capital are sources of funds. The primary sources of working capital for a firm include:

1. Current operations (inflows from revenues less outflows for expenses).
2. The sale of noncurrent assets.
3. Borrowing from long-term lenders.
4. The sale of capital stock.

Funds from Operations

Net income of a firm for a particular period has been defined as the excess of its revenues over its expenses. Revenues generally result in an increase in current assets. For example, sales usually cause an increase in either cash or accounts receivable. Similarly, most expenses require either that a current outlay of cash be made or that a current liability be incurred. Thus, the operations of a firm are a source of funds if the inflow of working capital from revenues exceeds the outflow of working capital for expenses during the period.

The reported net income of a firm, however, is not necessarily equal to the amount of funds provided. This is because not all expenses require a current expenditure or the incurrence of a liability. Certain types of expenses enter into the determination of net income but have no effect on working capital. For example, depreciation of fixed assets is an expense which reduces income but does not require an outlay of funds and therefore does not affect working capital. In order to determine working capital provided by operations, it is necessary to deduct from revenues only those expenses which required an expenditure of funds and therefore caused a decrease in working capital. A convenient way of determining working capital from operations is simply to add back to net income all those expenses which did not require an outlay of funds, i.e., working capital. It is important to note that the adding back of expenses which did not require the use of working capital to net income is not a source of funds in and of itself, but instead is simply a means of determining the amount of working capital generated by operations. Other expenses which do not affect working capital include amortization of the cost of intangible assets and amortization of discount on bonds payable.

Certain items included in the income statement decrease expenses (thereby increasing income) without increasing working capital. For example, the amortization of premium on bonds payable causes interest expense to be less than the amount of the cash paid. Therefore, these items should be deducted from net income in computing the amount of working capital provided by operations.

To illustrate, assume that Martin Company had net income of $1,000 during 19x1, determined as follows:

Martin Company
Income Statement
For the Year Ending December 31, 19x1

Sales		$20,000
Cost of goods sold		10,000
Gross margin		$10,000
Operating expenses:		
Salaries	$6,000	
Rent	1,000	
Depreciation	2,000	9,000
Net Income		$ 1,000

In this example, Martin Company had an inflow of $20,000 of working capital from sales, and outflows of $10,000 for cost of goods sold, $6,000 for salaries, and $1,000 for rent. Since the $2,000 depreciation expense did not require an outlay of funds, the increase in working capital is equal to sales of $20,000 less $17,000 of expenses which did cause an outflow of working capital. In other words, a total of $3,000 of funds was provided by operations. Alternatively, funds generated by operations can also be obtained by adding the $2,000 depreciation expense to the $1,000 net income, for a total of $3,000.

A firm that experiences a net loss for the period may still generate working capital from its operations if the total expenses which did not require the use of working capital exceed the amount of the loss. Thus, a firm with a net loss of $10,000 which included depreciation of $15,000 among its expenses would generate working capital of $5,000 from its operations. If the loss exceeds such adjustments, the difference constitutes a use of working capital during the period.

Additional adjustments may be required in order to obtain working capital provided by operations if net income includes either nonoperating gains or losses. For example, if land that had an original cost of $1,000 is sold for $1,500 during the period, a $500 gain on the sale of land is included in net income for the period. Since the $1,500 received from the sale represents the total funds provided and is shown in the statement as a separate item, it would be double counting to also include the $500 gain as a part of working capital provided by operations. Thus, in order to determine the amount of working capital provided by operations, it is necessary to deduct any nonoperating gains and add back any nonoperating losses.

The computation of the working capital provided by operations may be summarized as follows:

> Net Income
>
> \+
>
> Items Reducing Net Income Which Do Not Affect Working Capital
>
> \+
>
> Nonoperating Losses
>
> −
>
> Nonoperating Gains
>
> −
>
> Items Increasing Net Income Which Do Not Affect Working Capital
>
> =
>
> Working Capital Provided by Operations

Other Sources of Funds

The treatment of nonoperating sources of funds is fairly straightforward. Borrowing on long-term loans, for example, increases current assets without a corresponding increase in current liabilities, and therefore represents a source of funds. Similarly, the sale of additional capital stock or the sale of fixed assets results in a net inflow of current assets without an increase in current liabilities.

Uses of Funds

Transactions that decrease working capital are classified as uses of funds. Typical uses of working capital include:

1. Purchase of noncurrent assets.
2. Repayment of long-term debt.
3. Repurchase of capital stock.
4. Declaration of cash dividends.

Again, most uses of funds are fairly obvious. When noncurrent assets such as buildings, equipment, or land are purchased, a firm will usually make an outlay of cash, and/or increase its liabilities. In these instances, working capital is reduced and, thus, there is a use of funds. Similarly, the repayment of long-term debt such as a mortgage or bond, or the repurchase of outstanding capital stock, usually requires an outlay of funds.

The declaration of a cash dividend to be paid at a later date is also a use of funds. Working capital is reduced at the time the declaration is made because a current liability, dividends payable, is incurred and recorded at that time. The subsequent payment of the cash dividend does not affect working capital because cash, a current asset, and dividends payable, a current liability, are reduced by equal amounts.

17 | The Statement of Changes in Financial Position 525

DETERMINING SOURCES AND USES OF WORKING CAPITAL

The amounts of individual sources and uses of working capital necessary in order to prepare the statement of changes in financial position may be determined as follows:

1. Compute changes in current asset and current liability (working capital) accounts;
2. Compute changes in all the noncurrent accounts;
3. Analyze changes in the noncurrent accounts.

It is usually necessary to have comparative balance sheets for the beginning and end of the period and an income statement and retained earnings statement for the period available to determine sources and uses of working capital.

The following basic data will be used to illustrate the steps required for the preparation of a statement of changes in financial position.

Kraton Company
Income Statement
For the Year Ended December 31, 19x1

Net sales		$1,000
Cost of goods sold		400
Gross margin		$ 600
Operating expenses:		
Depreciation	$100	
Wage expense	100	
Other expenses	200	400
Net Income from Operations		$ 200
Gain on sale of land		100
Net Income		$ 300

Kraton Company
Retained Earnings Statement
For the Year Ended December 31, 19x1

Retained earnings at beginning of year	$250
Add: Net income	300
	$550
Subtract: Cash dividends	100
Retained earnings at end of year	$450

Kraton Company
Comparative Balance Sheet

	December 31		
ASSETS	19x1	19x0	Change
Cash	$ 250	$ 100	+150
Accounts receivable	350	200	+150
Inventories	200	250	− 50
Building	600	400	+200
Accumulated depreciation—building	(200)	(100)	+100
Land	100	200	−100
Total Assets	$1,300	$1,050	
LIABILITIES AND STOCKHOLDERS' EQUITY			
Accounts payable	$ 300	$ 200	+100
Accrued wages payable	50	100	− 50
Bonds payable—long-term	100	200	−100
Capital stock	400	300	+100
Retained earnings	450	250	+200
Total Liabilities and Equities	$1,300	$1,050	

Assume that the following additional information is available:

1. During the year, a building was purchased for $200 and land was purchased at a cost of $100.
2. Land with a cost of $200 was sold at a gain of $100.
3. All common stock was issued for cash.
4. A long-term bond was retired for $100.
5. A $100 dividend was paid during the year.

CHANGES IN WORKING CAPITAL

An increase in a current asset balance causes an increase in working capital. For example, if cash increases, current assets exceed current liabilities by a larger amount, other factors being equal. Similarly, a decrease in a current asset represents a reduction in working capital. An increase in a current liability, on the other hand, decreases working capital while a decrease in a current liability results in an increase in working capital. This is because current liabilities are deducted from current assets in determining working capital. Thus, the net change in working capital during the period can be easily computed by examining the changes in the current accounts in the comparative balance sheets.

The following illustration shows the changes in current assets, current liabilities, and working capital for Kraton Company from December 31, 19x0, to December 31, 19x1.

	December 31		Working Capital	
	19x1	19x0	Increase	Decrease
Current Assets:				
Cash	$250	$100	$150	—
Accounts receivable	350	200	150	—
Inventories	200	250	—	$ 50
Current Liabilities:				
Accounts payable	300	200	—	100
Accrued wages payable	50	100	50	—
			$350	$150
Increase in Working Capital				200
			$350	$350

In this situation, the statement of changes in financial position will disclose sources of working capital exceeding uses by $200. The next step is to determine the nature of the various sources and uses of working capital. This is accomplished by analyzing all changes in the noncurrent accounts.

Changes in Noncurrent Accounts

Once the change in working capital has been determined, the next step is to compute the changes in all noncurrent accounts (noncurrent assets, noncurrent liabilities, and stockholders' equity). An analysis of these changes will indicate the sources and the uses of working capital during the period.

All changes in the noncurrent accounts of Kraton Company from December 31, 19x0, to December 31, 19x1, are summarized below.

	December 31			
	19x1	19x0	Increase	Decrease
Building	$600	$400	$200	
Accumulated depreciation—building	200	100	100	
Land	100	200		$100
Bonds payable—long-term	100	200		100
Capital stock	400	300	100	
Retained earnings	450	250	200	

Once the amount of these changes has been determined, it is necessary to consider the effect that each change had on working capital. Each account must be considered in order to determine the cause of the change. If more than one transaction caused the change, the effect of each transaction must be analyzed separately.

Let us consider the changes in the noncurrent accounts of Kraton Company.

Building. The increase in the building account was the result of a single transaction in which a building was acquired at a cost of $200. The effect of this purchase on working capital was as follows:

> Use of Funds:
> Purchase of building $200

Land. The comparative balance sheet indicates that the land account decreased by $100 during 1982. This net decrease was a result of two transactions: one for the sale of land and another in which land was purchased. The source of funds from the sale of land is the total proceeds received from the sale. Thus, $300 of working capital was provided by the sale, the $200 book value of the land plus the $100 gain:

> Source of Funds:
> Sale of land $300

As previously indicated, in order to avoid double counting, the $100 gain on the sale must be deducted from net income in the calculation of working capital provided by operations.

The cost of the land acquired during the year affected working capital as follows:

> Use of Funds:
> Purchase of land $100

Accumulated Depreciation. The $100 increase in the Accumulated Depreciation—Building account resulted from recording depreciation expense for the year (see the income statement). The effect of depreciation on working capital will be considered in determining working capital provided by operations.

Bonds Payable. The next noncurrent item, bonds payable, decreased by $100 during the year. An analysis of the additional information provided indicates that this decrease resulted from the retirement of a bond at its face value. The effect on working capital is as follows:

> Use of Funds:
> Retirement of bonds payable $100

Capital Stock. The increase in the capital stock account resulted from the issuance of additional stock for $100 in cash during the year. This amount would be included in the statement as follows:

> Source of Funds:
> Issuance of capital stock $100

Retained Earnings. An examination of the comparative balance sheets reveals that retained earnings increased by $200 during 19x1. An analysis of the statement of retained earnings indicates that net income for 19x1 was $300, and that dividends of $100 were declared and paid during the year. These two transactions account for the net change in retained earnings. The effect of the net income of the period on working capital is included in the calculation of working capital from operations described below. Declaration of the cash dividend affected working capital as follows:

```
             Use of Funds:
                Cash dividend . . . . . . . . . . . . . . .  $100
```

WORKING CAPITAL PROVIDED BY OPERATIONS

As previously indicated, net income of Kraton Company is not equivalent to working capital from operations. One expense included in the income statement, depreciation, did not require either an outflow of current assets or an increase in a current liability. Therefore, it is necessary to add back depreciation expense of $100 to the net income of the period.

A second adjustment is required to eliminate the nonoperating gain on the sale of land from net income. The $100 gain was included in the proceeds from the sale of land as a separate source of working capital, and must be excluded from working capital provided by operations.

Thus, the working capital from operations is determined as follows:

```
    Source of Funds:
    Operations:
       Net Income . . . . . . . . . . . . . . . . . . . . . . . . . . . .  $300
       Add:  Expense not requiring outlay of working
                capital during the period—depreciation . . . . . . . .   100
       Deduct: Nonoperating gain . . . . . . . . . . . . . . . . . . .   (100)
       Working Capital from Operations . . . . . . . . . . . . . .   $300
```

It is only a coincidence that the working capital provided by operations is equal to the net income for the period.

FORM OF THE STATEMENT OF CHANGES IN FINANCIAL POSITION

All information which is necessary to prepare the statement of changes in financial position has now been analyzed. The 19x1 statement for the Kraton Company prepared from this information is shown on the following page.

Kraton Company
Statement of Changes in Financial Position
For the Year Ended December 31, 19x1

Sources of Funds:		
Operations:		
Net income	$300	
Add: Depreciation	100	
Less: Gain on sale of land	(100)	
Working Capital Provided by Operations		$300
Sale of land	$300	
Sale of capital stock	100	400
Total Funds Provided		$700
Uses of Funds:		
To acquire land	$100	
To acquire building	200	
To retire long-term bonds	100	
To pay dividends	100	500
Increase in Working Capital		$200

The statement identifies and analyzes the sources and uses of working capital which resulted in the $200 net increase in working capital during 19x1.

The statement of changes in financial position described above was simplified for purposes of illustration. Illustration 1 presents the actual statement of changes in financial position for General Motors Corporation.

TRANSACTIONS NOT AFFECTING CURRENT ACCOUNTS

In the Kraton Company illustration, all financing and investing activities occurred through transactions that involved either a current asset or current liability account and a nonworking capital account. It is possible, however, to have transactions which affect only noncurrent accounts. For example, assume that $20,000 par value of capital stock is exchanged for a building with a fair market value of $20,000. Although this appears to be a significant financial transaction, it has no effect on the amount of working capital. Therefore, this exchange would be excluded from the statement of changes if a strict interpretation of the working capital definition of funds was used.

Because the strict application of working capital or cash definition of funds could omit the effect of certain significant transactions from the statement, APB *Opinion No. 19* broadens the concept underlying the statement of changes in financial position to include financing and investing activities not directly affecting working capital. Under this concept, a significant transaction involving changes in noncurrent accounts must be

Illustration 1

STATEMENT OF CHANGES IN CONSOLIDATED FINANCIAL POSITION

For the Years Ended December 31, 1985, 1984 and 1983 (Dollars in Millions)

	1985	1984	1983
Source of Funds			
Net income	$ 3,999.0	$ 4,516.5	$ 3,730.2
Depreciation of real estate, plants and equipment	2,777.9	2,663.2	2,569.7
Amortization of special tools	3,083.3	2,236.7	2,549.9
Amortization of intangible assets (Note 1)	347.3	69.1	.8
Deferred income taxes, undistributed earnings of nonconsolidated subsidiaries and associates, etc.—net	(471.7)	(1,316.1)	645.5
Total funds provided by current operations	9,735.8	8,169.4	9,496.1
Decrease (Increase) in other working capital items	866.2	1,964.6	(1,142.0)
Increase in long-term debt	965.9	1,074.1	3,177.1
Issuances of common stocks, less repurchases of preferred stocks	2,755.5	602.2	212.0
Other—net	222.1	2,010.6	772.0
Total	14,545.5	13,820.9	12,515.2
Use of Funds			
Cash dividends paid to stockholders (Note 14)	1,616.9	1,523.7	892.2
Expenditures for real estate, plants and equipment—Operations	6,099.2	3,595.1	1,923.0
—Hughes acquisition	1,948.7	—	—
Expenditures for special tools	3,075.0	2,452.1	2,083.7
Intangible assets acquired in acquisitions (Note 1)	4,244.7	2,006.3	—
Decrease in long-term debt	883.1	1,793.9	4,491.9
Investments in nonconsolidated subsidiaries and associates	130.9	99.3	33.7
Total	17,998.5	11,470.4	9,424.5
Increase (Decrease) in cash and marketable securities	(3,453.0)	2,350.5	3,090.7
Cash and marketable securities at beginning of the year	8,567.4	6,216.9	3,126.2
Cash and marketable securities at end of the year	$ 5,114.4	$ 8,567.4	$ 6,216.9
Decrease (Increase) in Other Working Capital Items by Element			
Accounts and notes receivable	$ 75.9	($ 393.7)	($ 4,099.7)
Inventories	(910.0)	(738.2)	(437.3)
Contracts in process	(1,453.8)	—	—
Prepaid expenses	(1,707.8)	568.9	871.0
Accounts payable	2,578.7	101.2	1,041.6
Loans payable	(430.8)	1,830.8	72.7
United States, foreign and other income taxes payable	(375.8)	416.6	131.5
Accrued liabilities and deferred income taxes	3,089.8	179.0	1,278.2
Decrease (Increase) in other working capital items	$ 866.2	$ 1,964.6	($ 1,142.0)

Reference should be made to notes on pages 28 through 38.
Certain amounts for 1984 and 1983 have been reclassified to conform with 1985 classifications.

reported as both a source and a use of funds. Of course, including this type of transaction does not affect the reported increase or decrease in working capital, but it does provide the user with a comprehensive view of the total inflow and outflow of all financial resources during the period. Among the most common of these nonworking capital transactions are:

1. The issuance of noncurrent debt or capital stock for noncurrent assets.
2. The issuance of capital stock to retire noncurrent debt.

To illustrate, again consider the case where a firm issued $20,000 par value of its capital stock for a building with a fair market value of $20,000. This transaction would have been recorded in the accounts as follows:

```
Building ...................................  20,000
    Capital Stock ...........................          20,000
```

Although this transaction did not affect working capital, it should be viewed as being comprised of two parts, the sale of stock for $20,000 and the purchase of a building for the same amount. Thus, it would be reported on the statement of changes in financial position as follows:

```
Source of Funds:
    Issuance of capital stock............  $20,000
Use of Funds:
    Purchase of building ..............  $20,000
```

CASH FLOW ANALYSIS

If funds are defined as cash, the statement of changes in financial position discloses individual sources and uses of cash. The analysis of cash flow is very similar to the analysis which was described for the working capital concept of funds. Additional adjustments, however, are necessary to convert the net income for the period to the amount of cash which was provided by operations.

Cash Flow from Operations

Several adjustments are required to convert a firm's net income to cash flow from operations. As illustrated previously, a nonfund expense, such as depreciation, is an allocation of a past cost and thus does not result in an outlay of cash during the current period. Therefore, nonfund expenses must be added back to net income in determining cash provided by operations. In addition, since income statement data are based on the accrual method of accounting, further adjustments are required to convert revenues and expenses to cash receipts and disbursements. The financial statements previously presented for Kraton Company will again be used as a basis for illustration.

Cash Received from Customers. Since many firms make sales on a credit basis, cash receipts depend on the collections from customers. If the accounts receivable balance increased during the period, credit sales must have exceeded collections from customers. Similarly, a decrease in accounts receivable during the year indicates that cash collected from customers exceeded net credit sales by the amount of the decrease in accounts receivable. Therefore, cash received from customers may be computed thus:

$$\text{Sales} \quad \begin{array}{c} + \text{ Decrease in Accounts Receivables} \\ \text{or} \\ - \text{ Increase in Accounts Receivables} \end{array} \quad = \text{Cash Receipts from Sales}$$

The 19x1 cash receipts from sales is computed as follows for Kraton Company:

Net sales	$1,000
Less: Increase in accounts receivable	150
Cash Receipts	$ 850

Cash Disbursements Associated with Cost of Goods Sold. The initial step in computing the cash disbursements associated with cost of goods sold is determining purchases for the period. Purchases will differ from cost of goods sold if the inventory balance increased or decreased during the year. If inventories decreased, then a part of the cost of goods sold came from the reduction of the beginning inventory and did not represent goods purchased during the year. Similarly, if inventories increased, purchases exceeded the cost of goods sold by the amount of the increase in the inventory balance.

$$\text{Cost of Goods Sold} \quad \begin{array}{c} + \text{ Increase in Inventory} \\ \text{or} \\ - \text{ Decrease in Inventory} \end{array} \quad = \text{Purchases}$$

Since purchases are often made on a credit basis, purchases for a period may differ from cash disbursements if the accounts payable balance increased or decreased during the year. For example, if a firm increases its accounts payable,[2] it paid out less cash than the amount of its purchases for the period.

Thus, the procedure for computing cash disbursements for purchases is as follows:

---

[2] In this example, it is assumed that all accounts payable were incurred for credit purchases.

Purchases $\begin{array}{c} \text{+ Decrease in Accounts Payable} \\ \text{or} \\ \text{− Increase in Accounts Payable} \end{array}$ = Cash Disbursements for Purchases

To illustrate, Kraton Company's inventory decreased by $50 while its accounts payable increased by $100 during the year. Cash disbursements for purchases is computed as follows:

Cost of goods sold	$400
Less: Decrease in inventory	50
Purchases	$350
Less: Increase in accounts payable	100
Cash Disbursements for Purchases	$250

Cash Disbursements for Expenses. Expenses incurred during the current period may differ from cash outlays because of changes in either prepaid expense or accrued liability balances.

If an accrued liability related to an expense increased during the year, then only a portion of the expense represented an expenditure of cash during the period. Thus, if an expense has a related accrued liability account, the cash disbursement associated with the expense may be determined as follows:

Expense $\begin{array}{c} \text{+ Decrease in Accrued Liability} \\ \text{or} \\ \text{− Increase in Accrued Liability} \end{array}$ = Cash Disbursement for Expenses

Similarly, if an expense has a related prepaid expense account, an increase in the prepaid account indicates that the cash outlay exceeded the amount of the expense. For example, assume that prepaid insurance was $500 on January 1 and $600 on December 31 and that insurance expense for the year was $200. The entry to record insurance expense would reduce the prepaid insurance account by $200 to a balance of $300. Therefore, an additional payment of $300 must have been made for insurance during the year.

Prepaid Insurance

Additional Insurance Purchased → 500
→ 300   200 ← Insurance Expense
600

Thus, if an expense account has a related prepaid expense account, the cash outlay is computed as follows:

$$\text{Expense} \begin{array}{c} \text{+ Increase in Prepaid Expense Account} \\ \text{or} \\ \text{- Decrease in Prepaid Expense Account} \end{array} = \text{Cash Disbursement for Expenses}$$

The Kraton Company had no prepaid expense accounts and the only accrued liability, wages payable, decreased by $50 during the year. Therefore, the only adjustment required is to determine the cash paid for wages during the year which is as follows:

Wages expense.	$100
Add: Decrease in wages payable	50
Cash Disbursements for Wages	$150

Cash from Operations. Conversion of the net income of Kraton Company to cash provided by operations is shown below. It is derived from the computations which were made in the previous paragraphs.

Kraton Company
Conversion of Net Income to Cash Provided by Operations
For the Year Ended December 31, 19x1

	Income Statement	Add (Subtract)	Cash Receipts and (Disbursements)
Sales	$1000		
Less: Increase in receivables		$(150)	$ 850
Cost of goods sold	400		
Less: Decrease in inventory		(50)	
Increase in accounts payable		(100)	(250)
Gross Margin	$ 600		$ 600
Operating expenses:			
Depreciation	$ 100	(100)	
Wage expense	100		
Add: Decrease in wages payable.		50	$(150)
Other expenses	200		(200)
Net Income from Operations	$ 200		
Cash Provided by Operations			$ 250

Cash Used for Dividends

The computation of the cash used for dividends may also differ if there was a change in the dividends payable account from the beginning to the end of the year. For example, assume that dividends were declared on December 15, 19x0, to be paid on January 15, 19x1. The declaration of dividends would constitute a decrease in working capital during 19x1 because a current liability, dividends payable, is increased. The use of cash, however, would occur during the following year when the dividends are actually paid.

Kraton Company
Cash Flow Statement
For the Year Ended December 31, 19x1

Sources of Cash:			
Operations			
Net income			$300
Add: Depreciation expense	$100		
Decrease in inventory	50		
Increase in accounts payable	100	250	
		$550	
Less: Gain on sale of land	$100		
Increase in receivables	150		
Decrease in wages payable	50	300	
Cash Provided by Operations			$250
Sale of land			300
Sale of capital stock			100
			$650
Uses of Cash:			
To acquire land		$100	
To acquire building		200	
To retire long-term bonds		100	
To pay dividends		100	500
Increase in Cash			$150

CASH FLOW STATEMENT

Cash flow statements may vary considerably in both their format and terminology. The cash flow statement is comparable in form to the statement of changes in financial position, with funds defined as working capital, which was prepared earlier in this chapter. The general format discloses the sources and uses of cash with the difference representing the increase or decrease in cash during the period. The statement of changes in financial position for the Kraton Company for 19x1, with funds defined as cash was shown above. This statement explains the $150 increase in the cash balance which occurred during 19x1.

SUMMARY OF MECHANICS ON THE STATEMENT OF CHANGES IN FINANCIAL POSITION

The mechanics of the statement of changes in financial position may be summarized as follows:

Statement of Changes in Financial Position

Sources of Working Capital:
  From operations:
    Income (as per the income statement).
    Add: Depreciation and amortization of fixed assets.
             Amortization of discount on bonds payable.
             Losses on the sale of noncurrent assets.
    Deduct: Gains on the sale of noncurrent assets.
               Amortization of premium on bonds payable.
  Other sources:
    Proceeds from the sale of noncurrent assets (show entire proceeds—gain or loss adjusted as above).
    Sale of stock (regular issue or treasury stock).
    Noncurrent borrowing.

Uses of Working Capital:
  Purchase of noncurrent assets.
  Retirement of noncurrent debt.
  Purchase of treasury stock.
  Declaration of dividends.

Note: The above format assumes that funds are defined as working capital (current assets less current liabilities). If you wish to define funds as CASH, one change required is to analyze the current accounts (other than cash) and add the following section to your statement (included in "Cash Provided from Operations"):

Changes in current accounts:
Decrease in current assets	+
Increase in current liabilities	+
Increase in current assets	−
Decrease in current liabilities	− (net + or − added to or deducted in obtaining total sources)

In addition to the above change, the uses of funds for dividends must be adjusted if there was a change in the dividends payable account.

Comprehensive Illustration

The following example is used to illustrate the process of preparing a funds statement under both the working capital and cash concepts which have been discussed earlier in this chapter. Assume that the comparative balance sheet, income statement, and supplementary data for Lucas, Inc., is as follows:

Lucas, Inc.
Comparative Balance Sheet
December 31, 19x1 and 19x0

ASSETS	19x1	19x0	Increase (Decrease)
Current Assets:			
Cash	$ 40,000	$ 35,000	$ 5,000
Accounts receivable	90,000	70,000	20,000
Inventories	60,000	70,000	(10,000)
Prepaid expenses	20,000	15,000	5,000
Total Current Assets	$210,000	$190,000	$ 20,000
Noncurrent Assets:			
Land	$100,000	$ 50,000	$ 50,000
Buildings	220,000	200,000	20,000
Accumulated depreciation–buildings	(60,000)	(50,000)	(10,000)
Equipment	100,000	80,000	20,000
Accumulated depreciation–equipment	(20,000)	(10,000)	(10,000)
Patents	50,000	60,000	(10,000)
Total Noncurrent Assets	$390,000	$330,000	$ 60,000
Total Assets	$600,000	$520,000	$ 80,000

LIABILITIES AND STOCKHOLDERS' EQUITY			
Current Liabilities:			
Accounts payable	$ 60,000	$ 50,000	$ 10,000
Notes payable	20,000	30,000	(10,000)
Dividends payable	5,000	-0-	5,000
Accrued expenses	35,000	30,000	5,000
Total Current Liabilities	$120,000	$110,000	$ 10,000
Long-term liabilities:			
Bonds payable	$100,000	$150,000	$(50,000)
Stockholders' Equity:			
Common stock ($100 par value)	$260,000	$200,000	$ 60,000
Additional paid-in capital	40,000	30,000	10,000
Retained earnings	80,000	30,000	50,000
Total Stockholders' Equity	$380,000	$260,000	$120,000
Total Liabilities and Stockholders' Equity	$600,000	$520,000	$ 80,000

Lucas, Inc.
Income Statement
For the Year Ended December 31, 19x1

Sales		$1,500,000
Cost of goods sold		900,000
Gross margin		$ 600,000
Operating expenses:		
Depreciation and amortization expense	$ 40,000	
Selling and administrative expense	270,000	
Miscellaneous expense	175,000	
Total Operating Expenses		485,000
Net income from operations		$ 115,000
Other revenue and expense		
Add: Gain on sale of land		15,000
		$ 130,000
Less: Loss on sale of building	$10,000	
Interest expense	12,000	22,000
Net income before taxes		$ 108,000
Less: Income taxes		48,000
Net Income		$ 60,000

Supplementary data:

1. Cash dividends of $10,000 were declared during 19x1.
2. Depreciation on buildings and equipment and amortization of patent costs during 19x1 were as follows:

Buildings	$20,000
Equipment	10,000
Patents	10,000
Total	$40,000

3. Land valued at $80,000 was acquired in exchange for cash of $50,000 and common stock with a par value of $30,000.
4. A building with an original cost of $40,000 and accumulated depreciation of $10,000 was sold for $20,000.
5. A building was acquired for $60,000 cash.
6. Equipment was acquired for $20,000 cash.
7. Land with a cost of $30,000 was sold for $45,000.
8. Bonds payable of $50,000 were retired.
9. Common stock with $30,000 par value was sold for $40,000.

Preparation of Statement—Funds Defined as Working Capital

In this section, it is assumed that funds are defined as working capital. Details of the change in the working capital of Lucas, Inc., during 19x1 are shown below.

Lucas, Inc.
Statement of Changes in Working Capital
December 31, 19x1 and 19x0

	19x1	19x0	Working Capital Increase	Working Capital Decrease
Current Assets:				
Cash	$ 40,000	$ 35,000	$ 5,000	—
Accounts receivable	90,000	70,000	20,000	—
Inventories	60,000	70,000	—	$10,000
Prepaid expenses	20,000	15,000	5,000	—
Total Current Assets	$210,000	$190,000	—	—
Current Liabilities:				
Accounts payable	$ 60,000	$ 50,000	—	10,000
Notes payable	20,000	30,000	10,000	—
Dividends payable	5,000	-0-	—	5,000
Accrued expenses	35,000	30,000	—	5,000
Total Current Liabilities	$120,000	$110,000	—	—
Working capital	$ 90,000	$ 80,000	—	—
Increase in Working Capital				10,000
			$40,000	$40,000

To explain the $10,000 increase in working capital during 19x1, it is necessary to analyze all changes in the noncurrent accounts shown in the comparative balance sheet. Of course, the effect of net income and dividends is included in the change in retained earnings for the year. Explanations of the individual sources and uses of working capital included in the Statement of Changes in Financial Position follow:

1. *Land.* The acquisition of land for $80,000 is reported as a use of funds. Under the all financial resources concept, the partial payment by issuance of $30,000 of common stock is reported as a source of funds. The sale of land for $45,000 is also reported as a source of funds, while the gain on the sale of $15,000 is deducted from net income in determining working capital provided by operations.
2. *Building.* The sale of a building for $20,000 is reported as a source of funds and the $10,000 loss on the sale is added back to net income in determining working capital provided by operations. The acquisition of a building for $60,000 is reported as a use of funds.

3. *Accumulated Depreciation—Building.* The change in this account was $10,000. This change consisted of depreciation expense of $20,000 recorded during the year less $10,000 of accumulated depreciation which was removed from the account when the building was sold.
4. *Equipment.* The acquisition of equipment at a cost of $20,000 represents a use of funds.
5. *Accumulated Depreciation—Equipment.* The $10,000 change in this account was caused by the depreciation expense for the year.
6. *Patents.* The $10,000 decrease in the patents account resulted from the amortization of the cost of the patents during the year.
7. *Bonds Payable.* The decrease in bonds payable of $50,000 is reported as a use of funds since bonds were retired.
8. *Common Stock.* The $60,000 increase in common stock was caused by two transactions. The $30,000 par value of stock which was issued for land was reported as a source of funds under the all financial resources concept. Additionally, the $30,000 par value common stock which was sold for $40,000 represented a source of funds.
9. *Additional Paid-in Capital.* The $10,000 increase in this account was caused by the sale of common stock mentioned above.
10. *Retained Earnings.* The net increase in retained earnings resulted from net income for the period of $60,000 less the $10,000 cash dividend declared. The dividend is reported as a use of funds. The working capital provided by operations is computed as follows:

Net income		$ 60,000
Add: Depreciation and amortization	$40,000	
Loss on sale of building	10,000	50,000
		$110,000
Less: Gain on sale of land		15,000
Working capital provided by operations		$ 95,000

On the basis of the analysis of the noncurrent accounts, the statement which follows would be prepared.

This statement shows that of the total funds provided, less than half were generated by working capital provided by operations. Thus, the working capital provided by operations was sufficient to pay the dividends, but only a portion of the expansion in assets. The firm experienced an increase in working capital because it obtained $135,000 of funds from nonrecurring sources.

>
> **Lucas, Inc.**
> *Statement of Changes in Financial Position
> For the Year Ended December 31, 19x1*
>
> Working Capital Provided by:
>   Operations:
>   Net income . . . . $ 60,000
>   Add: Expenses not requiring outlay of
>   working capital during the
>   current period:
>   Depreciation and amortization $40,000
>   Loss on sale of buildings 10,000   50,000
> $110,000
>   Less: Gain on sale of land   15,000
>   Working Capital Provided by Operations . . . . . . $ 95,000
>   Sale of land . . . . $ 45,000
>   Sale of building   20,000
>   Sale of common stock   40,000
>   Common stock issued as part payment
>   for land   30,000   135,000
> $230,000
> Working Capital Applied to:
>   Acquisition of:
>   Land $80,000
>   Building 60,000
>   Equipment 20,000 $160,000
>   Retirement of bonds   50,000
>   Declaration of dividends   10,000   220,000
> Increase in Working Capital . . . . $ 10,000

Preparation of Statement—Funds Defined as Cash

The procedures which are necessary to prepare a statement of changes in financial position using the cash concept of funds are similar to those described in the previous section of this chapter. Additional steps, however, are necessary in order to determine dividends in terms of cash and cash flow from operations. Cash applied to dividends during the period is determined by adjusting the reported dividends for the change in the Dividends Payable account during the period. The amount of cash applied to dividends for Lucas, Inc. during 19x1 is as follows:

                Dividends $10,000
                Less: Increase in dividends payable   5,000
                Cash applied to dividends . . . . $ 5,000

Net income from operations was adjusted for nonfund expenses and nonrecurring gains and losses in determining the amount of working capital provided by operations. To determine cash provided by operations, net income must also be adjusted for changes in current assets (other than cash) and in current liabilities (other than dividends payable). These adjustments are necessary to convert the income statement data from the accrual to the cash basis and are reflected in the following statement of changes in financial position using the cash concept of funds.

Lucas, Inc.
Statement of Changes in Financial Position
For the Year Ended December 31, 19x1

Cash Provided by:			
Operations:			
Net income		$ 60,000	
Add:			
Depreciation and amortization	$40,000		
Loss on sale of building	10,000		
Decrease in inventories	10,000		
Increase in accounts payable	10,000		
Increase in accrued expenses	5,000	75,000	
		$135,000	
Deduct:			
Gain on sale of land	$15,000		
Increase in accounts receivable	20,000		
Increase in prepaid expenses	5,000		
Decrease in notes payable.	10,000	50,000	
Cash provided by operations			$ 85,000
Other sources:			
Sale of land		$ 45,000	
Sale of building		20,000	
Sale of common stock		40,000	
Common stock issued as partial			
payment of land		30,000	135,000
			$220,000
Cash Applied to:			
Acquisition of:			
Land	$80,000		
Building	60,000		
Equipment	20,000	$160,000	
Retirement of bonds		50,000	
Payment of dividends		5,000	215,000
Increase in Cash			$ 5,000

SUMMARY

The statement of changes in financial position is included as one of the major financial statements in annual reports. This statement is intended to provide a summary of the financing and investing activities of a firm and to disclose the changes in financial position that occurred during the period. The statement is divided into two major segments, one listing the sources of funds and the other listing the uses of funds. Although the term "funds" may be correctly interpreted to mean either cash or working capital, the working capital definition is often used for preparing the statement of changes in financial position. Under the all financial resources concept, those transactions involving a significant change in non-current accounts are also included on the statement as both a source and a use of funds.

The primary sources of working capital are current operations, the sale of noncurrent assets, long-term loans, and the sale of capital stock. Of these major sources, only the funds provided by current operations presents a degree of difficulty in its computation. In general, to derive the amount of funds provided by operations the net income of the firm must be adjusted for (1) those items that affect income but do not affect working capital and (2) nonoperating gains and losses.

The typical uses of working capital include purchases of noncurrent assets, repayment of long-term debt, repurchase of capital stock, and declaration of cash dividends. None of these uses require special adjustments in their computation.

If funds are defined as cash, the statement of changes in financial position will disclose individual sources and uses of cash and is commonly referred to as a cash flow statement. Although the general procedures for preparing the statement are basically the same as when the working capital definition of funds is used, several additional adjustments are necessary to convert a firm's net income to cash flow from operations.

This chapter concludes the discussion of common methods used to analyze a firm's financial position as reported in its financial statements. The next chapter will discuss a related issue, the effect on financial statements of changes in value and in the purchasing power of the dollar.

KEY DEFINITIONS

All financial resources This concept modifies "funds" to include not only those transactions affecting cash or working capital, but also those transactions of significant amount that affect the financing and investing activities of the firm, even though they involve only noncurrent accounts.

Cash concept of funds This concept defines funds in terms of cash or near-cash, and utilizes the funds statement to point out changes in the cash flow of the firm.

Cash disbursement Any outflow of cash by the firm is a cash disbursement.

Cash flow Any transaction that increases or decreases the cash balance of the firm is a cash flow.

Cash flow statement A cash flow statement is a statement summarizing the cash flows of the firm. It normally discloses the beginning cash balance, sources of cash receipts, types of cash payments, and the ending cash balance.

Cash from operations The net of cash receipts and disbursements for a period resulting from the normal operating activities of the firm. It is determined by adjusting each item in the income statement to a cash basis.

Cash receipt Any transaction that increases the cash account of the firm is a cash receipt.

Funds According to APB Opinion 19, funds are either cash, near cash, or working capital.

Funds from operations The effect on funds caused by the normal operating activities of the firm.

Funds statement See "Statement of Changes in Financial Position."

Noncurrent account An account that is neither a current asset nor a current liability.

Sources of funds Sources of funds involve any transaction that has caused funds to flow into a firm, i.e., any transaction that has increased working capital or cash, depending upon the definition of funds.

Statement of changes in financial position A statement of changes in financial position is a statement summarizing the financing and investing activities of the firm and disclosing changes in financial position.

Uses of funds Any transaction that has caused funds to flow out of the firm, i.e., any transaction that has decreased working capital or cash.

Working capital Working capital is the excess of current assets over current liabilities.

Working capital concept of funds This concept defines funds in terms of working capital, and utilizes the funds statement to point out changes in the working capital of the firm.

Working capital provided by operations This is the net effect on working capital from the normal operations of the business.

QUESTIONS

1. What are the four primary sources of working capital? What are four typical uses of working capital?

2. What are the steps in determining the sources and uses of working capital?

3. Can a firm with a loss for a period still have a source of working capital from operations for the period? If so, how?

4. Explain why depreciation expense is added back into operating income when determining the funds from operations.

5. What are the objectives of the "Statement of Changes in Financial Position"?

6. What are the two main parts of a Statement of Changes in Financial Position?

7. Why does APB *Opinion 19* broaden the concept of funds to "all financial resources"?

8. How are the following amounts computed?

    a. cash receipts from sales
    b. purchases
    c. cash disbursements for purchases
    d. cash disbursements for expenses

9. Discuss the different connotations of the term "funds" and the resulting effects on the Statement of Changes in Financial Position.

10. What are two ways of computing working capital from operations?

11. How do nonoperating gains and losses affect the computation of working capital from operations?

12. Is the declaration of a cash dividend to be paid at a later date a use of funds? Why or why not? What about subsequent payment of the dividend?

EXERCISES

13. Consider the following income statement for Wills Company.

Sales		$1,000,000
Cost of goods sold		750,000
Gross margin		$ 250,000
Selling and administrative expenses		
Salary expense	$50,000	
Depreciation expense	25,000	
Administrative expense	25,000	100,000
Net Income		$ 150,000

Required:

Compute the working capital from operations.

14. Below is the income statement for Lopes Company for the year ending December 31, 19x2.

Lopes Company
Income Statement
For the Year Ended December 31, 19x2

Sales (net)................................		$500,000
Cost of goods sold:		
Beginning inventory................	$ 50,000	
Purchases........................	300,000	
Goods available for sale............	$350,000	
Ending inventory...................	40,000	
Cost of goods sold................		310,000
Gross margin.......................		$190,000
Expenses:		
Wages...........................	$ 35,000	
Depreciation	30,000	
Advertising......................	15,000	
Administrative...................	5,000	85,000
Income from operations...............		$105,000
Gain on sale of equipment............		50,000
Net income.........................		$155,000

The following balances were derived from the balance sheet.

	December 31	
	19x2	19x1
Accounts receivable..................	$100,000	$90,000
Accounts payable....................	30,000	50,000
Prepaid advertising expense............	5,000	3,000
Wages payable......................	5,000	4,000

Required:

Prepare a schedule showing cash provided by operations.

15. Your examination of the financial statements of Russell Company reveals the following data.

	19x2		19x1	
Sales (net)......................		$100,000		$75,000
Cost of goods sold:				
Beginning inventory.............	$17,000		$12,000	
Purchases (net)................	58,000		55,000	
Goods available...............	$75,000		$67,000	
Ending inventory..............	15,000		17,000	
Cost of goods sold...........		$60,000		$50,000
Accounts payable................		20,000		25,000
Accounts receivable..............		50,000		45,000

Required:

Compute the following for 19x2:

1. Cash receipts from sales.
2. Cash disbursements for purchases.

16. Consider the following information for the period ending December 31, 19x1, concerning the Cey Company.

    a. Net income for 19x1 was $250,000.
    b. Depreciation expense on its buildings was $25,000. Accumulated depreciation on the buildings is $200,000.
    c. Extraordinary (non-operating) gains and losses included a loss of $50,000 on an uninsured building destoryed by fire.
    d. Dividends paid during the year in cash—$50,000.

Required:

Compute working capital from operations.

17. An outline of a statement of changes in financial position appears below. You may assume that the company operated at a profit for the year.

Crawford Company
Statement of Changes in Financial Position

Funds provided by:	
Operations:	
Net income	
Add..................................	(1)
Deduct...............................	(2)
Other sources of funds.....................	(3)
Funds applied to:	
Uses of funds.............................	(4)
Difference—change in working capital.	

For each of the items listed below determine in which of the designated positions, if any, the item would appear. *If more than one position is appropriate, so indicate.*

Answer Choices:

(1) Position 1; *(2)* Position 2; *(3)* Position 3; *(4)* Position 4; *(5)* None of these.

Items:

1. Declaration of a cash dividend............................. ( )
2. Payment of cash dividend after above declaration............. ( )
3. Depreciation expense for the year........................... ( )
4. Fully depreciated equipment written off the books............ ( )
5. Amortization of premium on long-term bonds payable........ ( )
6. Semiannual coupon *payments* on bonds mentioned in item #5 above... ( )
7. Sale of common stock at a discount........................ ( )
8. Purchase of treasury stock at a price above the original issue price... ( )
9. Payment of wages accrued at the end of the prior year......... ( )
10. Sale of fixed assets at a loss................................ ( )
11. Discounting the company's own 90-day note at a bank......... ( )
12. Sale of 10-year bonds at a discount........................ ( )
13. Three for one (3-1) split of the preferred stock................ ( )
14. Sale of machinery at a price in excess of its book value......... ( )
15. Amortization of goodwill................................. ( )

18. Wynn, Inc., hired you as an independent accountant to analyze the reasons for their unsatisfactory cash position. The company earned $42,000 during the year (19x1) but their cash balance is lower than ever. Your assistant prepared a worksheet providing you with the following information:

   a. Additional capital stock was sold in 19x1; the proceeds of the sale were $40,000.
   b. Vacant land purchased in 19x0 at a cost of $27,000 was sold in 19x1 for $30,000.
   c. A payment of $22,000 was made in 19x1 on a long-term mortgage.
   d. Equipment costing $89,000 was purchased during the year.
   e. Included in the firm's expenses for 19x1 were depreciation charges of $7,500.
   f. The firm's Accounts Receivable increased by $4,000 and their Accounts Payable decreased by $4,500 during the year.

   Required:

   Prepare a Cash Flow Statement for the year ended December 31, 19x1, which reflects the reasons for the firm's unsatisfactory cash position.

19. Put a check in the appropriate column or columns for each of the following items to indicate whether it is an application, a source, or neither in terms of (a) funds flow, and (b) cash flow.

	(a) Funds Flow	(b) Cash Flow
	Application Source Neither	Application Source Neither

1. Net income from operations
2. Purchase of treasury stock by company
3. Sale of bonds payable
4. Issuance of bonds payable for land
5. Sale of equipment at a gain
6. Declaration (but not payment) of cash dividends

20. From the following information prepare a statement of changes in financial position for the Sabre Company to determine the increase in working capital for 19x1.

    a. Net income for 19x1 was $6,000.
    b. Dividends paid during 19x1 were $2,000.
    c. Capital stock sales amounted to $2,000.
    d. Depreciation for the year was $2,000.
    e. Long-term bonds of $1,000 were retired.
    f. Land was purchased for $3,000.
    g. Land was sold for $6,000, resulting in a $2,000 gain.
    h. A building was purchased for $4,000.

21. Determine the amount of purchases, the cash disbursements for rent expense, and the cash applied to dividends for the Maple Leaf Company for the month of March from the information given below.

Cost of goods sold	$2,579
Increase in prepaid rent	864
Dividends	4,953
Rent expense	970
Increase in inventory	1,240
Decrease in dividends payable	691

22. Compute the increase or decrease in working capital for the Penguin Company from 19x1 to 19x2 from the following information:

	19x1	19x2
Taxes payable	0	$ 3,050
Common stock	$150,000	175,000
Inventory	9,700	10,000
Cash	21,370	15,950
Accrued wages	1,985	6,540
Dividends payable	7,500	0
Fixed assets	90,000	80,000
Accounts receivable	4,373	1,568
Accounts payable	3,000	2,000
Prepaid insurance	3,500	3,000
Notes payable	22,000	17,000

PROBLEMS

23. The comparative balance sheet of Buckner Corporation is as follows:

Buckner Corporation
Comparative Balance Sheet
December 31, 19x1 and 19x2

	19x2	19x1
ASSETS		
Current Assets:		
Cash	$ 50,000	$ 35,000
Accounts receivable	100,000	90,000
Inventory	60,000	65,000
Prepaid expenses	10,000	8,000
Total Current Assets	$220,000	$198,000
Fixed Assets:		
Building and equipment (net)	$200,000	$220,000
Land	50,000	50,000
Total Assets	$470,000	$468,000
LIABILITIES AND STOCKHOLDERS' EQUITY		
Accounts payable	$100,000	$ 80,000
Interest payable	10,000	10,000
Notes payable (current)	50,000	40,000
Capital stock	200,000	200,000
Retained earnings	110,000	138,000
Total Liabilities and Stockholders' Equity	$470,000	$468,000

Required:

Prepare a schedule computing the change in working capital.

24. Below is the income statement for the Rau Company for the year ended December 31, 19x1.

Rau Company
Income Statement
For the Year Ended December 31, 19x1

Sales		$1,000,000
Cost of goods sold:		
Beginning inventory	20,000	
Purchases	500,000	
Goods available for sales	$520,000	
Ending inventory	25,000	
Cost of goods sold		495,000
Gross margin		$ 505,000
Operating expenses:		
Salaries	$ 50,000	
Depreciation	20,000	
Bad Debts	10,000	
Advertising	20,000	
Patent amortization	5,000	
Total operating expenses		105,000
Operating income		$ 400,000
Gain on sale of equipment		50,000
Net Income		$ 450,000

Required:

Prepare a schedule computing working capital from operations.

25. Consider the following noncurrent account balances for Messerschmidt, Inc.

	\multicolumn{2}{c}{December 31}		
	19x2	19x1	Increase	Decrease
Buildings	$800	$1,000		$200
Accumulated depreciation—				
building	175	150	$ 25	
Land	300	200	100	
Bonds payable—long-term	200	100	100	
Capital stock	200	300		100
Retained earnings	300	150	150	
Working capital from 19x2 operations:	$100			

Required:

Prepare a Statement of Changes in Financial Position for Messerschmidt, Inc., for the period ending December 31, 19x2, assuming, where it is necessary, that the changes in the noncurrent accounts are the result of cash transactions. Funds are defined as working capital.

26. Given below are the balance sheets for Zahn Company for 19x1 and 19x2.

Zahn Company
Comparative Balance Sheet
December 31, 19x1 and 19x2

	19x1	19x2
Cash	$ 100	$ 300
Accounts receivable	400	350
Inventories	300	500
Fixed assets	900	1,000
Less: Accumulated depreciation	(100)	(200)
	$1,600	$1,950
Accounts payable	$ 400	$ 600
Bonds payable (due in 19x7)	400	200
Capital stock	500	700
Retained earnings	300	450
	$1,600	$1,950

Additional information:

The corporation paid a 10% stock dividend on January 2, 19x2, when its capital stock was selling at par. Net income for 19x2 was $200. During the year, the company sold a fixed asset with an original cost of $100 (and a book value of $25 at the date of sale) for $50. All other changes in the account are the results of transactions typically recorded in such accounts.

Required:

Prepare a statement of changes in financial position for Zahn Comany (where funds are defined as working capital).

27. The condensed comparative balance sheet for Marshall Company is presented below.

	December 31	
	19x2	19x1
ASSETS		
Cash	$ 80,000	$ 65,000
Accounts receivable (net)	100,000	90,000
Inventory	40,000	45,000
Prepaid expenses	12,000	10,000
Fixed assets	173,000	150,000
Accumulated depreciation—fixed assets	(35,000)	(30,000)
Total Assets	$370,000	$330,000
LIABILITIES AND STOCKHOLDERS' EQUITY		
Accounts payable	$ 80,000	$ 60,000
Bonds payable	150,000	150,000
Capital stock	100,000	100,000
Retained earnings	40,000	20,000
Total Liabilities and Stockholders' Equity	$370,000	$330,000

Supplemental data for 19x2.

  Net income............................ $20,000
  Depreciation expense................... 5,000
  A building was purchased for $23,000 cash.

Required:

Prepare a statement of changes in financial position based on changes in working capital.

28. Following are financial statements for Brewer, Inc.:

Brewer, Inc.
Comparative Balance Sheet
December 31, 19x2 and 19x1

	19x2	19x1	Increase (Decrease)
ASSETS			
Current Assets:			
Cash	$ 5,000	$ 45,000	$(40,000)
Accounts receivable	100,000	75,000	25,000
Inventories	50,000	45,000	5,000
Prepaid expenses	30,000	35,000	(5,000)
Total Current Assets	$185,000	$200,000	$(15,000)
Noncurrent Assets:			
Land	$100,000	$ 75,000	$ 25,000
Buildings	200,000	175,000	25,000
Accumulated depreciation—			
buildings	(50,000)	(40,000)	(10,000)
Equipment	100,000	75,000	25,000
Accumulated depreciation—			
equipment	(35,000)	(15,000)	(20,000)
Patents	20,000	30,000	(10,000)
Total Noncurrent Assets	$335,000	$300,000	$ 35,000
Total Assets	$520,000	$500,000	$ 20,000
LIABILITIES AND STOCKHOLDERS' EQUITY			
Current Liabilities:			
Accounts payable	$ 50,000	$ 40,000	$ 10,000
Notes payable	25,000	25,000	0
Accrued expenses	40,000	35,000	5,000
Total Current Liabilities	$115,000	$100,000	$ 15,000
Long-Term Liabilities:			
Bonds payable	$100,000	$140,000	$(40,000)
Stockholders' Equity:			
Common stock ($100 par value)	$230,000	$200,000	$ 30,000
Additional paid-in capital	40,000	30,000	10,000
Retained earnings	35,000	30,000	5,000
Total Stockholders' Equity	$305,000	$260,000	$ 45,000
Total Liabilities and Stockholder's Equity	$520,000	$500,000	$ 20,000

Brewer, Inc.
Income Statement
For the Year Ended December 31, 19x2

Sales		$2,000,000
Cost of goods sold		1,500,000
Gross margin		$ 500,000
Operating expenses:		
Depreciation and amortization expense	$ 50,000	
Selling and administrative expense	265,000	
Miscellaneous expense	170,000	
Total Operating Expenses		485,000
Net income from operations		$ 15,000
Other revenue and expense		
Add: Gain on sale of building		20,000
		$ 35,000
Less: Loss on sale of land	$ 10,000	
Interest expense	15,000	25,000
Net income before income taxes		$ 10,000
Less: Income taxes		5,000
Net Income		$ 5,000

Supplementary data:

a. Depreciation and amortization of patents were as follows:

Building	$20,000
Equipment	20,000
Patents	10,000
Total	$50,000

b. A building which cost $50,000 and had accumulated depreciation of $10,000 was sold for $60,000.
c. Common stock with $30,000 par value was sold for $40,000.
d. Land with a cost of $25,000 was sold for $15,000.
e. Land was purchased for $50,000.
f. Bonds of $40,000 were retired.
g. A building was purchased for $75,000.
h. Equipment was acquired for $25,000 cash.

Required:

Prepare statements of changes in financial position for Brewer, Inc. assuming:

1. Funds are defined as working capital.
2. Funds are defined as cash.

29. Below is information pertinent to John Corp. for the period ending December 31, 19x1.

    a. Sales, $50,000.
    b. Cost of goods sold, $20,000.
    c. Expenses, $10,000 (of which $2,000 was depreciation).
    d. Increase in accounts payable, $5,000.
    e. Increase in accounts receivable, $5,000.
    f. Sold land which cost $500 for $1,000 cash.
    g. Purchased a building for $10,000 cash and $10,000 par value common stock.
    h. Cash dividends paid, $5,000.
    i. Retired bond payable of $500.

    Required:

    Prepare a Statement of Changes in Financial Position assuming "funds" are defined as working capital.

30. From the following information prepare a statement showing in detail the sources and uses of working capital for 19x1.

Ferguson Company
Trial Balances
(in thousands)

	December 31, 19x1		December 31, 19x0	
Account	Debit	Credit	Debit	Credit
Cash	$ 178		$ 84	
Accounts receivable	300		240	
Allowance for bad debts		$ 13		$ 10
Merchandise inventory	370		400	
Building and equipment	420		360	
Allowance for depreciation		180		190
Accounts payable		220		210
Mortgage bonds		300		300
Unamortized bond discount	18		21	
Capital stock		357		270
Retained earnings		125		90
Net sales		4,200		4,000
Cost of goods sold	2,300		2,100	
Salaries and wages	1,500		1,400	
Administrative expense	110		100	
Depreciation expense	20		20	
Maintenance expense	10		10	
Interest expense	16		15	
Bad debt expense	20		20	
Loss on equipment sales*	6		0	
Dividends paid†	127		300	
	$5,395	$5,395	$5,070	$5,070

* In 19x1, equipment costing $40,000 and having a net book value of $10,000 was sold for $4,000.
† Dividends paid in 19x1 include a stock dividend of $27,000.

31. The trial balances of Canuck Company revealed the following information.

	December 31	
Debits	*19x1*	*19x2*
Cash	$ 14,000	$ 15,400
Accounts receivable (net)	26,600	33,600
Inventory	72,800	70,000
Prepaid expenses	4,200	5,600
Permanent investments	14,000	0
Buildings	126,000	168,000
Machinery	56,000	86,800
Patents	7,000	5,600
	$320,600	$385,000

Credits		
Accounts payable	$ 16,800	$ 11,200
Notes payable—short-term (nontrade)	12,600	18,200
Accrued wages	4,200	2,800
Accumulated depreciation	56,000	54,600
Notes payable—long-term	42,000	49,000
Common stock	168,000	210,000
Retained earnings	21,000	39,200
	$320,600	$385,000

Additional data:

a. Net income for 19x2 was $33,600.
b. Recorded depreciation on fixed assets was $11,200.
c. Amortization of patents was $1,400.
d. Machiney was purchased for $21,000; one-third was paid in cash; an interest-bearing note was given for the balance.
e. Common stock was issued to purchase machinery costing $35,000.
f. Old machinery which originally cost $25,200 (one-half depreciated) was sold for $9,800; the gain or loss was reported on the income statement.
g. Cash was paid for the building addition—$42,000.
h. Common stock was issued to pay a $7,000 long-term note.
i. Cash was received for the sale of permanent investment—$16,800.
j. Paid cash dividends.
k. Credit sales were $168,000.
l. Collections of accounts receivable were $161,000.

Required:

Prepare a statement of changes in financial position (cash basis).

32. The trial balances of Islander Company revealed the following information.

	December 31	
	19x1	19x2
Cash	$ 3,200	$ 4,000
Accounts receivable (net)	4,000	7,200
Inventory	8,000	9,600
Permanent investments	1,600	0
Fixed assets	24,000	37,600
	$40,800	$58,400
Accumulated depreciation	$ 4,000	$ 5,600
Accounts payable	2,400	4,000
Notes payable—short-term	3,200	2,400
Notes payable—long-term	8,000	14,400
Common stock	20,000	23,200
Retained earnings	3,200	8,800
	$40,800	$58,400

Additional data:

a. Net income was $11,200.
b. Depreciation was $1,600.
c. Permanent investments were sold at cost.
d. Dividends of $5,600 were paid.
e. Fixed assets were purchased for $4,000 cash.
f. A long-term note payable for $9,600 was given in exchange for fixed assets.
g. Common stock was issued to pay a $3,200 long-term note payable.

Required:

Prepare a statement of changes in financial position (cash basis).

33. Below is the balance sheet for Ranger Company comparing the years 19x1 and 19x2.

	December 31	
	19x2	*19x1*
ASSETS		
Cash	$ 25,000	$ 20,000
Accounts receivable (net)	90,000	75,000
Marketable securities	50,000	55,000
Prepaid expenses	15,000	13,000
Buildings	150,000	120,000
Accumulated depreciation—buildings	(85,000)	(65,000)
Total Assets	$245,000	$218,000
LIABILITIES AND STOCKHOLDERS' EQUITY		
Accounts payable	$ 71,000	$ 50,000
Bonds payable	100,000	80,000
Capital stock	50,000	60,000
Retained earnings	24,000	28,000
Total Liabilities and Stockholders' Equity	$245,000	$218,000

Additional information for 19x2:

Net income	$ 6,000
Cash dividends paid	10,000

Required:

By comparing the balance sheet for 19x2 and 19x1 and with the help of the above data:

1. Prepare a schedule computing the change in working capital.
2. Prepare a statement of changes in financial position for the year ended December 31, 19x2.

34. The 19x1 financial statements for the Alston Company are:

Alston Company
Income Statement
For the Year Ended December 31, 19x1

Net sales		$ 50,000
Cost of goods sold		30,000
Gross margin		$ 20,000
Operating expenses:		
Depreciation	$ 2,000	
Wage expense	7,000	
Other expenses	1,000	10,000
Net income from operations		$ 10,000
Gain on sale of land		5,000
Net income		$ 15,000

Alston Company
Retained Earnings Statement
For the Year Ended December 31, 19x1

Retained earnings at beginning of year	$25,000
Add: Net income	15,000
	$40,000
Subtract: Dividends	5,000
Retained earnings at end of year	$35,000

Alston Company
Comparative Balance Sheet

	December 31	
	19x1	*19x0*
ASSETS		
Cash	$ 69,000	$ 60,000
Accounts receivable	25,000	20,000
Inventories	15,000	10,000
Building	100,000	100,000
Accumulated depreciation—building	(27,000)	(25,000)
Land	125,000	100,000
Total Assets	$307,000	$265,000
LIABILITIES AND STOCKHOLDERS' EQUITY		
Accounts payable	$ 35,000	$ 15,000
Accrued wages payable	7,000	5,000
Bonds payable—long-term	130,000	120,000
Capital stock	100,000	100,000
Retained earnings	35,000	25,000
Total Equities	$307,000	$265,000

The following information is also available:

a. Land with a cost of $25,000 was sold for $30,000.
b. Additional land was purchased for $50,000.
c. A long-term bond was issued for $10,000.
d. $5,000 cash dividends were paid during the year.

Required:

Prepare a statement of changes in financial position for the Alston Company for the year ending December 31, 19x1 based on the:

1. "Working capital" concept of funds.
2. "Cash" concept of funds.

35. From the following pre-closing trial balances, prepare an income statement and a statement of changes in financial position for the year ended December 31, 19x1.

Rockies Incorporated
Trial Balances
(in thousands)
For the Year Ended December 31, 19x1

Account	December 31, 19x1 Debit	December 31, 19x1 Credit	December 31, 19x0 Debit	December 31, 19x0 Credit
Cash	$ 373		$ 26	
Accounts receivable	980		589	
Allowance for bad debts		$ 6		$ 3
Inventory	960		612	
Buildings	495		560	
Allowance for depreciation		170		100
Accounts payable		105		86
Bonds payable, due in 19x9		300		300
Unamortized bond premium, due in 19x2		19		20
Mortgage bond payable		0		50
Capital stock		250		280
Retained earnings		948		399
Net sales		3,100		3,297
Cost of goods sold	1,100		1,600	
Salaries expense	850		980	
Depreciation expense	135		135	
Interest expense	5		5	
Bad debt expense	15		16	
Gain on sale of building		25		0
Dividends	10		12	
	$4,923	$4,923	$4,535	$4,535

Additional information:

a. In 19x1, a building costing $65,000 was sold for $25,000. The building had been fully depreciated.
b. Capital stock was repurchased and retired.

36. The trial balance of Canadiens Company revealed the following information.

	December 31	
	19x1	19x2
Cash	$20,400	$ 20,700
Accounts receivable (net)	7,200	10,200
Inventory	9,600	8,400
Permanent investments	3,600	0
Fixed assets	48,000	55,800
Treasury stock	0	6,900
	$88,800	$102,000
Accumulated depreciation	$28,800	$ 23,400
Accounts payable	$11,400	$ 7,200
Bonds payable	6,000	18,000
Common stock	30,000	36,600
Retained earnings	12,600	16,800
	$88,800	$102,000

Additional information:

a. Credit sales were $42,000.
b. Credit purchases were $24,000.
c. Depreciation was $3,000.
d. Cash disbursements for expenses were $10,800.
e. Inventory decreased by $1,200.
f. Fixed assets were sold for $3,600; their original cost was $12,600 and two-thirds of this cost had been depreciated.
g. Fixed assets were purchased for $2,400 cash.
h. Bonds payable were issued for $18,000 to purchase fixed assets.
i. Permanent investments were sold for $5,400 cash.
j. Treasury stock was purchased for $6,900.
k. Bonds payable of $6,000 were retired by issuing common stock.
l. Accounts receivable collections were $39,000.
m. Accounts payable of $28,200 were paid.
n. Unissued common stock was sold for $600.

Required:

Prepare a statement of changes in financial position (cash basis) for the year ended December 31, 19x2.

Refer to the Annual Report included in the Appendix at the end of the text:

37. What was the total current assets and current liabilities at the end of the most recent year?

38. Compute working capital at the end of the most recent year?

39. Compute working capital provided by operations in the most recent year?

40. By what amount did working capital from operations increase/decrease in the most recent year?

41. Which component of working capital increased the most in the most recent year? Which component decreased the most?

42. What was the largest source of working capital in the most recent year?

43. Which current liability changed the most in the most recent year?

Learning Objectives

Chapter 18 examines the issues relating to the inclusion of current value and constant dollar or price-level information in financial statements. Studying this chapter should enable you to:

1. Discuss the basic concepts involved in current value and price-level adjustments.

2. Explain how a price-level index is derived.

3. Describe the effects of current value and general price-level changes on financial statements.

4. Prepare constant dollar or price-level adjusted financial statements from conventional statements.

5. Examine the advantages and disadvantages of including current value and constant dollar or price-level information in financial statements.

18 Accounting for Changing Prices

INTRODUCTION

As discussed previously, conventional financial statements are based on both the historical cost and the stable dollar concepts. Consequently, accounting data reflects past transactions recorded in terms of the number of dollars exchanged. However, because of the steady decline in the general purchasing power of the dollar and significant fluctuations in the values of certain assets, it has been suggested that financial information would be more useful if the historical cost and stable dollar concepts were abandoned.

There are two basic kinds of price changes that may be reflected in the accounting process: (1) changes in the general level of prices of all goods and services and (2) changes in the prices of specific items. In this chapter, we will examine the basic issues involved in modifying financial statements in order to incorporate these two types of price changes.

CONSTANT DOLLAR ACCOUNTING

A basic assumption underlying conventional accounting practice is that the unit of measure, the dollar, is a stable common monetary denominator of the accounting process. The result of this assumption is that accounting systems record the inflows and outflows of historical, or original, dollars. Since the amounts represented in account balances are stated in terms of original dollar flows, the accounting system is valid only if the value of the dollar remains stable over time. If inflation or deflation occurs, the value of the dollar changes. As a result, dollars of different purchasing power are entered and combined in the same account (or accounts) over a period of time. Therefore, even though all accounts in the financial statements include "dollars" they do not represent dollars of equal purchasing power. Combining dollars of different purchasing power in the accounts affects both the balance sheet and the income statement. Assets purchased at different times are reported in the financial statements in terms of dollars at the date of purchase. Thus, the account balance for a particular asset group (e.g., machinery) represents an aggregate amount comprised of dollars of unequal purchasing power. The cost of these assets, stated in dollars of both current and prior years, are allocated to depreciation expense. This expense is deducted from revenues which are expressed in terms of dollars of relative current purchasing power.

Adherence to the stable unit of measure assumption implies that changes in the purchasing power of the dollar are not significant. Obviously, the greater the fluctuation in purchasing power of the dollar over time, the less valid the stable monetary unit assumption and the resulting financial statements are.

In the United States, the rate of change in the purchasing power of the dollar was not considered particularly important until around 1940. With the steady increase in the level of prices both during and after World War II, however, there has been a growing concern with the limitations of financial statements based on the assumption of a stable monetary unit. As a result, numerous proposals have been made for the use of "constant dollar" accounting (which is also referred to as "price-level" accounting) to take into consideration the effects of changes in the purchasing power of the dollar. The means of providing constant dollar information and certain problems involved in this process are examined in this chapter.

MEASURE OF THE INSTABILITY OF THE DOLLAR

The change in the value or purchasing power of the dollar is measured by the changes over time in the amount of goods and services which a given quantity of money will buy. These movements in the price structure of goods and services as a whole are often referred to as shifts in the *general price level*. The purchasing power of the dollar is, of course, inversely related to the general level of prices. Thus, during periods of inflation, the general level of prices increases and the purchasing power of the dollar decreases. Similarly, a period of deflation results in a decrease in the general level of prices and a corresponding increase in the value of the dollar. Although the general level of prices cannot be measured in absolute terms, a relative measure of general price changes can be obtained by computing an index of the prices of a collection of goods and services during one period compared with the prices of these same goods and services during a selected base period. The price index of the base year is set equal to 100, and the prices of all other periods are stated as a percentage of this amount. For example, if the prices of all goods and services totaled $100,000 for the base period and $200,000 for a subsequent period, the price-level index would be 100 for the base period and 200 for the latter period. The ratio of the current index of prices to the index in the base period shows the percentage change in the prices of all goods and services which were included in the index. The change in the value of the dollar or the change in purchasing power is the reciprocal of the ratio of the price level index of two different periods. In the above example, the general price-level index increased from 100 in the base year to 200 in a later year. During this period prices have doubled while the purchasing power of the dollar has declined by one half.

Price-level index numbers may be used to convert dollars of one period into an equivalent number of dollars of purchasing power in another period. The conversion ratio is determined as follows:

$$\text{Conversion Ratio} = \frac{\text{Index of Current Year}}{\text{Index for the Year from Which You Are Adjusting Purchasing Power}}$$

To illustrate the use of a price-level index, assume that Staubach obtained $100 in cash several years ago when the price-level index was 100 and held this cash during a period when the price-level index increased to 200. Therefore, in terms of the current purchasing power, Staubach would now need $200 to have the equivalent purchasing power he possessed when the cash was originally received. This amount of dollars of equivalent purchasing power was computed as follows:

$$\$100 \times \frac{200}{100} = \$200$$

Theoretically, the measurement of changes in the general price-level should be based upon the prices of all goods and services in the economy. As a practical matter, however, price indexes are usually based upon a sampling of selected commodities. Therefore, price-level indexes provide only an estimation of the extent of inflation or deflation during a given period. In the United States there are several published indexes that provide estimates of the change in the general level of prices. These index values differ because each index is computed on the basis of prices of a different group of goods and services. Although there is not complete agreement as to the index that should be used for accounting purposes, the Financial Accounting Standards Board in its *Statement No. 33* required the use of the Consumer Price Index for All Urban Consumers for restating financial data for general price-level changes.

The extent of price changes in the United States as measured by the Consumer Price Index prepared by the United States Department of Commerce, is shown in the following table. In this index, the value for 1967, the base year, is equal to 100.

Year	Average Annual Consumer Price Index
1945	53.9
1950	72.1
1955	80.2
1960	88.7
1965	94.5
1967 (base year)	100.0
1970	116.3
1975	161.2
1980	247.3

This shows that the general level of prices increased more than 50 percent from 1975 to 1980 and that the price-level more than doubled in the period from 1970 to 1980. Similarly, it indicates that the purchasing power of the dollar is less than half as great in 1980 as it was in 1970.

EFFECTS OF GENERAL PRICE-LEVEL CHANGES

In determining the effects of general price-level changes, it is necessary to classify assets and liabilities as either monetary or nonmonetary items. Monetary items are assets and liabilities that are fixed in terms of dollars either by law or by contract and thereby do not change in terms of dollars when a change in the general price-level occurs. Monetary assets, which are in essence claims to a fixed quantity of dollars, include such items as cash, accounts receivable, and long-term investments in bonds. Monetary liabilities, which are obligations to pay a fixed amount of dollars, include debts such as accounts payable and notes payable. All other assets and liabilities which are not fixed in amount either by contract or law are referred to as nonmonetary items. The most common nonmonetary items include assets such as inventories, land, buildings, and equipment. Let us consider the effects of price-level changes on monetary items first.

Monetary Items

The number of dollars to be received (monetary asset) or paid out or expended (monetary liability) in the future remains fixed for a monetary item regardless of changes in the price level. Thus, if the amount of the monetary claims and obligations remains constant, a change in the purchasing power of the dollar results in general price-level gains or losses. For example, assume that Morton Company held $100,000 in cash (monetary asset) during a period when the price level increased from 100 to 150 (an increase of 50 percent in the price level). At the end of the period, Morton Company would need $150,000 ($150/100 \times \$100,000$) to maintain the same purchasing power at the end of the period that it held at the beginning of the period. That is, $150,000 would purchase the same amount of goods and services, in general, at the end of the period as could have been purchased for $100,000 at the beginning of the period. However, the cash available at the end of the period is the $100,000, and the result is a purchasing power loss of $50,000.

Holding a monetary liability during a period of changing prices has exactly the opposite effect. Suppose that Hill Company had borrowed $10,000 at the beginning of a year on a note which was due at year-end. If the price level increased by 50 percent during the year (i.e., the index increased from 100 to 150), the company would require $15,000 at the end of the year to repay the equivalent purchasing power of the $10,000 cash originally borrowed. However, since the $10,000 debt is fixed in amount, this amount is all that is required to satisfy the obligation and therefore Hill Company will have realized a purchasing power gain of $5,000 during the year. In other words, if you incur a liability during a period of increase in the price level you have a "gain" since you are repaying your debt in dollars that are "worth" less (i.e., have less purchasing power).

Based on the previous illustrations, it is apparent that during a period of increasing prices, a general price-level loss results from holding monetary assets and a general price-level gain results from holding monetary liabilities. Both are caused by the loss in the purchasing power of the dollar. On the other hand, during a period of decreasing prices, a general price-level gain results from holding monetary assets and a general price-level loss results from maintaining monetary liabilities, because of the increase in the purchasing power of the dollar.

Nonmonetary Items

Nonmonetary assets include those items of which the dollar price may fluctuate over time with changes in the general level of prices. Since the price of a nonmonetary asset may fluctuate with changes in the purchasing power of the dollar, there will be no gains or losses from changes in the general price level.

To illustrate the effect of a change in the general level of prices on a nonmonetary asset, assume that Garrison Company purchased land at the beginning of a year for $100,000. Garrison Company held the land during the year, and the price-level index increased from 100 at the beginning of the year to 110 at year-end. Land, a nonmonetary asset, can be restated for the change in price level since its acquisition. This restatement converts the cost of the land from original dollars to dollars of equivalent purchasing power at the end of the year. In this illustration the $100,000 acquisition cost of the land is equivalent to $110,000 ($100,000 × 110/100) in current dollars.

It should be noted that restatement of the original cost of a nonmonetary asset in terms of current dollars does not indicate either the current value or cost of that asset. Due to specific factors of supply and demand for a particular asset, the actual current value of the asset may be more or less than its original cost restated for price-level changes. Changing the unit of measurement does not really change the "amount" of the item. The restated amount simply indicates the amount of current dollars that are equivalent to original cost in terms of a stable monetary unit or purchasing power. This restatement of nonmonetary assets does not result in a price-level gain or loss, but adjusts the original costs of these items, regardless of the time of purchase, to equivalent dollars of current purchasing power.

PRICE-LEVEL ADJUSTED FINANCIAL STATEMENTS

Restating financial statements for changes in the general level of prices requires converting the "dollars" in unadjusted historical cost statements to current dollars of equivalent purchasing power. As previously indicated, this restatement requires that a distinction be made between monetary and nonmonetary items.

In a price-level adjusted balance sheet, each nonmonetary item should be converted into dollars of current purchasing power at the end of the current period. In restating these items, it is necessary to recognize the price-level change which has taken place since the time that *each* item was acquired. Since this conversion simply adjusts the original costs of these items to their current purchasing power equivalent, the restatement does not result in either a price-level gain or loss. Because monetary assets and liabilities are fixed in terms of dollars which will be received or paid, they are already stated in terms of their current purchasing power. Therefore, these items do not require any restatement in the balance sheet. Since these monetary claims and obligations remain constant while the purchasing power of the dollar fluctuates, a separate gain or loss on monetary items should be reported in the price-level adjusted income statement.

Many of the amounts which are reported in conventional income statements are not stated in terms of dollars of current purchasing power. For example, the annual depreciation charge is an allocation to expense of the original cost of fixed assets which were acquired at different times. Therefore, each income statement item should be converted to dollars of equivalent purchasing power at the end of the period. The converted revenues less the converted expenses is equal to the income before adjustment for general price-level gain or loss. This income amount plus or minus any gain or loss on monetary items equals the price-level adjusted net income for the period.

Illustration of Price-Level Adjusted Financial Statements

The following illustration indicates the basic procedures which are required for the restatement of financial statements in terms of dollars of uniform purchasing power. This illustration is based on the operations of Typo Co., a company engaged in typing and copying services, for 19x6. Typo Co. began its operation on January 1, 19x2. The illustration assumes the following hypothetical general price-level index at the end of each year from 19x1 through 19x6 (19x5 is the base year).

End of Year	*Price Level*
19x1	60
19x2	65
19x3	70
19x4	80
19x5	100
19x6	120

A conventional income statement reporting the results of operations for 19x6 and conventional balance sheets indicating the financial position at the end of 19x5 and 19x6 are presented below.

Typo Co.
Income Statement
For the Year Ended December 31, 19x6

Service revenues....................		$110,000
Operating expenses:		
Salaries and wages	$ 55,000	
Supplies expense	22,000	
Depreciation of equipment	10,000	
Depreciation of building..............	10,000	
Total operating expenses		97,000
Net Income		$ 13,000

Typo Co.
Balance Sheets
December 31, 19x5 and 19x6

	December 31	
ASSETS	19x5	19x6
Cash	$ 5,000	$ 25,000
Accounts receivable..................	25,000	75,000
Equipment........................	120,000	120,000
Less: Accumulated depreciation...........	(10,000)	(20,000)
Building	250,000	250,000
Less: Accumulated depreciation...........	(40,000)	(50,000)
Total Assets	$350,000	$400,000
LIABILITIES		
Accounts payable....................	$ 13,000	$ 50,000
STOCKHOLDERS' EQUITY		
Capital stock......................	$275,000	$275,000
Retained earnings...................	62,000	75,000
Total Stockholders' Equity	$337,000	$350,000
Total Liabilities and Stockholders' Equity.....	$350,000	$400,000

The following additional information is assumed in the illustration:

1. The price-level increased uniformly during each year. Therefore, the average index for a year is the average of the index values at the end of the current year and the end of the previous year. For example, the average index for 19x6 is 110 or $\left(\frac{120 + 100}{2}\right)$.

2. It is assumed that the service revenues were earned uniformly or evenly throughout the year and that the wage and supplies expense were incurred evenly during the year.

3. The building was purchased on January 1, 19x2, for $250,000. It has an estimated useful life of 25 years, and depreciation was recognized at $10,000 per year. Therefore, the accumulated depreciation balance is $50,000 and the book value of the building is $200,000 at the end of 19x6.
4. The existing equipment was purchased on December 31, 19x4, for $120,000. It has an estimated useful life of 12 years, and depreciation is recognized at $10,000 per year. Since the equipment is two years old, accumulated depreciation at the end of 19x6 is $20,000 and the book value is $100,000.
5. The capital stock was issued at the date the firm was organized.

PREPARATION OF THE RESTATED INCOME STATEMENT

An income statement for the year ended December 31, 19x6, restated for changes in the general level of prices, is shown in Illustration 1. Each item included in the conventional income statement was converted to dollars of equivalent purchasing power at the end of 19x6.

Illustration 1

Typo Co.
Income Statement Adjusted for Price-Level Changes
For the Year Ended December 31, 19x6

	Conventional Income Statement	Conversion Ratio	Price-Level Adjusted Statement
Service revenues	$110,000	120/110	$120,000
Operating expenses:			
Salaries and wages	55,000	120/110	60,000
Supplies expense	22,000	120/110	24,000
Depreciation—equipment	10,000	120/80	15,000
Depreciation—building	10,000	120/60	20,000
Total Expenses	$ 97,000		$119,000
Income before price-level loss	$ 13,000		$ 1,000
General price-level loss (see Illustration 2)			(6,400)
Net Loss After Price-level Loss			($ 5,400)

Normally firms earn revenues and incur expenses at various times during the year. Theoretically each amount of revenue earned and expense incurred during the year should be separately converted to end-of-year dollars. However, for practical purposes, it is usually assumed that revenues are earned and expenses incurred uniformly throught the year. Therefore, the average price-level for the period may be used in making the conversion.

Revenues

Since services are assumed to be performed evenly throughout the year, the service revenue balance is restated in terms of dollars of the average purchasing power for the year. In order to restate the service revenues in dollars of equivalent purchasing power at the end of the year, the balance is multiplied by the ratio of the end of 19x6 index to the average index for the year $\frac{120 + 100}{2}$.

$$\$110,000 \times \frac{120}{110} = \$120,000$$

Expenses Which Affect Monetary Items

Wage expense and supplies expense were also assumed to have been incurred evenly throughout the year. Thus, these expenses are restated in terms of end-of-year dollars by multiplying them by the ratio of the end of 19x6 index to the average index for the year.

$$\text{Wage Expense:} \quad \$55,000 \times \frac{120}{110} = \$60,000$$

$$\text{Supplies Expense:} \quad \$22,000 \times \frac{120}{110} = \$24,000$$

Allocated Expenses

Depreciation expense on the conventional income statement represents an allocation of the cost of a building acquired five years ago and the allocation of the cost of equipment acquired two years ago. Therefore, conventional depreciation is stated in terms of the purchasing power at the time of the acquisition of the assets. The restated amount can be calculated by adjusting the depreciation on a historical cost basis to 19x6 dollars. To restate depreciation expense on equipment, the conventional amount is multiplied by the ratio of the index at the end of 19x6 to the index at the time the equipment was acquired in 19x4 (80). Similarly, the restated depreciation expense on the building is computed by multiplying the unadjusted depreciation expense by the ratio of the index at the end of 19x6 to the index at the date of acquisition, January 1, 19x2 (60). These calculations are as follows:

$$\text{Depreciation} - \text{Equipment} \quad \$10,000 \times \frac{120}{80} = \$15,000$$

$$\text{Depreciation} - \text{Building} \quad \$10,000 \times \frac{120}{60} = \$20,000$$

Monetary Gains and Losses

Restatement of revenue and expense items in the conventional income statement provides the income for the period before any adjustment for price-level gain or loss on monetary items. The net price-level loss of $6,400 included in Illustration 1 resulted because the loss in purchasing power from holding monetary assets exceeded the gain in purchasing power from holding monetary liabilities during a period of increasing prices. The price-level loss is computed by comparing the net monetary assets available to the firm during the year expressed in terms of end-of-year dollars with the actual net monetary items held at the end of the year. The restated net monetary items available to the firm during the year equal the monetary assets and liabilities at the beginning of the period (restated to end-of-year dollars) plus increases in monetary items from revenues and decreases in monetary items from expenses during the year (again restated to end-of-year dollars). The depreciation expense is omitted from this computation because it represents an allocation of a cost incurred in a previous period and does not affect monetary items during the current year.

Illustration 2

Typo Co.

Computation of Price-Level Loss

	Balance on Conventional Statement	Conversion Factor	Restated Amount
Beginning net monetary assets 12/31/x5:			
Cash	$ 5,000	120/100	$ 6,000
Accounts receivable	25,000	120/100	30,000
Accounts payable	(13,000)	120/100	(15,600)
	$ 17,000	120/100	$ 20,400
Add: Increase in monetary items during the year:			
From sales	110,000	120/110	120,000
Less: Decrease in monetary items during the year:			
Salaries and wages	(55,000)	120/110	(60,000)
Supplies expense	(22,000)	120/110	(24,000)
Net monetary items available during the year in end-of-year purchasing power			$ 56,400
Ending net monetary assets 12/31/x6:			
Cash	$ 25,000		
Accounts receivable	75,000		
Accounts payable	(50,000)		50,000
General Price-Level Loss			$ (6,400)

PREPARATION OF THE RESTATED BALANCE SHEET

A balance sheet at December 31, 19x6, restated for the general price-level change is presented below. Since monetary assets and liabilities are fixed in

Typo Co.
Balance Sheet Adjusted for Price-Level Changes
December 31, 19x6

ASSETS	Conventional Balance Sheet	Conversion Ratio	Price-Level Adjusted Statement
Cash	$ 25,000	NA	$ 25,000
Accounts receivable	75,000	NA	75,000
Equipment	120,000	120/80	180,000
Less: Accumulated depreciation	(20,000)	120/80	(30,000)
Building	250,000	120/60	500,000
Less: Accumulated depreciation	(50,000)	120/60	(100,000)
Total Assets	$400,000		$650,000
LIABILITIES			
Accounts payable	$ 50,000	NA	$ 50,000
STOCKHOLDERS' EQUITY			
Capital stock	$275,000	120/60	$550,000
Retained earnings	75,000		50,000
Total Stockholders' Equity	$350,000		$600,000
Total Liabilities and Stockholders' Equity	$400,000		$650,000

amount, the balances for cash, accounts receivable and accounts payable are the same in the price-level adjusted balance sheet as in the unadjusted balance sheet. The nonmonetary assets, equipment and buildings, are restated to end-of-year dollars by multiplying the conventional balances by the ratio of the current-year price index to the index at the time the assets were acquired. Similarly, capital stock is expressed in terms of original dollar investment at the date of organization of the firm. This amount is restated in terms of current dollars by multiplying the conventional balance by the ratio of the 19x6 price index to the index at the date the stock was issued.

$$\text{Equipment: } \$100,000 \times \frac{120}{80} = \$150,000$$

$$\text{Building: } \$200,000 \times \frac{120}{60} = \$400,000$$

$$\text{Capital Stock: } \$275,000 \times \frac{120}{60} = \$550,000$$

The retained earnings balance of $50,000 in the price-level-adjusted balance sheet is equal to the restated assets less the restated liabilities and capital stock. This amount can also be determined by deducting the net loss from the price-level adjusted income statement from the price-level adjusted beginning retained earnings in terms of end-of-year dollars. The beginning retained earnings in end-of-year dollars can be computed by converting the December 31, 19x5, balance sheet amounts to end-of-19x6 dollars.

	December 31, 19x5 Conventional Balance	Conversion Ratio	19x6 Dollars
Cash	$ 5,000	120/100	$ 6,000
Accounts receivable	25,000	120/100	30,000
Equipment	120,000	120/80	180,000
Less: Accumulated depreciation	(10,000)	120/80	(15,000)
Buildings	250,000	120/60	500,000
Less: Accumulated depreciation	(40,000)	120/60	(80,000)
Accounts payable	(13,000)	120/100	(15,600)
Capital stock	(275,000)	120/60	(550,000)
Retained earnings at 12/31/x5—the balancing amount	$ 62,000		$ 55,400

Note: Credit balances are indicated by parentheses.

Thus, the beginning and ending balances of retained earnings in the price-level adjusted balance sheet may be reconciled as follows:

```
Retained Earnings, January 1 (End-of-year Dollars) ............... $55,400
Net Loss After Price-Level Loss (Illustration 1) ................... (5,400)
Retained Earnings, December 31 ............................... $50,000
```

CURRENT STATUS OF GENERAL PRICE-LEVEL ADJUSTED STATEMENTS

A basic argument for the presentation of price-level adjusted financial statements as a supplement to conventional financial statements is that the effects of changes in the purchasing power of the dollar are eliminated in the adjusted statements. Specifically, in the supplementary income statement, all revenues and expenses are stated in terms of dollars of common size or purchasing power. Similarly, all items in the supplementary balance sheet are expressed in terms of uniform or "common size" dollars. In addition, adjusted statements reveal gains or losses from holding monetary assets or owing monetary liabilities. Obviously, the greater the change in the purchasing power of the dollar over time, the greater is the potential benefit of the supplementary price-level adjusted statements.

Currently, however, there is not complete agreement as to the need for and the usefulness of price-level adjusted statements even as supplements to conventional financial statements. A major point of opposition is that the presentation of two different sets of financial statements for one period could result in considerable confusion to the users of financial statements. A second argument against the presentation of restated data is that since the general level of prices has increased only moderately during the past decade in the United States, the adjusted statements would not differ significantly from conventional statements. Recently, however, this argument has been less and less true. In any case, it should be remembered that the cumulative effect of inflation or deflation since the acquisition of assets by a firm affects the adjustment of fixed assets in the balance sheet and the related depreciation expense in the income statement. Thus, moderate inflation over a period of several years could result in significant differences between historical and adjusted financial statements.

The issue of price-level adjusted financial statements is currently unresolved. The Accounting Principles Board, in its *Statement No. 3* issued in 1969, concluded that supplementary statements ". . . present useful information not available from basic historical statements." However, the Board also stated that price-level information is not required for fair presentation of financial data in conformity with generally accepted accounting principles at this time. As a result, very few firms have made an attempt to include price-level adjusted data in their annual reports.

The Financial Accounting Standards Board issued an exposure draft in late 1974 which proposed that general price-level adjusted statements be required as supplementary information in published annual reports. The adjustments required by this proposal followed essentially the same procedures given in APB *Statement No. 3*. However, the Board suspended action on this draft until after the public hearings, scheduled for 1977 and early 1978, on a discussion memorandum regarding the conceptual framework for financial accounting and reporting.

In September 1979, the FASB issued *Statement of Accounting Standards No. 33*, "Financial Reporting and Changing Prices" that requires certain large companies to disclose specified supplementary constant dollar information. *Statement No. 33* does not require a comprehensive application of historical cost/constant dollar accounting to each financial statement item. Instead, the Board decided to focus on those items most often affected by inflation — inventories, property, plant and equipment, and monetary assets and liabilities. Therefore, the *Statement* requires disclosure for the current year of only:

1. Historical income from continuing operations adjusted for average current year constant dollar measurements of cost of goods sold and depreciation, depletion and amortization. (Generally, a constant dollar adjustment for cost of goods sold would not be necessary for a company that uses LIFO.)
2. Purchasing power gain or loss on net monetary items.

The *Statement* calls for the use of the average current year index for making the required adjustments. The General Restatement Rule may be expressed by the following formula:

$$\frac{\text{Constant Dollar}}{\text{Amount}} = \frac{\text{Historical}}{\text{Cost Amount}} \times \frac{\text{Average-for-the-Year Index}}{\text{Date-of-Acquisition Index}}$$

The Board has chosen the Consumer Price Index for All Urban Consumers (CPI) to measure general inflation, principally because this index is made available on a monthly basis. The supplementary disclosures were required to be included in annual reports for all years ending after December 25, 1979. While the required disclosures are limited to certain items by *Statement No. 33*, companies may present comprehensive supplementary financial statements on a constant dollar basis, if they wish to do so.

CURRENT VALUE ACCOUNTING

Conventional financial statements reflect transactions recorded in terms of the number of dollars exchanged. Such historical-dollar statements generally measure exchange values at the transaction date and ignore changes in value until another transaction occurs. With the significant price changes occurring over the past several years (and a steady increase in the general level of prices), there has been a growing concern about the usefulness of historical-dollar statements. It has been argued that substantial differences between the current values and historical costs of certain assets reduces the validity of data provided by conventional statements. Consequently, various proposals have been made to generate financial data reflecting price changes.

Current Value Approaches

There are several different measurement methods for valuing assets (and liabilities). The three most commonly proposed concepts of value (in addition to historical cost) are: current cost—i.e., current input price, current exit value, and present value—i.e., discounted future cash flows. While all these alternatives fall under the general approach of reflecting current values in financial statements, both the techniques of application and the resulting financial statements differ under the various approaches. The basics of each of the alternative measurement methods are discussed briefly below.

1. Historical Cost. This method is based on actual transactions prices, and value changes are not recognized until a completed transaction takes place. The historical cost basis is well understood and is considered to be objective and verifiable. The most frequently cited disadvantages of the historical cost basis are that the income statement may reflect a matching of current revenues with "old" costs (i.e., the amortization of long-lived assets) and that certain assets may be substantially undervalued in the balance sheet. Conventional accounting practice is essentially based on a modified historical cost approach since some assets are valued at amounts other than historical cost (for example, lower of cost or market for marketable securities or inventories).

2. Current Cost. Current cost is the cost that would be currently required to obtain the same asset. The "same asset" may refer to either an identical asset or an asset with equivalent productive capacity. The primary advantages attributed to this approach are that the matching of current costs against current revenues provides a more meaningful income measure and that the current valuation yields a more realistic balance sheet. Since current costs are not based on actual transactions by the firm, varying degrees of subjectivity are necessary in obtaining the values. Another potential disadvantage of this basis is that current cost may not be relevant to the firm—particularly when technological changes have occurred in the production process.

3. Current Exit Value. Current exit value is the price at which an asset could be sold in an orderly liquidation (preferably the quoted market price for an asset of similar kind or condition). The use of current exit value results in reporting income or loss prior to the final exchange of the product or service. The potential limitation of this concept is the loss of objectivity—the fact that certain assets have no quoted market values. Also questionable is the relevance of asset liquidation value when there is no intention to liquidate the firm.

4. Present Value. The present value is the discounted amount of net cash inflows associated with an asset. The present value is often considered to be the best obtainable measure of an asset's value because it is directly related to future cash flows. This valuation concept requires estimation of three factors: (*a*) the net cash flows—inflows and outflows—resulting from the use or disposition of the asset; (*b*) the timing of the cash flows; and (*c*) an appropriate discount factor. The present value of an asset is equal to the sum of the net cash flows for each year multiplied by the present value of one dollar at the selected discount rate. The present value approach is generally not considered to be a realistic valuation model for several reasons: (*a*) it is usually impossible to predict the amount and timing of future cash flows with any reasonable degree of accuracy; (*b*) it is difficult to establish an appropriate discount factor; and (*c*) when two or more factors are involved in the production process, it is usually impossible to logically allocate the future cash flows to the separate assets.

Proponents of current value accounting argue that historical dollar statements do not adequately reflect the real economic position of a business. The balance sheet is considered inadequate because many of the assets are reported at historical costs, and the income statement is considered deficient because many of the expenses which are matched against current revenues are based on costs determined from historical transactions.

The primary argument of the opponents of the current value approach is that current values are too subjective—current values may not be available at a reasonable cost for many assets, and changes in technology of new assets further complicates the problem. Some contend that the impression resulting from the use of current values would destroy the reliability of financial statements. Others admit that current values may be of marginal use, but contend that the benefits are not worth the extra costs involved for both the preparers and users of financial data.

It should be apparent that there is no single concept or procedure for the valuation of assets that is generally considered to be ideal in generating financial information. Thus, one of the major issues to be resolved in accounting is: *In preparing financial statements, should accounting remain primarily on a historical cost basis, or should it shift to some measure of current value?* The resolution of this issue will, of course, have a profound effect on the nature of financial accounting and reporting in the future.

FASB Statement No. 33

FASB *Statement No. 33* which requires selected constant dollar disclosures (discussed previously in this chapter) also calls for certain current cost disclosures to be made in a company's annual report to shareholders and in its Form 10-K. The current cost disclosures focus on the specific price changes for individual assets rather than price changes caused by general inflation. The current cost measurements are generally based on the replacement cost of assets presently owned by the company.

As under the historical cost/constant dollar basis, the Board focuses upon current cost accounting for inventories and property, plant and equipment. Companies are required to disclose for the current year:

1. Historical income from continuing operations adjusted for current cost measurements for both cost of goods sold and depreciation expense.
2. Increases or decreases in current cost amounts of inventories and property, plant and equipment, net of the effects of general inflation.
3. Current cost of inventories and net current cost of property, plant and equipment as of the most recent balance sheet date.

The FASB's current cost basis includes elements of current cost/constant dollar accounting. For example, the inflation component of the increase or decrease in current costs is a current dollar concept, which enables a comparison of how the specific price changes of a company's resources fared against general inflation. Also, companies wishing to present comprehensive supplementary financial statements on a current cost/constant dollar basis may do so, if they wish.

The *Statement* allows companies considerable flexibility in selecting methods of determining current cost, ranging from indexing historical costs with specific price indexes to direct pricing techniques (e.g., invoices, unit pricing). Resources and income producing real estate properties are exempted from the current cost disclosures.

Companies are also required to present a five-year summary of selected financial data to assist users of financial statements in assessing trends. In addition to the required current year historical cost/constant dollar and current cost information discussed above, this summary must include the following information, all expressed in constant dollars:

1. Net assets at year-end under the historical cost/constant dollar basis and the current cost basis.
2. Per share amounts of income from continuing operations under the historical cost/constant dollar basis and the current cost basis.
3. Net sales and other operating revenues.
4. Cash dividends per share.
5. Market price per share at year-end.
6. Average consumer price index.

Only the sales, dividends, market price, and consumer price index disclosures are required to be reported for years prior to 1979.

Although all of the information included in the five-year summary must be presented in constant dollars, companies have a choice between using current year dollars or base period dollars (currently 1967). If companies present the information in current year dollars, the prior year information must be restated (rolled forward to current year dollars) each year. Companies that use base period dollars avoid the annual restatement problem but will show different amounts of income from continuing operations in the five-year summary and the current year disclosures (which must be in current dollars), perhaps a more confusing result.

These disclosures were effective for fiscal years ending after December 24, 1979. However, only public companies having *either* $1 billion of assets *or* $125 million of inventories and gross properties at the beginning of the year are required to present the supplemental information.

SUMMARY

Various proposals have been made to provide financial data which reflect changes in price. In general, these proposals have been of two fundamental types—general price level adjustments, and current value adjustments—because there are two types of price changes involved. One kind of price change is concerned with changes in the general price level for all goods and services in the economy. Changes in prices in general reflect the change in the value of money. A second kind of price change relates to the changes in prices of specific goods or services. Accounting for the general price changes is referred to as general price-level adjustments and accounting for changes in specific prices is referred to as current value accounting. Financial statements adjusted for changes in the general price level rely on historical cost data; price-level restatements merely restate cost figures in terms of dollars of equivalent purchasing power. Current value accounting, on the other hand, abandons the historical cost basis of accounting and reports an entity's assets and liabilities (and changes therein) on the basis of one of several means of determining current value. Although general price-level adjustments and current value accounting are by no means alternative or competing methods, they are often regarded as such by their proponents.

The basic accounting assumption regarding the stability of the dollar is currently under attack because of significant fluctuations in the purchasing power of the dollar. Financial statements prepared under price-level accounting are intended to consider the effect of these fluctuations in the purchasing power of the dollar. Such financial statements may provide useful information as supplements to the usual financial statements prepared on a historical cost basis, but are not required for fair presentation of financial position.

The change in the value or purchasing power of the dollar is reflected in shifts in the general price level which is determined by reference to a base year. A conversion ratio is used to convert dollars of one period into an equivalent number of dollars of purchasing power in another period. This conversion ratio concept is the basis for restating conventional financial statements into price-level adjusted statements. Only monetary assets and liabilities are already stated in terms of current purchasing power and therefore do not require conversion. However, since such items are fixed in terms of dollars, a monetary gain or loss can result from holding them during a period of changing prices.

Although price-level adjusted statements may be beneficial in eliminating the effects of changes in price levels, their presentation may be confusing to the typical financial statement user. Their inclusion in annual reports is not currently in widespread use.

Until recently, the primary emphasis in the United States was toward price-level accounting. The Accounting Principles Board recommended in

1969 that price-level statements be provided as supplemental to the basic historical cost statements. In 1974, the FASB issued an exposure draft which contained a requirement that financial statements include certain price-level data. However, just as it appeared that price-level accounting was going to be adopted, several developments occurred which appear to have shifted attention from general price-level adjustments to current value accounting.

In 1976, the FASB withdrew its exposure draft on price-level accounting explaining that the need for such data was not sufficiently demonstrated to justify the cost of implementation. At about the same time there was a noticeable increase in attention over current value reporting. This trend is evidenced by a recent decision of the SEC to require that certain replacement cost data be disclosed in the footnotes to financial statements of approximately 1,000 of the largest nonfinancial corporations in the United States. In addition, proposals were developed by authoritative organizations in both Britain and Australia suggesting a current-cost approach to the valuation of assets and the measurement of income.

In September 1979, the FASB issued *Statement No. 33*, "Financial Reporting and Changing Prices". This *Statement* requires certain large publicly held companies to disclose specified constant dollar *and* current cost information.

KEY DEFINITIONS

Consumer price index The consumer price index for all urban consumers is a measure of the general price level in the United States. It is required by FASB *Statement No. 33* for use in preparing constant dollar disclosures.

Conversion ratio The ratio of the price index in the current year to the price index for the year from which purchasing power is adjusted. It is used to convert dollars from one period into an equivalent number of dollars in terms of purchasing power at another time.

Current cost The cost that would be currently required to obtain the same asset.

Current exit value The price at which an asset could be sold in an orderly liquidation (preferably the quoted market price for an asset of similar kind or condition).

Deflation Deflation is a general decrease in the average prices of goods and services over time; consequently, there is a corresponding increase in the purchasing power of the dollar.

General price level This is the average price of a collection of goods and services in the economy during one period compared with the prices of the same goods and services during a selected base period.

General price-level gain or loss Gain or loss in general purchasing power from holding monetary assets and liabilities during a period of inflation or deflation.

General purchasing power of the dollar This concept involves the ability of the dollar to buy goods and services in general.

Inflation Inflation is a general increase in the average prices of goods and services over time; consequently, there is a corresponding decrease in the purchasing power of the dollar.

Monetary assets Monetary assets are cash or claims to a fixed number of dollars in the future.

Monetary items Cash and other balance sheet accounts which represent a fixed number of dollars to be received or paid in the future are monetary items.

Monetary liabilities Monetary liabilities are obligations of a fixed amount of dollars to be paid in the future; these include accounts payable, notes payable, and long-term debt.

Nonmonetary items Nonmonetary items are those items which do not represent a fixed number of dollars to be received or paid in the future. These include inventories, plant and equipment, and stockholders' equity.

Present value The discounted amount of net cash inflows associated with an asset.

Price index A price index is a relative measure of the general price-level over time. It is obtained by computing the ratio of the prices of a collection of goods and services during one period with the prices of the same goods during a selected base period.

Price-level adjusted financial statements These are financial statements adjusted for changes in the general level of prices.

Purchasing power gain or loss This is the same as general price-level gain or loss.

Restatement of nonmonetary items The amounts of nonmonetary items are restated to dollars of current general purchasing power at the end of the period for which general price-level adjusted statements are prepared.

Stable unit of measure The use of money as the unit of measure implies that the value of the dollar is constant over time and hence is a stable unit of measure.

QUESTIONS

1. What is a price index? How is it derived?

2. What is meant by general price-level adjusted financial statements? What are some of the arguments for price-level adjusted statements? Against them?

3. Distinguish between monetary assets and nonmonetary assets.

4. What general price index is recommended by the FASB for price-level accounting purposes and why was it chosen?

5. What are the effects of holding monetary assets and liabilities in periods of inflation and deflation?

6. What is the stable-dollar assumption in the traditional accounting process? Why may comparisons of dollar amounts in conventional financial statements be misleading?

7. What is a conversion ratio? What is its use?

8. What are the effects of holding nonmonetary assets in periods of inflation or deflation?

9. Does the restatement of the original cost of a nonmonetary asset in terms of current dollars indicate the current value or cost of that asset?

10. To what extent must monetary assets be adjusted on a restated balance sheet?

11. What is the theoretically correct treatment for the conversion of expenses and revenues in price-level adjusted income statements? What is the practical treatment?

12. Define the three most commonly advocated concepts of current value.

13. List three arguments in opposition to recognizing current values in financial statements.

EXERCISES

14. In 19x0 Shackleford Company received $400 which was placed in a safe and forgotten. Nine years later, the cash was found by a company secretary and reported to the controller. Out of curiosity, the controller wishes to determine the cash needed at present in order to have the equivalent purchasing power the company possessed when the cash was originally received. Determine the amount, given each of the following sets of price indexes.

    a.   19x0 = 120;   19x9 = 80.
    b.   19x0 = 75;   19x9 = 125.
    c.   19x0 = 120;   19x9 = 80.

15. Determine the price-level for 19x1 through 19x4 using 19x3 as the base year, given the following information.

Year	Prices of a Market Basket of All Goods and Services
19x1	$2,300
19x2	2,400
19x3	2,500
19x4	2,750
19x5	3,000
19x6	3,125

16. The Walton Company purchased a machine at the beginning of 19x1 when the price-level index was 150. The machine, which cost $20,000 and had no salvage value, was depreciated using the straight-line method over a period of 20 years. The company purchased a building on January 1, 19x2, at a cost of $100,000 when the index was 200. The building had an expected life of 40 years and no salvage value, and was depreciated using the straight-line method. The depreciation expense for 19x3 is $1,000 for the machine and $2,500 for the building. The price-level index at the end of 19x3 is 250. What is the depreciation expense for 19x3 restated for changes in the price-level?

17. Data for 19x2 and the two preceding years are given below.

	Sales	Price Index
19x2	$500,000	200
19x1	400,000	140
19x0	300,000	100

Restate the sales for each year in terms of current-year dollars. What is revealed by a comparison of the restated amounts?

18. Brown Corp. purchased land in 19x0 for $100,000. Adjust the asset to end-of-year prices for each year from 19x1 to 19x9. Assume the following price-level index.

Year	Index	Year	Index
19x0	100	19x5	150
19x1	110	19x6	160
19x2	115	19x7	180
19x3	125	19x8	190
19x4	140	19x9	200

19. The Patsy Company purchased equipment on January 1, 19x0, for $20,000 when the price index was 80. The equipment has a 10-year life, no salvage value, and straight-line depreciation is used. The price index increased to 100 on December 31, 19x0, 120 on December 31, 19x1, and 180 on December 31, 19x2. What was the adjusted depreciation expense for 19x0, 19x1, and 19x2? Convert the historical machine account and accumulated depreciation balances at December 31, 19x2, to 19x2 dollars.

20. The Pun Co. purchased a machine on December 31, 19x0, for $55,000 when the price-level index was 100. The machine had a salvage value of $5,000 and an estimated life of 20 years, and is to be depreciated using the straight-line method. Assume that the price-level index at the end of each of the subsequent five years was as follows:

Year	Index
19x1	110
19x2	120
19x3	140
19x4	130
19x5	150

From the above information determine the values at which the depreciation expense and the machine (net of depreciation) will be included in the price-level adjusted financial statements each year from 19x1 to 19x5.

21. Joe College borrowed $10,000 in 19x0 in order to pay for his college education. Joe will graduate in June 19x4 and the loan is due one year after graduation. No interest is paid until that time. What would be Joe's purchasing power gain or loss if he repaid the loan when it became due, assuming each of the following sets of price indexes:

a. 19x0 = 80;   19x4 = 110.
b. 19x0 = 75;   19x4 = 130.
c. 19x0 = 105; 19x4 = 90.

22. The sales for the last eight quarters of the Cowboy Company are listed below:

19x0
1st	$10,000
2nd	11,500
3rd	12,300
4th	13,200

19x1
1st	14,000
2nd	15,600
3rd	15,800
4th	16,000

The *average* price index for the first quarter of 19x0 was 110 and this *average* increased by 3 points in each of the next seven quarters. The price index as of the last day of 19x1 was 132.

Required:

1. Prepare a list of average price-level indexes for each of these eight quarters and calculate conversion ratios using the index for the last day of 19x1 as the base figure.

2. Adjust each quarter's sales figures to sales dollars as of the last day of 19x1 using the conversion ratio previously calculated. What do you notice about the last three quarters of 19x1?

23. From the following unadjusted information of the Redskin Company, compute the general price-level gain or loss for 19x1.

	December 31, 19x0	December 31, 19x1
Cash	$ 3,000	$10,500
Accounts receivable	6,000	8,000
Accounts payable	4,100	4,600
Sales	38,000	36,000
Expenses needing a cash outlay	29,000	27,000
General price-level index	140	160

PROBLEMS

24. The price index increased from 100 to 120 during 19x0 and from 120 to 140 during 19x1. Shown below is a condensed income statement of Hanna Company for 19x1.

Hanna Company
Income Statement
For the Year Ended December 31, 19x1

Revenues		$100,000
Expenses:		
Wages	$40,000	
Supplies expense	15,000	
Miscellaneous expense	5,000	
Depreciation expense	25,000	85,000
Net income		$ 15,000

The depreciation expense was recorded on equipment purchased at the beginning of 19x0. All other expenses were incurred evenly during the current year and revenues were earned evenly throughout the year. Adjust the company's income statement for price-level changes (assume that the general price-level loss from holding net monetary items was determined to be $2,400).

25. State whether there has been a purchasing power gain, loss, or no change in each of the following situations (also state the amount of the gain or loss).

  a. Sum of $50,000 cash held over a period when the price-level decreased from 125 to 75.
  b. Land purchased for $25,000 held over a period when the price-level increased from 95 to 105.
  c. Account payable for $950 incurred when the price-level was 120 and paid when the price-level was 150.
  d. Bonds worth $200,000 issued when the price-level was 100 and redeemed when the price-level was 85.

e. Purchase of $10,000 of inventory when the price-level was 87, held until the price-level was 103.
f. Sale of $4,500 of goods on account when the price-level was 95, and account receivable was collected when the price-level was 110.

26. The conventional financial statements for the FEE Corporation on December 31, 19x5, are presented below.

FEE Corporation
Income Statement
For the Year Ended December 31, 19x5

Service revenue............................		$220,000
Wage expense.............................	$85,000	
General and administrative expense............	82,000	
Depreciation expense—building................	15,000	
Depreciation expense—equipment..............	15,000	197,000
Net income.............................		$ 23,000

FEE Corporation
Balance Sheet
December 31, 19x5

ASSETS

Cash...	$ 40,000
Accounts receivable..................................	30,000
Prepaid expenses.....................................	15,000
Building (net of accumulated depreciation)..............	150,000
Equipment (net of accumulated depreciation)............	54,000
Total Assets......................................	$289,000

LIABILITIES AND SHAREHOLDERS' EQUITY

Accounts payable....................................	$ 50,000
Capital stock...	200,000
Retained earnings.....................................	39,000
Total Liabilities and Shareholders' Equity..............	$289,000

The equipment was purchased on December 31, 19x2, and the building on December 31, 19x0. All of the stock was issued on December 31, 19x0. Assume that all revenues and expenses are earned and incurred evenly throughout the year and that the price-level changed at a constant rate each year. Prepare a price-level adjusted income statement and balance sheet for December 31, 19x5, assuming the following price-level indexes at the end of each year:

Year	Index
19x0	80
19x1	95
19x2	90
19x3	95
19x4	120
19x5	100

Assume that the general purchasing power gain for the year was determined to be $20,000.

27. Assume the following price-level indexes at the end of each year from 19x0 through 19x4:

Year	Index
19x0	60
19x1	80
19x2	90
19x3	100
19x4	120

A conventional income statement for 19x4 and a conventional balance sheet for 19x3 and 19x4 for the Comp Company are presented below.

Comp Company
Income Statement
For the Year Ended December 31, 19x4

Sales revenues		$280,000
Operating expenses:		
Wage expense	$140,000	
Miscellaneous expense	70,000	
Depreciation of equipment	25,000	
Depreciation of building	25,000	260,000
Net income		$ 20,000

Comp Company
Balance Sheet
December 31, 19x3 and 19x4

	December 31	
	19x3	*19x4*
ASSETS		
Cash	$ 10,000	$ 50,000
Accounts receivable	20,000	30,000
Equipment (net of accumulated depreciation)	125,000	100,000
Building (net of accumulated depreciation)	225,000	200,000
Total Assets	$380,000	$380,000
LIABILITIES		
Accounts payable	$ 20,000	0
STOCKHOLDERS' EQUITY		
Capital stock	$300,000	$300,000
Retained earnings	60,000	80,000
Total Stockholders' Equity	$360,000	$380,000
Total Liabilities and Stockholders' Equity	$380,000	$380,000

Assume that all revenues and expenses were earned and incurred evenly throughout each year and that the price-level increased evenly in each year. The building was purchased on December 31, 19x1, and the equipment on December 31, 19x2. All stock was issued when the company was formed, at which time the index was 40.

Required:

Prepare the 19x4 income statement and balance sheet adjusted for price-level changes.

28. Assume that the price-level index is 100 at the end of 19x0 and 200 at the end of 19x1. The following balances existed at the beginning of 19x1:

Cash	$200,000
Accounts receivable	150,000
Accounts payable	100,000

During 19x1 revenues of $180,000 were earned and expenses of $150,000 were incurred. The ending balances are:

Cash	$250,000
Accounts receivable	175,000
Accounts payable	145,000

Compute the price-level gain or loss assuming revenues were earned and expenses incurred evenly throughout the period.

29. The following information was derived from the December 31, 19x1, balance sheet of Easy Company.

> Cash .... $ 20,000
> Accounts receivable 40,000
> Equipment 100,000
> Building 150,000
> Accounts payable 50,000
> Capital stock 200,000

The price-level index was 100 on December 31, 19x1, and 120 on December 31, 19x2. All capital stock was issued on December 31, 19x0 when the index was 80. The equipment was purchased on December 31, 19x1, and the building on December 31, 19x0. The net loss on the price-level adjusted income statement for 19x2 was $10,000. What is the price-level adjusted retained earnings at December 31, 19x2?

30. The conventional adjusted trial balance for the Viking Company is presented below:

Viking Company
Trial Balance
As of December 31, 19x4

	Dr.	Cr.
Cash	$ 14,000	
Accounts receivable	24,000	
Equipment	225,000	
Accumulated depreciation—equipment		$ 56,250
Interest payable		15,000
Long-term note payable		59,750
Capital stock		50,000
Retained earnings		25,125
Revenues		160,000
Salaries and wages	40,000	
Supplies expense	20,000	
Interest expense	15,000	
Depreciation expense	28,125	
	$366,125	$366,125

Additional information:

1. Revenues, salaries and wages, and supplies expense were incurred evenly throughout the year.
2. The equipment was purchased on January 1, 19x3. It has an estimated useful life of eight years and no salvage value.
3. The long-term note payable was issued on January 1, 19x2. Interest is paid once a year on January 1.

4. All the capital stock was issued on January 1, 19x1, when the corporation was formed.
5. The general price-level index at the end of each year from 19x0 through 19x4 is listed below:

End of Year	Price-Level
19x0	110
19x1	115
19x2	125
19x3	130
19x4	135

Required:

1. Prepare a restated income statement assuming the general price-level loss is $13,600.
2. Prepare a restated balance sheet by converting to dollars of equivalent purchasing power at the end of 19x4.

31. The conventional income statement for 19x6 and the conventional balance sheet for 19x5 and 19x6 for the Steeler Company are presented below.

Steeler Company
Income Statement
For the Year Ended December 31, 19x6

Revenues	$560,000
Operating expenses:	
Salaries and wages	280,000
Depreciation on equipment	14,000
Miscellaneous expense	200,000
Net income	$ 66,000

Steeler Company
Balance Sheet
December 31, 19x5 and 19x6

	19x6	19x5
ASSETS		
Cash	$100,000	$ 20,000
Accounts receivable	60,000	40,000
Equipment	400,000	400,000
Less: Accumulated depreciation	(38,000)	(24,000)
	$522,000	$436,000
LIABILITIES AND EQUITIES		
Accounts payable	$ 70,000	$ 50,000
Capital stock	324,000	324,000
Retained earnings	128,000	62,000
	$522,000	$436,000

All revenues, salaries and wages, and miscellaneous expenses were incurred evenly throughout the year. The price-level was 85 at the beginning of 19x6 and was 92 at the end of 19x6. The company owns two pieces of equipment. One was purchased for $240,000 on December 31, 19x3 when the price-level was 70. It is being depreciated over a period of 24 years. The other piece of equipment was purchased for $160,000 on December 31, 19x4 when the price-level was 78. It is being depreciated over 40 years. All stock was issued in 19x0 when the price-level was 62.

Required:

1. Prepare the 19x6 income statement adjusted for price-level changes and supported by the computation of the price-level gain or loss.
2. Prepare the 19x6 adjusted balance sheet and prove the balancing retained earnings figure.

32. Select the best answer for each of the following items:

a. The valuation basis used in conventional financial statements is

1. Market value.
2. Original cost.
3. Replacement cost.
4. A mixture of costs and values.
5. None of the above.

b. An unacceptable practice for presenting general price-level information is

1. The inclusion of general price-level gains and losses on monetary items in the general price-level statement of income.
2. The inclusion of extraordinary gains and losses in the general price-level statement of income.
3. The use of charts, ratios and narrative information.
4. The use of specific price indexes to restate inventories, plant and equipment.
5. None of the above.

c. When general price-level balance sheets are prepared, they should be presented in terms of

1. The general purchasing power of the dollar at the latest balance sheet date.
2. The general purchasing power of the dollar in the base period.
3. The average general purchasing power of the dollar for the latest fiscal period.
4. The general purchasing power of the dollar at the time the financial statements are issued.
5. None of the above.

d. The restatement of historical-dollar financial statements to reflect general price-level changes results in presenting assets at

1. Lower of cost or market values.
2. Current appraisal values.
3. Costs adjusted for purchasing power changes.
4. Current replacement cost.
5. None of the above.

e. During a period of deflation, an entity would have the greatest gain in general purchasing power by holding

1. Cash.
2. Plant and equipment.
3. Accounts payable.
4. Mortgages payable.
5. None of the above.

f. When preparing general price-level financial statements, it would not be appropriate to use

1. Cost or market, whichever is lower, in the valuation of inventories.
2. Replacement cost in the valuation of plant assets.
3. The historical cost basis in reporting income tax expense.
4. The actual amounts payable in reporting liabilities on the balance sheet.
5. Any of the above.

g. For comparison purposes general price-level financial statements of earlier periods should be restated to the general purchasing power dollars of

1. The beginning of the base period.
2. An average for the current period.
3. The beginning of the current period.
4. The end of the current period.
5. None of the above.

h. In preparing price-level financial statements, monetary items consist of

1. Cash items plus all receivables with a fixed maturity date.
2. Cash, other assets expected to be converted into cash and current liabilities.
3. Assets and liabilities whose amounts are fixed by contract or otherwise in terms of dollars regardless of price-level changes.
4. Assets and liabilities which are classified as current on the balance sheet.
5. None of the above.

i. In preparing price-level financial statements a nonmonetary item would be

1. Accounts payable in cash.
2. Long-term bonds payable.
3. Accounts receivable.
4. Allowance for uncollectible accounts.
5. None of the above.

(AICPA, adapted)

33. The conventional income statement for 19x2 and the conventional balance sheet for 19x1 and 19x2 for the Raider Company are presented below.

Raider Company
Income Statement
For the Year Ended December 31, 19x2

Revenues	$800,000
Expenses:	
Salaries	680,000
Rent expense	130,000
Depreciation expense	28,000
Net loss	($38,000)

Raider Company
Balance Sheet
December 31, 19x1 and 19x2

	19x2	19x1
ASSETS		
Cash	$ 200,000	$ 80,000
Accounts receivable	140,000	100,000
Investment in Chief Company bonds	60,000	60,000
Buildings	880,000	880,000
Less: Accumulated depreciation	(104,000)	(76,000)
	$1,176,000	$1,044,000
LIABILITIES AND EQUITIES		
Accounts payable	$ 274,000	$ 104,000
Capital stock	900,000	900,000
Retained earnings	2,000	40,000
	$1,176,000	$1,044,000

All revenues, salaries, and rent expenses were incurred evenly throughout the year. The price-level was 90 at the beginning of 19x2 and increased by 7 during the year. The company owns two buildings. Building 1 was purchased for $600,000 four years ago when the price-level measured 72. It is being depreciated over 30 years. Building 2 was purchased for $280,000 three years ago when the price-level was 77. It is being depreciated over 35 years. The investment in Chief Company bonds was made on December 31, 19x0 when the price-level was 85. All stock was issued at the same time Building 1 was purchased.

Required:

1. Prepare the 19x2 income statement adjusted for price-level changes and supported by the computation of the price-level gain or loss.
2. Prepare the 19x2 adjusted balance sheet and prove the balancing retained earnings figure.

34. Select the best answer for each of the following items.

a. Gains and losses on nonmonetary assets usually are reported in historical-dollar financial statements when the items are sold. Gains and losses on the sale of nonmonetary assets should be reported in general price-level financial statements

1. In the same period, but the amount will probably differ.
2. In the same period and the same amount.
3. Over the life of the nonmonetary asset.
4. Partly over the life of the nonmonetary asset and the remainder when the asset is sold.
5. None of the above.

b. If land were purchased in 19x0 for $100,000 when the general price-level index was 100 and sold at the end of 19x9 for $160,000 when the index was 170, the general price-level statement of income for 19x9 would show

1. A general price-level gain of $70,000 and a loss on sale of land of $10,000.
2. A gain on sale of land of $60,000.
3. A general price-level loss of $10,000.
4. A loss on sale of land of $10,000.
5. None of the above.

c. If land were purchased at a cost of $20,000 in January 19x0 when the general price-level index was 120 and sold in December 19x6 when the index was 150, the selling price that would result in no gain or loss would be

1. $30,000.
2. $24,000.
3. $20,000.
4. $16,000.
5. None of the above.

d. If the base year is 19x0 (when the price index = 100) and land is purchased for $50,000 in 19x6 when the general price-index is 108.5, the cost of the land restated to 19x6 general purchasing power (rounded to the nearest whole dollar) would be

1. $54,250.
2. $50,000.
3. $46,083.
4. $45,750.
5. None of the above.

e. Assume the same facts as in item d. The cost of the land restated to December 31, 19x9 general purchasing power when the price-index was 119.2 (rounded to the nearest whole dollar) would be

1. $59,600.
2. $54,931.
3. $46,083.
4. $45,512.
5. None of the above.

The following information is applicable to items f through i: Equipment purchased for $120,000 on January 1, Year 1 when the price-index was 100, was sold on December 31, Year 3 at a price of $85,000. The equipment originally was expected to last six years with no salvage value and was depreciated on a straight-line basis. The price-index at the end of Year 1 was 125, at Year 2 was 150 and at Year 3 was 175.

f. The general price-level financial statements prepared at the end of the Year 1 would include

1. Equipment of $150,000, accumulated depreciation of $25,000 and a gain of $30,000.
2. Equipment of $150,000, accumulated depreciation of $25,000 and no gain or loss.
3. Equipment of $150,000, accumulated depreciation of $20,000 and a gain of $30,000.
4. Equipment of $120,000, accumulated depreciation of $20,000 and a gain of $30,000.
5. None of the above.

g. In general price-level comparative financial statements prepared at the end of Year 2, the Year 1 financial statements should show equipment (net of accumulated depreciation) at

1. $150,000.
2. $125,000.
3. $100,000.
4. $80,000.
5. None of the above.

h. The general price-level financial statements prepared at the end of Year 2 should include depreciation expense of

1. $35,000.
2. $30,000.
3. $25,000.
4. $20,000.
5. None of the above.

i. The general price-level income statement prepared at the end of Year 3 should include

1. A gain of $35,000.
2. A gain of $25,000.
3. No gain or loss.
4. A loss of $5,000.
5. None of the above.

(AICPA, adapted)

Refer to the Annual Report included in the Appendix at the end of the text:

35. What year's dollars were used to adjust for inflation?

36. What effect did adjusting depreciation and amortization expense to constant dollars have?

37. What effect did adjusting depreciation and amortization expense to current cost have?

38. What is the income for the most recent year in historical dollars? In constant dollars? In current dollars?

Learning Objectives

Chapter 19 discusses common techniques of analyzing information presented in financial statements. Studying this chapter should enable you to:

1. Distinguish between horizontal and vertical analyses and discuss the type of information that is provided by each.

2. Discuss the concept of ratio analysis and identify the problems that may be inherent in its use.

3. List the most commonly used standards against which a firm may be compared and explain the strengths and limitations associated with the use of these standards.

4. Describe and apply the basic techniques of financial analysis as they are used by common stockholders, long-term creditors, and short-term creditors.

19 Financial Statement Analysis

INTRODUCTION

The financial statements of a business enterprise are intended to provide much of the basic data used for decision-making and, in general, evaluation of performance by various groups such as current owners, potential investors, creditors, government agencies, and in some instances, competitors. Because general-purpose published financial statements are by their very nature issued for a wide variety of users, it is often necessary for particular user groups to extract the information in which they are particularly interested from the statements. For example, owners and potential investors are normally interested in the present earnings and future earnings prospects of a business. Similarly, short-term creditors are primarily concerned with the ability of a firm to meet its short-term obligations as they become due and payable. Consequently, a somewhat detailed analysis and interpretation of financial statements is usually required in order to obtain the information which may be relevant for the specific purposes of a particular user. In this chapter, several selected techniques which are useful in financial analysis will be described and discussed.

COMPARATIVE FINANCIAL STATEMENTS

In general, the usefulness of financial information is increased when it can be compared with related data. Comparison may be internal (i.e., within one firm) or external (i.e., with another firm). External comparisons may be difficult to make in practice since financial statements of firms may not be readily comparable because of the use of different generally acceptable accounting principles. However, some useful information may be obtained by comparison with industry averages, ratios, etc. (such as those compiled by *Moody's* and *Standard and Poor's*) or by direct comparison with the statements of another firm. Obviously, considerable caution must be exercised when making this type of analysis.

The financial statements of a particular firm are most useful when they can be compared with related data from within the current period, information from prior periods, or with budgets or forecasts. Comparative statements are useful in providing a standard which facilitates the analysis and interpretation of changes and trends which have occurred in elements of the financial statements. Generally, published annual reports of corporations provide comparative accounting statements from the previous period and often also include selected historical information for the firm for a longer period of time, such as ten years.

Assume that the income statement of a firm for the year ended December 31, 19x2, disclosed net income of $100,000. This information, in and of itself, provides a user with only a single indicator of the absolute amount of income for the year. If an income statement for 19x1, disclosing net income of $80,000 was also presented, 19x2 net income would become much more meaningful information to the user. The 25 percent increase of 19x2 income over that for 19x1 indicates a significant improvement in performance that could not be determined from the 19x2 statements alone.

BASIC ANALYTICAL PROCEDURES

Comparisons of financial statement data are frequently expressed as percentages or ratios. These comparisons may represent:

1. Percentage increases and decreases in an item in comparative financial statements;
2. Percentage relationships of individual components to an aggregate total in a single financial statement; or
3. Ratios of one amount to another in the financial statements.

Application of each of these three methods will be illustrated by the use of the comparative financial statements of Dolbey Company which follow. These comparative statements will also serve as a basis for the analysis presented in the remainder of this chapter.

Dolbey Company
Comparative Balance Sheet
December 31, 19x2 and 19x1

	19x2 Dollars	19x2 Percent of Total Assets	19x1 Dollars	19x1 Percent of Total Assets	Increase (Decrease) Dollars	Increase (Decrease) Percent
ASSETS						
Current assets:						
Cash	$ 80,000	5.0	$ 40,000	2.8	$ 40,000	100.0
Net accounts receivable	100,000	6.3	80,000	5.5	20,000	25.0
Inventories	200,000	12.5	160,000	11.1	40,000	25.0
Prepaid expenses	20,000	1.2	8,000	.6	12,000	150.0
Total Current Assets	$ 400,000	25.0	$ 288,000	20.0	$112,000	38.9
Land, buildings, and equipment (Net)	1,200,000	75.0	1,152,000	80.0	48,000	4.2
Total Assets	$1,600,000	100.0	$1,440,000	100.0	$160,000	11.1
LIABILITIES						
Current liabilities:						
Accounts payable	$ 200,000	12.5	$ 130,000	9.0	$ 70,000	53.8
Notes payable	100,000	6.3	60,000	4.2	40,000	66.7
Total Current Liabilities	$ 300,000	18.8	$ 190,000	13.2	$110,000	57.9
Bonds payable	200,000	12.5	200,000	13.9	-0-	-0-
Total Liabilities	$ 500,000	31.3	$ 390,000	27.1	$110,000	28.2
STOCKHOLDERS' EQUITY						
Common stock ($30 par)	$ 900,000	56.2	$ 900,000	62.5	-0-	-0-
Retained earnings	$ 200,000	12.5	$ 150,000	10.4	$ 50,000	33.3
Total Liabilities and Stockholders' Equity	$1,600,000	100.0	$1,440,000	100.0	$160,000	11.1

Horizontal Analysis

Analysis of increases or decreases in a given financial statement item over two or more accounting periods is often referred to as horizontal analysis. Generally, this type of analysis discloses both the dollar and percentage changes for the corresponding items in comparative statements. An example of horizontal analysis is included in the comparative financial statements presented for Dolbey Company. These statements include data with regard to income, retained earnings, and financial position for a two-year period with the dollar and percentage changes for each item listed in the final two columns.

Dolbey Company
Comparative Income Statement
For the Years Ended December 31, 19x2 and 19x1

	19x2 Dollars	19x2 Percent of Sales	19x1 Dollars	19x1 Percent of Sales	Increase (Decrease) Dollars	Increase (Decrease) Percent
Net sales	$2,000,000	100.0	$1,500,000	100.0	$500,000	33.3
Cost of goods sold	1,400,000	70.0	1,080,000	72.0	320,000	29.6
Gross profit on sales	$ 600,000	30.0	$ 420,000	28.0	$180,000	42.9
Operating expenses:						
Selling expenses	$ 300,000	15.0	$ 240,000	16.0	$ 60,000	25.0
Administrative expenses	180,000	9.0	129,000	8.6	51,000	39.5
Total Operating Expenses	$ 480,000	24.0	$ 369,000	24.6	$111,000	30.1
Operating income	$ 120,000	6.0	$ 51,000	3.4	$ 69,000	135.3
Interest expense	10,000	.5	9,000	.6	1,000	11.1
Income before income taxes	$ 110,000	5.5	$ 42,000	2.8	$ 68,000	161.9
Income taxes	30,000	1.5	12,000	.8	18,000	150.0
Net Income	$ 80,000	4.0	$ 30,000	2.0	$ 50,000	166.7

Dolbey Company
Comparative Statement of Retained Earnings
For the Years Ended December 31, 19x2 and 19x1

	19x2	19x1	Increase (Decrease) Dollars	Increase (Decrease) Percent
Retained earnings, January 1	$150,000	$135,000	$15,000	11.1
Net income	80,000	30,000	50,000	166.7
	$230,000	$165,000	$65,000	39.4
Less: Dividends	30,000	15,000	15,000	100.0
Retained earnings, December 31	$200,000	$150,000	$50,000	33.3

Data from the 19x0 statements:
- Total assets (December 31, 19x0) $1,160,000
- Stockholders' equity (December 31, 19x0) 1,035,000
- Net receivables (December 31, 19x0) 70,000
- Inventory (December 31, 19x0) 110,000

Interpretation of the increases or decreases in individual statement items cannot be completely evaluated without additional information. For example, the comparative balance sheet discloses an increase in inventory during 19x2 of $40,000, to an amount 25 percent greater than in 19x1. This increase may have been required in order to support a higher sales volume as net sales increased by a third during 19x2. Alternatively, this increase could have resulted from a buildup of an obsolete inventory item. Obviously, the point to be made here is that additional information is often useful and sometimes absolutely necessary for meaningful interpretation.

Percentage changes included in the statements for Dolbey Company were stated in terms of the data for two years. When a comparison is made between statements of two periods, the earlier statement is normally used as a base in computing percentage changes. For statements which include more than two years, there are two methods which may be used in selecting a base year. One alternative is to use the earliest year as a base. If this alternative is selected, each amount on all succeeding statements will be expressed as a percentage of the base year amount. Since this procedure results in a constant base, percentage changes for more than two years can be interpreted as trend values for individual components of the financial statements. A second alternative is to compare each statement with the statement which immediately precedes it. Adoption of this procedure results in a changing base that may make comparisons of percentage changes over a period of several years more difficult.

Vertical Analysis

The percentage relationship of an individual item or component of a single financial statement to an aggregate total in the same statement often discloses significant relationships. These relationships may be useful information for decision-making purposes. For example, in reporting income data, it may be useful to indicate the relationship between sales and other elements of the income statement for a period. This analysis of the elements included in the financial statements of a single period is often referred to as vertical analysis.

Vertical analysis is also illustrated in the financial statements presented for Dolbey Company. In the comparative balance sheet, the total assets balance and the total liabilities and stockholders' equity balance for each year are used as a base. Each item in the statement is then expressed as a percentage of this base. For example, the statements indicate that current assets increased from 20 percent of total assets in 19x1 to 25 percent at the end of 19x2. An analysis of the composition of the current asset balance provides additional details of the changes in various individual categories of current assets.

Vertical analysis may also be employed in presenting a comparative income statement. In the Dolbey Company illustration, each individual item is stated as a percent of net sales for the period.

Common-Size Statements

Horizontal and vertical analyses are frequently useful in disclosing certain relationships and trends in individual elements included in the financial statements. The analysis of these relationships may be facilitated by the use of common-size statements, i.e.,—statements in which all items are stated in terms of percentages or ratios. Common-size statements may be prepared in order to compare data from the current period with that from one or more past periods for a firm. These statements may also be used to compare data of two or more business firms for the same period or periods, subject to the limitations mentioned previously.

A common-size statement comparing income statement data for Dolbey Company with that of Nutt Company is presented below. The column for Dolbey Company is prepared by using the percentage figures that were included in the comparative income statement previously given. Net sales of each firm are set as a base of 100 percent and each individual item included in the statement is shown as a percentage of net sales. Consequently, use of this statement format provides a comparison of the relationships of the income statement items for the two firms regardless of the absolute dollar amount of sales and expenses of either company. It can be seen, for example, that Dolbey Company obtained $.04 of net income from each dollar of net sales, while Nutt Company netted only $.01 of net income from each sales dollar.

Dolbey Company and Nutt Company
Condensed Common-Size Income Statement
For the Year Ended December 31, 19x2

	Dolbey Company	Nutt Company
Net sales	100.0%	100.0%
Cost of goods sold	70.0	72.5
Gross profit on sales	30.0%	27.5%
Operating expenses:		
Selling expense	15.0%	17.5%
Administrative expense	9.	7.5
Total Operating Expenses	24.0%	25.0%
Operating income	6.0%	2.5%
Interest expense	.5	1.0
Income before income taxes	5.5%	1.5%
Income taxes	1.5	.5
Net Income	4.0%	1.0%

RATIO ANALYSIS

A ratio is an expression of the relationship of one numerical item to another. Significant interrelationships which may be present in financial statements are often identified and highlighted by the use of ratio analysis. A simple example of such a relationship would be the ratio of cash to current liabilities for Dolbey Company at the end of 19x2. The ratio would be calculated or computed as follows:

$$\text{Ratio of Cash to Current Liabilities} = \frac{\text{Cash}}{\text{Current Liabilities}}$$

$$.27 = \frac{\$80,000}{\$300,000}$$

Ratios may be expressed in several different ways. Generally, ratios are stated in relation to a base of one. For example, for the ratio computed above, it could be stated that the ratio of cash to current liabilities is .27 to 1 (which is sometimes simply stated as .27 with the "to 1" omitted). In any case, a ratio is a method used to describe a relationship between two financial statement amounts. The meaningful use of ratio analysis requires that there be a logical relationship between the figures compared, and that this relationship be clearly understood by the user.

Comparison with Standards

The analytical procedures employed in computing percentage changes (horizontal analysis), component percentages (vertical analysis), and ratios convert financial statement items into a form which may be comparable to various standards. It is comparisons made among the relationships derived from the financial statements and selected standards that allow the user to draw meaningful conclusions concerning the firm. Among the most commonly used standards of comparison against which the position of a particular firm may be measured are the following:

1. Past performance of the firm.
2. Financial data of similar or competing firms.
3. Average performance of a number of firms in the industry.

A major deficiency of comparison with the past performance of the firm is that there is no indication of what *should* have occurred given the nature of the firm, the economy of the period, etc. For example, the fact that the net income of a firm increased by 3 percent from the previous year may initially appear to be favorable. However, if there is evidence that net income *should* have increased by 6 percent, the performance for the current year would be regarded as unfavorable.

The weakness of comparisons with past performance of the firm may be overcome somewhat by using the performance of a similar firm or firms or an industry average as an additional standard for comparison. A problem with this approach, however, is that it is often difficult to identify firms which are truly comparable, both because of the nature of the firms themselves and because of the use of alternative "generally accepted accounting principles." In spite of these limitations, a careful analysis of comparative performance, both internal and external, often provides meaningful input for use in decision-making.

ANALYSIS FOR COMMON STOCKHOLDERS

Common stockholders and potential investors purchase securities of a firm in an attempt to earn a return on their investment through increases in the market price of the stock and by dividends. Because each of these factors is influenced by net income, the analysis of financial statements made by, or on behalf of, an investor is focused primarily on the company's record of earnings. Certain of the more important relationships which are of interest to the stockholder-investor are discussed in the following sections of this chapter.

Rate of Return on Total Assets

The rate of return on total assets provides a measure of management's ability to earn a return on the firm's assets. The income figure used in this computation should be income before the deduction of interest expense, since interest is the return to creditors for the resources that they provide to the firm. Thus, the rate of return on total assets is computed by dividing net income plus interest expense by the average investment in assets during the year.

$$\frac{\text{Rate of Return}}{\text{on Total Assets}} = \frac{\text{Net Income (after taxes)} + \text{Interest Expense}}{\text{Average Total Assets during the Year}}$$

Although assets are continually acquired and disposed of throughout a period, an average of asset balances at the beginning and end of the period is generally used for this calculation. The calculation for Dolbey Company would be as follows:

	19x2	19x1
Net income	$ 80,000	$ 30,000
Add interest expense	10,000	9,000
Net income before interest expense	$ 90,000	$ 39,000
Total assets		
Beginning of year	$1,440,000	$1,160,000
End of year	1,600,000	1,440,000
Total	$3,040,000	$2,600,000
Average total assets	$1,520,000	$1,300,000
Rate of return on assets	5.9%	3.0%

This ratio indicates that the earnings per dollar of assets invested have almost doubled in 19x2. It appears that the management of Dolbey Company has increased its efficiency in the use of the firm's assets to generate income.

Rate of Return on Common Stockholders' Equity

The rate of return on common stockholders' equity is a measure of a firm's ability to earn a profit for its residual owners, the common stockholders. Because interest paid to creditors and dividends paid to preferred stockholders are normally fixed in amount, the return on common stockholders' equity may not be equal to the return on total assets. If management is able to earn a higher return on assets than the cost (i.e., interest expense) of assets contributed by the creditors, the excess benefits the owners. This is often referred to as using debt as favorable "leverage" in order to increase the owners' rate of return or as "trading on equity." Of course, if the cost of borrowing funds exceeds the return on assets, leverage will be unfavorable and will reduce the rate of return to the residual owners. The rate of return on common stockholders' equity is computed by dividing net income, less preferred dividends, by the average equity of the common stockholders.

$$\text{Rate of Return on Common Stockholders' Equity} = \frac{\text{Net Income (after taxes)} - \text{Preferred Dividends}}{\text{Average Common Stockholders' Equity}}$$

Since Dolbey Company has no preferred stock, the rate of return on common stockholders' equity would be computed as follows:

	19x2	19x1
Net income	$ 80,000	$ 30,000
Common stockholders' equity:		
Beginning of the year	$1,050,000	$1,035,000
End of the year	1,100,000	1,050,000
Total	$2,150,000	$2,085,000
Average common stockholders' equity	$1,075,000	$1,042,500
Rate of return on common stockholders' equity	7.4%	2.9%

The rate of return on the common stockholders' equity is higher than the rate of return on assets for 19x2 because the cost of funds contributed by creditors is less than the rate earned on assets. Thus the company is experiencing favorable "leverage," using borrowed funds to earn a return in excess of their cost.

Earnings Per Share of Common Stock

Since the owners of a business invest in shares of stock, they are usually interested in an expression of earnings in terms of a per share amount. If a company has only a single class of common stock outstanding, the earnings per share figure is computed by dividing net income for the period by the average number of common shares outstanding.[1] If the firm has other securities outstanding which have certain characteristics similar to

---
[1] The calculation of earnings per share was discussed in Chapter 14.

those of common stock (such as convertible bonds), the usefulness of earnings per share data is enhanced if these other securities are also considered in the computation of earnings per share. These securities are often referred to as common stock equivalents. While a discussion of the inclusion of common stock equivalents in the computation of earnings per share is beyond the scope of this text, the basic principle involved is that earnings per share figures are calculated so as to indicate the effects of the conversion of these securities into common stock.

When there is both common and preferred stock outstanding, net income must be reduced by preferred dividend requirements in order to determine net income available to common stockholders.

$$\text{Earnings Per Share} = \frac{\text{Net Income} - \text{Preferred Dividends}}{\text{Average Number of Common Shares Outstanding}}$$

In the case of Dolbey Company, which has no preferred stock, the earnings per share of common stock would be calculated as follows:

	19x2	19x1
Net income	$80,000	$30,000
Number of common shares outstanding	30,000	30,000
Earnings per share of common stock	$ 2.67	$ 1.00

Earnings per share is a ratio frequently mentioned in the financial press in relation to the earnings performance of business firms. In addition, earnings per share data is reported on the income statement, and usually in various other sections of corporate annual reports. Although the concept of earnings per share has received a great deal of attention, particularly in recent years, it should be viewed with some caution. As a minimum, it should be recognized that all of the significant aspects of a firm's performance simply cannot be reduced to a single figure. This point cannot be overemphasized.

Price-Earnings Ratio on Common Stock

Each investor must allocate his limited resources among various investment opportunities which are available to him. For this reason the rate of earnings in relation to the current market price of his investment often provides a useful basis for comparing alternative investment opportunities. This ratio is commonly referred to as the price-earnings ratio. It is computed by dividing the current market price per share of common stock by earnings per share.

$$\text{Price-Earnings Ratio} = \frac{\text{Market Price Per Share of Common Stock}}{\text{Earnings Per Share}}$$

Assuming that the market price per common share of Dolbey Company at the end of 19x2 was $24 and at the end of 19x1 was $8, price-earnings ratios would be calculated as follows:

	19x2	19x1
Market price per share at the end of the year	$24.00	$8.00
Earnings per share	$ 2.67	$1.00
Price-earnings ratio	9	8

The price-earnings ratio may be interpreted as the value that investors in the stock market place on every dollar of earnings for a particular firm. An investor may compare the price-earnings ratio of a firm to that of other companies in an attempt to estimate whether a firm's stock is overpriced or underpriced.

Debt-to-Equity Ratio

The debt-to-equity ratio measures the proportion of funds supplied to the firm by its stockholders as opposed to funds provided by creditors. It is computed by dividing total debt by stockholders' equity.

$$\text{Debt-to-Equity Ratio} = \frac{\text{Total Debt}}{\text{Stockholders' Equity}}$$

The debt-to-equity ratio provides a measure of the risk incurred by common stockholders. Since debt consists of fixed obligations, the larger the debt-to-equity ratio, the greater is the chance that a firm may face a situation in which it is unable to meet its obligations. At the same time, however, a high debt-to-equity ratio can increase the rate of return on stockholders' equity through the use of favorable financial leverage. This can occur because interest on debt is fixed in amount, regardless of the amount of earnings. Consequently there is no ideal debt-to-equity ratio. Rather, each investor must define a satisfactory debt-to-equity ratio based on his desired degree of risk.

For Dolbey Company, the debt-to-equity ratios are calculated as follows:

	19x2	19x1
Total debt	$ 500,000	$ 390,000
Stockholders' equity	$1,100,000	$1,050,000
Debt-to-equity ratio	45.5%	37.1%

ANALYSIS FOR LONG-TERM CREDITORS

Bondholders and other long-term creditors, like stockholders and investors, are also concerned with measures of the profitability of a business. In addition, however, long-term creditors are particularly interested in a firm's ability to meet its interest requirements as they become due and payable. A good indicator of a firm's ability to pay interest is the margin between income and interest payments. A common measure of this margin is the ratio of net income available for interest payments to annual interest expense. This ratio, which is referred to as the number of times interest earned, is computed by dividing net income before interest expense and income taxes by the interest requirement for the period. Income taxes are added back to net income because interest charges are an expense which is deducted in computing income taxes. Similarly, interest charges are added back to net income because the ratio provides a measure of the ability of the firm to pay fixed interest charges.

$$\frac{\text{Number of Times}}{\text{Interest Earned}} = \frac{\text{Net Income + Interest Expense + Income Taxes}}{\text{Interest Expense}}$$

The computation for Dolbey Company would be as follows:

	19x2	*19x1*
Net income	$ 80,000	$30,000
Add back:		
Income taxes	30,000	12,000
Interest expense	10,000	9,000
Amount available for interest requirements	$120,000	$51,000
Number of times interest earned	12.0	5.7

The increase in the ratio from 5.7 times in 19x1 to 12.0 times in 19x2 would appear to be favorable with respect to a long-term creditor of Dolbey Company.

ANALYSIS FOR SHORT-TERM CREDITORS

Short-term creditors are also concerned with the earnings prospects of a firm. Of primary importance to the short-term creditor, however, is a firm's ability to pay its current debt on a timely basis and to meet its current operating needs. This is often referred to as the current position of the firm.

The ability of a firm to pay its current debts as they fall due depends largely upon the relationship between its current assets and its current liabilities. The excess of a firm's current assets over its current liabilities is termed working capital. Adequate working capital enables a firm to meet its current needs and obligations on a timely basis. However, an analysis of the components of working capital and the flow of working capital is necessary in order to determine the adequacy of the working capital position of a specific firm.

Current Ratio

The absolute amount of working capital may be an inadequate measure of a firm's ability to meet its obligations. As an illustration, consider the following data for two companies:

	Reed Company	Frazier Company
Current assets	$20,000	$50,000
Current liabilities	10,000	40,000
Working capital	$10,000	$10,000

In this example, both companies have $10,000 of working capital. However, the current assets of Reed Company could be reduced by 50 percent and still be equal to the current liabilities, while the current assets of Frazier Company could only shrink by 20 percent and remain equal to current liabilities.

Another means of evaluating working capital is to evaluate the relationship between current assets and current liabilities. This ratio is referred to as the current ratio.

$$\text{Current Ratio} = \frac{\text{Current Assets}}{\text{Current Liabilities}}$$

The use of the current ratio for the example given would disclose a ratio of 2 to 1 for Reed Company and 1.25 to 1 for Frazier Company. This clearly indicates the stronger current position of Reed Company.

The current ratio for Dolbey Company is calculated as follows:

	19x2	19x1
Current assets	$400,000	$288,000
Current liabilities	300,000	190,000
Current ratio	1.3	1.5

Although the working capital of Dolbey Company increased from $98,000 in 19x1 to $100,000 in 19x2, current assets per dollar of current liabilities declined from $1.50 to $1.30. This is an unfavorable trend from the viewpoint of short-term creditors because the margin of safety has declined.

A satisfactory current ratio for a particular firm depends, of course, upon the nature of its business. Although short-term creditors generally feel safer as the current ratio increases in amount, this may not be efficient from a business standpoint. For example, a firm with excess cash in relation to its current needs is inefficient since cash is a nonproductive asset. A good measure of the adequacy of a firm's current ratio is often a comparison with the current ratios of similar firms or industry averages.

Acid-Test or Quick Ratio

In analyzing the ability of a firm to meet its obligations, the distribution of current assets is also important. For example, a firm with a large proportion of cash to current assets is better able to meet its current debts than a firm with a larger proportion of inventories. This is because inventories usually require more time for conversion into cash than do other current assets. Assets with a longer conversion period are usually referred to as being less liquid. For this reason, a ratio which excludes the less liquid assets is often used as a supplement to the current ratio. The ratio of the highly current assets—cash, marketable securities, and receivables—to current liabilities is known as the acid-test or quick ratio.

$$\text{Acid-Test Ratio} = \frac{\text{Cash + Marketable Securities + Receivables}}{\text{Current Liabilities}}$$

Since Dolbey Company owns no marketable securities, its acid-test ratio would be calculated as follows:

	19x2	19x1
Cash	$ 80,000	$ 40,000
Net accounts receivables	100,000	80,000
Total	$180,000	$120,000
Current liabilities	$300,000	$190,000
Acid-test ratio	.60	.63

In evaluating the acid-test ratio, again the nature of the business must be considered. The .6 acid-test ratio for Dolbey Company in 19x2 may indicate a serious problem as there may not be sufficient liquid assets to meet current liabilities as they become due.

Analysis of Accounts Receivable

It is obvious that the rate at which non-cash current assets may be converted into cash is an important determinant of the firm's ability to meet its current obligations. Because neither the current nor the acid-test ratio considers this movement in current assets, short-term creditors should use additional tests in considering the liquidation of two significant working capital items, receivables and inventories.

An approximation of the average time which is required by a firm in order to collect its receivables may be determined by first computing the turnover of accounts receivable. Receivables turnover is computed by dividing net credit sales by the average accounts receivable balance. Ideally, a monthly average of receivables should be used, but generally only the balances at the beginning and end of the year are available to the user of the financial statements.

$$\frac{\text{Accounts Receivable}}{\text{Turnover}} = \frac{\text{Net Sales on Account}}{\text{Average Accounts Receivable}}$$

The accounts receivable turnover is an approximation of the number of times accounts receivable were converted into cash during the period. Therefore, the higher the turnover, the more liquid are the firm's receivables.

Accounts receivable turnover of Dolbey Company is computed below. Assume that all sales were made on a credit basis and that only the beginning and end of the year balances of receivables are available.

	19x2	19x1
Net sales on account	$2,000,000	$1,500,000
Net receivables:		
Beginning of year	$ 80,000	$ 70,000
End of year	100,000	80,000
Total	$ 180,000	$ 150,000
Average	$ 90,000	$ 75,000
Accounts receivable turnover per year	22.2 times	20.0 times

This increase in the receivables turnover for Dolbey Company during 19x2 indicates that the average collection period for receivables has decreased. This could be a result of more successful collection practices or a change in credit policies, or a combination of both factors.

The receivables turnover may be used to determine the average collection period, which can be readily compared with the firm's credit terms. The average number of days to collect receivables is computed by dividing 365 days by the receivables turnover.

$$\frac{\text{Average Number of Days}}{\text{to Collect Receivables}} = \frac{365 \text{ Days}}{\text{Accounts Receivable Turnover}}$$

If the average number of days required to collect receivables significantly exceeds the credit terms of the firm, this would indicate that the credit department may be ineffective in its credit granting and collecting activities.

The average number of days to collect receivables is calculated for the Dolbey Company as follows:

	19x2	19x1
Receivables turnover	22.2 times	20.0 times
Average number of days to collect receivables	16.4 days	18.3 days

Analysis of Inventories

A procedure similar to that used for evaluating receivables may be employed in evaluating the inventories of a firm. One indication of the liquidity of inventories is obtained by determining the relationship between the cost of goods sold and the average balance of inventories on hand during a period. Cost of goods sold is used because it represents the cost (rather than selling price) of goods that have been sold from the inventories during the period.

Inventory turnover is calculated by dividing cost of goods sold by the average inventory. Again, if possible, monthly figures should be used to determine average inventory. Usually, however, only the beginning and end of the year inventory balances are available.

$$\text{Inventory Turnover} = \frac{\text{Cost of Goods Sold}}{\text{Average Inventory}}$$

A low inventory turnover may indicate management inefficiency in that excess cash has been committed to the investment in inventory. Although inventories are necessary to meet the demands of a firm, there are advantages in maintaining the investment in inventory at the minimum level necessary to service customers, thus minimizing carrying costs, risks of loss or obsolescence, etc.

Assuming that only the beginning and ending inventories are available, the computation of inventory turnover for Dolbey Company is as follows:

	19x2	19x1
Cost of goods sold	$1,400,000	$1,080,000
Inventory:		
Beginning of the year	$ 160,000	$ 110,000
End of the year	200,000	160,000
Total	$ 360,000	$ 270,000
Average inventory	$ 180,000	$ 135,000
Inventory turnover	7.8 times	8 times

It appears that the trend of the inventory turnover for Dolbey Company is somewhat unfavorable, since inventories were turned over more slowly in 19x2 than in 19x1. Again, the analyst would want to obtain additional information before making a definitive judgment.

INTERPRETATION OF ANALYSES

The user must exercise considerable caution in the use of ratios in order to analyze the financial statements of a business enterprise. Some of the problems inherent in ratio analysis are summarized below:

1. Comparisons of items for different periods or for different companies may not be valid if different accounting practices have been used. For example, one firm may use straight-line depreciation and the Fifo inventory method while a similar company may use accelerated depreciation and Lifo for its inventories.
2. Financial statements represent only one source of financial information

concerning a firm and its environment. Consequently, other information not disclosed in financial statements may have an impact on the evaluation of the statements.
3. Most financial statements are not adjusted either for changes in market values or in the general price level. This may seriously affect comparability between firms over time.
4. As ratio analysis has increased in popularity, there has sometimes been a tendency to develop ratios which have little or no significance. A meaningful ratio can be developed only from items which have a logical relationship.

All of the ratios and measurements developed in this chapter need not be used as input in a particular decision. In determining the financial strengths and weaknesses of a particular firm, relevant measurements need to be selected, developed, and interpreted in view of the conditions relating to the business.

SUMMARY

Financial statements provide a variety of external users with essential data regarding a firm's financial position and the results of its operations. However, most users of financial statements must make a detailed analysis and interpretation of the data presented to obtain evaluative information useful in making decisions.

The actual evaluative techniques used by an individual will vary according to personal preference and the nature of the individual's relationship to the reporting firm. Most techniques involve some type of comparison with related data. The data may relate to the firm's past performance, to similar or competing firms, or to an industry average. Comparisons are often expressed in terms of percentages or ratios, although there are certain problems inherent in ratio analysis.

Firms may present a horizontal or vertical analysis of relevant data along with their regular financial statements. A horizontal analysis usually presents both the dollar and percentage changes for corresponding items for two or more accounting periods. Vertical analysis discloses the percentage relationship of an individual item or component of a single financial statement to an aggregate total included in the same statement. Presentation of these analyses may be facilitated by the use of common-size statements in which all items are stated in terms of percentages and ratios.

Since current and potential stockholders are primarily interested in earning an acceptable return on their investments through increases in the market price of the stock and by dividends, their analyses focus on the company's record of earnings. Examples of earnings relationships of interest to the stockholder-investor are the rate of return on total assets, the rate of return on common stockholders' equity, the earnings per share of common stock, and the price-earnings ratio on common stock. The stockholders may also be interested in the debt to equity ratio as a measure of the risk incurred by the common stockholders as opposed to the risk incurred by creditors.

In addition to their interest in the profitability of the business, bondholders and other long-term creditors are concerned with the firm's ability to meet its interest requirements as they become payable. A common measure of such ability is the ratio of net income available for interest payments to annual interest expense. This measure is generally referred to as the number of times interest is earned.

Short-term creditors are primarily interested in the firm's ability to pay its current debt on a timely basis and to meet its current operating needs. Although the absolute amount of working capital available to a firm may provide useful information to a creditor, the ratio of current assets to current liabilities (referred to as the current ratio) is generally thought to provide better evaluative data. If only the more liquid current assets are used in the ratio, it is referred to as an acid-test ratio. Other evaluation methods used by short-term creditors include the analysis of accounts receivable and the analysis of inventories.

KEY DEFINITIONS

Accounts receivable turnover Accounts receivable turnover is an approximation of the number of times accounts receivable were converted into cash during the period. It is defined as net sales on account divided by average accounts receivable.

Acid-test ratio This ratio is a measure of a firm's ability to pay its current liabilities as they come due with the more liquid current assets. It is usually the ratio of cash, marketable securities, and receivables to total current liabilities.

Average collection period This is a measure of the average time required by a firm to collect a receivable. Collection period is computed by dividing 365 days by the receivables turnover.

Common-size statements In common-size financial statements, all items are stated in terms of percentages or ratios.

Current ratio This ratio measures a firm's ability to pay current liabilities as they come due. It is defined as the ratio of current assets to current liabilities.

Debt-to-equity ratio Debt-to-equity measures the proportion of funds supplied by stockholders as opposed to the funds provided by creditors. It is computed by dividing total debt by total stockholders' equity.

Horizontal analysis The analysis of the increase or decrease in a given financial statement item over two or more accounting periods.

Inventory turnover Inventory turnover gives an indication of the liquidity of inventories. Its computation involves dividing cost of goods sold by the average inventory.

Number of times interest earned This measure of a firm's ability to pay interest is computed by dividing net income before interest expense and income taxes by the interest expense.

Price-earnings ratio The current market price of a share of stock divided by the earnings per share.

Rate of return on common stockholders' equity This measure of the firm's ability to earn a profit for its common stockholders is computed by dividing net income after taxes and preferred dividends by the average common stockholders' equity.

Rate of return on total assets This measure of the ability of the firm's management to earn a return on the assets without regard to variations in the method of financing is computed by dividing net income plus interest expense by the average investment in assets during the year.

Ratio analysis The analysis of items in a financial statement expressing the relationship of one numerical item to another.

Vertical analysis The percentage relationship between an individual item or a component of a single financial statement to an aggregate total in the statement.

QUESTIONS

1. How is the financial statement analysis related to the needs of the various users of financial statements?

2. Distinguish between vertical analysis and horizontal analysis.

3. What are common-size statements?

4. How are each of the following computed?

    a. Rate of Return on Total Assets.
    b. Rate of Return on Common Stockholders' Equity.
    c. Earnings per Share of Common Stock.
    d. Price-Earnings Ratio on Common Stock.
    e. Debt-to-Equity Ratio.
    f. Number of Times Interest Earned.
    g. Current Ratio.
    h. Acid-Test Ratio.
    i. Accounts Receivable Turnover.
    j. Average Number of Days to Collect Receivables.
    k. Inventory Turnover.

5. Each of the ratios (in Question 4 above) are utilized by one user group more than others. Indicate whether each item is utilized most by (1) common shareholders (or investors), (2) long-term creditors, or (3) short-term creditors.

6. What are the most commonly used standards against which to measure the position of a particular firm? What are the weaknesses inherent in these standards?

7. Business corporations usually provide comparative statements in their annual reports. What is a comparative statement? How do they enhance the usefulness of financial information?

8. What will be the effect (increase, decrease, none) on the rate of return on assets of each of the following?

    a. Cash purchase of a new machine.
    b. Increase in the tax rate.
    c. Reduction of accounts payable.
    d. Cash sale of a fully depreciated machine.

9. What is indicated if the average number of days to collect receivables significantly exceeds the credit terms of the firm?

10. What are the principal limitations that should be considered in evaluating ratios?

11. When percentage changes are given in comparative statements for more than two years, there are two methods for selecting the base year. What are they?

EXERCISES

12. Which of the methods in Question 11 makes comparison of percentage changes over several years more difficult? Why?

13. The acid-test ratio at the beginning of 19x0 was 2 to 1 for the Gilly Company.

    Required:

    How would the following transactions affect the acid-test or quick ratio?

    1. Collection of note receivable from Silly Co. The note was due in 19x3.
    2. Collection of accounts receivable.
    3. Sales on account.
    4. Purchase of inventory on account.
    5. Payment of accounts payable.
    6. Collection of an account receivable.
    7. Cash purchase of common stock of ABC Co. as a temporary investment.
    8. Purchase of a new machine on a credit basis, the purchase price payable in 6 months.

14. The following information has been extracted from the financial statements of Cozeb Corp.

Common stock, $5 par	$ 5,000,000
Common stock, $10 par	5,000,000
Preferred stock, $100 par	10,000,000
Net income	3,000,000
Preferred dividends	1,000,000

    Required:

    Compute earnings per share assuming the number of shares outstanding did not change during the year.

15. The December 31, 19x1 financial statement of Flunkart Company included the following data:

Cash	$ 60,000
Accounts receivable	200,000
Marketable securities	100,000
Prepaid expenses	25,000
Accounts payable	200,000
Notes payable (current)	85,000
Inventory	115,000
Bonds payable (due in 5 years)	300,000
Wages payable	15,000

    Required:

    1. What is the current ratio? Acid-test ratio? Working capital?
    2. Comment on the significance of this current ratio.

16. Using the information given, complete the balance sheet below.
    a. The "quick" ratio is 2:1.
    b. Notes payable are long-term liabilities and are four times the dollar amount of the marketable securities.
    c. Accounts receivable are $2,000 and are one-half of the "quick" assets, one-fourth of the current assets, and equal to plant and equipment.
    d. Total stockholders' equity is equal to the working capital and contributed capital is twice the dollar amount of the net accumulation of earnings.

Assets		Liabilities and Stockholders' Equity	
Cash	_____	Accounts payable	_____
Marketable securities	_____	Notes payable	_____
Accounts receivable	_____		
Inventories	_____	Capital stock	_____
Plant and equipment	_____	Retained earnings	_____

17. Consider the following information concerning the 19x1 and 19x2 operations of ABC Co.

	19x1	19x2
Sales	$800,000	$1,000,000
Purchases	400,000	450,000
Beginning inventory	80,000	90,000
Ending inventory	90,000	90,000
Selling expense	40,000	50,000
Administrative expenses	10,000	40,000
Income taxes	100,000	200,000

Required:

Prepare a comparative income statement for the years ending December 31, 19x1 and 19x2. Indicate the changes both in percentages and dollars.

18. Small Company is a manufacturer of widgets. Industrywide averages (expressed in percentages of sales) for the production and sale of widgets are as follows:

Sales	100%
Cost of goods sold	70%
Selling expenses	10%
Administrative expenses	7%

In order to compare its own performance with industrywide standards, the Small Company has computed the following percentages:

Sales	100%
Cost of goods sold	60%
Selling expenses	20%
Administrative expenses	15%

Required:

1. Comment on the performance of Small Company.
2. What are the problems relating to the use of industrywide standards as a basis for evaluating an individual company's performance?

19. The current ratio of Lap Co. on December 31, 19x1 was 2 to 1 ($200,000 to $100,000). In 19x2 the following transactions occurred:

   a. Payment of accounts payable, $125,000.
   b. Collection of accounts receivable, $50,000.
   c. Sales of $200,000, ¾ of which was cash; cost of goods sold was $125,000.
   d. Purchase of goods, all on credit, $150,000.
   e. A loan for $100,000, due in 5 years.
   f. Cash purchase of marketable securities, $10,000.

   Required:

   On the basis of the preceding information, compute the current ratio at December 31, 19x2.

20. The Hawks Company decided to change its credit policy in 19x3, from 2/10, n/30, the policy in effect during 19x2, to 5/10, n/30. Using the information given below, evaluate whether or not this was a beneficial change.

	19x2	19x3
Total sales	$350,000	$400,000
Cash sales	75,000	85,000
Accounts receivable, 12/31/x1	25,000	
Accounts receivable, 12/31/x2	28,000	
Accounts receivable, 12/31/x3	18,000	

21. The ending inventory for each month of 19x1 is listed below for the Expo Company:

1/31	$21,998		7/31	$35,000
2/28	33,000		8/31	40,000
3/31	28,000		9/30	47,000
4/30	29,500		10/31	48,600
5/31	34,200		11/30	47,300
6/30	29,000		12/31	49,100

   During the last half of the year, the company decided to order inventory in larger quantities to take advantage of a quantity discount. The company was able to pass this discount on to its customers in the form of a price decrease. Cost of goods sold for the first half of the year was $224,000 and for the last half of the year was $410,000, reflecting an increase in demand.

   Required:

   Compute inventory turnover for both halves of the year and decide whether this new inventory policy is beneficial.

22. What would Phillie Company's working capital be after the occurrence of *each* of the following consecutive transactions during March? Working capital as of March 1 was ($10,000).

Mar.	2	Sold $15,000 of merchandise. Cost of goods sold was $13,500.
	8	Paid $11,000 on accounts payable.
	10	Purchased $6,000 of inventory for cash.
	15	Collected $3,000 on accounts receivable.
	18	Issued a $10,000, 8 percent bond for $12,000.
	21	Purchased a building with the proceeds from the bond.
	26	Issued 25 shares of $10 par value capital stock for $13.
	31	Adjustment for $200 accrued interest payable.
	31	Adjustment for $500 accrued rent receivable.

PROBLEMS

23. The comparative income statement for Joe Company and John Company is presented below.

Joe Company and John Company
Comparative Income Statement
For the Year Ending December 31, 19x1

	Joe Company	John Company
Net sales	$500,000	$250,000
Cost of goods sold	350,000	150,000
Gross profit on sales	$150,000	$100,000
Operating expenses:		
Selling expense	$ 50,000	$ 10,000
Administrative expense	10,000	7,000
Total Operating Expenses	$ 60,000	$ 17,000
Operating income	$ 90,000	$ 83,000
Interest expense	30,000	5,000
Income before income taxes	$ 60,000	$ 78,000
Income taxes	20,000	25,000
Net income	$ 40,000	$ 53,000

Required:

Using the above information, prepare a common-size statement comparing income data for Joe Company and John Company.

24. The income statements for 19x2 for Spahn Company and Sain Company are presented below.

Spahn Company
Income Statement
For the Year Ended December 31, 19x2

Sales		$225,000
Cost of goods sold		140,000
Gross profit from sales		$ 85,000
Expenses:		
Selling expense	$18,000	
Administrative expense	20,000	
General expenses	15,000	
Total Expenses		53,000
Income from operations		$ 32,000
Interest expense		2,000
Income before taxes		$ 30,000
Income taxes		7,000
Net Income		$ 23,000

Sain Company
Income Statement
For the Year Ended December 31, 19x2

Sales		$300,000
Cost of goods sold		195,000
Gross profit from sales		$105,000
Expenses:		
Selling expense	$15,000	
Administrative expense	30,000	
General expenses	21,000	
Total Expenses		66,000
Income from operations		$ 39,000
Interest expense		6,000
Income before taxes		$ 33,000
Income taxes		4,000
Net Income		$ 29,000

Required:

Prepare a common-size income statement comparing Spahn Company with Sain Company.

25. The following information was taken from the financial statements of Maker Company on December 31, 19x2.

Cash	$ 75,000
Accounts receivable	125,000
Inventory	100,000
Fixed assets (net)	500,000
	$800,000
Accounts payable	$100,000
Bond payable (due December 31, 19x27)	300,000
Capital stock ($10 par)	300,000
Retained earnings	100,000
	$800,000
Net income	$ 50,000

Required:

Compute the following:

1. Current ratio
2. Working capital
3. Acid-test ratio
4. Earnings per share
5. Debt-to-equity ratio

26. Following is the condensed common-size income statement for Francis Co.:

Francis Company
Condensed Common-Size Income Statement
For the Year Ended December 31, 19x2

Net sales	100.0%
Cost of goods sold	68.0
Gross profit on sales	32.0%
Operating expenses:	
Selling expense	16.0%
Administrative expense	6.0
Total Operating Expense	22.0%
Operating income	10.0%
Interest expense	0.5
Income before income taxes	9.5%
Income taxes	2.0
Net income	7.5%

Net sales for the period were $3,000,000.

Required:

Prepare the income statement for Francis Company.

27. Your examination of the balance sheet for Reswarts Corp. on December 31, 19x1, 19x2, and 19x3 reveals the following information:

	19x1	19x2	19x3
Cash	$ 50,000	$ 75,000	$100,000
Accounts receivable (net)	150,000	100,000	150,000
Inventory	175,000	200,000	225,000
Prepaid expenses	25,000	25,000	40,000
Land	45,000	45,000	45,000
Buildings (net)	170,000	155,000	200,000
Machinery and equipment (net)	70,000	60,000	50,000
Accounts payable	120,000	140,000	130,000
Notes payable	50,000	40,000	50,000
Capital stock	400,000	400,000	400,000
Retained earnings	115,000	80,000	230,000

Required:

Prepare comparative balance sheets for the three years using (1) the first year presented as a base and (2) the previous year as a base. Include both percentage and dollar changes.

28. Given below are the balance sheets for Meyers, Inc., for 19x1 and 19x2.

Meyers, Inc.
Comparative Balance Sheet
December 31, 19x2 and 19x1

	19x2	19x1
ASSETS		
Current assets:		
Cash	$ 20,000	$ 17,000
Accounts receivable (net)	45,000	60,000
Supplies inventory	8,000	6,000
Prepaid expenses	7,000	5,000
Total Current Assets	$ 80,000	$ 88,000
Land	120,000	70,000
Buildings (net)	200,000	100,000
Total Assets	$400,000	$258,000
LIABILITIES		
Current liabilities:		
Accounts payable	$ 10,000	$ 7,000
Taxes payable	9,000	3,000
Total Current Liabilities	$ 19,000	$ 10,000
Bonds payable	115,000	70,000
Total Liabilities	$134,000	$ 80,000
STOCKHOLDERS' EQUITY		
Common stock ($5 par)	$ 50,000	$ 45,000
Additional paid-in capital	125,000	80,000
Retained earnings	91,000	53,000
Total Liabilities and Stockholders' Equity	$400,000	$258,000

Required:

Prepare a horizontal and vertical analysis of the balance sheets of Meyers, Inc. for 19x1 and 19x2.

29. Shown below are partially completed comparative financial statements of Neil Company.

Required:

1. Complete the statements.
2. Compute the following for 19x2:
   a. Rate of Return on Total Assets
   b. Rate of Return on Common Stockholders' Equity
   c. Earnings per Share of Common Stock
   d. Debt-to-Equity Ratio
   e. Number of Times Interest Earned
   f. Working Capital
   g. Current Ratio
   h. Acid-Test Ratio
   i. Inventory Turnover
   j. Average Number of Days to Collect Receivables

Neil Company
Comparative Balance Sheet
December 31, 19x2 and 19x1

	19x2 Dollars	19x2 Percent of Total Assets	19x1 Dollars	19x1 Percent of Total Assets	Increase (Decrease) Dollars	Increase (Decrease) Percent
ASSETS						
Current assets:						
Cash	$ 55,000		$ 50,000			
Net accounts receivable	200,000		175,000			
Inventories	300,000		225,000			
Prepaid expenses	45,000		50,000			
Total Current Assets	$ 600,000		$ 500,000			
Land, buildings and equipment (net)	1,400,000		1,250,000			
Total Assets	$2,000,000		$1,750,000			
LIABILITIES						
Current liabilities:						
Accounts payable	$ 300,000		$ 350,000			
Notes payable	200,000		100,000			
Total Current Liabilities	$ 500,000		$ 450,000			
Bonds payable	500,000		500,000			
Total Liabilities	$1,000,000		$ 950,000			
STOCKHOLDERS' EQUITY						
Common stock ($20 par)	$ 600,000		$ 600,000			
Retained earnings	400,000		200,000			
Total Liabilities and Stockholders' Equity	$2,000,000		$1,750,000			

Neil Company
Comparative Income Statement
For Years Ended December 31, 19x2 and 19x1

	19x2 Dollars	19x2 Percent of Sales	19x1 Dollars	19x1 Percent of Sales	Increase (Decrease) Dollars	Increase (Decrease) Percent
Net sales	$3,000,000		$2,000,000			
Cost of goods sold	2,100,000		1,500,000			
Gross profit on sales	$ 900,000		$ 500,000			
Operating expenses:						
Selling expenses	$ 400,000		$ 200,000			
Administrative expenses	100,000		50,000			
Total Operating Expenses	$ 500,000		$ 250,000			
Operating income	$ 400,000		$ 250,000			
Interest expense	40,000		30,000			
Income before income taxes	$ 360,000		$ 220,000			
Income taxes	90,000		45,000			
Net Income	$ 270,000		$ 175,000			

Neil Company
Comparative Statement of Retained Earnings
For Years Ended 12/31/x2 and x1

	19x2	19x1	Increase (Decrease) Dollars	Increase (Decrease) Percent
Retained earnings, January 1	$200,000	$ 75,000		
Net income	270,000	175,000		
	$470,000	$250,000		
Less: Dividends	70,000	50,000		
Retained earnings, December 31	$400,000	$200,000		

30. Met Wholesale Company has in recent prior years maintained the following relationships among the data on its financial statements:

1.	Gross profit rate on net sales	35%
2.	Net profit rate on net sales	5%
3.	Rate of selling expenses to net sales	25%
4.	Accounts receivable turnover	8 per year
5.	Inventory turnover	6 per year
6.	Times interest earned in 19x4	2
7.	Current ratio	2.5
8.	Rate of return on total assets	3%
9.	Quick-asset composition:	
	Cash	10%
	Marketable securities	30%
	Accounts receivable	60%

The company has a net income of $240,000 for 19x4. The resulting earnings per share was $0.48 per share on common stock. Additional information follows:

a. Capital stock issued (all in 19x2) and outstanding:

> Common, $20 per share par value, issued at 2 percent premium.
> Preferred, 8 percent nonparticipating, $100 per share par value, issued at an 8 percent premium.

b. Long-term debt issued at par value in 19x0 has an interest rate of 5 percent and is due in 19x10. Total debt is $5,408,000.
c. The company owns no depreciable assets.
d. All sales were on account. Assume the ending accounts receivable, fixed assets, and inventory balances are the average for the year.
e. The preferred dividend's obligation for 19x4 totaled $8,000 and was paid on December 31, 19x4. There had been no dividends in arrears for years prior to 19x4.

Required:

1. Prepare an income statement.
2. Prepare a balance sheet for the Met Wholesale Company for the year ending December 31, 19x4 from the ratios and information given above. Ignore taxes. The two statements will only include the accounts divulged in this problem. (Hint: Retained Earnings is a balancing figure in this problem.)

31. Joe Stockholder is contemplating buying stock in one of the following companies, both in the same business. Below is financial data relating to each company:

	Pirate Company	Cardinal Company
Sales	$ 6,000	$18,000
Cost of goods sold	3,800	13,884
Depreciation expense	800	1,400
Interest expense	200	800
Other expenses	44	110
Income taxes	480	600
Cash	1,000	4,000
Accounts receivable	3,500	10,000
Inventory	800	1,900
Fixed assets	10,000	38,000
Accumulated depreciation	4,000	14,000
Accounts payable	1,800	4,000
Income taxes payable	480	600
Bonds payable	200	3,600
Common stock ($20 par value)	6,000	36,000
Retained earnings	2,820	(4,300)
Current market value per share	$ 33	$ 5.35

Required:

Compute the ratio that would best give the answer to each of the following questions, then answer the question. Make all necessary assumptions.

1. Which company has the best current position?
2. Which company has the most effective credit department?
3. Which company is doing the best job at keeping the most appropriate inventory level?
4. Which firm has the best ability to make their interest payments?
5. Which firm is earning the best return on the firm's assets?
6. Which stock is the best buy?

32. From the following stockholders' equity portion of the balance sheet and additional information calculate these ratios for the year ended December 31, 19x2:

a. Earnings per share.
b. Rate of return on common stockholders' equity.
c. Price-earnings ratio.

	December 31 19x1	December 31 19x2
Stockholders' Equity:		
6 percent preferred stock, $90 par value, 10,000 shares authorized, 5,000 shares issued and outstanding in 19x1; 6,000 in 19x2 (callable at $110)	$ 450,000	$ 540,000
Common stock, $8 par value, 100,000 shares authorized, 45,000 shares issued and outstanding in 19x1; 54,000 in 19x2	360,000	432,000
Additional paid-in capital:		
Common stock issued	135,000	270,000
Preferred stock issued	105,000	126,000
Total contributed capital	$1,050,000	$1,368,000
Retained earnings	48,000	89,000
Total Stockholders' Equity	$1,098,000	$1,457,000

Additional information:

No dividends were paid during 19x2. Preferred stock has no dividends in arrears from previous years and is nonparticipative. The market price per share of common stock at the end of 19x2 is $13.50.

33. The following are financial statements of ZYX Corporation for 19x1.

ZYX Corporation
Balance Sheet
December 31, 19x1

ASSETS

Current assets:		
Cash	$100,000	
Accounts receivable (net)	200,000	
Prepaid expenses	50,000	
Inventory	110,000	
Total Current Assets		$ 460,000
Fixed assets:		
Land	$ 50,000	
Machinery (net)	100,000	
Building (net)	250,000	
Total Fixed Assets		400,000
Total Assets		$ 860,000

LIABILITIES AND STOCKHOLDERS' EQUITY

Accounts payable	$ 50,000
Wages payable	5,000
Interest payable	2,000
Bonds payable (due December 31, 19x6)	200,000
Capital stock ($2 par value)	400,000
Retained earnings	203,000
Total Liabilities and Stockholders' Equity	$ 860,000

ZYX Corporation
Income Statement
For the Year Ended December 31, 19x1

Sales (net)		$1,000,000
Cost of goods sold:		
Beginning inventory	$ 90,000	
Purchases	600,000	
Goods available for sale	$690,000	
Ending inventory	110,000	
Cost of goods sold		580,000
Gross profit on sales		$ 420,000
Operating expenses:		
Sales salaries expense	$ 75,000	
Depreciation expense	20,000	
Insurance expense	5,000	
Interest expense	10,000	
Total operating expense		110,000
Income before taxes		$ 310,000
Income taxes		100,000
Net Income		$ 210,000

January 1, 19x0 data:

    Common shares outstanding............ 200,000

Required:

Compute the following:

1. Earnings per Share of Common Stock
2. Debt-to-Equity Ratio
3. Number of Times Interest Earned
4. Current Ratio
5. Acid-Test or Quick Ratio
6. Inventory Turnover

34. Orioles Retail Company has maintained the following relationships in recent years among the data on its financial statements:

1.	Gross profit rate on net sales............	30%
2.	Net profit rate on net sales..............	6%
3.	Rate of selling expenses to net sales......	6%
4.	Accounts receivable turnover...........	10 per year
5.	Inventory turnover....................	7 per year
6.	Times interest earned in 19x4...........	4 times
7.	Current ratio.........................	3.2
8.	Rate of return on total assets............	5%
9.	Quick-asset composition:	
	Cash............................	15%
	Marketable securities................	25%
	Accounts receivable.................	60%
10.	Tax rate............................	40%

The company has a net income after taxes of $450,000 for 19x4. The resulting earnings per common share was $2.50. Additional information follows:

a. Capital stock issued (all in 19x2) and outstanding:

   Common, $10 per share par value, issued at 10 percent premium.
   Preferred, 7 percent nonparticipating, $100 per share par value, issued at a 10 percent premium.

b. Preferred dividends were paid up through 19x3; 19x3 dividends of $4,900 were paid on July 1, 19x4.

c. The only long-term debt, an 8 percent bond payable, was issued at par in 19x0 and is due in 19x10. Total debt is $3,750,000.

d. All sales were on account. Assume that accounts receivable and inventory balances were the same on January 1, 19x4 as they are on December 31, 19x4.

e. Fixed assets have been owned for five years and are depreciated at a rate of 5 percent on their original cost per year.

Required:

1. Prepare an income statement.
2. Prepare a balance sheet for the Orioles Retail Company for the year ending December 31, 19x4. The two statements will only include the accounts divulged in this problem. (Hint: Retained Earnings is a balancing figure.)

Refer to the Annual Report included in the Appendix at the end of the text:

35. Compute the accounts receivable turnover for the most recent year.

36. Compute the average collection period for the most recent year.

37. Compute the current ratio for the most recent year.

38. Compute the acid-test ratio for the most recent year.

39. Compute the debt-to-equity ratio for the most recent year.

40. Compute the average inventory for the most recent year.

41. Compute the number of times interest was earned in the most recent year.

42. Compute the return on total assets in the most recent year.

Learning Objectives

Chapter 20 presents a general discussion of the federal income tax. Studying this chapter should enable you to:

1. Identify the primary objectives of the federal income tax.

2. Discuss the process of determining an individual and corporate taxpayer's tax liability.

3. Recognize the important differences in the taxation of corporations versus the taxation of individuals.

4. Describe the purpose of interperiod tax allocation and the accounting procedures involved.

5. Illustrate how intraperiod tax allocation is generally accomplished.

20 Income Tax Considerations*

*This chapter was originally written by Professors Thomas L. Dickens of Clemson University and Kenneth R. Orbach of the Louisiana State University. The sixth edition was revised by Bob G. Kilpatrick of Texas A&M University.

INTRODUCTION

Income taxes are periodic charges levied by federal, state, and city governments on the taxable income of both individuals and business corporations. Taxable income is a statutory concept, i.e., it is defined by law and is equal to gross income minus all allowable deductions. For businesses organized as corporations, income taxes are accounted for as an expense which is deducted in computing the net income for the period. The amount of taxes owed, but not paid, is a liability which is included in the balance sheet. Because income taxes normally represent a significant cost to a business enterprise, an awareness of the tax laws and how they are applied is essential to a complete understanding of accounting information.

Data which is required for the determination of income taxes is usually found in the accounting records. Taxable income, however, may not be the same as the income reported in the income statement even though both are determined from the identical set of accounting records. This difference often occurs because income tax law is not always the same as the basic concepts which are used for financial accounting purposes.

This chapter is devoted to a general discussion of the federal income tax and its implication for the financial reporting process of a business. Although many states and cities also impose income taxes, which may differ in application from the federal income tax, the tax liability to all governmental units is treated similarly in the accounting records. For this reason, the following discussion is limited to the federal income tax.

THE FEDERAL INCOME TAX

The modern era of federal income taxation originated in 1913 with the adoption of the Sixteenth Amendment to the Constitution. This amendment gives Congess the power to ". . . lay and collect taxes on incomes, from whatever source derived, without apportionment among the several States, and without regard to any census or enumeration." Soon after the Sixteenth Amendment was adopted, Congress enacted the Revenue Act of 1913, which provided for a general yearly income tax. Since that time, Congress has passed numerous income tax statutes amending the various Revenue Acts so that there has been a continuous development of income tax law in the United States. In 1939 the Internal Revenue Code was enacted. This code was thoroughly revised in 1954 and extensively amended and supplemented by the Tax Reform Act of 1969, the Revenue Act of 1971, the Tax Reduction Act of 1975, the Tax Reform Act of 1976, the Tax Reduction and Simplification Act of 1977, the Revenue Act of 1978, the Economic Recovery Act of 1981, the Tax Equity and Fiscal Responsibility Act of 1982, and the Deficit Reduction Act of 1984. Tax law is also supplemented by interpretations of the Internal Revenue Code by both the courts and the Treasury Department. The Treasury Department, operating through a branch known as the Internal Revenue Service, is charged with the enforcement and collection of income taxes.

The original purpose of the income tax was stated as simply to obtain revenues for the use of the federal government. The income tax on individuals under the 1913 Act consisted of a flat one percent tax on taxable income in excess of $4,000 for married persons plus a progressive surtax of one to seven percent on income in excess of $20,000. A progressive tax is one in which tax rates increase as taxable income increases.

Since 1916, both the objectives of the income tax and income tax rates have undergone a significant change. The purpose of the federal income tax today includes such diverse objectives as controlling inflation, influencing economic growth, decreasing unemployment, redistributing national income, and encouraging the growth of small businesses. All of these purposes are in addition to the original objective of raising revenue to finance the operations of the government. Similarly, there have been substantial changes in tax rates. The current rates for married taxpayers are presented in Illustration 1.

CLASSES OF TAXPAYERS

Income taxes are levied upon four major types of taxable entities: individuals, corporations, estates, and trusts. Business entities organized as sole proprietorships or partnership are not taxable entities. Instead, their income is included in the gross income of the individual owner or owners, whether or not it is actually withdrawn from the business and distributed to these owners. A partnership, however, is required to prepare an information return which indicates the items of its gross income, deductions, and credits and how these are allocated to the partners. The partners then report these amounts in their own tax returns.

A corporation is treated as a separate entity for tax purposes and must pay taxes on its taxable income. In addition, individual corporate stockholders must include any dividends received from the corporation as a part of their taxable income. For this reason, it is often argued that the profits of a corporation are taxed twice—once to the corporation when the income is reported and again to its stockholders when dividends are distributed. Under limited circumstances, a corporation meeting certain qualifications may avoid this "double taxation" of corporate income by making an S Corporation election; the shareholders are then taxed on undistributed income on a current basis.[1]

An estate is a separate legal entity which is created to take charge of the assets of a deceased person to pay the decedent's debts and distribute any remaining assets to the heirs. A trust is a legal entity which is created when a person by gift or devise transfers assets to a trustee for the benefit of designated persons. The tax rules that apply to estates and trusts will not be discussed in this chapter, as they are beyond the scope of this text.

---

[1] These entities are referred to as "S Corporations." Numerous changes in the tax treatment of S Corporations were made in the "Subchapter S Revision Act of 1982." Subchapter S Corporations are now called S Corporations.

Illustration 1

Rate Schedule for Married Individuals Filing Joint Returns

Taxable Income		Tax Liability		
Over—	But Not Over—	1982	1983	1984 and Later	of the Amount Over—
$ 3,400	$ 5,500	0 + 12%	0 + 11%	0 + 11%	$ 3,400
5,500	7,600	$ 252 + 14	$ 231 + 13	$ 231 + 12	$ 5,500
7,600	11,900	546 + 16	504 + 15	483 + 14	7,600
11,900	16,000	1,234 + 19	1,149 + 17	1,085 + 16	11,900
16,000	20,200	2,013 + 22	1,846 + 19	1,741 + 18	16,000
20,200	24,600	2,937 + 25	2,644 + 23	2,497 + 22	20,200
24,600	29,900	4,037 + 29	3,656 + 26	3,465 + 25	24,600
29,900	35,200	5,574 + 33	5,034 + 30	4,790 + 28	29,900
35,200	45,800	7,323 + 39	6,624 + 35	6,274 + 33	35,200
45,800	60,000	11,457 + 44	10,334 + 40	9,772 + 38	45,800
60,000	85,600	17,705 + 49	16,014 + 44	15,168 + 42	60,000
85,600	109,400	30,249 + 50	27,278 + 48	25,920 + 45	85,600
109,400	162,400	42,149 + 50	38,702 + 50	36,630 + 49	109,400
162,400	215,400	68,649 + 50	65,202 + 50	62,600 + 50	162,400
215,400	—	95,149 + 50	91,702 + 50	89,100 + 50	215,400

INDIVIDUAL FEDERAL INCOME TAX

The cash basis of measuring taxable income is used by almost all individuals in preparing their tax returns. Generally, revenue is recognized upon the actual or constructive receipt of cash; and expenses are recognized as cash is expended.

Individual income tax rates depend on the status of the taxpayer. There are different tax rate schedules for married taxpayers who file a joint return, married individuals who file separate returns, unmarried taxpayers, and single taxpayers qualifying as a "head of household." Generally, "head of household" status applies to certain unmarried or legally separated persons who maintain the principal residence for a relative.

The federal income tax for individuals is a progressive tax. A progressive tax is one in which each increment of taxable income is subject to a higher rate than the preceding increments of income. Such a tax is designed to accomplish certain objectives of the federal income tax which were mentioned previously.

The amount of federal income tax that an individual must pay is generally determined by knowledge of gross income, deductions for adjusted gross income, adjusted gross income, zero bracket amount, itemized deductions (deductions from adjusted gross income), personal exemptions, tax table income or taxable income, and credits. The relationship of these concepts and the procedures for determining taxable income are summarized in Illustration 2. A more detailed explanation of the items outlined in the determination of taxable income is given in the following paragraphs.

Gross Income. Basically, gross income is defined as all income from whatever source derived, unless expressly excluded by law or by the U.S. Constitution. This includes income from sources such as wages, dividends, interest, partnership income, rents, and numerous other items. Among the more important classes of income which are currently excludable from gross income by law are gifts, life insurance proceeds received at the insured's death, social security benefits (up to certain amounts), inheritances (but not income from trusts and life estates), workmen's compensation, interest on certain state and municipal bonds, and up to $100 of dividends from domestic corporations ($200 on a joint return).

Deductions for Adjusted Gross Income. The deductions for adjusted gross income are business expenses and other expenses connected with earning certain types of revenue. These include ordinary and necessary expenses incurred by the taxpayer in the operation of his unincorporated business or profession, certain business expenses of an employee, losses from the sale or exchange of certain property, expenses incurred in connection with earning rent or royalty income, payments to an individual retirement arrangement or to a Keogh retirement plan, 60 percent of the excess of the net long-term capital gain over net short-term capital loss, and periodic payments of alimony made under a court decree.

Illustration 2

*Process of Determining
Tax Liability for Individuals*

Gross Income = Includes income from all sources except those specifically excluded by law or by the U.S. Constitution

Minus

Deductions for Adjusted Gross Income = Includes business expenses and certain other expenses

Equals

Adjusted Gross Income

Minus

Excess Itemized Deductions = Itemized deductions for certain personal expenses such as charitable contributions, taxes, interest, casualty losses, and medical expenses, less the zero bracket amount

Minus

Personal Exemptions = Deduction of $1,040 each for the taxpayer, his spouse, and qualified dependents, and additional exemptions for the taxpayer and spouse who are over 65 and/or blind

Equals

Taxable Income → Tax Table or Tax Rate Schedule → Tax

Minus

Credits

Equals

Tax Liability

*If taxable income is not greater than $50,000 then the tax can generally be found using the tax tables. For certain taxpayers, the unused zero bracket must be added to arrive at taxable income.

Deductions from Adjusted Gross Income (Itemized Deductions). Itemized deductions include such items as a limited amount of charitable contributions, interest payments, certain taxes paid by the taxpayer, a limited amount of medical expenses, a limited amount of casualty and theft losses, and nonbusiness expenses (other than expenses incurred in connection with earning rent or royalty income). These nonbusiness expenses are the necessary expenses incurred in producing income, for the management of income-producing property, or in connection with the determination, collection or refund of any tax. These include such items as certain legal fees relating to investments, dues to professional organizations, and expenses incurred for the preparation of tax returns.

Under prior law, a taxpayer could either deduct the sum of itemized deductions or take the standard deduction. For tax years beginning after December 31, 1976, individual taxpayers may no longer elect a standard deduction. In its place the 1977 Tax Reduction and Simplification Act substituted the new zero bracket amount (this is simply that initial range of income on which there is a zero tax, e.g., 0-$3,540 for married taxpayers filing jointly). The zero bracket amount is presently $3,540 for married taxpayers filing jointly, $1,770 for a married taxpayer filing separately, and $2,390 for single taxpayers and heads of household. The zero bracket amount is not a deduction; rather it is incorporated into the tax tables and the tax rate schedules. As a result, a taxpayer who itemizes must deduct from adjusted gross income the excess itemized deductions (i.e., the difference between the itemized deductions and the relevant zero bracket amount).

Taxable income may now be computed. Generally, taxable income equals adjusted gross income reduced by excess itemized deductions and personal exemptions.[2] If taxable income is not more than $50,000 then the tax can usually be found in the tax tables.

If taxable income is greater than $50,000, or for some other reason prescribed by law, the tax tables may not be used; the tax must then be found by using the proper tax rate schedule. This tax is reduced by the relevant credits (see below).

Personal Exemption. A taxpayer is allowed a $1,040 deduction for each personal exemption to which he or she is entitled. Personal exemptions may be taken for the following individuals:

1. *The taxpayer.* An additional exemption is allowed in case the taxpayer is blind or at least 65 years of age (2 additional exemptions if both blind and at least 65).
2. *The taxpayer's spouse if a joint return is filed.* As in (1), one or two additional exemptions may be taken in case the spouse is blind and/or at least 65 years old.

---

[2] Some taxpayers must add a certain additional amount (unused zero bracket amount) in order to arrive at taxable income.

3. *The taxpayer's spouse if a joint return is not filed, but only if the spouse has no gross income and is not a dependent of another taxpayer.* As in (1), one or two additional exemptions may be taken in case the spouse is blind and/or at least 65 years old.
4. *Certain dependents.* A dependent is an individual (a) more than ½ of whose support is provided by the taxpayer, (b) who is related to the taxpayer or whose principal place of abode is with the taxpayer, and (c) who is either a U.S. citizen or national or a resident of the U.S., Canada, or Mexico. The taxpayer may take a $1,040 personal exemption for each dependent who does not file a joint return (unless the return is not required but is filed merely to receive a refund of tax withheld) and whose gross income is less than $1,040 (unless the dependent is taxpayer's child and is either less than 19 years old or is a full time student).

Credits. A credit is an amount by which the tax liability is reduced. At the time of this writing, the most commonly used credits included the earned income credit, credit for the elderly, credit for child and dependent care expenses, the investment credit, and the foreign tax credit.

Withholding and Estimated Tax. Taxpayers are generally required to make payments on their estimated tax liability during the year. This is accomplished by two principal procedures:

1. Employers withhold income tax on compensation to their employees.
2. Individuals who have income not subject to withholding (such as self-employed individuals) or who have income from which not enough is withheld should file a declaration of estimated tax. This estimated tax is generally paid in four equal installments.

In either instance, any difference between the amounts paid and the actual tax liability at the end of the year is settled when the tax return is filed.

Capital Gain and Losses. Gains from the sale of certain property defined by the tax law as capital assets are given special treatment for income tax purposes. Capital assets most commonly held by taxpayers include stocks, bonds, personal residences, and land. To qualify for special tax treatment, capital gains must be long-term. Long-term capital gains or losses result from the sale of capital assets held by the taxpayer for more than six months, and short-term gains or losses result from the sale of those held six months or less. Short-term capital gains do not qualify for special tax treatment and are taxed as ordinary income.

The special tax treatment applies to the taxpayer's net capital gain, i.e., the excess of the net long-term capital gain (long-term capital gains less long-term capital losses) over the net short-term capital loss (short-term capital losses less short-term capital gain);[3] 60 percent of the net capital gain is a deduction for adjusted gross income.

To illustrate this concept, assume that a taxpayer had the following capital gains and losses:

Long-term capital gains	$11,000
Long-term capital losses	2,000
Short-term capital gains	5,000
Short-term capital losses	6,000

In this case, the taxpayer has a net long-term capital gain of $9,000 ($11,000 − $2,000) and a net short-term capital loss of $1,000 ($6,000 − $5,000). The taxpayer's net capital gain of $8,000 ($9,000 − $1,000) is included in computing adjusted gross income. In addition, the taxpayer enjoys a $4,800 (60% × $8,000) deduction for adjusted gross income. Therefore, there is a net increase of $3,200 ($8,000 − $4,800 or 40% × $8,000) in adjusted gross income due to the capital transactions.

Computation of Individual Income Tax-An Illustration. The example included in Illustration 3 details the computation of the income tax for an individual filing a joint return. This individual, who owns a drug store organized as a sole proprietorship, is married and has two minor children. In practice, the information would be reported on standard tax forms provided by the Federal government.

CORPORATE INCOME TAX

A corporation is a taxable entity which is separate and distinct from its stockholders. In general, the taxable income of a corporation is computed by deducting its ordinary business expenses and special deductions from its gross income. Although a corporation is taxed in generally the same manner as individuals, there are several important differences:

1. The concepts of itemized deductions, zero bracket amount, and personal exemptions are not applicable to corporations.
2. Corporations may ordinarily deduct 85 percent of all dividends received on investments in stocks of other taxable domestic corporations.
3. The deduction for charitable contributions is limited to ten percent of taxable income (before charitable contributions, before the 85 percent dividend deduction and before certain other deductions) in any one year.
4. Corporations are not allowed a net capital gain deduction. However, such gain is subject to tax at a maximum of 28 percent.

---

[3] If total capital losses exceed capital gains, individual taxpayers may generally deduct up to $3,000 of capital losses in a year with any excess subject to certain carry-forward rules.

Illustration 3

Income Tax Computation for Married Taxpayer Filing Jointly

Gross Income and Deductions from Gross Income

Sales			$100,000
Less:			
Cost of goods sold		$50,000	
Business expenses		30,000	80,000
Net business income			$ 20,000
Interest on savings accounts			1,000
Rents received		$ 5,000	
Less: Expenses		2,000	
Net rental income			3,000
Net capital gain		$10,000	
Less: Net capital gain deduction		6,000	4,000
Adjusted Gross Income			$ 28,000
Itemized deductions:			
Charitable contributions	$ 500		
Interest paid	1,100		
Property taxes	2,000		
Sales taxes	100		
Casualty loss (in excess of $100)	300	$ 4,000	
Less: Zero bracket amount		3,540	460
Less: Exemptions (4 × $1,040)			4,160
Taxable Income			$ 23,380
Total Tax			$ 3,116
Less: Payments on estimated taxes			3,500
Amount of refund			$ 384

5. An excess of capital losses over capital gains may not be deducted in the year of the loss. The net loss, however, may be used to offset capital gains of the preceding three years and the following five years, in chronological order.

The corporate tax rate also differs from the rate applied to individual taxpayers. A corporation pays a tax of 15 percent of the first $25,000 of taxable income, 18 percent of the second $25,000, 30 percent of the third $25,000, 40 percent of the fourth $25,000, and 46 percent of taxable income in excess of $100,000. Corporations also have available the alternative tax of 28 percent (mentioned above) on net capital gains.

Example: X Corporation has taxable income of $150,000 including $20,000 of net capital gains. The tax liability before credits is the lower of:

1. (15% × $25,000) + (18% × $25,000) + (30% × $25,000) + (40% × $25,000) + (46% × $50,000) = $48,750

or

2. (15% × $25,000) + (18% × $25,000) + (30% × $25,000) + (40% × $25,000) + (46% × $30,000) + (28% × $20,000) = $45,150

X Corporation's tax liability before credits is $45,150.

DIFFERENCES BETWEEN ACCOUNTING INCOME AND TAXABLE INCOME

The taxable income of a corporation often differs from the net income reported in its financial statements. Taxable income is determined by tax law while accounting income is based on generally accepted accounting principles. The rules and regulations comprising the income tax laws reflect the objectives of income taxation as well as administrative rulings which have been made to implement the law. Financial accounting, on the other hand, is concerned with the proper determination and matching of revenues and expenses in order to measure income.

Some differences between taxable income and accounting income occur because of special tax rules that differ from generally accepted accounting principles. Certain items of revenue are excluded by law from taxable income. For example, interest on state and municipal bonds is included in accounting income but not in taxable income. Similarly, certain expenses may not be treated as deductions for tax purposes. For example, goodwill is amortized as an expense for accounting purposes but it is not subject to amortization under current tax regulations. These items represent permanent differences between taxable and accounting income and are referred to as such.

Other differences between taxable income and accounting income are not permanent. These result from timing differences in the recognition of revenues and expenses. Timing differences occur because, in some instances, one method or procedure may be used for tax purposes and a different method or procedure for financial accounting purposes. The underlying reason why different methods are used is because of the differences in the objectives of accounting and taxation. The objective of financial accounting is a fair and accurate measurement of income and financial position, while the objective of a business in selecting tax methods is usually to minimize taxable income and postpone the payment of taxes. Although over a long enough period of time the timing differences should "wash out" so that total taxable income and total accounting income are the same, the difference during any one year may be significant. Two major examples of timing differences are as follows:

1. *Depreciation.* Prior to 1981, the tax laws allowed the use of several depreciation methods. A firm could use an accelerated depreciation method such as double-declining balance or sum-of-the-years'-digits for tax purposes, and straight-line depreciation for purposes of financial accounting. The accelerated methods resulted in larger depreciation expense than the straight-line method in the earlier years of the life of an asset, and smaller depreciation charges in the later years. Thus, the use of the different methods resulted in lower taxable income than accounting income during the early years, but had the opposite effect in later years.

    The 1981 Economic Recovery Tax Act overhauled the system of tax depreciation through the introduction of the Accelerated Cost Recovery System (ACRS). ACRS generally provides for the use of a statutory accelerated method approximating the declining balance method. Assets are depreciated over periods of time which are usually much shorter than their estimated useful lives.[4] Taxpayers not wanting the faster write-off may elect straight-line depreciation and longer lives. In either event, salvage value is no longer considered in the depreciation calculation. Because ACRS has not been approved as a generally accepted method for financial reporting purposes, the reporting difference between accounting income and taxable income will continue.
2. *Installment basis.* Businesses that sell merchandise on the installment basis may recognize revenue for financial accounting purposes at the time of sale but report the income for tax purposes as cash is actually received.

There are also several different methods of accounting for inventories. During periods of increasing prices, the last-in, first-out (Lifo) method results in higher costs and, thus, lower net income than the other acceptable inventory pricing methods. Consequently, with the general increase in prices in recent years, many firms have adopted the Lifo method for tax purposes. The use of Lifo for tax purposes, however, has not resulted in significant differences between taxable and accounting income because the tax law requires generally that a business must use this method for financial accounting if it is used for tax purposes.

---

[4] ACRS provides: (1) *Personal property* — Generally over 3, 5, 10 or 15 year recovery period, (2) *Real property* — Generally over 15 year recovery period.

Interperiod Tax Allocation

When one accounting method is used for tax purposes and a different method for financial accounting, revenues or expenses may be reported on the income statement and the tax return in different periods. Although the same total revenue and expenses (ignoring permanent differences) eventually are reported for both tax and financial accounting purposes, taxable income and accounting income during any one period may differ significantly. Therefore, as a result of timing differences, a part of the income tax liability during one period is caused by revenues and expenses reported during some other year for financial accounting purposes. Consequently, if income tax expense reported in the income statement is based on income taxes actually paid, there is a mismatching of revenues and expenses. That is, earnings may be included in the income statement of one period, and the related tax expense reported in a different period.

To illustrate this situation, assume that Ruth Company purchased several light trucks on January 1, 19x2, for $120,000. The firm plans to use the straight-line depreciation method for both tax and financial accounting purposes. No salvage value is anticipated and the trucks are assigned a four-year useful life for accounting purposes and a three-year life for tax purposes. Assume further that the income before taxes and depreciation remains constant at $100,000 for the years 19x2 through 19x5, and that the applicable tax rate is 50 percent (to simplify the illustration). Under these circumstances, the depreciation expense on the income statement will be $30,000 ($120,000 ÷ 4) each year, 19x2 through 19x5. The deduction for depreciation on the tax return, on the other hand, will be $40,000 ($120,000 ÷ 3) each year, 19x2 through 19x4 with no depreciation for tax purposes in 19x5, since the trucks were assigned a three-year life for tax purposes. The firm's taxable income and actual tax liability for the four-year period are as follows:

	19x2	19x3	19x4	19x5	Total
Income before depreciation and taxes	$100,000	$100,000	$100,000	$100,000	$400,000
Deduction for depreciation	40,000	40,000	40,000	0	120,000
Taxable income	$ 60,000	$ 60,000	$ 60,000	$100,000	$280,000
Income tax paid (50%)	$ 30,000	$ 30,000	$ 30,000	$ 50,000	$140,000

Using the income tax due the government for the year as the income tax expense on the income statement would result in the following determination of accounting income.

	19x2	19x3	19x4	19x5	Total
Income before depreciation and taxes	$100,000	$100,000	$100,000	$100,000	$400,000
Depreciation expense	30,000	30,000	30,000	30,000	120,000
Income before taxes	$ 70,000	$ 70,000	$ 70,000	$ 70,000	$280,000
Income tax expense	30,000	30,000	30,000	50,000	140,000
Net income	$ 40,000	$ 40,000	$ 40,000	$ 20,000	$140,000

It should be noted that even though Ruth Company had identical operating results during each year, the tax expense and the net income figures vary.

To correct this improper matching of revenues and expenses, tax expense in the income statement should be matched against the income reported therein, regardless of when the income will be included in taxable income and the tax actually paid. This procedure, known as interperiod tax allocation, relates the income tax expense for the period to accounting income rather than to taxable income. Thus, the tax expense reported on the income statement is equal to the tax rate applied to accounting income rather than the actual tax liability (tax rate × taxable income) for the period (after adjustments to reflect permanent differences have been made). If the timing differences cause the tax expense to exceed the taxes actually owed for the period, the excess represents a deferred credit—deferred income taxes. With regard to a particular timing difference, this deferred credit will eventually be eliminated in future periods when the tax liability exceeds the tax expense.

Using interperiod tax allocation, Ruth Company would report tax expense equal to the tax rate (50%) applied to the accounting income before taxes. The resulting income statements for the four-year period would be as follows:

	19x2	19x3	19x4	19x5	Total
Income before depreciation and taxes	$100,000	$100,000	$100,000	$100,000	$400,000
Depreciation expense	30,000	30,000	30,000	30,000	120,000
Income before taxes	$ 70,000	$ 70,000	$ 70,000	$ 70,000	$280,000
Income tax expense	35,000	35,000	35,000	35,000	140,000
Net income	$ 35,000	$ 35,000	$ 35,000	$ 35,000	$140,000

Thus, under tax allocation procedures, the tax expense in the income statement of $35,000 in each year is logically related to the earnings before taxes of $70,000 (given a tax rate of 50 percent). Note that the tax expense over the four-year period is still $140,000, and the total tax liability is also $140,000. The entries to record the tax expense for the year are:

19x2	Income Tax Expense.....................	35,000		
	Income Taxes Payable..................		30,000	
	Deferred Tax.........................		5,000	
19x3	Income Tax Expense.....................	35,000		
	Income Taxes Payable..................		30,000	
	Deferred Tax.........................		5,000	
19x4	Income Tax Expense.....................	35,000		
	Income Taxes Payable..................		30,000	
	Deferred Tax.........................		5,000	
19x5	Income Tax Expense.....................	35,000		
	Deferred Tax...........................	15,000		
	Income Taxes Payable..................		50,000	

In this example, the difference between accounting income and taxable income is eliminated over the four-year period. Therefore, the deferred tax account has a zero balance at the end of the four years. In practice, the differences between accounting and taxable income may last for a considerable number of years or even indefinitely since the company is continually replacing its assets and seldom, if ever, would all assets be fully depreciated. The balance in the deferred tax account may, therefore, become a significant amount.

The situation can also occur where taxable income exceeds accounting income in earlier years. Under interperiod tax allocation, the excess of the tax liability over tax expense would be considered a prepayment of income taxes. The difference would be debited to an asset, Deferred Tax Charges, representing income taxes paid on accounting income that will be recognized in a later period. For example, assume that Marion Company agrees to rent a portion of its office space to Dean Company on a one-time basis for 19x2 and receives its annual rent of $3,600 for the year 19x2 on December 31, 19x1. None of this amount would be included in accounting income for 19x1 since it will not be earned by Dean Company until 19x2. For tax purposes, however, the entire amount would be included in taxable income for 19x1 since prepaid rent is taxed as it is received rather than as it is earned. Assume that the income of Marion Company from all sources other than rentals was $10,000 for both 19x1 and 19x2. Its taxable income would be $13,600 (accounting income of $10,000 plus the $3,600 rent received) in 19x1 and $10,000 in 19x2. Further assume that the tax rate in both years was 50 percent. The entries to record the tax expense for 19x1 and 19x2 would be as follows:

19x1	**Tax Expense**	5,000		
	Deferred Tax Charge.........................	1,800		
	Income Taxes Payable.....................		6,800	
19x2	**Tax Expense**	6,800		
	Deferred Tax Charge.........................		1,800	
	Income Taxes Payable.....................		5,000	

In this example, the difference between accounting income and taxable income due to the timing difference in recognizing the rental income was eliminated by the end of 19x2.

In general, interperiod tax allocation for timing differences consists of charging income tax expense for an amount equal to accounting income × tax rate, crediting income tax payable for an amount equal to taxable income × tax rate, and debiting or crediting the difference to a deferred tax account. This "rule" assumes that there are only timing and not permanent differences between accounting income and taxable income.

Allocation of Income Tax Within a Period

According to Accounting Principles Board *Opinions No. 9* and *30*, the income statement should disclose separate income figures for: (1) income from continuing operations; (2) income from any segment or division of the business which has been, or is to be discontinued or sold—referred to as discontinued operations; and (3) income from unusual, nonrecurring item-referred to as extraordinary items. Income from continuing operations, income or losses from discontinued operations, and extraordinary gains or losses may be included in taxable income and, hence, affect the tax liability for the period. For this reason, it is believed that allocation of the total amount of income taxes for the period among income from continuing operations, discontinued operations, and extraordinary gains or losses provides a more meaningful income statement.

This allocation, called intraperiod tax allocation, is accomplished by deducting from income from continuing operations taxes related to that amount, showing income or losses from discontinued operations and extraordinary gains and losses net of the tax applicable to the gain or income and less the related tax reduction due to losses.

To illustrate, assume that Cobb Company, which uses the same methods for tax purposes and for financial accounting purposes (so that there are no timing difference), determined its tax liability for 19x2 as follows:

Revenues.	$100,000
Operating expenses	60,000
Operating income before taxes.	$ 40,000
Income from discontinued operations.	20,000
Extraordinary gain.	30,000
Taxable Income.	$ 90,000

Further, assume that the tax rate is 40 percent. The total tax liability would be $36,000 ($90,000 × 40%). Of this amount, $16,000 ($40,000 × 40%) is applicable to normal operating income; $8,000 ($20,000 × 40%) is due to discontinued operations; and $12,000 ($30,000 × 40%) is applicable to the extraordinary gain. The following statement illustrates the intraperiod tax allocation.

Cobb Company
Income Statement
For the Year Ended December 31, 19x2

Revenues	$100,000
Operating expenses	60,000
Income from continuing operations before taxes	$ 40,000
Provisions for income taxes	16,000
Income from continuing operations	$ 24,000
Discontinued operations:	
Income from discontinued operations	
(less related taxes of $8,000)	12,000
	$ 36,000
Extraordinary items:	
Extraordinary gain (less related taxes of $12,000)	18,000
Net Income	$ 54,000

INCOME TAXES AND MANAGEMENT DECISIONS

Because money has a "time value," it is rational for corporate management to defer as long as possible the incurrence and payment of corporate income taxes. Thus, a major consideration in tax planning is the timing of income and deductions. Management will normally attempt to minimize the current tax liability by deferring income or accelerating deductions to the extent possible under the tax laws. Successful tax planning is dependent upon a timely selection of the most advantageous tax alternatives.

While a detailed review of management decision making regarding corporate income taxes is beyond the scope of this text, the following are major areas of importance in tax planning:

1. Selecting the form of business organization
2. Acquisition, use, and disposition of fixed assets
3. Employee compensation
4. Corporate reorganizations
5. Financing arrangements

SUMMARY

Income taxes represent a significant expense of doing business for both corporate and noncorporate business enterprises. The four major classes of taxpayers are individuals, corporations, estates, and trusts. Sole proprietorships and partnerships are not taxable entities, although the income from these enterprises is taxed as income to their owners.

The individual federal income tax is computed by appropriately utilizing the tax tables or the tax rate schedules. Before calculating one's tax liability, an individual should be aware of the amount of gross income, deductions for adjusted gross income, adjusted gross income, itemized deductions, zero bracket amount, personal exemptions, taxable income, and credits.

Although the general procedure for determining a corporation's income tax is similar to that used by an individual, the treatment of specific items may differ significantly. In addition, the tax rate structure for corporations is greatly simplified from that for individuals. Since taxable income is determined by tax law while accounting income is based on generally accepted accounting principles, the tax liabilities based on the two amounts may differ. Tax expense in the income statement should be matched against the income reported therein, regardless of when the income is included in taxable income and the tax actually paid. The process of matching tax expense to the appropriate accounting periods is referred to as interperiod tax allocation. This process is used only when the difference in tax liabilities is due to timing. If a difference is permanent, no allocation is appropriate or necessary. An additional allocation of income tax within a period is made on the income statement to income from continuing operations, from discontinued operations, and from extraordinary items. This is referred to as intraperiod tax allocation.

KEY DEFINITIONS

Accounting income Accounting income is the amount of income determined using generally accepted accounting principles.

Adjusted gross income (for individuals) Adjusted gross income is gross income less deductions for adjusted gross income.

Capital assets Capital assets generally include all property except such items as trade receivables, inventories, copyrights or compositions in the hands of their creator, and government obligations issued on a discount basis and due within one year without interest. Real or depreciable property used in a trade or business may be treated as capital assets under certain circumstances.

Capital gain or loss A capital gain or loss is a realized gain or loss incurred from the sale or exchange of a capital asset.

Deductions for gross income (for individuals) Deductions for gross income in computing adjusted gross income include business and other expenses connected with earning certain types of revenue. These include ordinary and necessary expenses incurred by the taxpayer in the operation of his business or profession and certain employee expenses.

Deductions from adjusted gross income (for individuals) Deductions from adjusted gross income are legally allowable deductions that may be classified as either itemized deductions or personal exemptions.

Deferred tax Deferred tax is the cumulative difference between income tax expense and the income tax liability resulting from interperiod tax allocation.

Double taxation The corporation is taxed on its reported income and stockholders are taxed upon the receipt of dividends from the corporation. This is sometimes referred to as double taxation.

Estate An estate is a separate legal entity created to take charge of the assets of a deceased person, paying the decedent's debts and distributing the remaining assets to heirs.

Gross income Gross income includes all income from whatever source derived unless expressly excluded by law or the U.S. Constitution.

Head of household The title of head of household is a tax status that applies to certain unmarried or legally separated persons who maintain a residence for a relative.

Itemized deductions Deductions for certain employee business expenses and for personal expenses and losses such as charitable contributions, taxes, interest, casualty losses, and medical expenses are referred to as itemized deductions.

Interperiod tax allocation Interperiod tax allocation is a procedure used to apportion tax expense among periods so that the income tax expense reported for each period is in relation to the accounting income.

Intraperiod tax allocation Intraperiod tax allocation is the allocation of the total amount of income tax expense for a period among income from normal operations, discontinued operations, extraordinary items, and prior period adjustments.

Long-term capital gains or losses Long-term capital gains or losses are gains or losses which result from the sale or exchange of capital assets and certain productive assets of a business held by the taxpayer for more than twelve months. A special tax rate applies to net long-term capital gains.

Permanent difference A permanent difference is a difference between taxable income and accounting income which occurs because of tax rules which differ from generally accepted accounting principles and which will not be offset by corresponding differences in future periods.

Personal exemptions A personal exemption is a deduction of $1,000 from adjusted gross income for the taxpayer, his spouse, and qualified dependents. There are additional exemptions for the taxpayer and his spouse who are over 65 or blind.

Progressive tax This is a tax in which the tax rates increase as taxable income increases.

Taxable income Generally, taxable income is obtained by reducing adjusted gross income by the sum of (i) the difference between the taxpayer's itemized deductions and the zero bracket amount, and (ii) the deduction for personal exemptions.

Timing differences These are differences between taxable income and accounting income which occur because an item is included in taxable income in one period and in accounting income in a different period.

Trust A trust is a legal entity which is created when a person transfers assets to a trustee for the benefit of designated persons.

Zero bracket amount The zero bracket amount is presently $3,400 for married taxpayers filing jointly, $1,700 for a married taxpayer filing separately, and $2,300 for single taxpayers and heads of household. The zero bracket amount was introduced by the 1977 Tax Reduction and Simplification Act as a replacement for the old standard deduction. It is that initial amount of income which is subject to zero tax.

QUESTIONS

1. Explain how the net earnings of the following types of business entities are taxed by the federal government: (a) sole proprietorships, (b) partnerships, and (c) corporations.

2. The earnings of a corporation are subject to a "double tax." Explain.

3. Certain factors may cause the income before taxes in the accounting records to differ from taxable income. These factors may be either permanent differences or timing differences. Explain.

4. Does a corporation electing partnership treatment for tax purposes (Subchapter S) pay federal income taxes? Discuss.

5. What are the four major classes of taxable entities?

6. What is the objective of using the interperiod tax allocation procedures?

7. Does it make any difference in computing income taxes whether a given deduction is for computing adjusted gross income or an itemized deduction? Explain.

8. For an individual taxpayer, it is better to have a net long-term capital gain than an equal amount of ordinary income; but it is better to have an ordinary loss instead of an equal amount of net capital losses. Explain.

9. What are some of the differences between the tax rules for corporations and those for individuals?

10. What are some of the objectives of the federal income tax?

EXERCISES

11. Indicate the income tax status for each of the items listed below. For each item, state whether it is (a) included in gross income, (b) a deduction from gross income to determine adjusted gross income, (c) an itemized deduction, or (d) none of the above.

    1. Property taxes paid on personal residence.
    2. Interest paid on mortgage on personal residence.
    3. Damages of $500 to personal residence from a storm.
    4. Capital loss on the sale of stock.
    5. Insurance on home.
    6. Sales taxes.
    7. Inheritance received upon death of a relative.
    8. Interest received on municipal bonds.
    9. Share of income from partnership.
    10. Salary received as an employee.
    11. Rental income.
    12. Expenses incurred in earning rental income.
    13. Contributions to church.

12. James and Martha Gentry, filing a joint return, are entitled to one personal exemption each and two additional exemptions for dependent children. James Gentry owns a business organized as a sole proprietorship. Additional information related to their income tax return is as follows:

Revenues	$100,000
Cost of goods sold	60,000
Business expenses	20,000
Life insurance proceeds (death of father)	10,000
Interest on city of Bowro Bonds	500
Rental income	5,000
Allowable itemized deductions	1,800
Salary—Martha Gentry	6,000

Determine the following:

   a. Adjusted gross income
   b. Taxable income
   c. Income tax liability. (Use the tax table provided in this chapter.)

13. Don Looney had the following capital gains and losses in 1982.

Long-term losses	$ 3,000
Long-term gains	12,000
Short-term losses	8,000
Short-term gains	6,000

Determine the tax on Looney's capital gain assuming his marginal tax rate is 27 percent.

14. The following differences enter into the reconciliation of financial net income and taxable income of A.P. Baxter Corp. for the current year:

   a. Tax depreciation exceeds book depreciation by $30,000.
   b. Estimated warranty costs of $6,000 applicable to the current year's sales have not been paid. (Not deductible for tax purposes until paid.)
   c. Percentage depletion deducted on the tax return exceeds cost depletion by $45,000.
   d. Unearned rent revenue of $25,000 was deferred on the books but appropriately included in taxable income.
   e. A book expense of $2,000 for life insurance premiums on officers' lives is not allowed as a deduction on the tax return. (Note: this is not a timing difference.)
   f. A $7,000 tax deduction resulted from expensing research and development costs for tax purposes while such costs were capitalized for financial reporting.
   g. Gross profit of $80,000 was excluded from the taxable income because Baxter had appropriately elected the installment sale method for tax reporting while recognizing all gross profit from installment sales at the the time of the sale for financial reporting.

Required:

Consider each reconciling item independently of all others and explain whether each item would enter into the calculation of income taxes to be allocated. For any which are included in the income tax allocation calculation, explain the effect of the item on the current year's income tax expense and how the amount would be reported on the balance sheet. (Tax allocation calculations are not required.)

15. From the following information, calculate corporate income tax for the Brown Company.

   a. Sales were $990,000; cost of goods sold was 70 percent of sales.
   b. Dividends from domestic corporations totaled $30,000.
   c. Selling and miscellaneous expenses were 10 percent of sales.
   d. Assume that the corporate tax rate is 15 percent of the first $25,000 of taxable income; 18 percent of the second $25,000; 30 percent of the third $25,000; 40 percent of the fourth $25,000; and 46 percent of taxable income in excess of $100,000.

16. The partial tax return is shown below for Bengal, Inc. for the year 19x2.

Operating income before taxes	$ 80,000
Income from discontinued operations	45,000
Extraordinary gain (capital gain)	25,000
Taxable income	$150,000

   Assume that the tax rate is 40 percent. Bengal, Inc. uses the same methods for tax and financial accounting purposes.

   Required:

   Reflect the application of intraperiod income tax allocation procedures as they would be reported on the financial statements.

17. The taxable income for the Saints Corporation for 19x1 was $12,000, $15,000 for 19x2 and $10,000 for 19x3. Due to timing differences of reporting income for book purposes and tax purposes, the following differences occurred in these three years: 19x1—Book income exceeded income per tax return by $2,000; 19x2—Income per tax return exceeded book income by $3,500; 19x3—Book income exceeded income per tax return by $5,000. The tax rate is 40 percent.

   Required:

   Prepare journal entries to record the tax accrual and to reflect tax allocation procedures.

20 | Income Tax Considerations   661

18. Mary and Harry Jones have two children and file a joint return. In addition, they provide for the full support of Harry's mother and Mary's father, both over 65. Mary earns a gross salary of $10,000 a year and Harry earns $8,000. Mary received $250 in dividends and Harry received $70. Together they earned $500 interest on their joint savings account and $700 interest on municipal government bonds. On December 1, one of their children died and they received $5,000 in life insurance proceeds.

Required:

1. How many personal exemptions can the Jones' claim?
2. What is their adjusted gross income (or gross income in this case)?
3. What is their taxable income?
4. How much must they pay in federal income taxes?

19. The taxable income for the Patriot Corporation is $150,000 before capital gains and losses are taken into consideration. Determine the company's corporate income tax under each of the following independent assumptions involving capital gains and losses:

a. Long-term capital gains, $10,000.
    Long-term capital losses, $15,000.
b. Long-term capital gains, $12,000.
    Long-term capital losses, $9,000.
c. Long-term capital gains, $13,000.
    Long-term capital losses, $5,000.
    Short-term capital gains, $3,000.
    Short-term capital losses, $6,000.

Assume that the corporate tax rate is 17 percent of the first $25,000 of taxable income; 20 percent of the second $25,000; 30 percent of the third $25,000; 40 percent of the fourth $25,000; and 46 percent of taxable income in excess of $100,000. Corporations also have available an alternative tax of 28 percent on net capital gains.

PROBLEMS

20. Jim Simmons and his wife are both 63 years old and own a dry cleaning store. His wife has been legally blind since she was in a car accident when she was 55. In reviewing the books of his dry cleaning store, Jim finds that it had revenues of $95,000 and expenses of $80,000. During the year, Jim rented a vacant lot to a friend at an annual rental of $3,000. Jim paid property taxes of $300 on the lot.

Jim and his wife have a $7,000 savings account and earned interest at six percent compounded annually on this amount. On July 30, Jim realized a $1,000 capital gain on stocks purchased January 1 of the *preceding* year, and a $250 capital gain on other securities purchased June 1 of the *present* year. In examining his personal records, Jim found that he had made charitable contributions of $275 and had paid interest on his mortgage of $300. Also, he had paid $300 of property taxes.

Required:

Compute Jim's taxable income for the year assuming he filed a joint return with his wife.

21. In each of the following cases, determine the amount of capital gains to be included in adjusted gross income or the amount of capital loss to be deducted for an individual taxpayer. Assume taxpayer's taxable income from noncapital sources is $100,000.

	A	B	C
Long-term capital gains	$20,000	$20,000	$15,000
Long-term capital losses	15,000	15,000	20,000
Short-term capital gains	4,000	6,000	4,000
Short-term capital losses	6,000	4,000	6,000

22. Seahawk Company sells directly to its customers and uses the installment basis of revenue recognition on its tax return. However, the company recognizes revenue at the point of sale for accounting purposes. During the year, the following two sales were made and were to be paid in installments as indicated:

Date	Sale	Cost of Sale	Terms of Sale
2/1	$500	$300	$25/month for 20 months
4/1	800	680	$80/month for 10 months

The first payment was due on the first day of the month following the sale. All payments were made when due. Income taxes *payable* for 19x2 totaled $1,500 and $1,700 for 19x3. The income tax rate is 50 percent.

Required:

1. Calculate the difference between accounting income and taxable income for 19x2 and 19x3 resulting from the above transactions.
2. Make the entries to record the tax expense for 19x2 and 19x3.

23. An individual taxpayer had the following capital gains and losses during the year:

	Gains	Losses
Short-Term	$ 6,000	$11,000
Long-Term	20,000	5,000

Required:

Compute the amount of income tax on the capital gains assuming that the taxpayer has a marginal tax rate of: (a) 32 percent and (b) 50 percent.

24. The Hall Company uses accelerated depreciation for tax purposes and straight-line depreciation for its financial accounting records. Its taxable income and accounting income (before income taxes) for a four-year period are shown below:

	19x1	19x2	19x3	19x4
Taxable income	$ 70,000	$100,000	$140,000	$210,000
Accounting income	100,000	120,000	150,000	200,000

Assume that the corporate tax rate is 50 percent.

Required;

1. Compute the net income after taxes in the financial statement for Hall Company (a) assuming that interperiod tax allocation procedures are not used and (b) assuming the tax allocation procedure is used.
2. Determine the balance in the "Deferred Tax" account at the end of 19x4 in 1(b) above.

Refer to the Annual Report included in the Appendix at the end of the text:

25. Are the stockholders being taxed twice?

26. What is the amount of deferred taxes "owed" at the end of the most recent year?

27. What was the effective tax rate for the most recent year?

28. Was there a capital gain or loss in the most recent year?

29. What was the amount of this gain or loss (if any)?

30. What was the amount of the investment tax credits in the most recent year?

Appendix to Chapter 20

1985 Tax Table
Your zero bracket amount has been built into the Tax Table.

Based on Taxable Income

For persons with taxable incomes of less than $50,000.

Example: Mr. and Mrs. Brown are filing a joint return. Their taxable income on line 37 of Form 1040 is $25,325. First, they find the $25,300-25,350 income line. Next, they find the column for married filing jointly and read down the column. The amount shown where the income line and filing status column meet is $3,545. This is the tax amount they must write on line 38 of their return.

At least	But less than	Single	Married filing jointly*	Married filing separately	Head of a household
			Your tax is—		
25,200	25,250	4,513	3,523	5,614	4,177
25,250	25,300	4,528	3,534	5,633	4,191
→ 25,300	25,350	4,543	(3,545)	5,652	4,205
25,350	25,400	4,558	3,556	5,671	4,219

If line 37 (taxable income) is—		And you are—				If line 37 (taxable income) is—		And you are—				If line 37 (taxable income) is—		And you are—			
At least	But less than	Single	Married filing jointly*	Married filing separately	Head of a household	At least	But less than	Single	Married filing jointly*	Married filing separately	Head of a household	At least	But less than	Single	Married filing jointly*	Married filing separately	Head of a household
			Your tax is—						Your tax is—						Your tax is—		
$0	$1,775	$0	$0	$0	$0	2,400	2,425	2	0	71	2	3,400	3,450	114	0	188	114
1,775	1,800	0	0	2	0	2,425	2,450	5	0	73	5	3,450	3,500	119	0	194	119
						2,450	2,475	8	0	76	8	3,500	3,550	125	0	200	125
						2,475	2,500	11	0	79	11	3,550	3,600	131	4	206	130
1,800	1,825	0	0	5	0	2,500	2,525	13	0	82	13	3,600	3,650	137	9	212	136
1,825	1,850	0	0	7	0	2,525	2,550	16	0	84	16	3,650	3,700	143	15	218	141
1,850	1,875	0	0	10	0	2,550	2,575	19	0	87	19	3,700	3,750	149	20	224	147
1,875	1,900	0	0	13	0	2,575	2,600	22	0	90	22	3,750	3,800	155	26	230	152
						2,600	2,625	24	0	93	24	3,800	3,850	161	31	236	158
						2,625	2,650	27	0	95	27	3,850	3,900	167	37	242	163
1,900	1,925	0	0	16	0	2,650	2,675	30	0	98	30	3,900	3,950	173	42	248	169
1,925	1,950	0	0	18	0	2,675	2,700	33	0	101	33	3,950	4,000	179	48	254	174
1,950	1,975	0	0	21	0	2,700	2,725	35	0	104	35	**4,000**					
1,975	2,000	0	0	24	0	2,725	2,750	38	0	106	38						
2,000						2,750	2,775	41	0	109	41	4,000	4,050	185	53	261	180
						2,775	2,800	44	0	112	44	4,050	4,100	191	59	268	185
												4,100	4,150	197	64	275	191
2,000	2,025	0	0	27	0	2,800	2,825	46	0	115	46	4,150	4,200	203	70	282	196
2,025	2,050	0	0	29	0	2,825	2,850	49	0	117	49						
2,050	2,075	0	0	32	0	2,850	2,875	52	0	120	52	4,200	4,250	209	75	289	202
2,075	2,100	0	0	35	0	2,875	2,900	55	0	123	55	4,250	4,300	215	81	296	207
												4,300	4,350	221	86	303	213
						2,900	2,925	57	0	126	57	4,350	4,400	227	92	310	218
2,100	2,125	0	0	38	0	2,925	2,950	60	0	129	60						
2,125	2,150	0	0	40	0	2,950	2,975	63	0	132	63	4,400	4,450	233	97	317	224
2,150	2,175	0	0	43	0	2,975	3,000	66	0	135	66	4,450	4,500	239	103	324	229
2,175	2,200	0	0	46	0	**3,000**						4,500	4,550	245	108	331	235
												4,550	4,600	251	114	338	240
2,200	2,225	0	0	49	0	3,000	3,050	70	0	140	70	4,600	4,650	258	119	345	246
2,225	2,250	0	0	51	0	3,050	3,100	75	0	146	75	4,650	4,700	265	125	352	252
2,250	2,275	0	0	54	0	3,100	3,150	81	0	152	81	4,700	4,750	272	130	359	258
2,275	2,300	0	0	57	0	3,150	3,200	86	0	158	86	4,750	4,800	279	136	366	264
2,300	2,325	0	0	60	0	3,200	3,250	92	0	164	92	4,800	4,850	286	141	373	270
2,325	2,350	0	0	62	0	3,250	3,300	97	0	170	97	4,850	4,900	293	147	380	276
2,350	2,375	0	0	65	0	3,300	3,350	103	0	176	103	4,900	4,950	300	152	387	282
2,375	2,400	0	0	68	0	3,350	3,400	108	0	182	108	4,950	5,000	307	158	394	288

*This column must also be used by a qualifying widow(er).

Continued on next page

1985 Tax Table—Continued

If line 37 (taxable income) is—		And you are—				If line 37 (taxable income) is—		And you are—				If line 37 (taxable income) is—		And you are—			
At least	But less than	Single	Married filing jointly*	Married filing sepa-rately	Head of a house-hold	At least	But less than	Single	Married filing jointly*	Married filing sepa-rately	Head of a house-hold	At least	But less than	Single	Married filing jointly*	Married filing sepa-rately	Head of a house-hold
		Your tax is—						Your tax is—						Your tax is—			
5,000						**8,000**						**11,000**					
5,000	5,050	314	163	401	294	8,000	8,050	746	519	858	680	11,000	11,050	1,218	939	1,412	1,159
5,050	5,100	321	169	408	300	8,050	8,100	754	526	866	687	11,050	11,100	1,226	946	1,423	1,167
5,100	5,150	328	174	415	306	8,100	8,150	761	533	874	694	11,100	11,150	1,234	953	1,434	1,176
5,150	5,200	335	180	422	312	8,150	8,200	769	540	882	701	11,150	11,200	1,242	960	1,445	1,184
5,200	5,250	342	185	429	318	8,200	8,250	776	547	890	708	11,200	11,250	1,250	967	1,456	1,193
5,250	5,300	349	191	436	324	8,250	8,300	784	554	898	715	11,250	11,300	1,259	974	1,467	1,201
5,300	5,350	356	196	443	330	8,300	8,350	791	561	906	722	11,300	11,350	1,268	981	1,478	1,210
5,350	5,400	363	202	450	336	8,350	8,400	799	568	915	729	11,350	11,400	1,277	988	1,489	1,218
5,400	5,450	370	207	457	342	8,400	8,450	806	575	924	736	11,400	11,450	1,286	995	1,500	1,227
5,450	5,500	377	213	464	348	8,450	8,500	814	582	933	743	11,450	11,500	1,295	1,002	1,511	1,235
5,500	5,550	384	218	471	354	8,500	8,550	821	589	942	750	11,500	11,550	1,304	1,009	1,522	1,244
5,550	5,600	391	224	478	360	8,550	8,600	829	596	951	757	11,550	11,600	1,313	1,016	1,533	1,252
5,600	5,650	398	229	485	366	8,600	8,650	836	603	960	764	11,600	11,650	1,322	1,023	1,544	1,261
5,650	5,700	405	235	492	372	8,650	8,700	844	610	969	771	11,650	11,700	1,331	1,030	1,555	1,269
5,700	5,750	412	240	499	378	8,700	8,750	851	617	978	778	11,700	11,750	1,340	1,037	1,566	1,278
5,750	5,800	419	246	506	384	8,750	8,800	859	624	987	785	11,750	11,800	1,349	1,044	1,577	1,286
5,800	5,850	426	252	513	390	8,800	8,850	866	631	996	792	11,800	11,850	1,358	1,051	1,588	1,295
5,850	5,900	433	258	520	396	8,850	8,900	874	638	1,005	799	11,850	11,900	1,367	1,058	1,599	1,303
5,900	5,950	440	264	527	402	8,900	8,950	882	645	1,014	806	11,900	11,950	1,376	1,065	1,610	1,312
5,950	6,000	447	270	534	408	8,950	9,000	890	652	1,023	813	11,950	12,000	1,385	1,072	1,621	1,320
6,000						**9,000**						**12,000**					
6,000	6,050	454	276	541	414	9,000	9,050	898	659	1,032	820	12,000	12,050	1,394	1,079	1,632	1,329
6,050	6,100	461	282	548	420	9,050	9,100	906	666	1,041	827	12,050	12,100	1,403	1,086	1,643	1,337
6,100	6,150	468	288	555	426	9,100	9,150	914	673	1,050	836	12,100	12,150	1,412	1,093	1,654	1,346
6,150	6,200	475	294	562	432	9,150	9,200	922	680	1,059	844	12,150	12,200	1,421	1,100	1,665	1,354
6,200	6,250	482	300	570	438	9,200	9,250	930	687	1,068	853	12,200	12,250	1,430	1,107	1,676	1,363
6,250	6,300	489	306	578	444	9,250	9,300	938	694	1,077	861	12,250	12,300	1,439	1,114	1,687	1,371
6,300	6,350	496	312	586	450	9,300	9,350	946	701	1,086	870	12,300	12,350	1,448	1,121	1,698	1,380
6,350	6,400	503	318	594	456	9,350	9,400	954	708	1,095	878	12,350	12,400	1,457	1,128	1,709	1,389
6,400	6,450	510	324	602	462	9,400	9,450	962	715	1,104	887	12,400	12,450	1,466	1,135	1,720	1,398
6,450	6,500	517	330	610	468	9,450	9,500	970	722	1,113	895	12,450	12,500	1,475	1,143	1,731	1,407
6,500	6,550	524	336	618	474	9,500	9,550	978	729	1,122	904	12,500	12,550	1,484	1,151	1,742	1,416
6,550	6,600	531	342	626	480	9,550	9,600	986	736	1,131	912	12,550	12,600	1,493	1,159	1,753	1,425
6,600	6,650	538	348	634	486	9,600	9,650	994	743	1,140	921	12,600	12,650	1,502	1,167	1,764	1,434
6,650	6,700	545	354	642	492	9,650	9,700	1,002	750	1,149	929	12,650	12,700	1,511	1,175	1,775	1,443
6,700	6,750	552	360	650	498	9,700	9,750	1,010	757	1,158	938	12,700	12,750	1,520	1,183	1,786	1,452
6,750	6,800	559	366	658	505	9,750	9,800	1,018	764	1,167	946	12,750	12,800	1,529	1,191	1,797	1,461
6,800	6,850	566	372	666	512	9,800	9,850	1,026	771	1,176	955	12,800	12,850	1,538	1,199	1,809	1,470
6,850	6,900	574	378	674	519	9,850	9,900	1,034	778	1,185	963	12,850	12,900	1,547	1,207	1,822	1,479
6,900	6,950	581	384	682	526	9,900	9,950	1,042	785	1,194	972	12,900	12,950	1,556	1,215	1,834	1,488
6,950	7,000	589	390	690	533	9,950	10,000	1,050	792	1,203	980	12,950	13,000	1,565	1,223	1,847	1,497
7,000						**10,000**						**13,000**					
7,000	7,050	596	396	698	540	10,000	10,050	1,058	799	1,212	989	13,000	13,050	1,574	1,231	1,859	1,506
7,050	7,100	604	402	706	547	10,050	10,100	1,066	806	1,221	997	13,050	13,100	1,583	1,239	1,872	1,515
7,100	7,150	611	408	714	554	10,100	10,150	1,074	813	1,230	1,006	13,100	13,150	1,592	1,247	1,884	1,524
7,150	7,200	619	414	722	561	10,150	10,200	1,082	820	1,239	1,014	13,150	13,200	1,601	1,255	1,897	1,533
7,200	7,250	626	420	730	568	10,200	10,250	1,090	827	1,248	1,023	13,200	13,250	1,610	1,263	1,909	1,542
7,250	7,300	634	426	738	575	10,250	10,300	1,098	834	1,257	1,031	13,250	13,300	1,619	1,271	1,922	1,551
7,300	7,350	641	432	746	582	10,300	10,350	1,106	841	1,266	1,040	13,300	13,350	1,628	1,279	1,934	1,560
7,350	7,400	649	438	754	589	10,350	10,400	1,114	848	1,275	1,048	13,350	13,400	1,637	1,287	1,947	1,569
7,400	7,450	656	444	762	596	10,400	10,450	1,122	855	1,284	1,057	13,400	13,450	1,646	1,295	1,959	1,578
7,450	7,500	664	450	770	603	10,450	10,500	1,130	862	1,293	1,065	13,450	13,500	1,656	1,303	1,972	1,587
7,500	7,550	671	456	778	610	10,500	10,550	1,138	869	1,302	1,074	13,500	13,550	1,666	1,311	1,984	1,596
7,550	7,600	679	462	786	617	10,550	10,600	1,146	876	1,313	1,082	13,550	13,600	1,676	1,319	1,997	1,605
7,600	7,650	686	468	794	624	10,600	10,650	1,154	883	1,324	1,091	13,600	13,650	1,686	1,327	2,009	1,614
7,650	7,700	694	474	802	631	10,650	10,700	1,162	890	1,335	1,099	13,650	13,700	1,696	1,335	2,022	1,623
7,700	7,750	701	480	810	638	10,700	10,750	1,170	897	1,346	1,108	13,700	13,750	1,706	1,343	2,034	1,632
7,750	7,800	709	486	818	645	10,750	10,800	1,178	904	1,357	1,116	13,750	13,800	1,716	1,351	2,047	1,641
7,800	7,850	716	492	826	652	10,800	10,850	1,186	911	1,368	1,125	13,800	13,850	1,726	1,359	2,059	1,650
7,850	7,900	724	498	834	659	10,850	10,900	1,194	918	1,379	1,133	13,850	13,900	1,736	1,367	2,072	1,659
7,900	7,950	731	505	842	666	10,900	10,950	1,202	925	1,390	1,142	13,900	13,950	1,746	1,375	2,084	1,668
7,950	8,000	739	512	850	673	10,950	11,000	1,210	932	1,401	1,150	13,950	14,000	1,756	1,383	2,097	1,677

* This column must also be used by a qualifying widow(er).

Continued on next page

1985 Tax Table—Continued

If line 37 (taxable income) is—		And you are—				If line 37 (taxable income) is—		And you are—				If line 37 (taxable income) is—		And you are—			
At least	But less than	Single	Married filing jointly *	Married filing sepa- rately	Head of a house- hold	At least	But less than	Single	Married filing jointly *	Married filing sepa- rately	Head of a house- hold	At least	But less than	Single	Married filing jointly *	Married filing sepa- rately	Head of a house- hold
		Your tax is—						Your tax is—						Your tax is—			
14,000						**17,000**						**20,000**					
14,000	14,050	1,766	1,391	2,109	1,686	17,000	17,050	2,408	1,879	2,903	2,255	20,000	20,050	3,131	2,419	3,829	2,898
14,050	14,100	1,776	1,399	2,122	1,695	17,050	17,100	2,420	1,888	2,917	2,265	20,050	20,100	3,144	2,428	3,845	2,910
14,100	14,150	1,786	1,407	2,134	1,704	17,100	17,150	2,431	1,897	2,931	2,275	20,100	20,150	3,157	2,437	3,862	2,922
14,150	14,200	1,796	1,415	2,147	1,713	17,150	17,200	2,443	1,906	2,945	2,285	20,150	20,200	3,170	2,446	3,878	2,934
14,200	14,250	1,806	1,423	2,159	1,722	17,200	17,250	2,454	1,915	2,959	2,295	20,200	20,250	3,183	2,455	3,895	2,946
14,250	14,300	1,816	1,431	2,172	1,731	17,250	17,300	2,466	1,924	2,973	2,305	20,250	20,300	3,196	2,464	3,911	2,958
14,300	14,350	1,826	1,439	2,184	1,740	17,300	17,350	2,477	1,933	2,987	2,315	20,300	20,350	3,209	2,473	3,928	2,970
14,350	14,400	1,836	1,447	2,197	1,749	17,350	17,400	2,489	1,942	3,001	2,325	20,350	20,400	3,222	2,482	3,944	2,982
14,400	14,450	1,846	1,455	2,209	1,758	17,400	17,450	2,500	1,951	3,015	2,335	20,400	20,450	3,235	2,491	3,961	2,994
14,450	14,500	1,856	1,463	2,222	1,767	17,450	17,500	2,512	1,960	3,029	2,345	20,450	20,500	3,248	2,500	3,977	3,006
14,500	14,550	1,866	1,471	2,234	1,776	17,500	17,550	2,523	1,969	3,043	2,355	20,500	20,550	3,261	2,509	3,994	3,018
14,550	14,600	1,876	1,479	2,247	1,785	17,550	17,600	2,535	1,978	3,057	2,365	20,550	20,600	3,274	2,518	4,010	3,030
14,600	14,650	1,886	1,487	2,259	1,794	17,600	17,650	2,546	1,987	3,071	2,375	20,600	20,650	3,287	2,527	4,027	3,042
14,650	14,700	1,896	1,495	2,272	1,803	17,650	17,700	2,558	1,996	3,085	2,385	20,650	20,700	3,300	2,536	4,043	3,054
14,700	14,750	1,906	1,503	2,284	1,812	17,700	17,750	2,569	2,005	3,099	2,395	20,700	20,750	3,313	2,545	4,060	3,066
14,750	14,800	1,916	1,511	2,297	1,821	17,750	17,800	2,581	2,014	3,113	2,405	20,750	20,800	3,326	2,554	4,076	3,078
14,800	14,850	1,926	1,519	2,309	1,830	17,800	17,850	2,592	2,023	3,127	2,415	20,800	20,850	3,339	2,563	4,093	3,090
14,850	14,900	1,936	1,527	2,322	1,839	17,850	17,900	2,604	2,032	3,141	2,425	20,850	20,900	3,352	2,572	4,109	3,102
14,900	14,950	1,946	1,535	2,334	1,848	17,900	17,950	2,615	2,041	3,155	2,435	20,900	20,950	3,365	2,581	4,126	3,114
14,950	15,000	1,956	1,543	2,347	1,857	17,950	18,000	2,627	2,050	3,169	2,445	20,950	21,000	3,378	2,590	4,142	3,126
15,000						**18,000**						**21,000**					
15,000	15,050	1,966	1,551	2,359	1,866	18,000	18,050	2,638	2,059	3,183	2,455	21,000	21,050	3,391	2,599	4,159	3,138
15,050	15,100	1,976	1,559	2,372	1,875	18,050	18,100	2,650	2,068	3,197	2,465	21,050	21,100	3,404	2,610	4,175	3,150
15,100	15,150	1,986	1,567	2,384	1,884	18,100	18,150	2,661	2,077	3,211	2,475	21,100	21,150	3,417	2,621	4,192	3,162
15,150	15,200	1,996	1,575	2,397	1,893	18,150	18,200	2,673	2,086	3,225	2,485	21,150	21,200	3,430	2,632	4,208	3,174
15,200	15,250	2,006	1,583	2,409	1,902	18,200	18,250	2,684	2,095	3,239	2,495	21,200	21,250	3,443	2,643	4,225	3,186
15,250	15,300	2,016	1,591	2,422	1,911	18,250	18,300	2,696	2,104	3,253	2,505	21,250	21,300	3,456	2,654	4,241	3,198
15,300	15,350	2,026	1,599	2,434	1,920	18,300	18,350	2,707	2,113	3,268	2,515	21,300	21,350	3,469	2,665	4,258	3,210
15,350	15,400	2,036	1,607	2,447	1,929	18,350	18,400	2,719	2,122	3,284	2,525	21,350	21,400	3,482	2,676	4,274	3,222
15,400	15,450	2,046	1,615	2,459	1,938	18,400	18,450	2,730	2,131	3,301	2,535	21,400	21,450	3,495	2,687	4,291	3,234
15,450	15,500	2,056	1,623	2,472	1,947	18,450	18,500	2,742	2,140	3,317	2,545	21,450	21,500	3,508	2,698	4,307	3,246
15,500	15,550	2,066	1,631	2,484	1,956	18,500	18,550	2,753	2,149	3,334	2,555	21,500	21,550	3,521	2,709	4,324	3,258
15,550	15,600	2,076	1,639	2,497	1,965	18,550	18,600	2,765	2,158	3,350	2,565	21,550	21,600	3,534	2,720	4,340	3,270
15,600	15,650	2,086	1,647	2,511	1,975	18,600	18,650	2,776	2,167	3,367	2,575	21,600	21,650	3,547	2,731	4,357	3,282
15,650	15,700	2,098	1,655	2,525	1,985	18,650	18,700	2,788	2,176	3,383	2,585	21,650	21,700	3,560	2,742	4,373	3,294
15,700	15,750	2,109	1,663	2,539	1,995	18,700	18,750	2,799	2,185	3,400	2,595	21,700	21,750	3,573	2,753	4,390	3,306
15,750	15,800	2,121	1,671	2,553	2,005	18,750	18,800	2,811	2,194	3,416	2,605	21,750	21,800	3,586	2,764	4,406	3,318
15,800	15,850	2,132	1,679	2,567	2,015	18,800	18,850	2,822	2,203	3,433	2,615	21,800	21,850	3,599	2,775	4,423	3,330
15,850	15,900	2,144	1,687	2,581	2,025	18,850	18,900	2,834	2,212	3,449	2,625	21,850	21,900	3,612	2,786	4,439	3,342
15,900	15,950	2,155	1,695	2,595	2,035	18,900	18,950	2,845	2,221	3,466	2,635	21,900	21,950	3,625	2,797	4,456	3,354
15,950	16,000	2,167	1,703	2,609	2,045	18,950	19,000	2,858	2,230	3,482	2,646	21,950	22,000	3,638	2,808	4,472	3,366
16,000						**19,000**						**22,000**					
16,000	16,050	2,178	1,711	2,623	2,055	19,000	19,050	2,871	2,239	3,499	2,658	22,000	22,050	3,651	2,819	4,489	3,378
16,050	16,100	2,190	1,719	2,637	2,065	19,050	19,100	2,884	2,248	3,515	2,670	22,050	22,100	3,664	2,830	4,505	3,390
16,100	16,150	2,201	1,727	2,651	2,075	19,100	19,150	2,897	2,257	3,532	2,682	22,100	22,150	3,677	2,841	4,522	3,402
16,150	16,200	2,213	1,735	2,665	2,085	19,150	19,200	2,910	2,266	3,548	2,694	22,150	22,200	3,690	2,852	4,538	3,414
16,200	16,250	2,224	1,743	2,679	2,095	19,200	19,250	2,923	2,275	3,565	2,706	22,200	22,250	3,703	2,863	4,555	3,426
16,250	16,300	2,236	1,751	2,693	2,105	19,250	19,300	2,936	2,284	3,581	2,718	22,250	22,300	3,716	2,874	4,571	3,438
16,300	16,350	2,247	1,759	2,707	2,115	19,300	19,350	2,949	2,293	3,598	2,730	22,300	22,350	3,729	2,885	4,588	3,450
16,350	16,400	2,259	1,767	2,721	2,125	19,350	19,400	2,962	2,302	3,614	2,742	22,350	22,400	3,742	2,896	4,604	3,462
16,400	16,450	2,270	1,775	2,735	2,135	19,400	19,450	2,975	2,311	3,631	2,754	22,400	22,450	3,755	2,907	4,621	3,474
16,450	16,500	2,282	1,783	2,749	2,145	19,450	19,500	2,988	2,320	3,647	2,766	22,450	22,500	3,768	2,918	4,637	3,486
16,500	16,550	2,293	1,791	2,763	2,155	19,500	19,550	3,001	2,329	3,664	2,778	22,500	22,550	3,781	2,929	4,654	3,498
16,550	16,600	2,305	1,799	2,777	2,165	19,550	19,600	3,014	2,338	3,680	2,790	22,550	22,600	3,794	2,940	4,670	3,510
16,600	16,650	2,316	1,807	2,791	2,175	19,600	19,650	3,027	2,347	3,697	2,802	22,600	22,650	3,807	2,951	4,687	3,522
16,650	16,700	2,328	1,816	2,805	2,185	19,650	19,700	3,040	2,356	3,713	2,814	22,650	22,700	3,820	2,962	4,703	3,534
16,700	16,750	2,339	1,825	2,819	2,195	19,700	19,750	3,053	2,365	3,730	2,826	22,700	22,750	3,833	2,973	4,720	3,546
16,750	16,800	2,351	1,834	2,833	2,205	19,750	19,800	3,066	2,374	3,746	2,838	22,750	22,800	3,846	2,984	4,736	3,558
16,800	16,850	2,362	1,843	2,847	2,215	19,800	19,850	3,079	2,383	3,763	2,850	22,800	22,850	3,859	2,995	4,753	3,570
16,850	16,900	2,374	1,852	2,861	2,225	19,850	19,900	3,092	2,392	3,779	2,862	22,850	22,900	3,872	3,006	4,769	3,582
16,900	16,950	2,385	1,861	2,875	2,235	19,900	19,950	3,105	2,401	3,796	2,874	22,900	22,950	3,885	3,017	4,786	3,594
16,950	17,000	2,397	1,870	2,889	2,245	19,950	20,000	3,118	2,410	3,812	2,886	22,950	23,000	3,898	3,028	4,802	3,606

* This column must also be used by a qualifying widow(er).

Continued on next page

1985 Tax Table—*Continued*

If line 37 (taxable income) is—		And you are—				If line 37 (taxable income) is—		And you are—				If line 37 (taxable income) is—		And you are—			
At least	But less than	Single	Married filing jointly *	Married filing separately	Head of a household	At least	But less than	Single	Married filing jointly *	Married filing separately	Head of a household	At least	But less than	Single	Married filing jointly *	Married filing separately	Head of a household
		Your tax is—						Your tax is—						Your tax is—			
23,000						**26,000**						**29,000**					
23,000	23,050	3,911	3,039	4,819	3,618	26,000	26,050	4,753	3,712	5,918	4,401	29,000	29,050	5,653	4,462	7,058	5,241
23,050	23,100	3,924	3,050	4,835	3,630	26,050	26,100	4,768	3,724	5,937	4,415	29,050	29,100	5,668	4,474	7,077	5,255
23,100	23,150	3,937	3,061	4,852	3,642	26,100	26,150	4,783	3,737	5,956	4,429	29,100	29,150	5,683	4,487	7,096	5,269
23,150	23,200	3,950	3,072	4,868	3,654	26,150	26,200	4,798	3,749	5,975	4,443	29,150	29,200	5,698	4,499	7,115	5,283
23,200	23,250	3,963	3,083	4,885	3,666	26,200	26,250	4,813	3,762	5,994	4,457	29,200	29,250	5,713	4,512	7,134	5,297
23,250	23,300	3,976	3,094	4,901	3,678	26,250	26,300	4,828	3,774	6,013	4,471	29,250	29,300	5,728	4,524	7,153	5,311
23,300	23,350	3,989	3,105	4,918	3,690	26,300	26,350	4,843	3,787	6,032	4,485	29,300	29,350	5,743	4,537	7,172	5,325
23,350	23,400	4,002	3,116	4,934	3,702	26,350	26,400	4,858	3,799	6,051	4,499	29,350	29,400	5,758	4,549	7,191	5,339
23,400	23,450	4,015	3,127	4,951	3,714	26,400	26,450	4,873	3,812	6,070	4,513	29,400	29,450	5,773	4,562	7,210	5,353
23,450	23,500	4,028	3,138	4,967	3,726	26,450	26,500	4,888	3,824	6,089	4,527	29,450	29,500	5,788	4,574	7,229	5,367
23,500	23,550	4,041	3,149	4,984	3,738	26,500	26,550	4,903	3,837	6,108	4,541	29,500	29,550	5,803	4,587	7,248	5,381
23,550	23,600	4,054	3,160	5,000	3,750	26,550	26,600	4,918	3,849	6,127	4,555	29,550	29,600	5,818	4,599	7,267	5,395
23,600	23,650	4,067	3,171	5,017	3,762	26,600	26,650	4,933	3,862	6,146	4,569	29,600	29,650	5,833	4,612	7,286	5,409
23,650	23,700	4,080	3,182	5,033	3,774	26,650	26,700	4,948	3,874	6,165	4,583	29,650	29,700	5,848	4,624	7,305	5,423
23,700	23,750	4,093	3,193	5,050	3,786	26,700	26,750	4,963	3,887	6,184	4,597	29,700	29,750	5,863	4,637	7,324	5,437
23,750	23,800	4,106	3,204	5,066	3,798	26,750	26,800	4,978	3,899	6,203	4,611	29,750	29,800	5,878	4,649	7,343	5,451
23,800	23,850	4,119	3,215	5,083	3,810	26,800	26,850	4,993	3,912	6,222	4,625	29,800	29,850	5,893	4,662	7,362	5,465
23,850	23,900	4,132	3,226	5,101	3,822	26,850	26,900	5,008	3,924	6,241	4,639	29,850	29,900	5,908	4,674	7,381	5,479
23,900	23,950	4,145	3,237	5,120	3,834	26,900	26,950	5,023	3,937	6,260	4,653	29,900	29,950	5,923	4,687	7,400	5,493
23,950	24,000	4,158	3,248	5,139	3,846	26,950	27,000	5,038	3,949	6,279	4,667	29,950	30,000	5,938	4,699	7,419	5,507
24,000						**27,000**						**30,000**					
24,000	24,050	4,171	3,259	5,158	3,858	27,000	27,050	5,053	3,962	6,298	4,681	30,000	30,050	5,955	4,712	7,438	5,523
24,050	24,100	4,184	3,270	5,177	3,870	27,050	27,100	5,068	3,974	6,317	4,695	30,050	30,100	5,972	4,724	7,457	5,539
24,100	24,150	4,197	3,281	5,196	3,882	27,100	27,150	5,083	3,987	6,336	4,709	30,100	30,150	5,989	4,737	7,476	5,555
24,150	24,200	4,210	3,292	5,215	3,894	27,150	27,200	5,098	3,999	6,355	4,723	30,150	30,200	6,006	4,749	7,495	5,571
24,200	24,250	4,223	3,303	5,234	3,906	27,200	27,250	5,113	4,012	6,374	4,737	30,200	30,250	6,023	4,762	7,514	5,587
24,250	24,300	4,236	3,314	5,253	3,918	27,250	27,300	5,128	4,024	6,393	4,751	30,250	30,300	6,040	4,774	7,533	5,603
24,300	24,350	4,249	3,325	5,272	3,930	27,300	27,350	5,143	4,037	6,412	4,765	30,300	30,350	6,057	4,787	7,552	5,619
24,350	24,400	4,262	3,336	5,291	3,942	27,350	27,400	5,158	4,049	6,431	4,779	30,350	30,400	6,074	4,799	7,571	5,635
24,400	24,450	4,275	3,347	5,310	3,954	27,400	27,450	5,173	4,062	6,450	4,793	30,400	30,450	6,091	4,812	7,590	5,651
24,450	24,500	4,288	3,358	5,329	3,967	27,450	27,500	5,188	4,074	6,469	4,807	30,450	30,500	6,108	4,824	7,609	5,667
24,500	24,550	4,303	3,369	5,348	3,981	27,500	27,550	5,203	4,087	6,488	4,821	30,500	30,550	6,125	4,837	7,628	5,683
24,550	24,600	4,318	3,380	5,367	3,995	27,550	27,600	5,218	4,099	6,507	4,835	30,550	30,600	6,142	4,849	7,647	5,699
24,600	24,650	4,333	3,391	5,386	4,009	27,600	27,650	5,233	4,112	6,526	4,849	30,600	30,650	6,159	4,862	7,666	5,715
24,650	24,700	4,348	3,402	5,405	4,023	27,650	27,700	5,248	4,124	6,545	4,863	30,650	30,700	6,176	4,874	7,685	5,731
24,700	24,750	4,363	3,413	5,424	4,037	27,700	27,750	5,263	4,137	6,564	4,877	30,700	30,750	6,193	4,887	7,704	5,747
24,750	24,800	4,378	3,424	5,443	4,051	27,750	27,800	5,278	4,149	6,583	4,891	30,750	30,800	6,210	4,899	7,723	5,763
24,800	24,850	4,393	3,435	5,462	4,065	27,800	27,850	5,293	4,162	6,602	4,905	30,800	30,850	6,227	4,912	7,742	5,779
24,850	24,900	4,408	3,446	5,481	4,079	27,850	27,900	5,308	4,174	6,621	4,919	30,850	30,900	6,244	4,924	7,761	5,795
24,900	24,950	4,423	3,457	5,500	4,093	27,900	27,950	5,323	4,187	6,640	4,933	30,900	30,950	6,261	4,937	7,780	5,811
24,950	25,000	4,438	3,468	5,519	4,107	27,950	28,000	5,338	4,199	6,659	4,947	30,950	31,000	6,278	4,949	7,799	5,827
25,000						**28,000**						**31,000**					
25,000	25,050	4,453	3,479	5,538	4,121	28,000	28,050	5,353	4,212	6,678	4,961	31,000	31,050	6,295	4,962	7,818	5,843
25,050	25,100	4,468	3,490	5,557	4,135	28,050	28,100	5,368	4,224	6,697	4,975	31,050	31,100	6,312	4,974	7,837	5,859
25,100	25,150	4,483	3,501	5,576	4,149	28,100	28,150	5,383	4,237	6,716	4,989	31,100	31,150	6,329	4,987	7,856	5,875
25,150	25,200	4,498	3,512	5,595	4,163	28,150	28,200	5,398	4,249	6,735	5,003	31,150	31,200	6,346	5,001	7,875	5,891
25,200	25,250	4,513	3,523	5,614	4,177	28,200	28,250	5,413	4,262	6,754	5,017	31,200	31,250	6,363	5,015	7,894	5,907
25,250	25,300	4,528	3,534	5,633	4,191	28,250	28,300	5,428	4,274	6,773	5,031	31,250	31,300	6,380	5,029	7,915	5,923
25,300	25,350	4,543	3,545	5,652	4,205	28,300	28,350	5,443	4,287	6,792	5,045	31,300	31,350	6,397	5,043	7,936	5,939
25,350	25,400	4,558	3,556	5,671	4,219	28,350	28,400	5,458	4,299	6,811	5,059	31,350	31,400	6,414	5,057	7,957	5,955
25,400	25,450	4,573	3,567	5,690	4,233	28,400	28,450	5,473	4,312	6,830	5,073	31,400	31,450	6,431	5,071	7,978	5,971
25,450	25,500	4,588	3,578	5,709	4,247	28,450	28,500	5,488	4,324	6,849	5,087	31,450	31,500	6,448	5,085	7,999	5,987
25,500	25,550	4,603	3,589	5,728	4,261	28,500	28,550	5,503	4,337	6,868	5,101	31,500	31,550	6,465	5,099	8,020	6,003
25,550	25,600	4,618	3,600	5,747	4,275	28,550	28,600	5,518	4,349	6,887	5,115	31,550	31,600	6,482	5,113	8,041	6,019
25,600	25,650	4,633	3,612	5,766	4,289	28,600	28,650	5,533	4,362	6,906	5,129	31,600	31,650	6,499	5,127	8,062	6,035
25,650	25,700	4,648	3,624	5,785	4,303	28,650	28,700	5,548	4,374	6,925	5,143	31,650	31,700	6,516	5,141	8,083	6,051
25,700	25,750	4,663	3,637	5,804	4,317	28,700	28,750	5,563	4,387	6,944	5,157	31,700	31,750	6,533	5,155	8,104	6,067
25,750	25,800	4,678	3,649	5,823	4,331	28,750	28,800	5,578	4,399	6,963	5,171	31,750	31,800	6,550	5,169	8,125	6,083
25,800	25,850	4,693	3,662	5,842	4,345	28,800	28,850	5,593	4,412	6,982	5,185	31,800	31,850	6,567	5,183	8,146	6,099
25,850	25,900	4,708	3,674	5,861	4,359	28,850	28,900	5,608	4,424	7,001	5,199	31,850	31,900	6,584	5,197	8,167	6,115
25,900	25,950	4,723	3,687	5,880	4,373	28,900	28,950	5,623	4,437	7,020	5,213	31,900	31,950	6,601	5,211	8,188	6,131
25,950	26,000	4,738	3,699	5,899	4,387	28,950	29,000	5,638	4,449	7,039	5,227	31,950	32,000	6,618	5,225	8,209	6,147

* This column must also be used by a qualifying widow(er).

Continued on next page

1985 Tax Table—Continued

If line 37 (taxable income) is— At least / But less than	Single	Married filing jointly *	Married filing sepa-rately	Head of a house-hold	If line 37 (taxable income) is— At least / But less than	Single	Married filing jointly *	Married filing sepa-rately	Head of a house-hold	If line 37 (taxable income) is— At least / But less than	Single	Married filing jointly *	Married filing sepa-rately	Head of a house-hold
32,000					**35,000**					**38,000**				
32,000 32,050	6,635	5,239	8,230	6,163	35,000 35,050	7,655	6,079	9,490	7,123	38,000 38,050	8,777	6,989	10,750	8,159
32,050 32,100	6,652	5,253	8,251	6,179	35,050 35,100	7,672	6,093	9,511	7,139	38,050 38,100	8,796	7,005	10,771	8,176
32,100 32,150	6,669	5,267	8,272	6,195	35,100 35,150	7,689	6,107	9,532	7,155	38,100 38,150	8,815	7,022	10,792	8,194
32,150 32,200	6,686	5,281	8,293	6,211	35,150 35,200	7,706	6,121	9,553	7,171	38,150 38,200	8,834	7,038	10,813	8,211
32,200 32,250	6,703	5,295	8,314	6,227	35,200 35,250	7,723	6,135	9,574	7,187	38,200 38,250	8,853	7,055	10,834	8,229
32,250 32,300	6,720	5,309	8,335	6,243	35,250 35,300	7,740	6,149	9,595	7,203	38,250 38,300	8,872	7,071	10,855	8,246
32,300 32,350	6,737	5,323	8,356	6,259	35,300 35,350	7,757	6,163	9,616	7,219	38,300 38,350	8,891	7,088	10,876	8,264
32,350 32,400	6,754	5,337	8,377	6,275	35,350 35,400	7,774	6,177	9,637	7,235	38,350 38,400	8,910	7,104	10,897	8,281
32,400 32,450	6,771	5,351	8,398	6,291	35,400 35,450	7,791	6,191	9,658	7,251	38,400 38,450	8,929	7,121	10,918	8,299
32,450 32,500	6,788	5,365	8,419	6,307	35,450 35,500	7,808	6,205	9,679	7,267	38,450 38,500	8,948	7,137	10,939	8,316
32,500 32,550	6,805	5,379	8,440	6,323	35,500 35,550	7,827	6,219	9,700	7,284	38,500 38,550	8,967	7,154	10,960	8,334
32,550 32,600	6,822	5,393	8,461	6,339	35,550 35,600	7,846	6,233	9,721	7,301	38,550 38,600	8,986	7,170	10,981	8,351
32,600 32,650	6,839	5,407	8,482	6,355	35,600 35,650	7,865	6,247	9,742	7,319	38,600 38,650	9,005	7,187	11,002	8,369
32,650 32,700	6,856	5,421	8,503	6,371	35,650 35,700	7,884	6,261	9,763	7,336	38,650 38,700	9,024	7,203	11,023	8,386
32,700 32,750	6,873	5,435	8,524	6,387	35,700 35,750	7,903	6,275	9,784	7,354	38,700 38,750	9,043	7,220	11,044	8,404
32,750 32,800	6,890	5,449	8,545	6,403	35,750 35,800	7,922	6,289	9,805	7,371	38,750 38,800	9,062	7,236	11,065	8,421
32,800 32,850	6,907	5,463	8,566	6,419	35,800 35,850	7,941	6,303	9,826	7,389	38,800 38,850	9,081	7,253	11,086	8,439
32,850 32,900	6,924	5,477	8,587	6,435	35,850 35,900	7,960	6,317	9,847	7,406	38,850 38,900	9,100	7,269	11,107	8,456
32,900 32,950	6,941	5,491	8,608	6,451	35,900 35,950	7,979	6,331	9,868	7,424	38,900 38,950	9,119	7,286	11,128	8,474
32,950 33,000	6,958	5,505	8,629	6,467	35,950 36,000	7,998	6,345	9,889	7,441	38,950 39,000	9,138	7,302	11,149	8,491
33,000					**36,000**					**39,000**				
33,000 33,050	6,975	5,519	8,650	6,483	36,000 36,050	8,017	6,359	9,910	7,459	39,000 39,050	9,157	7,319	11,170	8,509
33,050 33,100	6,992	5,533	8,671	6,499	36,050 36,100	8,036	6,373	9,931	7,476	39,050 39,100	9,176	7,335	11,191	8,526
33,100 33,150	7,009	5,547	8,692	6,515	36,100 36,150	8,055	6,387	9,952	7,494	39,100 39,150	9,195	7,352	11,212	8,544
33,150 33,200	7,026	5,561	8,713	6,531	36,150 36,200	8,074	6,401	9,973	7,511	39,150 39,200	9,214	7,368	11,233	8,561
33,200 33,250	7,043	5,575	8,734	6,547	36,200 36,250	8,093	6,415	9,994	7,529	39,200 39,250	9,233	7,385	11,254	8,579
33,250 33,300	7,060	5,589	8,755	6,563	36,250 36,300	8,112	6,429	10,015	7,546	39,250 39,300	9,252	7,401	11,275	8,596
33,300 33,350	7,077	5,603	8,776	6,579	36,300 36,350	8,131	6,443	10,036	7,564	39,300 39,350	9,271	7,418	11,296	8,614
33,350 33,400	7,094	5,617	8,797	6,595	36,350 36,400	8,150	6,457	10,057	7,581	39,350 39,400	9,290	7,434	11,317	8,631
33,400 33,450	7,111	5,631	8,818	6,611	36,400 36,450	8,169	6,471	10,078	7,599	39,400 39,450	9,309	7,451	11,338	8,649
33,450 33,500	7,128	5,645	8,839	6,627	36,450 36,500	8,188	6,485	10,099	7,616	39,450 39,500	9,328	7,467	11,359	8,666
33,500 33,550	7,145	5,659	8,860	6,643	36,500 36,550	8,207	6,499	10,120	7,634	39,500 39,550	9,347	7,484	11,380	8,684
33,550 33,600	7,162	5,673	8,881	6,659	36,550 36,600	8,226	6,513	10,141	7,651	39,550 39,600	9,366	7,500	11,401	8,701
33,600 33,650	7,179	5,687	8,902	6,675	36,600 36,650	8,245	6,527	10,162	7,669	39,600 39,650	9,385	7,517	11,422	8,719
33,650 33,700	7,196	5,701	8,923	6,691	36,650 36,700	8,264	6,543	10,183	7,686	39,650 39,700	9,404	7,533	11,443	8,736
33,700 33,750	7,213	5,715	8,944	6,707	36,700 36,750	8,283	6,560	10,204	7,704	39,700 39,750	9,423	7,550	11,464	8,754
33,750 33,800	7,230	5,729	8,965	6,723	36,750 36,800	8,302	6,576	10,225	7,721	39,750 39,800	9,442	7,566	11,485	8,771
33,800 33,850	7,247	5,743	8,986	6,739	36,800 36,850	8,321	6,593	10,246	7,739	39,800 39,850	9,461	7,583	11,506	8,789
33,850 33,900	7,264	5,757	9,007	6,755	36,850 36,900	8,340	6,609	10,267	7,756	39,850 39,900	9,480	7,599	11,527	8,806
33,900 33,950	7,281	5,771	9,028	6,771	36,900 36,950	8,359	6,626	10,288	7,774	39,900 39,950	9,499	7,616	11,548	8,824
33,950 34,000	7,298	5,785	9,049	6,787	36,950 37,000	8,378	6,642	10,309	7,791	39,950 40,000	9,518	7,632	11,569	8,841
34,000					**37,000**					**40,000**				
34,000 34,050	7,315	5,799	9,070	6,803	37,000 37,050	8,397	6,659	10,330	7,809	40,000 40,050	9,537	7,649	11,590	8,859
34,050 34,100	7,332	5,813	9,091	6,819	37,050 37,100	8,416	6,675	10,351	7,826	40,050 40,100	9,556	7,665	11,611	8,876
34,100 34,150	7,349	5,827	9,112	6,835	37,100 37,150	8,435	6,692	10,372	7,844	40,100 40,150	9,575	7,682	11,632	8,894
34,150 34,200	7,366	5,841	9,133	6,851	37,150 37,200	8,454	6,708	10,393	7,861	40,150 40,200	9,594	7,698	11,653	8,911
34,200 34,250	7,383	5,855	9,154	6,867	37,200 37,250	8,473	6,725	10,414	7,879	40,200 40,250	9,613	7,715	11,674	8,929
34,250 34,300	7,400	5,869	9,175	6,883	37,250 37,300	8,492	6,741	10,435	7,896	40,250 40,300	9,632	7,731	11,695	8,946
34,300 34,350	7,417	5,883	9,196	6,899	37,300 37,350	8,511	6,758	10,456	7,914	40,300 40,350	9,651	7,748	11,716	8,964
34,350 34,400	7,434	5,897	9,217	6,915	37,350 37,400	8,530	6,774	10,477	7,931	40,350 40,400	9,670	7,764	11,737	8,981
34,400 34,450	7,451	5,911	9,238	6,931	37,400 37,450	8,549	6,791	10,498	7,949	40,400 40,450	9,689	7,781	11,758	8,999
34,450 34,500	7,468	5,925	9,259	6,947	37,450 37,500	8,568	6,807	10,519	7,966	40,450 40,500	9,708	7,797	11,779	9,016
34,500 34,550	7,485	5,939	9,280	6,963	37,500 37,550	8,587	6,824	10,540	7,984	40,500 40,550	9,727	7,814	11,800	9,034
34,550 34,600	7,502	5,953	9,301	6,979	37,550 37,600	8,606	6,840	10,561	8,001	40,550 40,600	9,746	7,830	11,821	9,051
34,600 34,650	7,519	5,967	9,322	6,995	37,600 37,650	8,625	6,857	10,582	8,019	40,600 40,650	9,765	7,847	11,842	9,069
34,650 34,700	7,536	5,981	9,343	7,011	37,650 37,700	8,644	6,873	10,603	8,036	40,650 40,700	9,784	7,863	11,863	9,086
34,700 34,750	7,553	5,995	9,364	7,027	37,700 37,750	8,663	6,890	10,624	8,054	40,700 40,750	9,803	7,880	11,884	9,104
34,750 34,800	7,570	6,009	9,385	7,043	37,750 37,800	8,682	6,906	10,645	8,071	40,750 40,800	9,822	7,896	11,905	9,121
34,800 34,850	7,587	6,023	9,406	7,059	37,800 37,850	8,701	6,923	10,666	8,089	40,800 40,850	9,841	7,913	11,926	9,139
34,850 34,900	7,604	6,037	9,427	7,075	37,850 37,900	8,720	6,939	10,687	8,106	40,850 40,900	9,860	7,929	11,947	9,156
34,900 34,950	7,621	6,051	9,448	7,091	37,900 37,950	8,739	6,956	10,708	8,124	40,900 40,950	9,879	7,946	11,968	9,174
34,950 35,000	7,638	6,065	9,469	7,107	37,950 38,000	8,758	6,972	10,729	8,141	40,950 41,000	9,898	7,962	11,989	9,191

* This column must also be used by a qualifying widow(er).

Continued on next page

20 | Income Tax Considerations 669

1985 Tax Table—*Continued*

If line 37 (taxable income) is—		And you are—				If line 37 (taxable income) is—		And you are—				If line 37 (taxable income) is—		And you are—			
At least	But less than	Single	Married filing jointly *	Married filing separately	Head of a household	At least	But less than	Single	Married filing jointly *	Married filing separately	Head of a household	At least	But less than	Single	Married filing jointly *	Married filing separately	Head of a household
			Your tax is—						Your tax is—						Your tax is—		
41,000						**44,000**						**47,000**					
41,000	41,050	9,917	7,979	12,010	9,209	44,000	44,050	11,090	8,969	13,270	10,259	47,000	47,050	12,350	9,959	14,604	11,344
41,050	41,100	9,936	7,995	12,031	9,226	44,050	44,100	11,111	8,985	13,291	10,276	47,050	47,100	12,371	9,975	14,627	11,365
41,100	41,150	9,955	8,012	12,052	9,244	44,100	44,150	11,132	9,002	13,312	10,294	47,100	47,150	12,392	9,992	14,649	11,386
41,150	41,200	9,974	8,028	12,073	9,261	44,150	44,200	11,153	9,018	13,333	10,311	47,150	47,200	12,413	10,008	14,672	11,407
41,200	41,250	9,993	8,045	12,094	9,279	44,200	44,250	11,174	9,035	13,354	10,329	47,200	47,250	12,434	10,025	14,694	11,428
41,250	41,300	10,012	8,061	12,115	9,296	44,250	44,300	11,195	9,051	13,375	10,346	47,250	47,300	12,455	10,041	14,717	11,449
41,300	41,350	10,031	8,078	12,136	9,314	44,300	44,350	11,216	9,068	13,396	10,364	47,300	47,350	12,476	10,058	14,739	11,470
41,350	41,400	10,050	8,094	12,157	9,331	44,350	44,400	11,237	9,084	13,417	10,381	47,350	47,400	12,497	10,074	14,762	11,491
41,400	41,450	10,069	8,111	12,178	9,349	44,400	44,450	11,258	9,101	13,438	10,399	47,400	47,450	12,518	10,091	14,784	11,512
41,450	41,500	10,088	8,127	12,199	9,366	44,450	44,500	11,279	9,117	13,459	10,416	47,450	47,500	12,539	10,107	14,807	11,533
41,500	41,550	10,107	8,144	12,220	9,384	44,500	44,550	11,300	9,134	13,480	10,434	47,500	47,550	12,560	10,124	14,829	11,554
41,550	41,600	10,126	8,160	12,241	9,401	44,550	44,600	11,321	9,150	13,502	10,451	47,550	47,600	12,581	10,140	14,852	11,575
41,600	41,650	10,145	8,177	12,262	9,419	44,600	44,650	11,342	9,167	13,524	10,469	47,600	47,650	12,602	10,157	14,874	11,596
41,650	41,700	10,164	8,193	12,283	9,436	44,650	44,700	11,363	9,183	13,547	10,486	47,650	47,700	12,623	10,174	14,897	11,617
41,700	41,750	10,183	8,210	12,304	9,454	44,700	44,750	11,384	9,200	13,569	10,504	47,700	47,750	12,644	10,193	14,919	11,638
41,750	41,800	10,202	8,226	12,325	9,471	44,750	44,800	11,405	9,216	13,592	10,521	47,750	47,800	12,665	10,212	14,942	11,659
41,800	41,850	10,221	8,243	12,346	9,489	44,800	44,850	11,426	9,233	13,614	10,539	47,800	47,850	12,686	10,231	14,964	11,680
41,850	41,900	10,240	8,259	12,367	9,506	44,850	44,900	11,447	9,249	13,637	10,556	47,850	47,900	12,707	10,250	14,987	11,701
41,900	41,950	10,259	8,276	12,388	9,524	44,900	44,950	11,468	9,266	13,659	10,574	47,900	47,950	12,728	10,269	15,009	11,722
41,950	42,000	10,278	8,292	12,409	9,541	44,950	45,000	11,489	9,282	13,682	10,591	47,950	48,000	12,749	10,288	15,032	11,743
42,000						**45,000**						**48,000**					
42,000	42,050	10,297	8,309	12,430	9,559	45,000	45,050	11,510	9,299	13,704	10,609	48,000	48,050	12,770	10,307	15,054	11,764
42,050	42,100	10,316	8,325	12,451	9,576	45,050	45,100	11,531	9,315	13,727	10,626	48,050	48,100	12,791	10,326	15,077	11,785
42,100	42,150	10,335	8,342	12,472	9,594	45,100	45,150	11,552	9,332	13,749	10,644	48,100	48,150	12,812	10,345	15,099	11,806
42,150	42,200	10,354	8,358	12,493	9,611	45,150	45,200	11,573	9,348	13,772	10,661	48,150	48,200	12,833	10,364	15,122	11,827
42,200	42,250	10,373	8,375	12,514	9,629	45,200	45,250	11,594	9,365	13,794	10,679	48,200	48,250	12,854	10,383	15,144	11,848
42,250	42,300	10,392	8,391	12,535	9,646	45,250	45,300	11,615	9,381	13,817	10,696	48,250	48,300	12,875	10,402	15,167	11,869
42,300	42,350	10,411	8,408	12,556	9,664	45,300	45,350	11,636	9,398	13,839	10,714	48,300	48,350	12,896	10,421	15,189	11,890
42,350	42,400	10,430	8,424	12,577	9,681	45,350	45,400	11,657	9,414	13,862	10,731	48,350	48,400	12,917	10,440	15,212	11,911
42,400	42,450	10,449	8,441	12,598	9,699	45,400	45,450	11,678	9,431	13,884	10,749	48,400	48,450	12,938	10,459	15,234	11,932
42,450	42,500	10,468	8,457	12,619	9,716	45,450	45,500	11,699	9,447	13,907	10,766	48,450	48,500	12,959	10,478	15,257	11,953
42,500	42,550	10,487	8,474	12,640	9,734	45,500	45,550	11,720	9,464	13,929	10,784	48,500	48,550	12,980	10,497	15,279	11,974
42,550	42,600	10,506	8,490	12,661	9,751	45,550	45,600	11,741	9,480	13,952	10,801	48,550	48,600	13,001	10,516	15,302	11,995
42,600	42,650	10,525	8,507	12,682	9,769	45,600	45,650	11,762	9,497	13,974	10,819	48,600	48,650	13,022	10,535	15,324	12,016
42,650	42,700	10,544	8,523	12,703	9,786	45,650	45,700	11,783	9,513	13,997	10,836	48,650	48,700	13,043	10,554	15,347	12,037
42,700	42,750	10,563	8,540	12,724	9,804	45,700	45,750	11,804	9,530	14,019	10,854	48,700	48,750	13,064	10,573	15,369	12,058
42,750	42,800	10,582	8,556	12,745	9,821	45,750	45,800	11,825	9,546	14,042	10,871	48,750	48,800	13,085	10,592	15,392	12,079
42,800	42,850	10,601	8,573	12,766	9,839	45,800	45,850	11,846	9,563	14,064	10,889	48,800	48,850	13,106	10,611	15,414	12,100
42,850	42,900	10,620	8,589	12,787	9,856	45,850	45,900	11,867	9,579	14,087	10,906	48,850	48,900	13,127	10,630	15,437	12,121
42,900	42,950	10,639	8,606	12,808	9,874	45,900	45,950	11,888	9,596	14,109	10,924	48,900	48,950	13,148	10,649	15,459	12,142
42,950	43,000	10,658	8,622	12,829	9,891	45,950	46,000	11,909	9,612	14,132	10,941	48,950	49,000	13,169	10,668	15,482	12,163
43,000						**46,000**						**49,000**					
43,000	43,050	10,677	8,639	12,850	9,909	46,000	46,050	11,930	9,629	14,154	10,959	49,000	49,050	13,190	10,687	15,504	12,184
43,050	43,100	10,696	8,655	12,871	9,926	46,050	46,100	11,951	9,645	14,177	10,976	49,050	49,100	13,211	10,706	15,527	12,205
43,100	43,150	10,715	8,672	12,892	9,944	46,100	46,150	11,972	9,662	14,199	10,994	49,100	49,150	13,232	10,725	15,549	12,226
43,150	43,200	10,734	8,688	12,913	9,961	46,150	46,200	11,993	9,678	14,222	11,011	49,150	49,200	13,253	10,744	15,572	12,247
43,200	43,250	10,754	8,705	12,934	9,979	46,200	46,250	12,014	9,695	14,244	11,029	49,200	49,250	13,274	10,763	15,594	12,268
43,250	43,300	10,775	8,721	12,955	9,996	46,250	46,300	12,035	9,711	14,267	11,046	49,250	49,300	13,295	10,782	15,617	12,289
43,300	43,350	10,796	8,738	12,976	10,014	46,300	46,350	12,056	9,728	14,289	11,064	49,300	49,350	13,316	10,801	15,639	12,310
43,350	43,400	10,817	8,754	12,997	10,031	46,350	46,400	12,077	9,744	14,312	11,081	49,350	49,400	13,337	10,820	15,662	12,331
43,400	43,450	10,838	8,771	13,018	10,049	46,400	46,450	12,098	9,761	14,334	11,099	49,400	49,450	13,358	10,839	15,68	12,352
43,450	43,500	10,859	8,787	13,039	10,066	46,450	46,500	12,119	9,777	14,357	11,116	49,450	49,500	13,379	10,858	15,707	12,373
43,500	43,550	10,880	8,804	13,060	10,084	46,500	46,550	12,140	9,794	14,379	11,134	49,500	49,550	13,400	10,877	15,729	12,394
43,550	43,600	10,901	8,820	13,081	10,101	46,550	46,600	12,161	9,810	14,402	11,155	49,550	49,600	13,421	10,896	15,752	12,415
43,600	43,650	10,922	8,837	13,102	10,119	46,600	46,650	12,182	9,827	14,424	11,176	49,600	49,650	13,442	10,915	15,774	12,436
43,650	43,700	10,943	8,853	13,123	10,136	46,650	46,700	12,203	9,843	14,447	11,197	49,650	49,700	13,463	10,934	15,797	12,457
43,700	43,750	10,964	8,870	13,144	10,154	46,700	46,750	12,224	9,860	14,469	11,218	49,700	49,750	13,484	10,953	15,819	12,478
43,750	43,800	10,985	8,886	13,165	10,171	46,750	46,800	12,245	9,876	14,492	11,239	49,750	49,800	13,505	10,972	15,842	12,499
43,800	43,850	11,006	8,903	13,186	10,189	46,800	46,850	12,266	9,893	14,514	11,260	49,800	49,850	13,526	10,991	15,864	12,520
43,850	43,900	11,027	8,919	13,207	10,206	46,850	46,900	12,287	9,909	14,537	11,281	49,850	49,900	13,547	11,010	15,887	12,541
43,900	43,950	11,048	8,936	13,228	10,224	46,900	46,950	12,308	9,926	14,559	11,302	49,900	49,950	13,568	11,029	15,909	12,562
43,950	44,000	11,069	8,952	13,249	10,241	46,950	47,000	12,329	9,942	14,582	11,323	49,950	50,000	13,589	11,048	15,932	12,583

* This column must also be used by a qualifying widow(er).

50,000 or over—use tax rate schedules

Learning Objectives

Chapter 21 is concerned with basic accounting theory. Studying this chapter should enable you to:

1. Discuss a conceptual framework of accounting.

2. Describe the objectives of financial reporting.

3. Discuss the qualitative characteristics of accounting information.

4. Define and discuss the elements of financial statements.

5. Explain recognition and measurement in financial statements.

6. Trace the process of developing generally accepted accounting principles.

7. Discuss the accounting standard setting process.

8. Describe international aspects of accounting.

21
Basic Accounting Theory

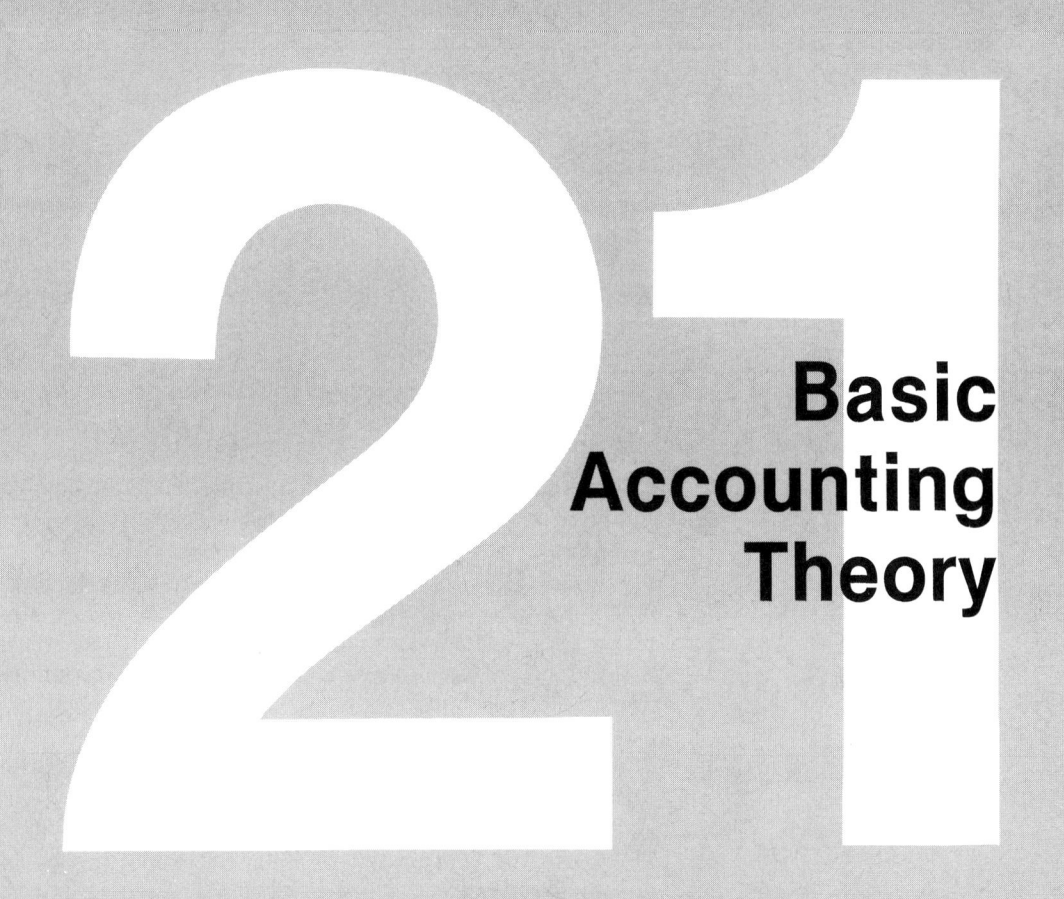

The objective of this chapter is to introduce and discuss the objectives of financial reporting, the qualitative characteristics of accounting information, the elements of financial statements, recognition and measurement in financial statements, the development of generally accepted accounting principles, and certain of the basic accounting concepts which underlie financial reporting and the preparation of financial statements. It should be noted that the objectives, qualitative characteristics, elements, and recognition and measurement concepts are an integral part of the FASB's conceptual framework project.

The conceptual framework project is an attempt by the FASB to develop a system of coherent interrelated objectives and fundamental principles that will enable the FASB to issue more useful and consistent standards in the future. To date, the Board has issued a total of six Statements of Financial Accounting Concepts (SFAC). These are:

1. SFAC No. 1, "Objectives of Financial Reporting by Business Enterprises"

2. SFAC No. 2, "Qualitative Characteristics of Accounting Information"

3. SFAC No. 3, "Elements of Financial Statements of Business Enterprises"

4. SFAC No. 4, "Objectives of Financial Reporting by Nonbusiness Organizations"

5. SFAC No. 5, "Recognition and Measurement in Financial Statements of Business Enterprises"

6. SFAC No. 6, "Elements of Financial Statements"

A CONCEPTUAL FRAMEWORK

For a long time, accountants have attempted to develop a coherent set of conceptual principles to form a general frame of reference for accounting and financial reporting purposes. When in place, this frame of reference could serve as a foundation for the establishment of consistent accounting standards.

There have been numerous attempts to develop such a frame of reference. Both the AICPA and the American Accounting Association issued documents intended to initiate this process during the 1960's. These efforts failed to have a significant impact on the profession, however. Then in 1970, the APB issued its Statement No. 4, "Basis Concepts and Accounting Principles Underlying Financial Statements of Business Enterprises." This

Statement has two broad purposes: (1) to provide a basis for an increased understanding of accounting fundamentals, and (2) to provide a basis for the development of financial accounting. Statement No. 4 is primarily descriptive, not prescriptive, and is based primarily on observation of accounting practice. The Statement's intent is to provide a framework within which accounting problems could be solved rather than to provide solutions to the problems themselves.

In 1971, the AICPA established the Study Group on the Objectives of Financial Statements. On the basis of the Study Group's report, the FASB subsequently issued two pronouncements which led to the issuance of the six Statements of Financial Accounting Concepts.

The components of the FASB's conceptual framework project are presented below in a diagram published by the FASB and included in its "Financial Statements and Other Means of Financial Reporting." *These objectives, which are derived from the needs of the of the users of the financial statements, are the most basic components of the conceptual framework. The qualitative characteristics are the criteria to be used in the selection and evaluation of accounting and reporting policies. The elements are the components of the financial statements (e.g., assets, liabilities, revenues, and expenses).* These elements must meet the criteria for recognition and possess characteristics which can be measured reliably. Reporting considerations include the information which is provided and the manner in which the information should be presented.

**Conceptual Framework
for Financial Accounting and Reporting**

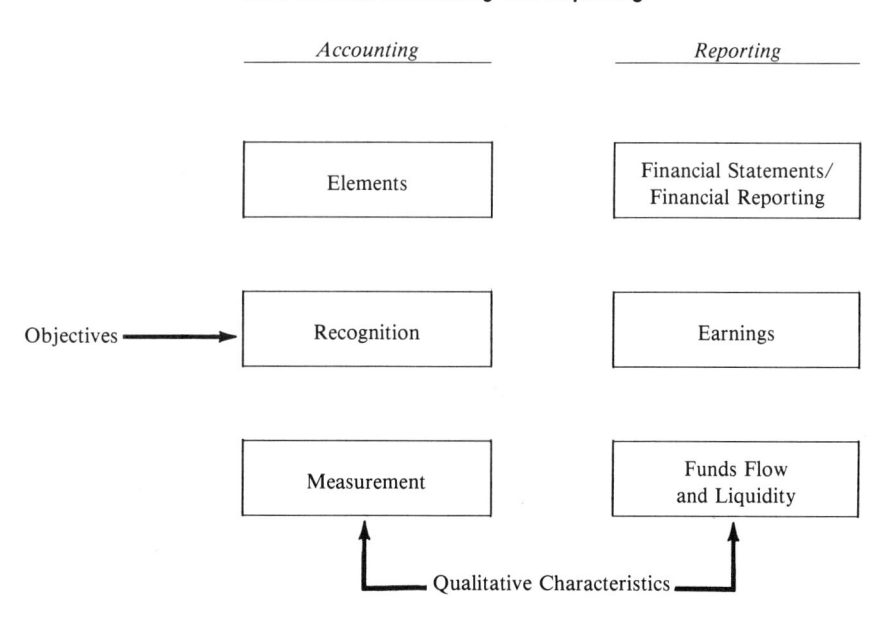

Accounting	*Reporting*
Elements	Financial Statements/Financial Reporting
Recognition ← Objectives	Earnings
Measurement	Funds Flow and Liquidity

Qualitative Characteristics

A *conceptual framework* may be defined as follows:

> A conceptual framework is a constitution, a coherent system of interrelated objectives and fundamentals that can lead to consistent standards and that prescribes the nature, function, and limits of financial accounting and financial statements. The objectives identify the goals and purposes of accounting. The fundamentals are the underlying concepts of accounting, concepts that guide the selection of events to be accounted for, the measurement of those events, and the means of summarizing and communicating them to interested parties. Concepts flow from them and repeated reference to them will be necessary in establishing, interpreting, and applying accounting and reporting standards.[1]

The FASB expected that the conceptual framework would provide many benefits:

1. *Guide the FASB in the establishment of accounting standards*—accounting standards, which are general solutions to identified accounting problems, stand between underlying concepts and accounting practices in specific situations.

2. *Provide direction for resolving accounting questions for which no specific standard exists*—guide the analysis by focusing considerations on some solutions while eliminating others.

3. *Determine the bounds for judgment in the preparation of financial statements*—the conceptual framework should not be so detailed as to eliminate any judgment and should not be so abstract that a high degree of subjectivity is needed in applying the concepts.

4. *Increase users' understanding of financial statements and the users' confidence in these statements*—users will recognize that the definitions and measures of the elements of financial statements are consistent from company to company and will understand the limitations of accounting information.

5. *Enhance the comparability of financial statements*—a conceptual framework should narrow the range of acceptable accounting methods and should prevent the proliferation of methods.

The Board decided not to issue the conceptual pronouncements as FASB Statements, because these concepts would fall under the required disclosures of Rule 203 of the Rules of Conduct of the Code of Professional

---

[1] FASB, "Conceptual Framework for Financial Accounting and Reporting: Elements of Financial Statements and Their Measurement," *FASB Discussion Memorandum* (Stamford: FASB, 1976), p. 2 of the section "Scope and Implications of the Conceptual Framework Project."

Ethics of the AICPA which requires that all disclosures made in the financial statements be in accordance with generally accepted accounting principles. Such a situation could cause numerous problems. Each element in the financial statements would have to be reviewed by both management and the auditors to make certain that it conformed with the definition in the conceptual pronouncement.

OBJECTIVES OF FINANCIAL REPORTING

The objectives of financial reporting are discussed in SFAC No. 1. *Financial reporting includes not only the financial statements but also such other forms of communicating financial information as annual reports filed with the SEC, news releases, and management forecasts.*

The users of financial information may be divided into internal and external groups. Internal users such as managers and directors can specify the information that they want, can receive additional and more detailed information than is appropriate or necessary for external reports, and can receive information pertaining to planning and control operations. External users include owners, lenders, suppliers, potential investors, potential creditors, employees, customers, stockbrokers, financial analysts, employees, taxing authorities, regulatory authorities, trade associations, and teachers. Certain of these external users (e.g., taxing authorities) can specify and obtain both the form and content of the information desired; others lack the authority to prescribe the financial information desired.

Investors and creditors are the most obvious external groups who use financial information and cannot obtain all the information that they may wish to have. Their decisions significantly affect the allocation of resources in the economy. In addition, information which meets the needs of investors and creditors is likely to meet the needs of those other external users who rely on external financial reporting.

A primary objective of financial reporting is to "... provide information that is useful to present and potential investors and creditors and other users in making rational investment, credit, and similar decisions."[2] In order to accomplish this goal, it is necessary that the information which is communicated must be understood; it "... should be comprehensible to those who have a reasonable understanding of business and economic activities and are willing to study the information with reasonable diligence."[3]

The users of financial information are concerned not only with past and current performance but also with the future expectations of a business. Recognizing these needs, *the primary focus of financial reporting is on the disclosure of information concerning the earnings of a business*, although

---

[2] FASB Statement of Financial Accounting Concepts No. 1, "Objectives of Financial Reporting By Business Enterprises," (Stamford: FASB, 1978), para. 34.
[3] *Ibid.*

information concerning the resources of an enterprise also is emphasized. Consequently, two other important objectives which are stated in FASB Statement of Financial Accounting Concepts No. 1, "Objectives of Financial Reporting by Business Enterprises," are as follows:

> Financial reporting should provide information to help present and potential investors and creditors and other users in assessing the amounts, timing, and uncertainty of prospective cash receipts from dividends or interest and the proceeds from the sale, redemption, or maturity of securities or loans. The prospects for those cash receipts are affected by an enterprise's ability to generate enough cash to meet its obligations when due and its other cash operating needs, to reinvest in operations, and to pay cash dividends and may also be affected by perceptions of investors and creditors generally about that ability, which affect market prices of the enterprise's securities. Thus, financial reporting should provide information to help investors, creditors, and others assess the amounts, timing, and uncertainty of prospective net cash inflows to the related enterprise.[4]
>
> Financial reporting should provide information about the economic resources of an enterprise, the claims to those resources (obligations of the enterprise to transfer resources to other entities and owners' equity), and the effects of transactions, events, and circumstances that change its resources and claims to those resources.[5]

The Board emphasized that accrual accounting is a superior indicator of an enterprise's performance than is accounting on a cash basis. *The measurement of income under the conventions of accrual accounting is intended to provide users with more useful information concerning an enterprise's present and future ability to generate desirable cash flows than is indicated by the income measured on a cash basis. Investors, creditors, and other users of financial information are interested in the current and future cash flows of an enterprise.* Therefore, these users of financial information prefer that information concerning an enterprise's performance to be measured on an accrual rather than a cash basis.

QUALITATIVE CHARACTERISTICS OF ACCOUNTING INFORMATION

In order to be useful, accounting information should possess certain qualitative characteristics. These qualitative characteristics are described in detail in SFAC No. 2. A hierarchy of these qualitative characteristics of accounting information is presented in this section of the chapter.

---

[4] *Ibid.*, para. 37.
[5] *Ibid.*, para. 38.

Pervasive Constraint

Benefits and Costs. *In order to justify providing accounting information, the benefits which may be derived from the use of this information must exceed the costs of providing the data.* There are several costs of providing information, including: (1) costs of collecting, processing, and disseminating; (2) costs of auditing; (3) costs associated with dangers of litigation and loss of competitive advantage; and (4) costs to the user for analysis and interpretation. Also, there are benefits to the preparers of the information as well as to the users; these benefits include improved access to capital markets and favorable impact on public relations.

User-Specific Qualities

Understandability. *The information which is provided by financial reporting should be understandable to those who have a reasonable understanding of business and economic activities* and who are willing to study the information with reasonable diligence. Useful information which is difficult to understand should not be excluded. In this context, understandability is the quality which enables users to perceive the significance of information.

Decision Usefulness. The determination as to whether or not information is useful is dependent upon the particular decision to be made, the manner in which the decision is to be made, the other information which already is available, and the ability of the decision maker to process and use the information. *SFAC No. 2 identifies usefulness for decision-making as the most important quality of accounting information.* Usefulness provides the benefits from information to set against the costs of providing the information; without usefulness, there would be no benefits. Decision usefulness may be separated into the qualities of *relevance* and *reliability*, both of which are defined below.

Relevance. *In order to be relevant, accounting information must be capable of making a difference in a particular decision* by helping users to form predictions concerning the outcomes of past, current, or future events or to confirm or correct prior expectations. In this context, an "event" is a happening of consequence to an enterprise (for example, receipt of a sales order or a change in the price of a good which is bought or sold), while an "outcome" is the effect or result of a series of events (for example, the amount of last year's profit or the expected profit for the current year). Relevant information does not necessarily mean that a new decision should be made; the information may support the decision which was made previously.

Reliability. *Reliable information is information which is reasonably free from both error and bias and which faithfully represents what it is intended to represent.* To be reliable, accounting information must be verifiable, neutral and possess representational faithfulness.

Reliability and relevance often conflict with one another in the standard setting process. The type of information which is most desired by users of

A Hierarchy of Accounting Qualities*

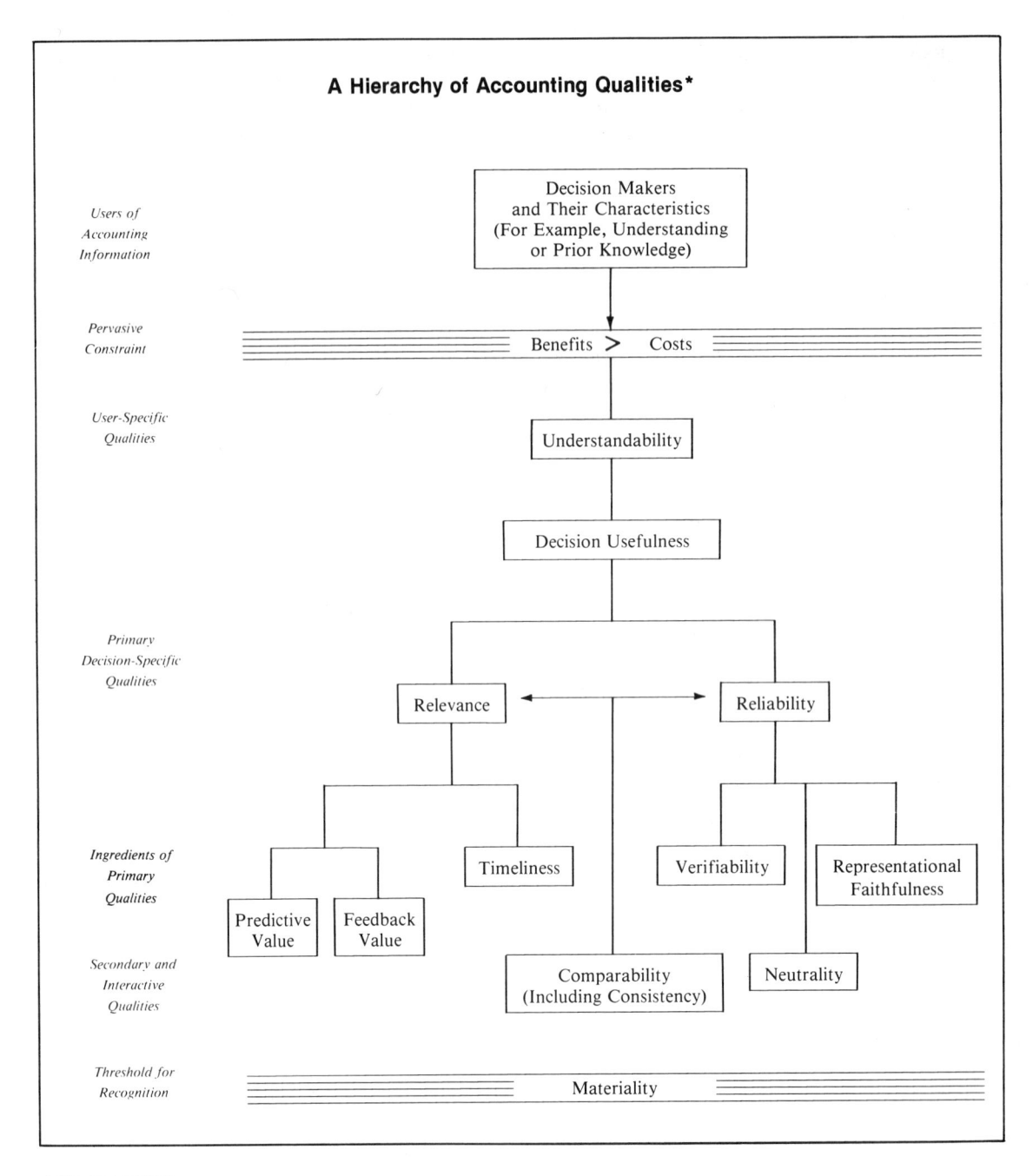

Users of Accounting Information	Decision Makers and Their Characteristics (For Example, Understanding or Prior Knowledge)
Pervasive Constraint	Benefits > Costs
User-Specific Qualities	Understandability
	Decision Usefulness
Primary Decision-Specific Qualities	Relevance ↔ Reliability
Ingredients of Primary Qualities	Predictive Value, Feedback Value, Timeliness / Verifiability, Representational Faithfulness
Secondary and Interactive Qualities	Comparability (Including Consistency), Neutrality
Threshold for Recognition	Materiality

*"Qualitative Characteristics of Accounting Information," FASB Statement of Financial Accounting Concepts No. 2 (Stamford, Conn. FASB, 1980).

financial accounting information (relevance) is often the most difficult information to obtain in a reliable fashion. Traditionally, standard setters have favored reliability over relevance in those situations in which the two are in conflict.

Ingredients of Primary Qualities

Predictive and Feedback Value. *Accounting information has predictive value when it assists the decision maker in correctly forecasting the outcomes of past or present events.* It possesses feedback value when it assists the decision maker in either confirming or correcting prior expectations.

Timeliness. *Timeliness means having information available to decision makers before the information loses its capacity to influence decisions.* Timeliness by itself does not make information relevant. However, information may lose relevance if it is not communicated on a timely basis. Often, a gain in relevance from increased timeliness may involve, for example, a sacrifice of reliability; therefore, trade-offs in the qualitative characteristics of accounting information must be considered by decision makers.

Verifiability. *Verifiability (sometimes referred to as objectivity) of accounting information means that several measurers are likely to obtain the same measure, so that measurement results may be duplicated independently.* The Certified Public Accountant (CPA) is an independent accountant who examines or audits financial statements and attests to or reports as to whether or not the financial statements "present fairly" financial position, results of operations and changes in financial position of an entity. In accounting, verification is a primary concern of auditing and the CPA.

Representational Faithfulness. *Representational faithfulness means that there is correspondence or agreement between the accounting numbers and the resources or events that those numbers are supposed to represent.* For example, if a firm reports that its cash account has a balance of $50,000 when the correct balance is actually $35,000, the concept of representational faithfulness is violated. Information that is biased (consistently too high or too low) is not representationally faithful. Bias may arise because the measurement method is not used properly or the measurement method does not represent what it is supposed to represent.

Secondary and Interactive Qualities

Neutrality. *Accounting information should be free from any bias toward or against a predetermined result.* The effect of an accounting rule on the interests of a particular user should not be a major consideration in its selection. The primary concern here is the relevance and reliability that results from the application (or the formulation) of accounting standards.

Comparability. *The significance of information is enhanced greatly when it can be contrasted with similar information concerning other enterprises and with similar information about the same enterprise for some other period or point in time.* Information, especially quantitative information, is most useful when it can be compared with such benchmarks. The purpose of these comparisons is, of course, to detect and explain similarities and differences.

Consistency. The concept of consistency is linked closely to comparability. *Consistency is conformity from one period to another in the use of accounting methods and procedures.* A more detailed discussion of the concept of consistency as it relates to financial reporting was included in Chapter 1.

Threshold for Recognition

Materiality. *Materiality indicates that the amount involved is sufficiently large to affect or make a difference in a decision.* The concept of materiality was discussed in detail in Chapter 1.

ELEMENTS OF FINANCIAL STATEMENTS OF BUSINESS ENTERPRISES

Financial statements require certain elements to be reported or disclosed in order to measure the performance and status of an enterprise. SFAC No. 6, which replaced SFAC No. 3, has identified and defined ten interrelated elements of financial statements.

Elements[6]

Assets. *Assets are probable future economic benefits obtained or controlled by a particular entity as a result of past transactions or events.* For example, an acre of land purchased by a company is considered to be an asset, because the company can obtain the future economic benefits, can control others' access to these benefits, and has completed the transaction for the purchase of the land. If access to the land cannot be controlled by the company because the city can use it as a right-of-way or if the transaction has not occurred yet but will in the future, then the land is not considered to be an asset.

Liabilities. *Liabilities are probable future sacrifices of economic benefits arising from present obligations of a particular entity to transfer assets or provide services to other entities in the future as a result of past transactions or events.* An obligation to pay an account which arose on the credit purchase of inventory or the use of electricity in advance of payment are examples of liabilities. An obligation to pay an executive a bonus in cash is a liability; an obligation to pay an executive a bonus in the company's own stock is not a liability because it does not involve a commitment of assets. An agreement to purchase inventory in the future is not considered to be a liability because no transaction has taken place.

Equity. *Equity is the residual interest in the assets of an entity that remains after deducting its liabilities (i.e., Equity = Assets − Liabilities).* In

---

[6] FASB Statement of Financial Accounting Concepts No. 6, "Elements of Financial Statements," (Stamford: FASB, December, 1985).

a business enterprise, the equity is the ownership interest. Equity is the source of distributions to the owners of an enterprise. These distributions are made at the discretion of the owners after any restrictions imposed by law, regulation, or agreements with other entities have been satisfied. Equity is increased by owners' investments and by comprehensive income. The division between liabilities and equity is clear in concept but not always in practice. For example, securities such as convertible bonds and preferred stock have characteristics of both liabilities and equity.

The illustration on the next page distinguishes between the sources of changes in equity (Class B) and the other transactions, events, and circumstances affecting an enterprise during a period (Class A and Class C). The changes in assets and liabilities under Class A do not produce changes in equity—examples include purchasing inventories for cash, issuing a note payable to settle an account payable, purchasing equipment on account, and repaying bonds payable. The changes in assets and liabilities under Class B produce changes in equity—examples include comprehensive income (revenues, expenses, gains, and losses) and changes in equity due to investments by owners and distributions to owners. Changes which affect the composition of equity but not the amount are represented by Class C—examples include stock dividends and the conversion of preferred stock into common stock.

Investments By Owners. Investments by owners are increases in equity of a particular business enterprise resulting from transfers to the enterprise from other entities of something of value to obtain or increase ownership interests (or equity) in it. Assets are most commonly received as investments by owners, but that which is received may also include services or satisfaction or conversion of liabilities of the enterprise.

Distributions to Owners. Distributions to owners are decreases in equity of a particular business enterprise resulting from transferring assets, rendering services, or incurring liabilities by the enterprise to owners. Distributions to owners decrease ownership interest (or equity) in an enterprise.

Comprehensive Income. *Comprehensive income is the change in equity (net assets) of a business enterprise during a period from transactions and other events and circumstances from non-owner sources.* It includes all changes in equity during a period except those resulting from investments by owners and distributions to owners.

Revenues. *Revenues are inflows or other enhancements of assets of an entity or settlements of its liabilities (or a combination of both) from delivering or producing goods, rendering services, or other activities that constitute the entity's ongoing major or central operations.* For example, a sale of furniture by a furniture manufacturer is considered to be revenue, whereas the sale of one of its short-term investments at a price exceeding its cost is not considered to be revenue.

Effects on an Enterprise During a Period

All transactions and other events and circumstances that affect a business enterprise during a period

A. All changes in assets and liabilities not accompanied by changes in equity

1. Exchanges of assets for assets
2. Exchanges of liabilities for liabilities
3. Acquisitions of assets by incurring liabilities
4. Settlements of liabilities by transferring assets

B. All changes in assets or liabilities accompanied by changes in equity

1. Comprehensive income
   a. Revenues
   b. Gains
   c. Expenses
   d. Losses

2. All changes in equity from transfers between a business enterprise and its owners
   a. Investments by owners
   b. Distributions to owners

C. Changes within equity that do not affect assets or liabilities

Source: Statement of Financial Accounting Concepts No. 6

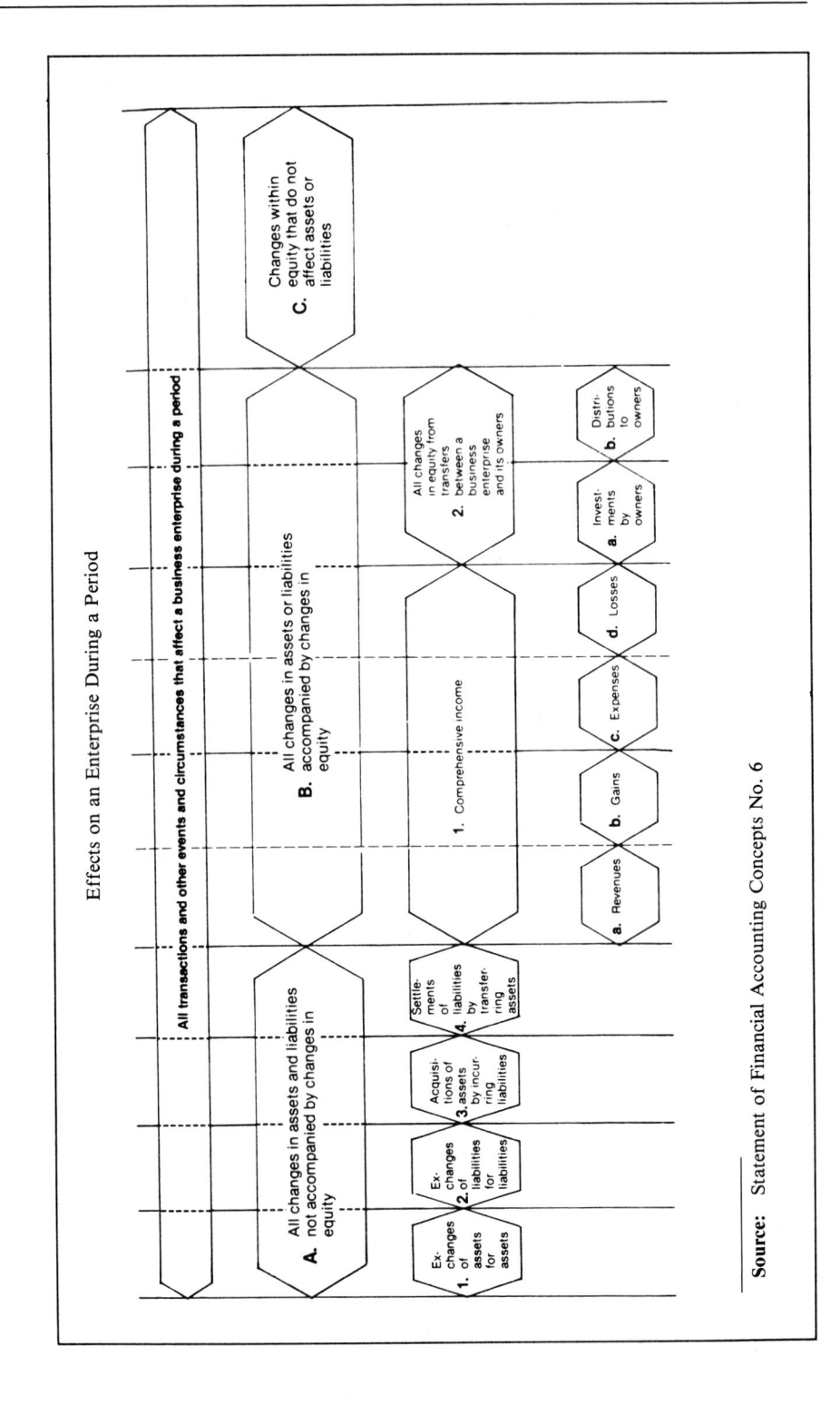

Expenses. *Expenses are outflows or other consumption or using up of assets or incurrences of liabilities (or a combination of both) from delivering or producing goods, rendering services, or carrying out other activities that constitute the entity's ongoing major or central operations.* For example, the cost of the furniture sold by the furniture manufacturer above is considered to be an expense, whereas the sale of one of its short-term investments at a price less than its cost is not considered to be an expense.

Gains. *Gains are increases in equity (net assets) from peripheral or incidental transactions of an entity and from all other transactions and other events and circumstances affecting the entity during a period except those that result from revenues or investments by owners.* The sale of the short-term investment by the furniture manufacturer at a price exceeding its cost is considered to be a gain.

Losses. *Losses are decreases in equity (net assets) from peripheral or incidental transactions of an entity and from all other transactions and other events and circumstances affecting the entity during a period except those that result from expenses or distributions to owners.* The sale of the short-term investment by the furniture manufacturer at a price less that its cost is considered to be a loss.

RECOGNITION AND MEASUREMENT IN FINANCIAL STATEMENTS OF BUSINESS ENTERPRISES

Since financial statements are the principal means by which financial accounting information is communicated, it is essential to know what information should be incorporated into the financial statements. *SFAC No. 5 identifies this formal incorporation of information as the process of recognition.* For items that meet the criteria for recognition, disclosure by such other means as notes to the financial statements and supplementary information is not a substitute for recognition in the financial statements.

The Role of Financial Statements

According to SFAC No. 5, financial statements should contribute to meeting the objectives of financial reporting both individually and collectively. A complete set of financial statements for a period should include:

1. Financial position at the end of the period;

2. Earnings for the period;

3. Comprehensive income for the period;

4. Cash flows during the period; and

5. Investments by and distributions to owners during the period.[7]

---

[7] FASB Statement of Financial Accounting Concepts No. 5, "Recognition and Measurement in Financial Statements of Business Enterprises," (Stamford: FASB, December, 1984), p. vii.

Statement of Financial Position. *A statement of financial position (balance sheet) is designed to provide information concerning an entity's assets, liabilities, and equity and their relationship among one another at a moment in time.* It is not designed to present the value of a business enterprise but should assist users in assessing this value.

Statements of Earning and of Comprehensive Income *Together, these two statements show the degree to which and the ways in which the equity of an entity increased or decreased.* The concept of *earnings is defined as a measure of entity performance based on the extent to which asset inflows (revenues and gains) associated with cash-to-cash cycles substantially completed during the period exceed asset outflows (expenses and losses).* Earnings is similar to net income for a period but, unlike comprehensive income, excludes the effects of certain accounting adjustments of earlier periods that are recognized in the current period—primarily the cumulative effect of a change in accounting principle—as well as changes in net assets attributable to certain types of holding gains and losses.

Statement of Cash Flows. An entity should report its sources of cash receipts and uses of cash payments in a statement of cash flows. Cash flow information should also be provided concerning an entity's operating, financing, and investing activities.

Statement of Investments By and Distributions to Owners. This statement is designed to reflect an entity's capital transactions during a period, including the extent and ways to which the equity of the entity was changed from capital transactions with the owners.

Recognition and Measurement

According to SFAC No. 5, an item and information about it should meet four criteria subject to the cost-benefit constraint and materiality threshold to be recognized. These are:

1. The item fits one of the definitions of elements in SFAC No. 6 (formerly SFAC No. 3);

2. The item has a relevant attribute measurable with sufficient reliability;

3. The information is relevant; and

4. The information is reliable.

The item can be measured by different attributes (e.g., historical cost, current market value, replacement cost, net realizable value, and present value of future cash flows), depending on the nature of the item and the relevance and reliability of the attribute measured.

SFAC No. 5 provides guidance for the recognition of revenues and gains and of expenses and losses. As a reaction to uncertainty, more stringent requirements are imposed for recognizing revenues and gains than for recognizing expenses and losses.

Recognition of revenues and gains involves the consideration of two factors:

1. Revenues and gains are generally not recognized until realized (assets or services exchanged for cash or claims to cash) or realizable (assets are readily convertible to known amounts of cash or claims to cash).

2. Revenues are not recognized until earned (the entity has substantially accomplished what is needed to be entitled to the benefits); being earned is generally less significant for gains than being realized or realizable.

Recognition of expenses and losses also involves the consideration of two factors:

1. Consumption of economic benefits are recognized by matching the expense with revenues (e.g., cost of the goods sold), by recognizing the expense in the period in which cash is spent or liabilities are incurred (e.g., administrative salaries), and by systematically allocating expenses to the periods during which the related assets are expected to provide benefits (e.g., depreciation).

2. An expense or loss is recognized if an asset no longer has a future economic benefit or if a liability has been incurred without associated economic benefits.

DEVELOPING GENERALLY ACCEPTED ACCOUNTING PRINCIPLES

Generally accepted accounting principles (GAAP) are concerned with the measurement and disclosure of economic activity. GAAP determines the manner in which the accounting process is to be applied in specific situations. *Generally accepted accounting principles is defined by the APB in its Statement No. 4 as follows:*

> ... Generally accepted accounting principles incorporate the consensus at a particular time as to which economic resources and obligations should be recorded as assets and liabilities by financial accounting, which changes in assets and liabilities should be recorded, when these changes should be recorded, how the assets and liabilities and changes in them should be measured, what information should be disclosed and how it should be disclosed and which financial statements should be prepared.
>
> Generally accepted accounting principles therefore is a technical term in financial accounting. Generally accepted accounting principles encompass the conventions, rules, and procedures necessary to define ac-

cepted accounting practice at a particular time. The standard of "generally accepted accounting principles" includes not only broad guidelines of general application, but also detailed practices and procedures.

Generally accepted accounting principles are conventional—that is, they become generally accepted by agreement (often tacit agreement) rather than by formal derivation from a set of postulates or basic concepts. The principles have developed on the basis of experience, reason, custom, usage, and, to a significant extent, practical necessity.[8]

There are two basic sources of GAAP. The first source is the *authoritative bodies (e.g., the APB and the FASB)* which have developed specific principles. These authoritative (sometimes called promulgated) principles must be followed by all accountants. The second source is the *nonauthoritative bodies (e.g., committess of the AICPA)* which have developed principles and the practitioners who have used principles which have evolved over time.

The FASB, as was the case with its predecessors the CAP and the APB, and the SEC are authoritative bodies with the power to set accounting standards. *The FASB and APB pronouncements which must be followed, as prescribed by Rule 203 of the AICPA's Rules of Conduct of the Code of Professional Ethics, are FASB Statements and Interpretations, APB Opinions, and Accounting Research Bulletins.* Any deviations from these principles require an auditor either to qualify the opinion or to explain the reasons for the departures and their effect on the financial statements. The SEC is empowered to establish the rules and procedures regarding filings to the Commission by the Securities Exchange Act of 1934.

Positions contained in AICPA Industry Audit and Accounting Guides, AICPA Statements of Position, AICPA Accounting Interpretations, and FASB Technical Bulletins are considered to be preferable, rather than mandatory, accounting principles. They may be departed from, but an auditor must justify the use of a different accounting principle. These pronouncements have been concerned with specialized principles for particular industries; these positions may not apply to all industries.

The FASB's Statements of Financial Accounting Concepts and the APB's Statements are included in GAAP. These documents provide a framework within which solutions to accounting problems may be found.

Some accounting principles have become part of accounting practice without being included in authoritative standards. For example, FIFO and LIFO are acceptable methods for costing inventories and determining cost of goods sold; however, there are no APB or FASB pronouncements which deal with the bases for these methods.

---

[8] APB Statement No. 4, "Basic Concepts and Accounting Principles Underlying Financial Statements of Business Enterprises," (New York: AICPA, 1970), para. 137-139.

THE ACCOUNTING STANDARD SETTING PROCESS

A well-accepted view of the accounting standard-setting process asserts that it is essentially a political process involving various user groups each of which is attempting to advance its own self-interests.[15] User groups often react negatively to those proposed standards which are perceived to be damaging to them and positively to those proposed standards which they perceive to be favorable for them.

User groups are able to politicize the standard setting process by means of their lobbying efforts with Congress, the SEC, and the President. Since the SEC has both the authority and power to enact accounting standards, the FASB must remain responsive to these user groups or assume the risk of having its standard setting power usurped. Therefore, accounting standards sometimes lack the theoretical background one might expect as greater emphasis is given to the economic consequences of a proposed standard on various user groups.

Some accountants believe that the FASB should not only take accounting theory and the usefulness of accounting information into consideration, but also should support the economic goals of our government. Others believe that if accounting standards are promulgated to achieve macroeconomic objectives, then the confidence in these standards would be destroyed.

Most accounting standards have a definite economic impact. For example, the requirement to expense rather than to capitalize research and development costs has been considered to be a threat to technological progress. The requirement to use the method initially required by the FASB for accounting for the exploration and development costs of oil and gas companies was believed to be injurious to these enterprises.

At the time that the FASB issues a Discussion Memorandum, Invitation to Comment, or Exposure Draft, those companies that would be most affected submit their comments. There are always companies that dislike and oppose a proposed standard, and these companies may appeal to the government to become involved. If a standard is adopted that a company does not feel is beneficial, that company may not follow the standard on the basis of immateriality, or the company may alter its behavior in order to circumvent the effect of the standard. In addition, the company may increase its lobbying efforts in an attempt to have the standard modified or repealed.

International Aspects

Accounting principles and practices vary widely across countries. Accounting practices in certain countries (e.g., the United States and Canada) are prescribed by private organizations (e.g., FASB and the Canadian Institute of Chartered Accountants); accounting practices in other countries (e.g., France) are prescribed by the government.

---

[15] Charles Horngren, "The Marketing of Accounting Standards," *Journal of Accountancy*, (October, 1973), pp. 61-66.

Some accounting organizations have attempted to standardize practices across national boundaries. Two such organizations are the European Economic Community Commission, which has issued several directives on accounting practices for members of the Common Market, and the International Accounting Standards Committee (IASC), which has issued numerous International Accounting Standards.

Although professional accounting institutes in several countries have conformed their accounting requirements to these International Accounting Standards, the IASC members in many countries (e.g., the AICPA in the United States) have not been able to ensure that the accounting organization responsible for prescribing accounting practices in those countries (e.g., the FASB in the United States) issue standards which parallel the requirements stated in the International Accounting Standards. Therefore, in the United States, as well as in many other countries, there are differences between the requirements under the International Accounting Standards and domestic generally accepted accounting principles.

The financial statements of a foreign subsidiary may be included in the consolidated financial statements of a U.S. company. This foreign subsidiary may have prepared its financial statements in conformity with the requirements of the country in which it is located. Such requirements may or may not have been in agreement with the International Accounting Standards, the European Economic Community Commission, or some other multi-national organization. Before the financial statements of this foreign subsidiary are included in the consolidated financial statements of the U.S. company, the foreign statements must be prepared in accordance with the generally accepted accounting principles for the United States.

Although a knowledge of accounting requirements in other countries and by multi-national organizations is useful to practicing accountants in the United States, an examination of such requirements is beyond the scope of this text. International aspects of accounting are typically covered in advanced accounting courses.

KEY DEFINTIONS

Assets Assets are probable future economic benefits obtained or controlled by a particular entity as a result of past transactions or events.

Benefits and costs In order to justify providing accounting information, the benefits which may be derived from the use of this information must exceed the costs of providing the data.

Bias Bias in measurement is the tendency of a measure to fall more often on one side than the other of what it represents instead of being equally likely to fall on either side. Bias in accounting measures means a tendency to be consistently too high or too low.

Comparability Comparability is the quality of information that enables users to identify similarities in and diferences between two sets of economic phenomena.

Completeness Completeness is the inclusion in reported information of everything material that is necessary for faithful representation of the relevant phenomena.

Comprehensive income Comprehensive income is the change in equity (net assets) of a business enterprise during a period from transactions and other events and circumstances from non-owner sources.

Concept of earnings The concept of earnings is defined as a measure of entity performance based on the extent to which asset inflows (revenues and gains) associated with cash-to-cash cycles substantially completed during the period exceed asset outflows (expenses and losses).

Conceptual framework The conceptual framework project is an attempt by the FASB to develop a system of coherent interrelated objectives and fundamental principles that will enable the FASB to issue more useful and consistent standards in the future.

Elements of Financial Statements The elements are the components of the financial statements (e.g., assets, liabilities, revenues, and expenses).

Equity Equity is the residual interest in the assets of an entity that remains after deducting its liabilities (i.e., Equity = Assets − Liabilities).

Expenses Expenses are outflows or other consumption or using up of assets or incurrences of liabilities (or a combination of both) from delivering or producing goods, rendering services, or carrying out other activities that constitute the entity's ongoing major or central operations.

Feedback value Feedback value is the quality of information that enables users to confirm or correct prior expectations.

Financial reporting Financial reporting includes not only the financial statements but also such other forms of communicating financial information as annual reports filed with the SEC, news releases, and management forecasts.

Gains Gains are increases in equity (net assets) from peripheral or incidental transactions of an entity and from all other transactions and other events and circumstances affecting the entity during a period except those that result from revenues or investments by owners.

Liabilities Liabilities are probable future sacrifices of economic benefits arising from present obligations of a particular entity to transfer assets or provide services to other entities in the future as a result of past transactions or events.

Losses Losses are decreases in equity (net assets) from peripheral or incidental transactions of an entity and from all other transactions and other events and circumstances affecting the entity during a period except those that result from expenses or distributions to owners.

Materiality concept This concept indicates that the accountant should be primarily concerned with those transactions which are of real significance to the users of his report. No specific value can be assigned to any transaction to determine materiality, but if the information would affect a financial statement user's decisions, then it is material. It is the magnitude of an omission or misstatement of accounting information that, in the light of surrounding circumstances, makes it probable that the judgment of a reasonable person relying on the information would have been changed or influenced by the omission or misstatement.

Neutrality Neutrality is the absence in reported information of bias intended to attain a predetermined result or to induce a particular mode of behavior.

Objective of financial reporting A primary objective of financial reporting is to ". . . provide information that is useful to present and potential investors and creditors and other users in making rational investment, credit, and similar decisions. In order to accomplish this goal, it is necessary that the information which is communicated must be understood; it ". . . should be comprehensible to those who have a reasonable understanding of business and economic activities and are willing to study the information with reasonable diligence."

Objectives of Financial Statements The objectives of financial statements which are derived from the needs of the users of the financial statements, are the most basic components of the conceptual framework.

Predictive value Predictive value is the quality of information that helps users to increase the likelihood of correctly forecasting the outcome of past or present events.

Primary focus of financial reporting The primary focus of financial reporting is on the disclosure of information concerning the earnings of a business.

Qualitative characteristics of financial statements The qualitative characteristics are the criteria to be used in the selection and evaluation of accounting and reporting policies.

Relevance Relevance is the capacity of information to make a differnece in a decision by helping users to form predictions about the outcomes of past, present, and future events or to confirm or correct prior expectations.

Reliability Reliability is the quality of information that assures that information is reasonably free from error and bias and faithfully represents what it purports to represent.

Representational faithfulness Representational faithfulness is the correspondence or agreement between a measure or description and the phenonmenon that it purports to represent (sometimes called validity).

Revenues Revenues are inflows or other enhancements of assets of an entity or settlements of its liabilities (or a combination of both) from delivering or producing goods, rendering services, or other activities that constitute the entity's ongoing major or central operations.

Statement of cash flows An entity should report its sources of cash receipts and uses of cash payments in a statement of cash flows.

Statement of financial position A statement of financial position (balance sheet) is designed to provide information concerning an entity's assets, liabilities, and equity and their relationship among one another at a moment in time.

Statement of investments by and distributions to owners This statement is designed to reflect an entity's capital transactions during a period, including the exent and ways to which the equity of the entity was changed from capital transactions with the owners.

Statements of earnings and of comprehensive income These two statements show the degree to which and the ways in which the equity of an entity increased or decreased.

Timeliness Timeliness is having information available to a decision maker before it loses it capacity to influence decisions.

Understandability Understandability is the quality of information that enables users to perceive its significance.

Verifiability Verifiability is the ability through consensus among measurers to ensure that information represents what it purpots to represent or that the chosen method of measurement has been used without error or bias.

QUESTIONS

1. What is the purpose of the FASB's conceptual framework project?

2. What are the most basic components of the conceptual framework project? How are these derived?

3. What are the qualitative characteristics?

4. What are the elements of financial statements? Define each element.

5. What are the anticipated benefits of the conceptual framework?

6. Is financial reporting limited to issuing financial statements? Comment.

7. Discuss the primary objective of financial reporting? What is its focus?

8. Comment on the measurement of income under the conventions of accrual accounting and the cash flows of an enterprise.

9. How do "benefits and cost" impact on the disclosure of accounting information?

10. Comment on the relationship of "relevance" and "reliability" in the standard setting process.

11. Define each of the following terms:

    a. Assets
    b. Liabilities
    c. Equities

12. Differentiate between:

    a. Revenues and gains
    b. Expenses and losses

13. List the statements that are normally included in a complete set of financial statements.

14. Does a balance sheet "value" a business? Comment.

15. What are the criteria an item should meet for recognition?

16. Define generally accepted accounting principles. How are they derived?

17. What are the sources of generally accepted accounting principles? Discuss.

Appendix:

General Motors Corporation and Consolidated Subsidiaries

CONSOLIDATED FINANCIAL STATEMENTS

General Motors Corporation and Consolidated Subsidiaries
RESPONSIBILITIES FOR FINANCIAL STATEMENTS

The following financial statements of General Motors Corporation and consolidated subsidiaries were prepared by the management which is responsible for their integrity and objectivity. The statements have been prepared in conformity with generally accepted accounting principles and, as such, include amounts based on judgments of management. Financial information elsewhere in this Annual Report is consistent with that in the financial statements.

Management is further responsible for maintaining a system of internal accounting controls, designed to provide reasonable assurance that the books and records reflect the transactions of the companies and that its established policies and procedures are carefully followed. From a stockholder's point of view, perhaps the most important feature in the system of control is that it is continually reviewed for its effectiveness and is augmented by written policies and guidelines, the careful selection and training of qualified personnel, and a strong program of internal audit.

Deloitte Haskins & Sells, independent certified public accountants, are engaged to examine the consolidated financial statements of General Motors Corporation and its subsidiaries and issue reports thereon. Their examination is conducted in accordance with generally accepted auditing standards which comprehend a review of internal accounting controls and a test of transactions. The Accountants' Report appears on page 38.

The Board of Directors, through the Audit Committee (composed entirely of non-employe Directors), is responsible for assuring that management fulfills its responsibilities in the preparation of the financial statements. The Committee selects the independent public accountants annually in advance of the Annual Meeting of Stockholders and submits the selection for ratification at the Meeting. In addition, the Committee reviews the scope of the audits and the accounting principles being applied in financial reporting. The independent public accountants, representatives of management, and the internal auditors meet regularly (separately and jointly) with the Committee to review the activities of each and to ensure that each is properly discharging its responsibilities. To ensure complete independence, Deloitte Haskins & Sells have full and free access to meet with the Committee, without management representatives present, to discuss the results of their examination, the adequacy of internal accounting controls, and the quality of the financial reporting.

Chairman

Chief Financial Officer

STATEMENT OF CONSOLIDATED INCOME

For the Years Ended December 31, 1985, 1984 and 1983 (Dollars in Millions Except Per Share Amounts)

	1985	1984	1983
Net Sales and Revenues (Notes 1 and 2)			
Manufactured products	$95,268.4	$83,699.7	$74,581.6
Computer systems services	1,103.3	190.2	—
Total Net Sales and Revenues	96,371.7	83,889.9	74,581.6
Costs and Expenses			
Cost of sales and other operating charges, exclusive of items listed below	81,654.6	70,217.9	60,718.8
Selling, general and administrative expenses	4,294.2	4,003.0	3,234.0
Depreciation of real estate, plants and equipment	2,777.9	2,663.2	2,569.7
Amortization of special tools	3,083.3	2,236.7	2,549.9
Amortization of intangible assets (Note 1)	347.3	69.1	.8
Total Costs and Expenses	92,157.3	79,189.9	69,073.2
Operating Income	4,214.4	4,700.0	5,508.4
Other income less income deductions—net (Note 6)	1,299.2	1,713.5	815.8
Interest expense (Note 1)	(892.3)	(909.2)	(1,352.7)
Income before Income Taxes	4,621.3	5,504.3	4,971.5
United States, foreign and other income taxes (Note 8)	1,630.3	1,805.1	2,223.8
Income after Income Taxes	2,991.0	3,699.2	2,747.7
Equity in earnings of nonconsolidated subsidiaries and associates (dividends received amounted to $100.5 in 1985, $706.1 in 1984 and $757.3 in 1983)	1,008.0	817.3	982.5
Net Income	3,999.0	4,516.5	3,730.2
Dividends on preferred stocks	11.6	12.5	12.9
Earnings on Common Stocks	$ 3,987.4	$ 4,504.0	$ 3,717.3
Earnings attributable to:			
$1-2/3 par value common stock	$ 3,883.6	$ 4,498.3	$ 3,717.3
Class E common stock (issued in 1984)	$ 103.8	$ 5.7	—
Average number of shares of common stocks outstanding (in millions):			
$1-2/3 par value common	316.3	315.3	313.9
Class E common (issued in 1984)*	66.5	36.3	—
Earnings Per Share Attributable to (Note 9):			
$1-2/3 par value common stock	$12.28	$14.27	$11.84
Class E common stock (issued in 1984)*	$1.57	$0.16	—

Reference should be made to notes on pages 28 through 38. Certain amounts for 1984 and 1983 have been reclassified to conform with 1985 classifications.

Earnings and earnings per share attributable to common stocks have been restated to reflect the Class E common stock amendment approved by the stockholders in December 1985.

*Adjusted to reflect the two-for-one stock split in the form of a 100% stock dividend distributed on June 10, 1985.

CONSOLIDATED BALANCE SHEET

December 31, 1985 and 1984 (Dollars in Millions Except Per Share Amounts)

ASSETS	1985	1984
Current Assets		
Cash	$ 179.1	$ 467.5
United States Government and other marketable securities and time deposits—at cost, which approximates market of $4,933.1 and $8,108.7	4,935.3	8,099.9
Total cash and marketable securities	5,114.4	8,567.4
Accounts and notes receivable (including GMAC and its subsidiaries—$4,038.7 and $3,868.5)—less allowances (Note 10)	7,282.0	7,357.9
Inventories (less allowances) (Note 1)	8,269.7	7,359.7
Contracts in process (less advances and progress payments of $2,525.3 in 1985) (Note 1)	1,453.8	—
Prepaid expenses	2,136.1	428.3
Total Current Assets	24,256.0	23,713.3
Equity in Net Assets of Nonconsolidated Subsidiaries and Associates (principally GMAC and its subsidiaries—Note 10)	5,718.5	4,603.0
Other Investments and Miscellaneous Assets—at cost (less allowances)	3,069.8	2,344.4
Common Stocks Held for the GM Incentive Program (Note 3)	190.2	144.2
Property		
Real estate, plants and equipment—at cost (Note 11)	47,267.1	39,354.1
Less accumulated depreciation (Note 11)	24,325.0	21,649.8
Net real estate, plants and equipment	22,942.1	17,704.3
Special tools—at cost (less amortization)	1,710.9	1,697.2
Total Property	24,653.0	19,401.5
Intangible Assets—at cost (less amortization) (Note 1)	5,945.3	1,938.5
Total Assets	$63,832.8	$52,144.9

LIABILITIES AND STOCKHOLDERS' EQUITY		
Current Liabilities		
Accounts payable (principally trade)	$ 7,322.2	$ 4,743.5
Loans payable (Note 13)	2,655.2	3,086.0
United States, foreign and other income taxes payable	243.1	618.9
Accrued liabilities and deferred income taxes (Note 12)	12,078.0	8,988.2
Total Current Liabilities	22,298.5	17,436.6
Long-Term Debt (Note 13)	2,500.2	2,417.4
Capitalized Leases (including GMAC and its subsidiaries—$76.1 and $113.2)	367.0	355.5
Other Liabilities (including GMAC and its subsidiaries—$300.0 in 1985 and 1984)	7,179.8	5,971.9
Deferred Credits (including investment tax credits—$1,328.8 and $1,259.9)	1,962.6	1,749.2
Stockholders' Equity (Notes 3, 4 and 14)		
Preferred stocks ($5.00 series, $169.3 and $169.8; $3.75 series, $81.4 and $85.8)	250.7	255.6
Common stocks:		
$1-2/3 par value common (issued, 318,853,315 and 317,504,133 shares)	531.4	529.2
Class E common (issued, 66,227,137 and 29,082,382 shares)	6.6	2.9
Class H common (issued, 65,495,316 shares in 1985)	6.6	—
Capital surplus (principally additional paid-in capital)	6,667.8	3,347.8
Net income retained for use in the business	22,606.6	20,796.6
Subtotal	30,069.7	24,932.1
Accumulated foreign currency translation and other adjustments (Note 1)	(545.0)	(717.8)
Total Stockholders' Equity	29,524.7	24,214.3
Total Liabilities and Stockholders' Equity	$63,832.8	$52,144.9

Reference should be made to notes on pages 28 through 38.

STATEMENT OF CHANGES IN CONSOLIDATED FINANCIAL POSITION

For the Years Ended December 31, 1985, 1984 and 1983 (Dollars in Millions)

	1985	1984	1983
Source of Funds			
Net income	$ 3,999.0	$ 4,516.5	$ 3,730.2
Depreciation of real estate, plants and equipment	2,777.9	2,663.2	2,569.7
Amortization of special tools	3,083.3	2,236.7	2,549.9
Amortization of intangible assets (Note 1)	347.3	69.1	.8
Deferred income taxes, undistributed earnings of nonconsolidated subsidiaries and associates, etc.—net	(471.7)	(1,316.1)	645.5
Total funds provided by current operations	9,735.8	8,169.4	9,496.1
Decrease (Increase) in other working capital items	866.2	1,964.6	(1,142.0)
Increase in long-term debt	965.9	1,074.1	3,177.1
Issuances of common stocks, less repurchases of preferred stocks	2,755.5	602.2	212.0
Other—net	222.1	2,010.6	772.0
Total	14,545.5	13,820.9	12,515.2
Use of Funds			
Cash dividends paid to stockholders (Note 14)	1,616.9	1,523.7	892.2
Expenditures for real estate, plants and equipment—Operations	6,099.2	3,595.1	1,923.0
—Hughes acquisition	1,948.7	—	—
Expenditures for special tools	3,075.0	2,452.1	2,083.7
Intangible assets acquired in acquisitions (Note 1)	4,244.7	2,006.3	—
Decrease in long-term debt	883.1	1,793.9	4,491.9
Investments in nonconsolidated subsidiaries and associates	130.9	99.3	33.7
Total	17,998.5	11,470.4	9,424.5
Increase (Decrease) in cash and marketable securities	(3,453.0)	2,350.5	3,090.7
Cash and marketable securities at beginning of the year	8,567.4	6,216.9	3,126.2
Cash and marketable securities at end of the year	$ 5,114.4	$ 8,567.4	$ 6,216.9
Decrease (Increase) in Other Working Capital Items by Element			
Accounts and notes receivable	$ 75.9	($ 393.7)	($ 4,099.7)
Inventories	(910.0)	(738.2)	(437.3)
Contracts in process	(1,453.8)	—	—
Prepaid expenses	(1,707.8)	568.9	871.0
Accounts payable	2,578.7	101.2	1,041.6
Loans payable	(430.8)	1,830.8	72.7
United States, foreign and other income taxes payable	(375.8)	416.6	131.5
Accrued liabilities and deferred income taxes	3,089.8	179.0	1,278.2
Decrease (Increase) in other working capital items	$ 866.2	$ 1,964.6	($ 1,142.0)

Reference should be made to notes on pages 28 through 38.
Certain amounts for 1984 and 1983 have been reclassified to conform with 1985 classifications.

NOTES TO FINANCIAL STATEMENTS

NOTE 1. Significant Accounting Policies

Principles of Consolidation
The consolidated financial statements include the accounts of the Corporation and all domestic and foreign subsidiaries which are more than 50% owned and engaged principally in manufacturing or wholesale marketing of General Motors products as well as defense, electronics and computer services. General Motors' share of earnings or losses of nonconsolidated subsidiaries and of associates in which at least 20% of the voting securities is owned is included in consolidated income under the equity method of accounting.

Revenue Recognition
Sales are generally recorded by the Corporation when products are shipped to independent dealers. Provisions for normal dealer sales incentives and returns and allowances are made at the time of sale. Costs related to special sales incentive programs are recognized as sales deductions when these incentive programs are announced.

Certain sales under long-term contracts, primarily in the defense business, are recorded using the percentage-of-completion method of accounting. Under this method, sales are recorded equivalent to costs incurred plus a portion of the profit expected to be realized on the contract, determined based on the ratio of costs incurred to estimated total costs at completion. Profits expected to be realized on contracts are based on the Corporation's estimates of total sales value and cost at completion. These estimates are reviewed and revised periodically throughout the lives of the contracts, and adjustments to profits resulting from such revisions are recorded in the accounting period in which the revisions are made. Estimated losses on contracts are recorded in the period in which they are first identified.

Inventories
Inventories are stated generally at cost, which is not in excess of market. The cost of substantially all domestic inventories other than the inventories of GM Hughes Electronics Corporation (GMHE) is determined by the last-in, first-out (LIFO) method. If the first-in, first-out (FIFO) method of inventory valuation had been used for inventories valued at LIFO cost, such inventories would have been about $2,196.3 million higher at December 31, 1985 and $2,183.0 million higher at December 31, 1984. As a result of decreases in LIFO eligible U.S. inventories, certain LIFO inventory quantities carried at lower costs prevailing in prior years, as compared with the costs of current purchases, were liquidated in 1985. These inventory adjustments favorably affected income before income taxes by approximately $20.9 million. The cost of inventories outside the United States and the inventories of GMHE is determined generally by FIFO or average cost methods.

Major Classes of Inventories

(Dollars in Millions)	1985	1984
Productive material, work in process and supplies	$5,591.5	$5,264.2
Finished product, service parts, etc.	2,678.2	2,095.5
Total	$8,269.7	$7,359.7

Contracts in Process
Contracts in process are stated at costs incurred plus estimated profit less amounts billed to customers and advances and progress payments received. Engineering, tooling, manufacturing and applicable overhead costs, including administrative, research and development and selling expenses are charged to cost of sales when they are incurred. Contracts in process include amounts relating to contracts with long production cycles. Although shown as a current asset, approximately $98.6 million in 1985 is not expected to be collected within one year. Under certain contracts with the United States Government, progress payments are received based on costs incurred on the respective contracts. Title to the inventories related to such contracts (included in contracts in process) vests with the United States Government.

Depreciation and Amortization
Depreciation is provided on groups of property using, with minor exceptions, an accelerated method which accumulates depreciation of approximately two-thirds of the depreciable cost during the first half of the estimated lives of the property.

Expenditures for special tools are amortized over short periods of time because the utility value of the tools is radically affected by frequent changes in the design of the functional components and appearance of the product. Amortization is applied directly to the asset account. Replacement of special tools for reasons other than changes in products is charged directly to cost of sales.

Income Taxes
Investment tax credits are generally deferred and amortized over the lives of the related assets (the "deferral method"). In 1985, Electronic Data Systems Corporation changed its method of accounting for investment tax credits from the flow-through method to the deferral method used by the Corporation. The effect of the change was to reduce 1985 earnings attributable to Class E common stock by $0.41 per share and defer the recognition to earnings attributable to Class E common stock in future years. The tax effects of timing differences between pretax accounting income and taxable income (principally related to depreciation, sales and product allowances, vehicle instalment sales, and benefit plans expense) are deferred. Provisions are made for estimated United States and foreign taxes, less available tax credits and deductions, which may be incurred on remittance of the Corporation's share of subsidiaries' undistributed earnings less those deemed to be permanently reinvested. Possible taxes beyond those provided would not be material.

Pension Program
The Corporation and its subsidiaries have several pension plans covering substantially all of their employes. Benefits under the plans are generally related to an employe's length of service, wages and salaries, and, where applicable, contributions. The costs of these plans are determined on the basis of actuarial cost methods and include amortization of prior service cost over periods not in excess of 30 years, generally from the later of October 1, 1979 or the date such costs are established. With the exception of certain Canadian and overseas subsidiaries, pension costs accrued are funded within the limitations set by the Employee Retirement Income Security Act.

Product Related Expenses
Expenditures for advertising and sales promotion and for other product related expenses are charged to costs and expenses as incurred; provisions for estimated costs related to product warranty are made at the time the products are sold. Expenditures for research and development are charged to expenses as incurred and amounted to $3,625.2 million in 1985, $3,075.8 million in 1984 and $2,602.2 million in 1983.

Interest Cost
Total interest cost incurred in 1985, 1984 and 1983 amounted to $944.9 million, $932.5 million and $1,401.8 million, respectively, of which $52.6 million, $23.3 million and $49.1 million, related to certain real estate, plants and equipment acquired in those years, was capitalized.

Foreign Currency Translation
As required by the Financial Accounting Standards Board, effective January 1, 1983, the Corporation implemented Statement of Financial Accounting Standards (SFAS) No. 52, Foreign Currency Translation. Under SFAS No. 52, all assets and liabilities of operations outside the United States, except for operations in highly inflationary economies (principally in Latin America) or those that are highly integrated with operations of the Corporation (principally in Canada), are translated into U.S. dollars using current exchange rates, and the effects of foreign currency translation adjustments are deferred and included as a component of stockholders' equity. For operations in highly inflationary economies or that are highly integrated, foreign currency translation adjustments are included in income. The effect of adopting SFAS No. 52 was to reduce net income for 1983 by about $422.5 million ($1.35 per share of $1-2/3 par value common stock). Exchange and translation gains (losses) included in net income in 1985, 1984 and 1983 amounted to $54.1 million, ($114.8) million and ($52.3) million, respectively.

(continued)

NOTES TO FINANCIAL STATEMENTS (continued)

NOTE 1. (concluded)

Acquisitions

Effective December 31, 1985, the Corporation acquired Hughes Aircraft Company (Hughes) and its subsidiaries for $2.7 billion in cash and cash equivalents and 50 million shares of General Motors Class H common stock having an estimated total value of $2,561.9 million. Hughes is one of the leading defense electronics firms in the world and specializes in high-technology electronics for military, scientific and commercial use. In addition, the Corporation has contingently agreed to pay the Howard Hughes Medical Institute (Institute) on December 31, 1989, for each share of Class H common stock issued in connection with the acquisition and held by the Institute on that date, the amount, if any, by which the market value per share of Class H common stock is below $60; provided that such payment shall not be greater than $40 per share. Any payment required under this contingency provision will be charged to capital surplus.

The acquisition has been accounted for as a purchase. In view of the current policy of the Department of Defense and a recent decision of the Armed Services Board of Contract Appeals, there is substantial uncertainty as to the recoverability through contracts with the U.S. Government of any increase in the book values of the net assets of a defense contractor as a result of a business combination accounted for as a purchase. Accordingly, the amounts assigned to the tangible net assets of Hughes do not differ materially from the historical net book values. The purchase price exceeded the net book value of Hughes by $4,244.7 million, which was assigned as follows: $500.0 million to patents and related technology, $125.0 million to the future economic benefits to the Corporation of the Hughes Long-Term Incentive Plan, and $3,619.7 million to other intangible assets. The amounts assigned to the various intangible asset categories are to be amortized on a straight-line basis; patents and related technology over 15 years, the future economic benefits of the Hughes Long-Term Incentive Plan over 5 years and other intangible assets over 40 years. Amortization is to be applied directly to the asset accounts. For the purpose of determining earnings per share and amounts available for dividends on common stocks, the amortization of these intangible assets is to be charged against earnings attributable to $1-2/3 par value common stock.

Because the acquisition was made effective December 31, 1985, the Statement of Consolidated Income does not include any operations of Hughes for 1985. Pro forma results of operations as though the acquisition of Hughes had been effective at the beginning of 1985 and 1984 are as follows:

(Dollars in Millions)	Pro Forma 1985	1984
Net Sales and Revenues	$102,537.1	$89,706.2
Net Income	$ 4,023.5	$ 4,476.4
Earnings Per Share Attributable to:		
$1-2/3 par value common stock	$11.89	$13.61
Class E common stock	$ 1.57	$ 0.16
Class H common stock	$ 2.44	$ 2.59

On October 18, 1984, the Corporation acquired Electronic Data Systems Corporation (EDS) and its subsidiaries, whose activities include the design of large-scale data processing systems and the operation of data centers and communications networks, for $2,501.9 million. The acquisition was consummated through an offer to exchange EDS common stock for either (a) $44 in cash or (b) $35.20 in cash plus two-tenths of a share of Class E common stock plus a nontransferable contingent promissory note issued by GM. Certain EDS stockholders elected to receive fluctuating rate GM notes due in 1985 in lieu of cash. The nontransferable contingent promissory note is payable seven years after closing in an amount equal to .2 times the excess of $62.50 (post-split) over the market price of the Class E common stock at the maturity date of the note. Holders may tender their notes for prepayment at discounted amounts beginning five years after closing. If the market price of Class E common stock at the maturity date of the notes were to equal the market price at December 31, 1985, $40.88 a share, the aggregate additional consideration would be $483 million. Any additional consideration will be charged to goodwill and amortized over the remaining life of that asset.

The acquisition was accounted for as a purchase. The purchase price in excess of the net book value of EDS, $2,179.5 million, was assigned principally to existing customer contracts, $1,069.9 million, computer software programs developed by EDS, $646.2 million, and other intangible assets, including goodwill, $290.2 million. The cost assigned to these assets is being amortized on a straight-line basis over five years for computer software programs, about seven years for customer contracts, ten years for goodwill and varying periods for the remainder. Amortization is applied directly to the asset accounts.

The Statement of Consolidated Income includes the operations of EDS since October 18, 1984. For the purpose of determining earnings per share and amounts available for dividends on common stocks, the amortization of these assets is charged against earnings attributable to $1-2/3 par value common stock. The effect on the 1985 and 1984 earnings attributable to $1-2/3 par value common stock was a net charge of $241.0 million and $31.7 million, respectively, consisting of the amortization of the intangible and other assets arising from the acquisition less related income tax effects, the profit on intercompany transactions and the earnings of EDS attributable to $1-2/3 par value common stock. Earnings per share of $1-2/3 par value common stock would have been reduced by $0.66 in 1984 and $0.83 in 1983 if the acquisition had been consummated at the beginning of those years.

NOTE 2. Net Sales and Revenues

Net sales and revenues includes sales to:

(Dollars in Millions)	1985	1984	1983
Nonconsolidated subsidiaries and associates	$ 289.1	$ 121.6	$ 111.2
Dealerships operating under dealership assistance plans	$2,090.1	$1,917.4	$1,634.3

Unrealized intercompany profits on sales to nonconsolidated subsidiaries and to associates are deferred.

NOTE 3. General Motors Incentive Program

The General Motors Incentive Program consists of the General Motors Bonus Plan, the General Motors Stock Option Plans and the General Motors Performance Achievement Plan. The By-Laws provide that the Plans in which directors or officers of the Corporation may participate shall be presented for action at a stockholders' meeting at least once in every five years. The Program was last approved by stockholders at the 1982 Annual Meeting, while amendments to the Stock Option Plans were approved at the 1984 Annual Meeting and in conjunction with the acquisition of Hughes.

The Corporation maintains a reserve for purposes of the Bonus Plan. Under the current Plan provisions, for any year a maximum credit may be made to the reserve equal to the amount which the independent public accountants of the Corporation determine to be 8% of the net earnings which exceed $1 billion, but not in excess of the amount paid out as dividends on the common stock during the year. The Incentive and Compensation Committee may, at its discretion, direct that for any year an amount less than the maximum amount available under the formula be credited. Further the Committee may, but is not obligated to, award as bonus in any year the full amount available in the reserve for such awards, or it may award less than the amount available. Bonus awards under the Bonus Plan and such other amounts arising out of the operation of the Bonus Plan as the Committee may determine are charged to the reserve.

The Incentive and Compensation Committee has determined that the credit for 1985 to the reserve shall be $260.7 million. The credit so determined was, as required by the Bonus Plan, less than the amount distributed as dividends to holders of common stock in 1985. On February 3, 1986, the Committee granted awards to 5,749 employes of $218.6 mil-
(continued)

NOTES TO FINANCIAL STATEMENTS (continued)

NOTE 3. (continued)

lion. These awards consisted of 1,486,771 shares of $1-2/3 par value common stock valued at an average of $72.50 per share for award purposes in accordance with the Bonus Plan, and $110.8 million in cash. The balance of $42.1 million was made available in the reserve for future awards. A credit of $269.2 million was made to the reserve in 1984, an amount $35.0 million less than the maximum which could have been credited under the formula; actual 1984 awards totaled $224.1 million. A credit of $180.0 million was made to the Bonus Plan reserve in 1983. This was less than the maximum which could have been credited to the reserve. Substantially all of the credit was awarded to participants for that year. No credits or awards were made for 1982 and 1981.

Under the Performance Achievement Plan approved by stockholders in 1982, the Committee established performance achievement levels for the initial three-year phase-in period ending in 1984 and for the first five-year period ending in 1986. In 1984, the Committee established performance achievement levels for a new five-year period ending in 1988. Under the Plan, the annual average of the aggregate final awards relating to the aggregate target awards granted in the years 1982 through 1986 shall not exceed $60 million. Payment of these awards is contingent upon achievement of earnings in relation to average worldwide industry sales volume targets over the term of the performance period related to each grant. In the future, it is anticipated that new grants will be made every two years. Employes selected to participate in the Plan are granted target awards payable in cash and/or $1-2/3 par value common stock which are, in general, expressed as a percentage of the participant's salary at the beginning of the performance period. Accruals of $12.2 million and $9.3 million were made in 1985 to recognize progress toward achieving the 1982-1986 and 1984-1988 earnings targets, respectively. Awards for the 1982-1984 grant, representing an average of $9.3 million for the three-year period, were paid in early 1985. The awards for the 1982-1986 and 1984-1988 periods will not be paid until 1987 and 1989, respectively, with the ultimate amounts dependent on actual performance. Accruals of $12.3 million and $20.9 million were made in 1984 to recognize progress toward achieving the three-year and five-year earnings targets, respectively. Another $15.5 million and $11.0 million were accrued for these two periods in 1983. There was no accrual for the Plan in 1982.

Under the provisions of the Bonus Plan, participants receive their awards in instalments in as many as three years. Performance Achievement Plan awards are to be paid as soon as is practicable following completion of the performance period. If participants in the Plans fail to meet conditions precedent to receiving undelivered instalments of bonus and performance achievement awards (and contingent credits related to the Stock Option Plan prior to 1977), the amount of any such instalments is credited to income.

On April 2, 1984, October 1, 1984 and October 7, 1985, the Committee granted Stock Appreciation Rights (SARs) to certain officers of the Corporation in conjunction with incentive and nonqualified stock options granted. SARs provide officers with the right to receive payment equal in value to the appreciation in the Corporation's common stock over the option exercise price of the shares under option. Such payment would be made in lieu of the exercise of the related option, with the corresponding options cancelled and not available for regrant under the Plan. SARs are exercisable at such time as determined by the Committee, but only upon surrender of the related option and only to the extent that the related option is exercisable. SARs expire no later than the date of the underlying option, are not transferable under any circumstances and may be exercised only when the market value of the stock subject to the related option exceeds the applicable option price.

The utilization of SARs requires an accrual each year for the appreciation on the rights expected to be exercised. The amount of such accrual is dependent upon the amount, if any, by which the fair market value of common stock exceeds the related option price and changes in fair market value during the period. An accrual of ($2.7) million was made for SARs in 1985 and $13.9 million in 1984.

Changes during 1983, 1984 and 1985 in the status of options granted under the Stock Option Plans are shown in the following table. The option prices are 100% of the average of the highest and lowest sales prices of $1-2/3 par value common stock on the dates the options were granted, as reported on the Composite Tape of transactions on all major exchanges and nonexchange markets in the U.S. for options granted in 1976 and subsequent years. Incentive stock options expire ten years from date of grant. Nonqualified stock options granted prior to 1982 expire ten years from date of grant, and nonqualified stock options granted in 1982 and thereafter expire ten years and two days from date of grant. Options are subject to earlier termination under certain conditions.

	Years Granted	Option Prices	Shares Under Option
Outstanding at Jan. 1, 1983	1973-1982	$38.25-$73.38	3,252,139
Granted	1983	72.88	586,820
Exercised	1974-1982	38.25-66.57	(627,318)
Terminated	1973-1983	38.25-72.88	(111,347)
Outstanding at Dec. 31, 1983	1974-1983	38.25-72.88	3,100,294
Granted	1984	77.19	615,355
Exercised: Options	1974-1983	38.25-72.88	(794,828)
SARs	1984	38.25-72.88	(231,539)
Terminated	1974-1983	38.25-72.88	(48,039)
Outstanding at Dec. 31, 1984	1976-1984	38.25-77.19	2,641,243
Granted	1985	67.94	1,132,605
Exercised: Options	1976-1983	38.25-72.88	(365,798)
SARs	1977-1983	38.25-72.88	(35,970)
Terminated	1976-1985	38.25-72.88	(30,692)
Outstanding at Dec. 31, 1985	1976-1985	38.25-77.19	3,341,388

The Corporation intends to deliver newly issued $1-2/3 par value common stock upon the exercise of any of the stock options. The maximum number of shares for which additional options might be granted under the Plans was 6,760,945 at January 1, 1983, 6,195,185 at December 31, 1983, 5,595,283 at December 31, 1984 and 4,482,229 at December 31, 1985. Options outstanding at December 31, 1985 consisted of:

	Years Granted	Option Prices	Shares Under Option
1972 Plan	1976	$65.19	29,766
1977 Plan	1977	66.57	111,663
	1978	63.75	128,385
	1979	59.50	136,648
	1980	53.25	152,504
	1981	50.00	144,649
	1982	38.25	132,328
1982 Plan	1982	46.50	232,463
	1983	72.88	539,747
	1984	77.19	602,715
	1985	67.94	1,130,520
Total $1-2/3 Par Value Shares Under Option			3,341,388

In connection with the 1985 acquisition of Hughes, the General Motors stockholders approved certain modifications to the Stock Option Plans to permit adjustments of options outstanding to reflect dividends of one class of common stock to holders of another class of common stock. As modified, the Plans permit adjustments to the shares issuable on exercise of the options outstanding to include the shares that would have been issued in the dividend if the shares under option had been outstanding at the dividend record date. Stock Appreciation Rights may be similarly adjusted.

On December 2, 1985, the Committee approved the related Stock
(continued)

NOTES TO FINANCIAL STATEMENTS (continued)

NOTE 3. (concluded)

Option Plan amendment, subject to a favorable Internal Revenue Service ruling, and the adjustment of the shares under option to reflect the December 1984 dividend of Class E common stock and the December 1985 dividend of Class H common stock. The adjustment will have the effect of replacing options on $1-2/3 par value common shares as of the close of business on the record date for each dividend with options on units comprised of $1-2/3 par value common shares and the applicable Class E common and/or Class H common shares attributable to the dividends. The number of Class E common and Class H common shares to be included in such units are estimated at 260,000 and 170,000, respectively.

Common stocks held for the Incentive Program are stated substantially at cost and used exclusively for payment of Program liabilities.

(Dollars in Millions)	1985		1984	
	Shares	Amount	Shares	Amount
Bal. at Jan. 1	2,072,694	$144.2	828,273	$ 56.3
Acquired: $1-2/3	1,629,809	118.7	1,869,391	133.1
Class E*	29,427	1.0	38,268	.7
Delivered: $1-2/3	(1,023,688)	(73.0)	(663,238)	(45.9)
Class E*	(38,578)	(.7)	—	—
Bal. at Dec. 31: $1-2/3	2,640,547	189.2	2,034,426	143.5
Class E*	29,117	1.0	38,268	.7
Total	2,669,664	$190.2	2,072,694	$144.2

*Post-split basis.

NOTE 4. EDS Incentive Plans

At its meeting on December 3, 1984, the GM Board of Directors approved and adopted the 1984 Electronic Data Systems Corporation Stock Incentive Plan in accordance with stockholder approval obtained in connection with GM's acquisition of EDS. Under this Plan, which covers up to 40 million shares (post-split) of Class E common stock during the 10-year life of the Plan, shares, rights or options to acquire shares, which may be subject to restrictions, may be granted or sold.

In 1985, the incentive and compensation committee of the EDS board of directors granted the right to purchase a total of 6,219,186 shares of Class E common stock at a price of $0.10 per share to key employes under the provisions of the 1984 Plan. The Class E shares sold under the provisions of the 1984 Plan are subject to restrictions and will vest over a ten-year period from the date of grant. An expense of $13.2 million was recorded for these awards in 1985.

In 1985, the committee also granted incentive stock options under the provisions of the 1984 Plan. The option price is 100% of the average of the highest and lowest sales prices of Class E common stock on the date the options were granted, as reported on the Composite Tape of transactions on all major exchanges and nonexchange markets in the U.S. These incentive stock options expire six years from date of grant and are subject to earlier termination under certain conditions.

	Year Granted	Option Price	Shares Under Option
Granted	1985	$35.82	4,082,500
Terminated	1985	35.82	(38,300)
Outstanding at Dec. 31, 1985	1985	$35.82	4,044,200

With regard to the unvested shares under the EDS 1977 Stock Incentive Plan, as a part of the acquisition agreement the 2,270,160 unvested shares of EDS common stock issued under the 1977 Plan were converted at the date of the acquisition into an equal number of unvested shares of Class E common stock (4,540,320 shares on a post-split basis). In addition, EDS employes holding unvested shares under the 1977 Plan may receive deferred compensation payments under certain conditions. These payments are intended to provide each participant with the same after Federal income tax proceeds that would have been realized after seven years if the employe had received an amount equal to the product of (a) the excess of $62.50 (post-split) over the then average market price per share of Class E common stock and (b) one-half of the number of unvested shares of Class E common stock received by the employe, and had been eligible for long-term capital gain income tax treatment.

EDS has a bonus plan under which awards are granted to key executives and employes. The amount accrued in 1985 was $16.9 million. The amount to be awarded and the individual awards will be determined at a later date.

NOTE 5. Hughes Incentive Plans

Prior to the acquisition of Hughes, the Hughes board of directors adopted the Hughes Long-Term Incentive Plan (the "LTIP"). The LTIP was developed by the Institute and Hughes to provide incentives to employes to remain with Hughes, a factor considered significant in preserving the value of Hughes for a buyer. The LTIP provided approximately 1,000 key scientists, engineers and managers of Hughes with restricted cash units ("Units"), which entitle participants to receive payments from a trust established and funded pursuant to the terms of the LTIP (the "Trust"). Such payments will be paid in equal annual instalments at the end of the third, fourth and fifth years following the date of award. Forfeiture occurs if the participant is discharged for cause or, other than for good reason, voluntarily terminates employment with Hughes within five years of the date of grant and prior to normal retirement. The value of a Unit at any time is its pro rata portion of the value of the Trust's assets. The LTIP provided that, upon the sale of Hughes, the Trust was to be funded by Hughes with $250 million. Such funds were obtained by Hughes through a combination of short-term notes payable to banks and long-term debt, and Hughes incurred a nonrecurring preacquisition charge of about $125 million (net of the related income tax effects).

Hughes maintains supplemental compensation plans under which awards are currently granted to officers and other key employes. The aggregate amount and the individual awards are determined by the Hughes board of directors, subject to certain limitations based upon net income.

NOTE 6. Other Income Less Income Deductions

(Dollars in Millions)	1985	1984	1983
Other income: Interest	$1,328.3	$1,466.8	$719.5*
Other	143.6	302.4	161.7*
Income deductions	(172.7)	(55.7)	(65.4)
Net	$1,299.2	$1,713.5	$815.8

*Includes a gain of $13.9 million from early retirements of long-term debt.

NOTE 7. Pension Program and Postemployment Benefits

Total pension expense of the Corporation and its consolidated subsidiaries amounted to $1,674.8 million in 1985, $1,618.4 million in 1984, and $1,714.2 million in 1983. Of the 1985 expense, $22.3 million was attributable to EDS. For purposes of determining pension expense, the Corporation uses a variety of assumed rates of return on pension funds in accordance with local practice and regulations, which rates average approximately 7%. The following table compares accumulated plan benefits and plan net assets for the Corporation's defined benefit plans in the
(continued)

NOTES TO FINANCIAL STATEMENTS (continued)

NOTE 7. (concluded)

United States, other than for EDS and Hughes, as of October 1 (the plans' anniversary date):

(Dollars in Millions)	1985	1984
Actuarial present value of accumulated plan benefits:		
Vested	$21,982.1	$20,216.2
Nonvested	3,351.9	1,814.2
Total	$25,334.0	$22,030.4
Net assets available for benefits:		
Trustees	$20,033.0	$16,245.5
Insurance companies	3,276.3	3,211.8
Total	$23,309.3	$19,457.3

The assumed rates of return used in determining the actuarial present value of accumulated plan benefits shown in the table above were based upon those published by the Pension Benefit Guaranty Corporation, a public corporation established under the Employee Retirement Income Security Act (ERISA), adjusted to reflect a fixed income management technique under which an immunized rate is being earned on certain pension fund assets. Such rates averaged approximately 8¾% for 1985 and approximately 10¼% for 1984. The effect of the immunized rate adjustment was to reduce the unfunded liability by $732.3 million in 1985 and $663.5 million in 1984.

The EDS retirement plan provides for pension payments to its eligible employes upon retirement. The market value of the net assets available for benefits under this plan exceeded the actuarial present value of accumulated plan benefits by $58.5 million in 1985 and $29.4 million in 1984.

Hughes retirement plans cover substantially all of its employes and provide for monthly pension payments to eligible employes upon retirement. As of the most recent actuarial valuation dates, January 1, 1985 and 1984, a comparison of Hughes accumulated plan benefits and net assets available for benefits is as follows:

(Dollars in Millions)	1985	1984
Actuarial present value of accumulated plan benefits:		
Vested	$1,386.4	$1,189.6
Nonvested	22.0	64.7
Total	$1,408.4	$1,254.3
Net assets available for benefits, at market value	$2,176.4	$2,097.7

The weighted average rate of return used in determining the actuarial present value of accumulated plan benefits shown above was 8.5% in 1985 and 8.25% in 1984.

The pension plans of subsidiaries outside the United States are not required to report to governmental agencies pursuant to ERISA, and the actuarial present value of accumulated benefits for these plans has not been determined in the manner calculated and shown above. The total of these plans' pension funds and balance sheet accruals, less pension prepayments and deferred charges, exceeded the actuarially computed value of vested benefits by approximately $785 million at December 31, 1985 and $340 million at December 31, 1984.

In addition to providing pension benefits, the Corporation and certain of its subsidiaries provide certain health care and life insurance benefits for retired employes. Substantially all of the Corporation's employes, including employes in some foreign countries, may become eligible for those benefits if they reach normal retirement age while working for the Corporation. The Corporation recognizes the cost of providing those benefits by expensing the cost as incurred. The cost of such benefits amounted to $836.5 million in 1985 and $806.1 million in 1984.

NOTE 8. United States, Foreign and Other Income Taxes

(Dollars in Millions)	1985	1984	1983
Taxes estimated to be payable currently:			
United States Federal	$1,465.4	$1,151.7	$254.4
Foreign	287.3	662.5	146.0
State and local	147.9	140.1	126.0
Total	1,900.6	1,954.3	526.4
Taxes deferred—net:			
United States Federal	(386.7)	8.3	1,241.3
Foreign	54.9	(170.6)	192.7
State and local	(4.6)	32.1	142.0
Total	(336.4)	(130.2)	1,576.0
Investment tax credits deferred—net:			
United States Federal	49.0	(15.1)	47.7
Foreign	17.1	(3.9)	73.7
Total	66.1	(19.0)	121.4
Total taxes	$1,630.3	$1,805.1	$2,223.8

Investment tax credits entering into the determination of taxes estimated to be payable currently amounted to $427.6 million in 1985, $311.6 million in 1984 and $406.2 million in 1983.

The deferred taxes (credit) for timing differences consisted principally of the following: 1985—$269.0 million for depreciation, ($608.1) million for sales and product allowances and $125.1 million for pollution control bonds; 1984—$762.6 million for benefit plans expense, ($305.5) million for sales and product allowances, $387.6 million for vehicle instalment sales, ($240.3) million for interest, ($125.1) million for pollution control bonds and ($435.7) million for the domestic international sales corporation (DISC); and 1983—$519.2 million for benefit plans expense, ($438.0) million for sales and product allowances, $379.5 million for vehicle instalment sales and $707.5 million for depreciation.

Income before income taxes included the following components:

(Dollars in Millions)	1985	1984	1983
Domestic income	$3,690.5	$4,513.6	$4,387.6
Foreign income	930.8	990.7	583.9
Total	$4,621.3	$5,504.3	$4,971.5

The consolidated income tax was different than the amount computed at the United States statutory income tax rate for the reasons set forth in the table below.

(Dollars in Millions)	1985	1984	1983
Expected tax at U.S. statutory income tax rate	$2,125.8	$2,532.0	$2,286.9
Investment tax credits amortized	(361.5)	(330.6)	(284.8)
Foreign tax rate differential	(7.2)	135.9	43.9
State and local income taxes	77.4	93.0	144.7
Deferred income tax reversal on the DISC	—	(421.3)	—
Taxes on undistributed earnings of subsidiaries	—	(112.2)	54.4
Research and development credit	(147.0)	(73.5)	(18.0)
Other adjustments	(57.2)	(18.2)	(3.3)
Consolidated income tax	$1,630.3	$1,805.1	$2,223.8

NOTES TO FINANCIAL STATEMENTS (continued)

NOTE 9. Earnings Per Share Attributable to and Dividends on Common Stocks

Earnings per share attributable to common stocks have been determined based on the relative rights of $1-2/3 par value common, Class E common and Class H common stocks to participate in dividends. The effect on earnings per share resulting from the assumed exercise of outstanding options and delivery of bonus awards and contingent credits is not material.

Dividends on the $1-2/3 par value common stock are to be declared out of the earnings of GM and its subsidiaries, excluding the Available Separate Consolidated Net Income of EDS and GMHE.

In connection with the authorization of the Class H common stock issued in the acquisition of Hughes, the stockholders of the Corporation approved certain amendments to the General Motors Certificate of Incorporation to redefine the earnings available for payment of dividends on Class E common stock. As a result of the amendment, earnings attributable to Class E common stock are determined and reported on a basis consistent with the earnings that the GM Board of Directors had previously treated as available for payment of dividends on that class. Because the amendment was retroactive to the date that the Class E common shares were first issued, previously reported earnings and earnings per share attributable to common stocks have been restated. The amendment had the effect of increasing earnings per share attributable to $1-2/3 par value common stock by $0.27 per share in 1985 and $0.05 per share in 1984.

Dividends on the Class E common stock are to be declared out of the Available Separate Consolidated Net Income of EDS earned since the acquisition of EDS by GM. The Available Separate Consolidated Net Income of EDS is determined quarterly and is equal to the separate consolidated net income of EDS, excluding the effects of purchase accounting adjustments arising from the acquisition of EDS, multiplied by a fraction, the numerator of which is the weighted average number of shares of Class E common stock outstanding during the period and the denominator of which is currently 121.9 million shares.

Dividends on the Class H common stock are to be declared out of the Available Separate Consolidated Net Income of GMHE earned after December 31, 1985, the date the Hughes acquisition was made effective. The Available Separate Consolidated Net Income of GMHE will be determined quarterly and will be equal to the separate consolidated net income of GMHE, excluding the effects of purchase accounting adjustments arising from the acquisition of Hughes, multiplied by a fraction, the numerator of which is the weighted average number of shares of Class H common stock outstanding during the period and the denominator of which initially will be 200 million shares.

The denominators used in determining the Available Separate Consolidated Net Income of EDS and GMHE will be adjusted as deemed appropriate by the Board of Directors to reflect subdivisions or combinations of the Class E common and Class H common stocks and to reflect certain transfers of capital to or from EDS and GMHE.

Dividends may be paid on common stocks only when, as and if declared by the Board of Directors in its sole discretion. The Board's policy with respect to $1-2/3 par value common stock is to distribute from current earnings such amounts as the outlook and the indicated capital needs of the business permit. The current policy of the Board of Directors with respect to the Class E common and Class H common stocks is to pay cash dividends approximately equal to 25% of the Available Separate Consolidated Net Income of EDS and GMHE, respectively, for the prior year.

NOTE 10. General Motors Acceptance Corporation and Subsidiaries

Condensed Consolidated Balance Sheet (Dollars in Millions)		1985	1984
Cash and investments in securities		$ 2,787.7	$ 2,100.1
Finance receivables—net (including GM and affiliates—$300.0 in 1985 and 1984)		66,025.7	50,051.5
Other assets		6,634.8	2,291.5
Total Assets		$75,448.2	$54,443.1
Short-term debt		$42,642.9	$27,629.5
Accounts payable and other liabilities (including GM and affiliates—$4,038.7 and $3,868.5)		8,548.0	6,931.4
Long-term debt		19,110.5	15,715.5
Stockholder's equity		5,146.8	4,166.7
Total Liabilities and Stockholder's Equity		$75,448.2	$54,443.1
Condensed Statement of Consolidated Income (Dollars in Millions)	1985	1984	1983
Gross Revenue	$9,755.8	$8,098.6	$7,391.1
Interest and discount	5,121.8	4,772.4	4,099.1
Other expenses	3,613.0	2,541.4	2,290.0
Total Expenses	8,734.8	7,313.8	6,389.1
Net Income	$1,021.0	$ 784.8	$1,002.0

Interest is paid to General Motors on settlements of wholesale financing of product sales which are made beyond transit time.

NOTES TO FINANCIAL STATEMENTS (continued)

NOTE 11. Real Estate, Plants and Equipment and Accumulated Depreciation

(Dollars in Millions)	1985	1984
Real estate, plants and equipment (Note 13):		
Land	$ 599.2	$ 414.9
Land improvements	1,297.8	1,170.0
Leasehold improvements—less amortization	79.4	59.7
Buildings	9,545.6	8,162.6
Machinery and equipment	29,580.9	26,269.9
Furniture and office equipment	1,407.8	752.5
Satellites and related facilities	270.0	—
Capitalized leases	968.0	814.6
Construction in progress	3,518.4	1,709.9
Total	$47,267.1	$39,354.1
Accumulated depreciation:		
Land improvements	$ 759.9	$ 665.5
Buildings	4,453.6	4,120.3
Machinery and equipment	18,149.5	16,207.9
Furniture and office equipment	479.4	289.8
Capitalized leases	482.6	366.3
Total	$24,325.0	$21,649.8

Gross property increased in 1985 by $1,478.1 million as a result of foreign currency translation adjustments. Net book value increased $509.5 million because of such adjustments.

NOTE 12. Accrued Liabilities and Deferred Income Taxes

(Dollars in Millions)	1985	1984
Taxes, other than income taxes	$ 1,158.3	$ 990.0
Payrolls	2,353.5	1,764.3
Employe benefits	571.1	630.4
Dealer and customer allowances, claims, discounts, etc.	4,659.7	3,896.7
Other, including deferred income taxes	3,335.4	1,706.8
Total	$12,078.0	$8,988.2

NOTE 13. Long-Term Debt

(Dollars in Millions)	Interest Rate	Maturity	1985	1984
GM:				
U.S. dollars:				
Notes	10.00 %		$ —	$ 50.0
Notes	12.20	1987-88	150.0	200.0
Notes	10.00	1991	250.0	250.0
Debentures	8.625	2005	102.4	102.4
Other	4.76	1987-2001	57.8	69.1
Other currencies	7.41	1987	21.9	17.7
Consolidated subsidiaries:				
U.S. dollars	9.77	1987-2011	987.1	960.6
Spanish pesetas	12.58	1987-91	629.1	527.8
German marks	6.27	1987-96	70.9	143.5
Austrian schillings	5.90	1987-89	84.1	17.6
Other currencies	Various	1987-95	241.3	182.6
Total			2,594.6	2,521.3
Less unamortized discount (principally on 10% notes due 1991)			94.4	103.9
Total			$2,500.2	$2,417.4

At year-end 1985, the Corporation and its consolidated subsidiaries had unused short-term credit lines of approximately $2.6 billion and unused long-term credit agreements of approximately $1.5 billion. Long-term debt at December 31, 1985 and 1984 included approximately $702 million and $624 million, respectively, of short-term obligations which are intended to be renewed or refinanced under long-term credit agreements. Long-term debt (including current portion) bore interest at a weighted average rate of approximately 12.5% at December 31, 1985 and 12.3% at December 31, 1984.

In 1981, the Corporation and a subsidiary arranged a private financing of $500 million in 10% notes due 1991. The difference between the 10% stated interest rate and the 14.7% effective rate reflects the discount which is being amortized over the lives of the notes. An option to acquire certain real estate in 1991 was also granted. The option holder may deliver the notes in payment for the real estate.

Under the sinking fund provisions of the trust indenture for the Corporation's 8⅝% Debentures due 2005, the Corporation is to make annual sinking fund payments of $3.0 million in 2002 and $11.8 million in each of the years 2003 and 2004.

Maturities of long-term debt in the years 1986 through 1990 are (in millions) $446.9 (included in loans payable at December 31, 1985), $540.5, $421.1, $228.4 and $152.7. Loans payable at December 31, 1984 included the current portion of long-term debt in the amount of $735.5 million.

NOTE 14. Stockholders' Equity

The preferred stock is subject to redemption at the option of the Board of Directors on any dividend date on not less than thirty days' notice at the redemption prices stated in the table on the next page plus accrued dividends.

Holders of $1-2/3 par value common stock, Class E common stock and Class H common stock are entitled to one, one-quarter and one-half vote per share, respectively, on all matters submitted to the stockholders for a vote. The liquidation rights of common stockholders are based on per share liquidation units of the various classes and are subject to certain adjustments if outstanding common stock is subdivided, by stock split or otherwise, or if shares of one class of common stock are issued as a dividend to holders of another class of common stock. At December 31, 1985, each share of $1-2/3 par value common, Class E common and Class H common stock was entitled to a liquidation unit of approximately one, one-quarter and one-half, respectively.

After December 31, 1994 or December 31, 1995, the Board of Directors may exchange $1-2/3 par value common stock for Class E common stock or for Class H common stock, respectively, if the Board has declared and paid certain minimum cash dividends during each of the five years preceding the exchange. If GM should sell, liquidate, or otherwise dispose of EDS or Hughes (or substantially all of the other business of GMHE), the Corporation will be required to exchange $1-2/3 par value common stock for Class E common or Class H common stock, respectively. In the event of any exchange, the Class E common or Class H common stockholders will receive $1-2/3 par value common stock having a market value at the time of the exchange equal to 120% of the market value of the Class E common or Class H common stock exchanged.

The Certificate of Incorporation provides that no cash dividends may be paid on the $1-2/3 par value common stock, Class E common stock, Class H common stock or any series of preference stock so long as current assets (excluding prepaid expenses) in excess of current liabilities of the Corporation are less than $75 per share of outstanding preferred stock. Such current assets (with inventories calculated on the FIFO basis) in excess of current liabilities were greater than $75 in respect of each share of outstanding preferred stock at December 31, 1985 and 1984.

The equity of the Corporation and its consolidated subsidiaries in the accumulated net income or loss, since acquisition, of associates has been included in net income retained for use in the business.

At December 31, 1985, consolidated net income retained for use in the business attributable to $1-2/3 par value common and Class E common stocks was $22,510.7 million and $95.9 million, respectively.

(continued)

NOTES TO FINANCIAL STATEMENTS (continued)

NOTE 14. (continued)

(Dollars in Millions Except Per Share Amounts)	1985	1984	1983
Capital Stock:			
Preferred Stock, without par value, cumulative dividends (authorized, 6,000,000 shares):			
$5.00 series, stated value $100 per share, redeemable at Corporation option at $120 per share:			
Outstanding at beginning of the year (1,698,294 shares in 1985 and 1,835,644 in 1984 and 1983)	$ 169.8	$ 183.6	$ 183.6
Reacquired on the open market (5,000 shares in 1985 and 137,350 in 1984)	(.5)	(13.8)	—
Outstanding at end of the year (1,693,294 shares in 1985, 1,698,294 in 1984 and 1,835,644 in 1983)	169.3	169.8	183.6
$3.75 series, stated value $100 per share, redeemable at Corporation option at $100 per share:			
Outstanding at beginning of the year (858,000 shares in 1985 and 1,000,000 in 1984 and 1983)	85.8	100.0	100.0
Reacquired on the open market (43,900 shares in 1985 and 142,000 in 1984)	(4.4)	(14.2)	—
Outstanding at end of the year (814,100 shares in 1985, 858,000 in 1984 and 1,000,000 in 1983)	81.4	85.8	100.0
Preference Stock, $0.10 par value (authorized, 100,000,000 shares in 1984), no shares issued	—	—	—
Common Stock, $1-2/3 par value (authorized, 1,000,000,000 shares):			
Issued at beginning of the year (317,504,133 shares in 1985, 315,711,299 in 1984 and 312,363,657 in 1983)	529.2	526.2	520.6
Newly issued stock used for bonus deliveries, sold under provisions of the Stock Option Plans, Employe Stock Ownership Plans, Savings-Stock Purchase Programs and the Dividend Reinvestment Plan (1,349,182 shares in 1985, 1,792,834 in 1984 and 3,029,593 in 1983) and exchanged for long-term debt (318,049 shares in 1983)	2.2	3.0	5.6
Issued at end of the year (318,853,315 shares in 1985, 317,504,133 in 1984 and 315,711,299 in 1983)	531.4	529.2	526.2
Class E Common Stock, $0.10 par value (authorized, 190,000,000 shares in 1984):			
Issued at beginning of the year (29,082,382 shares in 1985)	2.9	—	—
Issued as a public offering (3,125,000 shares)	.3	—	—
Two-for-one stock split in the form of a 100% stock dividend (31,742,670 shares)	3.2	—	—
Reacquired on the open market (651,804 shares)	(.1)	—	—
Issued in the acquisition of EDS in 1984 (11,371,268 shares)	—	1.1	—
Issued in conjunction with the EDS 1977 and 1984 Stock Incentive Plans (2,928,889 shares in 1985 and 2,270,160 in 1984) (Note 4)	.3	.2	—
Issued to $1-2/3 par value common stockholders as a dividend (15,440,954 shares in 1984)	—	1.6	—
Issued at end of the year (66,227,137 shares in 1985 and 29,082,382 in 1984)	6.6	2.9	—
Class H Common Stock, $0.10 par value (authorized, 600,000,000 shares in 1985):			
Issued in the acquisition of Hughes in 1985 (50,000,000 shares)	5.0	—	—
Issued to $1-2/3 par value common stockholders as a dividend (15,495,316 shares)	1.6	—	—
Issued at end of the year (65,495,316 shares in 1985)	6.6	—	—
Total capital stock at end of the year	795.3	787.7	809.8
Capital Surplus (principally additional paid-in capital):			
Balance at beginning of the year	3,347.8	2,136.8	1,930.4
Stated value in excess of repurchase price of preferred stock reacquired in open market transactions	2.9	16.2	—
Proceeds in excess of par value of newly issued $1-2/3 par value common stock used for bonus deliveries, sold under provisions of the Stock Option Plans, Employe Stock Ownership Plans, Savings-Stock Purchase Programs and the Dividend Reinvestment Plan and, in 1983, exchanged for long-term debt	90.7	109.7	206.4
Amounts in excess of par value of Class E common stock:			
Issued as a public offering	193.3	—	—
Two-for-one stock split in the form of a 100% stock dividend	(3.2)	—	—
Repurchase price in excess of par value of stocks reacquired in open market transactions	(125.8)	—	—
Issued in the acquisition of EDS	—	499.2	—
Issued in conjunction with EDS employe stock plans	34.7	.8	—
Issued as a dividend	—	585.1	—
Amounts in excess of par value of Class H common stock:			
Issued in the acquisition of Hughes	2,556.9	—	—
Issued as a dividend	570.5	—	—
Balance at end of the year	$6,667.8	$3,347.8	$2,136.8

(continued)

NOTES TO FINANCIAL STATEMENTS (continued)

NOTE 14. (concluded)

(Dollars in Millions Except Per Share Amounts)	1985	1984	1983
Net Income Retained for Use in the Business:			
Balance at beginning of the year	$20,796.6	$18,390.5	$15,552.5
Net income	3,999.0	4,516.5	3,730.2
Total	24,795.6	22,907.0	19,282.7
Dividend of one Class E common share for each 20 shares of $1-2/3 par value common outstanding	—	586.7	—
Dividend of one Class H common share for each 20 shares of $1-2/3 par value common outstanding	572.1	—	—
Cash dividends:			
Preferred stock, $5.00 series, $5.00 per share	8.4	8.9	9.2
Preferred stock, $3.75 series, $3.75 per share	3.2	3.6	3.7
$1-2/3 par value common stock, $5.00 per share in 1985, $4.75 in 1984 and $2.80 in 1983	1,581.2	1,497.5	879.3
Class E common stock, $0.195 per share in 1985 and $0.045 in 1984 (post-split basis)	12.4	1.2	—
Cash payments in lieu of fractional shares of common stock issued as a dividend:			
Class E common	—	12.5	—
Class H common	11.7	—	—
Total cash dividends	1,616.9	1,523.7	892.2
Balance at end of the year	22,606.6	20,796.6	18,390.5
Accumulated Foreign Currency Translation and Other Adjustments:			
Balance at beginning of the year:			
Accumulated foreign currency translation adjustments	(789.5)	(661.8)	(668.0)
Net unrealized gains on marketable equity securities	71.7	91.3	68.1
Changes during the year:			
Accumulated foreign currency translation adjustments	114.5	(127.7)	6.2
Net unrealized gains (losses) on marketable equity securities	58.3	(19.6)	23.2
Balance at end of the year	(545.0)	(717.8)	(570.5)
Total Stockholders' Equity	$29,524.7	$24,214.3	$20,766.6

NOTE 15. Segment Reporting

General Motors is a highly vertically-integrated business operating primarily in a single industry consisting of the manufacture, assembly and sale of automobiles, trucks and related parts and accessories classified as automotive products. Because of the high degree of integration, substantial interdivisional and intercompany transfers of materials and services are made.

Substantially all of General Motors' products are marketed through retail dealers and through distributors and jobbers in the United States and Canada and through distributors and dealers overseas. To assist in the merchandising of General Motors' products, GMAC and its subsidiaries offer financial services and certain types of automobile insurance to dealers and customers.

Net sales and revenues, net income (loss), total and net assets and average number of employes in the U.S. and in locations outside the U.S. for 1985, 1984 and 1983 are summarized below. Net income (loss) is after provisions for deferred income taxes applicable to that portion of the undistributed earnings not deemed to be permanently invested, less available tax credits and deductions, and appropriate consolidating adjustments for the geographic areas set forth below. Interarea sales and revenues are made at negotiated selling prices.

1985	United States	Canada	Europe	Latin America	All Other	Total*
Net Sales and Revenues:			(Dollars in Millions)			
Outside	$80,204.7	$ 5,283.7	$7,671.6	$1,841.9	$1,369.8	$96,371.7
Interarea	8,893.8	8,494.6	322.8	995.5	483.7	—
Total net sales and revenues	$89,098.5	$13,778.3	$7,994.4	$2,837.4	$1,853.5	$96,371.7
Net Income (Loss)	$ 3,624.3	$ 473.7	($ 372.1)	$ 308.3	$ 9.1	$ 3,999.0
Total Assets	$50,796.0	$ 2,920.1	$5,960.6	$3,054.2	$1,634.6	$63,832.8
Net Assets	$26,710.0	$ 1,906.4	($ 765.7)	$1,327.8	$ 572.2	$29,524.7
Average Number of Employes (in thousands)	561	44	125	59	22	811

*After elimination of interarea transactions.

(continued)

NOTES TO FINANCIAL STATEMENTS (continued)

NOTE 15. (concluded)

1984	United States	Canada	Europe	Latin America	All Other	Total*
Net Sales and Revenues:			(Dollars in Millions)			
Outside	$69,355.6	$ 4,411.6	$6,735.7	$1,642.0	$1,745.0	$83,889.9
Interarea	7,276.5	8,170.0	242.2	823.6	401.7	—
Total net sales and revenues	$76,632.1	$12,581.6	$6,977.9	$2,465.6	$2,146.7	$83,889.9
Net Income (Loss)	$ 3,872.0	$ 762.2	($ 291.1)	$ 94.4	$ 61.5	$ 4,516.5
Total Assets	$41,692.7	$ 2,833.5	$4,425.7	$2,874.0	$ 932.0	$52,144.9
Net Assets	$22,149.7	$ 1,628.9	($ 439.2)	$1,016.7	$ 41.7	$24,214.3
Average Number of Employes (in thousands)	511	41	122	49	25	748
1983						
Net Sales:						
Outside	$59,668.7	$ 3,866.4	$7,761.7	$1,742.7	$1,542.1	$74,581.6
Interarea	6,493.4	7,366.0	208.6	653.1	295.4	—
Total net sales	$66,162.1	$11,232.4	$7,970.3	$2,395.8	$1,837.5	$74,581.6
Net Income (Loss)	$ 3,469.0	$ 592.3	($ 228.3)	($ 15.0)	($ 91.1)	$ 3,730.2
Total Assets	$34,670.4	$ 2,385.5	$5,379.1	$2,834.3	$ 813.9	$45,694.5
Net Assets	$18,749.3	$ 1,332.9	($ 120.5)	$ 919.6	$ 8.9	$20,766.6
Average Number of Employes (in thousands)	463	39	123	41	25	691

*After elimination of interarea transactions.

NOTE 16. Profit Sharing Plans

Profit Sharing Plans were established, effective January 1, 1983, under which eligible United States hourly and salaried employes will share in the success of the Corporation's U.S. operations. Under the Plans' provisions, 10% of profits, as defined, will be shared when the Corporation's U.S. income before income taxes plus equity in U.S. earnings of non-consolidated subsidiaries (principally GMAC) exceeds 10% of the net worth of U.S. operations plus 5% of the difference between total assets of U.S. operations and net worth of U.S. operations. Amounts applicable to subsidiaries incorporated in the U.S. that are operating outside of the U.S., as well as amounts applicable to associates, are excluded from the calculation. Ten percent of the profits in excess of the minimum annual return, less a diversion for the Guaranteed Income Stream Benefit Program and Income Protection Plan and that portion of profit sharing allocable to non-participating employes, will be distributed to eligible U.S. employes by March 31 following the year earned. The accrual for profit sharing was $180.3 million in 1985, $281.9 million in 1984 and $322.2 million in 1983. The calculation of the profit sharing accrual for 1985 is shown below.

(Dollars in Millions)   1985

Minimum Annual Return	January 1, 1985	December 31, 1985	Average		
Total Assets in the U.S.	$41,692.7	$50,796.0			
Deduct assets of excluded subsidiaries and associates	2,018.5	6,368.2			
Total Assets of U.S. operations as defined in the Plans	$39,674.2	$44,427.8	$42,051.0		
Net Assets in the U.S.	$22,149.7	$26,710.0			
Deduct net assets of excluded subsidiaries and associates	1,609.3	3,263.8			
Net Worth of U.S. operations as defined in the Plans	$20,540.4	$23,446.2	21,993.3 X 10% =		$2,199.3
Other assets of U.S. operations			$20,057.7 X 5% =		1,002.9
Minimum Annual Return as defined in the Plans					$3,202.2

(continued)

NOTES TO FINANCIAL STATEMENTS (concluded)

NOTE 16. (concluded)

(Dollars in Millions)			1985
Profits as Defined in the Plans			
Net Income in the U.S.			$3,624.3
Add (Deduct): Net income of excluded subsidiaries and associates			(45.3)
Income taxes of U.S. operations			1,275.1
Provision for the General Motors Incentive Program applicable to U.S. operations			239.0
Profit sharing accrual			180.3
Profits as defined in the Plans			$5,273.4
Profit Sharing Accrual			
Profits as defined in the Plans	$5,273.4		
Deduct Minimum Annual Return as defined in the Plans	3,202.2		
Profits in excess of Minimum Annual Return	$2,071.2	X 10% =	$ 207.1
Deduct:			
Diversion for Guaranteed Income Stream Benefit Program and Income Protection Plan		$ 20.1	
Portion of profit sharing allocable to non-participating employes		6.7	26.8
Profit Sharing Accrual			$ 180.3

NOTE 17. Contingent Liabilities

There are serious potential liabilities under government regulations pertaining primarily to environmental, fuel economy and safety matters, but the ultimate liability under these regulations is not expected to have a material adverse effect on the Corporation's consolidated financial position. There are also various claims and pending actions against the Corporation and its subsidiaries with respect to commercial matters, including warranties and product liability, civil rights, antitrust, patent matters, taxes and other matters arising out of the conduct of the business. Certain of these actions purport to be class actions, seeking damages in very large amounts. The amounts of liability on these claims and actions at December 31, 1985 were not determinable but, in the opinion of the management, the ultimate liability resulting should not have a material adverse effect on the Corporation's consolidated financial position.

ACCOUNTANTS' REPORT

Deloitte Haskins+Sells
CERTIFIED PUBLIC ACCOUNTANTS

1114 Avenue of the Americas
New York, New York 10036

General Motors Corporation, its Directors and Stockholders:

February 3, 1986

We have examined the Consolidated Balance Sheet of General Motors Corporation and consolidated subsidiaries as of December 31, 1985 and 1984 and the related Statements of Consolidated Income and Changes in Consolidated Financial Position for each of the three years in the period ended December 31, 1985. Our examinations were made in accordance with generally accepted auditing standards and, accordingly, included such tests of the accounting records and such other auditing procedures as we considered necessary in the circumstances.

In our opinion, these financial statements present fairly the financial position of the companies at December 31, 1985 and 1984 and the results of their operations and the changes in their financial position for each of the three years in the period ended December 31, 1985, in conformity with generally accepted accounting principles applied on a consistent basis.

Deloitte Haskins + Sells

SUPPLEMENTARY INFORMATION

Selected Quarterly Data
(Dollars in Millions Except Per Share Amounts)

	1985 Quarters 1st	2nd	3rd	4th	1984 Quarters 1st	2nd	3rd	4th
Net sales and revenues	$24,182.5	$25,056.9	$22,491.7	$24,640.6	$22,886.4	$21,583.3	$18,542.6	$20,877.6
Operating income (loss)	1,529.3	1,467.8	(20.9)	1,238.2	2,424.7	1,546.8	306.9	421.6
Income before income taxes	1,632.2	1,664.4	74.8	1,249.9	2,487.4	1,786.5	526.0	704.4
United States, foreign and other income taxes (credit)	781.8	716.5	(172.4)	304.4	1,097.5	384.7	277.8	45.1
Income after income taxes	850.4	947.9	247.2	945.5	1,389.9	1,401.8	248.2	659.3
Equity in earnings of nonconsolidated subsidiaries and associates	221.3	211.4	269.3	306.0	224.1	207.0	168.6	217.6
Net income	1,071.7	1,159.3	516.5	1,251.5	1,614.0	1,608.8	416.8	876.9
Dividends on preferred stocks	2.9	2.9	3.0	2.8	3.2	3.2	3.1	3.0
Earnings on common stocks	$ 1,068.8	$ 1,156.4	$ 513.5	$ 1,248.7	$ 1,610.8	$ 1,605.6	$ 413.7	$ 873.9
Earnings attributable to:								
$1-2/3 par value common stock	$ 1,048.6	$ 1,132.8	$ 485.1	$ 1,217.1	$ 1,610.8	$ 1,605.6	$ 413.7	$ 868.2
Class E common stock (issued in 1984)	$ 20.2	$ 23.6	$ 28.4	$ 31.6	—	—	—	$ 5.7
Average number of shares of common stocks outstanding (in millions):								
$1-2/3 par value common	316.2	316.4	316.4	316.3	315.2	315.5	315.3	315.3
Class E common (issued in 1984)*	64.7	67.8	66.7	67.0	—	—	—	36.3
Number of shares of Class H common outstanding (issued in December 1985)	—	—	—	65.5	—	—	—	—
Earnings per share attributable to:								
$1-2/3 par value common stock**	$3.32	$3.58	$1.53	$3.85	$5.11	$5.09	$1.31	$2.76
Class E common stock (issued in 1984)*	$0.32	$0.35	$0.43	$0.47	—	—	—	$0.16
Cash dividends per share of common stocks:								
$1-2/3 par value common	$1.25	$1.25	$1.25	$1.25	$1.00	$1.25	$1.25	$1.25
Class E common (issued in 1984)*	$0.045	$0.05	$0.05	$0.05	—	—	—	$0.045
Stock price range:								
$1-2/3 par value common***								
High	$85.00	$75.13	$73.88	$77.25	$80.50	$68.25	$80.25	$82.75
Low	$72.50	$66.00	$65.75	$64.25	$62.63	$61.00	$64.25	$73.38
Class E common (issued in 1984)****								
High*	$36.00	$42.00	$46.50	$43.63	—	—	—	$21.25
Low*	$20.63	$29.75	$35.00	$32.88	—	—	—	$16.50
Class H common (issued in 1985)*****								
High	—	—	—	$50.00	—	—	—	—
Low	—	—	—	$38.00	—	—	—	—

Earnings and earnings per share attributable to common stocks have been restated to reflect the Class E common stock amendment approved by the stockholders in December 1985. Previously reported earnings and earnings per share, respectively, attributable to common stocks for the first three quarters of 1985 and the fourth quarter of 1984, respectively, were as follows (in millions and in dollars): $1-2/3 par value common stock—$1,030.8 [$3.26], $1,113.9 [$3.52], $461.6 [$1.46] and $855.2 [$2.71]; Class E common stock—$38.0 [$0.63], $42.5 [$0.67], $51.9 [$0.78] and $18.7 [$1.03].

*Adjusted to reflect the two-for-one stock split in the form of a 100% stock dividend distributed on June 10, 1985.

**Includes favorable (unfavorable) effects on earnings per share of: foreign exchange/translation activity [1985: first quarter—($0.18), second quarter—($0.23), third quarter—$0.38, fourth quarter—$0.28; 1984: first quarter—$0.24, second quarter—($0.23), third quarter—($0.45), fourth quarter $0.24] and an adjustment of income taxes of $1.34 in the 1984 second quarter reflecting a change in the provisions covering domestic international sales corporations (DISC) in accordance with the Deficit Reduction Act of 1984.

***The principal market is the New York Stock Exchange and prices are based on the Composite Tape. $1-2/3 par value common stock is also listed on the Midwest, Pacific and Philadelphia stock exchanges. As of December 31, 1985, there were 914,905 holders of record of $1-2/3 par value common stock.

****The principal market is the New York Stock Exchange and prices are based on the Composite Tape. As of December 31, 1985, there were 482,345 holders of record of Class E common stock. Market prices were on a "when issued" basis prior to December 12, 1984.

*****The principal market is the New York Stock Exchange and prices are based on the Composite Tape. As of December 31, 1985, there were 592,345 holders of record of Class H common stock. Market prices were on a "when issued" basis prior to December 31, 1985.

The effective income tax rates and credit for the 1985 quarters reflect the favorable impact of U.S. investment tax credits. The effective income tax rate for the 1984 second quarter reflects the $421.3 million reversal of deferred income taxes related to DISC legislation; the rate for the third quarter reflects losses at overseas subsidiaries where no applicable tax credits were available; and the rate for the fourth quarter reflects higher investment tax credits due to increased capital expenditures and the effect of foreign tax credits on dividends declared by subsidiaries, applied to lower pretax earnings.

(continued)

SUPPLEMENTARY INFORMATION (concluded)

Selected Financial Data
(Dollars in Millions Except Per Share Amounts)

	1985	1984	1983	1982	1981
Net sales and revenues	$96,371.7	$83,889.9	$74,581.6	$60,025.6	$62,698.5
Earnings attributable to $1-2/3 par value common stock	$ 3,883.6	$ 4,498.3	$ 3,717.3	$ 949.8	$ 320.5
Cash dividends on $1-2/3 par value common stock	1,592.9	1,510.0	879.3	737.3	717.6
Dividend of Class E common shares	—	586.7	—	—	—
Dividend of Class H common shares	572.1	—	—	—	—
Net income (loss) retained in the year	$ 1,718.6	$ 2,401.6	$ 2,838.0	$ 212.5	($ 397.1)
Earnings per share attributable to $1-2/3 par value common stock	$12.28	$14.27	$11.84	$3.09	$1.07
Cash dividends per share of $1-2/3 par value common stock	5.00	4.75	2.80	2.40	2.40
Per share dividend of Class E common shares	—	1.90	—	—	—
Per share dividend of Class H common shares	1.94	—	—	—	—
Net income (loss) per share retained in the year	$ 5.34	$ 7.62	$ 9.04	$0.69	($1.33)
Earnings attributable to Class E common stock (issued in 1984)	$ 103.8	$ 5.7	—	—	—
Cash dividends on Class E common stock (issued in 1984)	12.4	1.2	—	—	—
Net income retained in the year	$ 91.4	$ 4.5	—	—	—
Earnings per share attributable to Class E common stock*	$1.57	$0.16	—	—	—
Cash dividends per share of Class E common stock*	0.195	0.045	—	—	—
Net income per share retained in the year*	$1.375	$0.115	—	—	—
Average number of shares of common stocks outstanding (in millions):					
$1-2/3 par value common	316.3	315.3	313.9	307.4	299.1
Class E common (issued in 1984)*	66.5	36.3	—	—	—
Cash dividends on capital stocks as a percent of net income	40.4%	33.7%	23.9%	77.9%	219.1%
Expenditures for real estate, plants and equipment	$ 8,047.9**	$ 3,595.1	$ 1,923.0	$ 3,611.1	$ 6,563.3
Expenditures for special tools	$ 3,075.0	$ 2,452.1	$ 2,083.7	$ 2,601.0	$ 3,178.1
Cash and marketable securities	$ 5,114.4	$ 8,567.4	$ 6,216.9	$ 3,126.2	$ 1,320.7
Working capital	$ 1,957.5	$ 6,276.7	$ 5,890.8	$ 1,658.1	$ 1,158.8
Total assets	$63,832.8	$52,144.9	$45,694.5	$41,397.8	$38,979.0
Long-term debt and capitalized leases	$ 2,867.2	$ 2,772.9	$ 3,521.8	$ 4,745.1	$ 4,044.0

Earnings and earnings per share attributable to common stocks have been restated to reflect the Class E common stock amendment approved by the stockholders in December 1985.

Financial data for years prior to 1983 have not been restated for the adoption of Statement of Financial Accounting Standards No. 52, Foreign Currency Translation.

*Adjusted to reflect the two-for-one stock split in the form of a 100% stock dividend distributed on June 10, 1985.

**Includes $1,948.7 million of net property acquired in Hughes acquisition.

EFFECTS OF INFLATION ON FINANCIAL DATA

The accompanying Schedule displays the basic historical cost financial data adjusted for changes in specific prices (current cost) for use in the evaluation of comparative financial results.

The current cost of inventories was estimated based on costs in effect at December 31, 1985. Cost of sales for inventories maintained on a first-in, first-out basis was restated to a current cost basis using the specific level of prices at the time the goods were sold.

The current cost of property owned and the related depreciation and amortization expense for U.S. operations were calculated by applying (1) selected producer price indices to historical book values of machinery and equipment and (2) the Marshall Valuation Service index to buildings, and the use of assessed values for land. For locations outside the United States, such amounts were calculated generally by applying indices closely related to the assets being measured and translating the resulting amounts using year-end foreign currency exchange rates. Depreciation and amortization were calculated on a straight-line basis.

The purpose of this type of restatement is to furnish estimates of the effects of price increases for replacement of inventories and property on the potential future net income of the business and thus assess the probability of future cash flows. A more meaningful estimate of the effects of such costs on future earnings is the estimated level of future capital expenditures which is set forth on page 16 in the Financial Review: Management's Discussion and Analysis.

Under the current cost method, the net income of General Motors is lower (or the net loss is higher) than that determined under the historical cost method. This means that businesses, as well as individuals, are affected by inflation and that the purchasing power of business dollars also has declined. In addition, the costs of maintaining the productive capacity, as reflected in the current cost data (and estimate of future capital expenditures), have increased, and thus management must seek ways to cope with the effects of inflation through accounting methods such as the LIFO method of inventory valuation, which matches current costs with current revenues, and through accelerated methods of depreciation and amortization.

Selected Data Adjusted for Effects of Changing Prices
(Dollars in Millions Except Per Share Amounts)

Historical data adjusted for changes in specific prices (current cost)*:	1985	1984	1983	1982	1981
Net Sales and Revenues	$96,371.7	$86,883.1	$80,530.1	$66,898.1	$74,161.0
Cost of sales	81,717.8	72,777.3	65,613.7	57,859.0	65,544.2
Depreciation and amortization of property	6,577.1	5,177.8	5,817.6	5,504.6	6,150.8
Other operating and nonoperating items—net	3,226.6	2,537.9	3,011.7	3,584.5	3,426.4
United States and other income taxes	1,630.3	1,869.5	2,401.2	(281.1)	(145.6)
Total costs and expenses	93,151.8	82,362.5	76,844.2	66,667.0	74,975.8
Net Income (Loss)	$ 3,219.9	$ 4,520.6	$ 3,685.9	$ 231.1	($ 814.8)
Earnings (Loss) per share attributable to $1-2/3 par value common stock	$9.82	$14.32	$11.74	$0.75	($2.72)
Earnings per share attributable to Class E common stock (issued in 1984)	$1.57	$0.17	—	—	—
Cash dividends per share of $1-2/3 par value common stock	$5.00	$4.92	$3.02	$2.67	$2.84
Cash dividends per share of Class E common stock (issued in 1984)	$0.195	$0.047	—	—	—
Net assets at year-end	$39,780.9	$25,078.3	$22,422.9	$20,380.8	$20,960.9
Accumulated foreign currency translation adjustments	$ 118.9	($ 166.7)	($ 418.4)	—	—
Unrealized gain from decline in purchasing power of dollars of net amounts owed	$ 257.3	$ 162.8	$ 278.6	$ 420.6	$ 777.5
Excess of increase in general price level over increase in specific prices of inventories and property	$ 465.6**	$ 1,033.7	$ 252.6	$ 2,775.2	$ 1,994.5
Market price per $1-2/3 par value common share at year-end	$70.38	$81.18	$80.31	$69.52	$45.54
Market price per Class E common share at year-end (issued in 1984)	$40.88	$43.89	—	—	—
Market price per Class H common share at year-end (issued in 1985)	$38.25	—	—	—	—
Average Consumer Price Index	322.2	311.1	298.4	289.1	272.4

*Data have been adjusted to 1985 dollars.

**At December 31, 1985, current cost of inventories was $10,456.6 million and current cost of property (including special tools), net of accumulated depreciation and amortization, was $32,722.4 million.

Index

A

Accelerated Cost Recovery System (ACRS), 302-05
Accelerated depreciation, 299-305
Account, 60-63
Accounting as a process of communication, 5
Accountancy as a profession, 15-16
Accounting
  defined, 2
  financial, 4
  managerial, 4-5
Accounting changes
  changes in estimate, 406-07
  changes in principle, 405-06
  errors, 407
Accounting equation, 25
Accounting for cost of goods sold, 136-37
Accounting for merchandising operations, 136-41
Accounting for oil and gas, 329-30
Accounting Principles Board (APB), 13
Accounting system, 183-84
Accounting vs. bookkeeping, 4
Accounts payable, 244
Accounts receivable
  defined, 32
  subsidiary ledger, 176-78
  turnover, 616-17
Accrual basis, 113
Accrued expenses, 109-10
Accrued revenues, 112-13
Accumulated depreciation, 111
Acid-test ratio, 616
Additional paid-in capital, 384-85
Adjusted gross income, 643-45
Adjusting entries, 70-72, 106-13
Admission of a partner, 352-56
After-closing trial balance, 76
Aging accounts receivable, 240-42
Allocation of taxes, 651-54
Allowance for bad debts, 238-42
Allowance (inventory), 147-49

American Accounting Association (AAA), 16
American Institute of Certified Public Accountants (AICPA), 12
Amortization
  intangible assets, 330-32
  premium or discount on bonds payable, 442-44
  premium or discount on investment in bonds, 448-50
Analysis for common stockholders, 610-13
Analysis for long-term creditors, 613-14
Analysis for short-term creditors, 614
Analysis of accounts receivable, 616-17
Analysis of inventories, 617-18
Annuity, 472-73
Appropriation of retained earnings, 418-19
Articles of incorporation, 378-79
Assets
  cash, 32
  current, 32-33
  defined, 24, 32-33, 688
  fixed, 33
  inventories, 32-33
  marketable securities, 32
  other, 33
  prepaid expenses, 33
  receivables, 32
Audit trail, 182-83
Automated accounting systems, forms of, 183-84
Average cost method, inventory, 274-75
Average number of days to collect receivables, 616-17

B

Bad debts, 238-44
  balance sheet approach, 240-42
  balance sheet presentation, 242
  estimating expense, 238-42
  income statement approach, 239-40
  recovered, 243-44

write-off, 242-44
Balance sheet, 5, 24-25, 690
Balance sheet approach (bad debts), 240-42
Balance sheet classifications, 29-34
Bank reconciliation statement, 206-11
Basic accounting principles and underlying
    concepts, 7-12
        consistency concept, 9
        entity concept, 7
        going-concern concept, 7
        historical cost concept, 8
        matching concept, 9
        materiality concept, 10-11
        monetary concept, 8
        stable dollar concept, 8
Basic analytical procedures, 605-08
Benefits and costs, 677
Bonds, investments in, 448-50
Bonds payable
    callable, 445-46
    classes of, 439-40
    convertible, 445
    defined, 438-39
    determining price of, 474-76
    discount, 442-43
    interest method of amortization, 476-79
    issuance of, 440-44
    issued between interest dates, 441-42
    premium, 444
    retirement, 445-46
    straight-line method of
        amortization, 442-44
Bond sinking fund, 446
Bookkeeping, 4
Book value per share of
    common stock, 420-21

C

Callable bonds, 439
Capital, additional paid-in, 384-85
Capital, accounts, partners, 345
Capital expenditures, 309-11
Capital gains and losses, 646-47
Capital stock
    common, 380
    issuance of, 384-86
    nature of, 380
    no-par value, 383-84
    par value, 383-84
    preferred, 381-82
    subscriptions, 386-87

Capitalization of interest, 308-09
Cash
    basis, 155-56
    controlling cash disbursements, 205-06
    controlling cash receipts, 202-05
    defined, 32, 202
    disbursements, 205-06
    importance of, 202
    internal control, 202
    over and short, 205
    petty cash, 211-13
    receipts, 202-05
Cash disbursements
    control of, 205-06
    journal, 178-79
Cash dividends, 410-11
Cash flow
    analysis, 532
    from operations, 532-35
    illustration, 536
    statement, 536, 690
Cash receipts
    control of, 202-05
    journal, 178
Certified Public Accountant (CPA), 12
Change in accounting principle, 405-06
Change in estimate, 406-07
Changes in noncurrent accounts, 527-29
Changes in working capital, 526-27
Chart of accounts, 172-74
Checks
    Not Sufficient Funds, (N.S.F.), 207-08
    outstanding, 206-07
Classes of taxpayers, 641-42
Closing entries, 73-76
Common-size statements, 608
Common stock, 380
Comparability, 679, 688
Comparison with standards, 609-10
Comparative financial statements, 604
Completed production basis, 153-54
Completeness, 689
Comprehensive income, 689
Computer
    hardware, 184
    software, 184-85
Conceptual framework, 689
Consistency, 9
Consolidated statements
    balance sheet, 489-96
    income statement, 500-01
    minority interest, 502
    pooling of interest, 498-500
    usefulness of, 500

Constant dollar accounting, 566-67
Consumer price index, 567-68
Contra account, 111
Contributed capital, 380
Control accounts, 174-75
Convertible bonds, 445
Copyright, 330
Corporate officers, 377
Corporation
   articles of incorporation, 378-79
   capital of, 379
   characteristics, 376-78
   defined, 7, 376
   formation, 378-79
   income taxes, 647-49
   nature of capital stock, 380
   rights of stockholders, 380-83
Cost Accounting Standards Board
   (CASB), 16
Cost flow assumptions
   average cost, 274-75
   Fifo, 275
   Lifo, 275-76
Cost method for investments
   in stocks, 454-59
Cost of goods sold, 136-41
Cost of merchandise purchased, 137
Coupon rate, 439-40
Credit (Cr.), 60-63
Credit memorandum, 207
Creditors, 24
Cumulative preference, 381-82
Current assets, 32
Current cost, 580
Current exit value, 580
Current liabilities, 33-34
Current ratio, 615
Current value accounting, 579-82

Depletion base, 327
Deposit in transit, 209-10
Depreciation, 295-305
   Accelerated Cost Recovery System
     (ACRS), 302-05
   accelerated methods, 299-305
   adjusting entry, 110-11
   double-declining balance, 300-01
   methods, 298-305
   on assets acquired during
     a period, 306-08
   salvage value, 297-98
   straight-line, 299
   sum-of-the-years'-digits, 301-02
   useful life, 110-11, 297
Differences between accounting
   and taxable income
     permanent, 649-50
     timing, 650
Discontinued operations, 404
Discount
   on bonds, 442-43
   purchase, 144-47
   rate, 249-52
Discounted notes payable, 247-49
Discounting notes receivable, 247-49
Discounts lost account, 146-47
Dishonored note, 247
Dividends, 409-14
   cash, 410-11
   date of declaration, 410
   date of payment, 410
   date of record, 410
   stock, 411-14
Double-declining balance
   depreciation, 300-01
Double-entry, 60-63
Drawing account; see Withdrawals

D

Dates, for dividends, 410
Debenture bonds, 439
Debit (Dr.), 60-63
Debit memorandum, 207
Debt-to-equity ratio, 613
Decision usefulness, 677
Declaration, date of, 410
Deductions from adjusted
   gross income, 645
Deductions for adjusted gross income, 643
Deferred taxes, 651-54
Depletion, 327-29

E

Earnings (concept), 689
Earnings per share, 407-09, 611-12
Entity concept, 7
Equity, 689
Equity method for investment in
   stocks, 454-59
Errors, correction of, 407
Estimates, changes in, 406-07
Estimating bad debts,
   aging method, 240-42
   balance sheet approach (bad debts), 240-42
   income statement approach (bad debts),
     239-40

Exemptions, 645-46
Expenses, 35, 689
   recognition, 156-58
Extraordinary items, 402-04

F

Face value on bonds payable, 439-40
Federal income tax, 640-41
Federal unemployment tax, 253
Feedback value, 689
Financial accounting
   compared to managerial, 4-5
   defined, 4
Financial Accounting Standards Board
   (FASB), 14-15
   Statement No. 33, 581-82
Financial reporting and financial
   statements, 5-6, 689-90
Financial statement analysis, 604
   interpretation of analyses, 618-19
Financial statements, 76-79, 689-90
First-in, first-out (Fifo), 275
Fixed assets; *see* Long-term assets
F.O.B., 147
Formation of a corporation, 378-79
Formation of a partnership, 345-46
Freight-in, 147-49
Funds
   defined, 521
   from operations, 529
   sources of, 521-24
   uses of, 524

G

Gains, 689
Gains, extraordinary, 402-04
General journal, 174
General journal entries, 63-68
General ledger, 174
General price level, 569-70
General price level gain or loss, 575
Generally Accepted Accounting
   Principles, 7
Going-concern concept, 7
Goodwill, 330-32
Gross income, 643
Gross profit method, inventory, 278-79
Gross profit percentage, 278-79

H

Historical cost, 12, 579-80
Horizontal analysis, 606-07

I

Income statement, 6, 34-35
Income statement approach (bad debts),
   239-40
Income statement classifications, 41
Income summary account, 73-76
Income taxes,
   classes of taxpayers, 641-42
   corporation, 647-49
   credits, 646
   defined, 640
   federal, 640-41
   individual, 643-47
   interperiod allocation of, 651-54
   intraperiod allocation of, 654
   management decisions, 655
   sources of differences between
      accounting and taxable income, 651-54
   withholding, 253, 646
Individual income tax, 643-47
Inflation, 566-68
Influences on accounting principles, 14-15
   American Accounting Association, 15
   American Institute of Certified Public
      Accountants, 14
   Cost Accounting Standards Board, 15
   Financial Accounting Standards Board,
      14-15
   Internal Revenue Service, 15
   National Association of Accountants, 15
   Securities and Exchange Commission, 15
Installment basis, 155-56
Intangible assets, 330-32
Intercompany sales, 502-04
Intercorporate investments,
   consolidated statements for, 488-504
   cost method, 454-59
   equity method, 454-59
Interest
   calculation, 469-71
   compounded, 469-71
   costs (fixed assets), 308-09
   number of times earned, 613-14
Interest method of amortization, 476-79
Internal accounting control, 181-82
Internal Revenue Service (IRS), 15
Interperiod tax allocation, 651-54

Intraperiod tax allocation, 654
Inventory
   accounting objective, 141-42
   basis of accounting, 144, 273
   control over, 272
   cost of, 142-43
   defined, 32-33
   discounts, 147-48
   losses, 143-44
   lower of cost or market, 277-78
   objective of inventory accounting, 272-73
   periodic and perpetual, 143-44
   purchase discounts, 144-47
   returns and allowances, 147-49
   turnover ratio, 617-18
Inventory cost flow methods, 273-77
   average cost, 274-75
   differences in methods, 276-77
   Fifo, 275
   gross profit method, 278-79
   Lifo, 275-76
   retail method, 279-80
Investment in bonds,
   amortization of premium
     and discount, 448-50
   purchase, 448
   sale of bonds, 450
Investment in stock, 450-59
   cost method, 454-59
   equity method, 454-59
   long-term investments, 454-59
   temporary investments, 450-53
Issuance of bonds, 440-44
Issuance of par value stock, 384-86
Itemized deductions, 645

J

Journal
   cash disbursements, 178-79
   cash receipts, 178
   entry, 60-63
   form of special journals, 180
   payroll, 179-80
   purchases, 180
   sales, 176-78
   special, 175-80
Journal entry, defined, 62-63
Journalizing, 60-63

L

Last-in, first-out (Lifo), 275-76
Ledger, 174
Legal capital, 383-84
Liabilities, 689
   accounts payable, 34
   accrued, 109-10
   current, 33-34
   defined, 24, 33-34
   long-term, 34
   notes payable, 34
   taxes payable, 34
   unearned revenues, 34
Liquidation of a partnership, 358-61
Long-term assets
   acquired during the period, 306-08
   capital expenditures, 309-11
   control over, 292
   costs incurred after acquisition, 309-11
   cost of, 293-94
   defined, 33
   depreciation methods, 295-305
   disposition of, 322-27
   disclosure in the financial statements, 309
   intangible, 330-32
   interest costs, 308-09
   natural resources, 327-29
   revenue expenditures, 309-11
   recording, 305-11
   tangible, 293-311
   trade-ins, 324-27
   types of, 293
Long-term investments
   bonds, 448-50
   stock, 454-59
Long-term liabilities, 34, 438-47
Losses, 689
   extraordinary, 402-04
   inventory, 143-44
Lower of cost or market method
   inventories, 277-78
   temporary investments, 451-53

M

Managerial accounting
  defined, 5
  compared to financial, 4-5
Marketable securities, 32, 451-53
Matching concept, 9
Materiality, 10-11, 689
Measure of the instability of the
  dollar, 567-69
Minority interest, 502
Model of a financial accounting system, 170-72
Monetary concept, 8
Monetary gains or losses, 575
Monetary items, 569-70

N

National Association of Accountants (NAA), 15-16
Nature of earnings, 402
Natural resources, 327-30
Net income, 34-35
Neutrality, 679, 689
Nonmonetary items, 570
No-par value stock, 383-84
Notes payable
  accrual of interest, 246
  defined, 244
  discounting, 249-52
  issuance, 245-46
  issued at a discount, 247-49
  payment, 246-47
Notes receivable
  accrual of interest, 246
  calculation of interest, 245
  discounting, 249-52
  dishonored, 247
  issuance, 245-46
  issued at a discount, 247-49
  payment, 246-47
N.S.F. (Not Sufficient Funds) check, 207-08
Number of times interest earned, 613-14

O

Objective of inventory accounting, 141-42
Oil and gas accounting, 329-30
Opportunities in accounting, 17
Organization costs, 330
Other assets, 33
Outstanding checks, 206-07
Over-the-counter-sales, 203-05
Owners' equity
  appropriated retained earnings, 418-19
  defined, 25, 34
  retained earnings, 417-19
  statement of capital, 6, 42-43

P

Paid-in capital, 380
Par value, 383-84
Parent corporation, 488-89
Participating preference, 382
Partnership, 343-61
  accounting for, 345
  admission of a partner, 352-56
  advantages, 344-45
  agreement, 343-44
  characteristics, 343-45
  defined, 7, 342-43
  division of earnings, 346-51
  financial statements, 351-52
  formation, 345-46
  liquidation, 358-61
  statement of partners' capital, 351-52
  withdrawal of a partner, 356-58
Patents, 330
Payables
  accounts payable, 244
  classification, 235
  current, 235
  notes receivable and payable, 244-52
Payroll accounting, 252-54
Payroll journal, 179-80
Percentage-of-completion basis, 154-55
Perdictive value, 690
Periodic inventory procedure, 143-44
Permanent differences, 651-54
Perpetual inventory method, 143-44
Personal exemption, defined, 645-46
Petty cash, 211-13
Pooling of interest method, 498-500
Posting, 63, 68-69, 72
Preemptive right, defined, 380-81
Preferred stock, 381-83
Premium on bonds, 444
Prepaid expenses, 33, 107-09
Present value
  approach, 580-81
  bonds payable, 473-79
  of an annuity, 472-73
  of a future sum, 471-72
  tables, 480-83

Price-earnings ratio, 612-13
Price index, 567-68
Price level
    changes, 569-70
    gain or loss, 575
    statements, 570-74
Prior period adjustments, 405
Profit on intercompany sales, 502-04
Proprietorship, 7, 342-43
Proving the control accounts, 180
Purchases
    accounting for, 137
    discounts, 144-47
    journal, 180
    returns and allowances, 147-49

Q

Qualitative characteristics of accounting
    information, 676-80
        benefits and costs, 677
        comparability, 679
        decision usefulness, 677
        materiality, 680
        neutrality, 679
        relevance, 677
        reliability, 677
        understandability, 677
        verfiability, 679
Quick ratio, 616

R

Rate of return
    on stockholders' equity, 611
    on total assets, 610
Ratio
    acid test (quick), 616
    current, 615
    debt-to-equity, 613
    price-earnings, 612-13
Ratio analysis, 608-09
Receivables
    accounting for, 236-37
    aging of, 240-42
    classification, 234-35
    control, 235-36
    defined, 32
    notes, 244-52
    statement presentation, 252
    turnover, 616-17
Reciprocal accounts, 496
Recognition of expenses, 156-58

Reconciling bank statements with cash
    account balances, 206-11
Record, date of, 410
Recovery (bad debts), 243-44
Registered bonds, 439-40
Relevance, 677, 690
Reliability, 677, 690
Representational faithfulness, 690
Research and development, 332
Retail method, 279-80
Retailing operations, accounting
    for, 136-51
Retained earnings, 417-19
    appropriation, 418-19
    statement, 419
Returns (inventory), 147-49
Revenue, 35, 690
Revenue expenditures, 309-11
Revenue recognition, 152-53
    cash received, 155-56
    completed production, 153-54
    during production, 154-55
    time period, 152
Rights of stockholders, 380-83
Role of the accountant, 3

S

Sales
    discount, 144-47
    journal, 176-78
    merchandise, 137-38
    returns and allowances, 147-49
Salvage value, 297-98
Securities
    cost basis, 454-59
    equity basis, 454-59
    long-term investments in, 446-59
    marketable, 32, 451-53
Securities and Exchange Commission
    (SEC), 15
Social security taxes, 253
Sole proprietorship, 7, 342-43
Sources of working capital, 521-24
Special journals, 175-80
Stable dollar, 8
State unemployment tax, 253
Statement of capital, 6, 42-43
Statement of changes in financial
    position, 6
    basic objectives, 520
    definitions of funds, 521

    form of, 529-30
    illustration, 531
    summary of mechanics, 537
    transactions not affecting working
        capital, 530-32
Statement of financial position;
    (*see* balance sheet)
Statement of retained earnings, 419
Stock dividends, 411-14
Stock splits, 414-15
Stock subscribed account, 386-87
Stockholders, 380-83
Stockholders' equity in the balance sheet, 387
Straight-line method
    amortization of discount and
        premium, 442-44
    amortization of intangible assets, 330-32
    depreciation, 299
Subscriptions of capital stock, 386-87
Subsidiary
    accounts, 174-75
    corporation, 488-89
    ledger, 174-75
Sum-of-the-years'-digits
    depreciation, 301-02

T

T-account, 60
Tangible assets, 293-311
Tax allocation, (*see* Income taxes)
Taxable income, 649
Temporary accounts, 73-76
Temporary investments, 32, 451-53
Timeliness, 690
Timing differences in income tax
    allocation, 651-54
Trade-ins, accounting for, 324-27
Transaction, 25
Transaction analysis, 25-29, 35-41
Treasury stock
    acquisition and reissuance of, 415-17
    in statement of financial position, 417
Trial balance, 69-70
    after adjustment, 72-73
    after-closing, 76
True cash balance, 206-11
Turnover
    of accounts receivable, 616-17
    of inventory, 617-18

U

Uncollectible accounts, 238-44
Understandability, 677, 690
Unearned revenue, 111-12
Useful life, 110-11, 297
Uses of working capital, 524

V

Verifiability, 679, 690
Vertical analysis, 607
Voucher, 214-16
Voucher register, 216-17
Voucher system, 213-18

W

Withdrawal of a partner, 356-58
Withdrawals, 27
Withholding tax, 252-54
Working capital
    changes in, 526-27
    defined, 614
    from operations, 529
    sources of, 521-24
    uses of, 524
Worksheet, 96-106, 113-15
    defined, 96
    illustration, 96-106, 113-15
    merchandising firm, 149-51
    uses, 96
Write-off (bad debts), 242-44